HANDBOOK OF NEUROPSYCHOLOGY

HANDBOOK OF NEUROPSYCHOLOGY

Series Editors

FRANÇOIS BOLLER

Unit 324 INSERM, Centre Paul Broca, Paris, France

JORDAN GRAFMAN

Medical Neurology Branch, NINCDS, Bethesda, MD, U.S.A.

ELSEVIER

Amsterdam – New York – Oxford

HANDBOOK OF NEUROPSYCHOLOGY

Section Editors

R.D. NEBES
S. CORKIN

VOLUME 4

1991

ELSEVIER

Amsterdam – New York – Oxford

ISBN Series: 0-444-90492-1

First published (hardbound edition) by Elsevier Science Publishers B.V. (Biomedical Division), 1990.
ISBN: 0-444-81234-2.

This edition (paperback) published by Elsevier Science Publishers B.V., 1991.
ISBN: 0-444-89169-2.

This book is printed on acid-free paper

Published by:
ELSEVIER SCIENCE PUBLISHERS B.V.
P.O. BOX 211

Library of Congress Cataloging-in-Publication Data
(Revised for vol. 4)

Handbook of neuropsychology.

Includes bibliographies and indexes.
1. Clinical neuropsychology. 2. Neuropsychology.
[DNLM: 1. Neuropsychology.] I. Boller, Francois.
II. Grafman, Jordan.
RC343.H225 1988 616.8 88-21312
ISBN 0-444-90492-1 (set)

Printed in The Netherlands

Preface

In the preface to Volume 1 of the Handbook of Neuropsychology, we stated that in recent years there has been an enormous increase in interest in disorders of higher cortical functions and brain-behavior relationships. This interest is exemplified by the success met so far by the Handbook, which has already become an essential reference source for clinicians such as neurologists, psychiatrists and psychologists, as well as for all scientists engaged in research in the neurosciences.

The Handbook has been planned as a reference source in order to provide for the first time comprehensive and current coverage of experimental and clinical aspects of neuropsychology. To this end, the chapter authors have produced in-depth reviews that go beyond a summary of their own results and points of view. Each chapter is up-to-date, covering the latest developments in methodology and theory. Discussion of bedside evaluations, laboratory techniques and theoretical models are all to be found in the Handbook.

The first two volumes comprised an introductory section (edited by Boller and Grafman), and sections on attention (Rizzolatti), language, aphasia and related disorders (Goodglass) and visual behavior (Damasio). Volume 3 contains Section 5 dedicated to memory and its disorders (Squire) and Section 6 dedicated to emotional behavior and its disorders (Gainotti).

Volume 4, which we now present, also includes two sections. The first one (Section 7) has as Topic Editor Professor Robert Nebes and deals with the commissurotomized brain. Topics include a review of commissurotomy studies in animals, integrative functions of the cerebral commissures, sequelae of partial commissurotomy, and agenesis of the corpus callosum. Two chapters on the specific effects of commissurotomy on language, memory, and spatial cognition conclude this section.

The Topic Editor of the second part of this volume (Section 8) is Professor Suzanne Corkin. The section deals with aging, age-related disorders, and dementia. Owing to the considerable size of this section, only the first part will be found in Volume 4. Specific topics include animal models, brain imaging and cerebral metabolism, sensory systems (olfaction and vision), language, spatial abilities, memory, psychiatric symptoms and sleep. The first part of the section concludes with a chapter on longitudinal studies and one on statistical practice. The rest of the section, to be found in Volume 5, will cover epidemiology, the problem of possible subgroups in Alzheimer's disease, pathological and chemical correlates of dementia, disorders of attention and motor functions, as well as having additional chapters on memory. It concludes with reviews of specific disorders (Parkinson's disease, Huntington's disease and HIV infection) and a chapter on treatment strategies for cognitive impairments. Volume 5 will also include Section 9 (edited by Grafman and Boller) dealing with cognitive models, neurolinguistic approaches to aphasia, and contemporary trends in neuropsychology. This section ends the part of the Handbook dedicated to the neuropsychology of adulthood and aging. Two additonal volumes dealing with developmental neuropsychology are currently in preparation with Professors Isabelle Rapin and Sidney Segalowitz as Topic Editors.

Many people have contributed to the successful preparation of the Handbook. We again wish to emphasize our appreciation for the commitment of the Topic Editors, who have spent long hours in the planning stage and in the actual compiling of the various sections. Dr. Marie-Cécile Masure has painstakingly prepared the index of this volume as well as that of the three preceding volumes; we are most grateful to her for her efforts. Ms Annette Grechen in Pittsburgh and the editorial staff of Elsevier in Amsterdam continue to provide invaluable technical assistance.

François BOLLER
Jordan GRAFMAN

List of contributors

C.A. Barnes — Department of Psychology, University of Colorado, Campus Box 345, Boulder, CO 80309, U.S.A.

G. Berlucchi — Istituto di Fisiologia Umana, Strada Le Grazie, 37134 Verona, Italy

S. Corkin — Department of Brain and Cognitive Sciences, Massachusetts Institute of Technology, Cambridge, MA 02139, U.S.A.

A. Cronin-Golomb — Department of Psychology, Boston University, 64 Cummington St., Boston, MA 02215, U.S.A.

R.L. Doty — Smell and Taste Center, Department of Otorhinolaryngology and Human Communication, and Department of Physiology, School of Medicine, University of Pennsylvania, Philadelphia, PA 19104, U.S.A.

R.P. Friedland — Brain Aging and Dementia Section, Laboratory of Neurosciences, National Institute on Aging, National Institutes of Health, Bethesda, MD 20892, U.S.A.

H.W. Gordon — Western Psychiatric Institute and Clinic, University of Pittsburgh School of Medicine, 3811 O'Hara Street, Pittsburgh, PA 15213, U.S.A.

C.C. Hoch — Western Psychiatric Institute and Clinic, University of Pittsburgh School of Medicine, 3811 O'Hara Street, Pittsburgh, PA 15213, U.S.A.

F.J. Huff — Alzheimer's Disease Research Center, University of Pittsburgh, Suite 400, Iroquois Building, 3600 Forbes Avenue, Pittsburgh, PA 15213, U.S.A.

M.A. Jeeves Medical Research Council, Cognitive Neuroscience Research Group, University of St. Andrews, Fife, KY16 9JU, U.K.

R.D. Nebes Department of Psychiatry, University of Pittsburgh School of Medicine, 3811 O'Hara Street, Pittsburgh, PA 15213, U.S.A.

J.A. Ogden Department of Psychology, University of Auckland, Private Bag, Auckland, New Zealand

C. Owsley Department of Ophthalmology, School of Medicine/Eye Foundation Hospital, University of Alabama at Birmingham, Birmingham, AL 35294, U.S.A.

J.S. Poceta Sleep and Aging Research Program, American Lake VA Medical Center, Clinical Research Centre, University Hospital, Psychiatry and Behavioral Sciences, RP-10, University of Washington, Seattle, WA 98915, U.S.A.

P. Prinz Sleep and Aging Research Program, American Lake VA Medical Center, Clinical Research Centre, University Hospital, Psychiatry and Behavioral Sciences, RP-10, University of Washington, Seattle, WA 98195, U.S.A.

C.F. Reynolds III Western Psychiatric Institute and Clinic, University of Pittsburgh School of Medicine, 3811 O'Hara Street, Pittsburgh, PA 15213, U.S.A.

T.J. Rosen Department of Brain and Cognitive Sciences, Massachusetts Institute of Technology, Cambridge, MA 02139, and Department of Neurology, Massachusetts General Hospital, Boston, MA 02114, U.S.A.

H.J. Sagar Department of Neurology, Royal Hallamshire Hospital, Sheffield, S10 2JF, U.K.

M.E. Sloane Department of Psychology, University of Alabama at Birmingham, Birmingham, AL 35294, U.S.A.

M. Storandt Department of Psychology, Washington University, St. Louis, MO 63130, U.S.A.

C. Trevarthen Department of Psychology, University of Edinburgh, 7 George Square, Edinburgh, EH8 9JZ, U.K.

M.V. Vitiello Sleep and Aging Research Program, American Lake VA Medical Center, Clinical Research Center, University Hospital, Psychiatry and Behavioral Sciences, RP-10, University of Washington, Seattle, WA 98195, U.S.A.

D.W. Zaidel Department of Psychology, UCLA, Los Angeles, CA 90024-1563, U.S.A.

E. Zaidel Department of Psychology, UCLA, Los Angeles, CA 90024-1563, U.S.A.

Acknowledgements

The editors and publisher gratefully acknowledge Sandoz Ltd, Basle, Switzerland, CIBA-Geigy, Summit, NJ, U.S.A., Fondation IPSEN, Paris, France, and Farmitalia Carlo Erba, Milan, Italy, for partially supporting the publication of this volume.

Contents

Section 8: Aging and Dementia (Part 1) (Corkin)

Section 7

The Commissurotomized Brain

editor

R.D. Nebes

© 1990 Elsevier Science Publishers B.V. (Biomedical Division)
Handbook of Neuropsychology, Vol. 4
F. Boller and J. Grafman (Eds)

CHAPTER 1

The commissurotomized brain: introduction

Robert D. Nebes

Department of Psychiatry, University of Pittsburgh Medical School, Pittsburgh, PA, U.S.A.

The chapters in this section differ from others in the Handbook of Neuropsychology in that, rather than dealing with a particular area of cognition, (e.g., memory) or a particular disorder (e.g., dementia), they focus on the results of a unique surgical procedure – sectioning of the neocortical commissures. Research findings from studies on commissurotomized animals and humans have had a major impact on the neurosciences and neuropsychology, as is evident from the fact that the primary mover in these investigations, Dr. Roger Sperry, was awarded the Nobel prize in Physiology and Medicine in 1981 for his work in this area. However, it is not only the brain sciences that have been influenced by the commissurotomy work, but also fields as diverse as education (Zaidel, 1985), psychiatry (David, 1989), and even philosophy (Sperry et al., 1979). Much of the interest in these findings has sprung from the dramatic demonstration in human split-brain patients of the different cognitive specializations of the right and left cerebral hemispheres, and from the apparent ability of the two hemispheres of a single person to function relatively independently after commissurotomy. The dual brain concept has become so common that a cartoonist in a general circulation magazine can have a character say 'My left hemisphere couldn't agree more with what you are saying, but my right hemisphere intuits that it's all a load of rubbish' without fearing that the typical educated reader will fail to get the point. As might be expected with an area this popular, the scientific findings have, at times, been grossly over-interpreted and over-generalized. A regular cottage industry of techniques has sprung up proposing to train people how to release their supposedly repressed right-hemisphere abilities for fun and profit (Edwards, 1979; Harris, 1985). The chapters in this section will review the present state of our scientific knowledge in this area.

The initial studies on commissurotomized animals and humans were designed to examine the effects of the lesion itself. What was the organism unable to do after a commissurotomy that it had been able to do before? Early research focused on whether information presented to one hemisphere via lateralized sensory pathways was still accessible to the other hemisphere once the commissures were severed. It soon became clear that if a commissurotomized animal or human was allowed to blindly feel a stimulus with just one paw/hand or to see a stimulus in just one half visual field, then only the hemisphere contralateral to that paw/hand or field was aware of the identity of the stimulus (see the review by Bogen, 1985). Once this was established, it became possible to investigate a variety of broader questions about the functional organization of the brain. For example, after a commissurotomy do the two cerebral hemispheres become independent processing systems, each with its own separate memory traces, thoughts and perceptions? In humans, does a commissurotomy produce two conscious minds (Sperry, 1985) or is only the left hemisphere conscious, while the right is merely an automaton (Eccles, 1973)? An especially productive series of investigations focused on characterizing the different cognitive specializations shown by the right and left cerebral hemispheres in humans. Commissurotomized patients have a number of advantages for such studies (Nebes, 1974). Unlike individuals with unilateral focal lesions, in split-brain patients the two hemispheres are relatively intact and are available for independent testing. This allows a direct comparison of the performances of the right and left hemispheres of a single person on a given task. In these patients, it is thus possible to directly test the relative competence of the right and left hemispheres, rather than having to infer this competence from the relative amount of deficit that results from unilateral brain damage. Studies in commissurotomy patients have been especially important in establishing our present picture of the abilities of the right hemisphere. One of the difficulties with using unilateral lesion data to investigate right-hemisphere abilities is that there is always the possibility of a bias in selecting patients. Large left-hemisphere lesions often leave patients with such poor language comprehension that they are untestable, while the same is not true of large right-sided lesions. In the split-brain patients this is not an issue, as the relative *abilities* of each hemisphere are independently tested rather than their relative *disabilities* following unilateral damage. Lately, other issues have come to dominate commissurotomy research. Do the commissures have functions other than interconnecting the sensory and motor representations of the two sides of the brain? For example, are they important in regulating whole brain activities such as memory and attention? Dahlia Zaidel (Chapter 7) has argued that severing the commissures disrupts normal memory function. Levy (1985) and Trevarthen (Chapter 3) claim that the commissures play an important role in the regulation of attention, so that without them asymmetric attentional biases occur, leading to a fluctuating hemi-inattention toward one or the other side of space. The commissures are postulated to keep the arousal levels of the two hemispheres in balance, allocating processing resources efficiently to the right and left hemispheres. There is, however, contrasting work (Sergent, 1986) suggesting that the two hemispheres in split-brain subjects can work independently in parallel without showing the asymmetric arousal postulated by Levy and Trevarthen. This issue is one of many that remain to be settled in the area of commissurotomy research. Levy (1985) also claims that the commissures are important in the development of hemispheric specialization, although again the evidence for this is still controversial (Jeeves, Chapter 5). Another major question now under study is how commissurotomized animals and humans can operate as unitary beings despite all the disconnection symptoms that are so evident in tasks devised to examine interhemispheric transfer of information. In everyday life, the behavior of commissurotomized individuals is unremarkable and it is easy to see how the effects of a commissurotomy could be missed in the early surgical cases, such as those of Akelaitis (1944). Trevarthen (Chapter 3) describes factors, including subcortical systems, which act to unify visual-motor abilities, allowing commissurotomized subjects to function in an integrated fashion despite the fact that their representation of visual space is divided between their two hemispheres. Sergent (1986) also sees subcortical systems to be important in coordinating activities of the two hemispheres, thus allowing split-brain subjects to act as unified individuals. Furthermore, Sergent (1987) argues that much of the lack of integration seen in split-brain patients results from artificial test situations, and that if the test situation encourages interhemispheric integration in these patients, it will be found. Sperry (1985) has recently noted factors which act to produce an undivided consciousness in split-brain subjects, despite the lack of awareness of each hemisphere for much of the cognitive activity in the other. It is clear that questions about the independence of the processing systems in the two hemispheres of split-brain organisms and about the ways in which the divided hemispheres interact so as to produce unified action and consciousness still remain important areas of research.

The following chapters demonstrate the diversity of research questions involving the cerebral commissures, both in humans and in animals. They deal not only with the various functions of the commissures as revealed by deficits following commissurotomy, but also with what can be learned about hemispheric organization and specialization from studying commissurotomized humans. Other topics of investigation include the ability of the brain to compensate for an early loss of the commissures (agenesis) as well as the effects produced by division of various portions of the commissures (partial commissurotomy).

Chapter 2, by Dr. Berlucchi, reviews research on split-brain animals. Animal studies have played a central role in our understanding of the cerebral commissures. While research with commissurotomized humans often receives much of the attention in this area, it should not be forgotten that it was the animal studies of Sperry and Meyers in the early 1950s which first demonstrated the effects that severing the commissures has on interhemispheric transfer and integration. This work was crucial in stimulating and guiding the initial investigations into the effects that commissurotomy has in human patients (see Bogen, 1985, for an excellent review of the history of commissurotomy theory and research). Animal researchers have also carried out theoretically important studies which could not be performed in humans (e.g., combining commissurotomy with focal lesions of the hemispheres or neurophysiological recordings during behavioral tasks). Animal studies are the only way in which certain basic questions can be approached. For example, when sensory input is restricted to only one hemisphere in a learning task, do both hemispheres learn the task or is the memory engram restricted to the hemisphere that receives the direct sensory input?

Chapter 3, by Dr. Trevarthen, reviews the role that the commissures play in interhemispheric integration of perceptual information, as well as in the coordination of locomotion and fine motor control. This chapter also deals with factors that act to unify perception and action in split-brain subjects, including subcortical influences. A heavy emphasis is placed on the preservation in commissurotomized subjects of a unified perception of certain aspects of visual stimuli, such as their spatial position and relative movement. Dr. Trevarthen also argues that the cerebral commissures may be responsible for the distribution and allocation of selective attention between the hemispheres, and that this modulation of hemispheric activity may turn out to be one of the most important fuctions of the commissures.

In Chapter 4, Dr. Gordon reviews the literature on partial commissurotomies and what they reveal about the regional organization of the corpus callosum. Given the diversity of the known sensory, motor and cognitive functions of the various cortical areas interconnected by the corpus callosum, we might expect that the behavioral effects produced by severing different segments of the callosum would differ dramatically. However, this review makes it clear that section of the anterior two-thirds of the callosum has relatively little behavioral effect. Preservation of even a small portion of the splenium of the callosum is sufficient to prevent patients from developing the full commissurotomy syndrome. While there is some evidence for regional differentiation of callosal function in partial commissurotomy patients, this is relatively minor compared to the exquisite specificity of regional callosal interconnections (see Chapter 2 for an extensive review of these interconnections). These results pose a considerable problem for our understanding of how the commissures act.

Research on agenesis of the corpus callosum is reviewed by Dr. Jeeves in Chapter 5. Much of this work has focused on whether individuals born without a callosum show the same disconnection symptoms found in persons in whom the commissures are surgically severed in adulthood. The basic questions are: what limitations are there in an individual's ability to compensate for loss of the callosum early in life, and what mechanisms are responsible for the compensation that is seen (e.g., elaboration of ipsilateral pathways, increased use of subcortical cross-connections and the anterior commissure)? Another important line of research involving agenesis deals with the role that the cerebral commissures play in establishing hemispheric specialization and organization during development. If, as suggested by some researchers, interhemispheric inhibition acting across the commissures fosters the normal development of hemispheric specialization, then individuals born without a callosum should demonstrate an abnormal pattern of specialization. Even the development of normal brain organization within a given hemisphere might be altered by callosal agenesis.

Chapter 6, by Dr. Eran Zaidel, provides an up-to-date review of the language abilities of both the right and left hemispheres in commissurotomized patients, including a description of previously unpublished results. Commissurotomy studies have been crucial for determining the language potential of the right hemisphere. It soon became clear that only the left hemisphere of commissurotomized patients is capable of actual speech. However, this does not mean that the right hemisphere is devoid of other language abilities. The results reviewed in this chapter demonstrate that the right hemisphere has far more language ability than focal-lesion studies would suggest. It appears that many of the deficits seen in patients with left hemisphere lesions do not reflect an incompetence of the right hemisphere for language but, rather, nonadaptive attempts by the damaged left hemisphere to carry out language operations despite its injury. When the right hemisphere is examined independent of interference from the left (i.e., either in split-brain patients or in hemispherectomy patients), it is clear that the right hemisphere possesses a unique set of language abilities and makes a true contribution to language processing in the normal brain. While this view of right hemisphere language in commissurotomized man has been challenged in recent years (Gazzaniga, 1983; but see Myers, 1984, for a rebuttal), the vast majority of the evidence supports the characterization of right-hemisphere language advanced in this chapter.

In Chapter 7, Dr. Dahlia Zaidel provides a brief review of the visuospatial capacities of the separated right and left hemispheres. Her main focus, however, is not on lateralized abilities, but rather on the effect that commissurotomy has on memory function in the patient as a whole. Since for the most part the work reviewed examines patients' performance when tested with clinical memory tasks presented in the standard fashion (i.e., the information is not restricted to one hemisphere), a series of interpretative difficulties have to be dealt with. The most important of these is whether any memory deficit seen in commissurotomized patients results from extracallosal surgical damage to midline structures rather than from an actual loss of commissural connections. Given that a memory deficit is actually part of the commissurotomy syndrome, the nature and mechanism of this impairment still remain to be determined. Certainly, however, such a deficit would, like the attentional deficits suggested in Chapter 3, indicate that the cerebral commissures play a more complex role in regulating behavior than just serving as a pathway for the interhemispheric transmission of sensory-motor information.

At this point it should be acknowledged that some investigators feel that the impotance of the human commissurotomy findings for understanding normal brain function and organization has been greatly exaggerated (e.g., Whitaker and Ojemann, 1977). They point out that conclusions about the commissurotomy syndrome are based on results from a very few (often less than five in a study) patients in the California series studied by Sperry and his colleagues. While there have been other commissurotomy series since then, the patients have often received a partial commissurotomy, which does not produce the full split-brain syndrome (Gordon, Chapter 4). The cases of complete commissurotomy in these other series either have not been well described in the literature, or often have extensive presurgical brain damage (E. Zaidel, Chapter 6). Thus, much of our knowledge of the full commissurotomy syndrome in humans does, in fact, come from a relatively few patients.

It is also true that these individuals did not have normal brains to begin with. They all suffered from epileptic seizures, which in some cases began early in their lives, thus raising the possibility that their brains had undergone some compensatory reorganization prior to surgery. The surgery itself can produce extracallosal damage, a possibility that has complicated interpretation of some of the more generalized effects of commissurotomy such as those seen in memory (D. Zaidel, Chapter 7). Thus, the pattern of results in these patients might not be representative of what normal adults would show if they underwent a commissurotomy. However, it should be remembered that the human commissurotomy results are not our sole source of information about the functions of the commissures. There is a large literature on the behavioral effects that various split-brain procedures have on animals with no pre-existing brain damage (Berlucchi, Chapter 2). Since the pattern of deficits in interhemispheric transfer and integration following commissurotomy in animals is very similar to that found in humans, the animal work provides strong evidence that the human commissurotomy results are, in fact, useful for investigating normal brain function. Animal studies cannot, of course, corroborate the hemispheric specialization findings in commissurotomized humans. However, here too, the commissurotomy results do not stand alone. Studies on hemispherectomy patients provide converging evidence (E. Zaidel, Chapter 6), as do experiments on normal individuals (Beaumont, 1982) employing techniques such as lateralized tachistoscopic presentation and dichotic listening. While these latter approaches also have their problems, to the extent that studies on normals and hemispherectomy patients come to the same conclusions about hemispheric specialization as do the commissurotomy studies, our confidence in the commissurotomy findings is strengthened.

Finally, despite over thirty years of intense research on the neocortical commissures, our knowledge of these massive fiber tracts is still incomplete, as is evident from the chapters in this section. For example, given the apparent topographic organization of the callosum, why is it possible to sever the vast majority of the callosal fibers and still see so little of the syndrome found with a complete commissurotomy (Gordon, Chapter 4)? What are we missing? The failure of research to demonstrate dramatic behavioral symptoms after cutting the anterior two-thirds of the callosum may be due to the same reason that early studies did not find any effect at all from a total commissurotomy. That is, we are not testing the right thing in the right way. Much of the frontal lobe was once considered 'silent' because no obvious sensory, motor or cognitive problems followed lesions to this cortex. Now it is clear that these areas play a crucial role in behavior. Perhaps the same is true of the anterior part of the callosum. To date, much of the research has concentrated on the commissures' obvious use in interhemispheric transfer and integration of sensory and motor information. However, a number of the chapters in this section suggest that the functions of the commissures are far broader than this. Perhaps after another thirty years of research, interhemispheric transfer will be viewed as a relatively minor function of the commissures, in comparison to their importance for regulating attention, memory and even the normal development of cortical organization (Cook, 1986; Levy, 1985; D. Zaidel, Chapter 7).

References

Akelaitis AJ: A study of gnosis, praxis, and language following section of the corpus callosum and anterior commissure. *J. Neurosurg.: 1,* 94 – 102, 1944.

Beaumont JC: *Divided Visual Field Studies of Cerebral Organisation.* London: Acadamic Press, 1982.

Bogen JE: The Callosal Syndromes. In Heilman KM, Valenstein R (Editors), *Clinical Neuropsychology,* 2nd edition. New York: Oxford University Press, Ch. 11, pp. 295 – 338, 1985.

Cook ND: *The Brain Code.* London: Methuen & Co., 1986.

David AS: The split-brain syndrome. *Br. J. Psychiatry: 154,* 422 – 425, 1989.

Eccles JC: Brain, speech and consciousness. *Naturwissenschaften: 60,* 167 – 176, 1973.

Edwards B: *Drawing on the Right Side of the Brain.* Los Angeles: JP Tarcher, 1979.

Gazzaniga MS: Right hemisphere language following brain bisection: a 20-year perspective. *Am. Psychol: 38,* 525 – 537, 1983.

Harris LJ: Teaching the right brain: historical perspective on a contemporary educational fad. In Best CT (Editor), *Hemispheric Function and Collaboration in the Child.* Orlando: Academic Press, Ch. 8, pp. 231 – 274, 1985.

Levy J: Interhemispheric collaboration: single mindedness in the asymmetric brain. In Best CT (Editor), *Hemispheric Function and Collaboration in the Child.* Orlando: Academic Press, Ch. 2, pp. 11 – 31, 1985.

Myers JJ: Right hemisphere language: science or fiction. *Am. Psychol.: 39,* 315 – 320, 1984.

Nebes RD: Hemispheric specialization in commissurotomized man. *Psychol. Bull.: 81,* 1 – 14, 1974.

Sergent J: Subcortical coordination of hemispheric activity in commissurotomized patients. *Brain: 109,* 357 – 369, 1986.

Sergent J: A new look at the human split brain. *Brain: 110,* 1375 – 1392, 1987.

Sperry RW: Consciousness, personal identity and the divided brain. In Benson DF, Zaidel E (Editors), *The Dual Brain.* New York: Guilford Press, pp. 11 – 26, 1985.

Sperry RW, Zaidel E, Zaidel D: Self-recognition and social awareness in the deconnected hemisphere. *Neuropsychologia: 17,* 153 – 166, 1979.

Whitaker HA, Ojemann GA: Lateralization of higher cortical functions: a critique. *Ann. N. Y. Acad. Sci.: 299,* 459 – 473, 1977.

Zaidel E: Academic implications of dual-brain theory. In Benson DF, Zaidel E (Editors), *The Dual Brain.* New York: Guilford Press, pp. 393 – 397, 1985.

© 1990 Elsevier Science Publishers B.V. (Biomedical Division)
Handbook of Neuropsychology, Vol. 4
F. Boller and J. Grafman (Eds)

CHAPTER 2

Commissurotomy studies in animals

Giovanni Berlucchi

Istituto di Fisiologia Umana, Facoltà di Medicina e Chirurgia, Università di Verona, Italy

Introduction

Studies of the effects of sectioning the cerebral commissures in animals are important for neuropsychology on two counts. First, they can afford fundamental clues for understanding the functional significance of a major class of connections of the brain for psychological and behavioral activities in animals as well as in man. Second, animal models of experimental epilepsy based on commissurotomy can aid in the analysis of the pathophysiological mechanisms of the interhemispheric spread and generalization of abnormal neuronal discharges. As a consequence, such models have provided a rationale for employing commissurotomy in the treatment of select clinical cases of epilepsy, a category of neurological disorders which have a considerable effect on psychic functioning in man. Besides being therapeutically effective in most cases, this surgical approach has allowed the comparison and contrasting of the findings from commissurotomized animals with corresponding neuropsychological evidence from similarly commissurotomized people. Such comparative analyses have far-reaching implications not only for the clarification of several specific aspects of commissural function and hemispheric interaction, but also for a more complete view of the overall neural organization underlying complex behavior and consciousness.

Since this chapter deals chiefly with the behavioral and gross physiological effects of commissural sections in animals, a detailed description of the anatomy and specific functional properties of the commissures is beyond its scope. Commissurotomy has of course been very useful in anatomy for tracing the origin and termination of commissural fibers based on retrograde and anterograde degeneration, but neuronal labeling techniques have now made this approach largely dispensable. Extensive information about the neuronal organization of interhemispheric pathways can be found in several recent reviews (e.g. Berlucchi, 1981; Elberger, 1982; Innocenti, 1986; Manzoni et al., 1989), as well as in the books written or edited by Harnad et al. (1977), Gazzaniga and Ledoux (1978), Steele Russell et al. (1979), Reeves (1985), Lepore et al. (1986b) and Trevarthen (1989). The following section has the limited aims of defining the basic anatomic terms and stating some neurophysiological concepts which can help understand behavioral and physiological commissurotomy experiments.

Further anatomo-physiological notions will be presented in subsequent sections whenever they are relevant for the interpretation of specific clinical deficits of commissurotomized animals.

Anatomy and basic organization of commissural pathways

At all levels of the central nervous system, from forebrain to spinal cord, there are compact systems of fibers which cross the midline for connecting corresponding or functionally matched structures of the two sides. These bundles of fibers are called commissures. For present purposes consideration will be limited to the encephalic commissures, and especially to the forebrain commissures, which include the corpus callosum, the anterior commissure and the hippocampal commissure. The most massive and physiologically important of these commissures, the corpus callosum, is the commissure of the neocortex. It contains millions of myelinated and unmyelinated fibers of different sizes (Swadlow, 1985) which originate from a relatively tiny population of cortical neurons. Various facets of its main anatomical features will be dealt with in this and following sections.

The much smaller anterior commissure is the commissure of the paleocortex, the amygdalae and the olfactory bulbs, but it also contains fibers of neocortical origin. The neocortical component of the anterior commissure varies considerably from one mammalian species to another (Van Alphen, 1969; Doty and Negrao, 1973; Jouandet and Gazzaniga, 1979; Jouandet, 1982; Jouandet and Hartenstein, 1983; Jouandet et al., 1984, 1986). In mammals devoid of a corpus callosum, such as the monotremes and the marsupials, all interhemispheric connections of the neocortex run in the anterior commissure (Ebner, 1967; Heath and Jones, 1971; Granger et al., 1986). In monkeys, neocortical fibers of the anterior commissure originate from and terminate in relatively ample portions of the frontal and temporal lobes (Gazzaniga and Jouandet, 1979; Jouandet et al., 1984), and their terminals are adjacent to, but probably do not overlap with, those of callosal afferents to the same territories. In carnivores and rodents the neocortical contribution to the anterior commissure is comparatively more limited (Van Alphen, 1969; Jouandet, 1982; Jouandet and Hartenstein, 1983; Jouandet et al., 1984, 1986).

The hippocampal commissure is a predominantly archicortical commissure linking the hippocampal formations and related peri- and parahippocampal structures of the two sides (Voneida et al., 1981; Demeter et al., 1985). Other commissural connections are constituted by a relatively small number of fibers which are neither corticofugal nor corticopetal and serve to link subcortical centers on the two sides of the telencephalon (basal ganglia), diencephalon (thalamic, subthalamic and hypothalamic nuclei) and mesencephalon (pretectum and tectum). These subcortical commissures, called interthalamic commissure, supraoptic commissures, habenular commissure, posterior commissure and intertectal commissure, have not been studied in commissurotomy experiments as intensely as the forebrain commissures.

The forebrain commissures are connection systems endowed with a remarkable anatomical precision and highly differentiated functional actions. Genetic and experiential factors act together in ensuring the maturation of the commissural systems and in establishing their definitive pattern of organization (Innocenti, 1986), and the commissural connections can in turn play a role in the developmental course of non-commissural systems (Elberger, 1982, 1986). In each commissural system the constituent fibers are arranged in an orderly topographic manner which is just one aspect of their overall connection specificity (Pandya and Seltzer, 1986; Jouandet et al., 1986; Nakamura and Kanaseki, 1989). Histological, neurochemical and physiological criteria suggest that all neurons projecting to the corpus callosum have a direct synaptic facilitatory action on their immediate neuronal targets in the opposite hemisphere (Naito et al., 1970; Toyama et al., 1974; Innocenti, 1986; Voigt et al., 1988; Barbaresi et al., 1987; Conti et al., 1988), but powerful indirect inhibitions of cortical neurons by a commissural input can be effected by local interneurons directly activated by this input (Naito et al., 1970; Toyama et al., 1974; Innocenti, 1986). Highly organized spatial patterns of combined and concurrent excitatory and inhibitory effects on discrete target zones, rather than massive inhibitions or facilitations of entire cortical areas, are most probably the systematic physiological consequence of selective activations of commissural inputs (Asanuma and Okuda, 1962). The possibility that the commissural systems are involved in widespread or wholesale facilitatory or inhibitory actions, similar to those of the diffuse ascending brainstem pathways, does not seem realistic (Berlucchi et al., 1986), but if such a generic modulatory role is indeed a component of commissural function it must be minor compared to the precisely differentiated cross-midline transmission of sensory, motor and higher-order information.

Several principles have been proposed to account for the general plan of organization of the commissural connections. The homotopic principle, stating that commissural fibers interconnect homologous corresponding regions of the two sides in a reciprocal fashion, is supported by much histological and electrophysiological evidence. Yet it cannot be accepted in its most restrictive formulation, first because in all or most commissural systems there also exist numerous fibers linking definitely heterotopic sites, and second because even within a very precise homotopic arrangement the connections are not really reciprocal at the cellular level. This is due to the fact that commissural fibers often terminate in cortical layers different from those containing commissural projecting neurons, and even when they do they do not as a rule contact commissural neurons (Berlucchi, 1981; Innocenti, 1986).

According to the heterolateral principle, originally proposed by Mettler (1935), a cortical area is commissurally connected not only with its symmetrical opposite counterpart, but also with as many contralateral cortical areas as it is connected with in the ipsilateral hemisphere. Although the patterns of intra- and interhemispheric connections do indeed share many hodological features, the homolateral principle is only partially supported by the evidence insofar as intrahemispheric cortico-cortical connections are directed to more numerous and diffuse targets compared to interhemispheric connections (Innocenti, 1986).

Flechsig's general theory of the cortex (1989) has been used to account for the very uneven cortical distribution of commissural neurons and terminals, suggesting that commissural connections are restricted to association areas (Geschwind, 1965). However, while it is true that commissural connections seem to avoid extensive portions of primary sensory and motor cortex, all cytoarchitectural divisions of the cortex are now known to give rise to and receive interhemispheric projections in at least some of their subareas.

Sperry's principle of supplemental complementarity (1962) envisages the pattern of organization of the commissural connections as a means by which the activity of each cerebral hemisphere is supplemented in an orderly manner with different and complementary information about concurrent activities in the other hemisphere. The organization of the afferent and efferent neural projections is such that each cerebral hemisphere is in receipt of information from the opposite half of the sensory spaces and in control of the contralateral half of the musculature. The commissures provide the anatomical and functional continuity between the sensory and motor half maps on the two sides of the midline by establishing discrete connections between appropriate neuronal populations of the two hemispheres. For example, the representation of each hand in the contralateral hemisphere via specific afferent pathways can be supplemented and complemented at some stage of cortical processing by a callosally transmitted representation of the other hand. This arrangement is both supplementary, because the representations of the two hands add to one another in each hemisphere, and complementary, because this addition can provide a unitary substrate for the control of bimanual movements and active touch.

At the single-neuron level the principle of supplemental complementarity is best illustrated by the presence of neurons with homogeneous bilateral receptive fields in the visual system of cats (Berlucchi and Rizzolatti, 1968; Berlucchi et al., 1986, 1987; Berlucchi and Antonini, 1989) and monkeys (Gross and Mishkin, 1977). Such bilateral receptive fields extend continuously across the vertical midline of the general visual field, and are built up by a precise combination between an intrahemispheric input from the contralateral half field and an interhemispheric input from the ipsilateral half field. After severing the corpus callosum these receptive fields lose their portion lying in the ipsilateral visual field and become purely contralateral. As first proposed by Whitteridge (1965), the callosal connections which contribute to building up bilateral receptive fields in visual cortical areas must be limited to neurons 'looking at' visual field regions abutting or including the central vertical meridian. Such limitation is needed both for the continuity of the bilateral receptive fields and for the unification of the maps of the right and left visual hemifields which belong in different hemispheres (Berlucchi et al., 1986, 1987; Berlucchi and Antonini, 1989).

It has been argued that the commissural connections of the visual cortex obey the vertical midline rule because of developmental constraints which control the convergence of intra- and interhemispheric visual inputs on single neurons (Berlucchi, 1981). The developing brain is characterized by an excess of callosal fibers which is eliminated during a critical postnatal period (Innocenti, 1986). The elimination is assumed to be based on the acceptance by cortical neurons of callosal afferents transmitting visual information which is congruous and synchronous with that conveyed by the intrahemispheric afferents to the same neurons, and on the rejection of callosal afferents which do not undergo such coactivation. In a normal visual environment coactivation is highly probable for intra- and interhemispheric inputs from continuous visual field regions matched at the vertical meridian, and highly unlikely for intra- and interhemispheric inputs from totally disparate visual field regions. Visual information from visual field regions away from the vertical meridian can, however, be transmitted interhemispherically by callosal neurons with wide receptive fields extending from the meridian to the far visual periphery (Berlucchi et al., 1986, 1987; Berlucchi and Antonini, 1989).

The principle of supplemental complementarity and the vertical meridian rule can be shown to apply to the somatosensory system as well (Shanks et al., 1985; Lepore et al., 1986a; Ledoux et al., 1987; Manzoni et al., 1989), but there are some important differences with the visual system. For example, while in many somesthesic areas callosal connections conform to the vertical midline rule by being much more prominent in the representations of the axial parts of the body, in the second somatosensory area SII a region clearly unrelated to the midline such as the hand representation is also provided with dense callosal connections. This, however, in no way contradicts the supplemental complementarity principle and the postulated coactivation mechanism, insofar as the two hands are often submitted to synchronous and congruous somesthetic stimulation as they cooperate in bimanual stereognosis (Manzoni et al., 1984).

The supplemental complementarity principle, the vertical midline rule and the coactivation mechanism can probably also account for the pattern of callosal connections between cortical regions subserving other sensory modalities as well as between motor areas, but the available relevant evidence is very scanty. It is important to emphasize that supplemental complementarity is fully compatible with the proven existence of both homotopic and heterotopic commissural connections, inasmuch as the coactivation mechanism can link up both symmetric and non-symmetric homofunctional cortical sites of the two hemispheres.

It is perhaps naive, though not unreasonable, to state that the anatomical and physiological features of the forebrain commissures must be such as to allow the monitoring of information across the midline at all stages of cortical processing (Berlucchi, 1981; Hamilton, 1982; Innocenti, 1986). But after granting that learning processess, memory engrams, ideas, thoughts, emotions and motivations can be communicated between the hemispheres via the commissures along with elementary sensory signals and motor commands, it must be admitted that the analysis of the neuronal codes used in such interhemispheric exchanges of highly digested information is fraught with enormous conceptual and technical difficulties. Perhaps breaking the 'callosal code' (Gazzaniga, 1970) will help in breaking the complete 'brain code' (Cook, 1986), yet advances in the understanding of the mechanisms of commissural transmission of information are more likely to follow than precede advances in the knowledge of the general cerebral bases of psychological functions. At present, behavioral commissurotomy studies are still a tool of choice for inferring the functional significance of interhemispheric interaction and transfer and for guiding anatomical and physiological analyses of the underlying mechanisms.

Behavioral and physiological effects of commissurotomy in animals

Early assessments of the consequences of cutting the cerebral commissures in animals (reviews in Mingazzini, 1922; Bremer et al., 1956) failed in general to demonstrate specific behavioral deficits from hemisphere disconnection because the testing methods were usually inadequate and/or the symptomatology was contaminated by the effects of unintended extracommissural brain damage. It was only when the effects of commissurotomy began to be examined in relation to the capacity for bilateral sensory-sensory or sensory-motor integration, perceptual equivalence and transfer of training that selective impairments in interhemispheric integration and communication became evident.

Bilateral sensory-sensory integration, perceptual equivalence and transfer of training are special instances of stimulus generalization and sensory equipotentiality. These general terms allude to the fact that objects and images maintain their identity over space and time even when they are perceived through entirely different sensory channels, both within and across sensory modalities. As a special case of this integration, sensory inputs issuing from the two halves of the visual field or from receptors on opposite sides of the body can normally be compared, combined and fused into single percepts. Physiologically the extrapolation of the singleness and identity of an object from an array of heterogeneous and varying sensory signals is likely to be based on the convergence of all possible inputs generated by the object onto a functionally unitary brain mechanism which can integrate such inputs and ascribe them to a common external source. Inputs originating from opposite sides of the body or of the external space are usually conveyed by the largely lateralized sensory pathways to different hemispheres, so that as a rule their cross-midline integration occurs by an interhemispheric cooperation. In other words, the unitary cerebral substrate for representing an object projected in part to one hemisphere and in part to the other hemisphere must include a commissural component (Gross and Mishkin, 1977; Hamilton, 1982; Berlucchi and Marzi, 1982; Berlucchi and Antonini, 1989). A similar interhemispheric cooperation is bound to be required in bilateral sensory-motor integration, when a motor activity controlled by one hemisphere must be emitted to a sensory stimulus projected to the other hemisphere, and in bilateral motor coordination. Studies of the effects of commissurotomy on bilateral sensory-sensory, sensory-motor integration or motor coordination, perceptual equivalence and transfer of training attempt to demonstrate that the unity of the transhemispheric perceptual/representational mechanism or the cross-midline link between sensory input and motor output is indeed disrupted by sectioning the critical commissural component.

The experimental questions asked in these studies are rather direct. After an animal has acquired specific reactions or formed specific memories based on sensory inputs restricted to a single cerebral hemisphere, can those reactions or memories be retrieved when the same inputs are directed to the other hemisphere? Can an animal compare and contrast identical or different sensory signals simultaneously or successively delivered to different hemispheres, or cross-integrate motor reactions of the two sides, or couple motion on one side with sensory inputs from the other side? Can interhemispheric sensory-sensory, sensory-motor and motor integration, transfer and equivalence, if present, be selectively interfered with by sectioning appropriate components of the commissural systems? Bykov and Speranski's report (1924; see also Bykoff, 1924) that callosotomy rendered dogs incapable of transferring between flanks a conditioned alimentary response to a tactile stimulus made a good start toward providing affirmative answers to at least some of these questions. However, systematic studies on commissurotomy and interhemispheric communication were spawned only much later by the seminal experiments of Myers and Sperry (1953) and Myers (1955, 1956) on interocular transfer in the cat. These studies profitted from the superior opportunity offered by the visual modality compared to the other modalities for an absolute restriction of the relevant afferent inputs to a single hemisphere. The following account will therefore focus on experiments on interhemispheric interaction in vision.

Interhemispheric interactions in vision

The prototypic experiment is based on two facts: (1) in mammals with partially crossed optic pathways each retina projects to both cerebral hemispheres, and (2) visual pattern discriminations learned with one eye transfer successfully to the other eye. A midline section of the optic chiasm which interrupts all crossed fibers, thus leaving each retina connected solely to the ipsilateral hemisphere via the intact uncrossed fibers, does not interfere with interocular transfer (Myers, 1955). Since in these 'split-chiasm' animals inputs from different eyes go to different hemispheres, the convergence of the two monocular inputs onto a common substrate for interocular transfer must, as argued above, be ensured by interhemispheric connections. The above hypothesis was first proven, and the crucial interhemispheric connection indentified, by demonstrating that in split-chiasm cats with an additional sectioning of the corpus callosum ('split-brain' cats) interocular transfer failed (Myers, 1956), and discriminations acquired through one eye had to be completely relearned through the other eye (Sperry et al., 1956). Sectioning the corpus callosum in cats with an intact optic chiasm does not interfere with interocular transfer because the two monocular inputs can amply converge in each hemisphere owing to the existence of both crossed and uncrossed projections from each retina.

The callosal fibers mediating interocular transfer in the split-chiasm cat appear to be rather specific because a transection of the anterior two-thirds of the callosum leaves transfer unaffected whereas a selective section of the posterior third, including the splenium, causes the same effect as a complete callosal section, that is abolition of transfer (Myers, 1959). The posterior portions of the cat corpus callosum contain the interhemispheric connections of most if not all visual cortical areas (Jouandet et al., 1986; Nakamura and Kanaseki, 1989).

Since interocular transfer of learned responses can be observed in virtually all classes of vertebrates (Sperry, 1961; Cuénod, 1972; Doty and Negrao, 1973), experiments similar to those first performed in the cat were repeated in several other species, generally with comparable results. The presence of interocular transfer of visual pattern dicriminations in split-chiasm non-human primates, as well as its abolition by appropriate commissurotomy, were first demonstrated by Downer (1959, 1962) and Sperry (1961) using macaques, and by Black and Myers (1964) using chimpanzees. In contrast to the cat, both splenium and anterior commissure must be transected in these primates to obtain a complete suppression of interocular transfer (Black and Myers, 1964; Noble, 1968; Sullivan and Hamilton, 1973a,b; Doty and Negrao, 1973; Butler, 1979). The reason for this is that the commissural connections of all visual cortical areas run in the posterior corpus callosum in the cat, whereas in non-human primates visual areas in the inferior temporal lobes of the two sides are connected across the midline by fibers of both splenium and anterior commissure (Doty and Negrao, 1973; Zeki, 1973; Gross and Mishkin,

1977; Jouandet and Gazzaniga, 1979; Hamilton, 1982). Areas in the inferior temporal cortex are thought to be critical for object vision in primates (Gross and Mishkin, 1977; Mishkin, 1979), and it is not suprising that their commissural connections can have an important role in perceptual constancy across visual hemifields (Seacord et al., 1977; see below). Section of the splenium and anterior commissure has also been shown to interfere with the ability of monkeys with intact optic pathways to transfer learned visually guided responses from one visual hemifield to the other (Eacott and Gaffan, 1989).

Much less evidence is available for assessing the participation of discrete commissural pathways in the interhemispheric transfer of specific visual information in mammals lower than carnivores. Although surgical splitting of the chiasm has been performed successfully in rats (Cowey and Franzini, 1979) and rabbits (Steele-Russell et al., 1987), interocular transfer of visual discriminations has not been tested in these split-chiasm preparations, and therefore there are no data to be directly compared with the above findings in split-chiasm cats and monkeys. Contrasting results have been obtained in studies of the effect of callosotomy on interocular transfer of visual discriminations in rats with intact optic pathways, insofar as transfer has been found to be significantly impaired in some experiments (Sheridan, 1965; Levinson and Sheridan, 1969; Steele Russell and Safferstone, 1973) but not in others (Buresova and Bures, 1971; Cowey and Parkinson, 1973; Mohn and Russell, 1981). The discrepancy between results can be accounted for by variations in the number and functional significance of uncrossed optic fibers between albino and pigmented animals, the nearly complete absence of overlap between the two monocular visual fields in animals with laterally implanted eyes, and other contextual conditions which may affect performance on tests of interocular transfer (Cowey and Parkinson, 1973; Sheridan et al., 1980; Mohn and Russell, 1981; Mohn, 1984). All these factors have no direct bearing on the interpretation of commissurotomy effects for the understanding of commissural function, and a reasonable inference from the complex of the results is that, similar to the case in higher mammals, the posterior corpus callosum is the exclusive or predominant path for transferring highly specific visual information between the hemispheres of rodents (Mohn and Russell, 1981). The successful interocular transfer of brightness and pattern discriminations found in split-chiasm brush-tailed opossums is most likely to depend on the anterior commissure, which ensures the interhemispheric connectivity of the neocortex in the acallosal marsupials (Robinson, 1982). However, this hypothesis has not been crucially tested by cutting both optic chiasm and anterior commissure.

Experiments on interhemispheric transfer in fish and birds, reviewed by Cuénod (1972), Doty and Negrao (1973), Savage (1979) and Yeo (1979), take advantage of the fact that the optic pathways of these animals are completely crossed, so that the limitation of the visual input to a single hemisphere is a natural consequence of monocular stimulation. Interocular transfer of monocularly learned visual discriminations may not be present in fish and birds under all testing conditions (e.g. McCleary, 1960; Goodale and Graves, 1982; Gaston, 1983); when present, it must depend on an interhemispheric transfer via commissures that are functionally equivalent to the mammalian corpus callosum. The dorsal supraoptic decussation has been implied as the crucial pathway for visual interhemispheric transfer in birds (see e.g. Cuénod, 1972; Goodale, 1985), whereas the hypothalamic minor and horizontal commissures and the posterior commissure may constitute separate routes for interhemispheric transfer of, respectively, color and brightness, orientation, and shape information in fish (Hemsley and Savage, 1987). The tectal commissure has generally been regarded as uninvolved in interhemispheric visual transfer in fish (Ingle and Campbell, 1977), but other work suggests that it may be important for certain aspects of visual transfer in fish (Mark, 1966; Mark et al., 1973) as well as birds (Hamassaki and Britto, 1987).

With respect to the neuronal mechanisms, the supraoptic commissure may subserve interocular transfer in the pigeon because it generates binocular units in the visual Wulst, an avian counterpart of the mammalian visual cortex, just as the corpus callosum can sustain binocular interactions in visual cortical areas of split-chiasm mammals (Goodale, 1985). However, a bilateral lesion of the visual Wulst is not equivalent to a section of the supraoptic commissure, since it is compatible with a successful interocular transfer of visual discriminations (Francesconi et al., 1982). Perhaps the supraoptic commissure mediates binocular interactions not only in the visual Wulst, but also in other visual centers such as the superior colliculus.

Do subcortical commissures contribute to interhemispheric transfer of visual discriminations in mammals? The old idea that the recognition of patterned stimuli requires the cortex whereas the simple perception of the intensity of a sensory stimulus relies on subcortical substrates has been tested by examining interhemispheric transfer of different classes of visual discriminations. Earlier reports that the interocular transfer of brightness discriminations (Meikle and Sechzer, 1960) as well as the interocular comparison of brightnesses (Robinson and Voneida, 1964) persist in split-chiasm cats after transection of the corpus callosum, and their abolition requires an additional section of non-callosal commissures (Meikle, 1964; Robinson and Voneida, 1964), must be reconsidered on the basis of more recent experiments by Peck et al. (1979). These experiments point to the splenium of the corpus callosum as the essential pathway for interhemispheric transfer of not only pattern discriminations but also brightness and movement discriminations, and suggest that the previously reported persistence of the capacity for interhemispheric integration of brightness information in split-chiasm callosotomized cats might have been artefactual. Conversely, the relative unimportance of the posterior and intertectal commissures for interhemispheric transfer of pattern discriminations in split-chiasm cats is indicated by the high degree of transfer found after sectioning these commissures in the midbrain while leaving the corpus callosum intact (Berlucchi et al., 1987b).

In keeping with the above experiments on cats, many studies in macaques have implicated the corpus callosum as the main, and perhaps the only, route for interhemispheric transfer of brightness, color and movement discriminations (Downer, 1962; Hamilton and Gazzaniga, 1964; Hamilton et. al., 1968; Hamilton and Lund, 1970). The apparent survival of interocular transfer of brightness discriminations described by Trevarthen (1962) in split-brain monkeys was probably not due to a subcortical interhemispheric transmission of specific information, and is now attributed by Trevarthen himself (1987) to a relatively unspecific orientational and motivational modulation of bilateral cortical activities by undivided brainstem systems. The observation of a successful interocular transfer of brightness and color discriminations in split-chiasm, callosotomized chimpanzees (Black and Myers, 1968) still stands as the only evidence for an extracallosal interhemispheric transfer of non-spatial visual information in learning tasks in subhuman primates.

The hypothesis that under special training conditions some non-callosal, especially subcortical, commissures may be recruited for the interhemispheric transfer of at least some types of visual discrimination has been tested repeatedly. Sechzer (1964) found that interhemispheric transfer of the discrimination of line orientation, which is typically absent in split-chiasm cats trained with food reward, became successful if the reinforcement for learning and transfer was changed to shock-avoidance. An instrumentally conditioned limb flexion for avoiding a shock signaled by an intermittent light stimulus was similarly reported to transfer between the hemispheres of split-brain cats; this interhemispheric transfer was diminished but not abolished by an additional section of the commissure of the superior colliculi (Voneida, 1963). In contrast, no interhemispheric transfer was possible in split-brain cats when the emission of the shock-avoiding limb flexion required the discrimination between two different frequencies of intermittent light stimulation (Majkowski, 1967). Recent attempts to assess the role of subcortical commissures in the interhemispheric transfer of visuomotor responses for shock avoidance have met with failure mainly because of the erratic performance of cats trained with this procedure (Lepore et al., 1985). Some retention of learning with the second eye has been observed on tests of interocular transfer of pattern discriminations in split-brain cats with forebrain and thalamic commissurotomies which had to jump on, rather than walk toward, the discriminanda (Lepore et al., 1985). This low-degree capacity for interhemispheric transfer has been attributed to task-dependent motivational factors which encourage the use of secondary cues helping in the discrimination. Minor residual capacities for interhemispheric transfer that probably rely on subcortical commissures have also been reported in macaques (Tieman and Hamilton, 1973) and cats (Berlucchi et al., 1978a) submitted to an extensive practice with similar transfer tests before sectioning the cortical commissures. Extensive practice with transfer tests (Berlucchi et al., 1978a) and special training procedures employed during initial acquisition (e.g. Mascetti and Mancilla, 1984) have proved apt to facilitate subsequent transfers. It seems possible that practice may also induce a reorganization of the mechanisms for transfer in the presence of intact neocortical commissures, thereby allowing the maintenance of some capacity for transfer after severing the latter commissures.

The overwhelming majority of experiments on visual interhemispheric transfer have tested whether the forebrain commissures allow a cerebral hemisphere to perform a visual discrimination learned through an optic input restricted to the other hemisphere. A few other experiments have examined whether and which of the forebrain commissures are involved in the interhemispheric transfer of responses that depend on forms of learning other than the simple acquisition of visual discriminations. In split-chiasm monkeys which had 'learned to learn' several types of visual discrimination with the optic input restricted to one hemisphere, such a learning set appeared to be available to the other hemisphere only if the anterior portion of the corpus callosum was intact (Noble, 1973). Interhemispheric transfer was thus based on callosal information different from that transmitted by the posterior callosum in the interhemispheric transfer of simple visual discriminations. Mascetti et al. (1981) and Mascetti and Arriagada (1988) found that split-chiasm, but not split-brain, cats were capable of transferring between the eyes a set for reversal learning and an extinction response on visual discriminations, showing that the corpus callosum was essential for these types of transfer, as much as for the transfer of discrimination acquisition. Using a delayed matching-to-sample task and a running recognition task Doty et al. (1988) checked whether split-chiasm monkeys could recognize with one eye photographic slides after a single exposure to their other eye. These tasks differ from the usual discrimination tasks, which require the repeated presentation of the discriminanda, because they are intended to test for memory for 'events' rather than for memory for habits, a distinction now deemed very important for differentiating neural systems subserving memory in both man (Squire, 1987) and animals (Mishkin and Appenzeller, 1987). Nonetheless the essential commissural pathways for interhemispheric transfer on delayed recognition tasks proved to be the same as those involved in the interhemispheric transfer of discrimination habits, i.e. the anterior commissure and the splenium of the corpus callosum (Doty et al., 1988).

The above findings raise the problem of what and how many types of information are communicated by the commissures in experiments on interhemispheric transfer. Consider the successful interocular transfer of monocularly learned discriminations in the split-chiasm cats of the prototypic experiments of Myers (1955), or the successful monocular recognition of complex stimuli seen only once with the other eye in the split-chiasm monkeys of the experiment by Doty et al. (1988). The outstanding question is: During the acquisition period does the hemisphere connected to the exposed eye send an immediate duplicate of the visual input to the other hemisphere via the appropriate commissural connections, so that learning based on such information proceeds in parallel on both sides of the brain and each hemisphere forms its own memory trace or engram? Or is the engram laid down solely in the directly stimulated hemisphere, and made available through the commissures to the other hemisphere upon testing for interocular transfer, when the visual input is shifted to the other eye? In spite of more than three decades of ingenious theorizing and experimentation, there is no single definite answer to this question. Successful interocular transfer was found in some experiments in which commissurotomy was performed upon completion of the initial acquisition but before the test for interocular transfer, a finding compatible with the hypothesis of bilateral engrams and incompatible with the assumption of a transcommissural utilization of a unilateral engram (Myers, 1962, 1965; Gazzaniga, 1966; Butler, 1968; Sullivan and Hamilton, 1973b; Hamilton, 1977; Lepore et al., 1982). On the other hand there are also available several commissurotomy results which suggest a lateralization of memory to the hemisphere receiving the input and a subsequent commissural 'read-out' and/or 'write-in' of such unilateral engrams to the other hemisphere (Myers and Sperry, 1958; Myers, 1962; Gazzaniga, 1966; Doty and Negrao, 1973; Bures et al., 1988).

Evidence for a transcommissural utilization of unilateral engrams has been sought in elegant experiments by Doty et al. (1973, 1977). They cut the anterior commissure and the corpus callosum except the splenium in monkeys, and put a ligature around the intact splenium. The monkeys were then trained to press a lever in response to electrical stimulation of the striate visual cortex in one hemisphere. After completion of learning it was shown that a comparable stimulation of the opposite striate cortex elicited the same conditioned response. If, however, the ligature around the splenium was pulled, thus completing the callosal section, stimulation of the original cortical site could still produce the response, while contralateral stimulation could not, suggesting that the engram was confined to the originally stimulated hemisphere and was made continuously available to the other hemisphere through the splenium. The existence of bilateral engrams was instead indicated by similar experiments on completely callosotomized monkeys with an intact anterior commissure, in which pulling the ligature around the latter commissure did not prevent the contralateral generalization of the conditioned response after conditioning with unilateral electrical stimulation of the striate cortex. The conclusion that hemispheric interactions are associated with unilateral engrams when mediated by the splenium and with bilateral engrams when mediated by the anterior commissure (Doty et al., 1973, 1977) has been questioned by Hamilton (1977) and Bures et al. (1988) on account of the possible contaminating effects of an acute traumatic commissurotomy and the artificial nature of the learning situation.

On balance, it appears that the ability of the commissures to establish concurrent bilateral memories during learning has been proven beyond question, whereas the possibility of a commissural access by one hemisphere to memories fully lateralized to the other hemisphere has not been so well established in animals with surgical commissurotomies (see discussion in Hamilton, 1982). The delayed commissural transfer of fully lateralized engrams can perhaps be studied best in the reversible split-brain experimental system, which is obtained by temporarily inactivating one hemisphere with a chemical spreading depression. Although this system is a potentially viable alternative to the surgically split-brain animal for investigating various aspects of hemispheric interaction (Buresova and Bures, 1969; Bures et al., 1988), several problems of interpretation still exist, and the results are not easily amenable to direct neurophysiological analysis of the commissures involved in transfer.

Perhaps the commissural mechanisms of interhemispheric transfer of visual discrimination can be better understood within the framework of a general model of visual perception and memory. A currently popular model proposes that visual information is processed sequentially by hierarchies of cortical areas before being eventually relayed to limbic and motor structures which mediate learning and behavioral output (e.g. Mishkin, 1972, 1982; Mishkin and Appenzeller, 1987). In some experimental conditions callosal connections are shown to be essential for enabling visual information to progress from early stages in the cortical hierarchy to successive stages. For example, by isolating visual cortical areas in one hemisphere of the cat by sectioning all cortico-cortical intrahemispheric connections, Sperry et al. (1960) showed that this cortical island could still contribute to visual perception and memory provided its callosal connections with the other hemisphere were left intact. Successful visual control of behavior by the cortical island evidently required communication with the intact subsequent processing stages on the other side. A similar callosal participation in a sequential analysis of visual information has been described by Mishkin (1972, 1979) in the monkey. A removal of the first stage of the cortical hierarchy, the striate visual cortex, in one hemisphere and of the last stage of the hierarchy, the inferotemporal cortex in the other hemisphere, did not interfere with visual perception and memory so long as the corpus callosum was intact. Transection of the corpus callosum disrupted visually guided behavior presumably because visual information from the intact striate cortex could no longer be relayed to the remaining contralateral inferotemporal cortex, and perhaps also to other non-visual cortical areas (Nakamura and Mishkin, 1986).

Gross and Mishkin (1977) have argued that the interhemispheric transfer of visual discriminations in monkeys with intact cortices also requires a cross-midline transmission of visual information to the inferotemporal cortex. Their argument is based on the strong (though incomplete) reduction of interocular transfer in split-chiasm monkeys with bilateral inferotemporal lesions (Seacord et al., 1979) and on the already mentioned presence (pp. 11, 12) in the inferotemporal cortex of neurons that receive visual information from large portions of both halves of the visual field (Gross et al., 1977). The input which these neurons receive from the ipsilateral half field is removed by section of the splenium of the corpus callosum and of the anterior commissure, i.e. by the same commissural disconnection that disrupts behavioral interhemispheric transfer (Gross et al., 1977). Callosal connections between visual cortical areas earlier in the hierarchy, such as for example those between the prestriate cortices (Zeki, 1967, 1977; Hamilton and Vermeire, 1986), can, however, participate in interhemispheric transfer, as indicated by the abovementioned experiments (Mishkin, 1972) with contralateral striate and inferotemporal lesions, in which visual information conveyed across the midline to the remaining inferotemporal cortex obviously could not originate from the contralateral inferotemporal cortex.

The participation of different cortical areas and neuronal populations in interhemispheric transfer in the cat has been investigated with electrophysiological recordings in intact, split-chiasm and split-brain animals as well as in behavioral studies using circumscribed cortical lesions. Following the initial experiment of Berlucchi and Rizzolatti (1968), it has been repeatedly demonstrated that after the splitting of the chiasm and the consequent elimination of the crossed optic fibers, neurons in all known visual cortical areas (Lepore and Guillemot, 1982; Lepore et al., 1986a; Antonini et al., 1983, 1985; Cynader et al., 1981, 1986; Maffei et al., 1986; Ptito et al., 1986; Milleret and Buser, 1987; Berardi et al., 1987) and even in a subcortical center such as the superior colliculus (Antonini et al., 1978, 1979) can still receive visual information from the contralateral eye via specific callosal connections, and combine it with direct information from the ipsilateral eye in accord with the principle of supplemental complementarity (Berlucchi et al., 1986, 1987; see page 12). Responses of neurons in cortical areas 17 and 18 of split-chiasm cats to stimulation of the contralateral eye may be potentiated by a prolonged occlusion of the other eye at an early age (Cynader et al., 1981, 1986) or even in adulthood (Milleret and Buser, 1987), suggesting some kind of competition between the intrahemispheric and interhemispheric visual inputs.

The crucial proof of the callosal mediation of the input from the contralateral eye in split-chiasm cats is provided by the disappearance of that input, but not the input from the ipsilateral eye, after a posterior callosal transection. In addition, a callosal section in cats with intact optic pathways has been shown to abolish response to stimuli from the ipsilateral visual field, but not from the contralateral visual field, in several visual cortical areas (Dow and Dubner, 1971; Marzi et al., 1980, 1982; Lepore and Guillemot, 1982; Berlucchi et al., 1987) as well as in the superior colliculus (Antonini et al., 1979). Although the existence of callosal connections in the early stages of visual cortical processing such as areas 17, 18 and 19 has been proved beyond question (Berlucchi, 1972, 1981; Innocenti, 1986), the region of the visual field from which these connections transmit information is limited to a narrow strip running along the vertical meridian of the visual field (Berlucchi et al., 1967; Hubel and Wiesel, 1967; Shatz, 1977; Lepore and Guillemot, 1982; Antonini et al., 1985; Berlucchi et al., 1987), while behavioral visual interhemispheric transfer is liable to occur over the entire visual field.

Interhemispheric transfer of visual pattern discriminations has been studied in split-chiasm cats with lesions of areas 17 and 18, since such lesions do not abolish learning (Berlucchi, 1972; Berlucchi et al., 1978c; Berlucchi and Sprague, 1981; Berlucchi and Marzi, 1982). No deficits in interhemispheric transfer were found in these animals, and the capacity for transfer was subsequently eliminated by a callosal section; hence it was concluded that such ability depended on callosal connections of areas beyond 17 and 18. Comparable lesion studies attributed an essential role in interhemispheric transfer to a complex of visual cortical areas in the suprasylvian gyri (Berlucchi et al., 1979; Berlucchi and Sprague, 1981; Berlucchi and Marzi, 1982) and perhaps also to the superior colliculus (Berlucchi, 1982). The large bilateral receptive fields of neurons in these regions, whose ipsilateral component is mediated by the corpus callosum, are appropriate for collecting information from large portions of the visual field, in spite of their organization being in accord with the vertical meridian rule, and can thus provide a suitable substrate for behavioral interhemispheric transfer of visual dicriminations (Antonini et al ., 1983; Berlucchi et al., 1986). The callosum-dependent input from each visual hemifield to the ipsilateral superior colliculus (Antonini et al., 1979) can be accounted for by a serial connection between the cortico-cortical callosal pathway and the cortico-tectal pathway, in keeping with theories of cortico-subcortical interactions in visually guided behavior (Thompson, 1965; Sprague et al., 1971) and with a similar serial arrangement between interhemispheric cortico-cortical and intrahemispheric cortico-thalamic fibers in the somatosensory system (Landry et al., 1984).

If the callosal connections of the primary visual cortical areas are not involved in the interhemispheric transfer of visual discriminations, are they perhaps used for more basic visual functions (Pasik and Pasik, 1964; Berlucchi, 1975)? Commissurotomy studies have tested the possible role of these connections in interhemispheric interactions presumably necessary for some aspects of binocular stereopsis, binocular convergence and optokinetic nystagmus.

It is believed that the fundamental mechanism for the binocular perception of depth and appreciation of distance is provided by neurons that code for the horizontal disparity of the right and left monocular images of an object (Bishop, 1981). Object points lying directly behind or in front of the fixation point pose a special problem for binocular stereopsis to the extent that their monocular images are formed on heteronymous halves of the two retinae, i.e. either on both temporal or both nasal hemiretinae. Since the organization of the optic pathways is such that projections from heteronymous hemiretinae are largely directed to different cerebral hemispheres, neurons in each hemisphere that compare images falling on heteronymous hemiretinae must in principle receive both intra- and interhemispheric visual inputs (Blakemore, 1969). The evidence reviewed above proves that there exists an abundance of cortical visual neurons which receive intra- and interhemispheric (callosal) inputs from regions of both visual hemifields matched at the vertical meridian. In principle, binocular stereopsis in the central visual field should be expected to be deficient after a section of the corpus callosum which eliminates the input from the ipsilateral visual field to these neurons. This expectation has been at least partly confirmed by the finding of deficient binocular stereopsis in the vertical meridian region in patients with surgical callosal sections (Mitchell and Blakemore, 1970; Hamilton and Vermeire, 1986; Hamilton et al., 1987; Jeeves, 1989), as well as in patients with callosal agenesis (Jeeves, 1989). However, deficits in the tachistoscopic judgement of distance-in-depth were found over the whole visual field in split-brain and callosum-agenetic patients by Lassonde (1986). On the basis of these results Lassonde (1986) has argued in favor of a general unspecific facilitatory influence of the corpus callosum on stereopsis.

The effects of callosotomy in animals do not generally provide strong support for the hypothesis of a crucial role of the corpus callosum in binocular stereopsis. The threshold for binocular stereoacuity is not affected by a posterior callosal section in monkeys (Cowey, 1982) and cats (Timney et al., 1985), and no significant impairment in the binocular discrimination of random-dot stereograms follows callosotomy in either cat (Lepore et al., 1986c) or monkey (Hamilton and Vermeire, 1986). In contrast, massive deficits in stereoacuity and discrimination of random-dot stereograms are induced by a section of the optic chiasm in both monkey (Hamilton and Vermeire, 1986) and cat (Timney et al., 1985, 1989; Lepore et al., 1986c). It is possible that split-chiasm cats may have some extremely limited residual capacity for binocular stereopsis (Lepore et al., 1986c; Timney et al., 1989) and that this capacity is lost after callosotomy (Lepore et al., 1986c). No residual binocular stereopsis has been found after splitting of the chiasm in monkeys (Hamilton and Vermeire, 1986). The application to the same animals of tests of global and local and of fine and coarse stereopsis (Bishop, 1981), as well as due consideration of the enormous variability in binocular stereopsis in normal humans (Hamilton et al., 1987), will perhaps provide more satisfactory answers to the question of the commissural contribution to binocular stereoperception.

Controversial reports of the effects of a callosal disconnection on electrophysiological binocular interactions in areas 17 and 18 of cats with intact visual pathways have been published. The percentage of binocular neurons at the border between areas 17 and 18 was reported to fall significantly after an ablation of the contralateral corresponding cortical regions in some experiments (Dreher and Cottee, 1975; Blakemore et al., 1983) but not in others (Cynader et al., 1986). On the basis of the effects of unilateral visual cortical removals Gardner and Cynader (1987) have recently reaffirmed the participation of the corpus callosum in the generation of disparity-sensitive neurons in visual cortical areas 17 and 18 of the cat, but not in the generation of binocular interactions as such when the visual pathways are intact. However, the effects on the visual cortex of a removal of the contralateral corresponding areas may not be fully equivalent to section of the corpus callosum. Studies reviewed by Payne (1986) indicate that a callosal section caused a permanent reduction – from about 80% to about 40% – in the percentage of binocular neurons in those portions of areas 17 and 18 which represent the visual field near the vertical meridian. In contrast, Minciacchi and Antonini (1984) and Elberger and Smith (1985) found no effect of a callosal section on binocular interaction in areas 17 and 18 of cats callosotomized as adults, although the latter authors produced a significant reduction in the percentage of binocular neurons by performing the callosotomy early in life. Recently Berlucchi et al. (1987) confirmed that callosotomy does not disrupt binocular interaction in visual cortical areas 17 and 18 of adult cats with normal visual pathways, although it causes a significant reduction of receptive fields crossing the vertical meridian. Further experimentation in the cat as well as in other mammals is clearly needed for understanding the reasons for the discrepancies in these results.

The participation of the corpus callosum in cortical binocular interaction is well established only in albino animals with a genetically determined excessive crossing of the visual pathways, such as the Siamese cat. Neurons responding to photic stimulation of both eyes abound in the visual cortical suprasylvian areas of Siamese cats, in spite of the drastically reduced input from each eye to ipsilateral primary visual cortical areas 17 and 18. The corpus callosum is essential for the existence of a visual input from each eye to ipsilateral suprasylvian areas beyond 17 and 18, since this input is virtually lost after a posterior callosal section (Marzi et al., 1980, 1982; Zeki and Fries, 1980). Similar to Siamese cats, in normally pigmented cats submitted to an early surgical strabismus neurons in areas 17 and 18 are dominated by the input from the contralateral eye, in contrast with a balanced converging binocular input to visual suprasylvian neurons (Marzi et al., 1986). However, unlike Siamese cats, following callosotomy these strabismic cats show only a reduction, rather than an abolition, of the ipsilateral eye input to suprasylvian neurons, suggesting the existence of an alternative route for the interhemispheric conveyance of the latter input (Bedard et al., 1988). Binocular interactions found in areas 17 and 18 of albino rats have also been attributed to a callosal mediation, based on the disappearance of the response to stimulation of the ipsilateral eye during cooling of the contralateral cortex (Diao et al., 1983).

In mammals with frontal eyes, such as cat (Montarolo et al., 1981), monkey (Pasik and Pasik, 1964, 1972) and man (van Die and Collewijn, 1982, Ohmi et al., 1986), horizontal optokinetic nystagmus can be elicited in both directions from either eye and via both crossed and uncrossed retinal fibers. Optokinetic following of the stimulus in either direction can indeed be demonstrated when the visual inflow is appropriately channeled into a single hemifield of either eye of man, or restricted to a single hemiretina of monkeys or cats by monocular stimulation following either a midsagittal section of the optic chiasm or a transection of one optic tract. These analyses reveal only slight asymmetries in favor of stimulus movement in the temporonasal direction upon stimulation of either nasal hemiretina (crossed retinal fibers), and in favor of the nasotemporal direction upon stimulation of either temporal hemiretina (uncrossed retinal fibers). By contrast, in afoveate mammals with laterally placed eyes, optokinetic nystagmus upon monocular stimulation shows a strong predominance in favor of the temporonasal direction (Tauber and Atkin, 1986). This largely unidirectional nystagmic response appears to depend solely on the crossed fiber systems from the nasal hemiretinae, since the interruption of these systems by a chiasmatic section abolishes optokinetic nystagmus in both rat (Cowey and Franzini, 1979) and rabbit (Steele-Russell et al., 1987), in spite of the fact that the intact uncrossed fibers from the temporal hemiretinae prove capable of mediating other forms of visually guided behavior.

Bilateral ablations of occipital cortex in both cat (e.g. Montarolo et al., 1981) and monkey (e.g. Zee et al., 1987) cause a marked impairment in optokinetic nystagmus. Postoperative nystagmic responses resemble those of afoveate animals, particularly because of the emergence during monocular viewing of a conspicuous temporonasal preponderance due to a reduction of the response to nasotemporal motion. An essential component for optokinetic nystagmus is the nucleus of the optic tract in the pretectum: a lesion of this nucleus on one side abolishes optokinetic following of stimuli moving toward that side (Kato et al., 1986, 1988). While at least in the cat each nucleus of the optic tract may receive direct visual inputs from both hemiretinae of both eyes (Montarolo et al., 1981), these direct visual inputs, and especially the uncrossed input from ipsilateral temporal hemiretina, are reinforced by indirect inputs from visual cortical areas via cortico-pretectal projections (Montarolo et al., 1981; Hoffmann and Distler, 1986; Zee et al., 1987). One of the normal functions of these pathways is that of ensuring a balanced oculomotor reactivity to horizontal motion in both directions (Zee et al., 1987).

Experiments on monkeys strongly suggest that some of the cortico-pretectal pathways controlling the brainstem substrates for optokinetic nystagmus include an interhemispheric, predominantly callosal component. Horizontal optokinetic nystagmus elicited by stimulating each temporal hemiretina of split-chiasm monkeys occurs normally in either direction. If, however, the corpus callosum is sectioned in addition to the chiasm, optokinetic responses to temporonasal motion are normal in each eye, whereas responses to nasotemporal motion undergo a massive reduction (Pasik and Pasik, 1964, 1971, 1972). Similarly, monkeys submitted to a combined callosotomy and section of one optic tract exhibit a strong asymmetry in favor of optokinetic responses toward the lesioned side (Pasik and Pasik, 1972). Combined splitting of chiasm and corpus callosum also disturbs vertical optokinetic nystagmus from monocular stimulation, with paradoxical oblique downward movement evoked by upward motion and vice versa (Pasik et al., 1971).

These results in split-brain monkeys are not easy to explain on the basis of our present understanding of the pretectal substrates of optokinetic nystagmus. It can only be concluded that a normal optokinetic nystagmus requires that both hemispheres receive visual information. In the split-chiasm, monocularly occluded monkey the corpus callosum must supply at least part of this information to the hemisphere contralateral to the seeing eye. The neuronal mechanisms by which the corpus callosum can influence the brainstem substrates for optokinetic nystagmus are still largely unknown. A recent preliminary report by Hoffmann et al. (1988) indicates that neurons in the nucleus of the optic tract in the monkey receive visual information via the corpus callosum. Bilateral receptive fields, extending into both halves of the visual field, are typically recorded in the nucleus of the optic tract of normal monkeys. In two callosotomized monkeys receptive fields in the same nucleus were consistently restricted to the contralateral half field. This loss of ipsilateral receptive field components following callosotomy is akin to that described in the cat superior colliculus by Antonini et al. (1978, 1979). In conclusion, there is suggestive evidence that the callosal connections of primary visual cortical areas may partake in the mediation of rather elementary sensory functions such as binocular stereopsis, binocular convergence and optokinetic nystagmus, but more work is necessary for proving this functional involvement beyond question, as well as for differentiating such forms of interhemispheric interaction from those related to learning and memory.

Interhemispheric integration of non-visual sensory information

Somesthetic information from each side of the body is conveyed by crossed specific afferent pathways mainly but not exclusively to the contralateral hemisphere. Somatosensory cortical areas can receive inputs from the ipsilateral body half through uncrossed specific afferent pathways as well as via callosal connections. Afferent ipsilateral somatic representation is stronger for axial and proximal body parts and weaker or absent for distal extremities (Mountcastle, 1981). Homotopic and heterotopic commissural connections have been described in the somatosensory cortex of many species (see reviews by Killackey, 1985; Shanks et al., 1985; Innocenti, 1986; Cusick and

Kaas, 1986; Manzoni et al., 1989). The earlier belief that callosal connections are restricted to the representations of axial and proximal limb surfaces and avoid representations of distal extremities in all somatosensory areas (Jones and Powell, 1969; Pandya and Vignolo, 1969) has been substantially revised, since at best it applies only to the primary receiving area. The total absence of callosal connections between cortical regions representing the distal extremities would indeed be incompatible with behavioral results on somatosensory interhemispheric transfer.

As indicated previously, the era of split-brain research is thought to have begun with the famous experiment on tactile interhemispheric transfer performed by Bykov and Speranski (1924; see also Bykoff, 1924) in Pavlov's laboratory. It was known that dogs conditioned to salivate in response to tactile stimulation of a specific skin location on one side of the body were perfectly capable of transferring the response to a comparable stimulation of the corresponding point of the other side (see Pavlov, 1927). Bykov and Speranski (1924) showed that a transection of the corpus callosum suppressed contralateral generalization, and that different and independent reflexes could be established to identical stimuli applied to different sides of the body.

Confirming this pioneering study, subsequent experiments on cats trained with operant rather than classical conditioning demonstrated that callosotomy can totally abolish the normal transfer between the forelimbs of fairly simple motor responses to unilateral tactile or tactile-kinesthetic stimuli (Stamm and Sperry, 1957; Meikle et al., 1962). Abolition of the normal capacity for intermanual or interpedal transfer of unimanually or unipedally learned discriminations of several classes of somesthetic stimuli has also been generally observed in callosotomized monkeys (Glickstein and Sperry, 1960; Ebner and Myers, 1962; Lee-Teng and Sperry, 1966; Kohn and Myers, 1968; Hunter et al., 1975) and chimpanzees (Myers and Henson, 1960), but cases of persistence of somesthetic transfer after callosotomy have also been noted (Glickstein and Sperry, 1960; Ettlinger and Morton, 1966; Manzoni et al., 1972; Hunter et al., 1975). When transfer is abolished by partial callosal transections, the effective section is one which interrupts callosal fibers between the parietal lobes containing the somatosensory areas (Myers and Ebner, 1976). Direct electrophysiological recordings from callosal fibers in cats and monkeys proved that tactile and proprioceptive messages are readily transmitted across the midline upon peripheral natural or electric stimulation (Innocenti et al., 1974; Spidalieri et al., 1985; Guillemot et al., 1987b, 1988; Guandalini et al., 1989). Callosal fibers convey information from axial, proximal and distal parts of the body, but there is a relative overrepresentation of axial information, in accord with the concept of sensory midline fusion (Lepore et al., 1986a; Manzoni et al., 1989).

The persistence of transfer in callosotomized animals is most likely to depend on the incomplete crossing of the somatic sensory pathways, which allows the projection of unilateral sensory inputs to both hemispheres independent of interhemispheric connections (Ettlinger and Blakemore, 1969; Gazzaniga, 1970). Why the limited ipsilateral somatic input to each hemisphere should be used by callosotomized monkeys in some learning and/or transfer situations but not in others is not clear. Butler and Francis (1973) claimed that even normal monkeys could not transfer tactile discriminations between the hands, in spite of having an intact corpus callosum, when tactile information was carefully restricted to the fingers. Although at first sight this finding might be accounted for by the lack of callosal connections between the hand regions of the primary somatosensory cortical areas (SI) of the two sides, it is best attributed to procedural factors.

Several lines of evidence do indeed indicate that, as in the visual system, interhemispheric transfer in the somestheic system relies on cortical areas beyond the primary receiving area SI, and that the complement of callosal connections of these cortical areas is fully adequate for transfer between bilateral distal extremities such as the cat's forepaws or the monkey's hands. A most likely candidate is the second somatosensory area SII, which contains neurons with bilateral receptive fields on the distal forelimb extremities in both cat (Innocenti et al., 1973; Robinson, 1973) and monkey (Whitsel et al., 1969; Robinson and Burton, 1980). In the monkey SII these neurons are likely to receive the input from the ipsilateral hand via callosal projections from the contralateral hemisphere, since, contrary to earlier reports (Jones and Powell, 1969; Pandya and Vignolo, 1969), there is now definite anatomical evidence for a hand-related callosal input to SII from contralateral SI and SII (Manzoni et al., 1984). A section (Robinson, 1973; Guillemot et al., 1987a) or cathodal blockade of the corpus callosum (Innocenti et al., 1973) reduces, but does not annul, the number of bilateral fields in the cat SII by removing their ipsilateral input. The neurons having bilateral fields in the absence of the corpus callosum receive both their ipsilateral and contralateral inputs via the thalamus (Barbaresi et al., 1984; Manzoni et al., 1989). The effect of a callosal section on bimanual receptive fields in the monkey SII has not yet been tested; however, the important role of SII in tactile interhemispheric transfer in the monkey is indicated by the decrease in transfer after a lesion of SII (Garcha and Ettlinger, 1980; Garcha et al., 1982), in agreement with similar earlier findings in the cat (Teitelbaum et al., 1968).

Granted that in each modality sensory information is processed sequentially through a series of specific cortical areas before being relayed to the limbic system for memory storage and behavioral control, an analogy can be drawn between visual interhemispheric transfer and somatosensory transfer insofar as both depend on interhemispheric connections at levels well beyond the primary receiving cortical stages (Mishkin, 1979). Mishkin (1979) originally proposed that SII in the somatosensory system and the inferotemporal cortex in the visual system are the cortical sites specialized for interhemispheric transfer, but in more recent publications he has emphasized the primary or additional role of the insula in somesthetic perception and memory, including bilateral integration (Murray and Mishkin, 1984; Friedman et al., 1986; Pons et al., 1987). No specific function, other than a generic 'midline fusion' of right and left hemibody maps, has as yet been identified for the callosal connections of the primary somatosensory area SI. These connections appear to reinforce rather than create a bilateral representation of face and trunk which is already present at thalamic level (Barbaresi et al., 1984; Manzoni et al., 1989). It seems agreed that callosal connections are absent or sparse in the primary SI representations of those body parts which are normally used in environmental exploration, such as the whiskers in rodents and the hands in primates. The tendency of callosal connections to avoid mixing with somatic afferents having high resolving powers has been considered to be useful for the preservation of the 'purity' of basic sensory information at the first cortical processing station (Killackey, 1985; Ledoux et al., 1987; Manzoni et al., 1989).

Information about the role of the mammalian forebrain commissures in olfaction is limited to the demonstration of the primary importance of the anterior commissure for interhemispheric transfer. Afferent pathways from the olfactory mucosa in each nostril travel to ipsilateral olfactory centers, and the inter-nostril transfer of odorous information requires a cross-midline integration. Cutting the anterior commissure abolishes the inter-nostril transfer of olfactory discriminations in rats (Teitelbaum, 1972). Inter-nostril transfer of olfactory information used for orientation by homing pigeons has similarly been found to be absent after sectioning the anterior commissure (Foà et al., 1985). A normal inter-nostril transfer of habituation to odorous stimuli has instead been reported in pigeons with a section of the anterior commissure (Gagliardo and Teyssèdre, 1988).

Studies on the interhemispheric integration of auditory information in man have revealed an important role of the corpus callosum in performing dichotic listening tasks which involve a competition between different simultaneous inputs from the two ears. Because of the partial crossing of the auditory pathways in the brain stem, each cerebral hemisphere receives information from both ears, hence section of the forebrain commissures is plainly insufficient to separate the two monaural inputs into different hemispheres. However, there is evidence from both normal and brain-damaged subjects that at least under conditions of dichotic competition the crossed afferent pathway from each ear is functionally superior to the uncrossed pathway (Kimura, 1967; Sidtis, 1984). It appears that in these conditions transmission of information along the weaker uncrossed ascending pathway is virtually suppressed by the stronger crossed pathway, so that the corpus callosum becomes necessary for conveying the input from each ear to the ipsilateral hemisphere (Milner et al., 1968; Sparks and Geschwind, 1968). Does the corpus callosum subserve a comparable function in animals?

Among the scanty studies of the effects of commissurotomy on auditory perception in animals (see Wegener, 1965, for an earlier discussion), only one experiment employed dichotic stimulation. Kaas et al. (1967) trained cats to recognize a specific tonal change in one ear while disregarding different tonal changes occurring simultaneously in the other ear. Removal of the auditory cortex contralateral to the 'attentive' ear led to loss of the habit, whereas removal of the ipsilateral auditory cortex did not. If, however, the corpus callosum was sectioned prior to training, cortical ablation contralateral to the attentive ear did not abolish the habit, suggesting a compensation by the auditory cortex of the other hemisphere. It follows that in the intact brain the corpus callosum prevented rather than favored the access of the input from the attentive ear to the ipsilateral hemisphere. No confirmation of this putative role of the corpus callosum in audition in animals has so far been provided.

The concept that each hemisphere has a preferential or exclusive association with the contralateral auditory hemispace rather than with the contralateral ear (Jenkins and Masterton, 1982) may aid in investigating the participation of the corpus callosum to audition. Pavlov's (1927) claim that dogs conditioned to differentiate between sounds coming from the left and the right lost this ability after callosotomy could not be supported by Neff (1961), and the lack of effects from callosotomy on sound localization in cats has been reiterated in more recent investigations (e.g. Moore et al., 1974). It must be pointed out, however, that the above experiments employed rather crude tests of sound localization which have been shown to be inadequate for a precise mapping of the cerebral substrates of this ability (Masterton and Jenkins, 1982), and the possible contribution of the corpus callosum to sound localization should be reinvestigated by using several sound sources rather than only two. By analogy with the visual system, the hypothesis can also be made that auditory commissural connections are instrumental in uniting hemispace representations into whole-space representations. In the barn owl, for example, bilateral auditory space representation in the inferior colliculus appears to rely on commissural connections of this structure (Takahashi et al., 1989). It does not seem implausible that the mammalian corpus callosum may be similarly involved in unifying the right and left auditory hemispaces and more generally in transferring spatial auditory information between the two hemispheres. In this context it is noteworthy that callosal connections are concentrated in cortical regions which represent the midline of the sound space and contain neurons nonselective for sound direction, whereas cortical areas representing the contralateral sound space have few or no callosal connections (Imig et al., 1986). No physiological evidence as to the effects of a callosal section on the response of auditory cortical neurons to sound stimuli is yet available to match and interpret the above anatomical information.

Bilateral motor interactions

On the assumption of a complete crossing of the

motor pathways, a visual input restricted, say, to the right hemisphere can guide the motility of the left half of the body by an intrahemispheric visuomotor integration, while an interhemispheric interaction is required for the same input to guide motor responses on the right half of the body. In a split-chiasm animal a visual input from the right eye should elicit left-sided motor responses intrahemispherically and right-sided responses interhemispherically. To the extent that visuomotor control depends on cortico-cortical interactions, split-chiasm animals with an additional section of the cortical commissures should show impairments in the visual guidance of movements on the side of the eye receiving the input. Yet it has been found in split-brain cats that visual inputs to either eye could guide either foreleg in an essentially normal fashion (Schrier and Sperry, 1959; Voneida, 1963). Varying degrees of effective control over the motility of an arm by visual inputs to the ipsilateral eye have also been reported in split-brain monkeys (Downer, 1959; Myers et al., 1962; Gazzaniga, 1964; Hamilton, 1967; Lehman, 1968; Lund et al., 1970; Brinkman and Kuypers, 1973; Keating, 1973).

The cross-cuing model of Gazzaniga (1969) can account at least in part for the fact that commissurotomy does not abolish monocular visual reaching with the ipsilateral forelimb in split-chiasm animals. If in response to a visual input from the right eye the right hemisphere orients the head toward the visual target, bilaterally distributed spatial information from neck proprioceptors can then cue the 'blind' left hemisphere to align the right hand with the target. Gazzaniga (1969) saw that a mechanical immobilization of the head and the consequent blockade of the orienting reaction did indeed interfere with the ability of split-brain monkeys to reach with one hand under the visual guidance of the ipsilateral eye.

However, cross-cuing is not the only mechanism involved in successful ipsilateral eye-arm visuomotor control after commissurotomy. Anatomical, functional and clinical evidence suggests that the crossing of the central motor pathways for distal hand and finger muscles is virtually complete, whereas both crossed and uncrossed motor pathways can control axial and proximal limb muscles (Kuypers, 1981). Lund et al. (1970) observed motor abnormalities in the use of a hand ipsilateral to the seeing eye in monocularly occluded split-chiasm callosotomized monkeys, and argued that in the ipsilateral eye-hand condition of the experiment the corpus callosum is required for linking the visual input to the crossed corticospinal system, thus giving dexterity to visually controlled finger movements. These findings were confirmed and extended by Brinkman and Kuypers (1973), who found that on monocular tests of visual reaching with the forelimb ipsilateral to the seeing eye, split-brain monkeys could direct the arm toward the target, but were unable, if unaided by tactile cues, to make the discrete manual and digital actions required for the precise gripping of a small object. Such precise visually guided digital prehensions could, however, be accomplished successfully with the hand ipsilateral to the open eye by split-chiasm monkeys with an intact callosal splenium, as well as by both split-chiasm and split-brain monkeys using the hand contralateral to the open eye. These findings strongly support the notion that a visual input restricted to one hemisphere can access an uncrossed motor system of the same hemisphere for controlling the ipsilateral arm at proximal joints, but must be relayed via the corpus callosum to a crossed motor system in the other hemisphere for guiding the ipsilateral hand and fingers (Brinkman and Kuypers, 1973). Several portions of the corpus callosum in addition to the splenium are likely to subserve this interhemispheric transfer (Lehman, 1968).

Brinkman and Kuypers (1973) and Haaxma and Kuypers (1974) emphasized the importance for visuomotor guidance of a multi-stage serial cortico-cortical pathway between striate and motor cortex, with intermediate stations at prestriate, parietal and premotor cortex, and callosal connections linking up bilateral stations at all levels of the pathway. By contrast Glickstein (1989; see also Glickstein and May, 1982) has argued for an essential involvement of cortico-subcortical-cerebellar pathways in visual guidance of movements. These pathways run from many visual cortical areas, particularly in the parietal lobe, and from superior colliculus alike to ipsilateral pontine nuclei and thence to ipsilateral and contralateral cerebellum. Considering that each hemicerebellum has a predominant relationship with the musculature on the same side of the body, the pathway to a hemicerebellum from the ipsilateral cortex or colliculus could account for sight-guided movements of the ipsilateral forelimb when visual information is restricted to that side by forebrain commissurotomy (Glickstein, 1989). Cortico-ponto-cerebellar connections could also account for the surprisingly normal between-hand coordination that has been described in split-brain monkeys performing object manipulations and other skilled acts (Mark and Sperry, 1968), if one grants the cerebellum the ability to infer the position of either hand from the corollary discharges of cortical motor commands to the hand muscles, as well as to signal the inferred position of each hand to the other even in the absence of the commissures (Glickstein, 1989). Finally, in view of its role in various forms of learned visuomotor adjustments (Lisberger, 1988), the cerebellum could be involved in bilateral transfer of motor adaptation to a distorted unihemispheric visual input. A split-brain monkey wearing a light-deflecting prism in front of the open eye and trained to reach for a target with one arm transferred the learned motor adaptation between the eyes but not between the arms (Hamilton, 1967). The successful interocular transfer may be due to a convergence of binocular information, not disrupted by commissurotomy, onto cerebellar neurons feeding visual information into arm-specific neural substrates of motor learning.

Electrical microstimulation of the rostral corpus callosum in the cat induced discrete unilateral or bilaterally symmetrical movements of shoulder, whisker or eyelid muscles (Spidalieri and Guandalini, 1983). This pattern of motor responses from callosal stimulation was subsequently shown to be subject to a gradual postnatal maturation (Guandalini et al., 1989). The motor effects can only in part be attributed to orthodromic activation of callosal fibers synapsing on corticofugal neurons in motor cortex, since similar, though weaker, movements could be obtained through stimulation of a callosal stump after a chronic callosal section, or by callosal stimulation after unilateral motor cortex removal (Spidalieri et al., 1986). Motor responses observed under these conditions were attributed to an activation of motor cortex neurons pursuant to an antidromic excitation of surviving callosal fibers and a consequent orthodromic excitation of their recurrent collaterals. The pattern of results suggests that callosal connections of the motor cortices in the cat serve to ensure a self-strengthening bilateral activation of cortical motor neurons controlling axial and proximal muscles (Spidalieri et al., 1986).

Combined cortical stimulation and indentification of sites of callosal connectivity in primary and supplementary motor cortex and in frontal eye fields of the owl monkey revealed a rather diffuse callosal connectivity in the latter two areas. In the primary motor cortex, dense callosal connections tended to be associated with sites whose stimulation produced movements of axial and proximal body parts , and sparse callosal connections tended to be associated with sites whose stimulation produced movements of distal limbs. However, such relations were by no means exclusive, since the same body part, whether axial, proximal or distal, could be represented in both callosal and acallosal regions (Gould et al., 1986). In theory these callosal connections of motor cortical areas may serve (1) to mediate interhemispheric sensory guidance of unilateral movements, as discussed previously in relation to visuomotor control, (2) to help bilateral coordination during associated synchronous and symmetric movements of corresponding effectors on the two sides of the body, and/or (3) to allow an orderly dissociation between corresponding contralateral effectors during bilateral actions that require coordinated but different movements on the two sides.

Behavioral commissurotomy findings by Brinkman (1984) point to a clear-cut associative function of motor cortical callosal connections. A unilateral removal of the supplementary motor area in monkeys caused a chronic impairment in bimanual coordination, consisting in a tendency to make the same actions with the two hands in tasks which instead required an intermanual uncoupling and differentiation of labor. Since the deficit was alleviated or relieved by a subsequent callosal section, it was ascribed to a callosally transmitted influence of the intact supplementary motor area, overriding residual systems for motor control in the damaged hemisphere and imposing its own motor programs upon them. By inference it can be suggested that in the intact brain each supplementary motor area can function as an independent program generator for motor systems in the same hemisphere, but at the same time it can use callosal connections to make its activities known to its counterpart and related motor systems in the other hemisphere for the purpose of bilateral coordination (Brinkman, 1984). How interhemispheric influence of the supplementary motor areas can precisely interact with intrahemispheric influences in the target areas remains to be determined.

While the above study reported an amelioration of motor deficits by a callosal section, other studies addressing the problem of the neural organization of attention and motor intention have revealed detrimental influences of callosotomy. A severe but temporary contralateral polysensory neglect can be induced in monkeys by removal of the cortical eye field in one frontal lobe. Crowne et al. (1981) showed that section of the corpus callosum reinstated the hemineglect in monkeys which had recovered from a previous frontal lesion. This second hemineglect was also transitory. In a study by Watson et al. (1984), hemineglect from a unilateral frontal arcuate lesion was much more conspicuous in callosotomized than in callosum-intact monkeys, though the time course of the recovery was the same in the two groups. The callosal mechanisms underlying these commissurotomy findings in hemineglect are unknown, but certainly they cannot include the mutual interhemispheric inhibition postulated by Kinsbourne (1970) to account for at least some aspects of hemineglect in brain-damaged patients. On the hypothesis of a reciprocal interhemispheric inhibition a reduction or disappearance, rather than worsening, of hemineglect would indeed be expected following hemispheric disconnection. Extinction, i.e. the failure of subjects with unilateral brain damage to perceive stimuli on the affected side when another stimulus is concurrently presented to the normal side, can also be assumed to involve some kind of inhibition of the damaged hemisphere by the healthy hemisphere. Callosotomy experiments on monkeys with tactile extinction from unihemispheric lesions have shown that if such extinction does indeed involve an interhemispheric inhibition, the inhibition is *not* mediated by the corpus callosum, since its section leaves extinction unaffected (Eidelberg and Schwartz, 1971). Inhibitory side-to-side effects in visual orienting in cats with superior collicular lesions have been discovered by Sprague (1966) and replicated by Sherman (1977). Originally described as a reciprocal blocking influence between the superior colliculi via the intertectal commissure, this inhibition has now been attributed by Sprague and his colleagues to the action of non-commissural fibers decussating in the posterior part of the above commissure (Wallace et al., 1989).

Plasticity effects in commissurotomy experiments

Most commissurotomy experiments on interhemispheric transfer of learned responses have been carried out on adult animals, and one wonders whether immature animals might provide a more suitable model for revealing an experimental modifiability of the commissural substrates for transfer. An impressive amount of evidence from developmental behavioral studies in cats, reviewed by Berlucchi and Marzi (1982), leaves no doubt that the neural bases for the ability to transfer visual discriminations between the eyes are largely innate, and cannot be disrupted even by forcing the two eyes to receive asynchronous and incongrous information during the critical maturation period of the visual system. However, the interocular transfer examined in these developmental studies could not be taken as an index of interhemispheric transfer, since the experiments were performed on animals with an intact optic chiasm and a binocular visual input to each hemisphere. In recent studies on rats the interocular transfer of a spatial discrimination, presumably requiring interhemispheric communication, became apparent only after a postnatal practice period, suggesting that the substrates for interhemispheric transfer are provided not only by innate factors but also by a maturation process (Rudy and Stadler-Morris, 1987; Rudy and Paylor, 1987). Investigations on the influence of early experiential or direct manipulations of the nervous system on interhemispheric transfer are therefore in order.

Discordant results were obtained in four independent but similar experiments specifically designed to analyse the relative contribution of innate and experiential factors to the organization of the neural substrates for interhemispheric transfer in higher mammals, and more precisely to assess whether an early callosotomy can induce the utilization of alternative pathways for visual and tactual transfer. Jeeves and Wilson (1969) found no interpaw transfer of a tactile discrimination in cats with a neonatal section of the entire corpus callosum, although good transfer was observed in a cat with a neonatal incomplete callosal section presumably removing the interhemispheric connections between somesthetic cortical areas. They concluded that if a reorganization of the pathways for interhemispheric transfer is induced by an early callosal section, the section must be partial and the reorganization must affect the remaining portions of the corpus callosum itself rather than noncallosal commissures. Yamaguchi and Myers (1972) saw that forebrain commissurotomy blocked the interhemispheric transfer of brightness, color and pattern discriminations in split-chiasm macaques tested as adults, regardless of whether commissurotomy had been performed soon after birth or later in life. Ptito and Lepore (1983) compared interhemispheric transfer of visual pattern discriminations in two groups of cats, the corpus callosi of which had been sectioned at 20 days of age in one group and 45 days in the other. On anatomical and physiological criteria it was thought that maturation of the commissural connections was incomplete in the first age group and nearly complete in the second group. All cats were submitted to section of the optic chiasm and tested for interhemispheric transfer as adults. While there was no evidence for interhemispheric transfer in the group callosotomized at 45 days of age, the group with an earlier callosotomy proved to be endowed with some capacity for transfer. The hypothesis that this capacity was due to plasticity and reorganization of immature subcortical commissures pursuant to callosal disconnection must undergo further experimental confirmation and scrutiny in view of an opposite result reported by Mascetti (1983). He found that interhemispheric visual transfer was as bad in cats that had been callosotomized between the 22nd and the 28th postnatal day as in cats callosotomized as adults.

Elberger (1982, 1986) has described a series of behavioral and electrophysiological visual deficits in cats submitted to neonatal callosotomy. These deficits include a reduction in visual acuity, a reduction in cortical binocular interactions and a reduction in extent of visual field, and are probably due to the lack of a normal organizing action of the callosal connections on the functional architecture of the primary visual cortex. This organizing action occurs during an early postnatal period, because no such detrimental effects on visual behavior and electrophysiology occur in cats callosotomized as adults. An influence of the corpus callosum on the reorganization of the lateral visual suprasylvian cortex following early ablation of contralateral cortical areas 17, 18 and 19 has been reported by Tong et al. (1987). They found that in cats undergoing such unilateral cortical lesion at 8 weeks of age a callosal section interfered with the recuperation of directionally selective and binocularly driven neurons in the lateral suprasylvian area in the intact hemisphere.

Other authors have reported more general effects of early commissural sections. Sechzer et al. (1977) have argued that a neonatal callosal section in kittens results in widespread behavioral symptoms resembling those of the so-called minimal brain dysfunction syndrome in children. Denenberg (1981; see also Denenberg et al., 1986) has suggested that the corpus callosum is the agent of massive interhemispheric facilitations and inhibitions which may play a crucial role in the development of functional hemispheric specializations during the maturation of the brain in rats. Given that (a) the precise morphological brain changes attending neonatal callosotomy have not yet been worked out, (b) the possibility of a functional lateralization in the brain of non-human animals is a largely unsolved issue (see Glick, 1985; Hamilton and Vermeire, 1988, 1989), and (c) the basic physiology of the interhemispheric mechanisms presumably contributing to hemispheric specialization is unknown, the issue of the participation of the corpus callosum in the development and maturation of the rest of the central nervous system is completely open to further experimentation.

Commissurotomy effects in animal models of experimental epilepsy

Experimental epilepsy has been an active field of research in the neurosciences for well over a century (for a historical review see Moruzzi, 1950), and commissurotomy has consistently occupied a prominent position in it as an effective tool for investigating the mechanisms of epileptogenesis and the spread of epileptic activity through nervous tissue. The following discussion will be centered on the forebrain commissures and especially on the corpus callosum because of their major importance for experimental epilepsy.

It is essential to distinguish between three possible roles of the forebrain commissures in epileptic events. First, the commissures can almost instantaneously transmit epileptic discharges from a unilateral focus to healthy regions of the other hemisphere, thus arousing hypersynchronous activities in them. This is an important component of the mechanism for the generalization of an epileptic seizure. Second, if the projected discharges are prolonged and repeated, the commissures conveying them can inflict enduring damaging effects on their targets, with a resulting development of secondary autonomous foci. This induction of new foci is called secondary epileptogenesis. Third, the commissures can mediate interactions between independent foci of the two sides, usually generating a bilateral synchrony of ictal and interictal activity which increases the severity of the condition.

The role of the commissures in the rapid cross-midline projection of epileptic activities is well illustrated by the acute focal discharge model. Massive hypersynchronous firing of populations of neurons, resembling the ictal discharges of human epileptic attacks, can be promptly induced in discrete brain foci, such as circumscribed areas of neocortex or regions of hippocampus, either by direct tetanic electric stimulation or by local application of fast-acting chemical irritants. The tendency of the evoked discharges to outlast the triggering stimulus in a self-sustained fashion is expressed by the term 'afterdischarge'. A common feature of focal epileptic seizures, long known from both clinical practice and experimental investigations, is that they can quickly propagate from their primary location not only to adjacent tissue, as exemplified by the so-called Jacksonian march, but also to quite distant regions of the nervous system. That this long-distance fast propagation occurs chiefly over specific anatomic pathways is proven by the fact that it can be blocked by cutting the appropriate connections between the primary focus and its projection targets. Basically the mechanism of the propagation does not differ from the normal orthodromic conduction and transsynaptic transmission of impulses along the affected pathways, but some contribution from antidromic excitation and ephaptic transmission is probable (see below). The interhemispheric spread of discharges and afterdischarges has been tested repeatedly before and after total or partial and selective commissurotomy.

Although early observations (reviewed by Spiegel, 1931) indicated that unilateral tetanic stimulation of the motor cortex in dogs could give rise to convulsions on both sides of the body even after a complete transection of telencephalic, diencephalic and mesencephalic commissures, suggesting that bilateralization of seizure discharges in the central nervous system normally relies on ponto-bulbar or even spinal mechanisms rather than on direct interhemispheric connections, this view was radically revised after the application of electroencephalography (EEG) to the study of experimental epilepsy. Pioneering studies by Gozzano (1935) and Moruzzi (1939) led to the discovery that EEG epileptic discharges induced in the motor cortex of one side by local application of strychnine or tetanic electric stimulation promptly spread to the contralateral motor cortex with a latency that was compatible with the conduction speed of callosal fibers. Section of the corpus callosum abolished the appearance of epileptic activities in the EEG of the motor cortex contralateral to the side of stimulation. These results were soon replicated in macaque monkeys by Erickson (1940), who showed that the intactness of the corpus callosum was indispensable for the propagation of electrically evoked EEG afterdischarges from sites in the motor cortex in one hemisphere to mirror-symmetric cortical points in the other hemisphere. In addition to the EEG findings, this conclusion was also arrived at on the basis of behavioral and cerebral blood flow indexes of convulsive activity. The behavioral analysis revealed that after the callosal section typical tonic-clonic movements were no longer bilateral. Indeed they occurred solely in muscles contralateral to the side of stimulation, in contrast with the ipsilateral side, which exhibited only tonic contractions restricted to axial and proximal muscles. In good accord with present-day views about the organization of the cortico-spinal motor systems (Kuypers, 1981), Erickson (1940) attributed the ipsilateral tonic phenomena not abolished by callosotomy to the existence of uncrossed cortical motor pathways to motoneurons for muscles of the trunk and proximal limb segments, but not to motoneurons for distal muscles.

The early discoveries of Gozzano, Moruzzi and Erickson were later extended to several animal species as well as to a variety of cortical areas, firmly establishing the principle that direct commissural pathways are the preferential if not the exclusive route for the transfer of acutely induced epileptic activities from a cortical site in one hemisphere to a corresponding site in the other hemisphere. Evidence was obtained in cats, monkeys and chimpanzees (Bailey et al., 1941, 1943; McCulloch and Garol, 1941; Garol, 1942; Rosenblueth and Cannon, 1942) for a locus-specific, usually homotopic interhemispheric transfer of epileptic discharges following unilateral strychninization or electrical stimulation of neocortical areas endowed with abundant callosal connections. This contrasted with an absence of transfer between bilateral cortical areas lacking commissural connections. Interhemispheric transfer of seizures between acallosal temporal areas linked across the midline via the neocortical component of the anterior commissure was found to be mediated by the latter commissure (Bailey et al., 1941, 1943; McCulloch and Garol 1941; Garol, 1942; Poblete et al., 1959). In this vein, the method of 'strychnine physiological neuronography', assessing the existence of direct connections between two brain regions based on the possibility of firing one region by strichninizing the other (Dusser de Barenne and McCulloch, 1939), came to be regarded as a useful complement to classical neurohistology for mapping the exact origin and termination of callosal and other commissural fibers within various neural centers.

The chief contribution of the forebrain commissures to the contralateral spread of epileptic discharges was also demonstrated in commissurotomy studies employing gradually developing unilateral foci generated by the local application of slowly acting irritants such as aluminum hydroxide (e.g. Kopeloff et al., 1950) and penicillin (e.g. Isaacson et al., 1971), as well as in the reflex epilepsy model. Reflex epilepsy is usually induced through the summation of natural peripheral stimuli in one modality with subliminal local strychninization of the primary receiving cortical area in the same modality (Moruzzi, 1950). In a much-studied model of reflex epilepsy, the photosensitive baboon *Papio papio,* treatment of the cortex is not required for the triggering of seizures because of an inherent, probably innate epileptogenic tendency of the frontorolandic cortex. An ictal EEG symptomatology can be unleashed in this species by a 15 Hz intermittent light stimulation, and includes bisymmetrical and bisynchronous spike-and-waves, polyspikes and waves initially restricted to the frontorolandic cortex but subsequently diffusing to subcortical centers and other cortical areas. Generalized seizures which tend to outlast the light stimulation and eventually to recur spontaneously are thus generated, and are accompanied by myoclonic ocular, facial, collic and somatic contractions which may possibly give way to a grand-mal attack. Fukuda et al. (1988) saw that bilateral and bisynchronous EEG seizures could be precipitated by appropriate light stimulations in baboons with intact forebrain commissures, regardless of whether stimulation was delivered to the full visual field an thus to both hemispheres, or restricted to the right or left visual field and thus channeled into the contralateral hemisphere. Section of the anterior two-thirds of the corpus callosum and hippocampal commissure did not change the bilateral EEG pattern of photosensitive epilepsy upon full field stimulation; however, separate stimulation of each visual hemifield largely confined seizures to the contralateral hemisphere. It follows that upon stimulation of a single hemifield in intact baboons the anterior corpus callosum and possibly the hippocampal commissure are instrumental for projecting the seizure from the hemisphere receiving the visual input to the other hemisphere (Fukuda et al., 1988).

The old claim that the interhemispheric spread of epileptic events in the acute unilateral focus model may utilize extracommissural pathways (Spiegel, 1931) was reaffirmed based on findings of persisting contralateral afterdischarges in callosotomized cats after unilateral electric tetanization of motor (Hoefer and Pool, 1943) and ectosylvian cortex (Straw and Mitchell, 1967). The occurrence of an extracommissural interhemispheric spread after callosotomy might well depend on a very high intensity of the epileptic discharge (Hoefer and Poole, 1943), but in the case of the ectosylvian cortex it is likely that a non-callosal but commissural transfer was mediated by additional interhemispheric connections via the anterior commissure (Straw and Mitchel, 1967). A possible extracommissural pathway for the interhemispheric projection of epileptic discharges in the cat has been suggested by the discovery of an interhemispheric delayed response evoked in a cortical point by a single-shock stimulation of the corresponding point in the contralateral cortex. The response persists after a callosal section and is probably mediated by a multisynaptic pathway that may course through the brainstem reticular formation (Rutledge and Kennedy, 1960, 1961). However, the interhemispheric delayed response appears to be largely restricted to cortical regions in the suprasylvian gyri, thus making it unlikely that the pathway subserving it is an important component in the mechanisms for the interhemispheric propagation of epileptic discharges to all other cortical areas. Alternative cortical-subcortical-cortical routes for an interhemispheric epileptic spread in the absence of the forebrain commissures have also been suggested in other species (Isaacson et al., 1971; Nie et al., 1974) and in other experimental conditions (Kusske and Rush, 1978).

Secondary epileptogenesis can usually be subdivided into three stages: a first stage in which discharges at the secondary site are simple, synaptically mediated, responses to abnormal volleys from the discharging primary focus, as described previously; a second stage in which abnormal electrogenesis begins to develop at the secondary site, even in the absence of seizures within the primary focus, but subsides permanently following removal of the latter focus; and a final stage in which epileptic activity within the secondary site, now secondary focus, can no longer be suppressed by removing the primary focus or by disconnecting the two foci (see Moruzzi, 1950; Morrell, 1960, 1985). For still unknown reasons, secondary epileptogenesis is very often mediated in all its stages by interhemispheric pathways, and in accord with the predominantly homotopic character of these connections the most frequent localization of a secondary focus is at a specular position across the midline from the primary focus: the mirror focus. Among the interhemispheric pathways, the corpus callosum is a preferred route for the generation of a mirror focus in the hemisphere contralateral to that containing the primary focus, as proven by the fact that callosotomy performed soon after the establishment of the primary focus can prevent the development of a mirror focus, while a later callosotomy cannot (Morrell, 1960, 1985; McQueen and Dow, 1979). The hypothetical participation of non-commissural immunity-dependent mechanisms in the genesis of mirror foci (Ettlinger, 1979) is still to be proven.

Conceptually similar to secondary epileptogenesis is kindling. In this model, originally proposed by Goddard (1967, 1983; Goddard et al., 1969; see also Racine 1972a,b; Racine et al., 1972), an enduring predisposition to epilepsy is engendered by the stimulation of discrete telencephalic and diencephalic sites with recurring trains of electrical pulses of constant intensity. Although initially these stimuli are not strong enough to bring about behavioral or electric signs of epilepsy, they become overtly epileptogenic in the course of several days as a result of repeated intermittent applications separated by one or two days. Kindling stimulation is most effective within the limbic system, particularly in the amygdala and the hippocampus. The development of kindling is signalled by a gradual propagation of the electrical afterdischarge from the kindled site to increasingly more diffuse portions of cortex and subcortical centers, as well as by a progression of behavioral symptoms from focal to generalized, e.g. from facial twitching, head-turning and circling to jumping and standing, and eventually to falling down with diffuse clonic or clonic-tonic-clonic convulsions. Complete or even partial commissurotomies have been repeatedly observed to prevent or retard the bilateralization of electrical and clinical ictal phenomena evoked from a unilateral kindling site in rats (McCaughran et al., 1977, 1978; McIntyre and Stuckey, 1984; McIntyre et al., 1986; McIntyre and Edson, 1987), cats (Wada and Sato, 1975; Wada et al., 1982; Fukuda et al., 1987; Hiyoshi and Wada, 1988a,b), baboons (Wada and Mizoguchi, 1984; Wada and Komai, 1985) and macaques (Wada et al., 1978 , 1981). A positive interhemispheric transfer effect of kindling consists in a facilitation of kindling of a unilateral site such as the amygdala after kindling of the corresponding contralateral site. In contrast with the generation of cortical mirror foci, the interhemispheric transfer of kindling at limbic sites does *not* utilize the corpus callosum, but rather the hippocampal commissure (McIntyre and Edson, 1987; Fukuda et al., 1987) and/or the thalamic massa intermedia (Hiyoshi and Wada, 1988a,b). However, in the generalized seizures induced by kindling limbic stimulations a callosal section reduced the bilaterality and severity of ictal phenomena (Wada and Komai, 1985).

In the model with bilateral foci, if two independent epileptic foci are active in bilateral cortical sites interconnected by direct commissural pathways, mutual facilitation mediated by these pathways should be expected to result in an interfocal synchronization of epileptic discharges. Mattson and Bickford (1961) were the first to confirm this expectation by showing that pairs of epileptic foci acutely established by strychnine application in corresponding points of the two hemispheres of the cat cortex tended to produce bilaterally synchronous EEG spikes. Bilateral synchrony depended on a precise spatial symmetry between the foci and was disrupted by sectioning the corpus callosum. However, bilateral EEG coupling could be reestablished after callosotomy by increasing the depth of barbiturate anesthesia, obviously because of the recruitment of unknown extracallosal mechanisms for interhemispheric synchronization. The corpus callosum has long been suspected to be involved in the fine bilateral synchronization of normal EEG activities (Bremer and Stoupel, 1957; Berlucchi, 1966), but not in the gross bilateral symmetry of the EEG signs of the sleep-wake cycle (Berlucchi, 1966; Batini et al., 1967). Recent work on coherence patterns of the sleep EEG in infants with agenesis of the corpus callosum is in line with the old animal findings (Kuks et al., 1987).

The model with symmetrical foci has been most extensively utilized by Marcus and his associates (Marcus and Watson, 1966, 1968; Marcus et al., 1968; Marcus, 1985) in cats and monkeys with bilateral and symmetric topical application of estrogens or other fast-acting convulsants to several pairs of cortical areas. The resulting bilateral spike-slow wave complexes were found to be well synchronized in pairs of areas with abundant commissural connections, such as the frontal, precentral and parietal areas in monkeys, whereas in the same animals bilateral synchrony was less pronounced or absent in pairs of areas with few commissural connections, such as the primary visual cortex or the middle superior temporal area. In both cats and monkeys section of the forebrain commissures left each side with the capacity to produce independent discharges, but the discharges of the two sides were largely asynchronous. Occasional bilateral couplings of EEG spikes seen after complete forebrain commissurotomy were on a much coarser temporal scale than before commissurotomy: 40 – 200 ms as opposed to 0 – 20 ms (Marcus, 1985). In both cats and monkeys good and persistent bilateral synchrony was noted between EEG discharges of opposite foci established in cortical slabs surgically isolated from subcortical centers, but maintaining reciprocal interconnections via an intact corpus callosum. The dominant role played by the corpus callosum in the interactions between bilateral cortical foci was also supported by the failure of large diencephalic and mesencephalic lesions to disrupt bilateral synchrony of discharges in the presence of intact commissures (Marcus and Watson, 1966; Marcus et al., 1968; Marcus, 1985).

Results comparable with those of Marcus and coworkers were obtained by Isaacson et al. (1971) in rats with bilateral implants of penicillin into the cortex. Spike discharges in the two hemispheres were correlated within 20 ms of each other, the leading spike originating at random from either hemisphere. After a complete callosal section spike discharges from the two hemispheres became asynchronous and remained so for 75 minutes. Afterwards bilateral synchrony tended to reappear, but the time between correlated discharges in the two hemispheres increased to 80 – 100 ms. Musgrave and Gloor (1980) similarly described an uncoupling by callosotomy of bilateral epileptic activities induced by systemic injection of penicillin in cats.

However, there must exist a neural substrate for the partial synchronization of discharges of bilateral foci which occurs in commissurotomized animals. Ottino et al. (1971) proposed a thalamic and/or midbrain reticular substrate for this function. They established parallel foci in the sensorimotor cortex (anterior sigmoid gyrus) of the two sides of cats by local application of penicillin and/or strychnine. The continuous bilateral synchrony of discharges characterizing the preparation with intact commissures was markedly disrupted by severing the corpus callosum and the hippocampal commissure. The inconstant bilateral synchrony seen after this operation – covering on average 13% of the recording time – depended on a high intensity of the focal discharges, as signalled by the amplitude and frequency of the EEG epileptiform waves and by the appearance of clonic contractions of the limbs, as well as on a spread of the seizures from cortex to ipsilateral intralaminar thalamic nuclei and midbrain reticular formation. Bilateral synchrony was further reduced by an additional section of the anterior commissure and midline division of thalamus and hypothalamus, and permanently abolished by splitting the midbrain tectum and tegmentum.

A model with bilateral *asymmetric* foci, involving cortical sites not directly connected by commissural pathways, has been employed by Mutani and coworkers in cats (Mutani et al., 1972, 1973; Mutani and Durelli, 1980). Acute foci were induced by local applicaton of conjugated estrogens to the sigmoid gyrus on one side and the lateral gyrus on the other (Mutani et al., 1972; Mutani and Durelli, 1980); chronic foci were induced with intracortical injections of cobalt-alumina into the same areas (Mutani et al., 1973). While bilateral asynchrony was the rule for discharges from acute foci (Mutani et al., 1972; Mutani and Durelli, 1980), a clear-cut electric coupling between chronic foci of the two sides began to develop 5 – 7 days following treatment and became complete within 20 – 25 days. Each side could lead the other in random alternation by a time lag of 50 – 100 ms (Mutani et al., 1973). In keeping with the results with symmetric foci (Marcus, 1985), the bilateral coupling between asymmetric foci was lost upon sectioning the corpus callosum and the hippocampal commissure. The physiological mechanisms for this interhemispheric coupling between cortical areas lacking *direct* commissural connections remain to be clarified.

In summary, animal models of experimental epilepsy indicate that forebrain commissurotomy can (1) hinder the immediate bilateralization of initially unilateral seizures, (2) abolish or reduce the transhemispheric secondary epileptogenesis, i.e. the establishment of secondary mirror foci, and (3) decrease the severity of seizures in cases of bilateral symmetric or asymmetric foci by disrupting bilateral synergy and synchrony. To the extent that the results from animal models of experimental epilepsy are applicable to epilepsy in man, these effects of commissurotomy justify the employment of this surgical procedure for controlling drug-resistant forms of the disease in human patients. However, in addition to beneficial effects of callosotomy, the findings from models of experimental epilepsy may also reveal some limited adverse effects of the operation (e.g. Mutani and Durelli, 1980; Wada and Komai, 1985). While on balance the experimental evidence suggests that callosotomy may reasonably be regarded as a definite therapeutic possibility in carefully selected cases of human epilepsy, the final word on the advisability of its employment on a large scale will have to come from further clinical trials (e.g. Spencer, 1988).

In the present context it may be worthwhile to consider the possible cellular mechanisms which underlie commissurotomy effects in models of experimental epilepsy. As already mentioned, electrophysiological evidence undoubtedly indicates that callosal neurons are in all cases facilitatory to their immediate target neurons (Naito et al., 1970; Toyama et al., 1974; Innocenti, 1986), a characteristic which can reasonably be extrapolated to neurons of the anterior and hippocampal commissures. Callosal neurons most probably use excitatory amino acids as transmitters (Barbaresi et al., 1987; Conti et al., 1988). The various types of cortical neuron that project to the corpus callosum do not include the non-spiny stellate neurons belonging to the major GABA-ergic category of inhibitory cortical elements (Voigt et al., 1988). Inhibition of cortical neurons by callosal afferents can of course be mediated by interneurons (Naito et al., 1970; Toyama et al., 1974; Innocenti, 1986). Many callosal fibers give rise to recurrent collaterals which return to the cortex containing their parent cell bodies, and these collaterals may exert both inhibitory (Feeney and Orem, 1971) and facilitatory effects (Spidalieri et al., 1986). The conduction along callosal fibers of impulses underlying projected epileptic discharges is usually orthodromic, but there is some indication that callosal fibers terminating in, or running through, an epileptic focus can also be stimulated antidromically (Schwartzkroin et al., 1975). On these grounds, the following speculations can be offered. (1) The interhemispheric projection of epileptic discharges and the synchronization of bilateral epileptic activities can be ascribed to orthodromic transmission of predominantly facilitating callosal influences. (2) Occasional increases in partial epileptic seizures following callosal section (e.g. Mutani and Durelli, 1980; Wada and Komai, 1985; Spencer et al., 1988) may be due to a functional suppression of inhibitory recurrent actions of callosal fibers pursuant to axotomic depression of neurons projecting to the corpus callosum. (3) Secondary epileptogenesis may derive not from impulse conduction along commissural fibers, but from a secretion of toxic factors by these fibers. The establishment of mirror foci has indeed been reported to occur when axonal flow along callosal fibers is normal, but impulse generation is chemically prevented (Morrell, 1985). Experiments prompted by these speculations can increase our knowledge of both physiological and pathophysiological mechanisms of commissural activities.

Epilogue

The two facets of research on the effects of commissurotomy in animals – one concerned with physiological hemispheric interactions and the other with pathological epileptic mechanisms – are not as disparate as it may seem at first sight. It is a truism, but nevertheless true, that in every epoch of science researchers tend to produce results that fit the systems of ideas prevailing in the contemporary scientific community. When many decades ago the neuroscientific community seemed ready to substitute central nervous system models couched in terms of orthodox anatomical circuitry with field theories borrowed from physics, the alleged absence of dysfunctions produced by commissural section was as much a product of that frame of mind as an inspiration for it. Convinced that neural integration must be carried out *solely* by diffuse networks of short-axoned neurons, Lashley affirmed in 1951: "There are, of course, long association tracts in the cortex, such as the corpus callosum, the superior longitudinal fasciculus, and the temporo-frontal tracts. Once, 26 years ago, I suggested facetiously that these might be only skeletal structures, since I could find no function for them. No important functions of these tracts have yet been demonstrated. Section of the corpus callosum produces only a slight slowing of reaction time, ipsilateral as well as contralateral (Akelaitis, 1941) . . .".

Yet the patients studied by Akelaitis had had their forebrain commissures surgically transected, in an attempt to control their severe epileptic conditions, because animal experiments had already substantiated the involvement of the great cerebral commissures in the propagation of epileptic seizures. The latter notion was so solidly entrenched in neurological thinking that McCulloch could write in 1949: "I have laughingly said that, so far as I can see, it is the only demonstrable function of the corpus callosum, to spread seizures from one side to the other. I still do not know of anything else we can attribute to it safely." However, well before the times of Lashley and McCulloch's writings neurophysiologists had collected strong evidence that the separation between physiological and abnormal, epileptic, activities of the commissures was artificial and unwise, if not downright wrong. In 1939 Moruzzi had clearly shown in the rabbit that the masticatory cortex of each side normally exerted a physiological facilitatory action on the corresponding contralateral cortex via the corpus callosum, and had convincingly argued that the transhemispheric spread of epileptic discharges between the masticatory cortices of the two sides was due merely to an exaggerated intensification of the normal callosal activity. The fundamental notion that physiological and epileptogenic commissural actions differed in degree rather than kind, and that there could be a gradual transition between the two types of action, was extended to the entire cortex by Bremer (see Bremer et al., 1956) and elaborated into a conception of the forebrain commissures as key elements in the 'cerebral dynamogenesis'.

These germs for a paradigmatic shift in the way of thinking about commissural function were brought to fruition when Sperry, a staunch advocate of brain models founded on a strict selectivity of connections, and his student Myers combined proper behavioral tests with good neurosurgical techniques for linking the interhemispheric transfer of habits with specific commissural pathways in animals. From this Sperry and his colleagues went on to show that commissural section in epileptic human patients blocks normal interhemispheric communication as well as transhemispheric generalization of seizures. While the spectacular success, both clinical and scientific, of commissurotomy work on man is dealt with in other chapters of this volume, it is this writer's hope that the present review can provide the reader not with a complete survey of the field of commissurotomy studies in animals, which would be impossible anyway, but just with an impression of the magnitude and richness of the developments that have occurred in the 36 years following Myers and Sperry's publication of 1953. If, however, the review is to end on an advisory note, the message is that the search for the functional significance of the commissures and its place in an overall theory of the brain has still a long way to go, and the experimental uses of commissurotomy are by no means exhausted. Hypotheses about hemispheric interaction will have to be increasingly inspired by anatomy, physiology, neurochemistry, and even molecular biology, rather than by analysis of behavioral commissurotomy effects, but the latter analysis will continue to serve as the ultimate test of every assumption about commissural function.

References

Akelaitis AJ: Studies on the corpus callosum. II. The higher visual functions in each homonymous field following complete section of the corpus callosum. *Arch. Neurol. Psychiatry: 45,* 788 – 796, 1941.

Antonini A, Berlucchi G, Marzi CA, Sprague JM: Importance of corpus callosum for visual receptive fields of single neurons in cat superior colliculus. *J. Neurophysiol.: 42,* 137 – 152, 1979.

Antonini A, Berlucchi G, Sprague JM: Indirect, across-the-midline retinotectal projections and repesentation of ipsilateral visual field in superior colliculus of the cat. *J. Neurophysiol.: 41,* 285 – 304, 1978.

Antonini A, Berlucchi G, Lepore F: Physiological organization of callosal connections of a visual lateral suprasylvian area in the cat. *J. Neurophysiol.: 49,* 902 – 921, 1983.

Antonini A, Di Stefano M, Minciacchi D, Tassinari G: Interhemispheric influences on area 19 in the cat. *Exp. Brain Res.: 59,* 179 – 186, 1985.

Asanuma H, Okuda O: Effects of transcallosal volleys on pyramidal tract cell activity of cat. *J. Neurophysiol.: 25,* 198 – 208, 1962.

Bailey P, Garol HW, McCulloch WS: Cortical origin and distribution of corpus callosum and anterior commissure in chimpanzee (*Pan satyrus*). *J. Neurophysiol.: 4,* 564 – 571, 1941.

Bailey P, von Bonin G, Garol HW, McCulloch WS: Functional organization of temporal lobe of monkey (*Macaca mulatta*) and chimpanzee (*Pan satyrus*). *J. Neurophysiol.: 6,* 121 – 128, 1943.

Barbaresi P, Conti F, Manzoni T: Topography and receptive field organization of the body midline representation in the ventrobasal complex of the cat. *Exp. Brain Res.: 54,* 327 – 336, 1984

Barbaresi P, Fabri M, Conti F, Manzoni T: D-[^{3}H]Aspartate retrograde labeling of callosal and association neurones of somatosensory areas I and II of cats. *J. Comp. Neurol.: 263,* 159 – 178, 1987.

Batini C, Radulovacki M, Kado RT, Adey WR: Effect of interhemispheric transection on the EEG patterns in sleep and wakefulness in monkeys. *Electroencephalogr. Clin. Neurophysiol.: 22,* 101 – 112, 1967.

Bedard S, Di Stefano M, Lepore F, Marzi CA: Pathways subserving binocularity in the lateral suprasylvian area of callosum-sectioned strabismic cats. *Eur. J. Neurosci.: Suppl. 1,* 275, 1988.

Berardi N, Bisti S, Maffei L: The transfer of visual information across the corpus callosum: spatial and temporal properties in the cat. *J. Physiol.: 384,* 619 – 632, 1987.

Berlucchi G: Electroencephalographic studies in 'split-brain' cats. *Electroencephalogr. Clin. Neurophysiol.: 20,* 348 – 356, 1966

Berlucchi G: Anatomical and physiological aspects of visual functions of corpus callosum. *Brain Res.: 37,* 371 – 392, 1972.

Berlucchi G: Some features of interhemispheric communication of visual information in brain damaged cats and normal humans. In Michel F, Scott B (Editors), *Les Syndromes de Disconnexion Calleuse chez l'Homme.* Lyon: Colloque International Lyon, pp. 123 – 136, 1975.

Berlucchi G: Recent advances in the analysis of the neural substrates of interhemispheric communication. In Pompeiano O, Ajmone Marsan C (Editors), *Brain Mechanisms of Perceptual Awareness and Purposeful Behavior.* New York: Raven Press, pp. 133 – 152, 1981.

Berlucchi G: Interaction of visual cortical areas and superior colliculus in visual interhemispheric transfer in the cat. In Morrison AR, Strick PL (Editors), *Changing Concepts of the Nervous System.* New York: Academic Press, pp. 321 – 336, 1982.

Berlucchi G, Antonini A: The role of the corpus callosum in the representation of the visual field in cortical areas. In Trevarthen CB (Editor), *Brain Circuits and Functions of the Mind.*

Cambridge University Press, pp. 129 – 139, 1989.

Berlucchi G, Marzi CA: Interocular and interhemispheric transfer of visual discriminations in the cat. In Ingle DJ, Goodale MA, Mansfield RJW (Editors), *Analysis of Visual Behavior.* Cambridge, MA: The MIT Press, pp. 719 – 750, 1982

Berlucchi G, Rizzolatti G: Binocularly driven neurons in visual cortex of split-chiasm cats. *Science: 159:* 308 – 310, 1968.

Berlucchi G, Sprague JM: The cerebral cortex in visual learning and memory, and in interhemispheric transfer in the cat. In Schmitt FO, Worden FG, Adelman G, Deniss JG (Editors), *The Organization of the Cerebral Cortex.* Cambridge, MA: The MIT Press, pp. 415 – 440, 1981.

Berlucchi G, Gazzaniga MS, Rizzolatti G: Microelectrode analysis of transfer of visual information by the corpus callosum. *Arch. Ital. Biol.: 105,* 583 – 596, 1967.

Berlucchi G, Buchtel E, Marzi CA, Mascetti GG, Simoni A: Effects of experience on interocular transfer of pattern discriminations in split-chiasm and split-brain cats. *J. Comp. Physiol. Psychol.: 92,* 532 – 543, 1978a.

Berlucchi G, Buchtel HA, Lepore F: Successful interocular transfer of visual pattern discriminations in split-chiasm cats with section of intertectal and posterior commissure. *Physiol. Behav.: 20,* 331 – 338, 1978b.

Berlucchi G, Sprague JM, Lepore F, Mascetti GG: Effects of lesions of areas 17, 18 and 19 on interocular transfer of pattern discriminations in split-chiasm cats. *Exp. Brain Res.: 31* 275 – 297, 1978c.

Berlucchi G, Sprague JM, Antonini A, Simoni A: Learning and interhemispheric transfer of visual pattern discriminations following unilateral suprasylvian lesions in split-chiasm cats. *Exp. Brain Res.: 34,* 551 – 574, 1979.

Berlucchi G, Tassinari G, Antonini A: The organization of the callosal connections according to Sperry's principle of supplemental complementarity. In Lepore F, Ptito M, Jasper HH (Editors), *Two Hemispheres – One Brain: Functions of the Corpus Callosum.* New York: Alan R. Liss, pp. 171 – 188, 1986.

Berlucchi G, Antonini A, Mascetti GG, Tassinari G: Role of callosal connections in the representation of the visual field in the primary visual cortex of the cat. In Ottoson D (Editor), *Duality and Unity of the Brain.* London: MacMillan, pp. 349 – 366, 1987

Bishop PO: Binocular vision. In Moses RA (Editor), *Adler's Physiology of the Eye.* St.Louis: Mosby, pp. 575 – 649, 1981.

Black P, Myers RE: Visual functions of the forebrain commissures in the chimpanzee. *Science: 146,* 799 – 800, 1964.

Blakemore C: Binocular depth discrimination and the nasotemporal division. *J. Physiol.: 205,* 471 – 497, 1969.

Blakemore C, Diao Y, Pu M, Wang Y, Xiao Y: Possible functions of the interhemispheric connexions between visual cortical areas in the cat. *J. Physiol.: 337,* 331 – 349, 1983.

Bremer F, Stoupel N: Etude des mécanismes de la synergie bioélectrique des hémisphères cérébraux. *Acta Physiol. Pharmacol. Neerl.: 6,* 487 – 496, 1957.

Bremer F, Brihaye G, André-Balisaux G; Physiologie et pathologie du corps calleux. *Schweiz. Arch. Neurol. Psychiatrie: 78:* 51 – 87, 1956.

Brinkman C: Supplementary motor area of the monkey's cerebral cortex: short- and long-term deficits after unilateral ablation and the effects of subsequent callosal section. *J. Neurosci.: 4:* 918 – 929, 1984.

Brinkman H, Kuypers HGJM: Cerebral control of contralateral and ipsilateral arm, hand and finger movements in the split-brain rhesus monkey. *Brain: 96,* 653 – 674, 1973.

Bures J, Buresova O, Krivanek J: *Brain and Behavior. Paradigms for Research in Neural Mechanisms.* New York: Wiley, 1988.

Buresova O, Bures J: Can the brain be improved? *Endeavour: 28,* 139 – 145, 1969.

Buresova O, Bures J: Interocular and interhemispheric transfer of visual engrams in callosotomized rats. *Physiol. Bohemoslovenica: 20,* 557 – 563, 1971.

Butler CR: A memory-record for visual discrimination habits produced in both cerebral hemispheres of monkeys when only one hemisphere has received direct visual information. *Brain Res.: 10,* 152 – 167, 1968.

Butler CR, Francis AC: Split-brain behavior without splitting. Tactile discriminations in monkeys. *Isr. J. Med. Sci.: 9 (Suppl.)*: 79 – 84, 1973.

Butler SR: Interhemispheric transfer of visual information via the corpus callosum and anterior commissure in the monkey. In Steele Russell I, van Hof MW, Berlucchi G (Editors), *Structure and Function af Cerebral Commissures.* London: MacMillan, pp. 343-357, 1979.

Bykoff K: Versuche an Hunden mit Durchschneiden des Corpus callosum. *Zentralbl. gesamte Neurol. Psychiatrie: 39,* 199, 1924.

Bykov KM, Speranski AD: Observation upon dogs after section of the corpus callosum. In Pavlov IP (Editor), *Collected Papers Physiology Laboratories, Vol. I,* pp. 47 – 59, 1924.

Conti F, Fabri M, Manzoni T: Glutamate-positive corticortical neurons in the somatic sensory areas I and II of cats. *J. Neurosci.: 8,* 2948 – 2960, 1988.

Cook ND: *The Brain Code.* London: Methuen, 1986.

Cowey A: Sensory and non-sensory visual disorders in man and monkey. *Phil. Trans. R. Soc. Lond.: B 298:* 3 – 13, 1982.

Cowey A, Franzini C: The retinal origin of uncrossed optic nerve fibres in rats and their role in visual discriminations. *Exp. Brain Res.: 35,* 443 – 455, 1979.

Cowey A, Parkinson AM: Effects of sectioning the corpus callosum on interocular transfer in hooded rats. *Exp. Brain Res.: 18,* 433 – 445, 1973.

Crowne DP, Yeo CH, Steele Russell IS: The effects of unilateral frontal eye field lesion in the monkey: visual-motor guidance and avoidance behaviour. *Behav. Brain Res.: 2,* 165 – 187, 1981.

Cuénod M: Split-brain studies. Functional interaction between bilateral central nervous structures. In Bourne GH (Editor), *The Structure and Function of Nervous Tissue, Vol. V.* New York: Academic Press, pp. 455 – 506, 1972.

Cusick CG, Kaas JK: Interhemispheric connections of cortical sensory and motor representations in primates. In Lepore F, Ptito M, Jasper HH (Editors), *Two Hemispheres – One Brain: Functions of the Corpus Callosum.* New York: Alan R.Liss, pp. 83 – 102, 1986.

Cynader M, Gardner J, Dobbins A, Lepore F, Guillemot JP: Interhemispheric communication and binocular vision: Functional and developmental aspects. In Lepore F, Ptito M, Jasper HH (Editors), *Two Hemispheres – One Brain: Func-*

tions of the Corpus Callosum. New York: Alan R.Liss, pp. 189 – 209, 1986.

Cynader M, Lepore F, Guillemot J-P: Inter-hemispheric competition during postnatal development. *Nature: 290,* 139 – 140, 1981.

Demeter S, Rosene DL, Van Hoesen GW: Interhemispheric pathways of the hippocampal formation, presubiculum, and entorhinal and posterior parahippocampal cortices in the rhesus monkey: The structure and organization of the hippocampal commissures. *J. Comp. Neurol. 233,* 30 – 47, 1985

Denenberg VH: Hemispheric laterality in animals and the effects of early experience. *Behav. Brain Sci.: 4,* 1 – 49, 1981.

Denenberg VH, Gall JS, Berrebi A, Yutzev DA: Callosal mediation of cortical inhibition in the lateralized rat brain. *Brain Res.: 397,* 327 – 332, 1986.

Diao Y – C, Wang Y-K, Pu M-L: Binocular responses of cortical cells and the callosal projection in the albino rat. *Exp. Brain Res.: 49,* 410 – 418, 1983.

Doty RW, Negrao N: Forebrain commissures and vision. In Jung R (Editor), *Handbook of Sensory Physiology, Vol. VII.* Berlin: Springer, pp. 543 – 582, 1973.

Doty RW, Negrao R, Yamaga K: The unilateral engram. *Acta Neurobiol. Exp.: 33,* 711 – 728, 1973.

Doty RW, Ringo JL, Lewine JD: Forebrain commissures and visual memory: a new approach. *Behav. Brain Res.: 29,* 267 – 280, 1988.

Doty RW Sr, Overman WH Jr: Mnemonic role of forebrain commissures in macaques. In Harnad S, Doty RW, Goldstein L, Jaynes J, Krauthamer G (Editors), *Lateralization in the Nervous System.* New York: Academic Press, pp. 75 – 88, 1977.

Dow BM, Dubner R. Single unit responses to moving visual stimuli in middle suprasylvian gyrus of the cat. *J. Neurophysiol.: 34,* 47 – 55, 1971.

Downer JL de C: Changes in visually guided behaviour following midsagittal division of optic chiasm and corpus callosum in monkey (*Macaca mulatta*). *Brain: 82,* 251 – 259, 1959.

Downer JL de C: Interhemispheric integration in the visual system. In Mountcastle VB (Editor), *Interhemispheric Relations and Cerebral Dominance.* Baltimore: Johns Hopkins Press, pp. 87 – 100, 1962.

Dreher B, Cottee LJ: Visual receptive-field properties of cells in area 18 of cat's cerebral cortex before and after acute lesions in area 17. *J. Neurophysiol.: 38,* 735 – 750, 1975.

Dusser De Barenne JG, McCulloch WS: Physiological delimitation of neurones in the central nervous system. *Am. J. Physiol.: 127,* 620 – 628, 1939.

Eacott MJ, Gaffan D: Interhemispheric transfer of visual learning in monkeys with intact optic chiasm. *Exp. Brain Res.: 74,* 348 – 352, 1989.

Ebner FF: Afferent connections to neocortex in the opossum (*Didelphis virginians*). *J. Comp. Neurol.: 124:* 353 – 366, 1967.

Ebner FF, Myers RE: Corpus callosum and the interhemispheric transmission of tactual learning. *J. Neurophysiol.: 25,* 380 – 391, 1962.

Eidelberg E, Schwartz AS: Experimental analysis of the extinction phenomenon in monkeys. *Brain: 94,* 91 – 108, 1971.

Elberger AJ: The functional role of the corpus callosum in the developing visual system: a review. *Prog. Neurobiol.: 18,* 15 – 79, 1982.

Elberger AJ: The role of the corpus callosum in visual development. In Lepore F, Ptito M, Jasper HH (Editors), *Two Hemispheres – One Brain: Functions of the Corpus Callosum.* New York: Alan R.Liss, pp. 281 – 297, 1986.

Elberger AJ, Smith EL: The critical period of corpus callosum section to affect cortical binocularity. *Exp. Brain Res.: 57,* 213 – 223, 1985.

Erickson TC: Spread of the epileptic discharge. An experimental study of the after-discharge induced by electrical stimulation of the cerebral cortex. *Arch. Neurol. Psychiatry: 43,* 429 – 452, 1940.

Ettlinger G: Interhemispheric transmission of learning and of abnormal electrical discharges: why should there be differences? In Steele-Russell I, van Hof MW, Berlucchi G (Editors), *Structure and Function of Cerebral Commissures.* London: MacMillan, pp. 385 – 389, 1979.

Ettlinger G, Blakemore CB. The behavioural effects of commissural section. In Benton AL (Editor), *Contribution to Clinical Neuropsychology.* Chicago: pp. 30 – 72, 1969.

Ettlinger G, Morton HB: Tactile discrimination performance in the monkey. Transfer of training between the hands after commissural section. *Cortex: 2,* 30 – 49, 1966.

Feeney DM, Orem JM: Influence of antidromic callosal volleys on single units in visual cortex. *Exp. Neurol.: 33,* 310 – 321, 1971.

Flechsig P: *Gehirn und Seele.* Leipzig: Von Veit, 1896.

Foà A, Bagnoli P, Giongo F: Homing pigeons subjected to section of the anterior commissure can build up two olfactory maps in the deflector lofts. *J. Comp. Physiol.: A 159,* 465 – 472, 1986.

Francesconi W, Fogassi L, Musumeci D: Interocular transfer of visual discriminations in Wulst-ablated pigeons. *Behav. Brain Res. 5,* 399 – 406, 1982.

Friedman DP, Murray EA, O'Neill B, Mishkin M: Cortical connections of the somatosensory fields of the lateral sulcus of macaques: Evidence for a corticolimbic pathway for touch. *J. Comp. Neurol.: 252,* 323 – 347, 1986.

Fukuda H, Wada JA, Riche D, Naquet R: Role of the corpus callosum and hippocampal commissure on transfer phenomenon in amygdala-kindled cats. *Exp. Neurol.: 98,* 189 – 197, 1987.

Fukuda H, Valin A, Bryère P., Riche D., Wada JA, Naquet R. Role of the forebrain commissure and hemispheric independence in photosensitive response of epileptic baboon, *Papio papio. Electroencephalogr. Clin. Neurophysiol.: 69,* 363 – 370, 1988.

Gagliardo A, Teyssèdre A: Interhemispheric transfer of olfactory information in homing pigeon. *Behav. Brain Res.: 27,* 173 – 178, 1988.

Garcha HS, Ettlinger G: Tactile discrimination learning in the monkey: the effects of unilateral or bilateral removals of the second somatosensory cortex (area S2). *Cortex: 16,* 397 – 412, 1980.

Garcha HS, Ettlinger G, MacCabe JJ: Unilateral removal of the second somatosensory projection cortex in the monkey: evidence for cerebral predominance? *Brain: 105,* 787 – 810, 1982.

Gardner JC, Cynader MS: Mechanisms for binocular depth sensitiviy along the vertical meridian of the visual field. *Brain*

Res.: 413, 60 – 74, 1987.

Garol HW: Cortical origin and distribution of corpus callosum and anterior commisure in the cat. *J. Neuropathol. Exp. Neurol.: 1,* 422 – 429, 1942.

Gaston KE: Interocular transfer of pattern discrimination learning in chicks. *Brain Res.: 310,* 213 – 221, 1984.

Gazzaniga MS: Interhemispheric communication of visual learning. *Neuropsychologia: 4,* 183 – 189, 1966.

Gazzaniga MS: Cross-cuing mechanisms and ipsilateral eye-hand control in split-brain monkeys. *Exp. Neurol.: 23,* 11 – 17, 1969.

Gazzaniga MS: *The Bisected Brain.* New York: Appleton-Century-Crofts, 1970.

Gazzaniga MS: Ledoux JE: *The Integrated Mind.* New York: Plenum Press, 1978.

Geschwind N: Disconnexion syndromes in animals and man. *Part I. Brain, 88,* 237 – 294, 1965.

Geschwind N: Disconnexion syndromes in animals and man. *Part II. Brain, 88,* 585 – 644, 1965.

Glick SD (Editor): *Cerebral Lateralization in Nonhuman Species.* Orlando: Academic Press, 1985.

Glickstein M: Brain pathways in the visual guidance of movement and the behavioural function of the cerebellum. In Trevarthen CB (Editor), *Brain Circuits and Functions of the Mind.* Cambridge: Cambridge University Press, 1989.

Glickstein M, May JG III: Visual control of movement: the circuits which link visual to motor areas of the brain with special reference to the visual input to the pons and cerebellum. *Contrib. Sens. Physiol.: 7,* 103 – 145, 1982.

Glickstein M, Sperry RW: Intermanual somesthetic transfer in split-brain Rhesus monkeys. *J. Comp. Physiol. Phychol.: 53,* 322 – 327, 1960.

Goddard GV: Development of epileptic seizures through brain stimulation at low intensity. *Nature: 214,* 1020 – 1021, 1967.

Goddard GV: The kindling model of epilepsy. *Trends Neurosci., 6,* 275 – 279, 1983.

Goddard GV: McIntyre DC, Leech CK: A permanent change in brain function resulting from daily electrical stimulation. *Exp. Neurol.: 25,* 295 – 330, 1969.

Goodale MA: Interocular transfer in the pigeon after lesions of the dorsal supraoptic decussation. *Behav. Brain Res.: 16,* 1 – 7, 1985.

Goodale MA, Graves JA: Retinal locus as a factor in interocular transfer in the pigeon. In Ingle DJ, Goodale MA, Mansfield RJW (Editors), *Analysis of Visual Behavior.* Cambridge, MA: The MIT Press, pp. 211 – 240, 1982.

Gould HG III, Cusick CG, Pons TP, Kaas JH: The relationship of corpus callosum connections to electrical stimulation maps of motor, supplementary motor, and the frontal eye fields in owl monkey. *J. Comp. Neurol.: 247,* 297 – 325, 1986.

Gozzano M: Ricerche sui fenomeni elettrici della corteccia cerebrale. *Riv. Neurol.: 8,* 212 – 261, 1935.

Granger EM, Masterton RB, Glendenning KK: Origin of interhemispheric fibers in acallosal opossum (with a comparison to callosal origins in rat). *J. Comp. Neurol.: 241,* 82 – 98, 1986.

Gross CG, Mishkin M: The neural basis of stimulus equivalence across retinal translations. In Harnad S, Doty RW, Goldstein L, Jaynes J, Krauthamer G (Editors), *Lateralization of the Nervous System.* New York: Academic Press, pp. 109 – 122, 1977.

Gross CG, Bender DB, Mishkin M: Contribution of the corpus callosum and the anterior commissure to visual activation of inferior temporal neurons. *Brain Res.: 131,* 227 – 239, 1977.

Guandalini P. Franchi G, Semenza P, Spidalieri G: The functional development of input-output relationships in the rostral portion of the corpus callosum in kittens. *Exp. Brain Res.: 74,* 453 – 462, 1989.

Guillemot JP, Petit D, Lepore F: Relative contributions of the corpus callosum to the bilateral receptive field of cells in SII. *Soc. Neurosci. Abstr.: 13,* 44, 1987a.

Guillemot J-P, Richer L, Prevost L, Ptito M, Lepore F: Receptive field properties of somatosensory callosal fibres in the monkey. *Brain Res.: 402,* 293 – 302, 1987b.

Guillemot J-P, Lepore F, Prevost L, Richer l, Guilbert M: Somatosensory receptive fields of fibres in the rostral corpus callosum of the cat. *Brain Res.: 441,* 221 – 232, 1988.

Haaxma R, Kuypers HGJM: Intrahemispheric cortical connexions and visual guidance of hand and finger movements in the rhesus monkey. *Brain: 98,* 239 – 260, 1975.

Hamassaki DE, Britto LRG: Interocular transfer of habituation in pigeons: mediation by tectal and/or posterior commissures. *Behav. Brain Res.: 23,* 175 – 179, 1987.

Hamilton CR: Effects of brain bisection on eye-hand coordination in monkeys wearing prisms. *J. Comp. Physiol. Psychol.: 64,* 434 – 443, 1967.

Hamilton CR: Investigations of perceptual and mnemonic lateralization in monkeys. In Harnad S, Doty RW, Goldstein L, Jaynes J, Krauthamer G (Editors), *Lateralization in the Nervous System.* New York: Academic Press, pp. 45 – 62, 1977.

Hamilton CR: Mechanisms of interocular equivalence. In Ingle DJ, Goodale MA, Mansfield RJW (Editors), *Analysis of Visual Behavior.* Cambridge, MA: The MIT Press, pp. 693 – 717, 1982.

Hamilton CR: Hemispheric specialization in monkeys. In Trevarthen CB (Editor), *Brain Circuits and Functions of the Mind.* Cambridge: Cambridge University Press, 1989.

Hamilton CR, Gazzaniga MS. Lateralization of learning of colour and brightness discriminations following brain bisection. *Nature: 201:* 220, 1964.

Hamilton CR, Lund JS: Visual discrimination of movement. Midbrain or forebrain? *Science: 170,* 1428 – 1430, 1970.

Hamilton CR, Vermeire BA: Localization of visual functions with partially split-brain monkeys. In Lepore F, Ptito M, Jasper HH (Editors), *Two Hemispheres – One Brain: Functions of the Corpus Callosum.* New York: Alan R.Liss, pp. 315 – 333, 1986.

Hamilton CR, Vermeire BA: Complementary hemispheric specialization in monkeys. *Science: 242,* 1691 – 1694, 1988.

Hamilton CR, Hillyard SA, Sperry RW: Interhemispheric comparison of color in split-brain monkeys. *Exp. Neurol.: 21,* 486 – 494, 1968.

Hamilton CR, Rodriguez KM, Vermeire BA: The cerebral commissures and midline stereopsis. *Invest. Ophthalmol. Visual Sci.: 28,* 294, 1987.

Harnad S, Doty RW, Goldstein L, Jaynes J, Krauthamer G (Editors) : *Lateralization in the Nervous System.* New York: Academic Press, 1977.

Harris LR, Lepore F, Guillemot JP, Cynader M: Abolition of optokinetic nystagmus in the cat. *Science: 210,* 90 – 92, 1980.

Heath CJ, Jones EG: Interhemispheric pathways in the absence of a corpus callosum. An experimental study of commissural connexions in the marsupial phalanger. *J. Anat.: 109,* 253 – 270, 1971.

Hemsley JP, Savage GE: Interocular transfer of shape discrimination in the goldfish: a reassessment of the role of the posterior commissure. *Exp. Neurol.: 98,* 664 – 672, 1987.

Hiyoshi T, Wada JA: Midline thalamic lesion and feline amygdaloid kindling. I. Effect of lesion placement prior to kindling. *Electroencephalogr. Clin. Neurophysiol.: 70,* 325 – 338, 1988a.

Hiyoshi T, Wada JA: Midline thalamic lesion and feline amygdaloid kindling. II. Effect of lesion placement upon completion of primary site kindling. *Electroencephalogr. Clin. Neurophysiol.: 70,* 339 – 349, 1988b.

Hoefer PFA, Pool JF: Conduction of cortical impulses and motor management of convulsive seizures. *Arch. Neurol. Psychiatry: 50,* 381 – 400, 1943.

Hoffmann KP, Distler C: The role of direction selective cells in the nucleus of the optic tract of cat and monkey during optokinetic nystagmus. In Keller EL, Zee DS (Editors), *Adaptive Processes in Visual and Oculomotor Systems.* Oxford: Pergamon Press, pp. 261 – 266, 1986.

Hoffmann KP, Distler C, Ilg U: The corpus callosum is essential for the representation of the ipsilateral visual field in the pretectum of monkeys. *Eur. J. Neurosci.: Suppl. 1,* 274, 1988.

Hubel DH, Wiesel TN: Cortical and callosal connections concerned with the vertical meridian of visual fields in cats. *J. Neurophysiol.: 30,* 1561 – 1573, 1967.

Hunter M, Ettlinger G, Maccabe JJ: Intermanual transfer in the monkey as a function of amount of callosal sparing. *Brain Res.: 93,* 223 – 240, 1975.

Imig TJ, Reale RA, Brugge JF, Morel A, Adrian HO: Topography of cortico-cortical connections related to tonotopic and binaural maps of cat auditory cortex. In Lepore F, Ptito M, Jasper HH (Editors), *Two Hemispheres – One Brain: Functions of the Corpus Callosum.* New York: Alan R. Liss, pp. 103 – 115, 1986.

Ingle DJ, Campbell A: Interocular transfer of visual discriminations by goldfish with selective commissure lesions. *J. Comp. Physiol. Psychol.: 91,* 327 – 335, 1977.

Innocenti GM: General organization of callosal connections in the cerebral cortex. In Jones EG, Peters A (Editors), *Cerebral Cortex, Vol. 5.* New York: Plenum Press, pp 291 – 353, 1986.

Innocenti GM, Manzoni T, Spidalieri G: Relevance of the callosal transfer in defining the peripheral reactivity of somesthetic cortical neurones. *Arch. Ital. Biol.: 111,* 187 – 221, 1973.

Innocenti GM, Manzoni T, Spidalieri G: Patterns of somesthetic messages transferred through the corpus callosum. *Exp. Brain Res.: 19,* 447 – 466, 1974.

Isaacson RL, Schwartz H, Persoff N, Pinson L: The role of the corpus callosum in the establishment of areas of secondary epileptiform activity. *Epilepsia: 12,* 133 – 146, 1971.

Jeeves MA: Stereoperception in callosal agenesis and partial callosotomy. (in preparation)

Jeeves MA, Wilson AF: Tactile transfer and neonatal callosal section in the cat. *Psychonomic Sci.: 16,* 235 – 237, 1969.

Jenkins WM, Masterton RB: Sound localization: effects of unilateral lesions in central auditory system. *J. Neurophysiol.: 47,* 987 – 1016, 1982.

Jones EG, Powell TPS: Connexions of the somatic sensory cortex of the Rhesus monkey. II. Contralateral cortical connexions. *Brain: 92,* 717 – 730, 1969.

Jouandet ML: Neocortical and basal telencephalic origin of the anterior commissure of the cat. *Neuroscience: 7,* 1731 – 1752, 1982.

Jouandet ML, Gazzaniga MS: Cortical field of origin of the anterior commissure of the rhesus monkey. *Exp. Neurol.: 66,* 381 – 397, 1979.

Jouandet ML, Hartenstein V: Basal telencephalic origins of the anterior commissure in the rat. *Exp. Brain Res.: 50,* 183 – 192, 1983.

Jouandet ML, Garey LJ, Lipp HP: Distribution of the cells of origin of the corpus callosum and anterior commissure in the marmoset monkey. *Anat. Embryol.: 169,* 45 – 59, 1984.

Jouandet ML, Lachat J-J, Garey LJ: Topographic distribution of callosal neurons and terminals in the cerebral cortex of the cat. *Anat. Embryol.: 173,* 323 – 342, 1986.

Kaas J, Axelrod S, Diamond IT: An ablation study of the auditory cortex in the cat using binaural tonal patterns. *J. Neurophysiol.: 30,* 710 – 724, 1967.

Kato I, Harada K, Hasegawa T, Ikarashi T, Koike Y, Kawasaki T: Role of the nucleus of the optic tract in monkeys in relation to optokinetic nystagmus. *Brain Res.: 364,* 12 – 22, 1986.

Kato I, Harada K, Hasegawa T, Ikarashi T: Role of the nucleus of the optic tract of monkeys in optokinetic nystagmus and optokinetic after-nystagmus. *Brain Res.: 474,* 16 – 26, 1988.

Keating EG: Loss of visual control of the forelimb after interruption of cortical pathways. *Exp. Neurol.: 41:* 635 – 648, 1973.

Killackey HP: The organization of somatosensory callosal projections. A new interpretation. In Reeves AG (Editor), *Epilepsy and the Corpus Callosum.* New York: Plenum Press, pp. 41 – 51, 1985.

Killackey HP, Gould HJ III, Cusick CG, Pons TP, Kaas JH: The relation of corpus callosum connections to architectonic fields and body surface maps in sensorimotor cortex of new and old world monkey. *J. Comp. Neurol.: 219,* 384 – 419, 1983.

Kimura D: Functional asymmetry of the brain in dichotic listening. *Cortex: 3,* 163 – 178, 1967.

Kinsbourne M: A model for the mechanism of unilateral neglect of space. *Trans. Am. Neurol. Assoc.: 95:* 143 – 146, 1970.

Kohn H, Myers RE: Visual information and intermanual transfer of latch box problem solving in mokeys with commissures sectioned. *Exp. Neurol.: 23,* 303 – 309, 1969.

Kopeloff N, Kennard MA, Pacella BL, Kopeloff LM, Chusid JG: Section of corpus callosum in experimental epilepsy in monkey. *Arch. Neurol. Psychiatry: 63,* 719 – 727, 1950.

Kuks JBM, Vos JE, O'Brien MJ: Coherence patterns of the infant sleep EEG in absence of the corpus callosum. *Electroencephalogr. Clin. Neurophysiol.: 66,* 8 – 14, 1987

Kusske JA, Rush JL: Corpus callosum and propagation of afterdischarge to contralateral cortex and thalamus.

Neurology: 28, 905 – 912, 1978.

Kuypers HGJM: Anatomy of the descending pathways. In *Handbook of Physiology, Section I: The Nervous System* (Brookhart JM, Mountcastle VB, Editors), *Volume II: Motor Control* (Brooks VB, Editor), Part I, pp. 597 – 666. Bethesda, MD: American Physiological Society, 1981.

Landry P, Diadori P, Dykes RW: Interhemispheric reciprocal interaction between ventroposterolateral thalamic nuclei involving cortical relay neurons. *Brain Res.: 323,* 138 – 143, 1984.

Lashley KS: The problem of serial order in behavior. In Jeffress LP (Editor), *Cerebral Mechanisms in Behavior: The Hixon Symposium.* New York, Wiley, pp. 112 – 136, 1951.

Lassonde M: The facilitatory influence of the corpus callosum on intrahemispheric processing. In Lepore F, Ptito M, Jasper HH (Editors), *Two Hemispheres – One Brain: Functions of the Corpus Callosum.* New York: Alan R. Liss, pp, 385 – 401, 1986.

Ledoux MS, Whitworth RH, Gould HJ III: Interhemispheric connections of the somatosensory cortex of the rabbit. *J. Comp. Neurol.: 258,* 145 – 157, 1987

Lee-Teng E, Sperry RW: Intermanual sterognostic size discrimination in split-brain monkeys. *J. Comp. Physiol. Psychol.: 62,* 84 – 89, 1966.

Lehman RAW: Motor coordination and hand preference after lesions of the visual pathway and corpus callosum. *Brain: 91,* 525 – 538, 1968.

Lepore F, Guillemot JP: Visual receptive fields properties of cells innervated through the corpus callosum. *Exp. Brain Res.: 46,* 413 – 424, 1982.

Lepore F, Phaneuf J, Samson A, Guillemot J-P: Interhemispheric transfer of visual pattern discriminations: evidence for a bilateral storage of the engram. *Behav. Brain Res.: 5,* 359 – 374, 1982.

Lepore F, Ptito M, Provençal C, Bédard S, Guillemot J-P: Le transfert interhémisphérique d'apprentissages visuels chez le chat à cerveau divisé: effects de la situation expérimentale. *Rev. Can. Psychol.: 39,* 400 – 415, 1985.

Lepore F, Ptito M, Guillemot J-P: The role of the corpus callosum in midline fusion. In Lepore F, Ptito M, Jasper HH (Editors), *Two Hemispheres – One Brain: Functions of the Corpus Callosum.* New York: Alan R. Liss, pp. 211 – 229, 1986a.

Lepore F, Ptito M, Jasper HH (Editors), *Two Hemispheres – One Brain: Functions of the Corpus Callosum.* New York: Alan R.Liss, 1986b.

Lepore F, Ptito M, Lassonde M: Stereoperception in cats following section of corpus callosum and/or the optic chiasma. *Exp. Brain Res.: 61,* 258 – 264, 1986c.

Levinson DM: Interocular transfer in guinea pigs following section of the corpus callosum. *J. Comp. Physiol. Psychol.: 78,* 26 – 31, 1972.

Levinson DM, Sheridan CL: Monocular acquisition and interocular transfer of two types of pattern discrimination in hooded rat. *J. Comp. Physiol. Psychol.: 67,* 468 – 472, 1969.

Lisberger SG: The neural basis for motor learning in the vestibulo-ocular reflex in monkeys. *Trends Neurosci.: 11,* 147 – 152, 1988.

Lund JS, Downer L de C, Lumley JSP: Visual control of limb movement following section of optic chiasm and corpus callosum in the monkey. *Cortex: 6,* 323 – 346, 1970.

Maffei L, Berardi N, Bisti S: Interocular transfer of adaptation after effect in neurons of area 17 and 18 of split chiasm cats. *J. Neurophysiol.: 55,* 966 – 976, 1986.

Manzoni T, Barbaresi P, Conti F: Callosal mechanism for the interhemispheric transfer of hand somatosensory information in the monkey. *Behav. Brain Res.: 11,* 155 – 170, 1984.

Manzoni T, Barbaresi P, Conti F, Fabri M: The callosal connections of the primary somatosensory cortex and the neural bases of midline fusion. *Exp. Brain Res.: 76,* 251 – 266, 1989.

Manzoni T, Hunter M, MacCabe JJ, Ettlinger G: Tactile discrimination performance in the monkey: the effect of commissure section on transfer of training between the hands. *Cortex: 9,* 40 – 55, 1973.

Majkowski J: Electrophysiological studies of learning in split-brain cats. *Electroencephalogr. Clin. Neurophysiol.: 23,* 521 – 531, 1967.

Marcus EM: Generalized seizure models and the corpus callosum. In Reeves AG (Editor), *Epilepsy and the Corpus Callosum.* New York: Plenum Press, pp. 131 – 206, 1985.

Marcus EM, Watson CW: Bilateral synchronous spike wave electrographic patterns in the cat. *Arch. Neurol.: 14,* 601 – 610, 1966.

Marcus EM, Watson CW: Symmetrical epileptogenic foci in monkey cerebral cortex. *Arch. Neurol.: 19,* 99 – 116, 1968.

Marcus EM, Watson CW, Simon SA: An experimental model of some varieties of petit mal epilepsy. Electrical-behavioral correlations of acute bilateral epileptogenic foci in cerebral cortex. *Epilepsia: 9,* 233 – 248, 1968.

Mark RF: The tectal commissure and interocular transfer of pattern discrimination in cichlid fish. *Exp. Neurol.: 16,* 215 – 225, 1966.

Mark RF, Sperry RW: Bimanual coordination in monkeys. *Exp. Neurol.: 21,* 92 – 104, 1968.

Mark RF, Peer D, Steiner J: Integrative functions in the midbrain commissures of fish. *Exp. Neurol.: 39,* 140 – 156, 1973.

Marzi CA, Antonini A, Di Stefano M, Legg CK: Callosum-dependent binocular interactions in the lateral suprasylvian area of Siamese cats which lack binocular neurons in areas 17 and 18. *Brain Res.: 197,* 230 – 235, 1980.

Marzi CA, Antonini A, Di Stefano M, Legg CR: The contribution of the corpus callosum to receptive fields in the lateral suprasylvian visual area of the cat. *Behav. Brain Res.: 4,* 155 – 176, 1982.

Marzi CA, Di Stefano M, Lepore F, Bèdard S: Role of the corpus callosum for binocular coding in Siamese and early-strabismic cats. In Lepore F, Ptito M, Jasper HH, (Editors), *Two Hemispheres - One Brain: Functions of the Corpus Callosum.* New York: Alan R.Liss, pp. 299 – 313, 1986.

Mascetti GG: Absence of interocular transfer of visual pattern discriminations in cats submitted to early postnatal section of corpus callosum. *Res. Commun. Psychol. Psychiatry Behav.: 8,* 243 – 255, 1983.

Mascetti GG, Arriagada JR: Interocular transfer of extinction of visual pattern discriminations in split-chiasm and split-brain cats. *Exp. Neurol.: 101,* 276 – 287, 1988.

Mascetti GG, Mancilla F: Perfect interocular transfer of visual pattern discriminations in split-chiasm cats trained with fading. *Behav. Brain Res.: 14,* 255 – 261, 1984.

Mascetti GG, Wittver CM, Rojas FA, Arriagada JR: Interocular transfer of reversal learning in split-chiasm and split-brain cats. *Res. Commun. Psychol. Psychiatry Behav.: 8,* 243 – 255, 1981.

Mattson RH, Bickford RG: Firing patterns of strychnine spikes in the cortex of the cat. *Electroencephalogr. Clin. Neurophysiol.: 13,* 144 – 145, 1961.

McCaughran JA Jr: The role of the forebrain commissures in kindled seizure development. In Reeves AG (Editor), *Epilepsy and the Corpus Callosum.* New York: Plenum Press, pp. 207 – 233, 1985.

McCaughran JA Jr, Corcoran ME, Wada JA: Facilitation of secondary-site amygdaloid kindling following bisection of the corpus callosum and hippocampal commissure in rats. *Exp. Neurol.: 57,* 132 – 141, 1977.

McCaughran JA Jr, Corcoran ME, Wada JA: Role of the forebrain commissures in amygdaloid kindling in rats. *Epilepsia: 19,* 19 – 33, 1978.

McCleary RA: Type of response as a factor in interocular transfer in the fish. *J. Comp. Physiol. Psychol.: 53,* 311 – 321, 1960.

McCulloch W: Mechanisms for the spread of epileptic activation of the brain. *Electroencephalogr. Clin. Neurophysiol.: 1,* 19 – 24, 1949.

McCulloch WS, Garol HW: Cortical origin and distribution of corpus callosum and anterior commissure in the monkey (*Macaca mulatta*). *J. Neurophysiol.: 4,* 555 – 563, 1941.

McIntyre DC, Edson N: Facilitation of secondary site kindling in the dorsal hippocampus following forebrain bisection. *Exp. Neurol.: 96,* 569 – 579, 1987.

McIntyre DC, Stuckey GN: Dorsal hippocampal kindling and transfer in split-brain rats. *Exp. Neurol.: 87,* 86 – 95, 1985.

McIntyre DC, Stokes KA, Edson N: Status epilepticus following stimulation of a kindled hippocampal focus in intact and commissurotomized rats. *Exp. Neurol.: 94,* 554 – 570, 1986.

McQueen JK, Dow RC: Cobalt-induced epilepsy in the rat: Some studies on the mirror focus. In Steele-Russell I, van Hof MW, Berlucchi G (Editors), *Structure and Function of Cerebral Commissures.* London: MacMillan, pp. 155 – 163, 1979.

Meikle TH Jr: Failure of interocular transfer of brightness discrimination. *Nature: 202,* 1243 – 1244, 1964.

Meikle TH Jr, Sechzer JA: Interocular transfer of brightness discrimination in 'split-brain' cats. *Science: 132,* 734 – 735, 1960.

Meikle TH Jr, Sechzer JA, Stellar E: Interhemispheric transfer of tactile conditioned responses in corpus callosum sectioned cats. *J. Neurophysiol.: 25,* 530 – 542, 1962.

Mettler FA: Corticofugal fiber connections of the cortex of Macaca mulatta. The occipital region. *J. Comp. Neurol.: 61,* 221 – 256, 1935.

Milleret C, Buser P: Réorganisation de connexions interhémisphériques calleuses chez le chat adulte: effects de l'occlusion monocular après chiasmotomie. *C. R. Acad. Sci.: 305,* 325 – 330, 1987.

Milner B, Taylor L, Sperry RW: Lateralized suppression of dichotically presented digits after commissural section in man. *Science: 161,* 184 – 186, 1968.

Minciacchi D, Antonini A: Binocularity in the visual cortex of the adult cat does not depend on the integrity of the corpus callosum. *Behav. Brain Res.: 13,* 183 – 192, 1984.

Mingazzini G. *Der Balken. Eine anatomische, physiopathologische und klinische Studie.* Berlin: Springer, 1922.

Mishkin M: Cortical visual areas and their interactions. In Karczman AG, Eccles JC (Editors), *Brain and Human Behavior.* Berlin: Springer, pp. 187 – 208, 1972.

Mishkin M: Analogous neural models for visual and tactile learning. *Neuropsychologia: 17,* 139 – 151, 1979.

Mishkin M: A memory system in the monkey. *Phil. Trans. R. Soc. Lond. B: 298,* 85 – 95, 1982.

Mishkin, M., Appenzeller T. The anatomy of memory. *Sci. Am.: 256,* 62 – 71, 1987.

Mitchell DE, Blakemore C: Binocular depth perception and the corpus callosum. *Vision Res.: 10,* 49 – 54, 1970.

Mohn G: Visuomotor behaviour of normal and corpus callosum-sectioned rats during interocular transfer. *Behav. Brain Res.: 11,* 95-101, 1984.

Mohn G, Steele Russell IS: The role of the corpus callosum and some subcortical commissures in interocular transfer in the hooded rat. *Exp. Brain Res.: 42,* 467 – 474, 1981.

Montarolo PG, Precht W, Strata P: Functional organization of the mechanisms subserving the optokinetic nystagmus in the cat. *Neuroscience: 6,* 231 – 246, 1981.

Moore CN, Casseday JH, Neff WD: Sound localization: the role of the commissural pathways of the auditory system of the cat. *Brain Res.: 82,* 13 – 26, 1974.

Morell F: Secondary epileptogenic lesions. *Epilepsia: 1,* 538 – 560, 1960.

Morrell F: Callosal mechanisms in epileptogenesis. Identification of two distinct kinds of spread of epileptic activity. In Reeves AG (Editor), *Epilepsy and the Corpus Callosum.* New York: Plenum Press, pp. 99 – 130, 1985.

Moruzzi G: Contribution à l'electrophysiologie du cortex moteur. Facilitation, after-discharge et épilepsie corticale. *Arch. Int. Physiol.: 49* , 33 – 100, 1939.

Moruzzi G: L'Epilepsie Expérimentale. Paris: Hermann, 1950.

Mountcastle VB: Central nervous mechanisms in mechanoreceptive sensibility. In *Handbook of Physiology, Section I: The Nervous System* (Brookhart JM, Mountcastle VB, Editors), *Vol. III* (Darian-Smith I, Editor): *Sensory Processes, Part 2,* pp. 789 – 878. Bethesda, MD: American Physiological Society, 1984.

Murray EA, Mishkin M: Relative contributions of SII and area 5 to tactile discrimination in monkeys. *Behav. Brain Res.: 11,* 67 – 83, 1984.

Musgrave J, Gloor P: The role of corpus callosum in bilateral interhemispheric synchrony of spike and wave discharge in feline generalized penicillin epilepsy. *Epilepsia: 21,* 369 – 378, 1980.

Mutani R, Durelli L: Mechanisms of interaction of asymmetrical bilateral epileptogenic foci in neocortex. *Epilepsia: 21,* 549 – 556, 1980.

Mutani R, Bergamini L, Fariello R, Quattrocolo G: An experimental investigation on the mechanisms of interaction of asymmetrical acute epileptic foci. *Epilepsia: 13,* 597 – 608, 1972.

Mutani R, Bergamini L, Fariello R, Quattrocolo G: Bilateral synchrony of epileptic discharge associated with chronic asymmetrical cortical foci. *Electroencephalogr. Clin. Neurophysiol.: 34,* 53 – 59, 1973.

Myers RE: Interocular transfer of pattern discriminations in

cats following section of crossed optic fibers. *J. Comp. Physiol. Psychol.: 48,* 470 – 473, 1955.
Myers RE: Function of corpus callosum in interocular transfer. *Brain: 79,* 358 – 363, 1956.
Myers RE: Localization of function in the corpus callosum. Visual gnostic transfer. *Arch. Neurol.: 1,* 74 – 77, 1959.
Myers RE, Ebner FF: Localization of function in corpus callosum: tactual information transmission in *Macaca mulatta. Brain Res.: 103,* 455 – 462, 1976.
Myers RE, Henson CO: Role of corpus callosum in transfer of tactuokinesthetic learning in chimpanzee. *Arch. Neurol.: 3,* 404 – 409, 1960.
Myers RE, Sperry RW: Interocular transfer of a visual form discrimination habit in cats after section of the optic chiasma and corpus callosum. *Anat. Rec.: 115,* 351 – 352, 1953.
Myers RE, Sperry RW, McCurdy NM: Neural mechanisms in visual guidance of limb movement. *Arch. Neurol.: 7,* 195 – 202, 1962.
Naito H, Nakamura K, Kurosaki T, Tamura Y: Transcallosal excitatory postsynaptic potentials of fast and slow pyramidal tract cells in cat sensorimotor cortex. *Brain Res.: 19,* 299 – 301, 1970.
Nakamura H, Kanaseki T: topography of the corpus callosum in the cat. *Brain Res.: 485,* 171 – 175, 1989.
Nakamura RK, Mishkin M: Chronic 'blindness' following lesions of nonvisual cortex in the monkey. *Exp. Brain Res.: 63,* 173 – 184, 1986.
Neff WD: Neural mechanisms of auditory discrimination. In Rosenblith WA (Editor), *Sensory Communication.* New York: Wiley, pp. 259 – 278, 1961.
Nie V, Maccabe JJ, Ettlinger G, Driver MV: The development of secondary epileptic discharges in the rhesus monkey after commissure section. *Electroencephalogr. Clin. Neurophysiol.: 37,* 473 – 481, 1974.
Noble J: Interocular transfer in the monkey: Rostral corpus callosum mediates transfer of object learning set but not of single-problem learning. *Brain Res.: 50,* 147 – 162, 1973.
Ohmi M, Howard IP, Eveleigh B: Directional preponderance in human optokinetic nystagmus. *Exp. Brain Res.: 63,* 387 – 394, 1986.
Ottino CA, Meglio M, Rossi GF, Tercero E: An experimental study of the structures mediating bilateral synchrony of epileptic discharges of cortical origin. *Epilepsia: 12,* 299 – 311, 1971.
Pandya DP, Seltzer B: The topography of commissural fibers. In Lepore F, Ptito M, Jasper HH (Editors), *Two Hemispheres – One Brain: Functions of the Corpus Callosum.* New York: Alan R.Liss, pp. 47 – 73, 1986.
Pandya DN, Vignolo LA: Interhemispheric projections of the parietal lobe in the Rhesus monkey. *Brain Res.: 15,* 49 – 65, 1969.
Pasik P, Pasik T: Ocular movements in split-brain monkeys. *Adv. Neurol.: 18,* 125 – 135, 1977.
Pasik T, Pasik P: Optokinetic nystagmus: An unlearned response altered by section of chiasma and corpus callosum in monkeys. *Nature: 203,* 609 – 611, 1964.
Pasik T, Pasik P: Transmission of 'elementary' visual information through brain commissures as revealed by studies on optokinetic nystagmus in monkeys. In Cernacek J. (Editor), *Cerebral Interhemispheric Relations.* Bratislava: *The Publishing House of the Slovak Academy of Sciences,* pp. 269 – 285, 1972.
Pavlov IP: *Conditioned Reflexes.* Oxford: University Press, 1927.
Payne BR: Role of callosal cells in the functional organization of cat striate cortex. In Lepore F, Ptito M, Jasper HH (Editors), *Two Hemispheres - One Brain: Functions of the Corpus Callosum.* New York: Alan R.Liss, pp. 231 – 254, 1986.
Peck CK, Crewther SG, Hamilton CR: Partial interocular transfer of brightness and movement discrimination by split-brain cats. *Brain Res.: 163,* 61 – 75, 1979.
Poblete R, Ruben RJ, Walker AE: Propagation of after discharge between temporal lobes. *J. Neurophysiol.: 22,* 538 – 553, 1959.
Pons TP, Garraghty PE, Friedman DP, Mishkin M: Physiological evidence for serial processing in somatosensory cortex. *Science: 237,* 417 – 420, 1987.
Ptito M, Lepore F: Interocular transfer in cats with early callosal transection. *Nature: 301,* 513 – 515, 1983.
Ptito M, Tassinari G, Antonini A: Electrophysiological evidence for interhemispheric connections in the anterior ectosylvian sulcus in the cat. *Exp. Brain Res.: 66,* 90 – 98, 1987.
Racine RJ: Modification of seizure activity by electrical stimulation: I. After-discharge threshold. *Electroencephalogr. Clin. Neurophysiol.: 32,* 269 – 279, 1972.
Racine RJ: Modification of seizure activity by electrical stimulation: II. Motor seizure. *Electroencephalogr. Clin. Neurophysiol.: 32,* 281 – 294, 1972.
Racine R, Okujava V, Chipashvili S: Modification of seizure activity by electrical stimulation: III. Mechanisms. *Electroencephalogr. Clin. Neurophysiol.: 32,* 295 – 299, 1972.
Reeves AG (Editor): *Epilepsy and the Corpus Callosum.* New York: Plenum Press, 1985.
Robinson CJ. Burton H: Somatotopographic organization in the second somatosensory area of *M. fascicularis. J. Comp. Neurol.: 192,* 43 – 67, 1980.
Robinson DL: Electrophysiological analysis of interhemispheric relations in the second somatosensory cortex of the cat. *Exp. Brain Res.: 18,* 131 – 144, 1973.
Robinson JS, Voneida TJ: Central cross-integration of visual inputs presented simultaneously to separate eyes. *J. Comp. Physiol.: 57,* 22 – 28, 1964.
Robinson SR: Interocular transfer in a marsupial: The brushtailed possum (*Trichosurus vulpecula*). *Brain Behav. Evol.: 21,* 114 – 124, 1982.
Rosenblueth A, Cannon WB: Cortical responses to electric stimulation. *Am. J. Physiol.: 135,* 690 – 741, 1942.
Rudy JW, Paylor R: Development of interocular equivalence of place learning in the rat requires convergence sites established prior to training. *Behav. Neurosci.: 101,* 732 – 734, 1987.
Rudy JW, Stadler-Morris S: Development of interocular equivalence in rats trained on a distal-cue navigation task. *Behav. Neurosci.: 101,* 141 – 143, 1987.
Rutledge LT, Kennedy TT: Extracallosal delayed responses to cortical stimulation in chloralosed cats. *J. Neurophysiol.: 23,* 188 – 196, 1960.
Rutledge LT, Kennedy TT: Brain-stem and cortical interactions in the interhemispheric delayed response. *Exp. Neurol.: 4,* 470 – 483, 1961.

Savage GE: Interocular transfer and commissure function in lower vertebrates, with special references to fish. In Steele-Russell I, van Hof MW, Berlucchi G (Editors), *Structure and Function of Cerebral Commissures*. London: MacMillan, pp. 34 – 52, 1979.

Schwartzkroin PA, Futamachi KJ, Noebels JL, Prince DA. Transcallosal effects of a cortical epileptiform focus. *Brain Res.: 99,* 59 – 68, 1975.

Seacord L, Gross CG, Mishkin M: Role of inferior temporal cortex in interhemispheric transfer. *Brain Res.: 167,* 269 – 272, 1979.

Sechzer JA: Successful interocular transfer of pattern discrimination in 'split-brain' cats with shock-avoidance motivation. *J. Comp. Physiol. Psychol.: 58,* 76 – 83, 1964.

Sechzer JA, Folstein SE, Geiger EH, Mervis DF: Effects of neonatal hemispheric disconnections in kittens. In Harnad S, Doty RW, Goldstein L, Jaynes J, Krauthamer G (Editors), *Lateralization in the Nervous System*. New York: Academic Press, pp. 89 – 108, 1977.

Shanks MF, Pearson RCA, Powell TPS: The callosal connexions of the primary somatic sensory cortex in the monkey. *Brain Res. Rev.: 9,* 43 – 65, 1985.

Shatz C: Abnormal interhemispheric connections in the visual system of Boston Siamese cats: a physiological study. *J. Comp. Neurol.: 171,* 229 – 246, 1977.

Sheridan CL: Interocular transfer of brightness and pattern discriminations in normal and corpus callosum-sectioned rats. *J. Comp. Physiol. Psychol.: 59,* 292 – 294, 1965.

Sheridan CL, Levinson DM, Hottman TJ, Moore DR: Role of interproblem learning in interocular transfer. *Percept. Motor Skills: 50,* 343 – 355, 1980.

Sherman SM: The effect of superior colliculus lesion upon the visual fields of cats with cortical ablations. *J. Comp. Neurol.: 172,* 211 – 230, 1977.

Sidtis JJ: Music, pitch perception, and the mechanisms of cortical hearing. In MS Gazzaniga (Editor), *Handbook of Cognitive Neuroscience*. New York, Plenum Press, pp. 91 – 114, 1984.

Sparks R, Geschwind N: Dichotic listening in man after section of neocortical commissures. *Cortex: 4,* 3 – 16, 1968.

Spencer SS: Corpus callosum section and other disconnection procedures for medically intractable epilepsy. *Epilepsia: 29,* S85 – 99, 1988.

Spencer SS, Spencer DD, Williamson PD, Sass K, Novelly RA, Mattson RH: Corpus callosotomy for epilepsy. I. Seizure effects. *Neurology: 38,* 19 – 23, 1988.

Sperry RW: Cerebral organization and behavior. *Science: 133,* 1747 – 1757, 1961.

Sperry RW: Orderly function with disordered structure. In Foerster HV, Zopt GW (Editors), *Principles of Self-Organization*. New York: Pergamon Press, pp. 279 – 290, 1962.

Sperry RW, Stamm JS, Miner N. Relearning tests for interocular transfer following division of optic chiasm and corpus callosum in the cat. *J. Comp. Physiol. Psychol.: 49,* 529 – 533, 1956.

Sperry RW, Myers RE, Schrier AM: Perceptual capacity of the isolated visual cortex in the cat. *Q. J. Exp. Psychol.: 7,* 65 – 71, 1960.

Spidalieri G, Guandalini P: Motor representation in the rostral portion of the cat corpus callosum as evidenced by microstimulation. *Exp. Brain Res.: 53,* 59 – 70, 1983.

Spidalieri G, Guandalini P, Franchi G: Motor responses mediated by orthodromic and antidromic activation of the rostral portion of the cat corpus callosum. *Exp. Brain Res.: 64,* 133 – 142, 1986.

Spidalieri G, Franchi G, Guandalini P: Somatic receptive-field properties of single fibers in the rostral portion of the corpus callosum in awake cats. *Exp. Brain Res.: 58,* 75 – 81, 1985

Spiegel E: The central mechanism of generalized epileptic fits. *Am. J. Psychol.: 88,* 595 – 609, 1931.

Sprague JM: Interaction of cortex and superior colliculus in mediation of visually guided behavior in the cat. *Science: 153,* 1544 – 1547, 1966.

Sprague JM, Berlucchi G, Rizzolatti G: The role of the superior colliculus and pretectum in vision and visually guided behavior. In Jung R (Editor), *Handbook of Sensory Physiology, Vol. VII/3 B.* Berlin: Springer, pp. 27 – 101, 1973.

Squire LR. *Memory and Brain.* Oxford: Oxford University Press, 1987.

Stamm JS, Sperry RW: Function of corpus callosum in contralateral transfer of somesthetic discrimination in cats. *J. Comp. Physiol. Psychol.: 50,* 138 – 143, 1957.

Steele Russell IS, Safferstone JF: Lateralization of brightness and pattern discrimination learning in corpus callosum-sectioned rats. *Brain Res.: 49,* 497 – 498, 1973.

Steele-Russell I, van Hof MW, Berlucchi G (Editors): *Structure and Function of Cerebral Commissures.* London: MacMillan, 1979.

Steele-Russell I, van Hof MW, van der Steen J, Collewijn H: Visual and oculomotor function in optic chiasma-sectioned rabbits. *Exp. Brain Res.: 66,* 61 – 73, 1987.

Straw RN, Mitchell CL: Effect of section of the corpus callosum on cortical after-discharge patterns in the cat. *Proc. Soc. Exp. Biol. Med.: 125,* 128 – 132, 1967.

Sullivan MS, Hamilton CR: Interocular transfer of reversed and non-reversed discriminations via the anterior commissure in monkeys. *Physiol. Behav.: 10,* 355 – 359, 1973a.

Sullivan MS, Hamilton CR: Memory establishment via the anterior commissure of monkeys. *Physiol. Behav.: 11,* 873 – 879, 1973b.

Swadlow HA: The corpus callosum as a model system in the study of mammalian cerebral axons. A comparison of results from primate and rabbit. In Reeves AG (Editor), *Epilepsy and the Corpus Callosum.* New York: Plenum Press, pp. 55 – 71, 1985.

Takahashi TT, Wagner H, Konishi M: Role of commissural projections in the representation of bilateral auditory space in the barn owl's inferior colliculus. *J. Comp. Neurol.:* 281, 545 – 554, 1989.

Tauber ER, Atkin A: Optomotor response to monocular stimulation: relation to visual system organization. *Science: 160,* 1365 – 1367, 1968.

Teitelbaum H: Lateralization of olfactory memory in the split-brain rat. *J. Comp. Physiol. Psychol.: 75,* 51 – 56, 1971.

Teitelbaum H, Sharpless SK, Byck R: Role of somatosensory cortex in interhemispheric transfer of tactile habits. *J. Comp. Physiol Psychol.: 66,* 623 – 632, 1968.

Thompson R: Centrencephalic theory and interhemispheric

transfer of habits. *Psychol. Rev.: 72,* 385 – 398, 1965.

Tieman SB, Hamilton CR: Interocular transfer in split-brain monkeys following serial disconnection. *Brain Res.: 63,* 368 – 373, 1973.

Timney B, Elberger AJ, Vandewater ML: Binocular depth perception in the cat following early corpus callosum section. *Exp. Brain Res.: 60,* 19 – 26, 1985.

Timney B, Lansdown G: Binocular depth perception, visual acuity and visual fields in cats following neonatal section of the optic chiasm. *Exp. Brain Res.: 74,* 272 – 278, 1989.

Tong L, Spear PD, Kalil RE: Effects of corpus callosum section on functional compensation in the posteromedial lateral suprasylvian visual area after early visual cortex damage in cats. *J. Comp. Neurol.: 256,* 128 – 136, 1987.

Toyama K, Matsunami K, Ohno T, Tokashiki S: An intracellular study of neuronal organization in the visual cortex. *Exp. Brain Res.: 21,* 45 – 66, 1974.

Trevarthen C: Double visual learning in split brain monkeys. *Science: 136,* 258 – 259, 1962.

Trevarthen C: Subcortical influence on cortical processing in 'split' brains. In Ottoson D (Editor), *Duality and Unity of the Brain.* London: MacMillan, pp 382 – 415, 1987.

Trevarthen CB (Editor): *Brain Circuits and Functions of the Mind.* Cambridge: Cambridge University Press, 1989.

Van Alphen A: The anterior commissure of the rabbit. *Acta Anatom.: 57,* 1 – 112, 1969.

Van Die G. Collewijn H: Optokinetic nystagmus in man. *Human Neurobiol.: 1,* 11 – 119, 1982.

Voigt T, LeVay S, Stamnes SA: Morphological and immunocytochemical observations on the visual callosal projection in the cat. *J. Comp. Neurol.: 272,* 450 – 460, 1988.

Voneida TJ: Performance of a visual conditioned response in split-brain cats. *Exp. Neurol.: 8:* 493 – 504, 1963.

Voneida TJ, Vardaris RM, Fish SE, Reiheld CT: The origin of the hippocampal commissure in the rat. *Anatom. Rec.: 201,* 91 – 103, 1981

Wada JA, Komai S: Effects of anterior two-thirds callosal bisection upon bisymmetrical and bisynchronous generalized convulsions kindled from amygdala in epileptic baboon, *Papio papio.* In Reeves AG (Editor), *Epilepsy and the Corpus Callosum,* New York: Plenum Press, pp. 75 – 97, 1985.

Wada JA, Mizoguchi T: Effect of forebrain bisection upon amygdaloid kindling in epileptic baboon, *Papio Papio. Epilepsia: 25,* 278 – 287, 1984.

Wada JA, Sato M: The generalized convulsive seizure state induced by daily electrical stimulation of the amygdala in split brain cats. *Epilepsia: 16,* 417 – 430, 1975.

Wada JA, Mizoguchi T, Osawa T: Secondarily generalized convulsive seizure induced by daily amygdaloid stimulation in rhesus monkeys. *Neurology: 28,* 1026 – 1036, 1978.

Wada JA, Mizoguchi T, Komai S: Cortical motor activation in amygdaloid kindling: Observations in non-epileptogenic rhesus monkeys with anterior 2/3 callosal bisection. In Wada JA (Editor), *Kindling 2.* New York: Raven Press, pp. 235 – 248, 1981.

Wada JA, Nakashima T, Kaneko Y: Forebrain bisection and feline amygdaloid kindling. *Epilepsia: 23,* 521 – 531, 1982.

Wallace SF, Rosenquist AC, Sprague JM: Recovery from cortical blindness mediated by destruction of non-tectotectal fibers in the commissure of the superior colliculus in the cat. *J. Comp. Neurol.:* 1989 (in press).

Watson RT, Valenstein E, Day AL, Heilman KM: The effect of corpus callosum lesions on unilateral neglect in monkeys. *Neurology: 34,* 812 – 815, 1984.

Wegener JG: A note on auditory discrimination behaviour and the corpus callosum. In Ettlinger G (Editor), *Functions of Corpus Callosum.* London: Churchill, pp. 69 – 72, 1965.

Whitsel BL, Petruccelli CM, Werner G: Symmetry and connectivity in the map of the body surface in somatosensory area II of Primates. *J. Neurophysiol.: 32,* 170 – 183, 1969.

Whitteridge D: Area 18 and the vertical meridian of the visual field. In Ettlinger G (Editor), *Functions of Corpus Callosum.* Churchill, pp. 115 – 120, 1965.

Yamaguchi S, Myers RE: Age effect on forebrain commissure section and interocular transfer. *Exp. Brain Res.: 15,* 225 – 233, 1972.

Yeo CH: Interocular transfer in the goldfish. In Steele-Russell I, van Hof MW, Berlucchi G (Editors), *Structure and Function of Cerebral Commissures.* London: MacMillan, pp. 53 – 60, 1979.

Zee DS, Tusa RJ, Herdman SJ, Butler PH, Gücer G: Effects of occipital lobectomy upon eye movements in primate. *J. Neurophysiol.: 58,* 883 – 907, 1987.

Zeki SM: Visual deficits related to size of lesion in prestriate cortex of optic chiasm sectioned monkeys. *Life Sci.: 6,* 1627 – 1638, 1967.

Zeki SM: Comparison of the cortical degeneration in the visual regions of the temporal lobe of the monkey following section of the anterior commissure and the splenium. *J. Comp. Neurol.: 148:* 167 – 176, 1973.

Zeki SM: Simultaneous anatomical demonstration of the representation of the vertical and horizontal meridians in areas V2 and V3 of rhesus monkey visual cortex. *Proc. R. Soc. Lond. B: 195,* 517 – 523, 1977.

Zeki S, Fries W: Function of the corpus callosum in the Siamese cat. *Proc. R. Soc. Lond. B: 207,* 249 – 258, 1980.

Handbook of Neuropsychology, Vol. 4
F. Boller and J. Grafman (Eds)

CHAPTER 3

Integrative functions of the cerebral commissures

Colwyn Trevarthen

Department of Psychology, Edinburgh, Scotland

Introduction

The corpus callosum and the anterior commissure furnish the only direct links between the neocortices of the two cerebral hemispheres in the mammalian brain, and the only pathway through which the higher functions of perception and cognition, learning and voluntary motor coordination can be unified. There are estimated to be 10^9 axons in these commissures in the human brain. About half of these are comparatively large and myelinated, while the rest are unmyelinated, including some of very small diameter which are difficult to count (Innocenti, 1986). The position of their cell bodies in the cortex and the distribution of their terminals in the opposite cortex indicate that the commissural neurones perform functions similar to those of associative neurones that make medium- and long-range connections within each cortex. Indeed, cortical associative systems develop from cells whose axons first grow branches exuberantly both within the hemispheres and between them. Later, selective elimination of collaterals divides the cells into separate intrahemispheric and interhemispheric populations and a large proportion of axons, perhaps as many as 9/10 in the corpus callosum of a human being, are lost in early postnatal months (Innocenti, 1986). This sorting process, which is assisted by the patterning of stimuli, but is also gated by inputs from the reticular core of the brain, creates complementary sets of associative links between the cortical maps for various sensory and motor functions. It also refines the separation and interconnection of specialized cell networks for distinct modalities of perception (Innocenti, 1981). Commissural systems become organized to join together mirror projection fields in the two hemispheres, unifying perception over the midline of the body-centered field of experience (e.g., over the vertical meridian of the visual field), and assisting in the selection of unilateral motor adjustments, including orienting movements. Segregation of connections between parietal, temporal and frontal association cortices serves to form complementary hemispheric functions, including those asymmetrically distributed between the hemispheres (Innocenti, 1986; Goldman-Rakic, 1987).

The role of the interhemispheric commissures must be considered in relation to the functional maps in different parts of the cortex, and in a developmental context. Fig. 1 summarizes important phylogenetic and developmental trends in the commissures, and Figs. 2 and 3 outline the main features of the anatomy and function of the human commissures. Further information is to be found in the following: Bremer, 1956; Bremer et al., 1956; Yakovlev and Lecours, 1967; Rakic and Yakovlev, 1968; Berlucchi, 1972, 1981; Doty and Negrao, 1973; La Mantia and Rakic, 1974; Elberger, 1982; Innocenti, 1986; Bogen, 1987; Goldman-Rakic, 1987; Clarke et al., in press.

The effects of interruption of the corpus callosum on mental activities were, for long, obscure. Only scattered observations had been made before 1950. Among the most significant was Dejerine's identification of destruction of fibers in the splenium as a factor in 'verbal blindness' (Dejerine, 1892), an interpretation supported by visual deconnection effects following surgical sectioning of the splenium reported by Trescher and Ford (1937) and Maspes (1948). Another historic interpretation was the explanation for the symbolic apraxia of the left hand put forward by Liepmann and Maas (1908) in terms of disconnection of the voluntary control of the left hand in the right hemisphere from verbal comprehension in the left hemisphere (see Bremer et al., 1956; Geschwind, 1965; Bogen, 1978, 1987). In Pavlov's laboratory, Bykov (1925) showed that transfer of conditioned responses to tactile stimuli, from one flank of the body of a dog to the other, was stopped by cutting the corpus callosum. But there were many negative studies, and great uncertainty about the contribution of extracallosal damage to effects which some identified with interruption of the commissures (Bremer et al., 1956).

Then, 35 years ago, elegant experiments performed by Ronald Myers and Roger Sperry demonstrated that cutting the corpus callosum had profound effects on perception and learning (Myers, 1956; Myers and Sperry, 1953; Sperry, 1961). They first showed that visual discrimination learning was transferred from one eye of a cat to the other when the input that normally crossed from each eye to the cortex on the other side had been prevented by dividing the optic chiasma. This was presumed to be an interhemispheric transfer.

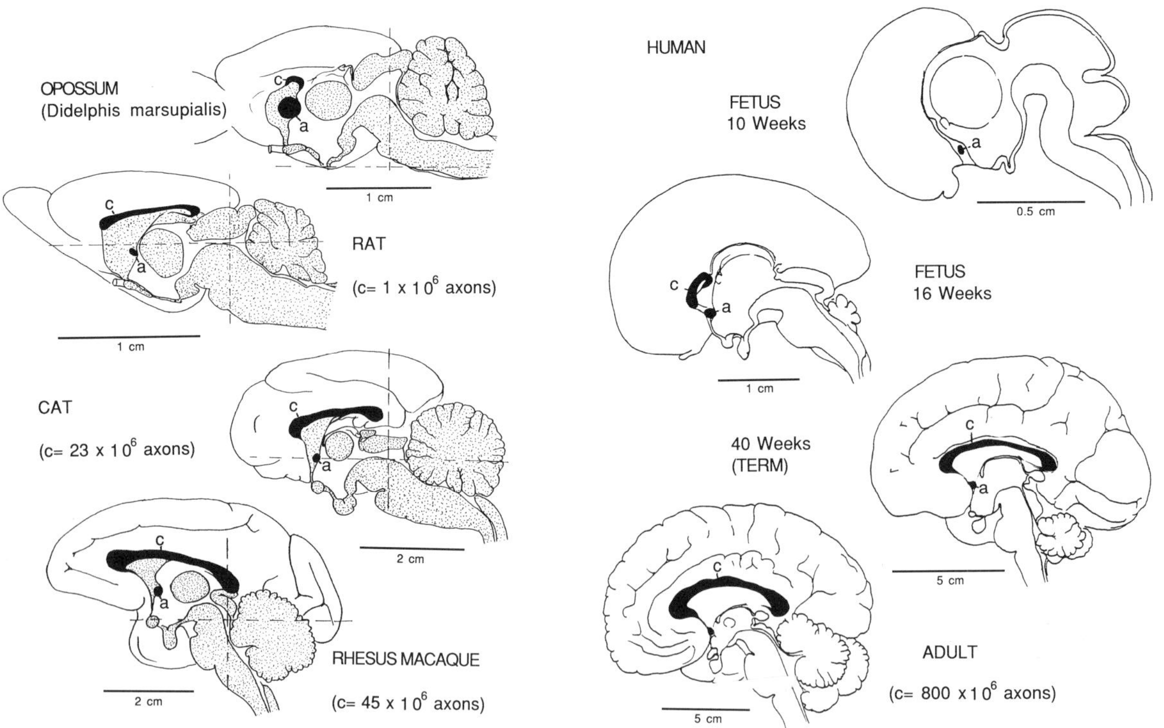

Fig. 1. Left: Sagittal sections of brains of a marsupial, a rodent, a carnivore and a primate show the evolutionary increase in size of the interhemispheric commissures. The corpus callosum (c) adds fibers towards the posterior (visual and auditory) parts in cat and monkey. The more primitive anterior commissure (a) is the major commissure in the marsupial, but a small part in eutherians. The number of callosal axons increases with evolution of visual and manual intelligence. The anterior part of the corpus callosum (genu) is large in the monkey, probably in relation to two-handed manipulation and the concepts of objects that go with this skill. Right: Development of forebrain commissures in a human. The corpus callosum grows in the fetus with the neocortex. The callosum of a newborn infant is proportionally more slender than in the adult, but has many times more axons.

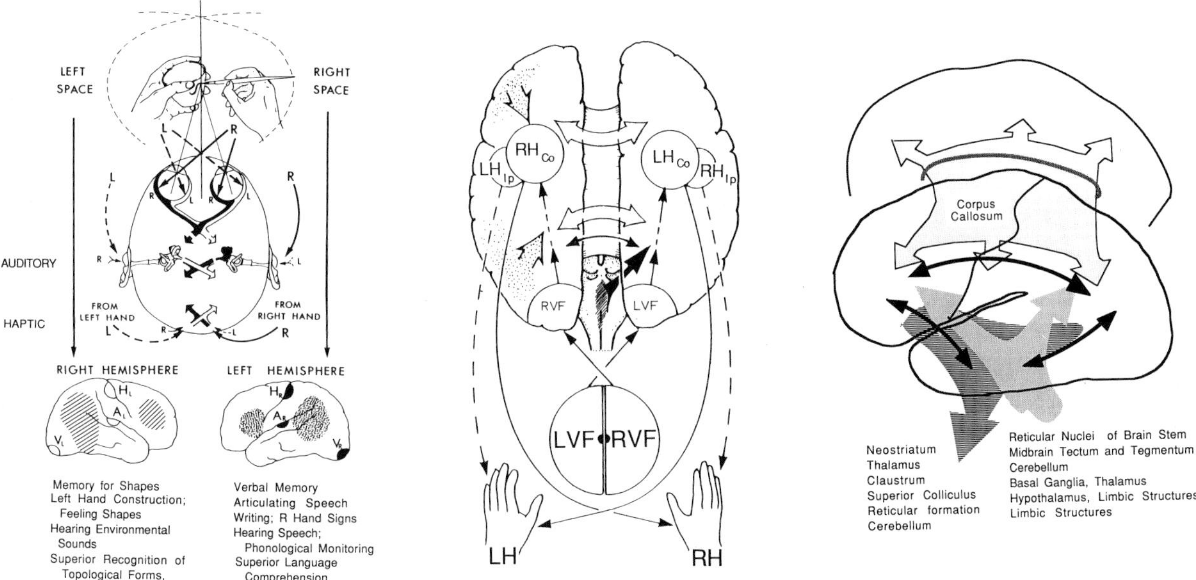

Fig. 2. Left: Sensory information from left and right halves of the body and of perceptual space enters by way of mirror cross-projections. The two hemispheres have complementary cognitive specializations. Center: In normal subjects, integrations between halves of the visual field (LVF and RVF) and manual responses (LH and RH) depend on intrahemispheric and callosal connections which are modulated by ascending projections from the brain stem (black arrows) and by intrahemispheric projections, e.g. from limbic cortex (dotted arrows). Connections to and from each half of the cortex are strong for the contralateral hand (Co) and weak for the ipsilateral hand (Ip). Right: Functions of intrahemispheric (black arrows) and interhemispheric (corpus callosum) connections are patterned by input from brainstem sites, most of which receive cortico-fugal projections. The commissures are only one mechanism integrating neocortical functions.

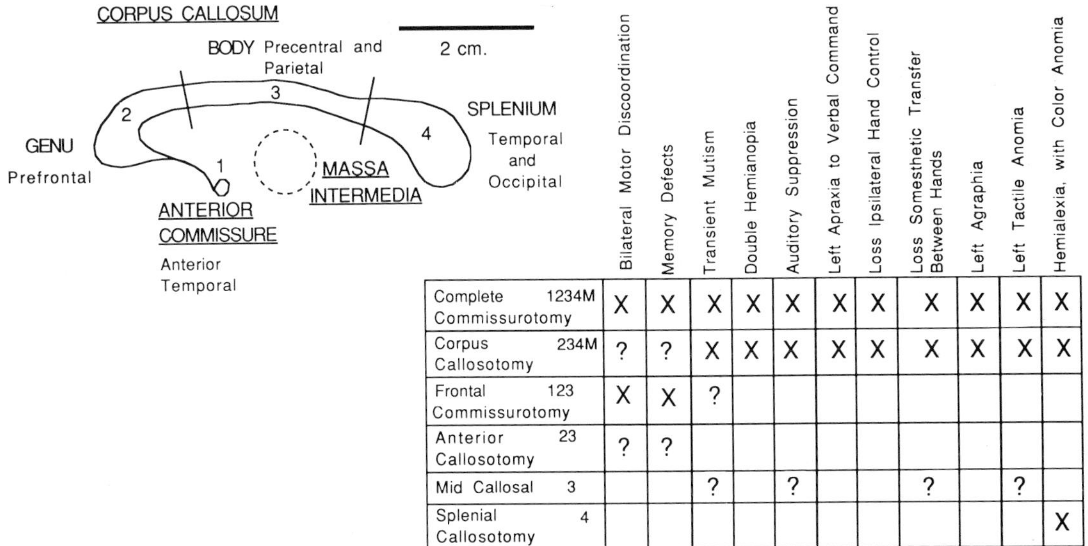

	Bilateral Motor Discoordination	Memory Defects	Transient Mutism	Double Hemianopia	Auditory Suppression	Left Apraxia to Verbal Command	Loss Ipsilateral Hand Control	Loss Somesthetic Transfer Between Hands	Left Agraphia	Left Tactile Anomia	Hemialexia, with Color Anomia
Complete Commissurotomy 1234M	X	X	X	X	X	X	X	X	X	X	X
Corpus Callosotomy 234M	?	?	X	X	X	X	X	X	X	X	X
Frontal Commissurotomy 123	X	X	?								
Anterior Callosotomy 23	?	?									
Mid Callosal 3			?		?			?		?	
Splenial Callosotomy 4											X

Fig. 3. Interruption of different parts of the commissures leads to different effects in perception, motor coordination, eupraxis, language and memory. The massa intermedia is a variable adhesion between midline thalamic nuclei; it is not a commissure.

When both the corpus callosum and the chiasma were cut, in what became known as the 'split brain', transfer was, indeed, abolished. Further experiments by Myers showed that transcallosal transfer of visual experience, though substantial and rapid for most tasks, was not complete. Some details of experience were not passed interocularly in animals in which the optic chiasma had been sectioned (Myers, 1962). Subsequent work has confirmed these findings (Berlucchi and Marzi, 1982).

A split-brain effect in somesthesis was shown when cats were tested for transfer of discrimination learning between paired textures or shapes mounted on pedals which the animal pushed with a forepaw to obtain food reward. Interpaw transfer of learning was abolished by callosum section (Stamm and Sperry, 1957). Soon afterwards, split-brain learning was demonstrated in monkeys, for both visual and haptic discriminations (Downer, 1959; Glickstein and Sperry, 1960; Sperry, 1961).

The splitting of perception and learning contrasted, in both cat and monkey, with retention of efficient, undivided, whole-body motor coordination (Myers et al., 1962). No disruption of movements was found in split – brain cats, and both forepaws could be directed to targets seen by one hemisphere (Schrier and Sperry, 1959). However, in training situations where orientation of the body was controlled, it was shown that fine coordinations of the two hands of a monkey were partly disrupted by the midline surgery. If a monkey with a divided optic chiasma, anterior commissure and corpus callosum was prevented from using preferred intrahemispheric systems for contralateral eye-hand combinations (left eye with right hand, and vice versa) and was forced to use ipsilateral (left-left or right-right) combinations which required interhemispheric coordination, then grasping and manipulating movements became clumsy and visual guidance of finger positioning and choice of target was impaired (Downer, 1959; Trevarthen, 1962, 1965; Lund et al., 1970; Brinkman and Kuypers, 1972.

Further experimentation showed that some features of visual experience could be transferred between the eyes of chiasm-callosum sectioned cats and monkeys, i.e. across the midplane of the brain below the level of the forebrain. Interocular transfer of brightness discriminations despite section of the optic chiasm, corpus callosum and anterior commissure was first reported in cats (Meikle and Sechzer, 1960). Subsequently Trevarthen, using a double learning technique with polarized stimuli to channel input separately to the two eyes and thus control for eye movements, showed that a number of discriminations, including some color discriminations, could be integrated between the inputs to the two eyes in split-brain monkeys (Trevarthen, 1962, 1965, 1968). Brainstem mechanisms could also transfer simple conditioned responses to light stimuli (Voneida, 1963).

In the 1960s, Los Angeles neurosurgeons Joseph Bogen and Philip Vogel, aiming to reduce interhemispheric spread of seizures in human beings who were suffering from severe intractable epilepsy, performed midline transection of both neocortical commissures, as well as the dorsal and ventral hippocampal commissures and, when it was present, the massa intermedia. Gazzaniga et al., (1962) described the results of tests with the first of these patients as a human split-brain condition. Simultaneously, Geschwind and Kaplan (1962) reported the case of a woman who had suffered an infarct of the corpus callosum. Her symptoms indicated a deconnection between the hemispheres – she wrote normally with her right hand but aphasically with her left. Geschwind and Kaplan interpreted their findings in the light of the experiments with split-brain animals (Geschwind, 1965). Intensive psychological testing of the patients of Bogen and Vogel after the operation resulted in the description of a condition of divided consciousness and learning known as the 'commissurotomy syndrome' (Sperry, 1968, 1974, 1982; Sperry et al., 1969; Gazzaniga, 1970; Bogen, 1978).

In general, the findings with commissurotomy patients confirmed those with split-brain animals.

Perceptual processes in commissurotomy patients are divided for vision, and for touch discrimination in the hands, as in the split-brain monkey, and under certain circumstances hearing and olfaction are also divided. Considerable debate has been generated around questions of the extent to which brain stem systems can provide transfer or coordination of attention, movement and motivation between the two cerebral cortices. The research has clarified the organization of intergrative processes of perception, learning and motor control, and has advanced understanding about the hierarchical organization of brain mechanisms. Commissurotomy patients have helped elucidate the role of arousal and orientation of attention in the acquisition by cortical processes of information through the special senses (Trevarthen, 1972, 1975). These findings lead to questions about intrinsic motivating processes generated in the core of the brain and how they affect cognitive processes and consciousness in the cortex (Trevarthen, 1987).

Most research has been done with vision. The organization of the visual system shows clearly the levels at which neocortical commissures operate. As is the case for primates generally, human vision depends upon the conjugate deployment of two foveal detectors of high resolution but limited spatial scope, which jointly activate the large and elaborately differentiated striate cortex areas. This central 'analyser' of the visual projection system is sharply divided down the midline. Stimulation from the left visual field (and right hemiretinae of the two eyes) is passed to the right optic tract, and thence to the right lateral geniculate body of the thalamus where separate layers of cells receive terminals from retinal ganglion cell axons of the two eyes. Beyond the thalamus, in the right striate cortex, a precise partial registration of inputs from the two eyes for the left visual field is achieved in binocular cells, which form the substrate for binocular vision, hyperacuity and steropsis by detection of interocular disparities. A mirror projection to the left lateral geniculate and left striate cortex carries foveal information for the left half of each eye, and the right visual field.

Functioning of this mirror-symmetrically divided geniculo-striate visual system of high acuity depends upon precise convergence of the two eyes, accurate focussing of the retinal image by accommodation of the lens, and precise conjugate displacement of the two eyes together by saccades, which separate intervals in which the retinal image is stabilized (i.e., displacing only by slow drift or microsaccades). This refined visual uptake of information also depends on stabilization of the head. This is the sensory-motor system of central, foveal or focal vision (Fig. 4). Its functions, though essentially cortical and unified at the vertical meridian by the corpus callosum, rely on subcortical oculomotor and postural systems acting in coordination with 'backstream' attentional activation of the visual cortex from the brain stem via the pulvinar nucleus of the thalamus and prestriate cortex (see Fig. 12).

Outside the foveal region of the retina, a set of larger-sized ganglion cells, increasingly numerous towards the retinal periphery, projects to the magnocellular laminae of the lateral geniculate nuclei, the roof of the midbrain (superior colliculus) and to a group of small nuclei about the dorsal mesencephalic/diencephalic boundary. These subcortical or brain stem sites of termination for visual input are generally assumed not to contribute to vision of local detail or to the buildup of a vividly conscious representation of the outside world in color. They have, however, phylogenetically ancient importance, being the essential components of the visual learning mechanisms of lower vertebrates, and they appear to retain, even in human beings, important special functions in preattentive vision and orienting of attention. They collaborate with auditory, somesthetic, vestibular and mechano-proprioceptive inputs to sustain a unified, body-referred context or frame for focal perception and an evaluative basis for selective consciousness. Diencephalic and mesencephalic (mid – brain) visual areas are linked with prestriate visual cortex by upward projections from the colliculus through the pulvinar, and by

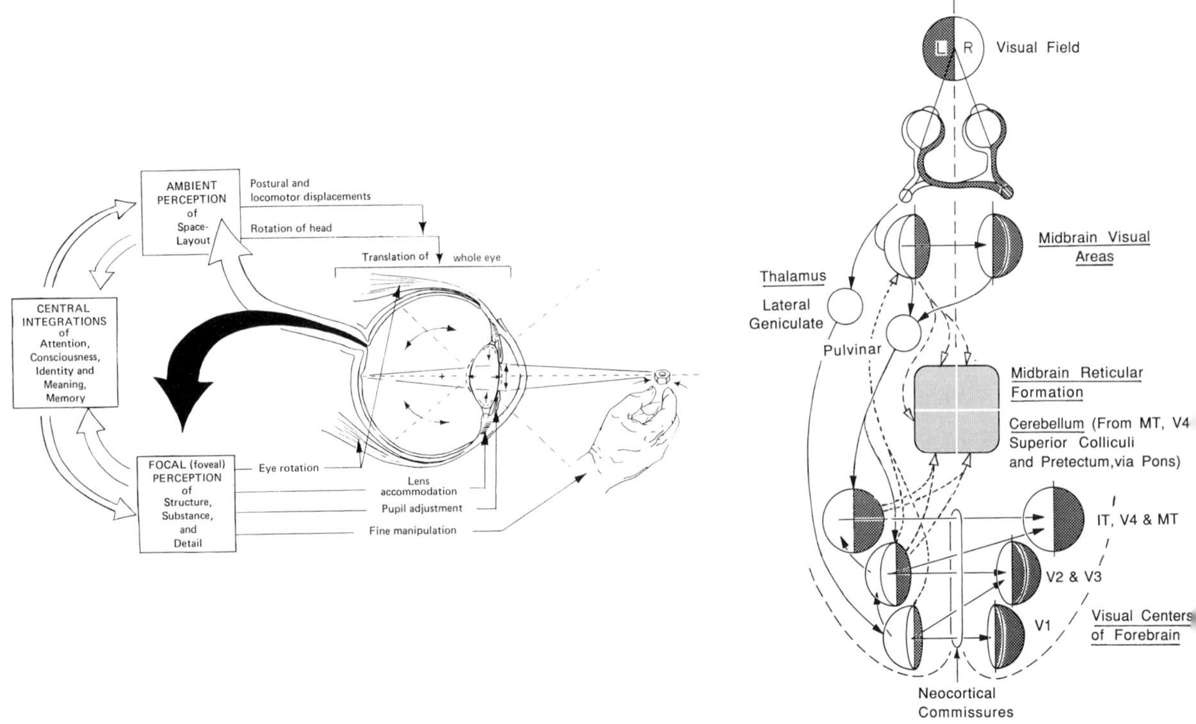

Fig. 4. Sensory-motor mechanisms for ambient and focal vision exemplify parallel and complementary systems for orienting the whole body and for discrimination. Rotation of the foveae to find objects is regulated from brain-stem oculomotor-systems. Focal information, for perception of detail necessary for accurate identification of objects and for fine guidance of manipulation, requires neocortical analysers with foveal input. The commissures inform a central, bilateral awareness in each hemisphere (Trevarthen, 1972). Memory stores for object recognition are separate from the bisymmetric, body-centered field of primary sensory reception and orienting movements, which are cross-integrated in brain-stem structures.

downward projections from the striate cortex by way of prestriate areas, to the superior colliculi (Fig. 12). Pattern recognition in the superior colliculi of cats and monkeys appears to depend largely on the latter striato-fugal projection. The input through the pulvinar to the posterior parietal cortex appears to have a key role in the regulation of selective attention and the eye movements that mediate it. In considering possible sites for visuomotor coordination below the hemispheres it is important not to forget the cerebellum, which receives a significant visual input from the striate cortex via the pons (Glickstein and Gibson, 1976; Glickstein, 1988).

The proximity of the midbrain visual areas to, and connections with, the motor nuclei of the eyes obviously relate to regulation of visual fixation with the head stabilized. However, it must also be noted that in humans, as in other animals, peripheral vision, outside the fovea and parafoveal zone, conveys information about surroundings when the head is being moved through space, i.e., when the eyes are translated rather than rotated. This ambient vision does not depend on precise conjugate fixation or accommodation (Fig. 4). Input of visual information through the system that serves the more extensive ambient visual field, from the flow of light patterns activated by movements which translate the head and eyes, is of great importance in setting up a visual frame for action. It guides locomotion, placement of limbs in space around the body, maintenance of stationary posture and selection of future foci for the foveal mechanism (Lee, 1980). With the aid of a few head and eye rotations, peripheral or extrafoveal vision can cover the whole sphere of space surrounding the subject. It informs the preattentive field for consciousness as well as guiding subconscious placement of the limbs. It can serve to give preliminary location for future objects of prehension, and it must, therefore, be capable of assisting the cerebral processes by which the arms and hands are aimed to off-center locations. Finally, the relations between the other modalities and vision are different for central and peripheral zones.

For all of the above reasons, we expect the visual input from central and peripheral retinas to be projected to different organized central cerebral systems. These will have differing relationships with the motor systems, differing dependence on attentional and orientational programs of central origin, and differing relations with other sensory modalities. As we shall see, split-brain animals and human commissurotomy patients have the capacity to cross-integrate activities of the two halves of their brains by way of brain-stem pathways. They have a degree of anatomic integrity in ambient awareness in spite of complete division of their focal awareness and memory (Trevarthen, 1987). The detailed evidence for these two levels of visual function is presented in the following.

Visual perception near the fovea, with fixed orientation of gaze

Following complete cerebral commissurotomy, all primary dimensions of visual discrimination, such as can be tested by exposing pictures or patterns of light within about 15° of the center of the visual field in a tachistoscope or on a computer screen, are perceived separately in the two hemispheres. While fixating gaze on a point, a commissurotomy patient cannot compare the form, color or orientation of small stimuli located to left and right of this point. There is no transfer of detailed, highly-resolved information across the vertical meridian (Fendrich and Gazzaniga, 1989). The same comparisons are easily made within each half of the field. In such experiments, the subjects signal their judgements by simple verbal report, by hand signals, or by pressing switches designated to represent different decisions. This evidence confirms that processing of retinal information in the striate cortex is entirely split in two by the operation. Verbal report is, in nearly all cases, accurate only for the right half of the visual field, the right hemisphere being incapable of producing speech. Some patients in whom the anterior commissure is intact, but corpus callosum divided, also show the full split-brain effect. In others an intact anterior commissure appears to transfer consciousness and learning.

Subjects with all commissures intact have no difficulty in making most visual comparisons or same-difference judgements across the vertical meridian. If the splenium of the corpus callosum (approximately the posterior fifth) is left intact and all anterior parts of the commissures are severed, visual perception is still not divided (Gordon et al., 1961). It may be concluded that part of the neocortical commissures, principally the splenium, serves as a sole and complete link of visual experience over the midline (Fig. 3). There is physiological support for this conclusion (Choudhury et al., 1965; Hubel and Wiesel, 1967; Rocha-Miranda et al., 1975; Van Essen et al., 1982). However, two qualifications are to be made. First, it has been found that information from stimuli of high spatial resolution and low contrast is not fully transmitted between the hemispheres of normal subjects with all commissures intact; be they cats or human beings, transfer is incomplete. This has been demonstrated by measuring the transfer of after-effects of stimulation over the vertical meridian (Maffei et al., 1986; Berardi et al., 1987; Berardi and Fiorentini, 1987). Evidently the highest degree of visual stimulus resolution or analysis depends on local intra-cortical circuits in the striate area. These circuits do not share information with callosal neurones, which are effective in representing intercellular processes only at a larger scale. The second point is that because callosal neurones interconnect striate cortex near the vertical meridian only (Berlucchi et al., 1986; Berlucchi and Antonini, 1988; Van Essen et al., 1982), callosal transfer of information more than a degree or two from the meridian must take place between prestriate visual areas; that is, after projection by a transcortical relay or several relays (Rocha-Miranda et al., 1975). Since the anterior commissure does not connect primary projection fields, its variable capacity to transfer visual experience may be due to the varying influence of motivational, activating or associational processes involving limbic and temporal lobe areas, which the anterior commissure does connect (McKeever and Sullivan, 1981; McKeever et al., 1981). If such an influence can determine visual transfer, the classical split-brain division of visual awareness may be due, in part, to unilateral activation of the brain when a stimulus is presented to one side, and not just the channelling of visual input to one side.

After commissurotomy, transfer of visual awareness can take place for events of low spatial resolution and high contrast which involve little pattern recognition, as demonstrated in experiments described below. As mentioned, commissurotomy patients with complete commissurotomy can, in most cases, speak accurately only about experiences presented in the right half of the visual field, their right hemispheres being mute. However, they can describe the experience of a flash of light, a shadow or some movement when patterns of low spatial resolution and high contrast are briefly exposed in the left field. When their attention is primed they can usually say, with accuracy and little hesitation, whether a stimulus was, or was not, presented in the left field. Motion appears to favor transfer of information to the speaking hemisphere. According to the verbal reports, displacements of light patterns can be detected in the left field, and the direction of motion can be perceived, indicating that the transferred vision can carry some spatial information. In tests of this kind, there will be a risk of transfer of information inside the eye over the vertical meridian of the retina, by scattering of light through the optic media. However, with appropriate controls, it is possible to prove that transfer of visual information has taken place in the brain.

Conflicting results have been reported for tests of the ability of commissurotomy patients to perceive apparent motion over the vertical meridian. Success was claimed with small lights appearing and disappearing at locations 9° apart (4½° either side of the vertical meridian) (Ramachandran et al., 1986). Indeed, the commissurotomy subjects were apparently normal in their ability to perceive apparent motion with interstimulus intervals up to 350 ms. An experiment under different controls, which produced negative results, used stimuli 2° apart (Gazzaniga, 1987). It is possible that apparent motion was seen in the first case because a 'long-range' motion system was excited; a 'short-range' motion system may have been broken at the meridian by sectioning of the splenium of the corpus callosum (Braddick, 1980).

When a small centrally placed stimulus, surrounding the fixation point, is caused to move off in different directions in a cinematographic presentation, a commissurotomy patient may report seeing a movement along the resultant vector of the two displacements (Fig. 5). There has been a central combination of impressions of feature displacement giving rise to an experience of motion, or a moving object is perceived to change in size (Levy and Trevarthen, unpublished). For such events, the subject can have a unified phenomenal awareness linking left and right halves of the perceived field over the center. Further cases of such perception are discussed below, for larger stimuli of longer duration.

Callosal neurones interconnecting the representation of the vertical meridian at the boundary of cortical areas 17 and 18 are capable of serving binocular stereopsis of relatively coarse resolution (Blakemore, 1969). Commissurotomy leads to loss of binocular stereopsis for parts of the visual field close to the vertical meridian and either nearer or further from the observer than the fixation point on which his or her eyes are converged (Mitchell and Blakemore, 1970). This is due to the deaf-

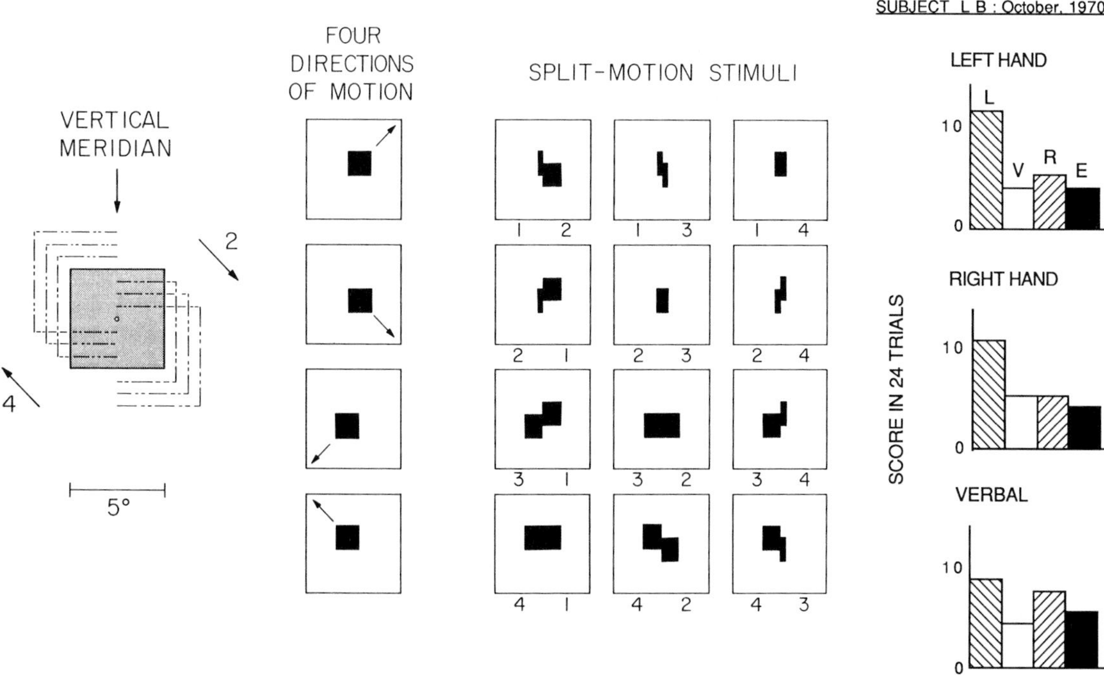

Fig. 5. A black square that appears centered on the fixation point, then moves off in two of four possible directions in the three frames of a cine projection (165 ms) before disappearing, may be perceived by a commissurotomy patient to move in the resultant, vector sum direction. Information in the two hemispheres about displacement in the two half-fields is integrated in one perception. The subject indicates responses by moving left or right index finger in a rectangular area, or by speaking. L = left half correct; R = right half correct; V = vectorial sum response; E = error (from Levy and Trevarthen, unpublished).

ferentiation of a set of binocular cells that must receive part of their input from callosal axons because the corresponding stimuli fall on different halves of the two eyes, one to the left and one to the right of the fovea (a condition known as 'crossed disparity').

We can conclude from these experiments with stimuli near the center of the visual field that the corpus callosum links near midline functions of the primary visual areas only below a certain level of spatial resolution and above a certain level of contrast. For stimuli of very low spatial resolution and high contrast, and for motion stimuli, absence of the callosal fibers does not divide awareness. For these stimuli sub-cortical areas, or bilateral inputs to the cortex outside the geniculo-striate system, must be responsible.

Attention and eye movements: subcortical expectancy

Although all reception of information for detailed, conscious vision is completely divided by commissurotomy involving the splenium, this does not mean that visual attention is also divided. Evidence that a potential field of visual consciousness extends both sides of the fovea in each of the disconnected hemispheres comes from studies where eye movements are directed into the deafferented half of the field by information transmitted to one hemisphere at a time. Both hemispheres can respond to a visual signal that indicates where a second stimulus may be expected to come a moment later. Both will follow instructions in the form of printed words or arrow heads that direct movement to either left or right, and the eye movements can be accurate in size and direction to reach a specified location in the ipsilateral half field, from which no visual information about the target had reached the hemisphere that was required to direct the movement (Trevarthen, 1974a; Fig. 6, upper panel). Thus input to the left hemisphere of a commissurotomy patient is capable of directing the eyes to look left, as well as right, and the right hemisphere can direct the eyes to the right, as well as left. In each case, normal conjugate saccades are made in both directions, but there are latency asymmetries, the ipsilateral direction being slower.

Holtzman used a cueing technique devised by

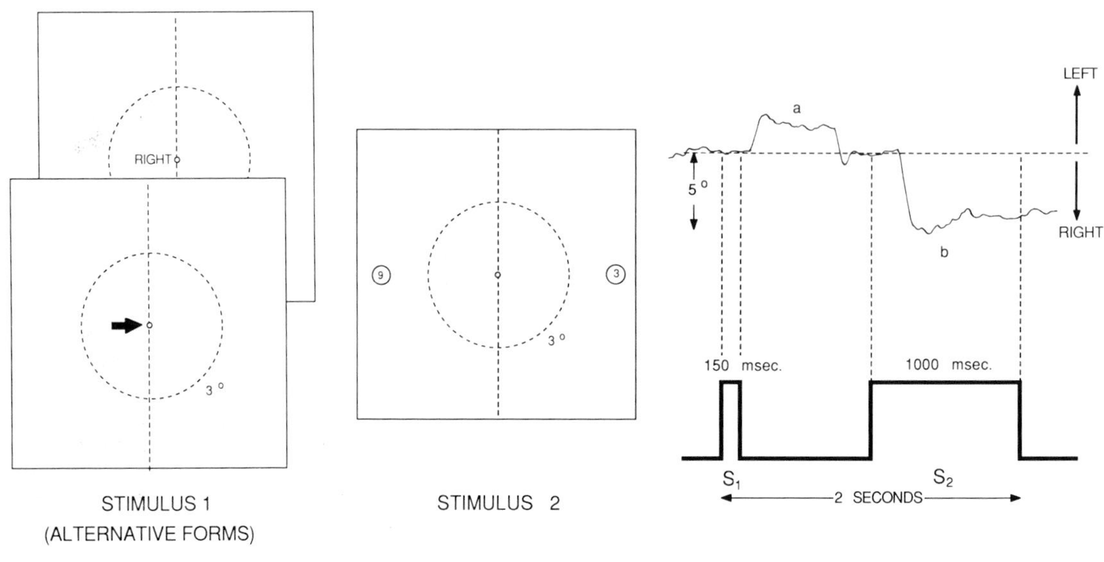

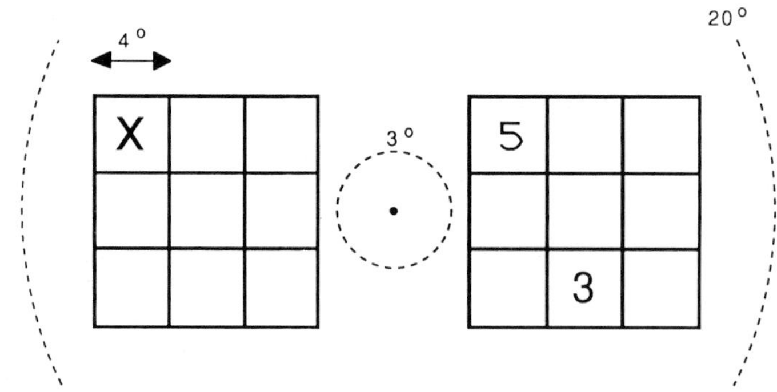

Fig. 6. Tests for sub-cortical processes orienting the two eyes in one spatial frame and linking perceptions in the hemispheres of commissurotomy patients. Upper panel: A word or arrow presented to one side of the fixation point directs the patient to one of two small circled numbers that appear later. The numbers can only be read by direct, foveal fixation and there is not time for two fixations. In the example, the EOG shows that an involuntary eye movement (a) was made to the 'iconic image' of S, in the left field, then gaze shifted correctly to the right side of S2 (b) and the patient correctly reported seeing the number '3' (Trevarthen, 1974a). Lower panel: Holtzman's test for transfer of spatial information across the vertical meridian (Holtzman et al., 1981). Two 3 × 3 grids either side of the fixation point serve as reference fields. The X in the left grid (S1) indicates that the correct target in the second stimulus (S2) on the right side is '5', not '3'. See text.

Posner et al. (1980) to test for transfer of attention to one of a small array of locations in the near central field (Fig. 6, lower panel; Holtzman et al., 1981). The observer, 50 cm from a microprocessor display, fixated a central dot, 4° on either side of which was a 3 x 3 grid of 9 squares each 4° x 4° in size. On each trial an 'x', 1° x 2° of visual angle, marked a position in the grid on one side of the fixation point. Following a 1.5-s interval, a target digit, which the subject had to look at and discriminate, was presented for 150 ms in the grid on the opposite side, either in the same position as the marker had indicated ('valid' trials) or in some other square ('invalid' trials). The displays were also presented with the marker and the digit appearing on the same side ('within field' condition). Eye movements were measured from a televized record. The subject had to indicate by pressing one of two keys whether the digit displayed was odd or even, and response latencies were obtained. In both 'within field' and 'between field' conditions the results showed that two commissurotomy patients were able to profit from information presented in one field to locate and identify a digit presented in the other field. Latencies of response to 'valid' cues were shorter that those to 'invalid' cues. Holtzman also demonstrated that information about the form of a stimulus in one field was not transferred to locate the same form in the other field. Observations with a subject lacking striate cortex in one hemisphere indicated that striatofugal fibers to the midbrain were essential to the direction of attention within the spatial field of the other intact hemisphere (Holtzman, 1984).

The conclusion from the above experiments is that each hemisphere of a commissurotomy patient can participate in a process that attends to, or expects to see, something in its 'hemianopic' field. It is probable that this kind of response is integrated in a unified brainstem oculomotor mechanism which draws on visual information about one and the same space frame from both hemispheres. The failure of the subject lacking striate cortex on one side shows that the brainstem mechanism requires appropriate corticofugal input from the striate cortex. The effects of parietal lesions on covert attention indicate that this part of the cortex is biased in each hemisphere to direct attention to the contralateral side (Posner et al., 1987). This effect complements evidence that each hemisphere can seek information by scanning both leftwards and rightwards.

Separate perceptions in disconnected hemispheres converge on one motor system: the question of parallel independent processing of perception

In vigilance tests, where commissurotomy patients indicate by hand movements the appearance of stimuli presented tachistoscopically on one or both sides of the vertical meridian, the operation results in an unstable visual neglect, or a decline of bilateral vigilance (Gazzaniga and Hillyard, 1973; Kinsbourne, 1974; Teng and Sperry, 1974; Trevarthen, 1975; Dimond, 1976). Ellenberg and Sperry (1979) obtained similar evidence of reduced vigilance following commissurotomy in a tactile signal detection task, involving attention to vibration of the fingertips to direct movements of both hands. Overall, the right hand performed worse than the left, indicating that in the competition for limited attentional resources, the right hemisphere dominated in this task.

When conflicting perceptual tasks are presented to the two visual fields, commissurotomy patients may not experience the perceptual conflict which normal subjects have with the same stimulation; hemispheric deconnection has given them a measure of 'enhanced perceptual processing capacity' (Holtzman and Gazzaniga, 1985). They may also show convergence of separate different perceptual judgements on a single resultant response, such as finger movement of one hand (Sergent, 1983, 1986), showing that, as Trevarthen (1962, 1965) found with monkeys, the separated hemispheres can have simultaneous awareness of conflicting information as long as one response is coordinated. However, reaction time measures show that, while attending to both hemispheres and receiving contradictory stimuli without perceptual conflict, commissurotomy subjects have responses that are slower than normal because bilateral attending is achieved with some cost even when the forebrain is divided (Trevarthen, 1974a, 1987). Similar results are obtained with split-brain monkeys (Guiard, 1980). These various findings show how the commissures normally function both in transferring perceptual information, and in assisting the distribution of central cerebral resources for attention and motor activation. Perceptual activity generated separately in the two hemispheres may converge to direct simple motor responses by one hand and motor decisions generated in the two hemispheres may be combined, but activation of the hemispheres is more competitive after they have been decoupled.

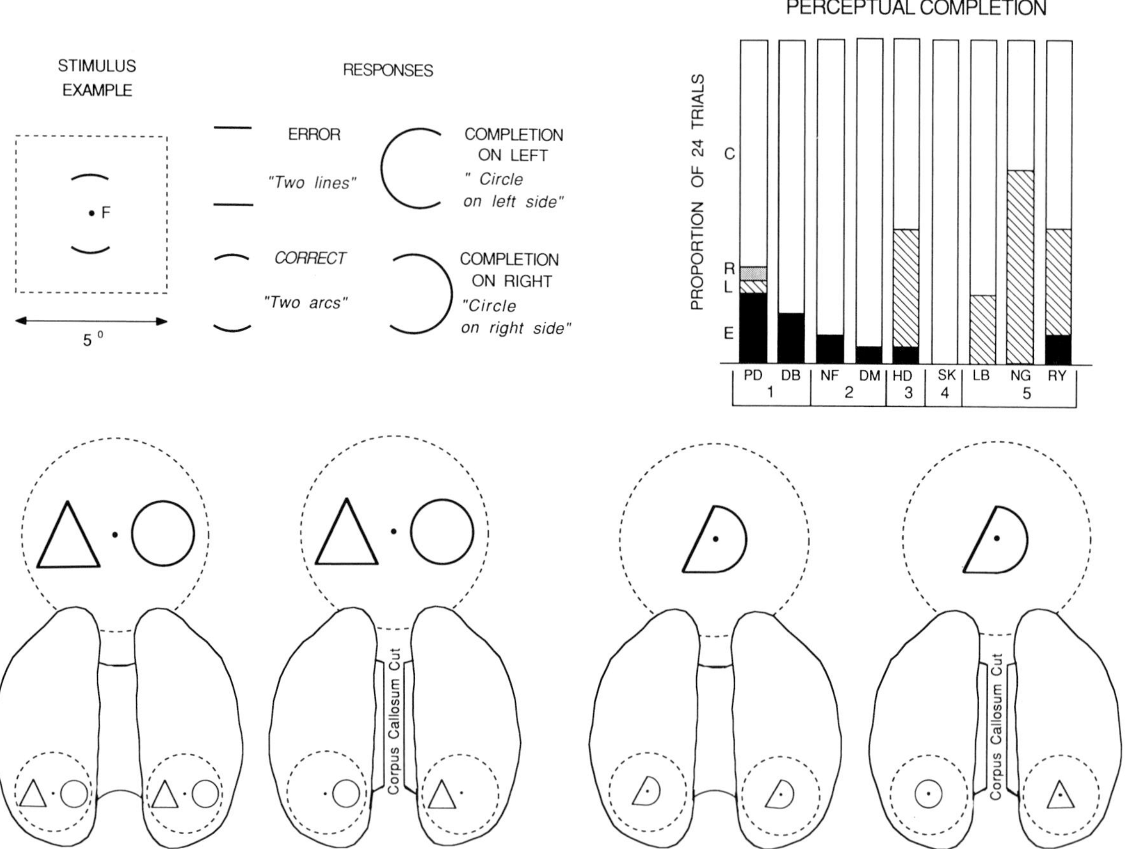

Fig. 7. Perceptual completion and neglect with tachistoscopic stimuli (150 ms). Upper panel: Commissurotomy patients fixating point F give non-viridical responses to visual stimuli that straddle the vertical meridian. Verbal responses (left hemisphere) are different with different brain conditions. Two unoperated epileptics (1) make errors (E), but few completions; two anterior commissurotomy patients (2) also make errors and no completions; a prosopagnosic with an abscess surgically removed from the right occipito-parietal region (3) shows many completions to the left (L); a congenital acallosal subject (4), as a normal subject would, makes no errors or completions, all responses being correct (C); and three epileptics with all forebrain commissures divided (5) show left-side completions (Trevarthen, 1974b). Lower panel: Diagrams showing how commissurotomy subjects (and split-brain monkeys) make mirror completions and neglects in left and right hemispheres. These perceptions are revealed by tests that evoke lateralized cerebral activity. Asymmetric 'chimeric' stimuli can lead to different perceptions located at the same point in the subjects' visual world (double consciousness).

Perceptual completion and neglect in deafferentiated visual half fields

Evidence that commissurotomy patients can be not only attentive or expectant for a bilateral visual field in each hemisphere but also bilaterally conscious of form, color, etc., comes from drawings and verbal descriptions they make of figures or pictures that have been presented to them juxtaposed along the vertical meridian (Trevarthen, 1974a,b, 1987). The evidence is that they can not only manifest perceptual neglect, failing to see, or attend to, details in the ipsilateral 'blind' field when responding with right or left hemisphere, but they also experience perceptual completion or image synthesis in which they see details in that field that were, in fact, not present in the stimulus. Perceptual completion is a normal process; for example, it is used to perceive a visual image through the area corresponding to the 'blind spot'. It permits us to see a variety of colors in far peripheral parts of the field where the retina and central visual system cannot resolve color that well.

A number of examples of neglect and completion by commissurotomy patients are given in Figs. 7 and 8, in which are also shown results of tests for completion and neglect in a variety of other conditions. The completed image can extend over a larger part of the central visual field, but is most striking when the foveal and parafoveal areas are involved, because then the subjects' reports give evidence that they experience refined detail and color in a part of space for which no striate input whatsoever exists. Visual consciousness is filled out where sensory information is lacking. When both directions of visual completion are possible, the direction of completion depends upon the relative activation of the two hemispheres – verbal activity favors activity of the left hemisphere and completion in the left field; drawing and visual matching favor the right hemisphere and lead to completion in the right field (Fig. 8). These effects are discussed further below.

When primed to expect a stimulus some degrees off the fovea, commissurotomy patients may be led to prevaricate verbally in extravagant detail, being unable to check their fabrication of awareness in the deafferented field because they have no evidence to the contrary. Comparable elaboration of drawings may indicate the same kind of 'invention' of images in the right field, leading to conflict with the realistic vision in this field when concurrent verbalization is requested.

Perceptual completion and neglect evidently cause problems for commissurotomy patients when they read. They make many reverse (right-to-left) saccades and tend to misread fixated words when the first left syllables or prefixes are not obvious. Patients have complained that reading is

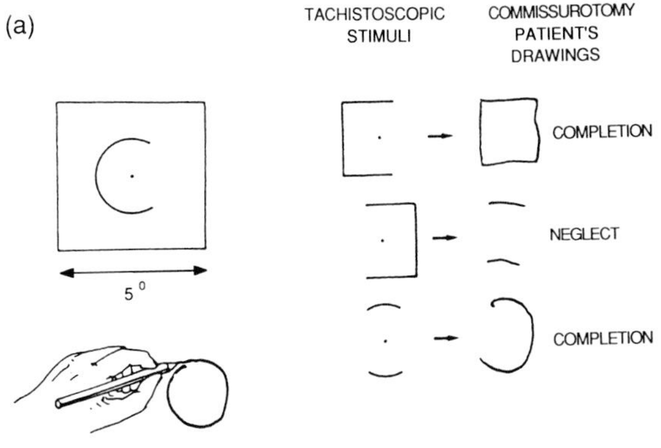

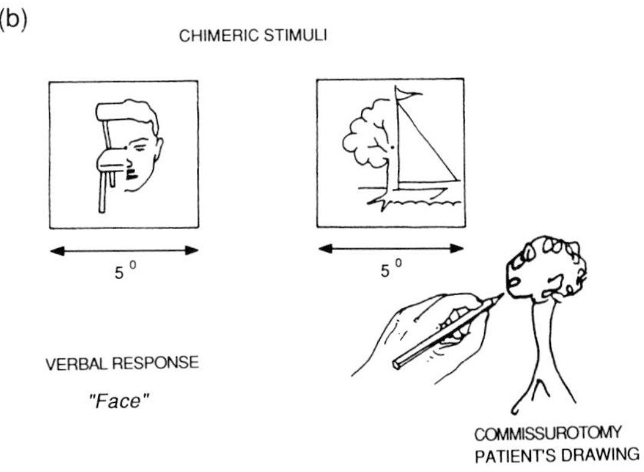

Fig. 8. (a) A commissurotomy patient drawing with the left hand shows perceptual completions and neglect in the right field. (b) With 'chimeric' stimuli, a commissurotomy patient making verbal responses reports only the right half. When drawing with the left hand she reproduces only the left half of the stimulus.

difficult and tiring. It follows that the corpus callosum normally participates in efficient reading, evidently because it has a role in all kinds of scanning for detail by horizontal saccadic eye movements. At a higher level of congitive process, reading is a bihemispheric skill, but with preponderant control from the left hemisphere. Commissurotomy patients, tested with Zaidel's contact lens occluder or with tachistoscopic exposure of words, can read at a moderately high level with input restricted to the left hemisphere, and less well with the isolated right hemisphere (Zaidel, E, 1973, in press).

Orientation of eyes and hands to reach targets on either side

Aiming of visual attention and of reaching and grasping to loci around the body is regulated by a cerebral system which resolves space less finely than the central mechanisms that are necessary for precise prehension, for accurate manipulation and for foveal scan and discrimination of fine detail. In reaching and grasping movement, two components with different spatial dimensions and time course can be distinguished, an 'open loop' transport of the hand towards the target location, and a visually guided approach phase giving refinement to prehension (Paillard and Beaubaton, 1976; Jeannerod, 1986). Similarly, oculomotor reorientations can be classed in two or three categories of differing size and speed. The correspondence observed between the angular magnitude and the time course of these mechanically very different motor activities – (i) head-and-eye movements and (ii) arm-and-hand movements – suggest that they are coupled under control of one and the same central hierarchy of orienting mechanisms that represent a unified body-centered space. Normally the 'partial orientations' of head-and-eye and arm-and-hand away from the main orientation of the trunk or body axis are synchronized, or they operate in precisely coordinated succession or alternation. All these basic patterns of motor coordination for selective orientation remain intact after commissurotomy. The two hands of a split-brain subject, human or monkey, can be brought together to meet at a target detected by one of them (Mark and Sperry, 1968). Evidently subcortical, brainstem and cerebellar, systems are sufficient to couple divided hemispheric systems; or, alternatively, each hemisphere is capable of coordinating both halves of motor space.

When tested for their ability to reach to or look at locations around the body, commissurotomy patients can register the spatial location of an off-center target in one visual field and then transport either left or right hand with moderate precision to that space. Critical experimental tests for this involved use of an apparatus in which reflected images of lights lasting 0.1 second signal target locations on paper spread over the surface of a table. (Fig. 9). Apart from the flashing spots of light, which are illuminated only while the subject is maintaining binocular fixation on a central spot, there are no features on the surface by which the subject can perceive the location of the targets. Responses are recorded by means of carbon paper concealed under the sheet of paper that the subject can see. The subject pinpoints with left or right hand the perceived location of the off-center lights with a stylus that leaves an invisible mark under the paper. Eye rotations were measured to $+0.5°$ by DC EOG, and head rotations by means of a counter-weighted, low-friction potentiometer accurate to $+0.25°$ (Fig. 10; Trevarthen, 1974, in press).

Commissurotomy patients located the position of a light with either hand with or without reorientation of gaze. The evidence from the pattern of errors in these location tests is that, in maintaining a representation of a space containing goals for future visual inspection or manipulative action, the central orienting mechanism adds together information from direct peripheral visual input of an event, proprioception of head or arm displacement, visual exproprioception of arm movement through the lower peripheral field and the remembered layout of the context and of the general form of target objects (Figs. 9 and 10).

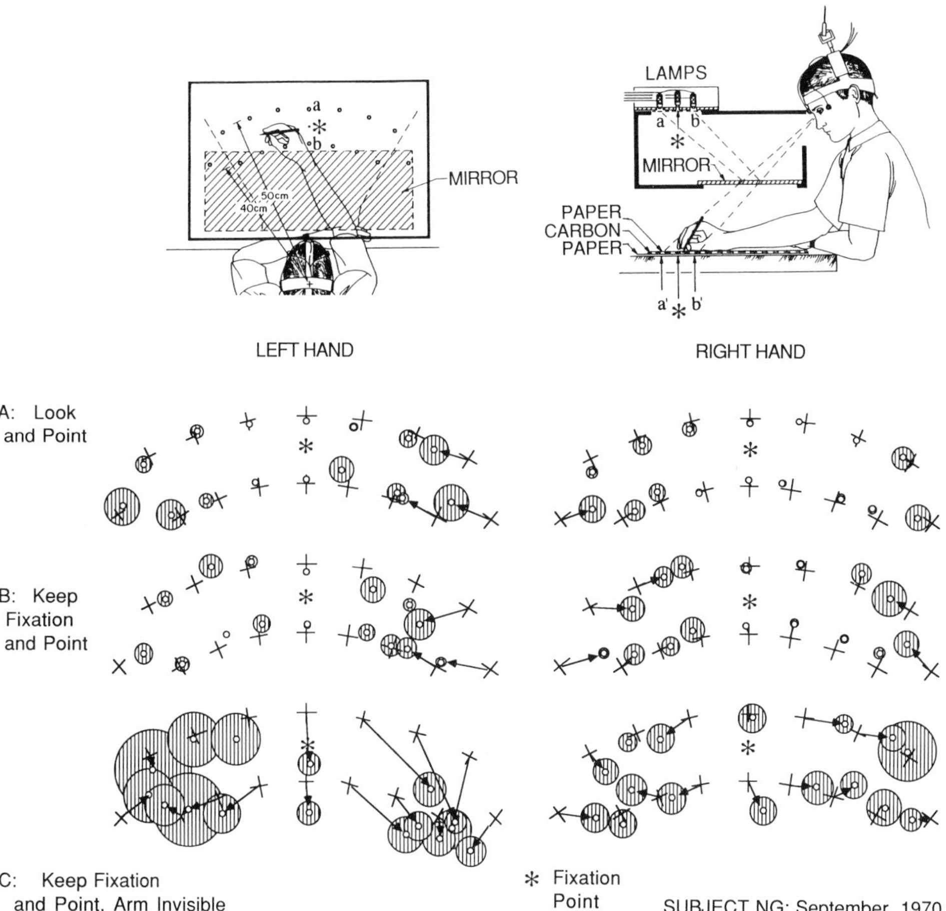

Fig. 9. Commissurotomy patient NG, pointing to lights in the peripheral field, directed eyes, head or either hand to stimuli appearing to left or right side. Positions of lights are marked by crosses. Accuracy of hand response was highest when she looked at the point where the light appeared before making her mark (A). When keeping fixation at the center (*) she was less accurate in the field contralateral to the hand she used (B). When a screen inserted under the mirror prevented sight of her hand she was less accurate with her left hand (C). Marks made by the subject were invisible to her. Circles respresent the mean scatter of four responses for each light. Centers of circles show deviation of the centroid of four responses from the target.

In reaching tests with commissurotomy patients, neglect and completion effects can distort the perception of reality, leading to false location of targets for reaching. One complete commissurotomy patient, NG, showed clear evidence of an attentional effect, transmitted between the hemispheres in the generation, or maintenance, of a spatial reference for target location at the moment she launched a reaching movement (Trevarthen, 1974, 1987). In this case the targets were rectangular or irregular polygonal pieces of white card subtending 5° to 30°, which were placed by the experimenter on a black table surface while the subject fixated a white spot a short distance in front of her waist. The subject used a felt-tip pen to mark the geometric center or 'balance point' (centroid) of the target. All object placements and responses were recorded on video by means of a camera mounted on the ceiling vertically above the fixation point. In several trials, the movement of her left arm from a rest position in the left field was aborted near its inception and, at or about the same instant, she described the target in the right visual field as 'disappearing' from vision. It remained invisible for several seconds while fixation was being maintained, even while the experimenter moved it gradually across the table towards the vertical meridian of the subjects' visual field. As soon as one corner, subtending a fraction of a degree, crossed the vertical meridian into her left field, her left hand made a very fast, ballistic, or uncontrolled, move which caused the tip of the pen forcefully to hit the exposed fragment of the object. This proves that the subject was maintaining a high level of vigilance in the left visual field while she held her left arm and hand ready to respond. The experience she described, of invisibility then sudden appearance of the object, was a vivid one which surprised her. She asked if a 'trick with mirrors' was involved.

In summary, the above experiments show that commissurotomy subjects retain a single attentional field linking left and right halves of pericorporal space, in which locations of targets for large eye movements (saccades of 5° and more) and for reaching arm movements (of comparable size and duration to the eye or head-and-eye orientations) are specified and coordinated together with an accuracy of to within a few degrees. Precision of locations in this field declines as soon as sensory information about body position and arm movement is reduced. The highest precision of orienting is achieved when a normally coordinated movement of head + eyes + arm and hand is allowed.

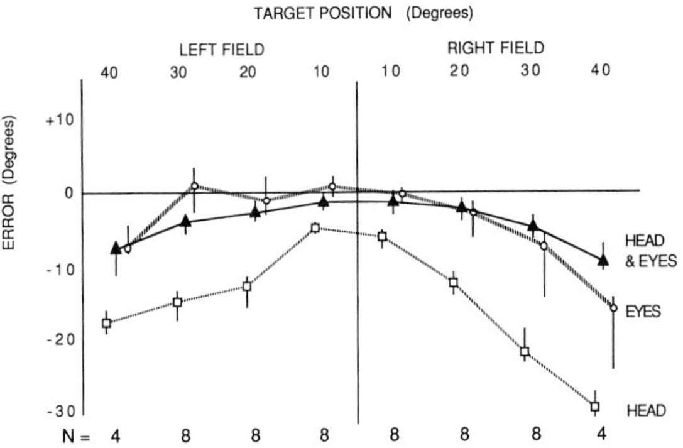

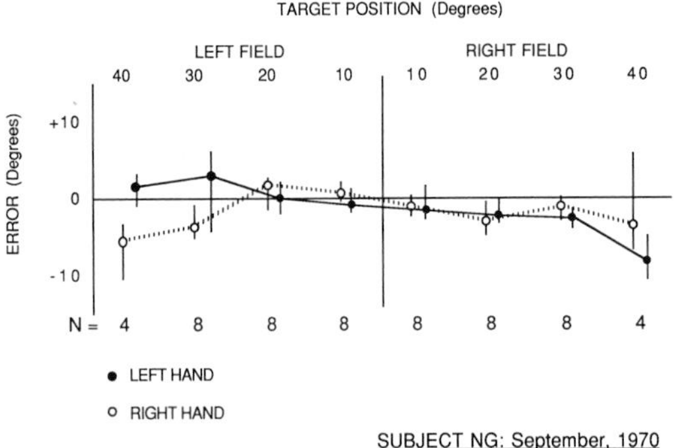

Fig. 10. Orientations of eyes (measured by DC electro-oculogram) and of head (measured by a potentiometer attached to her head as shown in Fig. 11) confirmed that commissurotomy patient NG was most accurate when movements of head, eyes and hand were combined, and she was also slightly more accurate in visual orientations in the left field when responding with her left hand.

Ambient vision of the peripheral field is undivided after commissurotomy

Interest in questions of consciousness and the perception of meaningful symbols led psychologists testing the vision of commissurotomy patients to work first in the central part of the visual field, where they could control allocation of clear and highly informative visual experiences between the two hemispheres. Such experiments require the subjects to be seated with head stationary and direction of gaze controlled. This kind of 'restricted field' procedure was used to demonstrate the profound divisions of consciousness described above. A different kind of question is posed when one considers freely moving vision. For a person whose head is in motion the peripheral parts of the visual field yield abundant evidence, requiring less conscious interpretation, about the layout of space and the position of objects or surfaces. Peripheral vision informs about goals for prehension, and guides and regulates posture and locomotor movements. Different experimental techniques are required to provide adequate stimulation of the peripheral parts of the 'total visual field' under conditions where visual orientation and the laterality of inputs are known.

Outside the central 30° or so, 15° either side of the fovea, the retina has relatively low capacity for resolving spatial detail or color, as was briefly discussed above. On the other hand, the peripheral retina is highly sensitive to brightness contrasts, and to stimulus change such as that due to motion. Vision in the peripheral parts of the field is only partly accessible to consciousness, but it responds rapidly and precisely to information from 'flow' or transformation in the light array, picking up evidence for control of movements about the form of surroundings at large and motion of its parts in three dimensions. Evidently the corresponding peripheral areas of the retinas project to brain systems with low spatial and contrast resolution, but with high capacity for resolving layout and depth from the motion parallax. This component of the visual mechanism has a capacity to derive a coherent spatial image, of stable masses and spaces and large objects in motion, by combining measures of flow vectors in different segments of the ambient field (Gibson, 1957). These are the kinds of stimuli generated by displacements of the head that carry the centers of the eyes along lines in space relative to the static array of matter at equilibrium in the gravitational field – head displacements such as those caused, for example, by locomotion and by being carried forward in a vehicle. It is also a vision which immediately distinguishes objects undergoing translation or rotation relative to the background. Peripheral parts of the retina also receive dynamic feedback information about movements of parts of the subject's body (arms and hands, legs and feet), or about large objects being moved by the subject. Thus, off-center vision serves as the main ex-proprioceptive system (Lee, 1980). All these kinds of events produce patterns of change, corresponding to the velocity and accelerations, periodicity, etc., of displacement, to which the peripheral retina is highly receptive, whether the change is self-produced or due to the activity of other beings, objects or media.

To test such peripheral 'ambient' vision in commissurotomy patients one needs to generate large stimuli of high contrast which are undergoing persistent change. To control the allocation of stimuli to the two hemispheres it is necessary to verify stability of the subject's gaze. This is more easily accomplished if stimuli that simulate displacements of the field at large are activated around a stationary, seated subject, rather than by causing the subject to displace his or her head relative to a field of reflected light and shadows from a fixed array of surfaces and spaces. A simple point-source shadow-casting technique devised by Gibson and Gibson (1957) to generate large, ecologically valid motion parallax displays is ideally suited to this purpose. A brilliant, very small (less than 1 mm) source of light is situated one side of a back-projection screen at a point that mirrors the locus of the center of the observer's eye, which is on the other side of the screen. Any opaque, or partially opaque, object placed between the light source and the screen will cast a pattern or form a shadow on the screen that exactly corresponds with the projection of a virtual object in the space between the observer's eye and the screen (Fig. 11). In fact, the observer perceives an object at this location, very clearly and in 3-D. All displacements and rotations of the actual objects are exactly reproduced by the perceived motions of the virtual object. Peripheral vision responds strongly to such kinematic and parallactically correct stimuli, and the subject easily perceives rigid or deforming objects that mirror whatever is put between the light source and the screen. If the geometry is incorrect, then distortions or plastic shape changes are perceived.

Tests using Gibson and Gibson's point-source shadow-casting technique were used by Trevarthen and Sperry (1973) to show that patients with complete commissurotomy had a unified bilateral apprehension of the peripheral spatial array. The patients were able to compare orientations and directions of motion in large kinematic stimuli in the two half fields outside central vision. Moreover,

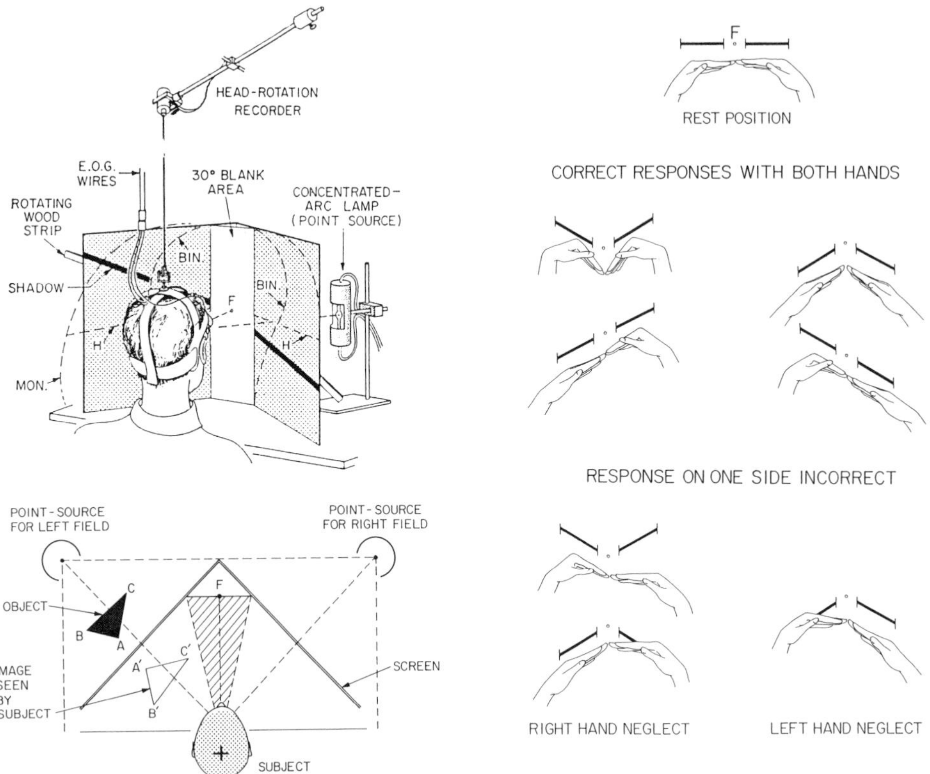

Fig. 11. Changing shadows projected in the peripheral visual field by a very small powerful source of light (point source) were used to show that commissurotomy patients can perceive and locate motion, and detect some form information, in the left visual field with the left, speaking hemisphere. They can also cross-integrate spatial information from the two fields. Hand movements to reproduce the positions of bar shadows stopping at different angles demonstrate unified ambient vision and its breakdown in some trials to result in neglect of either the left or right half (from Trevarthen and Sperry, 1973).

they could give immediate accurate *verbal descriptions* of the location, direction of displacement or rotation and approximate form of objects situated 45° from the center in the *left* visual field (Fig. 10).

These results prove that the lack of visual transfer demonstrated for static objects situated either side of the vertical meridian in the central visual field, and perceived with high resolution of form, color, etc., does not apply to shadows of large objects or textured sheets of material in motion in the peripheral field. As with normal subjects given peripheral stimuli, the verbal responses and actions of commissurotomy patients with the same stimuli, either side of the meridian, give report of experiences that lack clarity of detail. Even the normal subject cannot make local form discriminations such as would be required to read text beyond 15° lateral in the peripheral field. The commissurotomy patients were able to transfer, from left field to left speaking hemisphere, perceptions of the spatial location, size, approximate form and quality of motion of objects over 5° in size, promptly and accurately, even when the objects were 40° – 50° off-center.

As with normal peripheral vision, these perceptions of a commissurotomy subject quickly vanish when the object becomes stationary, and they show powerful rivalry within the subject's attention. If two stimuli are presented in one field moving together, their separation may not be detected, or, if they move differently, one may vanish. If two stimuli are presented in the peripheral to left and right of the midline at the same time, usually only one is seen. It is important to add that in the latter case, the subject may give verbal report, presumably with the left hemisphere, of disappearance of the *right* stimulus. Therefore, the rivalry of peripheral stimuli reflects an attentional selection within one united field of vision that can determine experimental access about equally from both its left and right halves to either hemisphere, in this case the left. Silent hand signs can be made by a commissurotomy patient to indicate that a comparable bidirectional rivalry can be experienced in the right hemisphere (Fig. 11). We can conclude that a considerable part of the input from the peripheral visual field is feeding into a single attentional mechanism that integrates its activities in one bilateral space in which movements are controlled by both hemispheres. This unified system persists in spite of the division of the commissures. Presumably it depends on commissural or partially decussating circuits of the brainstem (Fig. 12).

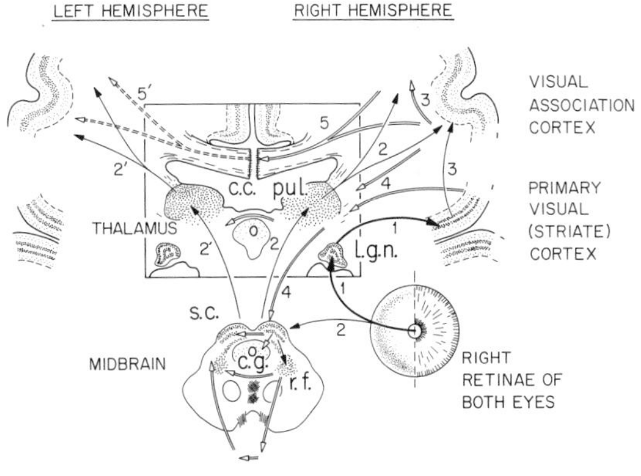

Fig. 12. Anatomical pathways which would permit cross-integration of ambient visual awareness when the corpus callosum is cut. Foveal (focal) input via the lateral geniculate nucleus (l.g.n.) to the striate cortex (1) is sharply divided at the vertical meridian. Midbrain visual centres (superior colliculus, S.C.) receive input serving ambient vision (2) and descending information from the visual cortex (4). The visual association cortex receives transcortical input from the striate cortex (3) and from the brain stem via the pulvinar (pul.). The corpus callosum (5) is cut, but midline transfer of some visual information may occur through the diencephalon (posterior commissure) in the midbrain between the colliculi, through the central gray (c.g.) or between sites in the reticular formation (r.f.). There may also be transfer through more posterior visual pathways involving the cerebellum. Transferred information (2′) is sufficient to unify ambient visual processes. Compare with Fig. 4.

There is evidence from experimental study of cats (Sprague, 1966) and from correlations between cognitive function and attentional orientation in humans (Kinsbourne, 1974) that the brainstem and cerebral cortices are linked in a bisymmetric coordinative system. Findings from commissurotomy patients indicate that left spatial neglect, usually consequent to a lesion of the right parietal cortex (Mesulam, 1981), may be contributed to by competing input to the orienting system of the brainstem from the intact left hemisphere (Plourde and Sperry, 1984).

Tests of peripheral color vision with the commissurotomy patients (Trevarthen and Sperry, 1973) point to the conclusion that the unified ambient space may carry information from a dichromatic system that assists in resolving spatial layouts by discriminating blue from not-blue (or reddish) parts of the spectrum. This would have ecological utility, helping to define the spatial layout, given that light from the sky, and reflected from such surfaces as the tops of bodies of water or the upward facing parts of leaves, is blue, and that the earth, most organic matter (including vegetation, wood, the fur of animals, and human skin, black or white) and many synthetic materials used in buildings and clothing reflect more strongly in the red half of the spectrum. Colored stimuli in the near-central parts of the field may also give rise to interactions over the midline, though most tests using colored stimuli in central vision show standard split-brain effects with commissurotomy patients (Levy and Trevarthen, 1981).

The experiments of Holtzman on attention in commissurotomy patients, reported above, indicate that a unified spatial vision of intermediate resolution extends to near-central parts not explored in the experiments with point-source shadow-casting (Holtzman et al., 1981; Holtzman, 1984).

Neuroanatomical implications of the unified

ambient vision and unified attention-distributing system in commissurotomy patients are illustrated in Fig. 12.

Split-brain effects in somesthesis, audition and olfaction

Commissurotomy patients cannot compare the 'feel' of objects held in their hands (Gazzaniga et al., 1962; Milner and Taylor, 1972; Nebes, 1972; Sperry et al., 1969). Crude differences in temperature, size and mass may transfer intermanually to be perceived in a unified mind, possibly with help of sensory effects crossing the midline of the body, but the form and texture of objects and the distribution of parts and masses are separately discriminated in the two hands. Unseen objects are intelligently handled by both hands, and held as befits their uses. However, whereas the right hand's experiences are spoken about correctly, those of the left hand are not named or described. The fact that objects may be retrieved by the left hand to match a word or picture shown in the left half of the visual field, and that they are manipulated appropriately, shows that the information reaching the right hemisphere is consciously perceived, even though no words are generated. In appreciation of the configuration of objects the left hand appears superior to the right, as it is for copying drawings. The right hand acts in exploring an object as if it is attracted to detailed features, and it tends to overlook the schema, gestalt or whole shape (Bogen, 1969a, Zaidel and Sperry, 1973, Levy, 1974; Nebes, 1974, 1978).

If a particular positioning of the fingers is impressed on one hand out of sight, the other hand cannot mimic the posture. If a picture of a hand position or sign is shown in one visual field it can be copied by the hand on the same side, but usually not by the other hand (Sperry et al., 1969; Bogen, 1987). Thus touch, as well as joint sensitivity and other kinds of proprioception, proves to be divided for the two hands. After complete commissurotomy the patient has lost part of the ability to name points touched on the left side of the body. This effect is clearest for the hands and especially for the fingertips. However, stimulation of either side of the face is perceived in both hemispheres (Sperry et al., 1969; Bogen, 1987).

In patients with the anterior commissure and the anterior 5 cm of the corpus cut, but the posterior one-fifth (splenium) intact, there are no split-brain effects in verbal identification of tactual stimuli, visuo-tactile matching, tactual-tactual matching, olfactory-tactual matching, hand movements to verbal command and cross-matching of cutaneous localization or hand postures (Gordon et al., 1971). This finding from commissurotomy patients with spenium intact does not agree with the condition of patients with vascular or neoplastic lesions who have similar lesions in the callosum sparing the splenium. The latter often show deconnection effects (anomia for manipulated objects, apraxia for verbal command and agraphia, all with the left hand). Evidently damage to parts neighboring the callosum can eliminate transfer through the splenium, possibly by reducing intermodal associations within the right hemisphere.

Mayer et al. (1988) have studied a right-handed patient who suffered a hematoma that destroyed the body of the corpus callosum, sparing the genu and ventral splenium. There was a complete disconnection syndrome with the exception of visual interhemispheric transfer, which was intact. Touch and deep pressure sensitivity were normal in the two hands, and haptic object recognition was unified. However, with two objects palpated at the same time, one in each hand, the left hand responses failed in verbal report. This 'extinction' of the left hand, without anomia, could be counteracted by cuing the subject to attend appropriately or by adding an appropriate haptic memory load. It was concluded that the callosal lesion had interfered with dynamic allocation of attention or activation of the two hemispheres. This resembles the effects of callosotomy on attention in the visual sphere, discussed above. McKeever et al.(1981) report that tactual anomia of the left hand after callosotomy may be reduced under hypnosis, which confirms that a dynamic setting of awareness or attention is involved in suppression of awareness of the left hand when verbal report is required. Division of the body of the corpus callosum, leaving splenium, genu and anterior commissure intact, produces dissociation of somesthesis in the two hands only for more taxing tasks (Jeeves, 1979; Bentin et al., 1984). The anterior commissure may not function effectively in transfer of stimulation effects in visual, auditory and tactile tasks when the corpus callosum and hippocampal commissure are sectioned (callosotmy) (McKeever et al., 1982).

Input from each ear is transmitted through a complex series of relays in the brainstem to both cerebral hemispheres, which permit multiple crossings of the brain midline. Nevertheless, commissurotomy does produce dissociation of auditory experiences on left and right when conflicting speech sounds are presented simultaneously to the two ears – the patient experiences a loss of the left ear input and gives accurate report only to words received by the right ear (Milner et al., 1968; Sparkes and Geschwind, 1968; Wale and Geffen, 1986). A reverse suppression effect favoring the left ear may be obtained with melodies, musical cords, rhythms and non-verbal voice sounds, which are evidently perceived best in the right hemisphere. Physiological studies show that the suppression of ipsilateral inputs, an effect which is observed in lesser degree with normal subjects when they are presented stimuli with dichotic conflict (Kimura, 1967), occurs in the brainstem.

Dichotic interference may sometimes be enhanced when only the middle (body) of the corpus callosum is sectioned (Bogen, 1987). Auditory deconnection effects due to interruption of the neocortical commissures are variable and may be hard to distinguish from suppression of one ear due to lesions in cortex or thalamus. With conflicting stimuli in the two ears, input from one ear is blocked at subhemispheric levels and the direction of blockage is influenced by orientation of attention to left or right. As for other modalities, the corpus callosum has a role to play in distributing attention or activation for auditory stimuli, as well as in transferring information for auditory perception.

Gordon (1974; Gordon and Sperry, 1969) tested transfer of olfactory perception in commissurotomy patients by stimulating one nostril at a time. In these subjects all crossing input from the olfactory epithelium of a nostril to the hemisphere on the other side was abolished by section of the anterior commissure. Correspondingly, naming of odors was accurate for the left nostril (connected to the left hemisphere) and inaccurate for the right nostril. Emotional reactions (to bad or pleasant smells) seemed not to transfer, except by 'cross-cuing' as a consequence of expressive movements of the face, or vocalizations. Even when such transfer of emotional quality occured, the precise identity of the odor did not transfer. Non-verbal tests showed that odors channelled through the right nostril were perceived with correct associations to tactile stimuli in the right hemisphere.

Bilateral coordination of manipulation, and drawing and writing, after commissurotomy

Immediately after complete forebrain commissurotomy, there are pronounced, but variable, defects in motor coordination (Bogen, 1987). The patients are slightly 'akinetic' and often mute. As Liepmann and Mass described in 1908, patients with the corpus callosum interrupted do not respond with their left hands to verbal command, and they may make competitive activities with the two hands (diagnostic dyspraxia; Akelaitis, 1945). These signs are usually much reduced within days or weeks after the operation (Bogen, 1987). Other effects persist for years.

D. Zaidel and Sperry (1977) gave the same patients a large battery of standardized tests of motor performance 5 – 10 years after surgery. They confirmed that the two hands were both quick and accurate when working separately, as long as there was no unilateral cerebral pathology impairing motor control on one side. The patients were, however, slower than normal, and sometimes they exhibited duplicate volition. But, for the most part, they were acting as single coherent agents.

Severe qualitative and quantitative impairment of bimanual coordination appeared in tasks that demanded alternation of the hands and independent control. This agrees with findings with split-brain baboons (Trevarthen, 1978). Kreuter et al. (1972) imposed double index-finger tapping at a maximum rate as a background task to test for duplication of cerebral processing capacity in the commissurotomy patients. Commissurotomy reduced the capacity of the subject to keep tapping with the fingers synchronized while doing mental arithmetic or reciting every third letter of the alphabet. Right-hand tapping was interfered with by moderate mental concentration on these verbal tasks. When the subject made a mistake or could not work out how to respond, both hands faltered, then stopped.

Ellenberg and Sperry (1979) had commissurotomy patients sort small objects for half an hour with two hands making synchronized movements as rapidly as possible. Most achieved good rates with the two hands (16 – 38 objects/minute) but both rates and errors showed evidence of two kinds of interference between the disconnected hemispheres. When one hemisphere had cortical damage affecting hand movements, this led to slowing of *both* hands when they moved together, and more errors. When both cortices were in good condition, activity of the right hemisphere (left hand) was interfered with by an idle left hemisphere (right hand doing nothing). When both hands were active, the sorting movements of the left hand accelerated. Subjects with complete commissurotomy frequently lost synchrony of hand movements, but anterior partials (anterior commissure and anterior 5 cm of the corpus callosum sectioned) did not. Evidently transmission of tactual afference through the posterior callosum was sufficient to maintain afference coordination in this task.

Preilowski (1975) applied a bimanual visual tracing task, a new skill in which the hands had to learn to crank on two handles collaboratively to guide a cursor along a diagonal line. Both complete and anterior partial commissurotomy patients performed badly, indicating that the genu region connecting the frontal lobes is important for bimanual coordination in a difficult joint visual guidance task. Evidence from monkeys indicates that commissural links between the two supplementary motor areas are important for bimanual collaboration (Goldberg, 1985). Well-practised bimanual coordinations, such as tying shoe laces, may be little affected by commissurotomy, possibly because the skill is in united subcortical systems such as the cerebellum, or because a coherent motor program is established in one hemisphere or in duplicate on both sides.

In spite of good verbal comprehension in the right hemisphere, the patients are inept in making symbolic gestures on command with the left hand (left ideomotor apraxia). The right hemisphere can recognize common objects, such as a toothbrush or spoon, grasped by the left hand, and can make proper use of them (ideational praxis), but the right hemisphere is poor at writing with this hand (left dysgraphia). Conversely, the right hand is inferior to the left in copying drawings (right dyscopia) (Bogen, 1969a; Gazzaniga et al., 1967; D. Zaidel and Sperry, 1977).

D. Zaidel and Sperry (1973) made a visuo-tactile version of Raven's progressive matrices test with images etched as raised metal lines as for a printing block. A pattern seen in free vision was matched to one of three fragments felt out-of-sight in the left or right hand. Scores of commissurotomy patients were low. The left hand (right hemisphere) performance was superior in accuracy as well as being 25% quicker. However, right hemisphere performance was interfered with by a preservering left hemisphere set that was evident in the subjects' verbalizations and their use of a sequential reasoning strategy to describe elements of the pattern. Subjects with anterior partial commissurotomy had higher scores, showing that normal performance is sustained by interhemispheric communication intergrating complementary search and recognition strategies in the two hemispheres.

In agenesis of the corpus callosum, motor coordination deficits are seen in absence of divided awareness (Milner and Jeeves, 1979). Jeeves et al., (1988) used Preilowski's tracking apparatus to test bimanual coordination in callosal agenesis and after section of the central third of the corpus callosum. Two adult acallosals performed poorly, like Preilowski's anterior partial commissurotomy patients, but the single case with the body of the callosum interrupted was indistinguishable from normals. Evidently bihemispheric integration of motor control for the hands requires the anterior parts of the corpus callosum. Slow performance in Preilowski's task may be guided by visual and proprioceptive information, but rapid performance needs precisely balanced activation of the two hemispheres, which is abolished if anterior parts of the corpus callosum are divided, or if they fail to develop.

Asymmetries in cognition

The most famous findings in studies of perception in commissurotomy patients involve their reactions to well-known real objects or meaningful symbols, rather than to abstract or simplified physical stimuli. The former are reactions that involve considerable cognitive work on the information given, and they reveal both complex associations inside each of the isolated cerebral hemispheres and differences between them in cognitive strategy or processing.

Tests requiring matching between different perceptual modalities (vision and touch) show how supra-modal concepts of objects are evoked by briefly presenting pictures to the left or the right of the vertical meridian, or by placing objects to be felt in one hand, out of sight of the patient. For example, the word 'KEY' shown on the screen is to be matched to a key chosen from a mix of objects presented out-of-sight for palpation by one hand; or a photograph of a dollar bill is to be matched to a coin felt in the hand. The commissurotomy patients can make such conceptual matches, or matches of meaning, between left visual field and left hand, or between right visual field and right hand; but they cannot do this crosswise, with contralateral field-hand combinations (Sperry et al., 1969).

Unlike psychophysical tests for sensory independence across the midline in the foveal or near parafoveal field, most tests for visual recognition of meaningful objects or symbols have used larger stimuli placed 5° to 15° left or right of the central fixation point and presented for less than 1/8 second by shuttered projectors or on computer screens. An alternative approach is Zaidel's contact lens arrangement, with collimator and screen focused in the plane of the stimulus and attached to one of the subject's eyes (E. Zaidel, 1975). This device occludes the half field of one eye but allows the eye to scan a picture or text, information being restricted to one hemisphere all the time by the screen, which moves with the eye. The other eye is closed by an eye patch.

Such methods, with complex stationary pictures or arrangements of letters, numbers, etc., invariably show that meaningful or realistic awareness is entirely split in two by the surgical division of the commissures. They also show that the identity or meaning of the stimuli can, in most cases, be reported verbally only by the left hemisphere. The few patients who are exceptions to this rule all appear to have had early left hemisphere damage followed by compensatory development of control from the right hemisphere. The most striking are left-handed patients whose histories reveal early injury to the left hemisphere. In one such case, PD, tested at Caltech, only the right hemisphere could speak after commissurotomy (Trevarthen and Sperry, 1973). This patient also had an exceptionally long post-surgical mutism (Bogen, 1987). In other cases some speech can be produced by both hemispheres (Levy et al., 1971). Important factors are the age of the subject at time of operation and the effects of post-surgical learning, which can lead to increased language comprehension, and even some speech, from the right hemisphere (E. Zaidel, 1978a,b, in press).

Commissurotomy patients can be vigilant with the hemisphere which the experimenter is trying to keep 'in the dark' or cut off from direct input of sensory information; and then, using this hemisphere, they sensitively and quickly pick up any escaping clue to identity of the object which the experimenter was intending to present only to the other half of their brain. This is the phenomenon of 'cross-cuing'. For example, the subject may transfer crucial information by shifting gaze to center on something in the room that matches a short-term memory of the stimulus given, thereby transferring the required information across the midline of the visual field; or an object of metal, glass, etc., moved in one hand can be caused to make a distinctive sound that is heard by both hemispheres.

The two cortices embody different cognitive systems. It has proved difficult to characterize the differences simply; all attempts to define a single principle by which hemispheric cognitive mechanisms differ have proved unable to satisfactorily predict all the response asymmetries of the subjects. Nor do they yet satisfactorily explain how such differences developed or evolved. Nevertheless, it is possible to list a number of differences between the hemispheres of commissurotomy patients comparable to those revealed in a very large number of studies of normal subjects in the past 25 years.

The asymmetric cognitive sets of the hemispheres may reflect different ways of moving to extract information from experience – different strategies for being conscious. In tests which involve scanning of forms, patterns or pictures, it has been found that the left hemisphere, separated from the right, is better at selecting meaningful elements from an array or configuration and that it prefers to match arrays or patterns by identifying distinctive features in a succession of experiences. When either the eyes or the hands are used to scan for the relevant information, this strategy of feature selection takes time – a 'chain' of focal attentions is made to locate information. Skilled manipulation involves rapid sequencing of finger movements, which alternate at high rates; and efficient oculomotor scan, as in rapid reading, reaches rates of 8 saccades/second. Similarly, speech involves sequencing of movements of the mouth and tongue at exceedingly high rates – up to 8 syllables/second. The control of motor sequencing at such high rates and the corresponding serial cognitive processes appear to reside more in the left hemisphere (Kimura, 1979; MacNeilage, 1986). Dichotic listening tests, with interaural conflict, have shown that the right ear (left hemisphere) is better at speech perception, particularly at discrimination of consonants that define different syllables carried by the same vowel (Levy and Trevarthen, 1977; E. Zaidel, 1978). The left hemisphere can perform rhyming tests, requiring matching of phoneme to phoneme, but in most cases the disconnected right hemisphere has not been able to do this. This indicates that the left hemisphere monitors the sounds produced by speaking. However, other evidence indicates that the right hemisphere tends to have predominant control over the prosody of speech and is responsible for the recognition of environmental sounds (Kimura, 1967; E. Zaidel, 1973; Gordon and Bogen, 1974; Heilman et al., 1974; Tucker et al., 1977; Bradshaw and Nettleton, 1983).

Commissurotomy patients also served in important demonstrations that the right hemisphere is better in appreciating the pattern or layout of an integral complex in visual space. The right hemisphere has better holistic or schematic awareness, including the discrimination of topological forms (Paterson and Zangwill, 1944; Hecaen, 1969; Nebes, 1971, 1972, 1974; Franco and Sperry, 1977; Hecaen and Albert, 1978; Trevarthen, 1984; Bradshaw and Nettleton, 1983; Benowitz et al., in press). It may be better, in general, at associating appearance and typical color of familiar objects, though colors are better named by the left hemisphere (Levy and Trevarthen, 1981). It is also better at emotional expression and at certain tasks related to the perception of persons and their states of motivation or emotion (Heilman et al., 1974; Tucker et al., 1977;

Sackheim et al., 1978; Gainotti, 1983; Buck and Duffy, 1980; Ley and Bryden, 1981; Moskovitch and Olds, 1981; Borod et al., 1981; Benowitz et al., 1983; Heilman and Satz, 1983; Ross, 1984).

These various asymmetries in motivation and cognitive processes may be consequences of differences in the motivations or emotions of brainstem and limbic origin that regulate activity, and development, of the cortex in the two hemispheres (Trevarthen, in press). Motives and emotions generated in the reticular core of the brain stem exercise regulatory influence over the balance of activity in the hemispheres.

Levy et al., (1972) used tachistoscopically presented stimulus chimeras, combinations of two different stimuli joined down the vertical meridian of the subjects' visual field, to give double, simultaneous stimulation of both left and right hemispheres of commissurotomy patients. This made it possible to determine which hemisphere the patient preferred to use to solve a given test. Whenever a verbal response was called for, to name or describe a stimulus, the right half of the chimera, seen by the left hemisphere, was chosen. But when direct matching of the appearance or form of stimuli was called for, the right hemisphere took over. The right hemisphere was also preferred for matching photographs of unfamiliar faces; the left hemisphere performed poorly at this task and resorted to checking through distinctive elements or features of the picture (such as moustache, glasses or dark hair) one at a time, and to naming the distinguishing features of one of the faces. Choices by the right hemisphere were indicated by the subject pointing silently at the appropriate matching face in an array viewed in free vision.

Levy and Trevarthen (1976) went on to show that hemispheric dominance for these chimeric perception tasks in commissurotomy patients was not a reflex consequence of a particular task exciting a more powerful or faster reaction in that hemisphere. They found that a readiness condition, which they called 'metacontrol', was involved, and this could be switched between the hemispheres so that it was possible for a subject to restrict processing, for a series of trials, to the hemisphere that was relatively incompetent at the given task. Chimeric pictures were used (Fig. 13) that could be matched by reference to Function or Meaning (e.g., bird with nest; scissors with sewing basket), or by similarity of Appearance (e.g., nest containing eggs with sewing basket containing bobbins). When scoring well, commissurotomy pa-

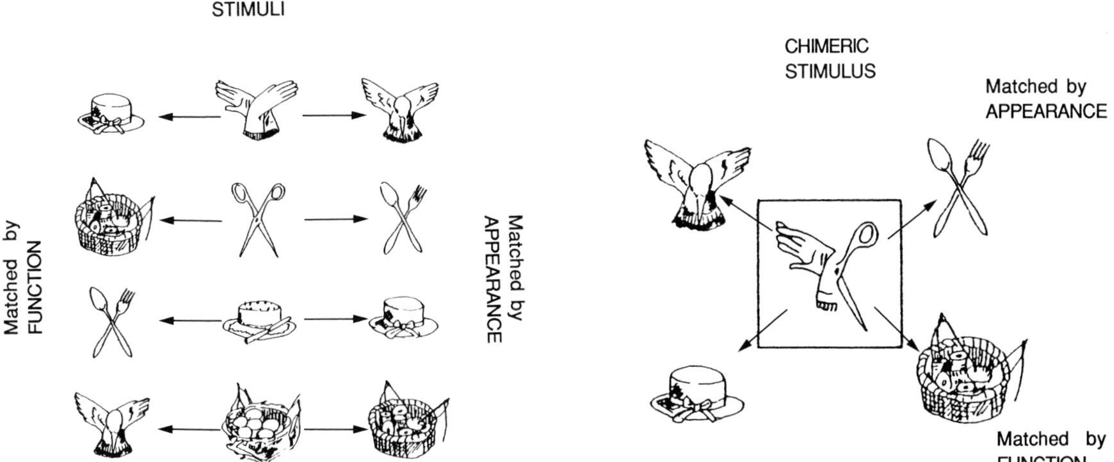

Fig. 13. Chimeric stimuli such as these, designed for matching to other stimuli either by 'appearance' or by 'function' or 'meaning', reveal cognitive asymmetries. They have also assisted in demonstrating 'metacontrol' activations that can channel cognitive activity to left or right hemisphere independently of hemispheric abilities (Levy and Trevarthen, 1976).

tients used the left hemisphere for Function matching and the right for Appearance matching. Runs in which many matches were unacceptable by either criterion were due to activation of the left hemisphere for Appearance matching or the right hemisphere for Function matching. Subsequently, Levy and her associates (Heller and Levy, 1981; Levy et al., 1983a, 1983b, in press; Levy and Kuek, 1983; Levine et al., 1987) have shown that the consistent differences in the cognitive activities of normal subjects on tests that activate processes which are asymmetrically represented in the two hemispheres, can be explained by habitual biases in the intrinsic activation of the hemispheres. Physiological and psychological tests show that metacontrol performs an important function in generating lasting individual differences of cognitive ability (Morgan et al., 1971; Shankweiler and Studdert-Kennedy, 1975; Furst, 1976; Rebert, 1977; Tucker and Suib, 1978; Davidson et al., 1979; Erlichman and Wiener, 1979; Dabbs and Choo, 1980; Gur and Reivitch, 1980; Heller and Levy, 1981; Gordon, in press; Levy, in press). The tests with commissurotomy patients prove that the metacontrol mechanism is still active when the neocortical midline pathways are removed, but there are indications that its functions are weakened. Bogen (in press) points out that normal subjects with fully intact commissures may show competition between different hemispheric modes of consciousness and this may be regarded as comparable with the more marked effects characteristic of commissurotomy patients.

Memory after commissurotomy

Hemispheric differences in consciousness are not simply due to in-built fixed asymmetries in activation from the brain stem. They also arise from the accumulated memories and associations built up within the two cortices through learning. Commissurotomy detaches the two cortical memory stores so they operate as independent associative systems. D. Zaidel (in press) has shown, in tests with commissurotomy patients and patients with unilateral lesions, that predilections to pick up and consolidate information in different ways result in the hemispheres seeing the world differently, recognizing different things as familiar and meaningful.

Both consolidation and retrieval of memories depend on the alertness, cerebral activation or motivation of parts of the brain that relate present and past experiences. Defective memory after commissurotomy indicates that the corpus callosum and anterior commissure have a role in such internal factors of learning and remembering.

Commissurotomy patients are forgetful, and this can cause them considerable daily inconvenience. Formal memory tests yield subnormal scores, below those to be expected in epileptics (D. Zaidel and Sperry, 1974). Deconnection of the hemispheres appears to prevent collaboration between the specialized memory systems of the two hemispheres (for example, objects or events recognized better by the right hemisphere cannot be talked about); and there is clearly an overall depletion of the motivating influences. Anterior partial commissurotomy causes memory loss, especially for highly verbal and semantically complex material.

Milner and Taylor (1972) showed that the right hemisphere of a commissurotomy patient has a better memory than the left for tactually perceived wire forms without names. However, they also recorded that memory was impaired, apparently by the separation of the hemispheres. The same conclusion comes from tests of the benefits of visual imagery in mediation of verbal paired-associate learning (Milner et al., in press). Experiments with monkeys show that the object recognition memory of the temporal lobes depends on limbic input and that the anterior commissure may act as an efficient conduit for this motivation or reinforcement and for associative memory linking, for example, visual and tactile memories (Mishkin, 1982; Mishkin and Phillips, in press).

Conclusions: neocortical commissures mediate in perception, cognition, attention, motivation and motor coordination

The simplest of mental integrations performed by the neocortical commissures is the transfer of primary perceptual information after early stages of cortical processing. This function is transferred through posterior parts of the body and splenium of the corpus callosum and it couples the mirror fields of sensory reception for left and right halves of experience at the midline of the body and of body-centered sensory space. When the splenium (about one-fifth of the commissures) is left intact and all more anterior commissural axons are cut, sensory impressions from the two halves of the visual field, the two hands and the two ears are efficiently transferred. This transfer probably benefits from intermodal translation of information and 'back-stream' projections within the hemispheres, connections across the splenium being essentially between visual areas. Somesthetic and auditory transfer occupies regions more towards the body of the callosum. We have seen that psychophysical studies of vision and touch indicate that there are limits to the refinement of discriminatory sense data transferred across the callosum.

In all modalities, less discriminating exteroceptive sensory information, especially information related to awareness of the relative displacement of body parts and transport of the whole body through surroundings (proprioceptive and ex-proprioceptive data), remains largely undivided after complete forebrain commissurotomy. Such perception and sensory-motor integration, partly subcortical, depends both on direct afference to brain-stem sensory fields and a corticofugal flow of information, taking information that came up the thalamo-cortical route and passing it back down to subcortical sites.

Distribution of centrally organized selective attention among the hemispheric mechanisms of perception, and between the hemispheres, depends on ascending activations from limbic and reticular systems. After commissurotomy, attention is abnormally unstable, leading to fluctuating neglect, loss of vigilance and unconstrained perceptual completion or image building (Kreuter et al., 1972; Dimond, 1976; Ellenberg and Sperry, 1979). Consciousness in the hemispheres may be profoundly changed by lateralized activation of the cortex and such 'metacontrol' can lead to poor cognitive performance in a commissurotomy patient if allocation of activity is to a hemisphere ill-equipped for a given task.

Coordination of locomotor, postural or reaching movements of the whole body are not much affected by total commissurotomy of the forebrain, but the programming of precisely synchronous and balanced or consecutive moves of the hands may be interfered with even when only the anterior one-third of the corpus callosum is cut. Commissurotomy also produces transient mutism and apraxia, and it leads to permanent speechlessness of the right hemisphere, as well as to complementary apractognosic disturbances in left and right hands. Evidently, refined voluntary motor programming of the two hands requires anterior callosal links. Loss of these in development, i.e., by agenesis of the corpus callosum, cannot be compensated for as easily as absence of the posterior sensory links. Acallosal patients have depleted bimanual coordination but show no split-brain effects in perception. This may be related to the order of development of commissural links in the early fetal stages, anterior axons growing across before posterior ones. The posterior parts of the hemispheres that the splenium interconnects may remain plastic to later fetal stages of development, allowing reorganization of a bilateral representation in each hemisphere, or the formation of compensatory sub-cortical cross-connections linking the two hemispheres.

Memory disorders after commissurotomy probably have two explanations. On the one hand, there will be poor coordination of retrieval and consolidation in the two halves of the cortex, with failure of cooperation between complementary semantic stores. In addition, there will be imbalance and reduced flexibility in motivation factors that implant or reactivate memories and facilitate the formation of associations. The anterior commissure, in particular, plays an important part in conveying motivating influences between limbic components of the memory and recognition systems.

The many integrative functions of the neocortical commissures will be performed by a number of neurochemical systems involving both excitatory and inhibitory synapses. It is not possible to reduce neocortical connections to a single physiological type, and the anatomy of commissural neurones and their dendrites and terminations in various cortical zones and cell layers confirms that they may have the full range of associative functions (Innocenti, 1986).

It has been reported that commissurotomy patients suffer from alexithymia. That is to say, thay fail to relate affectively loaded images and have weakened experience of self and poor memory for meaningful narratives (Hoppe and Bogen, 1977). Sperry et al., (1979) used Zaidel's scleral contact lens to lateralize input to one hemisphere at a time in tests of recognition for personal, affect-laden or social or politically significant pictures. They found both hemispheres of commissurotomy patients to be emotional, self-aware and socially experienced. But they also found evidence for transfer between the hemispheres of aspects of 'emotional or conative auras' generated by recognition of key items. They suggested that such mental states play an important part in mnemonic retrieval. These intriguing findings raise the possibility that while the corpus callosum has an important role in unifying or coordinating the emotional, motivational and associative processes that animate consciousness and memories, in doing so it supplements systems which are, at least partly, cross-unified in the brain stem. The studies of metacontrol point to the same conclusion.

There are two schools of thought regarding the complementary roles of disconnected hemispheres in consciousness. One identifies the ability to speak with consciousness and reason and concludes that only the left hemisphere has true human awareness and thinking (Eccles, 1965; Gazzaniga and Le Doux, 1978). The other draws on evidence that the right hemisphere can, in isolation, perform complex acts of reasoning, recognition or recall and can show evidence of practical and cultural knowledge, concluding that the hemispheres are naturally different but equally important partners in generation of human communication, thinking and creativity (Sperry, 1966, 1968, 1982a,b, 1983; Levy, 1969, in press; Bogen, 1969b; Bogen and Bogen, 1969; Benowitz, 1988; Gordon, 1988; Zaidel, 1983a, in press).

These perspectives see different roles for the commissures in integrating intelligence (Trevarthen, 1975). The former emphasizes the upgrading of primitive functions in the right hemisphere by human reason from the left. The latter regards the commissures as a two-way bridge that both contributes to and unites equally important components. In recent years this second theory has gained favor, with the growing realization that rational and verbal skills are dependent on linking or context-framing processes or judgements, which are disrupted by lesions of the right hemisphere, rather than the left.

Recently Doty (in press) has proposed that defective interhemispheric coordination may contribute to mental illness. Indeed, there is increasing evidence that emotional systems extending through limbic territories in the hemispheres and the two sides of the brain-stem core are asymmetrically constituted (Tucker and Williamson, 1984; Tucker and Frederick, 1987). Commissurotomy patients show asymmetries in emotional expression related to those brought to light by studies of patients with unilateral lesions (Benowitz et al., 1982, in press; Gainotti, 1983).

The asymmetries of the neocortex, so important in higher, culturally trained skills of human intelligence, may, in fact, be induced developmentally from sources of lateral differences in subcortical structures that differentiate before the cortices do. In evolution, the neocortical commissures of mammal species that were invading ever richer and more demanding environments, and moving from an intelligence dominated by oral transformation of objects under tactile, gustatory and olfactory control to bimanual manipulation under visual control, may have been selected to function in accordance with intergrative principles more primitively expressed in the reticular core of the brains of lower vertebrates (Trevarthen, 1972). The commissures of the cerebral cortex are the top level of a hierarchical set of commissural links in the CNS that permit flexible choice of behavioral sets and orientations. Their functions attain peak signifance in the integration of human cultural intelligence and learning, and in the psychological communication on which this intelligence and learning is founded (Trevarthen, in press).

Note on possible effects of epilepsy on psychological functions of commissurotomy patients

Epileptic activity impinging on the brain early in development, in the first few years after birth, can cause extensive change in the distribution of cerebral functions (Milner, 1974; Rasmussen and Milner, 1977; Trevarthen, 1984).

The commissurotomy patients discussed in this review have, in almost all cases, been operated upon to relieve severe epilepsy (Bogen and Vogel, 1963). In some cases the brain insult responsible for epilepsy occurred early in life or at birth. In a few, early damage to the left hemisphere has evidently led to transfer, or partial transfer, of speech control to the right hemisphere (Levy et al., 1971; 1972; Sidtis et al., 1981). Epilepsy can also contribute to an abnormal bihemispheric representation of perception or motor control for one half of extrapersonal space (Nebes et al., 1969; Gordon et al., 1971).

However, in the preceding review, integrative functions of the commissures were inferred from functions lost after surgical division of the commissures. These commissurotomy patients had unified visual experience before surgery but complete division of focal visual awareness down the vertical meridian after complete transection of the commissures of the forebrain. It is not likely that epilepsy, however early of onset and however longstanding, could have created a separation of functions and dependence on the commissures greater than in the normal brain.

It is also unlikely that bilaterally intact ambient visual functions, mediated through the early developing and relatively implastic brainstem, could have been created by epilepsy. Evidence of residual vision in the hemianopic field after early hemidecortication (Perenin, 1978; Perenin and Jeannerod, 1978), while leaving open the question of brain plasticity, supports the description of ambient vision obtained from commissurotomy patients (Trevarthen and Sperry, 1973).

Mutism, akinesia of the left hand, and conflicting actions of the two hands seen in early days or weeks after commissurotomy (Bogen, 1987) may have been exacerbated by effects of long-standing epilepsy, but these transient effects are probably consequences of the sudden loss of important coordinative or integrative links that normally sustain bihemispheric regulation of motor activity (Goldberg, 1985). The acute symptoms of commissurotomy may be taken as evidence that the corpus callosum normally acts as a major part of the mechanism for coordinating speech and collaboration between the two hands.

Commissurotomy patients, with no evidence for early left hemisphere pathology such as might cause transfer of language to the right hemisphere, have equal or superior cognitive functions of certain kinds in the right hemisphere. We believe that these reflect normal specializations of the right hemisphere. It has been claimed that all language-related functions, and all higher intellectual operations, that may have been detected in the right hemisphere of commissurotomy patients constitute a pathology resulting from epilepsy (Sidtis et al., 1981; Gazzaniga, 1983). Evidence presented in support of this claim does not stand up to critical examination (Levy, 1983; Zaidel, 1983a,b, Myers, 1984).

Epilepsy might have contributed to deficiencies of vigilance, memory and motor coordination observed after commissurotomy, but it will not be responsible for the metacontrol effects (Levy and Trevarthen, 1977), effects which help explain why patients with unilateral cortical lesions show severe symptoms, including complete loss of language comprehension with lesions confined to the left hemisphere (Bogen, 1974; Levy, 1989; Zaidel and Schweiger, 1984).

Finally, many of the findings in visual perception and visuo-motor coordination in human commissurotomy patients are confirmed by studies of split-brain cats and monkeys where there was no presurgical brain pathology (Trevarthen, 1965, 1968, 1987).

References

Akelaitis AJ: Studies of the corpus callosum IV. Diagnostic dyspraxia in epileptics following partial and complete section of the corpus callosum. *Am. J. Psychiatry: 101,* 594 – 599, 1945.

Benowitz LI, Bear DM, Rosenthal R, Mesulam M-M, Zaidel E, Sperry RW: Hemispheric specialization in nonverbal communication. *Cortex: 19,* 5 – 11, 1983.

Benowitz LI, Finklestein MD, Levine DNK, Moya K: the role of the right cerebral hemisphere in evaluating configurations. In Trevarthen C (Editor), *Brain Circuits and Functions of the Mind. Essays in Honor of RW Sperry.* New York: Cambridge University Press, in press.

Bentin S, Sahar A, Moscovitch M: Intermanual information transfer in patients with lesions in the trunk of the corpus callosum. *Neuropsychologia: 22,* 601 – 611, 1984.

Berardi N, Fiorentini A: Interhemispheric transfer of visual information in humans: Spatial characteristics. *J. Physiol.: 384,* 633 – 647, 1987.

Berardi N, Bisti S, Maffei L: The transfer of visual information across the corpus callosum: Spatial and temporal properties in the cat. *J. Physiol.: 384,* 619 – 635, 1987.

Berlucchi G: Anatomical and physiological aspects of visual functions of corpus callosum. *Brain Res.: 37,* 371 – 392, 1972.

Berlucchi G: Recent advances in the analysis of the neural substrates of interhemispheric communication. In Pompeiano O, Ajmone Marsan C (Editors), *Brain Mechanisms and Perceptual Awareness.* New York: Raven Press, pp. 133 – 152, 1981.

Berlucchi G, Antonini A: The role of the corpus callosum in the representation of the visual field in cortical areas. In Trevarthen C (Editor), *Brain Circuits and Functions of the Mind.* New York: Cambridge University Press, in press.

Berlucchi G, Marzi CA: Interocular and interhemispheric transfer of visual discrimination in the cat. In Ingle DJ, Goodale MA, Mansfield RJW (Editors), *Analysis of Visual Behavior.* Cambridge, MA: MIT Press, pp. 719 – 750, 1982.

Berlucchi G, Tassinari G, Antonini A: The organization of the callosal connections according to Sperry's principle of supplemental complementarity. In Lepore L, Ptito M, Jasper HH (Editors), *Two Hemispheres – One Brain.* New York: Alan R. Liss, pp. 171 – 188, 1986.

Blakemore C: Binocular depth perception and the optic chiasm. *Vision Res.: 10,* 43 – 47, 1969.

Bogen JE: The other side of the brain. I. Dysgraphia and dyscopia following cerebral commissurotomy. *Bull. Los Ang. Neurol. Soc.: 34,* 73 – 105, 1969a.

Bogen JE: The other side of the brain. 2. An appositional mind. *Bull. Los Ang. Neurol. Soc.: 34,* 73 – 105, 1969b.

Bogen JE: Dysfunction from defacilitation. Letter to the Editor. *Arch. Neurol.: 32,* 421 – 422, 1974.

Bogen JE: The callosal syndrome. In Heilman KM, Valenstein E (Editors), *Clinical Neuropsychology.* New York: Oxford University Press, pp. 308 – 359, 1978.

Bogen JE: Physiological consequences of complete or partial commissural section. In Apuzzo MLJ (Editor), *Surgery of the Third Ventricle.* Baltimore: Williams and Wilkins, pp. 175 – 194, 1987.

Bogen JE: Partial hemispheric independence with the neocommissures intact. In Trevarthen C (Editor), *Brain Circuits and Functions of the Mind.* New York: Cambridge University Press, in press.

Bogen JE, Bogen GM: The other side of the brain. 3. The corpus callosum and creativity. *Bull. Los Ang. Neurol. Soc.: 34,* 191 – 220, 1969.

Bogen JE, Vogel PJ: Treatment of generalized seizures by cerebral commissurotomy. *Surg. Forum: 14,* 431 – 433, 1963.

Borod JC, Caron HS, Koff E: Asymmetry of facial expression related to handedness, footedness, and eyedness: a quantitative study. *Cortex: 17,* 381 – 390, 1981.

Braddick OJ: Low and high level processes in apparent motion. *Phil. Trans. R. Soc. Lond. Ser. B: 290,* 137 – 151, 1980.

Bradshaw JL, Nettleton NC: *Human Cerebral Asymmetry.* Englewood Cliffs, NJ: Prentice-Hall, 1983.

Bremer F: Physiology of the corpus callosum. *Res. Publ. Assoc. Res. in Nerv. and Ment. Dis.: 36,* 424 – 428, 1956.

Bremer F, Brihaye J, Andre-Balisaux G: Physiologie et pathologie du corps calleux. *Schweiz. Arch. Neurol. Neurochir. Psychiatrie: 78,* 31 – 87, 1956.

Brinkman J, Kuypers HGJM: Split-brain monkeys: cerebral control of ipsilateral and contralateral arm, hand and finger movements. *Science: 176,* 536 – 539, 1972.

Buck R, Duffy RJ: Non-verbal communication of affect in brain-damaged patients. *Cortex: 16,* 351 – 362, 1980.

Bykov K: Versuche an Hunden mit Durchschneiden des Corpus callosum. Zentralblatt fur die ges. *Neurol. Psychiatrie: 39/40,* 199, 1925.

Choudhury BP, Whitteridge D, Wilson ME: The functions of the callosal connections of the visual cortex. *Q. J. Exp. Physiol.: 50,* 214 – 219, 1965.

Clarke S, Kraftsik R, Van der Loos H, Innocenti GM: Forms and measures of adult and developing corpus callosum: is there sexual dimorphism? *J. Comp. Neurol.:* in press.

Dabbs JM, Choo G: Left-right carotid blood flow predicts specialized mental ability. *Neuropsychologia: 18,* 711 – 713, 1980.

Davidson RJ, Taylor N, Saron C: Hemisphericity and styles of information processing: Individual differences in EEG asymmetry and their relationship to cognitive performance. *Psychophysiology: 16,* 197, 1979.

Dejerine J: Contribution a l'etude anatomo-pathologique et clinique de differents varietes de cecite varbale. *C. R. Soc. Biol. (Paris): 9,* 61 – 90, 1892.

Dimond SJ: Depletion of attentional capacity after total commissurotomy in man. *Brain: 99,* 347 – 356, 1976.

Doty RW: Some anatomical correlates of emotion and their bihemispheric coordination. In Gainotti G (Editor), *Emotions and the Dual Brain.* Berlin: Springer, in press.

Doty RW, Negrao N: Forebrain commissures and vision. In Jung R (Editor) *Handbook of Sensory Physiology VII/3.* Berlin: Springer-Verlag, 1972.

Downer JL de C: Changes in visually guided behaviour following mid-sagittal division of optic chiasma and corpus callosum in monkeys (*Macaca mulatta*). *Brain: 82,* 251 – 259, 1959.

Eccles JC: *The Brain and the Unity of Conscious Experience.* Cambridge: Cambridge University Press, 1965.

Elberger AJ: The functional role of the corpus callosum in the developing visual system: a review. *Prog. Neurobiol.: 18,* 15 – 79, 1982.

Ellenberg L, Sperry RW: Capacity for holding sustained attention following commissurotomy. *Cortex: 15,* 421 – 438, 1979.

Erlichman H, Wiener MS: EEG asymmetry during covert mental activity. *Psychophysiology: 17,* 228 – 235, 1980.

Fendrich R, Gazzaniga MS: Evidence for foveal splitting in a commissurotomy patient. *Neuropsychologia: 27,* 273 – 281, 1989.

Franco L, Sperry RW: Hemisphere lateralization for cognitive processing of geometry. *Neuropsychologia: 15,* 107 – 114, 1977.

Furst CJ: EEG asymmetry and visuospatial performance. *Nature: 260,* 254 – 255, 1976.

Gainotti E: *Emotions and the Dual Brain.* Berlin: Springer Verlag, 1979.

Gazzaniga MS: *The Bisected Brain.* New York: Appleton-Century-Crofts, 1970.

Gazzaniga MS: Right hemisphere language following brain bisection: a 20-year perspective. *Am. Psychol.: 38,* 525 – 537, 1983.

Gazzaniga MS: Perceptual and attentional processes following callosal section in humans. *Neuropsychologia: 25,* 119 – 122, 1987.

Gazzaniga MS, Hillyard SA: Attention mechanisms following brain bisection. *Attention Performance: 4,* 221 – 238, 1973.

Gazzaniga MS, Le Doux JE: *The Integrated Mind.* New York: Plenum, 1978.

Gazzaniga MS, Bogen JE, Sperry RW: Some functional effects of sectioning the cerebral commissures in man. *Proc. Natl. Acad. Sci. USA: 48,* 1765 – 1769, 1962.

Gazzaniga MS, Bogen JE, Sperry RW: Dyspraxia following division of the cerebral commissures. *Arch. Neurol.: 16,* 606 – 612, 1967.

Geschwind N: Disconnexion syndromes in animals and man, I and II. *Brain: 88,* 237 – 294, 585 – 644, 1965.

Geschwind N, Kaplan E: A human cerebral deconnection syndrome. *Neurology (Minneapolis): 12,* 675 – 685, 1962.

Gibson JJ: Optical motions and transformations as stimuli for visual perception. *Psychol. Rev.: 64,* 288 – 295, 1957.

Gibson JJ, Gibson EJ: Continuous perspective transformations and the perception of rigid motion. *J. Exp. Psychol.: 54,* 129 – 138, 1957.

Glickstein M: Brain pathways in visual guidance of movement and the behavioral functions of the cerebellum. In Trevarthen C (Editor), *Brain Circuits and Functions of the Mind.* New York: Cambridge University Press, in press.

Glickstein M, Gibson AR: Visual cells in the pons of the brain. *Sci. Am.: 234,* 90 – 98, 1976.

Glickstein M, Sperry RW: Intermanual somesthetic transfer in split-brain rhesus monkeys. *J. Comp. Physiol. Psychol.: 53,* 322 – 327, 1960.

Goldberg G: Supplementary motor area structure and function: Review and hypotheses. *Behav. Brain Sci.: 8,* 567 – 616, 1985.

Goldman-Rackic PS: Circuitry of the prefrontal cortex and the regulation of behavior by representational knowledge. In Plum F, Mountcastle V (Editors), *Handbook of Physiology, Vol. 5.* Bethesda, MD: American Physiological Society, pp. 373 – 417, 1987.

Gordon HW: Auditory specialization of the right and left hemispheres. In Kinsbourne M, Smith WL (Editors), *Hemispheric Disconnection and Cerebral Function.* Springfield, IL: Thomas, pp. 126 – 136, 1974.

Gordon HW: The neurobiological basis of hemisphericity. In Trevarthen C (Editor), *Brain Circuits and Functions of the Mind: Essays in Honor of RW Sperry.* New York: Cambridge University Press, in press.

Gordon HW, Bogen JE: Hemispheric lateralization of singing after intracortical sodium amylobarbitone. *J. Neurol. Neurosurg. Psychiatry: 37,* 727 – 738, 1974.

Gordon HW, Sperry RW: Lateralization of olfactory perception in the surgically separated hemispheres of man. *Neuropsychologia: 7,* 111 – 120, 1969.

Gordon HW, Bogen JE, Sperry RW: Absence of deconnexion syndrome in two patients with partial section of the neocommissures. *Brain: 94,* 327 – 336, 1971.

Guiard Y: Cerebral hemispheres and selective attention. *Acta Psychol.: 46,* 41 – 61, 1980.

Gur RC, Reivich M: Cognitive task effects on hemispheric blood flow in humans: evidence for individual differences in hemispheric activation. *Brain Lang.: 9,* 78 – 92, 1980.

Hecaen H: Aphasic, apraxic and agnosic syndromes in right and left hemisphere lesions. In Vinken PJ, Bruyn GW (Editors), *Handbook of Clinical Neurology, Vol. 4.* Amsterdam: North-Holland, pp. 291 – 311, 1969.

Hecaen H, Albert ML: *Human Neuropsychology,* New York: Wiley, 1978.

Heilman KM, Satz P (Editors): *Neuropsychology of Human Emotion.* London: Guildford Press, 1983.

Heilman KM, Scholes R, Watson RT: Auditory affective agnosia. *J. Neurol. Neurosurg. Psychiatry: 38,* 69 – 72, 1974.

Heller W, Levy J: Perception and expression of emotion in right-handers and left-handers. *Neuropsychologia: 19,* 263 – 272, 1981.

Holtzman JD: Interactions between cortical and subcortical visual areas: Evidence from human commissurotomy patients. *Vision Res.: 24,* 801 – 813, 1984.

Holtzman JD, Gazzaniga MS: Dual task interactions due exclusively to limits in processing resources. *Science: 218,* 1325 – 1327, 1985.

Holtzman JD, Sidtis JJ, Volpe BT, Wilson DH, Gazzaniga MS: Dissociation of spatial information for stimulus localization and the control of attention. *Brain: 104,* 861 – 872, 1981.

Hoppe ID, Bogen JE: Alexithymia in twelve commissurotomized patients. *Psychother. Psychosom.: 28,* 148 – 155, 1977.

Hubel DH, Wiesel TN: Cortical and callosal connections concerned with the vertical meridian of visual fields in the cat. *J. Neurophysiol.: 35,* 96 – 111, 1967.

Innocenti GM: The development of interhemispheric connections. *Trends Neurosci.: 4,* 142 – 144, 1981.

Innocenti GM: General organization of callosal connections in the cerebral cortex. In Jones EG, Peters A (Editors), *Cerebral Cortex, Vol. 5.* New York: Plenum, pp. 291 – 353, 1986.

Jeannerod M: Mechanisms of visuo-motor coordination: A study in normal and brain-damaged subjects. *Neuropsychologia: 24,* 41 – 78, 1986.

Jeeves MA, Silver PH, Jacobson I: Bimanual co-ordination in callosal agenesis and partial commissurotomy. *Neuropsychologia: 26,* 833 – 850, 1988.

Kimura D: Functional asymmetry of the brain in dichotic listening. *Cortex: 3,* 163 – 178, 1967.

Kimura D: Neuromotor mechanisms in the evolution of human communication. In Stecklis, Raleigh (Editors), *Neurobiology of Social Communication in Primates.* New York: Academic Press, pp. 197 – 219, 1979.

Kinsbourne M: Lateral interactions in the brain. In Kinsbourne M, Smith WL (Editors), *Hemispheric Disconnection and Cerebral Function.* Springfield, IL: C.C. Thomas, pp. 239 – 259, 1974.

Kreuter C, Kinsbourne M, Trevarthen C: Are deconnected cerebral hemispheres independent channels? A preliminary study of the effect of unilateral loading on bilateral finger tapping. *Neuropsychologia: 10,* 453 – 461, 1972.

LaMantia A-S, Rakic P: The number, size, myelination, and regional variation of axons in the corpus callosum and anterior commissure of the developing rhesus monkey. *Soc. Neurosci. Abstr.: 10,* 1373, 1984.

Lee DN: The optic flow field: the foundation of vision. *Phil. Trans. R. Soc. Lond. Ser. B: 290,* 169 – 179, 1980.

Levine SC, Banich MT, Kim H: Variations in arousal asymmetry: Implications for face processing. In Ottoson D (Editor), *Duality and Unity of the Brain.* London: Macmillan, pp. 207 – 222, 1987.

Levy-Agresti J, Sperry RW: Differential perceptual capacities of major and minor hemispheres. *Proc. Natl. Acad. Sci. USA: 61,* 1151, 1968.

Levy J: Possible basis for the evolution of lateral specialization of the human brain. *Nature (Lond.): 224,* 614 – 615, 1969.

Levy J: Cerebral asymmetries as manifested in split-brain man. In Kinsbourne M, Smith WL (Editors), *Hemispheric Disconnection and Cerebral Function.* Springfield, IL: Thomas, pp. 165 – 183, 1974.

Levy J: Language, cognition, and the right hemisphere: a response to Gazzaniga. *Am. Psychol.: 38,* 538 – 541, 1983.

Levy J: Regulation and generation of perception in the asymmetric brain. In Trevarthen C (Editor), *Brain Circuits and Functions of the Mind.* New York: Cambridge University Press, in press.

Levy J, Keuck L: A right hemispatial field advantage on a verbal free-vision task. *Brain Lang.: 27,* 224 – 37, 1986.

Levy J, Trevarthen C: Metacontrol of hemispheric function in human split-brain patients. *J. Exp. Psychol. Hum. Percept. Performance: 2,* 299 – 312, 1976.

Levy J, Trevarthen C: Perceptual, semantic and phonetic aspects of elementary language processes in split-brain patients. *Brain: 100,* 105 – 118, 1977.

Levy J, Trevarthen C: Color-matching, color-naming and color-memory in split-brain patients. *Neuropsychologia: 19,* 523 – 541, 1981.

Levy J, Nebes RD, Sperry RW: Expressive language in the surgically separated minor hemisphere. *Cortex: 7,* 49 – 58, 1971.

Levy J, Trevarthen C, Sperry RW: Perception of bilateral chimeric figures following hemispheric deconnection. *Brain: 95,* 60 – 78, 1972.

Levy J, Heller W, Banich MT, Burton L: Asymmetry of perception of free viewing of chimeric faces. *Brain Cognition: 2,* 404 – 419, 1983(a).

Levy J, Heller W, Banich MT, Burton L: Are variations among right-handed individuals in perceptual asymmetries caused by characteristic arousal differences between hemispheres? *J. Exp. Psych. Hum. Percept. Performance: 9,* 329 – 359, 1983(b).

Ley RG, Bryden MP: Hemispheric differences in processing emotions and faces. *Brain Lang.: 7,* 127 – 138, 1979.

Liepmann H, Mass O: Fal von Linksseitiger Agraphie und Apraxie bei rechtsseitiger Lahmung. *J. Psychol. Neurol.: 10,* 214 – 227, 1908

Lund JS, Downer JL, Lumley JSP: Visual control of limb movement following section of optic chiasm and corpus callosum in the monkey. *Cortex: 6,* 323 – 346, 1970.

MacNeilage PF: The evolution of hemispheric specialization for manuyal function and language. In Wise S (Editor), *Higher Brain Function: Recent Explorations of the Brain's Emergent Properties.* New York: Wiley, 1986.

Maffei L, Berardi N, Bisti S: Interocular transfer of adaptation after effect in neurones of area 17 and 18 of split chiasm cats. *J. Neurophysiol.: 55,* 966 – 1976, 1986.

Mark RF, Sperry RW: Bimanual coordination in monkeys. *Exp. Neurol.: 11,* 92 – 104, 1968.

Maspes PE: Le syndrome experimental chez l'homme de la section du splenium du corps calleux: Alexie visuelle pur hemianopsique. *Rev. Neurol.: 80,* 100 – 113, 1948.

Mayer E, Koenig O, Panchaud A: Tactual extinction without anomia: evidence of attentional factors in a patient with a partial callosal disconnection. *Neuropsychologia: 26,* 851 – 868, 1988.

McKeever WF, Sullivan KF: Typical cerebral hemisphere disconnection deficits following corpus callosum section despite sparing of the anterior commissure. *Neuropsychologia: 19,* 745 – 755, 1981.

McKeever WF, Larrabee GJ, Sullivan KF, Johnson HJ, Ferguson S, Rayport M: Unimanual tactile anomia consequent to corpus callosotomy: reduction of anomic deficit under hypnosis. *Neuropsychologia: 19,* 179 – 190, 1981.

McKeever WF, Sullivan KF, Ferguson SM, Rayport M: Right

hemisphere speech development in the anterior commissure-spared commissurotomy patient: a second case. *Clin. Neuropsychol.: 4,* 17–22, 1982.

Meike TH, Sechere JA: Interocular transfer of brightness discrimination in split-brain cats. *Science: 132,* 734–735, 1960.

Mesulam MM: A cortical network for directed attention and unilateral neglect. *Ann. Neurol.: 10,* 309–325.

Milner AD, Jeeves MA: A review of behavioral studies of agenesis of the corpus callosum. In Russel IS, van Hof MW, Berlucchi G (Editors), *Structure and Function of the Cerebral Commissures.* Baltimore: University Park Press, pp. 428–448, 1979.

Milner B: Hemispheric specialization: Scope and limits. In Schmitt FO, Worden FG (Editors), *The Neurosciences: Third Study Program.* Cambridge, MA: MIT Press, pp. 698–717, 1974.

Milner B, Taylor L: Right-hemisphere superiority in tactile pattern-recognition after cerebral commissurotomy: evidence for non-verbal memory. *Neuropsychologia: 10,* 1–15, 1972.

Milner B, Taylor LB, Sperry RW: Laterally suppressed dichotically presented digits after commissural section in man. *Science: 161,* 184–186, 1968.

Milner B, Taylor L, Jones-Gottman M: Lessons from commissurotomy: attention to sounds, memory for felt shapes and visual images in verbal associative-learning. In Trevarthen C (Editor), *Brain Circuits and Functions of the Mind: Essays in Honor of RW Sperry.* New York: Cambridge University Press, in press.

Mishkin M: A memory system in the monkey. *Phil. Trans. R. Soc. Lond. Ser. B: 298,* 85–95, 1982.

Mishkin M, Phillips RR: A cortico-limbic memory path revealed through its disconnection. In Travarthen C (Editor), *Brain Circuits and Functions of the Mind.* New York: Cambridge University Press, in press.

Mitchell DE, Blakemore CB: Binocular depth perception and the corpus callosum. *Vision Res.: 10,* 49–54, 1970.

Morgan AH, McDonald PJ, Macdonald H: Differences in bilateral alpha activity as a function of experimental task with a note on lateral eye movements and hypnotizability. *Neuropsychologia: 9,* 459–69, 1971.

Moscovitch M, Olds J: Asymmetries in spontaneous facial expressions and their possible relation to hemispheric specialization. *Neuropsychologia: 20,* 71–81, 1981.

Myers JJ: Right hemisphere language: science or fiction? *Am. Psychol.: 39,* 315–320, 1984.

Myers RE: Function of corpus callosum in interocular transfer. *Brain: 79,* 358–363, 1956.

Myers RE: Transmission of visual information within and between the hemispheres. In Mountcastle VB (Editor), *Interhemispheric Relations and Cerebral Dominance.* Baltimore: Johns Hopkins Press, pp. 51–73, 1962.

Myers RE, Sperry RW: Interocular transfer of a visual form discrimination habit in cats after section of the optic chiasum and corpus callosum. *Anat. Rec.: 115,* 351, 1953.

Myers RE, Sperry RW, McCurdy NM: Neural mechanisms in visual guidance of limb movement. *Arch. Neurol.: 2,* 195–202, 1962.

Nebes RD: Superiority of the minor hemisphere in commissurotomized man for the perception of part-whole relations. *Cortex: 7,* 333–349, 1971.

Nebes RD: Dominance of the minor hemisphere in commissurotomized man on a test of figural unification. *Brain: 95,* 633–638, 1972.

Nebes RD: Dominance of the minor hemisphere in commissurotomized man for the perception of part-whole relationships. In Kinsbourne M, Smith WL (Editors), *Hemisphere Disconnection and Cerebral Function.* Springfield, IL: C.C. Thomas, pp. 155–164, 1974.

Nebes RD: Direct examination of cognitive function in right and left hemispheres. In Kinsbourne M (Editor), *Asymmetrical Function of the Brain.* Cambridge: Cambridge University Press, pp. 99–137, 1978.

Nebes R, Bogen JE, Sperry RW: Variations of the human cerebral commissurotomy syndrome with birth injury in the domainant arm area. *Anat. Rec. 163:* 235, 1969.

Paillard J, Beaubaton D: Triggered and guided components of visual reaching: their dissociation in split-brain studies. In Shahani M (Editor), *Motor System: Neuropsychology and Muscle Mechanism.* Amsterdam: Elsevier, pp. 333–347, 1976.

Paterson A, Zangwill OL: Disorders of visual space perception associated with lesions of the right cerebral hemisphere. *Brain: 67,* 331–358, 1944.

Perenin MT: Visual function within the hemianopic field following early cerebral hemidecortication in man. II. Spatial localization. *Neuropsychologia: 16,* 697–708, 1978.

Perenin MT, Jeannerod M: Visual function within the hemianopic field following early cerebral hemidecortication in man. I. spatial localization. *Neuropsychologia: 16,* 1–13, 1978.

Plourde G, Sperry RW: Left hemisphere involvement in left spatial neglect from right lesions: a commissurotomy study. *Brain: 107,* 95–106, 1984.

Posner MI, Snyder CR, Davidson BJ: Attention and the detection of signals. *J. Exp. Psychol. (Gen.): 21,* 160–174, 1980.

Posner MI, Walker JA, Freidrich FA, Rafal RD. How do the parietal lobes direct covert attention? *Neuropsychologia: 25,* 135–145, 1987.

Preilowski B: Bilateral motor interaction: Perceptual-motor performance of partial and complete 'split-brain' patients. In Zuelch KJ, Creutzfeldt O, Galbraith GC (Editors), *Cerebral Localization.* Berlin: Springer, pp. 115–132, 1975.

Rakic P, Yakovlev PI: Development of the corpus callosum and cavum septi in man. *J. Comp. Neurol.: 132,* 45–72, 1968.

Ramachandran VS, Cronin-Golomb A, Myers JJ: Perception of apparent motion by commissurotomy patients. *Nature: 320,* 358–359, 1986.

Rasmussen T, Milner B: The role of early left-brain injury in determining lateralization of cerebral speech functions. *Ann. N.Y. Acad. Sci.: 299,* 355–369, 1977.

Rebert CS: Function cerebral asymmetry and performance. I. Reaction time to words and dot patterns as a function of EEG alpha asymmetry. *Behav. Neuropsychiatry: 8,* 90–98, 1977.

Rocha-Miranda CE, Bender DB, Gross CG, Mishkin M: Visual activation of neurones in inferotemporal cortex depends on striate cortex and forebrain commissures. *J. Neurophysiol.: 38,* 475–491, 1975.

Ross ED: Right hemisphere's role in language, affective

behavior and emotion. *Trends Neurosci.: 7,* 342 – 346, 1984.

Sackheim HA, Gur RC, Saucy MD: Emotions are expressed more intensely on the left side of the face. *Science: 202,* 434 – 436, 1978.

Schrier AM, Sperry RW: Visuo-motor integration in split-brain cats. *Science: 129,* 1275 – 1276, 1959.

Sergent J: Unified response to bilateral hemispheric stimulations by a split-brain patient. *Nature (Lond.): 305,* 800 – 802, 1983.

Sergent J: Subcortical coordination of hemisphere activity in commissurotomy patients. *Brain: 109,* 357 – 369, 1986.

Shankweiler D, Studdert-Kennedy M: A continuum of lateralization for speech perception? *Brain Lang.: 2,* 212 – 225, 1975.

Sidtis JJ, Volpe BT, Wilson DH, Rayport M, Gazzaniga MS: Variability in right hemisphere language function after callosal section: evidence for a continuum of generative capacity. *J. of Neurosci.: 1,* 323 – 331, 1981.

Sparkes R, Geschwind N: Dichotic listening in man after section of the neocortical commissures. *Cortex: 4,* 3 – 16, 1968.

Sperry RW: Cerebral organization and behavior. *Science: 133,* 1749 – 1757, 1961.

Sperry RW: Brain bisection and mechanisms of consciousness. In Eccles JC (Editor), *Brain and Conscious Experience.* New York: Springer, pp. 298 – 313, 1966.

Sperry RW: Hemispheric deconnection and unity in conscious awareness. *Am. Psychol.: 23,* 723 – 733, 1968.

Sperry RW: Perception in the absence of the neocortical commissures. *Res. Publ. Assoc. Res. Nerv. Ment. Dis.: 48,* 123 – 138, 1970.

Sperry RW: Lateral specialization in the surgically separated hemispheres. In Schmitt FO, Worden FG (Editors), *The Neurosciences: Third Study Program.* Cambridge: MIT Press, pp. 5 – 19, 1974.

Sperry RW: Consciousness, free will and personal identity. In Oakley DA, Plotkin HC (Editors), *Brain Behaviour and Evolution.* London: Methuen, pp. 219 – 228; 1223 – 1226, 1982a.

Sperry RW: Some effects of disconnecting the cerebral hemispheres. *Science: 217,* 1223 – 1226, 1982b.

Sperry RW: *Science and Moral Priority.* New York: Columbia University Press, 1983.

Sperry RW, Gazzaniga MS, Bogen JE: Interhemispheric relationships: the neocortical commissures; syndromes of hemispheric disconnection. Vinken PJ, Bruyn GW (Editors), *Handbook of Clinical Neurology, Vol. 4.* Amsterdam: North-Holland, pp. 273 – 290, 1969.

Sperry RW, Zaidel E, Zaidel D: Self-recognition and social awareness in the deconnected minor hemisphere. *Neuropsychologia: 17,* 152 – 166, 1979.

Sprague JM: Interaction of cortex and superior colliculus in mediation of visually guided behavior in the cat. *Science: 153,* 1544 – 1547, 1966.

Stamm JS, Sperry RW: Function of corpus callosum in contralateral transfer of somesthetic discrimination in cats. *J. Comp. Physiol. Psychol.: 50,* 138 – 143, 1957.

Teng EL, Sperry RW: Interhemispheric rivalry during simultaneous bilateral task presentation in commissurotomy patients. *Cortex: 10,* 111 – 120, 1974.

Trescher HH, Ford FR: Colloid cyst of the third ventricle: report of case. Operative removal with section of posterior half of the corpus callosum. *Arch. Neurol. Psychiatry: 37,* 959 – 973, 1937.

Trevarthen C: Double visual learning in split-brain monkeys. *Science: 136,* 258 – 259, 1962.

Trevarthen C: Functional interactions between the cerebral hemispheres of the split-brain monkey. In Ettlinger EG (Editor), *Functions of the Corpus Callosum* (Ciba Foundation, Study Group No. 20). London: Churchill, pp. 24 – 41 and discussions pp. 103 – 106, 111, 145 – 147, 1965.

Trevarthen C: Two mechanisms of vision in primates. *Psychol. Forsch.: 31,* 299 – 337, 1968.

Trevarthen C: Brain bisymmetry and the role of the corpus callosum in behavior and conscious experience. In Cernacek J, Podovinsky F (Editors), *Cerebral Interhemispheric Relations.* Bratislava: Slovak Academy of Sciences, pp. 00, 1972.

Trevarthen C: Analysis of cerebral activities that generate and regulate consciousness in commissurotomy patients. In Dimond SJ, Beaumont JG (Editors), *Hemisphere Function in the Human Brain.* London: Paul Elek, pp. 235 – 263, 1974a.

Trevarthen C: Functional relations of disconnected hemispheres with the brain stem and with each other: monkey and man. In Kinsbourne M, Smith WL (Editors), *Hemispheric Disconnection and Cerebral Function.* Springfield, IL: C.C. Thomas, pp. 187 – 207, 1974b.

Trevarthen C: Psychological activities after forebrain commissurotomy in man. Concepts and methodological hurdles in testing. In Michel F, Schott B (Editors), *Les Syndrômes de Disconnection Calleuse chez l'Homme.* Lyon: Hopital Neurologique, pp. 181 – 210, 1975.

Trevarthen C: Manipulative strategies of baboons and the origins of cerebral asymmetry. In Kinsbourne M (Editor), *The Asymmetrical Function of the Brain.* New York: Cambridge University Press, pp. 329 – 391, 1978.

Trevarthen C: Hemispheric specialization. In Darian-Smith I (Section Editor), *Handbook of Physiology (Section 1, The Nervous System); Vol. 2, Sensory Processes.* Washington, DC: American Physiological Society, pp. 1129 – 1190, 1984.

Trevarthen C: Subcortical influences on cortical processing in 'split' brains. In Ottoson D (Editor), *Duality and Unity of the Brain* (Wenner-Gren International Symposium Series, Vol. 47). London: Macmillan, 1987.

Trevarthen C: Growth and education of the hemispheres: In Trevarthen C (Editor), *Brain Circuits and Functions of the Mind: Essays in Honor of RW Sperry.* New York: Cambridge University Press, in press (a).

Trevarthen C: Grasping from the inside: intrinsic cerebral patterning for reach and grasp. In Goodale M (Editor), *Vision and Action: The Control of Grasping.* Norwood NJ: Ablex, in press (b).

Trevarthen C, Sperry RW: Perceptual unity of ambient visual field in human commissurotomy patients. *Brain: 96,* 547 – 570, 1973.

Tucker DM, Frederick SL: Emotion and brain lateralization. In Wagner H, Manstead T (Editors), *Handbook of Psychophysiology: Emotion and Social Behaviour.* New York: John Wiley, 1987.

Tucker DM, Williamson PA: Asymmetric neural control systems in human self-regulation. *Psychol. Rev.: 91,* 185 – 215, 1984.

Tucker GH, Suib MR: Conjugate lateral eye movement (CLEM) direction and its relationship to performance on verbal and visuospatial tasks. *Neuropsychologia: 16,* 251 – 254, 1978.

Tucker DM, Watson RT, Heilman KM: Discrimination and evocation of affectively informed speech in patients with right parietal disease. *Neurology: 27,* 947 – 950, 1977.

Van Essen DC, Newsome WT, Bixby JL: The pattern of interhemispheric connections and its relationship to extrastriate visual areas in the macaque monkey. *J. Neurosci.: 2,* 265 – 283, 1982.

Voneida RJ: Performance of a visual conditioned response in split-brain cats. *Exp. Neurol.: 8,* 493 – 504, 1963.

Wale J, Geffen G: Hemispheric specialization and attention: effects of complete and partial callosal section and hemispherectomy on dichotic monitoring. *Neuropsychologia: 24,* 483 – 496, 1986.

Yakovlev PI, Lecours A-R: The myelogenetic cycles of regional motivation of the brain. In Minkowsky A (Editor), *Regional Development of the Brain in Early Life.* Oxford: Blackwell, pp. 3 – 70, 1967.

Zaidel D: Long-term semantic memory in the two cerebral hemispheres. In Trevarthen C (Editor), *Brain Circuits and Functions of the Mind: Essays in Honor of RW Sperry.* New York: Cambridge University Press, in press.

Zaidel D, Sperry RW: Performance of Raven's colored progressive matrices test by subjects with cerebral commissurotomy. *Cortex: 9,* 34 – 39, 1973.

Zaidel D, Sperry RW: Memory impairment after commissurotomy in man. *Brain:* 97, 263 – 272, 1974.

Zaidel D, Sperry RW: Some long-term motor effects of cerebral commissurotomy in man. *Neuropsychologia: 15,* 493 – 504, 1977.

Zaidel E: Linguistic competence and related functions in the right cerebral hemisphere of man following commissurotomy and hemispherectomy. Doctoral dissertation, California Institute of Technology, 1973 (Dissertation Abstracts International 34, 2350B: University Microfilm No. 73 – 26, 481).

Zaidel E: A technique for presenting lateralized visual input with prolonged exposure. *Vision Res.: 15,* 283 – 289, 1975.

Zaidel E: Unilateral auditory language comprehension on the Token Test following cerebral commissurotomy and hemispherectomy. *Neuropsychologia: 15,* 1 – 18, 1977.

Zaidel E: Auditory language comprehension in the right hemisphere following cerebral commissurotomy and hemispherectomy. A comparison with child language and aphasia. In Caramazza A, Zurif EB (Editors), *Language Acquisition and Language Breakdown: Parallels and Divergences.* Baltimore: Johns Hopkins University Press, pp. 229 – 275, 1978a.

Zaidel E: Lexical organization in the right hemisphere. In Buser P, Rougeul-Buser A (Editors), *Cerebral Correlates of Conscious Experience.* Amsterdam: Elsevier, pp. 177 – 197, 1978b.

Zaidel E: Disconnection Syndrome as a model for laterality effects in the normal brain. In Hellige JB (Editor), *Cerebral Hemisphere Asymmetry: Method, Theory and Application.* New York: Praeger Publishers, pp. 95 – 151, 1983.

Zaidel E: A response to Gazzaniga: language in the right hemisphere, convergent perspectives. *Am. Psychol.: 38,* 542 – 546, 1983b.

Zaidel E: The saga of right hemisphere reading. In Trevarthen C (Editor), *Brain Circuits and Functions of the Mind: Essays in Honor of RW Sperry.* New York: Cambridge University Press, in press.

Zaidel E, Schweiger A: On wrong hypotheses about the right hemisphere: commentary on K Patterson and D Besner. Is the right hemisphere literate? *Cognitive Neuropsychol.: 1,* 351 – 364, 1984.

© 1990 Elsevier Science Publishers B.V. (Biomedical Division)
Handbook of Neuropsychology, Vol. 4
F. Boller and J. Grafman (Eds)

CHAPTER 4

Neuropsychological sequelae of partial commissurotomy

Harold W. Gordon

Western Psychiatric Institute & Clinic, University of Pittsburgh School of Medicine, Pittsburgh, PA, U.S.A.

Introduction

The corpus callosum is by far the most prominent commissural structure in the cerebrum. It contains some two hundred million axons cross-connecting both homologous and non-homologous cortical areas of the two cerebral hemispheres. Nevertheless, it was not until the 1950s and 1960s that R.W. Sperry and his colleagues demonstrated unequivocally that surgical division of some of this structure produced functional defects. This chapter examines a number of studies in which the corpus callosum has been partially divided by surgery for medical reasons. The goal is to provide insight into some of the functions that might be associated with parts of this large brain structure.

The anatomic distribution of the callosum has been well studied. It is known that there is little cross-connection between primary sensory areas. Instead, homotopic connections exist between the 'association' areas; heterotopic projections run *inter*hemispherically between cortical areas for which there are also *intra*hemispheric connections. This organization suggests that the callosum has a role in integrating information at varying levels of abstraction. Furthermore, the callosum is organized anteriorly – posteriorly in a way analogous to cortical representation of function; vision is transmitted through the posterior motor function more anteriorly. More importantly, there is wide individual variation in the gross structure of the corpus callosum, complicating the interpretation of any study of partial commissurotomy. One study purports that females have larger splenia (Lacoste-Utamsing and Holloway, 1982); another fails to support this sex difference, but demonstrates larger callosa in non-right handers (Witelson, 1985). The functional significance of these anatomical differences is still unclear.

In determining function for parts of the corpus callosum and other forebrain commissures in non-surgical cases, investigators have had to rely on evidence from patients with tumors or strokes (cerebral vascular accidents, CVAs) that impinge upon callosal fibers. Such pathology rarely, if ever, involves only the callosum. By contrast, surgical division of the commissures provides a circumscribed separation of the cross-connecting fibers. However, the 'cleaner' surgical division of commissural fibers mitigates, but does not eliminate, the effects of the extra-commissural neuropathology that led to the surgery in the first place. In some cases, the callosum is divided to gain access to a cyst or tumor in the underlying third ventricle or pineal body. In other cases, callosal surgery is recommended to alleviate pharmacologically intractable epilepsy due to multifocal or non-localizable seizure foci. Biological variability in humans produces individual differences in both the size and shape of the callosum, presence or absence of a massa intermedia, and differences in the number of fibers crossing in the anterior and other commissures. This variability further confounds attempts to analyse and interpret the effects of surgery. Unlike animal research where experimental investigations can be contrived, studies in humans depend on accidents of nature or medically indicated surgical intervention. The point to remember in the following is that the evidence for behavioral changes after commissurotomy is circumstantial. A function that is absent or deficient when a portion of brain has been damaged does not imply that the missing tissue is fully responsible for the behavior. Any neuroanatomical structure is invariably part of a larger system; thus lesions may act at a distance to produce behavioral changes. Finally, it should be noted that specific lesions, surgical or otherwise, usually affect more than one structure. The task of attributing function to structure is accordingly limited.

It is with these caveats in mind that functional changes following partial commissurotomy are discussed. (For a complete discussion of the physiological consequences of the surgery and a recent summary of the behavioral sequelae of complete and partial commissurotomy for patients with epilepsy see Bogen (1987)). In this chapter evidence is presented from a number of studies involving patients with different forms of pathology but with similar callosal involvement. Common deficits (or lack thereof) among these patients supply the converging evidence from which tentative conclusions may be drawn. Unfortunately, the data are limited because of the paucity of cases in which neuropsychological testing has been carried out pre- and postoperatively. On the fortunate side, there are a number of observations that have been made repeatedly with little or no contradiction. A broad summary would go something like this: functional cross-communication occurs largely in the splenium and posterior regions of the corpus callosum. In spite of concentrated efforts over the past 15 years, evidence continues to be sparse for behavioral deficits following surgical section of the anterior two-thirds of the corpus callosum. This conclusion remains unsettling for those who would expect to see greater functional loss after sectioning so much of the largest cerebral commissure.

Summary of studies

Anterior callosal section: preservation of functions attributable to the splenium and posterior callosum

It is quite likely that the behavioral consequences of anterior callosotomy were first described as behavioral outcomes of what were thought to be *complete* commissurotomies in the Akelaitis series of the early 1940s. In those patients, virtually no interhemispheric transfer deficits were reported; neither left visual field nor left (non-dominant) hand alexia was observed. The few transfer deficits that did emerge were explained away as extracallosal damage. It was concluded that complete surgical division of the corpus callosum did not disturb the ability to transmit primary sensory information from one hemisphere to the other. The observations suggested a fairly robust conclusion: sensory information was transferred between the hemispheres through other forebrain commissures or by subcortical routes (Akelaitis, 1943).

It was not until 27 years later, in a follow-up of one of the early patients, that the sparing of a little bit of splenial tissue was discovered as a sufficient interhemispheric communication channel (Goldstein and Joynt, 1969). The patient, a woman in her 40s at the retest, maintained a low (mid-70) Full Scale WAIS IQ, but performed quite well on tasks of complex bimanual coordination such as embroidery, making lace and playing the piano. More importantly, she could name and select objects, letters and geometric forms with *either* hand alone, suggesting tactile information was reaching the speech apparatus from either sensory field. Surgical notes stated that a small portion of the inferior splenium had remained intact. Apparently this remnant was sufficient for transmitting the information.

In contrast, this patient failed to cross-match and select an object with her right hand that was tachistoscopically flashed to her left visual field. Similarly, she could not select an object with her left hand flashed to her right field unless she first named it. Since all ipsilateral field/hand matches could be made without error, it was concluded that intermodal matching between the hemispheres was disrupted by the surgery. Although cross-field tactual-tactual and visual-visual matches were not reported, a tactual sorting task and tactual form board task were taught first to the right hand and then to the left without savings. This result further suggested that tasks involving tactual matching depended on structures anterior to the remaining splenial remnant. However, it is not clear how this patient could name objects felt only in the left hand. Either (tactile) naming and matching require different cortical functions, or the successful naming occurred because of cross-cueing, sometimes seen in commissurotomy patients.

There was no verification by autopsy or modern brain imaging procedures that other patients in the Akelaitis series, who reportedly were complete commissurotomies, actually had completely sectioned splenia. A case in point is A.M. who was originally described as having a complete commissurotomy (Van Wagenen and Herren, 1940), but later reported to have 1 cm of the splenium intact (Akelaitis, 1943). Case E.J.B. was also reported to have a complete callosal section, but another report of the same case allowed 'a few possible fibers in the tip of the splenium' (Akelaitis, 1941). The surgeries had been carried out through a single exposure anterior to the parietal suture of the skull which would preclude good visualization of the posterior corpus callosum even with present-day microscopic technology. Unless confirmed otherwise, a reasonable alternative explanation to the essentially negative behavioral disconnection symptoms of the reportedly complete commissurotomies of the early series is that the surgeries invariably spared a portion of the posterior splenium.

In cases where the splenium is intentionally left intact, very few deficits of interhemispheric matching of visual or tactual stimuli are observed. An extensive examination of two patients with intractable epilepsy, who had complete division in one operation of the anterior commissure and the anterior two-thirds of the corpus callosum revealed essentially the same results as the Akelaitis cases: complete absence of the 'classic' hemispheric disconnection symptomatology including a lack of deficits for visuotactual and tactuotactual cross-matching (Gordon et al., 1971). Contrary to the usual failures of cross-communication that had come to be expected from patients with complete commissurotomy (Bogen, 1985; Sperry et al., 1969), these two patients could name any object placed in their left (non-dominant) hand or describe any stimulus tachistoscopically flashed to their left visual field. Both patients demonstrated cross-modal transfer by retrieving objects with either hand that had been flashed to the ipsi- or contralateral visual field or placed in the opposite hand. Even complex shapes such as those from a jigsaw puzzle could be retrieved by either hand, even after simultaneous presentation to both hands. This general absence of symptomatology has been supported in subsequent studies of other patients with partial (anterior) commissurotomy for control of epilepsy (Gazzaniga et al., 1975; Lassande, 1986). In addition, more complete neuropsychological testing in non-epileptic patients whose anterior callosa had been sectioned for removal of cysts or tumors has confirmed the complete transfer of sensory information (Benes, 1982; Ozgur et al., 1977; Scarff, 1979; Shucart and Stein, 1978; Winston et al., 1979).

These studies can be summarized as demonstrating a complete interhemispheric transfer of all sensory information in patients with anterior callostomy with possible exceptions of olfaction (Gordon, 1974a) and taste. However, a number of studies described in the next section suggest that these patients do have other more subtle deficits.

Anterior callosal section: functional deficits

Depending on the extent of the surgery or extracallosal damage, deficits pertaining to anterior commissurotomy have been reported. One of the first was an impairment in memory that seemed to be just as severe as in patients with complete commissurotomy (Zaidel and Sperry, 1974). However, these conclusions were derived without the benefit of pre- and postoperative scores for any of the tests. In contradiction to this reported loss, memory improved in one patient following surgical section of the anterior corpus callosum to remove a tumor in the third ventricle (Winston et al., 1979). Additional patients with similar callosal surgeries sparing both the genu and splenium of the corpus callosum demonstrated few, if any, memory difficulties unless the surgery also involved the fornix (Geffen et al., 1980). In three recent cases of anterior callosotomy (the anterior commissure remained intact) for epilepsy, performance on verbal learning and spatial memory tasks was unchanged or improved in the 4-week postoperative period compared to preoperative levels (Gordon, unpublished data). The issue is not resolved since surgeries and types of memory tests are not always comparable (Dimond et al., 1977; Zaidel, Chapter 7, this volume), but the presence of extracallosal damage offers the most reasonable alternative explanation for conflicting reports of memory dysfunction following callosal surgery.

Anterior section of the corpus callosum has produced symptoms of auditory disconnection similar to those reported for complete commissurotomy. It is more difficult to lateralize auditory stimuli than visual or tactual stimuli because afferent auditory fibers project both ipsilaterally and contralaterally from each cochlea to both hemispheres. An experimental technique known as dichotic listening presents different auditory stimuli simultaneously through stereo headphones to the right and left ears of the subject. As a result, there appears to be a functional inhibition of the ipsilateral ear-to-cortex pathway by the contralateral. The effect in patients with complete commissurotomy is a complete extinction of verbal stimuli presented to the left ear (Milner et al., 1968) (although this has its qualifications) (Gordon, 1980). A similar extinction was reported for one case with almost complete commissurotomy; partial extinction was reported for another case with the splenium intact (Springer and Gazzaniga, 1975) and for two others with partial section for removal of tumors (Wale and Geffen, 1986).

Such asymmetries are not always observed, however. In a standard dichotic listening task, no ear extinction was observed in the two anterior-sectioned patients of the earlier Sperry series (Gordon, 1971). In that study, however, the pattern of the patients' responses differed from that of epileptic and normal controls. Instead of reporting first the items from one ear and then the items from the other, as normals usually do, the patients tended to report the items from the two ears jumbled together (Gordon, 1971). Thus, it can tentatively be concluded that cross-communication of auditory information occurs in the corpus callosum together with the crossing visual and tactual fiber tracts, but transfer of information important for organizing auditory input lies somewhat anteriorly. Confirmation of these conclusions and more definitive statements await future investigation.

A more definite deficit was found after anterior commissurotomy in bimanual motor coordination (Preilowsky, 1972). The task was to trace oblique lines with the pen of an $x-y$ plotter controlled by two crank handles, one for each hand. One crank controlled the x axis, the other the y axis. By altering the obliquity of the line, the relative contribution of each hand was changed. Patients with partial commissurotomy were able to trace the lines, albeit awkwardly, as long as they could see what they were doing. However, they could never improve the speed and facility of their performance with practice. With vision excluded, proprioceptive feedback was inadequate so that performance dropped markedly. This suggested that information regarding proprioceptive and corollary motor discharge is transmitted through some portion of the anterior two-thirds of the corpus callosum and/or the anterior commissure. In support of this view of motor dysfunction, it was reported that these same two patients performed as poorly as patients with left parietal excisions on tasks of copying arm and hand movements, and more poorly on tasks of copying facial movements and facial-movement sequences (Milner and Kolb, 1985). Other tactile and motor deficits have been reported for cases in which only portions of the trunk of the callosum were sectioned. These will be discussed later.

Although the most extensive neuropsychological studies were performed on epileptic patients who had anterior callosal sections for control of intractable seizures, there is another group of cases whose otherwise healthy callosa are partially sectioned in an effort to approach underlying tumors. These cases differ from the epileptics not only in that their corpora callosa connect healthy tissue and intact cortical circuitry, but also in that the associated tumors cause damage to specific, extracallosal cortex. Nevertheless, in spite of the differences in neuropathology, the absence of disconnection symptoms has been confirmed in these cases as well. Several examples can be cited. With the type of neuropsychological testing in the partially sectioned epileptics as a model, pre- and postoperative testing in one tumor patient clearly substantiated the preservation of interhemispheric communication of sensory information (Ozgur et al., 1977). Similarly, disconnection symptoms were generally absent in 25 patients with partial surgeries, although with a less extensive neuropsychological battery (Shucart and Stein, 1978), and in a study with four children (Winston et al., 1979).

On the other hand, these cases did demonstrate deficits in cross-communication of *tactual* and motor tasks. In the tumor case (Ozgur et al., 1977), the deficit was manifested by reduction in manual dexterity scores on the Purdue Pegboard and a minimal deficit in cross-finger localization. Other cases showed immediate deficits in copying complex drawings such as the Rey-Osterreith figure (Winston et al., 1979). Although not tested, these deficits resemble the bimanual coordination difficulties in the study with the anterior-sectioned epileptics (Preilowsky, 1972). Memory difficulties were also reported. Although these were similar to those reported for the epileptic patients (Zaidel and Sperry, 1974) they were not as severe. Also, the cause of the memory deficits was attributed to damage of the fornix or other structures rather than to the callosum per se.

While it is disconcerting to obtain essentially negative behavioral deficits in patients with extensive surgery, it is heartening that these results are confirmed in a large variety of epileptic and non-epileptic patients. The evidence converges to one conclusion: anterior callosal section does not disrupt transmission of visual stimuli, but may partially affect auditory transmission and probably affects some proprioceptive and motor feedback loops. Other deficits have been described for partial commissurotomies involving the mid-section of the callosum. These are described in the next section.

Circumscribed section of the corpus callosum preserving at least portions of the genu and posterior splenium

Partial resection of the trunk of the corpus callosum is not attempted for alleviation of epileptic seizures. Instead, all patients with such surgery have had tumors, cysts or arteriovenous malformations (AVMs) in the third ventricle, pineal body or other underlying structures. The transcallosal approach to these lesions provides the only cases of surgical disconnection of the body of the callosum. There have undoubtedly been hundreds of these operations performed, many of them fully reported in the last decade because of the compelling results of complete commissurotomies.

The first extensive description of a partial trunk commissurotomy involved the removal of an angioma that lay within the middle third of the corpus callosum (Dimond et al., 1977). In addition to parts of the medial aspect of the left posterior frontal lobe, about 2 – 3 cm of the corpus callosum was sectioned just anterior to the splenium. The patient initially had speech and sensory-motor difficulties but these eventually cleared, suggesting failures of interhemispheric communication. However, all the symptoms cleared after several weeks. These transient disconnection symptoms may well have been due to edema and bruising of the callosal areas surrounding the area of surgery. Once the insult of surgery healed, normal functioning of the otherwise intact callosum prevailed. In effect, the immediate post-surgical course produced symptoms resembling some, but not all, of those reported for complete commissurotomy. Another excellent example of recovery from disconnection symptoms was in a case of splenial incision to remove a pinealoma (Nagafuchi and Suzuki, 1973). The day following removal of the tumor through a 2-cm section in the anterior splenium, the patient developed auditory agnosia for both speech and music. Pure tone audiometry at 7 days postoperatively showed bilateral reduction for all but high frequencies and poor discrimination of monosyllabic words, especially in the left ear. By contrast, melodies could be identified normally in the *left* ear but defectively in the right. The patient had no difficulty with spontaneous speech, reading or writing. Other possible disconnection symptoms were not tested. The ear asymmetry for both words and melodies steadily improved toward normal in retests at 30 and 60 days. The ear asymmetry is what would be expected according to hemispheric specialization (Gordon, 1974b), and the recovery is consistent with post-neurosurgical healing.

Non-surgical cases have also been noted, on occasion, to produce temporary symptoms of complete commissurotomy. In one case of subarachnoid hemorrhage involving areas near the callosum (Wechsler, 1972), there was a left hemialexia and failure to cross-match the visual representation of letters presented tactually. Object naming and stereognosis were intact. In another case, an aneurysm in the anterior callosal area produced an agraphia, partial anomia and apraxia in the left hand similar to that reported with patients with complete commissurotomies (Beukelman et al., 1980). Of course, the most famous tumor case involving the anterior callosum produced the 'full-blown' commissurotomy pathology (Geschwind and Kaplan, 1962). In none of these cases was the splenium obviously involved. In light of the recovery from symptomatology in cases of partial callosotomy, it is reasonable to conclude that diaschises produced the initial behavioral deficit, by acting from a distance.

In addition to the transient deficits, some permanent effects of the partial section of the trunk of the corpus callosum have also been reported (Dimond et al., 1977). For reasons unexplained, the usual right ear dominance found in a dichotic listening task prior to the operation, reversed itself to produce a strong left ear dominance postoperatively in one patient. In a postoperative test with the same patient, geometric shapes separately flashed to the left and right visual fields could not be compared to each other, although they could be matched within one field. It was concluded that some complex visual information is transmitted in the body of the callosum. Finally, it was reported that the patient spontaneously increased use of the previously non-dominant left hand. These data were interpreted to suggest that the callosum provides a means for a functional balance between hemispheric systems – in this case, hand use and audition. When the callosum is intact, it provides a channel through which conflict and confusion are prevented. Sectioning of the callosum temporarily upset this balance until compensatory mechanisms could restore order.

Three patients with partial callosal sections in approximately the same place as that described above were reported in a study of cross-communication of tactile stimuli (Jeeves et al., 1979). Both single and multiple touches on the fingers of one hand could not be demonstrated by the other hand. These findings were corroborated by similar testing in other patients (Geffen et al., 1985). In fact, in the latter study, the amount of deficit for cross-localization following section of the body of the callosum was quantified at 28% reduction from normal.

An attempt to replicate the lack-of-transfer for tactile material failed in six carefully studied adults (Apuzzo et al., 1982). Tests included cross-location, light touches on the fingers, and transfer of learning on a finger maze and form board: no deficits were detected. It was suggested that the small size of the callosal resection (less than 2.5 cm) may have accounted for the discrepancy. In another study, tactile matching could be performed by one patient but not the other (Geffen et al., 1980). However, neither patient demonstrated a reversal of ear dominance (Geffen, 1980; Geffen et al., 1980). In fact, two of the three cases had suppression of the left ear as might be expected from complete commissurotomy. Finally, in a case whose extracallosal damage was due to an AVM fed by left anterior, middle and posterior arteries, none of the tactile tasks of naming, tachistoscopic reading, praxis or dichotic listening could demonstrate the disconnection effects (Sugishita et al., 1980). By contrast, the patient was agraphic for the left hand which was attributed to both extra-callosal damage and the surgical resection in the posterior trunk of the corpus callosum.

One possible explanation for these discrepancies is the differences in surgeries among patients. A systematic study using subtle tactile stimuli was performed on a number of patients who could be grouped according to the locus of the surgery (Bentin et al., 1984). These surgeries produced small sections of the body of the callosum for removal of underlying colloid cysts or tumors. Fine touch was tested by presenting small tactile patterns constructed from arrangements of five stick pins: a pattern felt with one hand had to be retrieved with the same or opposite hand. Patients who had 1.5 – 2.0 cm incisions in the body of the callosum, *posterior* to the foramen of Monro, had significantly more errors of intermanual transfer than patients with similar-sized lesions in other trunk locations. Patients with incisions anterior to the foramen of Monro or in the posterior body-anterior splenium region had no difficulty in intermanual transfer. In a test of finger sequencing in which the patients had to indicate the order in which fingers were touched, the same patients showed deficits of transfer. While these results are partially confirmed in another laboratory (Geffen et al., 1985), they do not explain the lack of transfer deficits in patients with more extensive lesions. There are often patients with all but the splenium divided who have low scores with both hands. It seems possible, therefore, that failure of tactile and visual transfer is due, at least in part, to extracallosal damage. This was precisely the conclusion of a study that followed-up nine patients several months after callosal surgery for tumors (Oepen et al., 1985). The location of the surgery ranged from anterior to posterior callosum. Some patients exhibited 'typical' disconnection effects, but most of these had the most extensive extracallosal damage. Those with the least damage had no failures of transfer or deficits in performance after extensive testing.

The difficulty in drawing conclusions from such few cases, especially with the complication of extracallosal damage, is best seen in two closely related cases of AVMs in the posterior callosum sparing the tip of the splenium (Greenblatt et al., 1980; Levine and Calvanio, 1980). Both AVMs were approached through right parietal craniotomies, and both surgeries resulted in a callosal excision of about 2 – 3 cm in length, starting about 1 cm anterior to the splenial tip. In one case (Levine and Calvanio, 1980), letter identification was significantly better in the right visual field (and presumably left hemisphere) for identifying one letter embedded in a 3-letter trigram flashed at 100 ms. In the other case (Greenblatt et al., 1980) there were virtually no asymmetries of accuracy, although the 'threshold' for 5-letter word identification was 30 ms higher for the left visual field than for the right field (110 vs. 80 ms). Since it is unlikely that threshold differences or speed of presentation explain the difference between the patients of the two studies, the failure of cross-communication in the one patient is more likely explained by extracallosal damage. Extracallosal damage is also the more parsimonious explanation in light of the absence of symptoms for extensive surgical sections for alleviation of epilepsy. The long-term follow-up case discussed above (Goldstein and Joynt, 1969) showed no alexia in the left visual field in spite of section of the entire callosum sparing no more than 1 cm of the splenium.

One final interpretation of these data deserves mention. In a third case of AVM removal in a Japanese patient, by essentially the same surgery in the splenium (sparing the tip), extensive studies were carried out to test the hypothesis that reduced performance in the left visual field is not entirely due to lack of transfer, but rather to a hemifield neglect (Sugishita et al., 1985). This conclusion was reached not only because there was poor reading and comprehension in the left field of both the logographic and phonographic script of written Japanese, but also because there was poor gap perception in the left field for different sizes of Landolt rings. Gap perception is not known to favor either hemifield, and hemiamblyopia was ruled out because gap detection was not dependent on the size of the ring. Thus, the deficit could only be explained on the basis of a left hemi*neglect* of tachistoscopically presented stimuli. This interpretation is consistent with a similar theory in which hemifield attention is directly related to cortical activation (Kinsbourne, 1973). The authors discuss the extreme possibility that *all* observed left visual field deficits, *including* those seen for splenial or complete commissurotomies, are due, all or in part, to left hemineglect.

Section of the posterior callosum including the splenium

The first description of the now well-known interhemispheric disconnection syndrome was presented in a clear report of splenial section for removal of a colloid cyst of the third ventricle in a 37-year-old woman (Trescher and Ford, 1937). After discharge from hospital, family complaints of the patient's disorientation to familiar surroundings prompted re-examination. Her inability to draw or describe her surroundings persisted, although improved over time. Of particular interest was the patient's failure to name or describe wooden letters displayed in her left visual field or placed in her left hand. By contrast, it was said she could recognize objects placed in her left hand, although it was not stated how she was tested. The testing method may be important. A patient with a complete commissurotomy can correctly select an examiner-named object from among other objects out of sight, as well as recognize and correctly manipulate such an object placed in the left hand. The disconnection syndrome is characterized by the failure to *name* objects placed in the left hand. In any case, it was concluded against strong conventional wisdom of the time, that the partial commissurotomy (complete section of the splenium) had caused the left field/left hand alexia as well as the spatial disorientation. Since the surgical approach to the cyst had been transcortical, through the right occipital or right parieto-occipital cortex, extracallosal damage from the surgery may have been a more likely source for the reported spatial dysfunction.

Two more early cases were reported with similar transcortical approaches for removal of third ventricular tumors (Maspes, 1948). With the specific purpose of contrasting the essentially negative findings of disconnection in the presumably complete commissurotomy for epilepsy reported in the Akelaitis series and the left field/hand alexia of the partial commissurotomy (Trescher and Ford, 1937), systematic tachistoscopic studies were carried out. The findings supported the visual alexia of the left field. The discrepancy between these cases and those with the supposedly complete commissurotomy cases (of Akelaitis) was explained on the basis of cerebral reorganization due to early damage in the epileptics.

Transcallosal surgical approaches and more exacting surgical techniques have reduced the number of cases with complete splenial section for extirpation of underlying tumors. Most surgeries now include parts of the body of callosum and only a portion of the splenium sparing the tip. The posterior and posterior-ventral fibers of the splenium are usually intact. However, the six or so cases of complete splenial section that have been reported since the early cases, support the initial reports of left field alexia (Damasio et al., 1980; Gazzaniga and Freedman, 1973; Iwata and

Toyokura, 1985; Sugishita et al., 1978). Details of the interhemispheric disturbances varied from case to case. In one case, digits and letters could be read from the non-dominant visual field while words could not (Damasio et al., 1980). In another, visual cross-matching could be performed while naming objects and reading in the non-dominant visual field could not (Gazzaniga and Freedman, 1973). In most cases, no disturbances from cross-transfer of tactile information were reported.

One case of splenial surgery for a pineal tumor was followed for a number of years (Sugishita et al., 1986; Sugishita and Yoshioka, 1987). Recovery in this case was observed when words could be read aloud or understood (as evidenced by pointing) in the left visual field at a better than chance level. The completeness of the splenial section was confirmed by magnetic resonance imaging (Sugishita et al., 1986). Since it is unlikely that the right hemisphere learned to read aloud, it was concluded that transfer of some of the visual information had become possible through intact portions of the callosum or other commissures (Sugishita and Yoshioka, 1987).

Surgeries involving the posterior callosum for AVMs were reported to have fewer symptoms of disconnection (Iwata and Toyokura, 1985). There are at least two possible explanations. Patients with AVMs often have associated, long-standing seizure disorders and it is not unreasonable that callosal reorganization has occurred in the face of early cortical necrosis. The other possibility is that the splenium of the callosum was not completely severed. The intent of the surgery was never to section the callosum per se but rather to remove the unwanted tissue in, and under, the callosum. In support of this possibility, there is at least one case that has come to autopsy that did not fulfill surgeons' impressions of complete splenial division (Gazzaniga and Freedman, 1973). It should also be noted that disconnection symptoms have been reported, even with part of the splenium intact (Levine and Calvanio, 1980). These studies highlight the difficulty in interpretation of functions of the corpus callosum in the face of associated extracallosal damage from either long-standing or acute lesions.

Although not immune from the criticism of extracallosal damage, patients with intractable epilepsy represent a population whose seizure loci are diffuse and not consistent from patient to patient. As an advantage, the extracallosal damage is more random and diffusely distributed than the damage associated with tumors underlying the callosum. Another advantage is that preoperative neuropsychological testing may occur without the acute effects of callosally associated tumors. In one case of surgical section of only the splenium for alleviation of intractable epilepsy, left visual field, left hand, and left ear performances for verbal material fell to chance level as is typically reported for epileptic patients with complete commissurotomy (Sidtis et al., 1981). However, contrary to the usual commissurotomy response, this patient gave the impression of awareness of objects flashed to the right hemisphere. In fact, with a dialogue of question and answer, the patient could sometimes correctly guess the object. Such was rarely reported for the complete commissurotomy cases. The implication is that, although sensory information had been blocked by the surgery, a sense of awareness was somehow being transferred in the anterior callosum. This awareness was lost in this patient after a second surgery in which the rest of the callosum was sectioned.

A few more cases of staged commissurotomy for intractable epilepsy have been reported (Wilson et al., 1982). The splenium was sectioned first, followed by the rest of the callosum within one to six months. Although the neuropsychological sequelae for most patients have not been described in the literature some 5 years after surgery, the general picture is consistent with the conclusion that the posterior splenium of the corpus callosum is necessary and sufficient to transfer at least visual information from one hemisphere to the other (Volpe et al., 1982).

One report of auditory processing in a splenium-sectioned patient who then had a complete callosotomy seemed puzzling. In dichotic and other auditory tests in which left ear suppression was expected, no suppression was found (Musiek et al., 1981). Possible explanations included cross-integration via the anterior callosum (while it was still intact) which allowed the development of alternate routes or independent hemispheric processing prior to the second surgery. It was also suggested that the anterior commissure, still intact after the complete callosotomy, might have prevented the expected left ear suppression. The notion of cerebral re-organization during the immediate postoperative period and the other speculations await validation, but it should be pointed out that even patients with complete commissurotomies *including* the anterior commissure, can attend to ipsilateral auditory pathways in certain testing situations (Gordon, 1980; Wale and Geffen, 1986).

Even though surgical division of the commissures provides a 'cleaner' lesion than space-occupying lesions or vascular infarct, criticism cannot be avoided that extracallosal damage complicates the interpretation of callosal function. It is true that some damage is localized, such as that from tumors in the third ventricle or pineal body. It is also true that, in patients with epilepsy, the damage is inconsistent from patient to patient and often multifocal, defying localization by behavioral, electrophysiological or imaging techniques. Common symptomatology among all these patients is good support that it can be directly related to the callosal surgery. But one can never be sure which of the symptoms described are enhanced or produced by associated non-callosal neuropathology.

There is, however, one case of partial callosal division in a Japanese subject with *no* known long-standing extracallosal brain damage. The case was an attempted suicide by means of an ice pick self-driven into the brain from 5 mm to the right of the mid-line of the forehead (Abe et al., 1986). The ice-pick severed the genu and inferior splenium of the callosum and extended into the right occipital lobe with possible minimal involvement of the right thalamus. The patient apparently never lost consciousness, slept all night and walked into the hospital the next day. The ice pick was surgically removed without measurable neurological sequelae. In testing with standard tachistoscopic techniques one and two years after the injury, the subject was found to have left hemialexia for Kana (the Japanese phonological script) and, to a lesser extent, for Kanji (the logographic script). The hemifield differences in script recognition reflect the same hemispheric differences reported previously in Japanese aphasics. Most importantly, these data support previous results by demonstrating that section of the inferior splenium of the corpus callosum with little extracallosal damage blocks interhemispheric transfer of visual stimuli. This case is the behavioral 'mirror image' of the epileptic patient in whom the entire corpus callosum was sectioned except for a fragment of the inferior splenium but who showed complete transfer of visual information (Goldstein and Joynt, 1969).

Callosal disconnection with non-surgical lesions involving the splenium

The interhemispheric disconnection discussed so far has resulted from partial surgical division of the corpus callosum. Disconnection of this sort has also been observed following infarcts, tumors, and aneurysms which have not involved callosal surgery. Because of the expanse of the extra callosal involvement, a full review of functional loss from callosal pathology would detract from the picture constructed after 'cleaner' callosal surgeries. Nevertheless, some cases offer enlightenment.

Patients who present with alexia without agraphia are especially interesting. These patients commonly have damage to the left occipital lobe and to the splenium of the corpus callosum, both of which are supplied by the posterior cerebral artery. Usually, there is a right homonymous hemianopia, although theoretically this is not a necessary condition for the alexia since the theory of disconnection requires only that the visual centers be cut off from the angular gyrus and other areas involved with language interpretation.

One 64-year-old male patient who had a severe infarction, affecting both the left occipital lobe and splenium, demonstrated no reading of words or naming of letters (Cumming et al., 1970). He could name objects and colors with no difficulty, and he could read numbers. Most notably, he could write to dictation or copy text (in block letters) but could not read what he had written. He did not have the difficulties in interhemispheric transfer of visual or tactual information that would be expected if he had had a complete surgical division of the splenium. It can be concluded from this case that visual information arriving at his intact right occipital lobe could not make its way across the callosum for language interpretation (i.e., reading). At the same time, there was sufficient transfer to visual recognition areas in both sides such that he could name objects and colors, and copy text (albeit without understanding).

In support of these observations, a 59-year-old male with cerebral infarcts presented with the same behavioral symptoms (Ajax et al., 1977). Speech and language were intact, as were object and color naming. His main difficulty was reading words. He wrote adequately to dictation, but could not copy. As reported for the previous case, the cerebral infarct invaded both the left occipital lobe and splenium of the callosum. Another patient, again with essentially the same behavioral presentation of alexia without agraphia, was a 50-year-old woman who did not have a cerebral infarct. Rather, her deficits seemed to be due to a left occipital glioblastoma that had also involved the splenium (Greenblatt, 1973). This case demonstrates that it is the disconnection that is crucial by whatever neuropathology. Whereas functions of the corpus callosum would be difficult to derive from these patients, the associated behavioral deficits give functional dimension to conclusions from the surgical cases.

Conclusion

It has taken 50 years to confirm that we have not learned anything new about the neurological sequelae of partial section of the corpus callosum. Complete division of the splenium including the tip is necessary and sufficient for preventing the transmission of visual information from one hemisphere to the other. Blockage of tactile information may require additional section of fibers just anterior to the splenium. However, if the slightest bit, a centimeter or so, of the posterior-most portion of the splenium is spared, disconnection symptoms are minimal or absent. As more of the splenium is preserved, disconnection symptoms are even more subtle. These symptoms have been described in a number of studies outlined in this chapter. But we cannot help being impressed with the paucity of consistently reported symptoms following surgical division of the anterior two-thirds of the corpus callosum – especially in light of the striking disconnection after surgical division of the posterior third. This is good news for patients who require an anterior callosotomy, but frustrating for students of neuropsychology who would expect dramatic changes after such a radical destruction of 200 million axons. Since anterior commissurotomy is a reasonable treatment for non-localizable, bilateral pathology causing atonic and other debilitating and intractable seizure patterns, the opportunity to learn functional significance of the anterior callosum remains a viable challenge for neuropsychology.

Acknowledgements

I deeply appreciate the career-long counsel of Joseph E. Bogen, M.D. whose work in this area has been a continued inspiration. I am grateful to Richard M. Dasheiff, Director, University of Pittsburgh Epilepsy Center and Robert J. Joynt, Dean, Rochester School of Medicine for advice and encouragement in preparation of this chapter.

References

Abe T, Nakamura H, Sugishita M, Kato Y, Iwata M: Partial disconnection syndrome following penetrating stab wound of the brain. *Eur. Neurol.: 25,* 233 – 239, 1986.

Ajax ET, Schenkenberg T, Kosteljanetz M: Alexia without agraphia and the inferior splenium. *Neurology: 27:* 685 – 688, 1977.

Akelaitis AJ: Studies on the corpus callosum. VII. Study of language function (tactile and visual lexia and graphia) unilaterally following action of the corpus callosum. *J. Neuropathol. Exp. Neurol.: 2,* 226 – 262, 1943.

Apuzzo MJ, Chikovani OK, Gott PS, Teng EL, Zee CS, Giannotta SL, Weiss MH: Transcallosal, interformical approaches for lesions affecting the third ventricle: surgical consideration and consequences. *Neurosurgery: 10*(5), 547 – 554, 1982.

Benes V: Sequelae of transcallosal surgery. *Child's Brain: 9,* 69 – 72, 1982.

Bentin S, Sahar A, Moscovitch M: Intermanual information transfer in patients with lesions in the trunk of the corpus callosum. *Neuropsychologia: 22*(5), 601 – 611, 1984.

Beuckelman DR, Flowers CR, Swanson PD: Cerebral disconnection associated with anterior communicating artery aneurysm: implications for evaluation of symptoms. *Arch. Phys. Med. Rehab.: 61,* 18 – 23, 1980.

Bogen JE: Split-brain syndromes. In Vinken PJ, Bruyn GW, Klawins HL (Editors) *Handbook of Clinical Neurology:* 1 (Revised Series), Amsterdam: Elsevier, pp. 99 – 106, 1985.

Bogen JE: Physiologic consequences of complete or partial commissural section. In: Apuzzo, M.L.J. (Editor) *Surgery of the third ventricle,* Baltimore: Williams & Wilkins, 1987.

Cuming WJA, Hurwitz LJ, Perl NT: A study of a patient who had alexia without agraphia. *J. Neurol. Neurosurg. Psychiatry: 33,* 34 – 39, 1970.

Damasio AR, Chui HC, Corbett J, Kassel N: Posterior callosal section in a non-epileptic patient. *J. Neurol. Neurosurg. Psychiatry: 43,* 351 – 356, 1980.

Dimond SJ, Scammell RE, Brouwers EYM, Weeks R: Functions of the centre section (trunk) of the corpus callosum in man. *Brain: 100,* 543 – 562, 1977.

Gazzaniga MS, Freedman H: Observations on visual processes after posterior callosal section. *Neurology: 23,* 1126 – 1130, 1973.

Gazzaniga MS, Risse GL, Springer SP, Clark AB, Wilson DH: Psychologic and neurologic consequences of partial and complete cerebral commissurotomy. *Neurology: 25,* 10 – 15, 1975.

Geffen G: Phenological fusion after partial section of the corpus callosum. *Neuropsychologia: 18,* 613 – 620, 1980.

Geffen G, Nilsson J, Quinn K, Teng EL: The effect of lesions of the corpus callosum on finger localization. *Neuropsychologia: 23*(4), 497 – 514, 1985.

Geffen G, Walsh A, Simpson D, Jeeves MA: Comparison of the effects of transcallosal and transcortical removal of intraventricular tumours. *Brain: 103,* 773 – 788, 1980.

Geschwind N: Disconnexion syndrome in animals and man, Part 1. *Brain: 88,* 237 – 294, 1965.

Geschwind H, Kaplan E: Human cerebral deconnection syndrome. *Neurology: 12,* 675 – 685, 1962.

Goldstein MN, Joynt RJ: Long-term follow-up of a callosal-sectional patient. *Arch. Neurol.: 20,* 96 – 102, 1969.

Gordon HW: *Functional deficits following partial surgical section of the forebrain commissures in man as determined by an auditory test.* Presented at the 79th Annual Convention of the American Psychological Association, Washington, D.C., 1971.

Gordon HW: Olfaction and cerebral separation. In Kinsbourne M, Smith, WL (Editors) *Hemispheric disconnection and cerebral function.* Springfield, IL: CC Thomas, pp. 137 – 154, 1974a.

Gordon HW: Auditory specialization of the right and left hemispheres. In Kinsbourne M, Smith WL (Editors) *Hemispheric disconnection and cerebral function.* Springfield, IL: CC Thomas, pp. 126 – 136, 1974b.

Gordon HW: Right hemisphere comprehension of verbs in patients with complete forebrain commissurotomy: use of the dichotic method and manual performance. *Brain Language: 11,* 76 – 86, 1980.

Gordon HW, Bogen JE, Sperry RW: Absence of deconnexion syndrome in two patients with partial sections of the neocommissures. *Brain: 94*(II), 327 – 336, 1971.

Greenblatt SH: Alexia without agraphia or hemianopia. *Brain: 96,* 307 – 316, 1973.

Greenblatt SH, Saunders RL, Culver CM, Bogdanowicz W: Normal interhemispheric transfer with incomplete section of the splenium. *Arch. Neurol.: 37,* 567 – 573, 1980.

Iwata M, Toyokura Y: Neuropsychological studies on partial split-brain patients in Japan. In Reeves AG (Editors) *Epilepsy and the corpus callosum.* New York: Plenum Press, pp. 401 – 415, 1985.

Jeeves MA, Simpson DA, Geffen G: *J. Neurol. Neurosurg. Psychiatry: 42,* 134 – 142, 1979.

Kinsbourne M: The control of attention by interaction between the cerebral hemispheres. In Kornblum S (Editor), *Attention and Performance, Vol. 4.* London: Academic Press, pp. 239 – 256, 1973.

Lacoste-Utamsing C de, Holloway RL: Sexual demorphism in the human corpus callosum. *Science: 216,* 1431 – 1432, 1982.

Lassande M: In Leporé F, Ptito M, Jasper HH (Editors) *Two Hemispheres – One Brain: Functions of the Corpus Callosum.* New York: Alan R Liss, pp. 385 – 401, 1986.

Maspes PE: Le syndrome expérimental chez l'homme de la section du splénium du corps calleux alexie visualle pure hémianopsique. *Rev. Neurol.: 80*(2), 100 – 113, 1948.

Milner B, Taylor L, Sperry RW: Lateralized suppression of dichotically presented digits after commissural section in man. *Science: 161,* 184 – 186, 1968.

Milner B, Kolb B: Performance of complex arm movements and facial-movement sequences after cerebral commissurotomy. *Neuropsychologia: 23*(6), 791 – 799, 1985.

Musiek FE, Wilson DH, Reeves AG: Staged commissurotomy and central auditory function. *Arch. Otolaryngol.: 107,* 233 – 236, 1981.

Nagafuchi M, Suzucki J: Auditory agnosia due to incision of splenium corporis callosi. *Acta Otolaryngol.: 76,* 109 – 113, 1973.

Oepen G, Schulz-Weiling R, Zimmermann P, Birg W, Straesser S, Gilsbach J: Long-term effects of partial callosal lesions. Preliminary report. *Acta Neurochirurg.: 77,* 22 – 28, 1985.

Ozgur MH, Johnson T, Smith A, Bogen JE: Transcallosal approach to third ventricle tumor: case report. *Bull. LA Neurol. Soc.: 42*(2), 57 – 62, 1977.

Preilowsky BFB: Possible contribution of the anterior forebrain commissures to bilateral motor coordination. *Neuropsychologia: 10,* 267 – 277, 1972.

Scarff TB: Life with a split brain. *Lancet: ii,* 828, 1979.

Shucart WA, Stein BM: Transcallosal approach to the anterior ventricular system. *Neurosurgery: 3*(3), 339 – 343, 1978.

Sidtis JJ, Volpe BT, Holtzman JD, Wilson DH, Gazzaniga MS: Cognitive interaction after staged callosal section: evidence for transfer of semantic activation. *Science: 212,* 344 – 346, 1981.

Sparks R, Geschwind N: Dichotic listening in man after section of neocortical commissures. *Cortex: 4,* 3 – 16, 1968.

Sperry RW, Gazzaniga MS, Bogen JE: Interhemispheric relationships: the neocortical commissures, syndromes of hemispheric disconnection. In Vinken PJ, Bruyn GW (Editors) *Handbook of Clinical Neurology. IV.* Amsterdam: North-Holland Publishing Co., pp. 272 – 290, 1969.

Springer SP, Gazzaniga MS: Dichotic testing of partial and complete split brain subjects. *Neuropsychologia: 13,* 341 – 346, 1975.

Sugishita M, Iwata M, Toyokura Y, Yoshioka M, Yamada R: Reading of ideograms and phonograms in Japanese patients after partial commissurotomy. *Neuropsychologia: 16,* 417 – 426, 1978.

Sugishita M, Shinohara A, Shimaji T, Ogawa T: In Reeves, AG (Editor) *Epilepsy and the Corpus Callosum.* New York: Plenum Press, pp. 417 – 434, 1985.

Sugishita M, Yoshioka M, Kamamura M: Recovery from hemialexia. *Brain Language: 29*(1), 106 – 118, 1986.

Sugishita M, Yoshioka M: Visual processes in a hemialexia patient with posterior callosal section. *Neuropsychologia: 25*(2), 317 – 460, 1987.

Sugishita M, Toyokura Y, Yoshioka M, Yamada R: Unilateral agraphia after section of the posterior half of the truncus of the corpus callosum. *Brain Language: 9,* 215 – 225, 1980.

Trescher JH, Ford FR: Colloid cyst of the third ventricle. Report of a case; operative removal with section of posterior half of corpus callosum. *Arch. Neurol. Psychiatry: 37,* 959 – 973, 1937.

Van Wagenen WP, Herren RY: Surgical division of commissural pathways in the corpus callosum. *Arch. Neurol. Psychiatry: 44,* 740 – 759, 1940.

Volpe BT, Sidtis JJ, Holtzman JD, Wilson DH, Gazzaniga MS: Cortical mechanisms involved in praxis: observations following partial and complete section of the corpus callosum in man. *Neurology: 32,* 645 – 650, 1982.

Wale J, Geffen G: Hemispheric specialization and attention: effects of complete and partial section and hemispherectomy on dichotic monitoring. *Neuropsychologia: 24*(4), 483 – 496, 1986.

Wechsler AF: Transient left hemislexia. *Neurology: 22,* 628 – 633, 1972.

Wilson DH, Reeves AG, Gazzaniga MS: 'Central' commissurotomy for intractable generalized epilepsy: Series two. *Neurology: 32,* 687 – 697, 1982.

Winston KR, Cavazzuti V, Arkins T: Absence of neurological and behavioral abnormalities after anterior transcallosal operation for third ventricular lesions. *Neurosurgery: 4*(5), 386 – 393, 1979.

Witelson SF: The brain connection: The corpus callosum is larger in left-handers. *Science: 229,* 665 – 668, 1985.

Zaidel D, Sperry RW: Memory impairment after commissurotomy in man. *Brain: 97*(II), 263 – 272, 1974.

© 1990 Elsevier Science Publishers B.V. (Biomedical Division)
Handbook of Neuropsychology, Vol. 4
F. Boller and J. Grafman (Eds)

CHAPTER 5

Agenesis of the corpus callosum

Malcolm A. Jeeves

Medical Research Council Cognitive Neuroscience Research Group, University of St Andrews, St Andrews, Fife, Scotland KY16 9JU

Introduction

As neuroencephalography was succeeded as a diagnostic technique first by computerized axial tomography and then by nuclear magnetic resonance (NMR), so more and more cases of agenesis of the corpus callosum have come to the notice of neurologists and neuropsychologists. This has resulted in an increase in detailed neuropsychological studies of these patients. Apart from their intrinsic interest as 'experiments of nature', these patients were, initially, of interest because of the apparent absence of the dramatic split-brain deficits exhibited in the classical studies of Sperry and his colleagues in the early 1960s. More recently, it has been recognized that they also afford a special opportunity to further our understanding of neural plasticity and to test some of the current theories of the role of the neocortical commissures both in normal development and at maturity.

Incidence and aetiology

Views about the aetiology of callosal agenesis are diverse. Familial incidence or chromosome anomalies are seen as indicating genetic determination (Warkany et al., 1966). The Aicardi syndrome (Aicardi et al. 1965) and reports by Andermann et al. (Andermann et al., 1972; Labrisseau et al., 1984; Menkes et al., 1964) indicate that dominant, recessive and sex-linked recessive inheritance must all be considered in cases of callosal agenesis. However, in most instances, agenesis would appear to carry no recurrence risk for sibs and is thus presumed to be due to environmental factors, non-dominant factors and/or polygenes.

Estimates of occurrence vary widely, from one case in 19 000 based on post-mortem records (Grogono, 1968) to 2% of mentally retarded patients presenting for neurological investigation. The latter groups included instances of the Aicardi and Andermann Syndromes (Aicardi et al., 1965; Andermann et al., 1972, 1975). There is no agreement about the relative incidence of total versus partial callosal agenesis (Lemire et al., 1975; Slager et al., 1957).

Associated brain abnormalities

The corpus callosum, like the anterior and hippocampal commissures, originates from the midline of the rostral end of the neural tube adjacent to the area of closure of the anterior neuropore. The commissure bearing fibres connecting the two halves of the brain thus arises from the lamina terminalis. One part of the lamina terminalis, the lamina reuniens, develops into the commissural plate which functions as a conducting system for the crossing of commissural axons from one hemisphere to the other. The first crossing is of the fibres that will form the anterior commissure at about the fiftieth day. This is in the lower part of the commissural plate. The second crossing, the hippocampal commissure, appears soon thereafter at the end of the second gestational month. Finally the corpus callosum begins its development at about the twelfth gestational week. There seems to be general agreement that the corpus callosum is formed in all its parts at 18 to 20 weeks after gestation. Callosal defects can thus vary in degree depending upon the time after conception that the presumed causative insult occurs (for a review see Warkany, J., 1981).

Most writers agree that the major features of the acallosal brain are (1) Probst's bundle (2) enlarged occipital and temporal horns and (3) radial patterning of the sulci on the medial surface of the brain. Probst's bundle is made up of uncrossed fibres which fail to reach the contralateral hemisphere and run within a hemisphere in a rostro-caudal direction. Terminating ipsilaterally these band-like formations of white matter are situated in the median walls of the hemispheres at the level of the callosum. Although Probst's bundle is almost always present it need not necessarily be so. As Loeser and Alvord (1968) note, the anterior commissure is usually present even though the corpus callosum is absent, but on occasion this may not be so. This becomes an important consideration when discussing the compensatory mechanisms at work in callosal agenesis. It is believed that where the anterior commissure as well as the corpus callosum is absent, this is an indication of severe cerebral damage with the involvement of the commissural plate (Loeser and Alvord, 1968). Some (e.g., Geschwind, 1974) but not all (e.g., Loeser and Alvord, 1968) report that when the anterior commissure is present it is hypertrophied due to the enclosure of heterotopic callosal fibres. The massa intermedia may be absent or stretched and thinned out as the third ventricle is enlarged.

Agenesis of the corpus callosum is not always total. Where it is partial, the splenium or rostrum may be absent. Whilst it is usually the posterior portion, the splenium, which is undeveloped, there are instances where anterior defects have been reported. More of these are coming to light with the use of NMR imaging techniques. The pathogenesis of partial agenesis has at times been attributed to vascular agenesis, to localized inflammation or to a dilated diencephalic pouch. Some cases of partial agenesis may, however, as noted above, also be due to genetic factors.

Whilst there are frequently associated cerebral malformations (Parrish et al., 1979), attempts to group them into systematic clusters have not been successful. It is, however, important to remember, as emphasised by Bossy (1970), that there exist asymptomatic cases of callosal agenesis. The general picture emerging from reviews of callosal agenesis is that someting like 10% of the cases which have been reported are asymptomatic during life, and the callosal agenesis has only come to light at routine necropsy. In one study, six of the 47 cases reported had associated pyramidal tract changes which, however, were not associated with obvious motor difficulties. This observation may be important in understanding some aspects of impaired perceptual – motor performance in acallosals. It has been suggested that where mental retardation occurs, it is due not to the absence of the corpus callosum per se but more likely to associated central nervous system anomalies. Certainly, where a diagnosis of callosal absence is made in adult life, reviews have shown that the patient's intelligence was almost always normal. Moreover, asymptomatic patients with agenesis found incidentally at autopsy were never reported to be retarded.

The presence of Probst's bundle noted above, together with the frequent hypertrophy of the anterior commissure, could be interpreted as indicating that callosal agenesis is not necessarily associated with absence of cortical neurones. The cells of origin of commissural fibres are present but the fibres fail to cross the midline and instead result in the Probst bundle. To settle this issue, detailed cytoarchitectural studies would be required. A small number have been reported. Bossy (1970) reported that microscopic study of the cortex of an acallosal asymptomatic during life did not show any marked differences from normal. Others (Akert et al., 1954; Shoumara et al., 1975) reported a reduction in cells in some cortical layers.

The neuropsychological profile

The frequent association of callosal agenesis with other brain anomalies dissuaded many investigators from undertaking detailed neuropsychological analyses of such cases. The problems of interpretation of test results seemed daunting. Reviewing the literature in 1980, Chiarello set three criteria for a study to be included in her survey: patients had to have an overall IQ of 70 or above; there could be no evidence of lipoma of the corpus callosum; behavioural tests had to be reported. Chiarello found that only 29 of 100 published cases met her criteria. Since Chiarello's review there has been a steady increase in the detailed case reports of acallosals. A good proportion of these reports originate from Lassonde and her co-workers investigating a large number of acallosal patients coming to notice in Quebec.

Most acallosals present initially for non-routine neurological tests because of signs suggestive of brain dysfunction. Some, however, appear purely by chance, for example, the asymptomatic patient reported by Bruyer et al. in 1985. More recently a surprisingly large number of children with identifiable callosal pathology have come to light in studies of children reported as having learning difficulties or behaviour disturbances. Amongst the cases reported in the past, the most commonly presenting cause is associated epilepsy.

Of the 29 cases reviewed by Chiarello, the average overall IQ was 89 (verbal IQ, 89, and performance IQ of 89). This apparent equality of mean verbal and performance IQs conceals the fact that there were actually very few patients whose verbal and performance IQs were approximately equal. The majority had high performance and low verbal IQs or vice versa. Whether the distribution of VIQ/PIQ discrepancies deviates from normal remains for the moment open to question and further investigation. That some have high IQs is without doubt. For example, Dennis (1976) reported a study of a 21-year-old female acallosal with IQ 110 (verbal 96, performance 119) and we have recently seen several children with IQs of 110 to 120.

Main lines of neuropsychological assessment

Strongly influenced by the now classical work on split-brain patients, the testing of acallosals has tended to focus round two issues concerned with that early work. First, can these patients integrate information presented separately to the two cerebral hemispheres through tactile, visual, motor and olfactory modalities? Second, does the learning of form boards and finger mazes transfer between the hemispheres. In addition there have been investigations which have studied cerebral lateralization in acallosals. These latter arose partly out of early speculation (Sperry, 1968) that functions which normally are lateralized may be bilaterally represented in acallosal brains as a means of compensating for the absence of the callosum. They were also aimed at investigating whether one of the functions of the neocortical commissures was to ensure that when one cerebral hemisphere was developing a specialized role it would, through the callosum, inhibit the development of the same specialization in the other hemisphere (e.g., Moscovitch, 1977). Assessments have been attempted of language lateralization in acallosals and most recently, of lateralization of motor control and visuospatial functions. The following section of this chapter summarizes the main features of the picture which has emerged from investigations carried out to address the issues listed above.

Integration: studies of inter- and intra-hemispheric performance

Tactile performance

The simplest procedure for testing interhemispheric transfer of tactile information requires the subject to sit with the backs of his hands resting on a table in front of him. The experimenter lightly touches the tip of a finger on one hand and the subject indicates which finger was touched either on the same hand or on the other hand by bringing together the thumb and the finger that was touched. Having ascertained that the subject can do this with his hands in view, the same procedure is followed either with the subject blindfolded or with his hands placed under a screen. This procedure has now been widely used. Numerous reports show that although some acallosals can occasionally perform at 100% accuracy, the majority perform below 100% both under the ipsilateral (uncrossed) condition and the contralateral (crossed) condition. Matched controls normally perform at 100% under both conditions. That this skill develops with age has been demonstrated by Quinn and Geffen (1986). They showed that the development appears to run parallel with the supposed myelination of the neocortical commissures. They have pointed out that because of the ceiling effect of 100% accuracy, the task needs to be made more difficult. They have done this by touching a sequence of fingers on one hand and requiring the subject to touch the same sequence on the other hand. This, however, changes the task considerably. Now it is no longer simply one of tactile localization but also involves a considerable spatial and sequential component. We have found this modified technique useful in testing acallosals if they initially perform at the 100% level ipsilaterally and contralaterally when only one finger is touched. It becomes evident that their performance now falls away from that of controls.

Nilsson (1983) concluded that the development of tactile transmission in acallosals paralleled normal development but that performance throughout was less efficient. She demonstrated that even by age 28 an acallosal given the more demanding task of transferring a 3-finger sequence showed below normal performance. Dennis (1976) has raised the question of whether the deficit in interhemispheric performance is due to lack of transfer of information or whether it is because the mapping of topography on the first hand is defective as compared with normals. She believes it is. She points out that topographic information arriving through the ipsilateral pathways is known to be less precisely represented than similar information arriving through crossed pathways. Recently Lassonde (1987) examined the intramanual and intermanual localization of touch and found that even when the *accuracy* of acallosals matches that of controls, the *speed* of their performance is significantly below that of the normals. Lassonde interprets this as evidence that whatever the alternative pathway being used, it is less efficient than the pathway employed in normal intact individuals.

Tactile cross-matching of cut-out letters, digits or small common objects is handled perfectly well by acallosals. They are normally also able to name objects and letters placed in the left hand as well as those placed in the right hand, a result which contrasts with the outcome when similar testing is done on split brain patients. Lassonde (1987) using a task requiring the intermanual matching of objects and shapes has shown that, as the complexity of the tactile patterns to be matched increases, the accuracy level may drop only slightly but the response latency will increase significantly with acallosals, again indicating that whatever alternative pathway is used it is less efficient than the normal. It thus seems clear that as regards tactile transfer, acallosals are able to perform successfully on these tasks, but that they do so with reduced efficiency. This reduced efficiency shows either in terms of longer latency even where the performance is accurate or, as the complexity of the tactile transfer increases, as both decreased accuracy and increased latency.

Visual

If one measures the time taken to press a key when a point source of light appears briefly in the left or right visual hemifield, one may confirm Poffenberger's (1912) observation that the uncrossed reaction time, e.g., when the right hand (RH) responds to a light in the right visual half-field (RVF), is systematically shorter than the crossed reaction time. Poffenberger estimated this to be of the order of 3 ms. The reason given for this is that, in the uncrossed condition, stimulus arrival and response initiation are confined to the same hemisphere. Jeeves (1969) applied this method to measure the interhemispheric transmission time (ITT) of acallosals and to compare them with normals. He replicated Poffenberger's findings with normals, reporting an ITT of 2 – 3 ms. By contrast, the acallosals gave lengthened ITTs sometimes in excess of 20 ms. That such lengthened crossed reaction times in acallosals are mediated by visually coded relay neurones has been supported by a study by Milner (1982) in which the ITT was found to vary as an inverse function of the intensity of the lateralized visual stimulus. Similar intensity effects are not found in normal subjects (Milner and Lines, 1982). It is generally believed (Berlucchi, 1978; Rizzolatti, 1979) that the ITT in normals measures a nonsensory callosal transmission. A recent report applying the same technique to the California commissurotomized patients has shown even longer ITTs than those reported in acallosals; for one patient the ITT was 28.8 ms and for the other 50.4 ms (Sergent and Myers, 1985). Since in the commissurotomized patients the effect was not influenced by stimulus intensity variations, it would appear that the route used by the acallosals was not available to the split brain subjects. The likelihood is (see below under Compensatory Mechanisms) that in the acallosals the anterior commissure is responsible for mediating the lengthened ITTs. Support for this comes from studies with monkeys (Hamilton and Vermeire, 1986).

When midline stereopsis has been studied using techniques similar to those employed reported by Mitchell and Blakemore (1970) on split brain patients, results have been varied. Some studies seem to show a deficit in midline stereopsis (Mackay, unpublished MA project report). However, more rigorous testing failed to replicate these early findings. Lassonde (1986) did find evidence for a depth perception deficit in acallosals. She gave acallosals the task of judging the distance between pairs of familiar objects which differed only in colour. Acallosals found greater difficulty in saying which object was nearer when the two objects were in different visual fields than when they were both within the same visual field. However, when compared with matched controls the acallosals also showed deficits in making correct judgements even when both objects were within one visual field and hence no interhemispheric communication was called for. Lassonde (1986) suggested that the corpus callosum in addition to integrating across the midline also exerts a facilitatory influence on the binocular cells receiving their monocular input from both retinae through the thalamocortical pathway. For our present purposes, however, the important point is that this is another report of difficulties in stereopsis. The other evidence that there may be difficulties in integrating over the vertical meridian comes from studies of acallosals presented with chimaeric faces. Jeeves (1979) reports that on first presentation the acallosals are unaware that they are observing chimaeric pictures and after the experimental session hotly deny that such was the case. During the experimental session they point with confidence to the face represented by one half of the chimaeric picture. However, there was no consistent trend, as in the case of the Californian split brain patients, to point to the picture of the person whose half face was on the left side of the chimaera and to name the person whose half face was on the right side.

As regards the integration of information from the two visual fields an earlier report of Ettlinger et al. (1972) has since been confirmed by others. They found that the visual matching of colour and form was performed by acallosals with little or no difficulty. Lassonde (1987) applied similar techniques in a study involving six acallosals. Her subjects were required to make same – different judgements of pairs of stimuli either of different colours or of different shapes. The stimuli were presented for 150 ms either both within the left visual field, both within the right visual field or one in each visual field (interhemispheric condition). In addition to reporting the percentage correct of same – different judgements she also reported the mean reaction times. She found that the acallosals, whilst making more errors than controls, nevertheless performed at a very high level of accuracy of 94%. The acallosals, however, responded slower than matched controls, both in the intra- and interhemispheric conditions, but to a greater extent in the interhemispheric condition.

She suggests that the anterior commissure is present and compensates for the absent callosum, but is less efficient than the splenium of the callosum and hence the slower speeds. Again we shall discuss this when considering compensatory mechanisms below. The recent reports by Johnson (1984) and by Sergent (1986) investigating the possible involvement of subcortical mechanisms in coordinating hemispheric activity in commissurotomized patients must alert us to the possibility that similar mechanisms may be at work in visual integration in acallosals. Certainly Johnson's report supports the view that brain stem interconnections may allow some commissurotomized patients to integrate bilateral visual stimuli and to make accurate same – different judgements. This points to subcortical mechanisms as candidates for compensatory integration.

There are conflicting reports about the ability of acallosals to integrate visual spatial information, by which we mean transmitting information from one hemisphere to the other about the location of a visual stimulus in space. Martin (1985) tested an acallosal patient who, whilst able to identify words, shapes and letters in either visual half field, was very poor at verbally reporting the spatial location of stimuli in his right visual half field, despite good performance on the left. Jeeves and Milner (1987) have attempted a replication of this, with a study of two acallosals. They could find no deficit in the right visual field in either patient. They did, however, confirm that the right visual field was superior to the left visual field for letter identification in these acallosals. There was thus no evidence of a qualitative limitation on interhemispheric integration of perceptual information in the acallosal patients studied.

Motor integration

Early observations (Jeeves, 1964, 1965) that acallosals experience problems in performing tasks which require bimanual coordination under a speed stress have since been confirmed by numerous workers (Dennis, 1976; Lassonde, 1986). Longitudinal studies (Jeeves, 1979) show that patients who showed such difficulties early in life, around the age of six, still experienced them 15 to 20 years later. That they are not related to factors such as general retardation or a low IQ was shown recently in a study of an acallosal boy of above average intelligence who nevertheless experienced marked difficulties in bimanual coordination (Jeeves et al., 1988). It has been observed by workers whose primary interest is in the study of skilled action that the organization of such skilled action is dependent upon the continuous use of feed-forward as well as feedback information about component movements. The problems experienced by acallosals may be due to one or both of two factors. First, the motor information may not be adequately distributed between the hemispheres due to the absence of the corpus callosum. Second, fine motor output may be compromised because of competition between contralateral and ipsilateral control systems. Those who have argued for an inhibitory function of the callosum at maturity see part of this as the suppression of ipsilateral, sensory and motor processes to prevent them competing with contralateral inputs and outputs. The importance of the first factor was strongly reinforced by Preilowski's (1972) studies of partial and total commissurotomy patients. Preilowski's task was, in effect, a sophisticated pantograph. Two handles controlled the movement of a pen. One handle produced vertical movement, the other horizontal movement. Thus if the handles were rotated at equal speeds a line was drawn at 45°. Patients were required to draw lines which stayed within parallel pairs of lines drawn on a vertical display. Even after extended practice patients in whom the anterior part of the callosum was sectioned were unable to achieve the speed or accuracy of matched controls. Preilowski attributed this to the lack of constant updating of activity between the hemispheres which normally occurs through the corpus callosum. In addition, he believed that feed-forward mechanisms postulated to be operating in the execution of fast, highly skilled bimanual activity could not operate effectively in such patients since these are presumed to occur by interhemispheric interaction through the corpus callosum (von Holst, Mittelstaedt, 1950; Teuber 1964). Studies using Preilowski's task have now been carried out with acallosals (Jeeves, 1986; Jeeves et al., 1988) and they report similar findings to those of Preilowski. The findings with acallosals support Preilowski's suggestion that motor fibres probably in the rostral part of the body of the corpus callosum are normally critical for integration of motor activity and that their absence cannot be compensated for.

As regards the second factor which we may call the disinhibition hypothesis, it receives support from a recent study of reaching and grasping behaviour in acallosals (Jeeves and Silver, 1988a). A 22-year-old acallosal woman was required to reach out and grasp objects seen for 150 ms to the left or right of a midline fixation point. Analysis of videofilms showed that control subjects displayed the typical opening and closing of the hand as described by Jeannerod (1986a, b). The acallosal, however, did not show normal prehension movements but, rather, the hand maintained an open, gaping configuration of the fingers and thumb until actual contact was made with the object. Measures of the rate of opening and closing of the hand in cm/s indicated that the acallosal was outside the range of the controls and differed significantly from their mean. This finding is consistent with the view that, whereas normally the callosum allows inhibition of the ipsilateral pathways so that they do not compete with the crossed pathways (Dennis, 1976), in acallosals this inhibition is absent. Competition ensues between crossed and uncrossed outputs and the uncrossed output, being uninhibited, maintains control of the arm movement to the detriment of the crossed output which normally acts to ensure the grasping movement of the fingers.

Olfactory

The few studies that have reported olfactory behaviour in acallosals have required the patient to name familiar odours such as peppermint or tobacco. No difficulty in naming stimuli presented to either nostril or in correctly cross-matching stimuli presented to both nostrils has been found. Anatomical considerations point to the anterior commissure as the interhemispheric pathway involved and one therefore tentatively concludes that it so happens that the acallosals so far tested have all possessed an anterior commissure. Once again NMR information should clarify this picture.

Transfer of learning

The deficits in performance on some tactile tasks when there is an appreciable spatial component involved makes the interpretation of performances on spatio-motor learning tasks ambiguous. Formboard learning has shown deficits in intermanual transfer in acallosals (Jeeves, 1965; Russell and Reitan, 1955; Solursh et al., 1965) but such deficits may be due to faulty spatial coding or imprecise motor control. Transfer of stylus maze training was impaired in the acallosals studied by Lehman and Lampe (1970) and Jeeves (1979) but was intact in another acallosal studied by Reynolds and Jeeves (1977).

Language in acallosals

Dennis (1981) presented data suggesting that the corpus callosum may be critical for the normal development of certain specific functions within the language domain. Her study of a 27-year-old right-handed female of average intelligence showed that the patient 'is impaired in syntactic comprehension, pragmatic use and understanding and metalinguistic knowledge, despite good capacity for phonological and lexical semantic processing.' Clearly the patient performed poorly in some of the language tests administered but whether the language deficits are 'highly specific' remains an open question. Whilst Dennis focussed on the syntactic and pragmatic impairment there is also evidence of phonological and semantic difficulties. The question remains of whether all acallosals show language deficits and if they do how are they to be explained. Jeeves and Temple (1987) studied two further acallosals, a 20-year-old man and a 22-

year-old woman, both of whom are right-handed, using a subset of the tests used by Dennis. The woman showed all the deficits exhibited by Dennis's patient with the exception that passive-negative sentences were correctly processed. However, she showed additional impairments, performing poorly on word retrieval from semantic cues, on constructing sentences and on comprehending active-affirmative sentences. The man performed well on almost all the language tests used, thus calling into question the generality of Dennis's findings. He showed only two deficits. He was poor at retrieving words from rhyming cues and produced more syntactic errors than controls in a task of sentence repetition. Since in these two patients the verbal IQ was lower than the performance IQ to the same degree as in Dennis's patient, one should pause before too readily concluding that specific language deficits are associated with callosal agenesis. Studies are required of acallosals with high verbal and low performance IQs. Early results from one such study (Jeeves and Temple, 1987) of an 11-year-old acallosal boy with a verbal IQ of 106 and a performance IQ of 68 underlines the need for such caution since most of his language skills are above normal. Sanders (personal communication, 1987) has studied a 6-year-old acallosal girl with a verbal IQ of 91 and a performance IQ of 70 and found that when compared with three other children matched for age and verbal IQ, she shows delayed or deficient syntactic development as well as impaired visual – spatial ability. This is an important finding since previous reports (Dennis, 1981) suggest that in acallosals *either* syntactic *or* visual-spatial ability is impaired but not both. Certainly current data do not support the notion that the corpus callosum is necessary for the normal development of certain language functions.

Hemispheric specialization in callosal agenesis

There is an ongoing debate as to whether after birth, a sharply asymmetrical development of the brain occurs or whether for a period during childhood and before the corpus callosum is fully myelinated both hemispheres develop in parallel as regards functions known to be lateralized in adulthood. There are certainly known morphological asymmetries in the cerebral hemispheres present at birth (Wada et al., 1975; Witelson and Palley, 1973). Moreover, studies using tachistoscopic and dichotic listening techniques have shown that behavioural asymmetries are already present in young children. Recent analyses have indicated that lesions that produce aphasia in children show a left side predominance, much as in adults (Carter et al., 1982). On the other hand, the view has been put forward by several workers (Moscovitch, 1973, 1977; Selnes, 1974; Galin, 1977; Davidson, 1978; Denenberg, 1981) that following the completion of myelogenesis in the corpus callosum, which is believed to take place by around the age of ten years, a relatively strong lateralized system in one hemisphere is able progressively to suppress the development of a similar functional specialization in the contralateral hemisphere and thus to produce the characteristic adult asymmetry of function. Sperry (1968a) suggested that in an acallosal brain there will be a failure to develop normal hemispheric specialization with resultant bilateral control of speech and other functions. Others (Milner and Jeeves, 1979, 1981; Chiarello, 1980; Milner, 1983; Jeeves, 1986) have argued that in fact no such demonstration has yet been convincingly achieved. The evidence which points to a picture of normal functional asymmetries in callosal agenesis may be summarized as follows:

The amytal test

Reports of the testing of three acallosals using this procedure have appeared. Milner, in a personal communication cited by Gazzaniga (1970), found that speech control was vested only in the right hemisphere. Two other reports claim to have shown bilateral control of speech (Gott and Saul, 1978; McGlone, 1985). Such an arrangement is found in only a small proportion of the general population (Rasmussen and Milner, 1977). However, it should be noted that among left handers the incidence of bilateral representation rises to 15% and amongst left handers who have suffered from early brain damage to 19% (Rasmussen and Milner, 1977). All three of the amytal tested acallosal patients reported were left handed and, since some acallosal patients show evidence of mild hemispheric pathology during childhood, this should be borne in mind in interpreting the data.

However, only one case of lateralized speech control in callosal agenesis is logically necessary to disprove the generalization that callosal processes are a necessary condition for such lateralization.

Visual half field recognition tests

In word recognition tests, there have been numerous reports that acallosal subjects demonstrate a normal right visual half field advantage. In one of the acallosals extensively tested over a number of years, recent new data (Jeeves and Milner, 1987) support this conclusion. It is further supported by a different type of visual half field study (Milner, 1982) in which simple vocal reaction times to lateralized light flashes were measured. The acallosal showed a highly significant right visual half field advantage. On a task of responding manually to the appearance of a lateralized spot of light there was no half field asymmetry (Milner, 1982). These indirect tests of both linguistic recognition and production clearly indicate moderate to strong cerebral asymmetries.

Dichotic testing

Chiarello (1980) has summarized the results of the 29 acallosals included in her review and presents clear evidence for a small, but reliable, dichotic asymmetry in these patients. One acallosal has been tested not only on traditional tasks of digit recall and serial syllable reproduction but also on the dichotic monitoring test devised by Geffen and Caudry (1981). She has shown a consistent right ear advantage on all methods of testing (Jeeves and Milner, 1987). In view of the variability of results of dichotic testing on normals, it is of particular interest that this patient, when tested on three occasions separated by several months, showed a clear and consistent right ear advantage in terms of correct identification and of response latencies. Successive testing on the three occasions gave a right ear advantage of 69% as compared with left ear 51% on the first occasion of testing, 77% compared with 60% on the second, and 65% compared with 51% on the third. Such evidence is consistent with a normal degree of asymmetry in at least some acallosal brains. This does not, however, necessarily imply a normal mechanism for left ear performance in agenesis cases (Geffen and Quinn, 1984).

Motor control

Surveys of the literature on acallosals (Milner and Jeeves, 1979; Chiarello, 1980) both showed that most of the acallosal patients studied have been right handed. Although a greater proportion than normal are described as non-right handed, this is not unusual for a neurological population. In bimanual testing, Preilowski studied two partially sectioned patients and reported an asymmetry of performance which led him to the conclusion that such a task confirmed the normal left hemisphere dominance for motor coordination. A similar study carried out on two acallosal patients (Jeeves et al., 1988) gave a pattern of results similar to that reported by Preilowski on his patients and to this extent it again can be interpreted as indicating normal motor specialization of the left hemisphere in these two acallosals.

Visuospatial functions

Martin (1985) in the study described above reported his patient well able to identify words, shapes and letters in either visual half field, but very poor at reporting spatial location of stimuli in his right visual half field, despite good performance on the left. Such a pattern of performance would be expected if there was a strong lateralization of visuospatial function in this patient, with spatial processing being dependent upon the right parietal region. An independent report by Meerwaldt (1983) could be interpreted in similar fashion. His acallosal patient, an 8-year-old child, was tested on the rod orientation test devised by De Renzi et al. (1971). In this test, the subject must set a movable hinged rod so as to match a model, both with respect to its orientation in a vertical plane and in the horizontal plane. Meerwaldt's patient, when tested in the tactile modality without visual information, performed very poorly with the right hand, whereas performance with the left hand was within the normal range. This pattern of results could be explained if there was a clear right parietal dependence for performing the task as indicated by other work on brain damaged patients (De Renzi et al., 1971; Meerwaldt and Harskamp, 1982). The generality of each of these findings is, however, in some doubt. As reported above, Milner and Jeeves (1987), though using a somewhat different technique, were unable to replicate Martin's findings. A recent attempt to test the generalizability of Meerwaldt's findings on a further series of acallosal patients produced a mixed picture. Some acallosals showed the same pattern of results as Meerwaldt's patient, although with a less marked asymmetry, whereas others showed no difference between the performance of the two hands (Jeeves and Milner, 1987; Jeeves and Silver, 1988b).

Conclusions concerning cerebral lateralization in acallosals

The evidence outlined above points to the conclusion that acallosals do not in general demonstrate bilateral representation of function but that lateralization develops much as it does in normals. This does not necessarily eliminate the possibility that the neocortical commissures, and in particular the corpus callosum, have an inhibitory role in ensuring that hemispheric asymmetry develops in ontogeny. It has been argued by some anatomists, for example (Bossy (1970), that at least some callosal fibres are re-routed and pass instead through the anterior commissure in acallosal brains. Also, the recent work by Innocenti (1980, 1981, 1986) has shown an elaboration of commissural fibres early in life in normal persons, followed by a decrease during later life. It may be that the elaboration of fibres passing through the anterior commissure continues in acallosals in a way in which it does not in normals. These fibres presumably could, to some extent, mediate the interhemispheric modulation hypothesized by Moscovitch and others. It would clearly be of great interest, with the increasing use of NMR imaging to determine directly the presence or absence and, if present, the size of the anterior commissure in acallosal individuals. If commissural interaction is necessary for lateralization, one would predict decreased specialization in patients lacking the anterior commissure as well as the corpus callosum. If, however, commissural interaction is not necessary one would expect increased or at least normal behavioural asymmetries in such patients. It is perhaps notable that there are isolated claims of grossly enlarged visual half field or hand asymmetries in particular acallosal patients (e.g., Field et al., 1978; Donoso and Santander, 1982; Meerwaldt, 1983). It would be of interest to know whether such patients are among that minority of acallosals who lack the anterior commissure (Lemire et al., 1975).

Compensatory mechanisms

Whatever the compensatory mechanisms are that may reduce the manifestation of typical split brain syndromes in acallosals, the fact remains that there are, in these patients, enduring deficits. Some of these may be due to undiagnosed extra callosal damage. No compensatory mechanism or mechanisms has fully made allowance for the absence from birth of the corpus callosum. Enduring sensory deficits are revealed by difficulties in stimulus topography (Dennis, 1976; Nilsson, 1983) and in midline stereopsis (Lassonde, 1986). There are enduring motor deficits evidenced by the presence of synkinetic movements (Dennis, 1976) and by bimanual coordination difficulties (Jeeves, 1965, 1979). There are deficits evident also in more sophisticated testing of bimanual coordination (Jeeves et al., 1988). There are enduring deficits of a cognitive kind, as is evidenced from the intelligence test profiles reviewed by Chiarello (1980). There appear to be an abnormally large number of high performance/low verbal WAIS profiles or the converse and relatively few where the performance and verbal IQs are similar. There are also enduring language deficits, though these are subtle and variable and have as yet received relatively little careful research (Dennis, 1976; Jeeves and Temple, 1987). It seems clear that whilst the information transmitting function of the corpus callosum may be served by alternate pathways such as the anterior commissure, the developmental callosal function is not so readily compensated for.

The presence of the corpus callosum during development appears to be essential not only for between-hand information transfer but, as Dennis has pointed out (1976), for the acquisition of finely differentiated sensation and movement *within* each hand. A poor coding of stimulus topography is typical of the way that sensory information is represented by uncrossed and extralemniscal pathways. Compared with the functions of the crossed tracts, the extralemniscal system shows larger receptive fields, more intermodal convergence and interaction and more corticofugal control. Adult congenital acallosals in many respects (Nilsson, 1983; Dennis, 1976) parallel, in their performance, young children in their apparent inability to suppress ipsilateral systems and there is evoked potential evidence to support the view that these ipsilateral systems are exceptionally well developed in acallosals (Laget, 1976, 1977).

In considering possible compensatory mechanisms, there are several candidates which may be at work individually or jointly and the way in which they combine in different individuals may vary. Those most strongly canvassed are (i) behavioural strategies, (ii) bilateral representation of function, (iii) ipsilateral pathways, (iv) the anterior commissure and subcortical commissural pathways. We shall consider each of these in turn:

Behavioural strategies

These were observed and reported frequently in the Californian studies of commissurotomy patients (Gazzaniga, 1970; Trevarthen, 1973) and have occasionally been observed in acallosals. Some have suggested that acallosals show an unusual amount of rapid eye movements scanning the visual field and it has been speculated that this may be to pull in information from both halves of the visual array. There is some evidence that, in an extended testing of touch localization, acallosal patients may flex the finger being touched in order to send information through the more proximal and uncrossed pathways which can be of use in identification with the other hand. There is also a hint of an attempt to use proximal information when doing the De Renzi rod task as when one acallosal held the wrist in a stiff posture and moved the whole forearm as he felt the orientation of the standard rods and set the test rods. This, however, appeared only after extended testing. Whilst there are these hints, it would seem that they play a very minor part as a compensatory mechanism. The fact remains that patients have had a lifetime to develop such compensatory behavioural strategies but they are not pronounced and are very difficult to detect. Moreover, it is also clear from longitudinal studies, e.g., Jeeves (1979) that where deficits are present early in life such as in bimanual coordination, they persist and are still evident 15 to 20 years later. If behavioural strategies could have compensated effectively then presumably over a 20-year period such compensation might be expected to have occurred, but did not.

Bilateral representation of function

Whilst this cannot be entirely ruled out, the whole thrust of the evidence reviewed above makes it an unlikely candidate. The possibility, however, remains that, in cases where the anterior commissure as well as the corpus callosum is absent, there might be a greater likelihood of bilateral representation occurring.

Elaboration of ipsilateral pathways

Dennis (1976) has argued for this possibility and certainly the evidence presented by her and others lends support to her arguments. It recognizes that sensory input accesses both hemispheres via the simultaneous use of crossed and uncrossed projection systems. It goes on to assume that normally the callosum serves as a pathway for the suppression of ipsilateral transmission in order to prevent competition between crossed and uncrossed projections. Dennis believes that the dissociation shown by acallosal patients between tasks of tactile discrimination and those of tactile localization lends further support to her hypothesis. The abnormal development of ipsilateral pathways helps to explain the difficulties which acallosals manifest on tasks requiring perceptual motor integration under speed stress but would suggest that the difficulty may be more the result of motor output than of perceptual integration. There may, however, be exceptions to this where rapid sensory feedback is at a premium. In those rare patients where there is a major deficit in perceptual integration (Donoso and Santander, 1982) it may be that both the anterior commissure and the corpus callosum are absent. In such cases, more dramatic sensori-motor deficits would be expected. Normal subjects achieve highly skilled performance on bimanual tasks by the use of motor feed-forward processes, which probably normally occur through the rostral parts of the corpus callosum. We might expect that in the early years of life when these pathways are not fully myelinated, there may be deficits as compared with performance at and after maturity as mentioned above. The evoked potential studies of Laget in 1976 and 1977 lend clear additional support for enhanced development and/or disinhibition of ipsilateral pathways in acallosals.

The anterior commissure and subcortical pathways

The evidence on tasks where, for example, a simple manual response was required to a lateralized point source of light produced results which could be attributed to the acallosal using an alternative sensory interhemispheric pathway rather than the normal callosal one. Thus, when the intensity of the stimulus was varied, interhemispheric transmission time covaried suggesting that when this task is done by acallosals we are measuring interhemispheric sensory transfer time and not motor transfer as is presumed to be the case in normals (Berlucchi, 1980; Rizzolatti, 1979). The most probable alternative pathways to consider are the anterior commissure or subcortical pathways. Sergent (1986) has presented evidence from studies designed to examine the capacity of commissurotomized patients to integrate information simultaneously received by each hemisphere, and then to produce a unified response. Her data suggest that subcortical structures subserve interhemispheric integration. In support of her view, she cites earlier work on animals (Trevarthen, 1965), as well as work by Trevarthen and Sperry (1973) and Holtzman (1984) on callosotomized subjects. There are, however, reasons for doubting that on the tasks most often administered the subcortical pathways are the most likely candidates in acallosals. Testing of surgically disconnected patients in whom both the corpus callosum and the anterior commissure were cut, revealed (a) that their interhemispheric transmission times were lengthened even more than those of the acallosals and (b) that there was no variation in ITTs as a function of stimulus intensity. If subcortical pathways mediated the transfer of visual sensory information in acallosal patients, then they should act similarly in both of these respects to the sectioned patients but, as we have seen, they do not.

As regards the transfer of visuo-spatial information, the anterior commissure remains the most likely candidate. Results of animal studies (Pohl,

1973; Ungerleider and Brody, 1977) indicate that in normal monkeys the anterior commissure may be capable of carrying information about location. There may also be a wider field of origin of cells contributing to the anterior commissure in the acallosal brain than is the case in the normal brain. In some cases, the anterior commissure is obviously larger than normal, possibly because it contains fibres which would normally be destined for the corpus callosum (Bossy, 1970). It may also be the case that the acallosal brain preserves some of the exuberant inputs which it receives early in foetal life (Innocenti, 1981, 1983) but which normally regress as the corpus callosum develops (Auroux and Roussel, 1967). Either way, the parietal regions in at least some acallosal brains may have interconnections through the anterior commissure which could mediate visuospatial integration. Lassonde et al. (1987) have observed that, even though acallosals can cross-integrate relatively complex visual and tactile information, they require more time to accomplish such integration than do normals.

Implications of callosal agenesis studies for theories of commissural functioning

A variety of functions have been proposed for the neocortical commissures. The list includes integration, inhibition, the switching of attention and facilitation. Of these functions the two which until recently have been most widely canvassed and intensively studied are those of integration, including interhemispheric transfer, and inhibition. The evidence reviewed earlier in this chapter would make it difficult to support unequivocally the claim that the corpus callosum plays an indispensable role in interhemispheric integration. Compensatory mechanisms are possible when the callosum is absent from birth but there do, nevertheless, appear to be certain residual integrative processes that are never fully compensated for either neurally or behaviourally. As regards the supposed inhibitory functions of the neocortical commissures these have been of two kinds. First, that the callosum plays an essential inhibitory role in the development of normal cerebral lateralization and, second, that at maturity it plays an essential role in the suppression of ipsilateral sensory and motor transmissions which would otherwise compete with the stronger crossed pathways. In the light of the evidence currently available, the contention that the corpus callosum performs an essential inhibitory role in normal development is not supported. The limited amount of available evidence, however, is consistent with the view that the callosum may play an important inhibitory role in preventing unnecessary competition between crossed and uncrossed sensory and motor pathways.

More recently, Lassonde et al. (1987) have presented persuasive evidence in support of an important facilitative role for the corpus callosum. She and her co-workers have shown that deficits in visual and visuomotor function are not limited to *inter*hemispheric processing but that *intra*hemispheric processing is also affected by the absence of callosal influx. They postulate ‘that in the intact cortex the corpus callosum exerts a facilitatory or modulating influence on the neural activity in both hemispheres’. In callosal agenesis this is assumed to be reduced or absent and hence the deficits in *intra*hemispheric as well as *inter*hemispheric processing. Lassonde (1987) speculates that such a function may have clinical implications. First, it may help to understand how callosal section not only abolishes interhemispheric propagation of seizure discharges but may also reduce abnormal activity in the initial focus. Second, through its modulating action the corpus callosum may actively participate in the functional reorganization that takes place after brain injury. If this is so, then presumably a brain-injured acallosal would have reduced prospects of functional reorganization, an hypothesis that could be tested (e.g., in animals). As far as the acallosal is concerned, the upshot of Lassonde's emphasis on a modulating role for the corpus callosum means that it is unlikely that either hemisphere will achieve its full potential.

Acknowledgements

I am pleased to acknowledge my indebtedness to my friend and colleague, Dr David Milner, for his comments on an early draft of this chapter; to my assistant Dr Priscilla Silver for her help in checking the references cited in this paper; to Mrs Marjorie Anderson for her patient retyping of successive drafts of the chapter and to the Medical Research Council and the Wellcome Foundation for their financial support which makes possible my continuing studies of acallosal patients.

References

Aicardi J, Lefebre J, Lerique-Koechlind: A new syndrome: spasms in flexion, callosal agenesis, ocular abnormalities. *Electroencephalogr. Clin. Neurophysiol.: 19,* 609 – 610, 1965.

Akert K, Puletti F, Erickson, TC: Abnormalities of the cerebral cortex associated with agenesis of corpus callosum and focal cortical seizures. *Trans. Am. Neurol. Assoc.: 79,* 151 – 153, 1954.

Andermann E, Andermann F, Joubert M. et al.: Three familial midline malformations of the central nervous system: Agenesis of the corpus callosum and anterior horn-cell disease; agenesis of the cerebellar vermis; and atrophy of the cerebellar vermis. *Birth Defects: 11,* 269 – 293, 1975.

Andermann F, Andermann E, Joubert M, Karpati S, Carpenter S, Melancon D: Familial agenesis of the corpus callosum with anterior horn cell disease. A syndrome of mental retardation, areflexia and paraplegia. *Trans. Am. Neurol. Assoc.: 97,* 242 – 244, 1972.

Auroux M, Roussel C: Relations neocorticales assurees par la commissure blanche anterieure chez le foetus humain. *Assoc. Anat. C.R.: 137,* 152 – 159, 1967.

Berlucchi G: Interhemispheric integration of simple visuomotor responses. In Buser PA, Rogeul-Buser A (Editors), *Cerebral Correlates of Conscious Experience.* Amsterdam: North Holland, pp. 83 – 94, 1978.

Bossy JG: Morphological study of a case of complete, isolated and asymptomatic agenesis of the corpus callosum. *Arch. Anat. Histol. Embryol.: 53,* 289 – 340, 1970.

Bruyer R, Dupuis M, Ophonen E, Rectem D, Reynart C: Anatomical and behavioural study of a case of asymptomatic callosal agenesis. *Cortex: 21,* 41 – 430, 1985.

Carter RL, Hohenegger MK, Satz P: Aphasia and speech organization in children. *Science: 218,* 797 – 799, 1982.

Chiarello C: A house divided? Cognitive functioning with callosal agenesis. *Brain Language: 11,* 128 – 158.

Davidson RJ: Lateral specialization in the human brain: speculations concerning its origins and development (Commentary). *Behav. Brain Sci.: 2,* 291, 1978.

De Renzi M, Faglioni P, Scotti G: Judgement of spatial orientation in patients with focal brain damage. *J. Neurol. Neurosurg. Psychiatry: 34,* 489 – 495, 1971.

Denenberg VH: Hemispheric laterality in animals and the effects of early experience. *Behav. Brain Sci.: 4,* 1 – 49, 1981.

Dennis M: Impaired sensory and motor differentiation with corpus callosum agenesis: a lack of callosal inhibition during ontogeny. *Neuropsychologia: 14,* 455 – 469, 1976.

Dennis M: Language in a congenitally acallosal brain. *Brain Language: 12,* 33 – 53, 1981.

Donoso A, Santander M: Hemialexia y afasia hemianoptica en agenesia del curepo calloso. *Rev. Chilena Neuropsiquiatria: 20,* 137 – 144, 1982.

Ettlinger G, Blakemore CB, Milner AD, Wilson J: Agenesis of the corpus callosum: a behavioural investigation. *Brain: 95,* 327 – 346, 1972.

Field M, Ashton R, White K: Agenesis of the corpus callosum: report of 2 pre-school children and a review of the literature. *Dev. Med. Child Neurol.: 20:* 47 – 61, 1978.

Freytag E, Lindenberg R: Neuropathological findings in patients of a hospital for the mentally deficient. A survey of 359 cases. *Johns Hopkins Med. J.: 121,* 379 – 392, 1967.

Galin D: Lateral specialization and psychiatric issues: speculations on development and the evolution of consciousness. *Ann. NY Acad. Sci.: 299,* 397 – 411, 1977.

Gazzaniga MS: *The Bisected Brain.* New York: Appleton Century Crofts, 1970.

Geffen G, Caudrey D: Reliability and validity of the dichotic monitoring test for language laterality. *Neuropsychologia: 19,* 413 – 423, 1981.

Geffen G, Quinn K: Hemispheric specialization and ear advantages in processing speech. *Psychol. Bull.: 96:* 273 – 291, 1984.

Geschwind N: Late changes in the nervous system: an overview. In Stein DG, Rasen JJ, Butters N (Editors), *Plasticity and Recovery of Function in the Central Nervous System.* New York: Academic Press, pp. 467 – 508, 1974.

Gott PS, Saul RE: Agenesis of the corpus callosum: limits of functional compensation. *Neurology: 28,* 1272 – 1279, 1978.

Grogono JL: Children with agenesis of the corpus callosum. *Dev. Med. Child Neurol.: 10,* 613 – 616, 1968.

Hamilton CR, Vermeire BA: Localization of visual functions with partially split-brain monkeys. In Lepore F, Ptito M, Jasper HH (Editors), *Two Hemispheres – One Brain.* New York: Alan R Liss, pp. 315 – 333, 1986.

Holst E Von, Mittelstaedt H: Das Reafferenzprinzip (Wechselwirkungen zwischen Zentralnervensystem and Peripherie). *Naturwissenschaften: 37,* 464 – 476, 1950.

Holtzman JD: Interactions between cortical and subcortical visual areas: evidence from human commissurotomy patients. *Vision Res.: 24:* 801 – 813, 1984.

Innocenti GM: Growth and reshaping of axons in the establishment of visual callosal connections. *Science: 212,* 824 – 827, 1981.

Innocenti GM: What is so special about callosal connections. In Lepore F, Ptito M, Jasper HH (Editors), *Two Hemispheres – One Brain: Functions of the Corpus Callosum.* New York: Alan R Liss, pp. 75 – 81, 1986.

Innocenti GM, Caminiti R: Postnatal shaping of callosal connections from sensory areas. *Exp. Brain Res.: 38,* 381 – 394, 1980.

Jeannerod M: The formation of finger grip during prehension.

A cortically mediated visuomotor pattern. *Behav. Brain Res.: 19,* 99 – 116, 1986.

Jeannerod M: The role of vision in the patterning of prehension movements. In Lepore F, Ptito M, Jasper HH (Editors): *Two Hemispheres – One Brain.* New York: Alan R Liss, pp. 369 – 383, 1986.

Jeeves MA: Psychological studies of three cases of congenital agenesis of the corpus callosum. In Ettlinger EG (Editor), *Functions of the Corpus Callosum.* CIBA Foundation Study Groups, Vol. 20. London: Churchill, pp. 73 – 94, 1965a.

Jeeves MA: Agenesis of the corpus callosum. Physiopathological and clinical aspects. *Proc. Aust. Assoc. Neurol. 3:* 41 – 48, 1965b.

Jeeves MA: A comparison of interhemispheric transmission times in acallosals and normals. *Psychonom. Sci.: 16,* 245 – 246, 1969.

Jeeves MA: Some limits to interhemispheric integration in cases of callosal agenesis and partial commissurotomy. In Russell IS, van Hof MW, Berlucchi G (Editors), *Structure and Function of Cerebral Commissures.* London: Macmillan, Ch. 37, pp. 449 – 474, 1979.

Jeeves MA: Callosal agenesis: neuronal and developmental adaptations. In: Lepore F, Ptito M, Jasper HH (Editors), *Two Hemispheres – One Brain.* New York: Alan R. Liss Inc., pp. 403 – 421, 1986.

Jeeves MA, Milner AD: Specificity and plasticity in interhemispheric integration: evidence from callosal agenesis. In: Ottoson D (Editor), *Duality and Unity of the Brain – Unified Functioning and Specialization of the Hemispheres.* London: Macmillan, pp. 416 – 441, 1987.

Jeeves MA, Silver PH: The formation of finger grip during prehension in an acallosal patient. *Neuropsychologia: 26,* 153 – 159, 1988a.

Jeeves MA, Silver PH: Interhemispheric transfer of spatial tactile information in callosal agenesis and partial commissurotomy. *Cortex: 24,* 601 – 604, 1988b.

Jeeves MA, Temple CM: A further study of language function in callosal agenesis. *Brain Language,* 1987, in press.

Jeeves MA, Silver PH, Jacobson I: Bimanual coordination in callosal agenesis and partial commissurotomy. *Neuropsychologia: 26,* 833 – 850, 1988.

Johnson LE: Bilateral visual cross-integration by human forebrain commissurotomy subjects. *Neuropsychologia: 22,* 167 – 175, 1984.

Kaplan P: X linked recessive inheritance of agenesis of the corpus callosum. *J. Med. Genet.: 20:* 122 – 124, 1983.

Laget P, Raimbault J, d'Allest AM, Flores-Guevara R, Mariani J, Thieriot-Prevost G: La maturation des potentiels evoques somesthesiqiues (PES) chez l'homme. *Electroencephalogr. Clin. Neurophysiol.: 40:* 499 – 515, 1976.

Laget P, d'Allest AM, Fihey R, Lortholary O: L'interet des potentials evoques somesthesiques homolateraux dans les agenesies du corps calleux. *Rev. Electroencephalogr. Neurophysiol. Clin.: 7:* 498 – 502, 1977.

Labrisseau A, Vanasse M, Brochu P, Gaetan J: The Andermann syndrome: agenesis of the corpus callosum associated with mental retardation and progressive sensorimotor neuronopathy. *J. Can. Sci. Neurol.: 11:* 257 – 261, 1984.

Lassonde M: The facilitatory influence of the corpus callosum on intrahemispheric processing. In Lepore F, Ptito M, Jasper HH (Editors), *Two Hemispheres – One Brain: Functions of the Corpus Callosum.* New York, Alan R Liss, pp. 385 – 401, 1986.

Lassonde M, Sauerwein H, McCabe N, Laurencelle L, Geoffroy G: Extent and limits. A cerebral adjustment to early section or congenital absence of the corpus callosum. *Behav. Brain Sci.:* 1987, in press.

Lemire RJ, Loeser JD, Leech RW, Alvord EC: *Normal and Abnormal Development of the Human Nervous System.* Hagerstown, MD: Harper & Row, 1975.

Lehman HJ, Lampe H: Observations on the interhemispheric transmission of information in 9 patients with corpus callosum defect. *Eur. Neurol.: 4:* 129 – 147, 1970.

Loeser JD, Alvord EC Jr: Clinico-pathological correlations in agenesis of the corpus callosum. *Neurology (Minneapolis): 18,* 745 – 756, 1968.

McGlone J: *Congenital absence of the corpus callosum: neuropsychological and sodium amytal findings.* Paper presented at INS annual meeting, San Diego, CA, 1985.

Martin A: A qualitative limitation on visual transfer via the anterior commissure. *Brain: 108,* 43 – 63, 1985.

Meerwaldt JD: Disturbance of spatial perception in a patient with agenesis of the corpus callosum. *Neuropsychologia: 21,* 161 – 165, 1983.

Meerwaldt JD, Harskamp F van: Spatial disorientation in right-hemisphere infarction. *J. Neurol. Neurosurg. Psychiatry: 45,* 586 – 590, 1982.

Menkes JH, Phillippart M, Clark DB: Hereditary partial agenesis of corpus callosum. *Arch. Neurol.: 11:* 198 – 208, 1964.

Milner AD: Simple reaction times to lateralized visual stimuli in a case of callosal agenesis. *Neuropsychologia: 20,* 411 – 419, 1982.

Milner AD, Lines CR: Interhemispheric pathways in simple reaction time to lateralized light flash. *Neuropsychologia: 20,* 171 – 179, 1982.

Mitchell DE, Blakemore C: Binocular depth perception and the corpus callosum. *Vision Res.: 10:* 49 – 54, 1970.

Moscovitch M: Language and the cerebral hemispheres: reaction-time studies and their implications for models of cerebral dominance. In Pliner P, Alloway T, Krames L (Editors), *Communication and Affect: Language and Thought.* New York: Academic Press, pp. 89 – 126, 1973.

Moscovitch M: The development of lateralization of language functions and its relation to cognitive and linguistic development: a review and some theoretical speculations. In Segalowitz SJ, Gruber FA (Editors), *Language Development and Neurological Theory.* New York: Academic Press, Ch. 15, pp. 193 – 211, 1977.

Nilsson J: *The effects of corpus callosum lesions and hemispheric specialization on tactile perception.* Unpublished PhD thesis. Flinders University, South Australia, 1983.

Parrish ML, Roessmann U, Levinsohn MW: Agenesis of the corpus callosum: a study of the frequency of associated malformations. *Ann. Neurol.: 6,* 349 – 354, 1979.

Pohl W: Dissociation of spatial discrimination deficits following frontal and parietal lesions in monkeys. *J. Comp. Physiol. Psychol.: 82,* 227 – 239, 1973.

Poffenberger AT: Reaction time to retinal stimulation with special reference to the time lost in conduction through nerve centers. *Arch. Psychol. (NY): 3,* 1 – 73, 1912.

Preilowski BFP: Possible contributions of the anterior forebrain commissures to bilateral motor coordination. *Neuropsychologia: 10,* 267 – 277, 1972.

Probst M: Uber den bau des vollstandigen balkenlosen groszhirns sowie uber heterotopie der grauen substanz. *Arch. Psychiatry: 34,* 709 – 686, 1901.

Quinn K, Geffen G: The development of tactile transfer of information. *Neuropsychologia: 24,* 793 – 804, 1986.

Rasmussen T, Milner B: The role of early left-brain injury in determining laterality of cerebral speech functions. *Ann. NY Acad. Sci.: 299,* 355 – 369.

Reynolds DM, Jeeves MA: Further studies of tactile perception and motor coordination in agenesis of the corpus callosum. *Cortex: 13,* 257 – 272, 1977.

Rizzolatti G: Interfield differences in RTs to lateralized visual stimuli in normal subjects. In Russell IS, Hof MW van, Berlucchi G (Editors), *Structures and Function of Cerebral Commissures.* London: Macmillan, Ch. 32, pp. 390 – 399, 1979.

Russell JR, Reitan RM: Psychological abnormalities in agenesis of the corpus callosum. *J. Nerv. Mental Dis.: 121,* 205 – 214, 1955.

Selnes OD: The corpus callosum: some anatomical and functional considerations with special reference to language. *Brain Language: 1,* 111 – 139, 1974.

Sergent J: Subcortical coordination of hemisphere activity in commissurotomized patients. *Brain: 109,* 357 – 369, 1986.

Sergent J, Myers JJ: Manual, blowing, and verbal simple reactions to lateralized flashes of light in commissurotomized patients. *Percept. Psychophys.: 37,* 571 – 578, 1985.

Shoumura K, Ando T, Kato K: Structural organization of 'callosal' OBg in human corpus callosum agenesis. *Brain Res.: 93,* 241 – 252, 1975.

Slager UT, Kelly AB, Wagner JA: Congenital absence of the corpus callosum. Report of a case and review of the literature. *New Engl. J. Med.: 256,* 1171 – 1176, 1957.

Solursh LP, Margulies AI, Ashem B, Stastiak EA: The relationships of agenesis of the corpus callosum to perception and learning. *J. Nerv. Mental Dis.: 141,* 180 – 189, 1965.

Sperry RW: Plasticity of neural maturation. *Dev. Biol.: Supplement 2,* 306 – 327, 1968a.

Sperry RW: Hemispheric deconnection and unity in conscious awareness. *Am. Psychol.: 23:* 723 – 733, 1968b.

Sperry RW: Mental unity following surgical disconnection of the cerebral hemispheres. *Harvey Lecture 6:* 293 – 323, 1980.

Teuber HL: The riddle of frontal lobe function in man. In Warren JM, Akert T (Editors), *The Frontal Granular Cortex and Behavior.* New York: McGraw Hill, pp. 410 – 444, 1964.

Trevarthen C: Functional interactions between the cerebral hemispheres of the split-brain monkey. In Ettlinger EG (Editor), *Functions of the Corpus Callosum.* London: Churchill, pp. 24 – 41, 1965.

Trevarthen C, Sperry RW: Perceptual of the ambient visual field in human commissurotomy patients. *Brain: 96,* 547 – 570, 1973.

Ungerleider LG and Brody BA: Extrapersonal spatial orientation: the role of posterior parietal, anterior frontal and inferotemporal cortex. *Exp. Neurol.: 56:* 265 – 280, 1977.

Wada JA, Clarke R, Hamm A: Cerebral hemispheric asymmetry in humans: cortical speech zones in 100 adult and 100 infant brains. *Arch. Neurol.: 32:* 239 – 246, 1975.

Warkany J: *Mental Retardation and Congenital Malformations of the Central Nervous System.* Chicago-London: Yearbook Medical Publishers, 1981.

Warkany J, Passarge E, Smith LB: Congenital malformations in autosomal trisomy syndromes. *Am. J. Dis. Children: 112,* 502 – 517, 1966.

Handbook of Neuropsychology, Vol. 4
F. Boller and J. Grafman (Eds)

CHAPTER 6

Language functions in the two hemispheres following complete cerebral commissurotomy and hemispherectomy

Eran Zaidel

Department of Psychology, University of California, Los Angeles, CA 90024-1563, U.S.A.

Introduction

There are three main behavioral approaches to the study of language functions in the two cerebral hemispheres: (1) the clinical neurological approach observes language deficits following hemispheric damage, (2) the disconnection approach taps directly the linguistic competence of the two disconnected hemispheres and compares them to each other, and (3) the experimental psychological approach measures behavioral responses to stimuli lateralized to one hemisphere in the normal brain. Each approach has its methodological difficulties and advantages and the results do not always agree. Resolution of the apparent conflicts is critical for the construction of a theory of language functioning in the brain. In this paper I will review evidence from the first two approaches. First, I will review behavioral data from patients with complete cerebral commissurotomy. Second, I will review the special case of patients with surgical removal of one complete cortical hemisphere.

Classic neurology regards language functions as exclusively specialized in the left hemisphere of the right-handed adult. In this view, the disconnection syndrome should result in no selective linguistic deficit. The disconnected left hemisphere should be linguistically normal, the disconnected right hemisphere should be language-free: word-deaf, word-blind and word-mute. For example, traditional accounts of pure alexia focus on primary visual deficits in the left hemisphere together with splenial visual disconnection but without any damage to the right hemisphere. In contrast, research with commissurotomy patients introduced the concept of hemispheric independence, in addition to complementary hemispheric specialization. In this view, each hemisphere has a fairly complete cognitive repertoire, adequate for processing most incoming stimuli and capable of controlling the behavior of the whole organism. In particular, the right hemisphere has some language functions necessary to complete its representation of the world, some other functions necessary for effective communication with the linguistic left hemisphere, and yet other functions complementing the communicative capabilities of the left hemisphere. Consequently, functional disconnection should reveal unique linguistic profiles in each hemisphere as well as loss of some linguistic competence because of the absence of right hemisphere contributions.

Language in the disconnected right hemisphere is of particular theoretical importance because it can clarify by contrast what is special about the biologically innate 'Language Acquisition Device' of the left hemisphere. Right hemisphere language may well be based on the general-purpose cognitive operations of that hemisphere which are not language-related whereas left hemisphere language determines not only language specialization but also cognitive specialization on the left. Thus, the relationships between language and cognition in the two hemispheres illustrate the two extreme philosophical positions on the nature of language: the right hemisphere illustrates the empiricist or cognitivist approach which says that language is but a species of general learning principles or symbolic cognitive operations, and the left hemisphere illustrates the rationalist or nativist approach which says that language is innate and unique. The nature, limits and optimal conditions of right hemisphere language functioning are, in turn, clinically important because they determine the extent of language recovery following left aphasiogenic lesions through right hemisphere takeover and compensation.

In this review I will emphasize new experiments with the California series, not reviewed elsewhere (e.g., Moscovitch, 1981; Lambert, 1982; Zaidel, 1985; Code, 1987). Data presented in Tables 2, 3 and 4 are new and not yet published. This is an active area of research and the experimental scene is likely to change substantially as new populations and methodologies for testing the disconnection syndrome become available, as long-term epidemiological follow-ups of hemispherectomy and hemisphere-damaged patients are undertaken, and as the nature of language-processing in the two normal hemispheres is clarified.

Disconnection syndrome

Initial testing of commissurotomy patients in the California series, who had been operated on by Phillip Vogel and Joseph Bogen at White Memorial Hospital, Los Angeles, quickly demonstrated a dramatic disconnection syndrome (Bogen and Vogel, 1962, 1975; Bogen et al., 1965; Sperry, 1982). Those patients who had complete cerebral commissurotomy, including the corpus callosum, anterior commissure and hippocampal commissure, were unable to name objects which were palpated by the left hand out of view (left-hand anomia) or whose pictures were flashed briefly to the left visual hemifield (LVF). At the same time, these patients could retrieve with the left hand objects whose picture was flashed in the LVF without being able to name them. More surprisingly, they could retrieve with the left hand an object named or described verbally by the experimenter. It was concluded that the disconnected right hemisphere (RH) is mute but not word-deaf.

Similar 'first-generation' experiments, where part of the stimulus (not necessarily the linguistic target itself) was lateralized either somesthetically or visually, led to the conclusion that the disconnected RH is not word-blind either. As long as responses were signaled nonverbally, the RH was seen to have at least a modest receptive vocabulary and functional associations among the lexical items (Gazzaniga and Sperry, 1967; Sperry and Gazzaniga, 1967). It could understand some phrases and obey some simple commands, and it seemed able to understand verbal task instructions. Initial reports that the RH can understand nouns, but not verbs, nor nouns derived from verbs, nor spoken commands (Gazzaniga, 1970) were challenged by Levy (1969), who showed that the RH understood the meaning of the command and was able to point to a corresponding picture or to select a corresponding object even when unable to execute the command. As concerns syntax, it was initially believed that the disconnected RH could understand simple active or negative sentences but not tense markings, plural inflections, or the relationship between subject, verb and object (Gazzaniga and Hillyard, 1971). This belief was also challenged later (see below).

These experiments focused largely on two patients with complete cerebral commissurotomy, L.B. and N.G.,* who had the least amount of extracallosal damage relative to the group as a whole. Neither of them had the kind of massive LH

* Initials identify commissurotomy patients (see Bogen and Vogel, 1975, for details of clinical background).

damage to the language area expected to result in an unusual language reorganization in the RH. Indeed, neither of them had a history of language deficit either in childhood or as adults. Thus these two patients were believed to be most representative of the true disconnection syndrome. Occasional 'second-generation' studies reported some language competence in the disconnected RHs of other patients as well. Those studies include auditory comprehension by A.A. (Nebes, 1971; Nebes and Sperry, 1971), RH execution of verbal commands by R.Y. (Gordon, 1980), phonological encoding in the RH of C.C. (Levy and Trevarthen, 1977), and auditory comprehension by the RH in N.W. and R.M. (Bogen, 1979).

Mutism following commissurotomy

Short-term mutism

Complete cerebral commissurotomy is usually immediately followed by a short-term mutism, with absent or sparse speech but with retained comprehension and writing. Mutism was not accompanied by paraphasia and recovery of speech was not accompanied by anomia, paraphasia or linguistic errors but did include hoarseness or whispering (Bogen, 1987). The duration of mutism in 10 cases varied from 3 days to 4 months. Patients with commissurotomy including the massa intermedia and anterior commissure but sparing the splenium had no postoperative mutism. This suggests that damage to the third ventricle or the right supplementary cortex was not the cause of the mutism (Bogen, 1987).

The cause of short-term postoperative mutism in patients with no extensive hemispheric damage or abnormal lateralization remains unknown. Bogen (1987) offers the following potential explanations. (1) The commissural fibers may have been acting in a compensatory fashion because of previous brain injury. (2) Speech may require some absolute number of relevant brain connections. In a marginal case, the callosotomy may be sufficient to bring the number of connections below the minimum required. (3) The callosotomy may produce a diaschisis in the speaking hemisphere, from which it recovers only slowly. (4) The callosum may carry a corollary discharge for speech output whose sudden loss results in downstream interhemispheric conflict. (5) Temporary circulatory alterations (particularly of the internal cerebral veins) may transiently derange the more sensitive functions of the basal ganglia. (6) Damage to one or the other fornix may be contributory. (7) Trauma to the anterior third ventricle during division of the anterior commissure or during division of the rostrum from in front may be relevant in some cases. (8) Supplementary motor cortex dysfunction may be contributory in some cases. (9) Decussating fibers (for example, from medial frontal cortex to opposite basal ganglia) may be relevant, in that their interruption plus medial frontal cortex edema combines to produce mutism when associated with a thalamic or striatal lesion.

Long-term mutism

Ferguson, Rayport and Corrie (1985) reported that 2 or 3 of 8 cases showed long-term loss of the ability to initiate spontaneous speech while still being able to repeat, give short responses and respond to cueing. Comprehension and singing were retained. Mutism occurred only after the second, posterior stage of the surgery. These authors, McKeever (personal communication) and Spencer et al. (1988) suggest that mutism follows complete corpus callosotomy in cases where manual and speech dominance are in opposite hemispheres. 'Discordant dominance' may reflect early brain damage and consequent unusual dependence on interhemispheric interaction for speech programming. Preoperative unilateral carotid amobarbital testing may disclose this condition (Bogen, 1987). Further evaluation of this 'syndrome' awaits sharper definition of the signs for manual and speech dominance and of the role of pre-existing damage.

Language deficits in the disconnected left hemisphere

Clinical impression

Though seemingly normal on clinical aphasiological tests, more subtle observation reveals persistent lacunae in the language repertoires of patients with cerebral commissurotomy. These lacunae include chronic impoverishment of verbal description of personal emotional experience (alexithymia, cf. TenHouten et al., 1986), long-term failure to sustain reading with adequate comprehension of paragraphs or extended text (Zaidel, 1982), and deficits in conversational interaction. The conversational inappropriateness is apparently especially striking on first encounters and tends to be less prominent with repeated meetings, as the examiner makes allowance for the deficit and rationalizes it in terms of the clinical/social consequences of epilepsy. These lacunae involve aspects of language use in context, i.e., pragmatics rather than phonology and syntax, and these aspects are not included in standard assessment batteries. The relationship of pragmatics to semantics, on the one hand, and to cognition and personality, on the other, is still unclear.

Conversational inappropriateness is highly variable across patients and is difficult to quantify, but it seems to involve pragmatic components. Curiously, those patients who are believed to have the most developed right hemisphere language seem to have the most severe pragmatic deficits. L.B., in particular, seems to exhibit social inappropriateness by failing to follow leads initiated by others, by using exaggerated or inappropriate rules of politeness, and by exhibiting a frequent tendency to rationalize mistakes and confabulate reasons for opaque performance patterns, even when they are not the clear results of right hemisphere processing. He rarely displays emotional outbursts and then they are short-lived, followed quickly by his normal mood. L.B. is self-centered in conversation and tends to initiate new topics of conversation rather than pursue a mutual exchange of an extended topic (C. Hamilton, personal communication). One tends to classify these conversational patterns as the results of an obsessive compulsive and repressed personality.

N.G. seems remarkably self-centered in conversation, yet surprisingly detached in her somewhat flippant, superficial style of discussing deeply personal topics. R.Y., too, is self-centered and tends to repeat the same stories and to invent new ones on the spur of the moment. He also tends to rationalize and confabulate, and once an 'explanation' is constructed it will acquire a reality of its own and be catalogued as history. A.A., like the rest of the patients, is remarkably brief about his ongoing life and emotional concerns. But he does seem to be more socially appropriate and able to carry out longer sustained exchanges (C. Hamilton, personal communication). Like L.B., N.G. and R.Y., he has a very poor episodic memory for the timing, both absolute and relative, of recent events.

To varying degrees, however, all four patients show a consistent and frequent use of humor in conversation. They both understand and employ it regularly, though with different levels of sophistication. They also use idioms and proverbs appropriately and frequently, and their gestures and intonation seem normal. L.B., in particular, makes frequent and clever use of puns, although this too was never assessed formally.

Formal testing of the linguistic competence of each disconnected hemisphere is possible with special techniques. But when one interacts linguistically with a complete commissurotomy patient or when one administers a standardized language test in free vision, the presumption is that one is interacting with the disconnected LH. Any deficits in free field testing of linguistic abilities must then reflect LH deficits, attributable to the absence of normal RH contribution. Even limited standardized assessment reveals surprisingly many such deficits. Two examples follow.

Wechsler intelligence and memory scales

Although the lateralizing significance of the Wechsler Verbal and Performance IQs remains controversial, some regard the Verbal subscale as tapping predominantly LH function and the Performance subscale as tapping mostly RH function (Lezak, 1983). When the Wechsler IQ is administered in free vision to patients with complete cerebral commissurotomy, verbal responses to verbal stimuli can be assumed to originate in the disconnected LH. Any selective postoperative deficits in verbal IQ may then be attributable to loss of RH contribution. Table 1 compares the pre- and postoperative verbal and performance IQs of six patients with complete and two patients with partial cerebral commissurotomy (Campbell et al., 1981). Performance IQ may show a postoperative decrease, depending on whether or not the RH controls the responses, and whether good performance normally depends on interhemispheric integration. A 15-point IQ difference corresponds to 1 standard deviation. The table shows that there is no general postoperative decrease in verbal IQ. Only the completely sectioned patient C.C. and the partially sectioned patient N.F. show consistent loss, which does not reach significance. Thus, there is no evidence that the RH contributes to any of the verbal subscales of the WAIS.

D. Zaidel and Sperry (1974) showed severe and selective deficits in both complete and partial commissurotomy patients on the two 'linguistic' subtests of the Wechsler Memory Scale: Associate Learning and Logical Memory (Table 2). Associate

TABLE 1

Pre- and postoperative Wechsler intelligence quotients in patients with complete and partial (P) cerebral commissurotomy from the Bogen-Vogel series.

Patient	Testing session	Preop IQ			Postop IQ			Pre – post verbal range (min – max)
		Full scale	Verbal	Performance	Full scale	Verbal	Performance	
L.B.	1.	113	119	108	106	110	100	
	2.	113	115	108	109	113	102	2 – 10
	3.				110	109	110	
N.G.	1.	76	79	74	77	83	71	
	2.				71	79	64	(–4) – 4
	3.				72	75	71	
R.Y.	1.				90	99	79	
	2.				82	94	69	
	3.				87	98		
N.W.	1.	93	97	89	93	97	89	
	2.				81	87	75	(–1) – 10
	3.				95	98	92	
A.A.	1.	74	80	72	78	77	82	
	2.				74	75	75	3 – 5
	3.				74	77	72	
C.C.	1.	76	73	83	65	61	70	
	2.				58	59	61	12 – 14*
M.K.	1.	88	89	88	74	80	72	9
J.M.	1.	102	106	95	90	104	74	
	2.				86	94	76	2 – 12
W.J.	1.	106	111	100	99	110	84	1
N.F. (P)	1.	101	93	108	80	77	86	
	2.				84	82	89	11 – 16*
D.M. (P)	1.	76	70	87	94	108	76	
	2.				71	68	77	(–38) – 2
	3.				73	72	78	

* = substantial postoperative loss of verbal IQ

Learning tests verbal retention through paired associate learning of easy and hard pairs. Good memory may depend on efficient associations with appropriate images and events, mediated by the RH. The logical memory task examines immediate free recall of two paragraphs following auditory presentation. The paragraphs depict strong emotional events and their proper recall may require RH integration. But it is also possible that the deficits are due to extracallosal surgical hippocampal damage rather than to disconnection per se (D.W. Zaidel, Ch. 7 of this volume). In either case, it is important to distinguish failure on the tests due to memory deficit from failure of integrative linguistic processes. In the Logical Memory subtest, failure of memory may result in loss of details, whereas linguistic failure of discourse processes may result in loss of theme. Commissurotomy patients, especially those with partial disconnection, lose both details and theme (D. Zaidel, personal communication). Loss of details may reflect loss of interhemispheric cooperation, whereas loss of theme may reflect loss of RH contribution.

While memory loss following cerebral commissurotomy may underlie some linguistic deficits, vigilance, attention or concentration deficits may account for the memory loss itself (Beniak et al., 1985). However, extensive long-term experience with the California series shows intact vigilance in numerous long and boring tests, including direct measures of concentration, such as the Rotary Motor Pursuit (D.W. Zaidel, personal communication). Dimond (1979a) did claim to have found failure of auditory vigilance in the disconnected left but not right hemisphere (see also Dimond, 1976). However, Ellenberg and Sperry (1979) did not replicate Dimond's finding and disputed his conclusions.

TABLE 2

Performance of complete and partial commissurotomy patients on the Logical Memory and Associate Learning subtests of the Wechsler Memory Scale. The mean is for 25-year-old normal subjects, taken from Wechsler, 1945

	Logical Memory			Associate Learning		
	A	B	Total	Easy	Hard	Total
Max score	24	22	23	9	12	21
Mean	9.8	8.76	7.99	8.56	7.16	15.48
SD	3.74	3.37	2.95	.45	2.63	3.48
Complete commissurotomy	6.62	4.37	10.99	7	1	8
Partial commissurotomy	4.0	1.5	5.5	6.25	1	7.25

Right hemisphere communication battery

The battery (Gardner and Brownell, 1986) is composed of ten separate subtests which assess the cognitive abilities required to integrate information, to understand nonliteral language, to appreciate humor, and to recognize emotion. All subtests show selective deficits following right hemisphere damage. Therefore, testing of the disconnected LH of patients with complete cerebral commissurotomy should show comparable deficits. Similar deficits might also be expected in free field testing of these patients, where the LH usually dominates the responses, especially in tests as linguistically complex as this battery.

Table 3 includes the free field performance of four commissurotomy patients on the battery. All patients showed deficits on at least some tests and good performance on others. There were large individual differences. There were consistently severe deficits across all patients in the appreciation of prosody, in understanding pictorial metaphor and in retelling stories, reflecting impaired recognition of emotional intonation, pragmatics and discourse, respectively. Performance on the battery depends on a good memory and presupposes intact intelligence and a fairly high educational level. For example, many items depend on lexical ambiguity and awareness of abstract or infrequent meanings (e.g., kid = boy, baby goat). Consequently, it is useful to focus on the profile of L.B., who is intellectually highest in the California series and of above-normal intelligence and linguistic awareness. His scores are included in Table 3.

TABLE 3

Percentage correct scores of commissurotomy and hemispherectomy patients on the Right Hemisphere Communication Battery in free vision

	Patient surgery IQ		L.B. split 106(110, 100)	N.G. split 77(83, 71)	A.A. split 78(77, 82)	R.Y. split 90(99, 79)	D.W. R hemidec 67(80, 60)	B.S. L hemidec 75(79, 71)
	Maximum score (number of items)	Chance score (%)						
I. Humor								
1. Cartoons	4	50	100	50	50	50	25	75
2. Verbal humor	8	20	87.5	25	62.5	37.5	25	75
3. Humor production	2	0	100	0	0	0	0	100
II. Emotion								
4. Prosody	8	25	50	37.5	37.5	37.5	100	87.5
III. Nonliteral language								
5. Indirect requests	8	25	37.5	25	25	75	37.5	62.5
6. Pictorial metaphor	8	25	75	75	12.5	50	75	62.5
7. Verbal metaphor	4	0	100	100	75	100	100	100
8. Sarcasm	6	8	50	17	17	50	50	83
sarcasm	4	8	50	0	0	25	25	100
truth	1	8	+	+	+	+	+	+
lie	1	8	–	–	–	+	+	–
9. Alternative word meanings	16	33	75	25	0	25	50	56
nouns	8	33	87.5	25	0	25	50	25
adjectives (metaphors)	8	33	62.5	25	0	25	50	87.5
IV. Integrative processes								
10. Inferences	8	6.25	62.5	12.5	50	12.5	0	12.5
correct infs	8	50	87.5	75	75	75	12.5	75
true facts	8	50	75	75	75	100	100	100
incorrect infs	8	50	25	87.5	50	37.5	37.5	12.5
false facts	8	50	0	50	25	62.5	62.5	87.5
11. Narrative comprehension	6	25	100	50	50	50	50	100
emotional	2	25	100	50	50	0	50	100
noncanonical	2	25	100	50	50	50	50	100
integrative	2	25	100	50	50	100	50	100
retelling	6	0	50	50	33	33	50	50
elements/ sequencing	4	0	75	50	50	50	75	75
emotional elts	2	0	0	50	0	0	0	0

From Zaidel E, Spence SJ, Kasher A, in preparation.

In addition to the deficits in common with other patients, L.B. made surprising mistakes in appreciating indirect requests (e.g., 'can you pass the salt?' interpreted as a request for the salt rather than as a yes/no question), in recognizing pictures of metaphors (heavy heart: sad or carrying a large heart-shaped object), and in differentiating ambiguous words (Alternative Word Meanings, e.g., shallow = not deep or stupid). L.B.'s difficulty with lexical ambiguity was not in recognizing both meanings simultaneously, which he did, but rather in preferring the literal meaning to a metaphor and in choosing word association when synonymy was called for (e.g., 'quick – horse,' instead of 'smart – quick'). This suggests that normal RH contribution is not to linguistic knowledge but rather to linguistic control.

L.B. had good performance on Humor, Verbal Metaphor, Inferences and Narrative Comprehension. For example, in the Inferences test, which requires a shift of interpretation, L.B. was correct on 8 out of 8 'correct inferences' but recalled only 7 out of 8 true facts (signalling some loss of memory), and was correct on only 2 out of 8 'incorrect inferences'. However, on a separate occasion, when allowed only one choice for each vignette, he chose 4 out of 8 true facts, 2 correct inferences and 2 incorrect inferences. In conclusion, some pragmatic functions that show deficit following right hemisphere damage (Foldi et al., 1983; Gardner et al., 1983; Heeschen and Reiches, 1979; Ross, 1981) do not appear to be impaired in the disconnected left hemisphere. These functions may be especially sensitive to cross-callosal inhibition or a malfunctioning interhemispheric interaction.

Reading passages

Several equivalent forms of the Davis Reading Test were administered to five commissurotomy patients in free field. This timed paper-and-pencil test uses multiple-choice questions to measure speed and depth of comprehension of reading passages of increasing length (Davis and Davis, 1962). Answers were marked with the dominant, right hand, on an answer sheet or designated verbally by the patient. Two patients, L.B. and N.G., received different forms at several-year intervals. In general, both level of comprehension and speed of comprehension were very low (Table 4). L.B.'s scores were the highest but his level and speed percentiles drop to 12 and 14, respectively, when

TABLE 4

Level and speed of comprehension of commissurotomy patients on Davis Reading Test (Davis and Davis, 1962)

Patient	Date	Age	Form	Raw score		Scaled score		11th grade percentile		Scaled score level – speed	
				level	speed	level	speed	level	speed		
L.B.	21/11/73	21	2A	28	20	70	62	56	24	8	*
	8/4/76	24	1C	10	10	68	66	47	36	2	ns
	8/6/81	29	1B	11	13	66	66	38	36	0	ns
	29/8/87	35	1A	11	15	66	67	38	42	−4	?
N.G.	15/11/73	40	2A	3	6	53	56	1	2	−3	?
	13/4/76	42	1C	4	2	63	60	19	5	3	?
	4/6/81	48	1A	0	0	59	59	4	3	0	ns
N.W.	13/12/73	43	1A	5	4	63	61	19	9	2	
R.Y.	30/11/73	50	2A	2	2	52	52	1	1	0	
A.A.	5/12/73	22	1A	5	4	63	61	19	9	2	

* Significant difference.

compared to freshmen entering college. He worked fast but had numerous errors. His first test (1973) showed a considerable advantage of level over speed of comprehension (8 points, 3 are significant at $p = 0.15$), but with subsequent administrations his level of comprehension decreased consistently while his speed of comprehension increased progressively. N.G. showed a significant improvement in level of comprehension from 1973 to 1976 (10 points, 8 are significant at $p = 0.15$) but dropped again in 1981, suggesting lability. These poor scores most probably reflect LH reading in the absence of RH input.

Systematic analyses of right hemisphere language

Both tachistoscopic and somesthetic stimulus lateralization severely restrict the complexity of the linguistic input that can be selectively presented to one hemisphere. They also limit the experimental paradigms that can be used. In addition, these paradigms introduce short-term memory effects that may be lateralized, and create increased opportunities for interhemispheric cross-cueing. Consequently, in 1970, a contact-lens technique for continuous hemispheric ocular scanning of complex visual arrays was developed, allowing visual guidance of manual control by one hemisphere (Zaidel, 1975). Standardized visual tests could now be administered to each hemisphere separately.

Psycholinguistic analysis

Initial testing of the disconnected RHs of the two selected complete commissurotomy patients, L.B. and N.G., who were fitted with contact lenses, disclosed little or no speech, much auditory comprehension, some reading, and little writing. Language comprehension, both auditory and visual, became the focus of study. Auditory language comprehension was studied by lateralizing visual multiple-choice arrays for left-hand pointing responses rather than by lateralizing the auditory messages themselves. It is more difficult to lateralize auditory stimuli to one hemisphere, since both ears are represented in both hemispheres. Although the disconnected RH has no speech it has access to articulatory control. Rather, its main deficit is that it has no phonetic ability and an impoverished output phonology. But it must have input phonology sufficient to recognize a large auditory vocabulary and many morphological constructions. Its limited phonology in turn prevents verbal rehearsal and results in a limited short-term verbal memory, which may restrict its ability to process certain complex syntactic constructions.

Sound (phonology) The disconnected RHs have large auditory vocabularies and smaller visual vocabularies. Thus the RH has acoustic access routes to its lexicon, but we know little about the abstract phonological structure available to it. There is indirect evidence that the acoustic representation of words in the RH is auditory rather than phonetic (see Liberman, 1974), where 'phonetic' refers to the coding of sounds by reference to the articulatory apparatus. Also, standardized auditory-comprehension tests with multiple-choice pictures which include both semantic and phonological decoys usually lead to semantic errors. This is in contrast to the LH, which rarely makes errors and, when it does, the errors tend to be phonological. We could interpret this to mean that the RH does not use phonological analysis as heavily as the LH.

The RHs performed poorly on an auditory-discrimination test where the names of the decoy pictures differ from the monosyllabic consonant-vowel-consonant or consonant-vowel names of the targets in only one phoneme, including a difference of one to three phonetic features. When background noise was added to the stimuli, reducing the signal-to-noise ratio, the disconnected RHs suffered more than the disconnected LHs (Zaidel, 1978b). It would seem that noise lacking specific phonetic information interferes more with the hypothesized auditory analysis by the RH, which would depend on general acoustic cues, than with phonetic analysis by the LH. If we take the RH to represent a nonphonetic or nonlinguistic processor, then the rank ordering of phonetic confusions in the RH can be taken to rank the linguistic codedness of these features. These confusion data do not support the view that place of articulation is linguistically more coded than voicing (cf. Molfese et al., 1983). The disconnected RHs are especially poor in decoding nonsense consonant-vowel syllables with initial stop consonants ('ba', 'da', 'ga', 'pa', 'ta', 'ka') by matching them with lateralized visual probes (the letters 'b', 'd', 'g', 'p', 't', or 'k') (Zaidel, 1976a). The stop consonants with their fast formant transitions are taken to be highly coded phonetic stimuli that require the specialized linguistic processing of the LH.

The argument that the RH is phonetically deficient because it has no access to a constructive speech mechanism has other circumstantial support in the apparent limitation of its short-term verbal memory (STVM). For example, the disconnected RH is poor at decoding Token Test instructions, which depend on memory more than on grammar (Zaidel, 1977). It would seem that the RH has an STVM with a capacity of 3 ± 1 items, whereas the LH has the normal capacity of 7 ± 2 items (cf. Goodglass et al., 1970).

The disconnected RH is poor at evoking the phonological image of an object name. When asked to point to two of four pictures 'whose names sound alike, but which mean different things' – for example a (finger)nail and a carpenter's nail, the RH of patient L.B. could occasionally point to the homonyms even though it could not name them (Zaidel and Peters, 1981). But no disconnected RH in the California series can construct the phonological image of a printed word; that is, the RH has no grapheme-phoneme conversion. This is illustrated by the inability of these RHs to match rhyming words that have different end-spellings or to point to the correct regular spelling of a spoken nonsense word. It thus appears that the RH can discern meaning directly from print, using perhaps some visual orthographic rules, but without intermediate phonological recoding (assembled phonology). Nor does the disconnected RH have good cognitive access to the phonological representation of the lexical item (addressed phonology).

Grammar (syntax) The Token Test contains a part that introduces grammatical and syntactic complexity (verbs, prepositions, conjunctions, dependent clauses, etc.). The disconnected RHs were more sensitive to memory load than to these linguistic variables (Zaidel, 1977). L.B. and N.G. were also given several tests designed expressly for comprehension of grammatical structures, where the responses consisted of pointing to multiple-choice pictures. The tests included Lee's Northwestern Syntax Screening Test, Carrow's Test for Auditory Comprehension of Language, Shewan's Sentence Comprehension Test, and Fraser, Bellugi and Brown's Test (Zaidel, 1973, 1978a,b, 1983b).

The results may be summarized as follows:

1. The disconnected RH can comprehend not only nouns, verbs and adjectives, but also a variety of grammatical and syntactic structures extending from functors to tense markers and to simple syntactic transformations such as the passive or negative.

2. Despite a large variability across subjects and linguistic structure, uninflected morphological constructions (free morphemes) are easier for the RHs to decode than inflected ones (bound morphemes). There is a relatively high error rate in the RH on lexical items involving numbers, adjectives of relative quantity, and quantifiers (such as 'four', 'many', 'middle'). By contrast, the RHs are adept at understanding spatial prepositions (such as 'on', 'in', 'under'). The RHs scored least well on constructions requiring the coordination of subject-object and direct-object – indirect-object relationships, which place a premium on word order, as well as making a heavy demand on memory.

3. The RH is affected by the length of the message more than by its syntactic complexity or by the difficulty of its vocabulary (Shewan's Test;

Zaidel, 1973, 1978a).

4. The RH finds syntactic structures (predication, complementation, etc.) more difficult than grammatical categories (case, number, gender, tense, etc.), which are in turn more difficult than morphological constructions (suffixes), with lexical items (nouns, verbs, adjectives, adverbs and prepositions) being relatively easiest (Carrow's Test; Zaidel, 1978b).

Lexical semantics The disconnected RH has a rich auditory lexicon which extends over diverse semantic fields and parts of speech. It recognizes some abstract nouns, many verbs, and spatial prepositions. It is facile in handling a variety of semantic relations, including synonymy, hoponymy (class membership) and antonymy. It is sensitive to word frequency and thus, presumably, to linguistic or communicative experience. It is sensitive to word associations (there is auditory semantic facilitation in a visual lexical-decision task lateralized to the LVF; Zaidel, 1983a), and it recognizes linguistic and nonlinguistic references to significant events and people. It shows linguistic access to what the cognitive psychologist calls 'episodic' (personal) and 'semantic' information (knowledge about the world). In picture vocabulary tests, the RHs of L.B. and N.G. scored at the level of normal children of ages 16 and 12, respectively. But, when the picture decoys in the multiple-choice arrays were all semantically associated with the target, these RHs made many errors (e.g., on Lesser's Test; Zaidel, 1973), more syntagmatic than paradigmatic. It would seem that the RH lexicon is characteristically connotative rather than denotative. That is, the semantic network in the RH is denser than in the LH, the arcs are longer (connect more distant concepts) and the organizing semantic relationships are more loosely associative and dependent on experience.

Both disconnected hemispheres of five commissurotomy patients of the California series can perform lexical decisions on orthographically regular English strings ('Is this a word or not?') (see next section). The RHs showed facilitation of decision when the targets were preceded by semantically related auditory primes, but not when preceded by the same printed primes. This may be because the visual vocabularies of the RHs seem to be proper subsets of the corresponding auditory vocabularies. The visual vocabularies of the RHs of L.B. and N.G. reach equivalent mental ages of only 10 and 7 years, whereas the auditory vocabularies of the RHs of these patients reached mental ages of 16 and 12, respectively (Zaidel, 1978). Moreover, the visual vocabulary of the RH seems to be organized differently from the auditory vocabulary in the same hemisphere, in the sense of showing a different pattern of deficits as a function of part of speech. For example, the RH visual vocabulary has selectively weaker representation for prepositions and verb forms in '-ing' as compared with nouns or adjectives (Zaidel, 1983b).

The disconnected RH does not seem to have a selective inability to decode actions or verbs, as claimed earlier (Gazzaniga, 1970). It often fails to execute a printed action flashed in the LVF, but can point to a picture depicting the action among multiple choices and can imitate manual actions when vision and feedback are restricted exclusively to the RH (Zaidel, 1982). It is suggested that under these circumstances LH dominance and usurping of control over the motor system can be minimized or bypassed (Levy, 1974). A similar 'release' of RH action is claimed to occur under conditions of simultaneous hemispheric activation and divided attention, as in dichotic listening (Gordon, 1980).

Lexical decision The lexical decision task is an attractive paradigm for tapping latent word recognition processes in the disconnected RH. The binary decision ('Is the stimulus string a real word or a nonword?') need not be verbal, and accurate response need not logically involve conscious access to the meaning. Indeed, Milberg and Blumstein (1981) showed that Wernicke aphasics who could neither read some words aloud, nor match them with pictures, could nonetheless accurately perform lexical decisions on them. This suggests that lexical decision can be pre-lexical. On the other hand, the task seems metalinguistic and could involve error monitoring competence that is independent of reading per se (Zaidel, 1987). Moreover, it is believed to involve post-lexical access components (Foss, 1989).

Using a set of lateralized concrete nouns and orthographically regular nonwords (Zaidel, 1989a), the disconnected RHs of five commissurotomy patients (four complete, one partial) could perform lexical decision above chance. The LHs were superior in accuracy but not in latency. Using signal detection measures, the LHs had greater sensitivity, but the bias in the RH (which tended to be less than 1, i.e., the RH tends to respond 'yes') varied independently of LH bias (which was both less and greater than 1). A model which posits that the lexical decision process in the RH is similar to that in the LH, but with a smaller vocabulary, predicts a consistently smaller sensitivity but larger bias in the RH. This model was not supported by the data. Rather, the results suggest independent and different lexical decision processes in the two hemispheres (Zaidel, 1989a). In fact, results with normal subjects (e.g., Measso and Zaidel, in press) suggest that words and nonwords may be identified by separate and parallel processes, at least in the normal RH. In that case, signal detection may be the wrong model to apply to the data because it presupposes a specific model of lexical decision by comparing a signal and a noise distribution. We also found that lexical decision underestimates the ability of the disconnected RH to read by matching the lateralized word with a picture.

In another lexical decision task which contrasted concrete and abstract nouns as well as 'active' and 'quiet' verbs, both disconnected hemispheres performed better on concrete nouns but not on active verbs (Eviatar et al., 1989). L.B.'s latencies showed no visual hemifield advantage for words rated as emotional by the subject after the test, but a large and significant right visual hemifield advantage for words rated as neutral.

A third lexical decision experiment presented abstract nouns of variable lengths (4, 5, 6 letters long) and emotionality ratings (emotional, neutral) to three complete commissurotomy patients (L.B., N.G. and R.Y.). Length affected accuracy in the LH but not consistently in the RH, probably because of the generally low accuracy with LVF presentations. Emotionality affected the accuracy of all patients in the RVF but only of R.Y. and L.B. in the LVF. Thus, there is no evidence for a selective sensitivity to concreteness, length or emotionality in the disconnected RH, at least from these difficult tasks.

Learning How did the RH acquire its spoken and visual vocabularies, and its linguistic repertoire? A plausible guess is that it learns from experience. If the RH is especially important for assimilating novel information (Zaidel, 1979a; Goldberg and Costa, 1981), and if vocabulary is acquired, as Chomsky believes, through one-trial learning, then the RH may be especially important in acquiring new vocabulary, by ostensive definition, as it were. Alternatively, the RH may acquire its vocabulary from the LH, through repeated exposure in context. Unfortunately, little is known about hemispheric differences in learning rates and styles. This remains a high-priority area for future study, with important theoretical as well as applied clinical implications.

An important element of learning by experience is the ability to benefit from error correction. There is some suggestive evidence that the RH may be competent in detecting certain linguistic errors, such as spelling violations in words (Zaidel, 1979c), but that it fails to take advantage of external error correction (Zaidel, 1987). As an exploratory step, we studied the short-term improvement in lexical decision by either hemisphere as a result of training. Specifically, following a standard tachistoscopic presentation of a lexical decision task using abstract nouns and manipulating word length and emotionality (Eviatar and Zaidel, 1989), we presented the same words for prolonged reading, asked the subject to respond verbally and by pointing with the left hand, corrected him/her if necessary, and repeated the correct response

TABLE 5

Lexical decision in the disconnected hemispheres before and after training

Patient	Measure	Presentation time (ms)	Before		After	
			LVF	RVF	LVF	RVF
R.Y.		150				
	RT (ms)		1313	1534	1182	1332
	Accuracy (%)		73	37.5	77	53
	Sensitivity (d prime)		0.23	0.47	−0.49	0.92
N.G.		150				
	RT (ms)		1414	1270	1299	944
	Accuracy (%)		59	79	62	76
	Sensitivity (d prime)		0	1.21	0.28	1.44
L.B.		80				
	RT (ms)		1260	909	1083	986
	Accuracy (%)		55	75	78	82.5
	Sensitivity (d prime)		−0.45	0.52	1.27	2.18

both verbally and by pointing. Table 5 shows the scores before and after training. The data indicate that training helped improve accuracy in both disconnected hemispheres but the RH nonetheless generally failed to reach above-chance performance. Training also failed to produce consistent effects as a function of either word length or emotionality in the disconnected RH.

This experiment focuses on abstract learning restricted to simple feedback. More effective learning may occur with illustration of meaning in context or by providing decision rules and criteria for responses. This remains to be explored in future research.

ERP correlates of semantic expectancy in sentential context Kutas et al. (1988) presented auditory sentences followed by a visual word which varied in 'cloze' probability (how likely is that word to be given as a completion to that sentence?). Words with a low cloze probability for a particular sentential context seem unexpected, incongruous and anomalous. An example is, 'Every Saturday morning he mows the *chair*.' They found an enhanced central parietal (roughly Wernicke's area) negativity (N400) which correlated highly with the cloze index of semantic anomaly (i.e., incongruity or unexpectedness), and showed a larger amplitude over the normal right hemisphere.

The task was administered to two commissurotomy patients of the California series (L.B. and N.G.) and to three of the Cornell series (J.W., V.P. and P.S.) by flashing two completing words to the two hemifields simultaneously (Kutas et al., 1988). All patients showed an N400 in response to anomalous completions in the right hemifield, but only P.S. and V.P., who can name left hemifield stimuli, showed an N400 to word completions in the left hemifield. In the corresponding behavioral task the patients could indicate by pointing whether the word completion made sense or not in the sentence context in both hemifields; performance in the left hemifield was worse than in the right hemifield, but still above chance.

Kutas believes that the N400 reflects a particular semantic organization of a lexicon designed to be used primarily for production, hence the absence of the ERP to left hemifield words in L.B. and N.G. and in J.W.

Speech in the right hemisphere or noncallosal interhemispheric transfer? Occasionally, split brain patients can name stimuli shown in the left hemifield (LVF) or palpated with the left hand

(Butler and Norsell, 1968; Levy et al., 1972; Teng and Sperry, 1973; Johnson, 1985; Myers, 1984). This could be due to (1) improper lateralization of the stimuli, (2) ipsilateral projection of sensory information from the LVF or left hand to the left hemisphere where verbalization occurs, (3) subcortical transfer of cognitive information sufficient to identify the stimulus to the LH following recognition by the RH, (4) cross-cueing from the RH to the LH using shared perceptual space (e.g., the RH may fixate a related item in the room, thus identifying it to the LH, or it may trace the shape of the object in question with the head so the movement can be 'read off' by the LH), (5) RH speech. Only when all other alternatives are ruled out can RH speech be considered seriously, given the weight of evidence so far. To date, there is no incisive evidence for RH speech in any of the patients in the California series (Myers, 1984). For example, it was never demonstrated that LVF or left hand stimuli could be named while nonverbal right hand identification of these stimuli failed.

Improper lateralization with tachistoscopic presentations can occur not only by failure to fixate the central mark (e.g., deviating all the way to the left so that both lateralized stimuli fall in the RVF), or by saccades to the stimuli that are too long, but also by fixating a point behind the plane of the image, by strabismus or by dyplopia, resulting in divergent fixations by the two eyes in binocular presentations. Improper lateralization with the contact lens or the lateral limits method can be due to faulty calibration.

Verbalization of left field stimuli due to ipsilateral sensory projection is limited to simple sensory features and to items uniquely identified by them, such as curved vs. straight contours or sharp vs. dull edges (Trevarthen and Sperry, 1973). Effective cross-cueing depends critically on the size of the stimulus set and on prior exposure to it, so that simple cues suffice to eliminate alternatives. L.B. often uses a verbal cross-cueing strategy where the LH seems to guess in turn each letter making up the name of the stimulus by going through the alphabet with the RH apparently signaling when the correct one is reached (D.W. Zaidel, 1988). Subcortical transfer of semantic features abstracted from the meaning of the stimulus may occur without necessarily identifying the stimulus uniquely. These features are thus not generally sufficient for naming. They include affective and connotative information (happy, sad, pleasant, etc.) (Zaidel, 1976b; Sperry et al., 1979), as well as associative (sensory and semantic) (Myers, 1984; Myers and Sperry, 1985), categorical ('animals that go in the water', one picture shown to each field simultaneously), functional ('shoe-sock') or abstract (communication: envelope-telephone) (Cronin-Golomb, 1984) features. Visual images do not seem to transfer subcortically. Thus, naming of left field stimuli in the absence of cross-field matching is not good evidence for RH speech. For example, cross-comparing may fail because of a tendency to neglect one hemifield with bilateral presentations.

D.W. Zaidel (1988) studied correct verbalizations and elegant examples of writing of the names of pictures restricted tachistoscopically to the LVF of complete commissurotomy patient L.B. She concluded that the verbalizations did not represent RH speech but that the RH could often write in cursive with the left hand the names of simple line drawings without being able to name them aloud. Thus, the disconnected RH has some writing but little or no speech (cf. also Levy et al., 1971).

Developmental analysis

In order to compare linguistic performance across hemispheres, tests and patients, we measured performance in terms of equivalent mental age scores on standardized developmental tests for first language acquisition. Although an identical total score does not guarantee identical solution strategies or error patterns, the resulting developmental profile of RH language could be relevant to the debate on the ontogenesis of language lateralization in the brain (cf. Segalowitz and Gruber, 1977). Furthermore, to the extent that the RH supports language in some aphasics, our data would also be relevant to the 'regression hypothesis' in aphasia; that is, whether the sequence of stages in language dissolution is the reverse of the sequence of normal language acquisition.

Lenneberg (1967) hypothesized that the two cerebral hemispheres are equipotential for language processing, but that during ontogenesis RH language competence is progressively inhibited as the LH becomes dominant for language by age 10. Such inhibition can only be removed with interference or malfunction in the LH, permitting RH compensation. In this view, latent RH competence for language should remain arrested at some uniform level of language development. However, this would not be required by a hypothesis of selective inhibition of specific RH functions such as speech in the adult brain. Curiously, the latter notion never seems to have been entertained in print.

Three facts are revealed by a systematic sampling of the developmental status of the disconnected RH on tests of diverse linguistic and paralinguistic skills as well as on tests of cognitive operations allegedly prerequisite for linguisitic skills. First, RH competence is locally 'developmentally coherent', in the sense that it often corresponds to a well-defined developmental stage in terms of total scores on specific tasks. Second, RH strategies and error patterns often diverge from those of normal children even when the total score is the same. Third, the general profile of RH language does not correspond uniformly to any stage in first language acquisition. Thus, the RH pattern of muteness with substantial auditory language comprehension is 'abnormal'. Similarly, no normal child who has learned how to read has a much smaller visual vocabulary than auditory vocabulary. Even for auditory language comprehension alone, the developmental profile of the disconnected RH is abnormal, with a rich auditory picture vocabulary but poor receptive grammar and poor comprehension of long, nonredundant phrases (Zaidel, 1978c).

Those local language functions that do show developmental coherence probably reflect 'processing modules' that are functionally relatively independent and are structurally separable or localizable. In general, the disconnected and (isolated) RHs tend to parallel the developmental pattern more in the semantic and acoustic analysis of single spoken words with well-specified denotations; the RHs tend to resemble the developmental pattern less well for auditory comprehension of grammatical structures and least for reading.

In sum, the level of competence of most components of RH language is in the range of that of 3 – 6-year-old normal children. It is likely that up to that age both hemispheres participate in and interact during language development. Thereafter, some RH components, such as speech, are functionally suppressed, whereas others, such as comprehension of lexical items, continue to develop in the RH into adulthood. Thus, different components of language lateralize to, or specialize in, the LH to different degrees and have different neurological histories. Since RH language does not correspond to a stage in first language acquisition, neither does the language of an aphasic who relies on the RH for recovery of language. For such aphasics, the 'regression hypothesis' is therefore false (Zaidel, 1978a).

Aphasiological analysis

A second measure for comparing RH language performance across hemispheres, patients and functions is in terms of percentile ranks relative to patients with acquired aphasia due to LH lesions. This, again, provides an independent measure in terms of another model of partial language structure – namely, language dissolution. Moreover, the comparison should help determine to what extent different aphasic syndromes represent compensatory language recovery by the intact RH. Does, then, the RH language profile parallel any known aphasic syndrome?

Reading Impressionistically, the total language profile of the disconnected RH comes closest perhaps to aphasic alexia associated with an anterior speech deficit. RH muteness really parallels global aphasia, but it may be said to approximate non-fluent aphasia. Anterior aphasics also resemble the disconnected RHs in their grammatical and phonological deficits and in their reliance on lexical semantics for decoding more complex phrases (Berndt et al., 1983). The RH reading deficit resembles sentence alexia, but this is not a powerful localizing symptom (Kertesz, 1979). Even more, RH reading resembles acquired deep dyslexia (Coltheart, 1983). Both syndromes show semantic errors in reading comprehension, as well as better reading of concrete content words than of abstract function words, and both lack grapheme-to-phoneme conversion. On the other hand, deep dyslexics are much less impaired linguistically than are the disconnected RHs. Deep dyslexics can speak and can read aloud, and their auditory vocabulary and sentence comprehension are superior to those of the disconnected RH. We now believe that deep dyslexics frequently resort to lexical semantic access by the RH during reading when LH mechanisms fail (Schweiger et al., 1989).

Auditory comprehension Neither aphasics nor the RH show the normal shared-features advantage in dichotic listening to nonsense stop consonant – vowel syllables (benefitting from shared phonetic features between the sounds in the two ears). Tests of phonemic discrimination using common words disclose good RH scores, again comparable to the mean of a heterogeneous aphasic population (ranging from the 36th to the 72nd percentiles) (Zaidel, 1978b). On the other hand, some studies of left brain-damaged aphasics show an increased left ear advantage in dichotic listening correlated with language recovery that surpasses the competence of the disconnected RH. For example, the Berlin et al. (1974) patient who had left temporal lobectomy was tested sequentially after the surgery and showed a fixed right ear score but a progressively increasing left ear score. The left ear advantage scores of aphasics with presumed RH language takeover (Johnson et al., 1977) are consistent only with the upper level of RH competence in the split brain, elicited under favorable conditions (pointing responses to picture probes, etc.). Thus the presence of the disconnected LH seems to prevent the disconnected RH from exhibiting its full phonetic potential.

On tests of auditory comprehension of single words, the disconnected and isolated RHs score around or below the mean of an unselected group of aphasics and show the same pattern of deficits for specific semantic word categories (in decreasing order of competence: objects, geometric shapes, actions, colors, numbers, letters) as fluent and nonfluent aphasics (Goodglass, 1982).

Grammar Tasks of auditory comprehension of grammar (Zaidel, 1973, 1978a) disclose that the disconnected RHs are more sensitive to length than to difficulty of vocabulary or to syntactic complexity, whereas mixed, unselected aphasics are most sensitive to syntactic complexity. On Carrow's Test the RHs are superior to receptive aphasics in morphology but inferior in syntax (Carrow, unpublished data, 1975). Interestingly, rank-order correlation of item difficulty on this test between the RHs and the receptive aphasics is higher with moderate than with severe aphasics and higher after speech therapy than before therapy, suggesting RH language compensation in the milder, chronic aphasics (Zaidel, 1978a). Other syntax tests suggest a higher correlation between the RH and Wernicke's aphasics than between the RH and Broca's aphasics (Zaidel, 1973). In general, aphasics seem more sensitive to linguistic variables of the task, whereas the disconnected RHs seem more sensitive to paralinguistic and perceptual constraints.

In sum, although the psychometric language competence of the disconnected RH is often comparable to that of a group of aphasics, the RH profile does not correspond to any classic syndrome. Actually, classic syndromes may apply to less than half of an unselected group of aphasics (Benson, 1979). The RH contribution to language in aphasia appears selective: it applies to some tasks, some of the time. The total aphasic syndrome more often than not probably reflects a complex, dynamic interhemispheric interaction with a frequently shifting locus of hemispheric control.

Pragmatics and paralinguistics So far, little has been learned of the possible contribution of the disconnected RH to the pragmatics of natural language, because so little spontaneous overt linguistic behavior is observed in these patients when communication is restricted to the RH. However, phenomenological observation reveals several important facts. Although the testing paradigms used to elicit language ability in the disconnected right hemisphere are artificial, the patients usually understand the instructions and respond appropriately, even when wrong. Most of the time, the disconnected right hemisphere takes appropriate turns in responding and occasionally it shows that it knows that it is unable to answer. Moreover, when the left hemisphere errs about stimuli available to the right hemisphere, the right hemisphere often shows awareness of the error and may even attempt to correct it nonverbally. This may be signalled by an emotional response showing dissatisfaction, or by temporary manual motor dominance and control in an attempt to reverse or erase a left hemisphere response.

Occasionally, especially in the beginning of a testing session with the contact lens system for continuous ocular scanning, patient N.G. fails to respond appropriately by manual pointing to multiple-choice pictures. Her left hand then tends to wander aimlessly over the page and point randomly where there are no stimuli. These occasions, however, seem limited to cases where the right hemisphere is unable to do the task.

Although the right hemisphere could match verbs with lateralized pictures describing the action (Levy, 1969; Zaidel, 1976b), it had limited ability to initiate responses to verbal commands (Zaidel, 1982). This is not due to the inability to form the appropriate motor patterns, since the disconnected right hemisphere can imitate those same patterns well (D. Zaidel and Sperry, 1977). The deficit may reflect conflicting hemispheric demands on the motor pathways, due to left hemisphere dominance over the left hand through ipsilateral control. Even so, this may reflect a right hemisphere pragmatic deficit in responding appropriately to commands.

Benowitz et al. (1983) administered parts of a standardized test for nonverbal communication (PONS – Profile of Nonverbal Sensitivity; Rosenthal et al., 1979) separately to the RH and LH of L.B. and in free vision with verbal responses to N.G., R.Y. and N.W. Forty video items showed 2-second emotional scenes, portrayed either by the facial expression alone or by conventional body movements alone. L.B.'s RH performed normally on the facial expressions but poorly on the body movements, whereas his LH was more impaired in facial expressions. All three other split-brain subjects scored extremely poorly on the face channel when verbally identifying freely viewed test items. This deficit presumably reflects LH processing. Responses to body movements and intonational qualities of voices varied from one patient to another (Benowitz et al., 1983). This result is consistent with findings in hemisphere-damaged patients and argues for a role for the RH in evaluating the significance of social interactions through nonverbal cues, particularly facial expressions.

Relationship of language to cognition in the disconnected right hemisphere

There is no doubt that the disconnected right hemisphere has a severely limited short-term verbal memory for both span and sequence (Zaidel, 1978c; see also review by D.W. Zaidel, Ch. 7 of this volume). We have argued above that this cognitive limitation constrains phonological and syntactic processing in the right hemisphere.

Could experimental data on right hemisphere language limitations reflect poorer performance due to attentional deficits during the tests? On the contrary, Dimond (1979a,b) found that a lateralized vigilance task showed decline in the disconnected left hemisphere but stable sustained attention in the right. However, these results were disputed and not replicated by Ellenberg and Sperry (1979). In fact, there is considerable circumstantial evidence that right hemisphere language is more labile over time, less deterministic across stimuli, and more variable across individuals than left hemisphere language, even when restricted to subsystems for which the hemispheres appear to have roughly equal competence. Thus, there are large interindividual differences in the absolute levels of competence of the disconnected right hemispheres, even though they all respect the same general pattern. Moreover, right hemisphere scores show a consistent short-term variability – that is, weak uniformity or concordance between subsequent administrations – even when the average long-term performance remains stable. This variability applies both to superior (e.g., auditory-picture vocabulary) and inferior (e.g., decoding nonredundant phrases, such as in the Token Test) component right hemisphere language functions (Zaidel, 1979b). It also applies to problem-solving strategies (such as in the Raven Progressive Matrices; Zaidel, 1981).

Can hemispheric differences in linguistic competence in turn be attributed to hemispheric differences in intelligence? That depends on which definition of intelligence is adopted. Most of the primary abilities in factorial theories of intelligence are hemispherically impure. For example, both Spearman's Hierarchical Abilities model and Thurstone's Mental Abilities model distinguish a verbal factor and a spatial factor. These factors involve components from both hemispheres. For example, Thurstone's analysis has revealed that verbal ability is indexed by size of vocabulary, as well as by syntactic skill. But we found that receptive vocabulary is largely bilaterally represented. Similarly, the spatial factor includes the ability to perform embedded figures tasks, which we found to be specialized in the left hemisphere (Zaidel, 1973).

When intelligence is defined with a nonverbal measure of 'g', the superordinate factor that is hypothesized to enter all intelligence tests, as with Raven's Progressive Matrices, both disconnected hemispheres have similar IQs (mean right hemisphere for L.B. and N.G. = 83, mean left hemisphere = 87) (Zaidel et al., 1981).

Nor can right hemisphere language deficits be accounted for in terms of the immaturity of putative prerequisite cognitive operations. A Piagetian analysis of spatial concepts in the disconnected hemispheres (Zaidel, 1978c) showed that neither hemisphere corresponds to a consistent cognitive stage and that there was no correlation between the syntactic competence of either hemisphere and its developmental stage in acquiring the concrete operational structures of reversibility, coordination and conservation.

One characterization of the cognitive styles of the two hemispheres borrowed from intelligence research does seem to capture the information-processing strategies that each disconnected hemisphere brings to bear on linguistic and visual-spatial problems alike. This is the characterization in terms of Thurstone's two visual-closure factors (Zaidel, 1978c). The right hemisphere seems to specialize in the first closure factor: the synthetic ability to integrate unrelated parts into a meaningful whole, as in figure completion. The left hemisphere seems to specialize in the second closure factor: the analytic ability to detect component features in more complex and distracting Gestalts, as in figure disembedding. From a linguistic point of view, the right hemisphere has the ability to label linguistic concepts by arbitrary, conventional linguistic Gestalts (words), but it does not seem to have the rich combinatorial generative capacity of the left hemisphere to operate on and combine these linguistic structures and to appreciate the associated grammars.

Certainly, the disconnected right hemisphere is remarkably passive during test situations, quite unlike the isolated right hemisphere in patients following dominant hemispherectomy. It can respond meaningfully by pointing with one hand to complex alternatives formulated by the experimenter and presented in a multiple-choice paradigm, but it seems incapable of generating spontaneous behavior, linguistic or otherwise. This makes assessment of competence difficult and of expressive abilities impossible. Most probably this right hemisphere 'passivity' reflects left hemisphere dominance over motor pathways in an attempt to ensure unified behavior. The dominance of the disconnected left hemisphere may apply even to tasks where its competence is inferior to that of the right. Similarly, the generally superior performance in the left is more resistant to cognitive perturbation, such as response delay, change in required strategy, ambiguity of possible answers, and change in stimulus modality (Zaidel, 1978c).

Other series

The Cornell series

Gazzaniga and his associates have documented some language testing in three patients who underwent a two-stage corpus callosotomy for intractable seizures, sparing the anterior commissure (Table 6). V.P. is a patient of M. Rayport and was tested earlier by McKeever and associates, who showed visual, auditory and tactile disconnection symptoms (McKeever et al., 1981), but also evidence for emerging RH speech (McKeever et al., 1982, 1985). What was originally interpreted in the latter paper as a reduction of left hemifield anomia under hypnosis is now believed to have reflected an early stage of speech development in the RH of patient V.P. (W. McKeever, personal communication, 1985). Indeed, standard disconnection symptoms may well have progressively decreased as well.

V.P., a right-handed female who was 27 years old at the time of testing, was six years old at onset of seizures, is presumed to have had early LH pathology, and has an IQ of 72 (Myers, 1984). She has evidence for both receptive and expressive RH language (Table 6). V.P. is reported to have car-

TABLE 6

Elements of right hemisphere language comprehension in five patients: this updates Gazzaniga, 1983

	Patient				
Skill	P.S.	V.P.	J.W.	N.G.	L.B.
Phonetic					
Rhyming (visual)	+	+	–	–	–
Rhyming (priming task)	n.a.	n.a.	+	n.a.	n.a.
CV discrimination (dichotic)	n.a.	+	–	–	–
Semantic					
Picture/word – word/picture	+	+	+	+	+
Synonym	+	+	+	+	+
Antonym	+	+	+	+	+
Function (clock-time)	+	+	+	+	+
Class membership:					
Superordinate	+	+	+	+	+
Subordinate	+	+	+	+	+
Verbal commands	+	+	–	–	–
Action verbs	+	+	+	+	+
Electrophysiological response to semantic violation (N400)	+	+	–	–	–
Behavioral response to semantic violation	+	+	+	+	+
Syntax					
Active/passive sentences	n.a.	+	–	+	+
Token test	+	+	+/–	–	–

n.a. = not available.

ried out written commands presented to her RH prior to the development of RH speech (Sidtis et al., 1981). Her RH could perform the Token Test (no data reported, Nass and Gazzaniga, 1987) and could disambiguate phrases such as 'peeling the skin' and 'the peeling skin' but had difficulty interpreting word order information. Her RH could also match printed high-frequency nouns for semantic relationships, and could detect a semantically incongruous word at the end of a visually presented sentence in either visual half-field, eliciting an N400 visual evoked potential bilaterally (Kutas et al., 1988). Thus, there is evidence for some phonetic, syntactic and semantic processing in the RH of V.P. There is also evidence for good reading and for speech, which is said to have developed progressively since surgery, although remaining inferior to that of her LH. By one year post-op V.P. could name 32% of LVF words and eventually her RH naming became perfect.

J.W., a right-handed male, was 26 years old at time of testing. He was 13 when seizures started, and had corpus callosotomy, sparing the anterior commissure, by D. Wilson at Dartmouth. His IQ is above 91. He showed consistent disconnection symptoms and evidence for modest auditory comprehension but no speech in the disconnected RH, though there is some conflicting data on the latter (cf. Myers, 1984). J.W. is said to best approximate L.B. and N.G. of the California series. His dichotic listening score in the RH was not above chance and his rhyming score was little better than chance, much inferior to V.P.'s. He could match printed words for semantic relationships and carry out printed commands above chance in his RH, though not as well as V.P. He could not match printed words for rhyming in the left visual half-field. J.W.'s RH was poor on the Token Test and could not disambiguate the printed noun phrases ('peeling skin'). But his RH could perform grammaticality judgments.

P.S., a right-handed man, was 15 when he underwent a two-stage corpus callosotomy sparing the anterior commissure. He first developed seizures with a left temporal lobe focus at age 2. He has RH comprehension and speech, which are said to have developed with time following surgery. His IQ is 89. At age 15, P.S. could already match printed verbs lateralized to the LVF with pictures of the corresponding actions, and he could match printed words presented in the LVF for various semantic relationships. He could also match LVF words for rhyming and could spell with his left hand the names of pictures lateralized to the LVF. Thus, early on, his RH showed phonological, syntactic and semantic competence in auditory comprehension and in reading, as well as in writing.

Moreover, like V.P., P.S. is said to have bilateral representation of speech, which developed especially between 20 and 36 months post-surgically. He is said to transfer phonetic or articulatory information from the RH to the LH, although this casts some doubt on claims for persisting auditory (and visual) disconnection. Like V.P., P.S. shows a bilateral N400 to semantic incongruities. His RH can define verbs and nouns, carry out printed commands, and perform the Token Test.

In sum, two of Gazzaniga's patients, V.P. and P.S., show evidence for extensive RH language, including speech. Gazzaniga and associates interpret these to reflect abnormal brain reorganization due to early LH damage. The damage must be much more extensive than in the California series and it probably involved language centers in the LH. The third patient, J.W., approximates the language competence of the disconnected RHs of L.B. and N.G. of the California series.

The Yale series

Spencer et al. (1988) summarize the neuropsychological changes of 18 out of 22 patients who underwent complete (10 patients, 8 with a 2-stage surgery) or partial (8 patients) callosal section for relief of intractable epilepsy. In no case was the anterior commissure sectioned. The neuropsychological battery included the Speech Sounds Perception Test (receptive speech), the controlled Word Production Test (fluency), an adaptation of the

Wechsler Memory Scale, and the Wechsler Adult Intelligence Scale. Patients with mild to moderate preoperative lateralized CNS dysfunction (indicated by unilateral impairment of grip strength or a memory deficit, but not both) showed post-operative deficits in language functions, irrespective of extent and location of section. Patients with opposite dominance for speech and handedness suffered particular expressive language deficits, including verbal dysfluency, dysnomia, conduction dysphasia and alexia with or without agraphia. Such deficits are attributed to the surgical interference with interhemispheric compensatory mechanisms associated with late-onset, left-hemisphere seizure disorders.

Unfortunately, no tests for disconnection or for language functions in each hemisphere are reported. Sass (1987) did describe one left-handed patient, K.K., with right hemisphere dominance for speech who is said to show no interhemispheric transfer of visual, tactile and auditory information, but no procedural details were provided. Indeed, the authors' interpretation of the post-operative linguistic deficits assumes abnormal language reorganization due to epilepsy. This conclusion is supported by the large number of patients (11) who showed right hemisphere dominance for language on amytal testing. Thus, in this view, the deficits do not reflect loss of normal right hemisphere contribution to language processing.

The Minneapolis series

Beniak et al. (1985) reported the pre- and post-operative neuropsychological status of 13 patients with corpus callosotomy, although 4 or 5 had inadvertently unsectioned remnants of the splenium. The battery included the Wechsler Adult Intelligence Scale, the Halstead-Reitan Aphasia Screening Test, the Wechsler Memory Scale, a verbal paired-associate learning task, and a test of Verbal Fluency. There were post-operative attentional deficits but no selective language decline. However, these patients also have low IQs (mean full scale 71, range 40 – 105) and extensive presurgical pathology likely to result in abnormal language organization. Again, no tests were undertaken for disconnection or for language functions in the disconnected hemispheres.

In sum, patients in the California series seem unique in their relatively high IQs, freedom from extracallosal damage and normal hemispheric organization for language.

Hemispherectomy

In principle, dominant, left hemispherectomy for lesions incurred in adulthood following normal language acquisition provides the best measure of the linguistic competence of the RH. In practice, the observed pattern in individual cases may be an overestimate reflecting abnormal reorganization of RH language due to early and undetected LH damage. However, the observed pattern may more likely be an underestimate due to undetected abnormality in the remaining hemisphere, or due to hemorrhage and clots created by the surgery itself (Trevarthen, 1984). In any case, the linguistic profile of the isolated RH does not necessarily reflect the contribution of the normal RH to processing natural language. Indeed, lateralization studies of reading in normal subjects reveal a greater contribution of the RH than could be inferred from either commissurotomy or hemispherectomy studies (Chiarello, 1988; Zaidel, 1989b).

Anatomical, physiological and behavioral evidence converge on the conclusion that functional hemispheric specialization is already present at birth (Segalowitz and Gruber, 1977), although functional maturation within each hemisphere may change the pattern of hemispheric specialization throughout development. Moreover, patterns of interhemispheric interaction may change with age because of increases of callosal connectivity with increasing myelinization up to puberty (Lecours, 1975). Still, brain plasticity, which decreases dramatically following puberty, permits language reorganization in the isolated RH following massive early damage to the dominant LH. Thus, persisting linguistic deficits following early RH takeover of language functions may reflect inherent limitations on RH language, and the resulting profile can be regarded as an upper limit on RH language competence (Zaidel, 1985). Unfortunately, here too, the residual deficit may reflect damage to the remaining hemisphere. Indeed, since the cause of the early injury is usually anoxia, infection or general and extensive mechanical insult to the head, the brain tissue of the supposedly healthy hemisphere is unlikely to be normal. Moreover, if the surgery is not done soon after the onset of epilepsy, bilateral damage is likely (Trevarthen, 1984). Conversely, failure to detect deficits may reflect insensitive or misdirected assessment. Thus, the relevance of language deficits following dominant left hemispherectomy due to early lesions to the linguistic profile of the RH remains theoretically ambiguous.

Perinatal lesions with infantile hemiplegia

Infantile hemiplegics form a heterogeneous population with widely different etiologies. Many have an arteriovenous malformation in one hemisphere (Sturge-Weber syndrome) and develop seizures in infancy. The affected hemisphere is atrophied to a greater or smaller extent at birth and it is removed sometime between early infancy and adulthood to check the spread of seizures to the other side. Thus, an important variable, usually unknown, is the extent of damage to the remaining hemisphere due to the original pathology or to subsequent epilepsy. Indeed, the extent of pathology in the surgically removed hemisphere may be inversely related to the degree of functional reorganization in the remaining hemisphere. Moreover, cases where the pathology is incomplete may show less reorganization the older the patient is when the surgical removal occurs. Certainly, with complete hemisphere atrophy, the critical variable is the age of onset of the disease rather than the age at which hemispherectomy is performed.

Left hemispherectomy in the first year is usually followed by grossly normal language development, consistent with the patient's general intellectual level. But more subtle psycholinguistic testing seems to reveal persistent deficits that do not accompany right, nondominant hemispherectomy. Interestingly, early removal of either hemisphere results in persistent visuo-spatial deficits. In the case of left, dominant hemispherectomy this is said to reflect the 'crowding effect' of language reorganization in the RH, and the priority language functions have in the competition for cortical space. Some find greater deficits to visuo-spatial functions specialized in the normal left hemisphere following early right hemispherectomy (Kohn and Dennis, 1974). Normal maturation of such functions in the adult LH presumably depends on earlier stages of development which are specialized in the child's RH (Trevarthen, 1984).

Curtiss (1985) reports that Hood and Perlstein (1955) and Bishop (1983) compared the consequences of left-sided versus right-sided injury in cases of infantile hemiplegics sustaining early damage but not involving hemispherectomy. They noted that right hemisphere damage led only to deficits in articulation and vocabulary acquisition, while left hemisphere injury led to widespread deficits and delays in language acquisition. Annett (1973), whose cases of infantile hemiplegia also involved early damage (before 13 months) without hemispherectomy, demonstrated that subsequent language impairments were far more frequently associated with left hemisphere damage than with right hemisphere damage. Assuming complete hemispheric atrophy, language asymmetry in cases of infantile hemiplegia without hemispherectomy could suggest that pathological inhibition by the diseased hemisphere is more detrimental to language development in the RH than in the LH.

Dennis series

Dennis and associates (Dennis, 1980a,b; Dennis and Kohn, 1975; Dennis et al., 1981; Dennis and Whitaker, 1976; Kohn and Dennis, 1974) followed up three infantile hemiplegics with Sturge-Weber-Dimitri syndrome whose diseased hemisphere was removed in infancy or who had no seizures during language acquisition. Dennis found that left but not right hemispherectomy patients had selective deficits in linguistic and metalinguistic syntactic tasks, such as detecting and correcting errors of surface syntactic structure, comprehending complex syntactic transformations, or producing tag questions to match the grammatical features of a heard statement. Moreover, she found that semantic space was both more lawful and more tightly organized in right hemispherectomy patients. That is, dimensions of semantic relatedness have a stronger and more consistent effect on lexical judgement tasks in the isolated left hemisphere than in the isolated right hemisphere. In reading, left hemidecorticates had grapheme-phoneme conversion deficits and were inferior on morphophonemic or orthographic processing, as well as in processing text (poor retention and fluency); they were superior in logographic or ideographic processing.

Dennis believes that these RH deficits reflect unique RH strategies rather than mere capacity limitations. In this view, RH strategies are limited to lexical sampling of the meaning and of the grammatical function-structure of single morphemes; the strategies exclude the integration of interpretative rules with surface syntax to derive thematic meaning. Thus, Dennis believes that RH strategies are characterized by strong lexical semantics and ideographic reading and by impoverished syntax, phonology and morphology, as well as by deficient integration of syntactic and semantic structures, but not by limited short-term verbal memory. Her view is generally consistent with the principle of a unique RH language profile based on commissurotomy studies.

Bishop (1983) pointed out methodological difficulties with Dennis's cases, arguing that the allegedly impaired syntactic skills in left hemidecorticates were actually within the normal range and reflected difficult tests. Thus, according to Bishop, Dennis and associates used inadequate experimental controls and inappropriate statistics. Specifically, the left and right hemidecorticates were few and not comparable in mental age and intelligence (Peabody estimate) at time of testing; their scores were not distinguishable from intelligence-matched controls (active-passive-negative test), or were not compared with age-matched controls (Token Test, letter cluster judgement task). Even more importantly, these patients need to be followed up to adulthood to rule out a developmental lag interpretation of the deficit following LH decortication (Verity et al., 1982).

Zaidel

In May 1988 we had the opportunity of studying word recognition in B.S., a 28-year-old infantile hemiplegic patient of Dr. Harry Chugani of UCLA who underwent left hemispherectomy at age 24 for intractable epilepsy. All members of his immediate family are right-handed. Neuropsychological and language tests were conducted by Susan Curtiss, Cathy Jackson, Roger Light and Avraham Schweiger of UCLA. B.S. shows general language retardation, general impairment in neuropsychological tests and variable performance on visuospatial tests, ranging from normal to severely deficient. His grammar and reading are at about the fourth grade level (Curtiss and Jackson, personal communication).

B.S. could match words for rhyming but had difficulty with nonwords. His word recognition showed an overwhelming effect of word frequency, a moderate effect of word length, a small effect of phonological regularity, and no effect of concreteness. This shows that B.S. is using both the lexical and non-lexical routes in reading (Patterson et al., 1985), but that his grapheme-phoneme conversion rules are rudimentary. His lexical route is dominated by orthographic addressing rather than by semantic addressing. This suggests that the part-of-speech effect and semantic paralexias characterize RH reading only when it is not constrained by phonology.

Other studies

Some investigators report no linguistic deficits in the isolated RH (Strauss and Verity, 1983) or even better language following dominant than non-dominant hemispherectomy (Verity et al., 1982). Others find supernormal verbal intelligence in the isolated LH (Griffith and Davidson, 1966). And many report a developmental lag in the acquisition of language but no specific linguistic deficits (Byrne and Gates, 1987). However, such claims are weak insofar as they constitute negative evidence and usually rely on a few uncomparable patients. What is clearly necessary is a large epidemiological study, controlling for residual function in the diseased hemisphere, age of removal, degree of pathology in the remaining hemisphere, age at testing, and using a standardized assessment battery which includes measures of syntax and pragmatics.

Strauss and Verity (1983), who reported no evidence of linguistic deficit (but impaired visuospatial and constructional abilities) in either isolated hemisphere (and better gesturing in the isolated right than left hemisphere), used the Boston Diagnostic Aphasia Examination – an aphasia battery not designed to detect syntactic or pragmatic disturbances. Moreover, the patients were a heterogeneous group (none with Sturge-Weber) with variable onset of seizures and age at hemidecortication and with CT and EEG indication of damage to the remaining hemispheres. Verity et al. (1982) also report that patients with an isolated right hemisphere had greater gestural fluency but lesser verbal fluency than patients with an isolated left hemisphere. The isolated RHs also performed better on a task requiring comprehension of complex ideas. Differences in intelligence and mental age may account for at least some of the asymmetries.

Day and Ulatowska (1979) studied two children, one with seizure onset at age 1 : 1 years, dominant left hemispherectomy at 3 : 11, and persisting seizures in the remaining RH, the other with seizure onset at age 3 : 6 and staged subtotal right hemispherectomy at ages 4 and 4 : 5. They found reduced intellectual functioning in both children and asymmetries consistent with adult specialization. The subject with left hemispherectomy showed metalinguistic deficits, preserving the ability to detect anomalous linguistic patterns but not to correct them.

Ogden (1988) studied two infantile hemiplegics. K.O'F. was a woman of 45 years of age when tested, and had had her left hemisphere removed at age 15 and 17. J.Sy was a 34-year-old man who had had a left hemispherectomy at age 18. Both had a higher verbal than performance IQ, and both patients had good spoken language and auditory comprehension (normal Token Test) though both made errors on an active-passive test. Significantly, both improved their scores on a written version of the test. Reading and writing were very slow and calculation was impaired. Word fluency was also impaired. Recent verbal memory was normal. K.O'F. has shown a remarkable progressive improvement in Wechsler IQ and recent verbal memory for 17 years following surgery. Her steadily improving recent verbal memory was accompanied by deteriorating recent nonverbal memory.

Thus, RH takeover of language functions 'at the expense of' nonverbal functions can continue well into adulthood but does not extend to some more recently evolved functions, such as calculation and reading. Moreover, some language functions associated with the RH, such as word fluency, remain impaired.

Comparison of language competence in the disconnected and normal RH with impaired language in some (e.g. global) aphasics suggests that the diseased LH may inhibit residual linguistic functions in the RH. Thus, in future studies it is best to concentrate on early hemispherectomies with complete perinatal lesions and no evidence of damage to the remaining hemisphere. The alternative is to develop systematic measures of degree of pathology in the removed and remaining hemispheres and to document the effects of differing age of onset of disease and age at surgery.

Hemispherectomy in cases with childhood lesions following language acquisition

The theoretical significance of hemispherectomy

for infantile hemiplegia to our understanding of RH language is that it represents an upper limit on possible competence: persisting deficits must reflect inherent limitations of RH language, which cannot be compensated for by plasticity. This depends on two assumptions: (1) that LH damage is complete, resulting in RH takeover of language, and (2) that there is no residual pathology in the remaining RH nor pathological inhibition of language development and functioning by the diseased LH. Often, neither assumption is true. For example, in Sturge-Weber's syndrome, angiomatosis and progressive calcification are initially restricted to the post-rolandic area with greatest involvement in the parieto-occipital lobes. At surgery there is variable hemispheric atrophy (Alexander and Norman, 1960). Furthermore, the onset of seizures can be accompanied by language loss (Alexander and Norman, 1960). Indeed, early onset of seizures and late surgeries are associated with poorer eventual intellectual status. Thus, the disease can be progressive.

Some of the methodological difficulties of perinatal lesions are avoided in hemispherectomy for lesions whose onset postdates normal language acquisition. Since plasticity decreases dramatically between ages 5 and 13, the resulting RH language profile is closer to normal.

Hillier

Hillier (1954) reports the case of a 14-year-old boy who had undergone left hemispherectomy in 1952. The boy disclosed no speech immediately following surgery but could utter simple words (mother, father, house) on the 6th postoperative day. At discharge, 36 days after surgery, he appeared to have 'normal powers of comprehension' and to enjoy music considerably. A constant improvement in the motor aphasia was noted even at 27 months postoperatively but occasional anomia persisted. He could read individual letters but not words.

Gott and Zaidel

Gott (1973a,b) and Zaidel (1973, 1979c, 1982) described two cases of hemispherectomy, one dominant, the other nondominant, with lesion onset following the normal acquisition of auditory comprehension and speech, but before the normal acquisition of reading.

Case R.S. R.S. was a normal, right-handed girl until age 7 : 8, when symptoms due to a left intraventricular ependymoma tumor first occurred. Following partial resection at age 8, the tumor recurred, leading to a total left hemispherectomy including the basal ganglia at age 10, when she was already pubescent. Following hemispherectomy, multiple shunt operations were performed.

R.S. was 14 and with a right hemiplegia when tested. She could read and write before and after the initial resections although some learning difficulties occurred. When tested, R.S. was essentially alexic, agraphic and acalculic. Auditory comprehension was better than expressive speech and semantic and pragmatic awareness seemed superior to syntactic competence. R.S. was mildly dysarthric, her ongoing speech was telegraphic, nonfluent and agrammatic and she had moderate-to-severe anomia. Her naming errors tended to be semantic and she often substituted a skillful nonverbal pantomime, a vocal imitation or relevant singing for an unavailable name. Some verbal or semantic paraphasias occurred in responsive naming but rarely in free speech. Literal paraphasias or neologisms were rare. Sentence repetition broke down after three items and showed a strong semantic focus, a prevalence of concrete and egocentric interpretations as well as a tendency to perseverate. Metalinguistic tests, such as defining words or performing sentential transformations on request, were particularly difficult.

Reading in R.S. was assessed with the reading tests in Schuell's Minnesota Test (S) and in Goodglass and Kaplan's Examination (G). She had no phonetic spelling and her limited reading vocabulary consisted of words she recognized on sight, as visual templates. She could match geometric forms and letters but only in the same case. Both on 'matching (printed) words to pictures' (S.B.3) and on 'matching printed to spoken words' (S.B.4) auditory confusions predominated over visual ones. This is in contrast to D.W. (with right hemispherectomy, see below), in whose reading performance visual errors predominated. Surprisingly, R.S. made 14 out of 32 errors (16 = chance) on 'matching (printed) words to pictures' but only 8 out of 32 errors on 'matching printed to spoken words'. Thus it seems that the acoustic representation of the word facilitated reading in R.S. more than did the corresponding pictures. This suggests that R.S. can make lexical judgements without semantic access, perhaps by generating an orthographic code from an acoustic one.

R.S. could not read sentences or paragraphs (S.B.5, S.B.7; G.IV.D). Thus, it seems that the isolated RH cannot acquire reading by itself. This contrasts with the disconnected RHs which show substantial reading competence, presumably acquired in association with the LH before the callosal section. The tendency toward auditory mediation in the limited reading of R.S. suggests that her RH was 'using' an LH reading strategy of phonetic recoding. This may be an example of 'crowding': a take-over of nonverbal 'space' by new language functions, and a 'usurpation' of RH style by LH strategies when the brain is young enough and the skill to be acquired is immature enough. In this case the use of an LH reading strategy was probably a suboptimal solution since it was thwarted by poor RH expressive ability. Some supporting evidence for the hypothesis that the reading strategy in R.S., such as it was, was different from the reading style of the disconnected RHs of N.G. and L.B. comes from their respective patterns of scores on 'matching printed to spoken words' (S.C.4) compared with 'matching words to pictures' (S.C.3; G.IV.C). R.S. was relatively better on the former, N.G. and L.B. were better on the latter.

Relation to aphasia There seemed to be no simple association between this patient and the commonly accepted classical aphasic syndromes. Like a Broca's aphasic, her speech was dysfluent, semantically appropriate and heavily stereotyped, frequently agrammatic and occasionally telegraphic. But unlike such an aphasic, R.S. had excellent intonation, which she often used as a syntactic cue. She also had high phrase length, good articulatory agility and relative variety (if simplication and malformation) of syntactic form. She also had more word-finding difficulties and verbal paraphasias. Unlike a Wernicke's aphasic, R.S. was not paragrammatic; she was relatively informative, had less frequent paraphasias in running speech, and had comparatively superior auditory language comprehension, naming and repetition. Finally, although she shared word-finding difficulties and paraphasic pattern with anomic aphasics, unlike them she was also dysfluent and agrammatic, had some verbal paraphasia in responsive speech, and had good recognition of her deficit, if not of her errors.

Relation to disconnected right hemisphere In general, the auditory comprehension of R.S. surpassed her speech ability when judged both clinically and developmentally (Zaidel, 1973, 1979c). We have already seen that her auditory comprehension profile was remarkably similar to that of the disconnected RH's. Indeed, her language development during 4 years of testing showed little improvement in Token Test scores, but rapid growth of auditory vocabulary (PPVT) comparable to that of normal children of similar mental ages. Increasing ability to handle metalinguistic tasks, partial remission of anomia and increasing syntactic competence were also observed. The two language components showing by far the widest discrepancy between the disconnected and isolated RH are clearly speech and reading. The disconnected RH seems mute but not illiterate, whereas the isolated RH of this patient could speak, albeit poorly and with a unique constellation of symptoms, but it could not read, write or perform simple arithmetic. R.S. also had a persisting visuospatial deficit which may be attributable to a parieto-occipital lesion in the RH for a shunt, or else due to the 'crowding' effect of RH language.

Case D.W. D.W. was left-handed, as are two of his siblings, when his right hemisphere was removed at age 7 : 9. However, right internal carotid amytal injection prior to surgery showed sustained speech and comprehension. D.W. has fluent speech with minor slurring and he also possesses relatively intact language comprehension. But longitudinal testing of his reading, writing and calculation skills has demonstrated severe, persisting and stable dyslexia, dysgraphia and dyscalculia which resist instruction. D.W. is aware of his deficits and often attempts to circumvent or camouflage them. In contrast to R.S.'s extremely small sight vocabulary, D.W. uses simplified phonetic rules in his spellings and misspellings. D.W. also has severe visuo-spatial and constructive impairments and his inability to carry a tune contrasts sharply with R.S.'s excellent melodic singing.

D.W. can read and correctly write to dictation individual letters with occasional reversals (e.g., reading 'p' for 'b', writing 's' for 'z' and 'i' for 'j'). Silent and oral reading are equally impaired and consist of laborious phonetic decoding syllable-by-syllable. Frequent confusions occur between words with similar visual frames, i.e., same initial or final letters (e.g., 'house' and 'horse') and reversals are common (e.g., 'was' and 'saw'). Phonetic spelling is verified by the preponderance of vowel as opposed to consonant errors (e.g., 'chire' for 'chair'). On subtests S.B.3 and S.B.4 of Schuell's aphasia battery, D.W. had mostly visual errors.

These deficits are paralleled by a severe visuo-spatial and constructive disorder which is characterized by poor spatial (e.g., 3-dimensional) representation and weak topographical orientation, in contrast to good attention to detail. There is a mild impairment or lability in left – right discrimination but no finger agnosia. D.W. does not have the Gerstmann Syndrome, and in general he corresponds better to a developmental dyslexic than to an adult with acquired alexia and agraphia. Indeed, D.W. matches well the clinical description of Boder's dyseidetic (as opposed to dysphonetic) dyslexic (Boder, 1971) or of Critchley's visual (as opposed to auditory) subsyndrome. It is as if, when trying to read a word, auditory information provided by subsequent guesses interferes with and modifies the contents of a labile, disordered short-term visual store which is interrogated regularly. The error patterns of D.W. during reading suggest that he uses a primitive visual strategy similar to non- or beginning readers. In summary, D.W. has good perceptual differentiation of written symbols and mapping of letters into sounds but poor integration of individual letters or phonemes into units by context-sensitive rules. The responsible mechanism may well be poor association of visual form with auditory linguistic units that are larger than phonemes (Zaidel, 1979c).

Comparison of D.W. with B.S. Both patients lost use of one hemisphere before reading acquisition. D.W. could not match nonwords for rhyme. His word recognition shows an effect of phonological regularity, an effect of word length and moderate effects of concreteness and frequency, suggesting reliance on both the nonlexical and the lexical routes of word recognition. There is an apparent interaction of word frequency with phonological regularity and length, suggesting that orthographic addressing becomes important when grapheme-phoneme conversion fails. In general, the reading of B.S., the infantile hemiplegic who lost use of his LH early, is better than the reading of D.W., who lost use of his RH relatively late. The two exceptions are concrete and regular low-frequency words, which are worse in B.S. Interestingly, D.W.'s reading aloud is sensitive to word concreteness, whereas B.S.'s is not. Thus, cortical plasticity has a stronger effect than innate hemispheric prewiring for reading control. Still, both hemispheres seem necessary for normal reading acquisition, if not maintenance.

The case of D.W. is theoretically important because it at once refutes Orton's theory that abnormal interhemispheric competition is the necessary neurological cause of developmental reading disability when accompanied by weak laterality and directional confusions. D.W. was indeed left-handed and he is visuo-spatially impaired and dyslexic, but, alas, he has no inter-hemispheric competition because he has a single hemisphere. It is logically possible that D.W. would have been a developmental dyslexic even had his RH remained intact. His mother insists, however, that before the onset of symptoms at age 6 : 1 he had precocious visuo-spatial and constructive abilities. It is also possible that D.W.'s left-handedness denotes an unusual cortical organization for language, with reading and speech localized in opposite hemispheres. The neurological possibility of such interhemispheric anatomical/functional dissociation is important and its demonstration here would be unique.

Patterson et al. (1989)
Case N.I. N.I. was a normal, right-handed girl, an average student until age 13, when lethargy and transient aphasic episodes led to generalized convulsions. By one year following onset she had a right hemiplegia, right homonymous hemianopsia, and some dyspraxia. A total left hemispherectomy was performed 30 months post onset of disease, diagnosed as Rasmussen's encephalitis with widespread abnormalities of the left neocortex. Presurgical periictal states included dysphasia but speech deteriorated radically 14 months post onset. Preoperative amytal testing was inconclusive but showed speech arrest only with RH injection.

Postoperative speech at age 17 is dysfluent, agrammatic and anomic. N.I. is a poor reader but shows a distinctive profile: she recognizes letters though she is poor at naming them and is unable to give their sound equivalents. She can discriminate very common words from orthographically similar nonwords but her lexical decision performance falls off quickly as word frequency declines. Her lexical decision is not sensitive to word imageability or part-of-speech, but her reading aloud is sensitive to these variables. She can comprehend concrete, common printed words by matching with pictures although she occasionally makes semantic errors. She has some success in oral reading of very familiar and highly imageable words, and here too she is prone to semantic paralexias. She can repeat but never read nonsense words and has poor phonological awareness: she cannot pronounce subcomponents of words, add or delete phonemes. Finally, N.I. can barely match words and is impaired in matching pictures when precise semantic distinctions are required.

The authors note that N.I.'s reading pattern closely resembles that of the disconnected RHs of L.B. and N.G., with the exception of her substantial as against their absent oral reading. N.I.'s reading performance is also identical in pattern, though not in level, to that of a deep dyslexic.

Case H.P. H.P. was the product of a normal pregnancy and delivery. Shortly after birth she was diagnosed as suffering from Turner's Syndrome. She was right-handed and an above-average student until almost 10 years old, when progressively severe seizures started. A total left hemispherectomy was performed at age 15, leading to the diagnosis of Rasmussen's encephalitis. Although the macroscopic histopathological examination revealed no focal lesions, the cortex showed varied and extensive degrees of damage and atrophy. Presurgical verbal IQ was 82, performance 67. Verbal memory was mildly impaired and spatial memory was severely deficient.

When tested at age 17 her general mental level was that of a normal 11-year-old. Her reading was delayed but not deviant. The authors concluded that the RH plays no necessary role in supporting reading skills involving single word recognition, comprehension and pronunciation.

In summary, hemispherectomy for lesions with onset following language acquisition but before adulthood reveals no selective deficits with right hemidecortication but severe language deficits and a characteristic profile with left hemidecortication.

The isolated RH supports auditory comprehension best, speech to a lesser extent and reading least. RH auditory comprehension is semantically based and pragmatically sensitive but syntactically and phonologically impoverished, with a limited short-term verbal memory. Melody and articulation are good. The RH may be necessary but certainly not sufficient for reading acquisition. The reading profile of the isolated RH following removal of the reading LH is characterized by ideographic reading, semantic errors and sensitivity to word familiarity and concreteness. This profile resembles that of the disconnected RH except for the presence of oral reading in the isolated RH.

Hemispherectomy with lesion onset in adulthood

Virtually all cases have had cursory, informal testing or some clinical assessment. None reports systematic, analytic neurolinguistic studies.

Early studies

Zollinger (1935) reports the case of a 43-year-old female with progressively severe aphasia (monosyllabic speech) preoperatively, and further reduced speech vocabulary following hemispherectomy. At least residual auditory language comprehension was indicated by her ability to show her teeth when asked to, several hours postoperatively. A small increase in vocubulary (from 'all right', 'yes', 'no', to 'thank you', 'please', 'sleep') was achieved through training before death on the seventeenth postoperative day. The author speculates on a gradual development of a speech center in the right hemisphere prior to surgery.

Crockett and Estridge (1951) describe the case of a 37-year-old male who had undergone left hemispherectomy sparing half of the globus pallidus, a third of the caudate nucleus and the entire thalamus. Immediately postoperatively he could comply with simple commands, distinguish left from right and say yes and no. Speech started deteriorating one month postoperatively due to recurrent tumor until death 117 days postoperatively.

French et al. (1955) report the case of a 38-year-old male with a severe preoperative global aphasia and improved postoperative language (fair speech comprehension and production). The authors believe that the right hemisphere had assumed language functions from the left preoperatively.

Smith and Burklund

Of the six cases of dominant hemispherectomy for tumor including the basal ganglia and the anterior dorsal portions of the thalamus in right-handed adult males reported by Burklund (1971), two (case 5, 21 years old when operated, and case 8, 37 years old when operated) demonstrated no postoperative language function, either expressive or receptive, until their death two and a half months and two days postoperatively, respectively. Two other cases (case 10, 48 years old; and case 12, 47 years old) demonstrated the ability to comprehend and carry out simple commands 24 hours and 4 hours following surgery, respectively, but not thereafter until death 7 and 6 months postoperatively, during which period they responded to no verbal or written stimuli. But Burklund believes these cases to be atypical.

Of the remaining two cases, one (case 4, 54 years old) who survived for one and a half months had expressive aphasia one year preoperatively although he then responded to simple commands and reacted appropriately to jokes. Following left hemidecortication the language functions were unchanged until only a few days before his death, when he was too ill to respond to verbal stimuli. Preoperative right hemisphere takeover of language functions is likely in this case.

The last case (47 years old , surgery in 1965) was studied extensively by Smith (Smith, 1966; Burklund and Smith, 1977) and showed expressive and receptive aphasia postoperatively. Immediately after surgery he attempted but was unable to speak and used solely expletives and short emotional phrases. He could not repeat words but could follow simple verbal commands. A pattern of gradual postoperative improvement of language functions together with improved attention span revealed the ability to sing complete familiar songs with good articulation 5 months after surgery, as well as better repetition and occasional propositional speech 10 months postoperatively. Five and a half months postoperatively this patient could perform simple arithmetic and could select colors from among five choices to aural or written names. He showed only minimal writing ('cow'), but was fairly accurate (85/112 items correct) on the Peabody Picture Vocabulary test six months postoperatively. This latter score improved to 98 by 13 months postoperatively.

Gott and Zaidel (Gott, 1973; Zaidel, 1973, 1979c, 1982)

Case G.E. Patient G.E. was a right-handed woman who had right, nondominant hemispherectomy for a glioma at age 28. She had lost her musical skill and presented severe visuo-spatial and constructive deficits but retained her reading, writing and arithmetical abilities apparently intact. Occasionally, she showed evidence of 'pseudoalexia', where her LVF deficit led her to ignore the left half of some initial words in the beginning of lines of print, especially when the retained portion actually spelled a common word. But, in general, G.E. appeared to read normally. Thus, although the RH cannot learn to read by itself, at least after age 5 (R.S.), and although the RH may be necessary for reading acquisition (D.W.), nonetheless the RH does not seem to be necessary for word and sentence reading once the skill has been acquired (G.E.). This view is consistent with models of normal RH reading functions which emphasize its role in learning to assign meaning to new linguistic symbols (e.g. Gordon and Carmon, 1976).

Conclusions

Summary

The overwhelming neuropsychological evidence suggests that the right hemisphere has a unique linguistic profile, although different experimental populations yield somewhat different profiles. When the left hemisphere is separated from the right, either through complete cerebral commissurotomy or through surgical removal of the left hemisphere, the emerging language profile is characterized by (1) much better language comprehension than speech, (2) better auditory comprehension than reading, (3) visual word recognition which proceeds ideographically or through orthographic rules, but without grapheme-phoneme translation, so that phonological representation is 'addressed' lexically rather than 'assembled', (4) a rich lexical semantic system but poor phonology and an impoverished syntax, (5) paralinguistic competence in appreciating the communicative significance of prosody, facial expressions and bodily postures.

In addition, although the disconnected left hemisphere possesses a normal linguistic repertoire in standardized clinical testing, with more analytic tests it reveals severe deficits in discourse analysis, reading, appreciation of prosody, and certain intersentential pragmatic functions.

What scant evidence exists on adult patients with hemidecortication for lesions of late onset supports the commissurotomy data. Earlier lesions show progressively diminishing plasticity from birth to adulthood. But even in infantile hemiplegics, some limits to plasticity are apparent. Early left hemisphere atrophy leads to lasting, if subtle, deficits in syntactic processing, phonological awareness and discourse analysis, in addition to visuospatial deficits.

Lacunae

To date, much is still unknown about language abilities in the disconnected and isolated hemispheres. Comprehensive analytic studies of patients with relatively healthy hemispheres and fairly normal intelligence are rare. Much more remains to be found about the language profile of each hemisphere in relation to the range of (1) auditory and visual word recognition, (2) phonological processes, (3) syntactic structures and parsing, (4) discourse analysis and (5) monitoring operations. Of special theoretical and clinical importance is an analysis of language learning styles and capabilities in the two hemispheres.

Representativity

The California series of commissurotomy patients is unique. These patients have relatively little extracallosal damage and relatively good intelligence. There is no evidence in any of these patients' neurological histories or subsequent language development for a massive lesion to the language area of the left hemisphere, for early or persisting linguistic deficits and, thus, for language reorganization due to early epileptogenic lesions.

Patients in the California series vary widely in IQ, etiology and localizing symptoms, and yet they conform to the same pattern of results. L.B. and N.G., who were analysed extensively with the contact-lens system for prolonged lateralized presentations, have EEG, MRI and clinical neurological evidence for, if anything, greater right hemisphere than left hemisphere damage. Moreover, the laterality of predominant extracallosal damage in these split-brain patients can at best predict somatosensory deficits and compensatory readjustments in ipsilateral manual transfer but not the observed visual or auditory laterality effects (Zaidel, 1978c).

Other experimental and clinical populations, most notably patients with temporary hemispheric anesthesia with sodium amobarbitol or hemispheric inactivation with unilateral electroconvulsive therapy, confirm the language profile observed in the surgically disconnected and isolated right hemisphere.

Generalizability

Relation to aphasia

Although the linguistic profile of the disconnected and isolated right hemisphere does not correspond to any classic aphasic syndrome, there is general agreement between the profile and the pattern of breakdown and preserved abilities in a majority of aphasics, as, for example, when auditory comprehension is more resistant to damage and recovers sooner than reading and speech (Nielsen, 1946). But some aphasics with lesions restricted to the left hemisphere, such as word-deaf, word-blind and global aphasic patients, do show devastating deficits inconsistent with residual language in the intact right hemisphere. Most likely, these syndromes represent maladaptive maintenance of control in the diseased left hemisphere and pathological inhibition of right hemisphere competence.

Acquired alexia illustrates the range of possible consequences of left hemisphere damage. In deep dyslexia (a form of alexia with agraphia characterized by prevalence of semantic paralexias, better reading of concrete nouns than abstract function words and inability to match words for rhyming) the symptomatology is consistent with intermittent right hemisphere contribution to lexical access together with retained phonological control in the left hemisphere. Indeed, Schweiger et al. (1989) described a deep dyslexic patient with intact visual fields who showed an intermittent shift of dominance for word recognition to the right hemisphere and a prevalence of semantic errors in reading aloud with left hemifield presentations.

Conversely, when patients who have alexia without agraphia (pure alexia) are deprived of their letter-by-letter reading strategy through the use of tachistoscopic word presentations, they can demonstrate significant comprehension by pointing to multiple-choice pictures, even while denying verbally being able to read the word. It has been suggested (Landis et al., 1980), but remains to be demonstrated, that this 'disconnection symptom' reflects 'released' right hemisphere reading.

Thus, evidence from aphasia tends to underestimate the linguistic competence of the right hemisphere. By the same token, recent evidence for pragmatic deficits following right hemisphere damage tends to overemphasize the linguistic deficit of the left hemisphere and thus to overestimate the linguistic competence of the right hemisphere. Much pragmatic deficit must reflect the loss of interhemispheric interaction.

Relation to the normal brain

Methods are now available for finding out when laterality effects in behavioral experiments in normal subjects reflect independent hemispheric processing (Zaidel, 1983a). Most of these experiments have used hemifield tachistoscopic presentations and were therefore restricted to simple stimuli, usually single words. Even so, there is a surprising range of lexical variables that show differential and independent effects in the two visual fields. Effects on lexical decision include length (orthographic); noun concreteness, emotionality, part-of-speech, and associative priming (semantic); and derivational morphology (semantic, phonological). Moreover, in a lateralized rhyming judgement task, the nonrhyme advantage was significant in the left but not the right hemifield (Rayman and Zaidel, submitted; probably an orthographic rather than a phonological effect) and in a noun-verb decision task, there was significant but independent grammatic priming in the two hemifields! Finally, both normal hemispheres appear to show a variety of semantic congruity and incongruity effects (orthographic-semantic 'Stroop-like' facilitation and interference, congruity effects in comparitive size judgement tasks with animal names and digits; Zaidel et al., 1988).

Thus, stimuli and tasks that are beyond the competence of the disconnected right hemisphere seem to be processed independently by the normal right hemisphere. This suggests that the performance of the disconnected right hemisphere is an underestimate of the contribution that the normal right hemisphere makes to language processing. What could be that contribution? Taken together, our data suggest the following functions as plausible candidates. (1) Provide orientation to the nonlinguistic context of the communicative situation, both cognitive and affective. (2) Facilitate reading through quick recognition of recurring visual lexical patterns. (3) Intergrate theme across sentences in discourse. (4) Provide a dynamic resource to complement left hemisphere processing: (i) perform lexical analysis when left hemisphere processes are overloaded; (ii) interpret novel stimuli when the left hemisphere cannot, and furnish alternative or supplementary connotative lexical interpretations on other occasions; (iii) monitor left hemisphere processes during critical tasks.

References

Alexander GI, Norman RM: *The Sturge-Weber Syndrome.* Bristol: John Wright & Sons, 1960.

Annett M: Laterality of childhood hemiplegia and the growth of speech and intelligence. *Cortex: 9,* 4 – 33, 1973.

Beniak TE, Gates JR, Risse GL: Comparison of selected neuropsychological test variables pre-and postoperatively on patients subjected to corpus callosotomy. *Epilepsia: 26,* 543 (Abstract), 1985.

Benowitz LI, Bear DM, Rosenthal R, Mesulam M, Zaidel E, Sperry RW: Hemispheric specialization in nonverbal communication. *Cortex: 19,* 5 – 11, 1983.

Benson DF: *Aphasia, Alexia, and Agraphia.* New York: Churchill Livingstone, 1979.

Berlin CI, Cullen JK, Lowe-Bell SS, Berlin HL: Speech perception after hemispherectomy and temporal lobectomy. Paper presented at the Speech Communications Seminar, Stockholm, 1 – 4 August 1974.

Berndt RS, Caramazza A, Zurif E: Language functions: syntax and semantics. In Segalowitz SJ (Editor), *Language Functions and Brain Organization.* New York: Academic Press, pp. 5 – 28, 1983.

Bishop DVM: Linguistic impairment after left hemidecortication for infantile hemiplegia? A reappraisal. *Q. J. Exp. Psychol.: 35A,* 199 – 208, 1983.

Boder E: Developmental dyslexia: prevailing diagnostic concepts and a new diagnostic approach. In Myklebust HR (Editor), *Progress in Learning Disabilities.* New York: Grune and Stratton, 1971.

Bogen JE: A systematic quantitative study of anomia, tactile cross-retrieval and verbal cross-clueing in the long term following complete cerebral commissurotomy. Invited address, Academy of Aphasia, San Diego, 1979.

Bogen JE: Physiological consequences of complete or partial commissural section. In Oppuzzo MLJ (Editor), *Surgery of the Third Ventricle.* Baltimore: Williams and Wilkins, pp. 175 – 194, 1987.

Bogen JE, Vogel PJ: Cerebral commissurotomy in man. *Bull. Los Ang. Neurol. Soc.: 27,* 169 – 172, 1962.

Bogen JE, Vogel PJ: Neurologic status in the long term following complete cerebral commissurotomy. In Michel F, Schott B, (Editors), *Les Syndromes de Disconnexion Calleuse chez l'Homme.* Lyon: Hopital Neurologique, pp. 227 – 251, 1975.

Bogen JE, Fisher D, Vogel DJ: Cerebral commissurotomy: a second case report. *J. Am. Med. Assoc.: 194,* 1328 – 1329, 1965.

Burklund CW: Cerebral hemisphere function in the human: fact vs. tradition. In Smith WL (Editor), *Drugs, Development, and Cerebral Function.* Springfield, IL: C.C. Thomas, pp. 8 – 36, 1972.

Burklund CW, Smith A: Language and the cerebral hemispheres: observations of verbal and nonverbal responses during 18 months following left ('dominant') hemispherectomy. *Neurology: 27,* 627 – 633, 1977.

Butler SR, Norsell U: Vocalization possibly initiated by the minor hemisphere. *Nature: 220,* 793 – 794, 1968.

Byrne JM, Gates RD: Single-case study of left cerebral hemispherectomy: Development in the first five years of life. *J. Clin. Exp. Neuropsychol.: 9,* 423 – 434, 1987.

Campbell AL, Bogen JE, Smith A: Disorganization and reorganization of cognitive sensorimotor functions in cerebral commissurotomy: compensatory roles of the forebrain commissures. *Brain: 104,* 493 – 511, 1981.

Chiarello C: Lateralization of lexical processes in the normal brain: a review of visual half-field research. In Whitaker HA (Editor), *Contemporary Reviews in Neuropsychology.* New York: Springer Verlag, pp. 36 – 76, 1988.

Code C: *Language, Aphasia and the Right Hemisphere.* Chichester: Wiley, 1987.

Coltheart M: The right hemisphere and disorders of reading. In Young AW (Editor), *Functions of the Right Cerebral Hemisphere.* London: Academic Press, pp. 171 – 120, 1983.

Crocket HG, Estridge NM: Cerebral hemispherectomy; a clinical, surgical, and pathological study of four cases. *Bull. Los Ang. Neurol. Soc.: 16,* 71 – 87, 1951.

Cronin-Golomb A: Intrahemispheric processing and subcortical transfer of non-verbal information in subjects with complete forebrain commissurotomy. Unpublished Doctoral Dissertation. Pasadena: California Institute of Technology, Division of Biology, 1984.

Curtiss S: The development of human cerebral lateralization. In Benson DF, Zaidel E (Editors), *The Dual Brain.* New York: Guilford Press, pp. 97 – 116, 1985.

Davis FB, Davis CC: *Davis Reading Test; Manual, Series 1 and 2.* New York: American Psychological Corporation, 1962.

Day P, Ulatowska H: Perceptual, cognitive, and linguistic development after early hemispherectomy: Two case studies. *Brain Lang.: 7,* 17 – 33, 1979.

Dennis M: Capacity and strategy for syntactic comprehension after left or right hemi-decortication. *Brain Lang.: 10,* 287 – 317, 1980a.

Dennis M: Language acquisition in a single hemisphere: semantic organization. In Caplan D (Editor), *Biological Studies of Mental Processes.* Cambridge: MIT Press, pp. 159 – 185, 1980b.

Dennis M, Kohn B: Comprehension of syntax in infantile hemiplegia after cerebral hemidecortication: left hemisphere superiority. *Brain Lang.: 2,* 472 – 482, 1975.

Dennis M, Whitaker HA: Language acquisition following hemidecortication: linguistic superiority of the left over the right hemisphere. *Brain Lang.: 3,* 404 – 433, 1976.

Dennis M, Lovett M, Weigel-Crump CA: Written language acquisition after left or right hemidecortication in infancy. *Brain Lang.: 12,* 54 – 91, 1981.

Dimond SJ: Depletion of attentional capacity after total commissurotomy in man. *Brain: 99,* 347 – 356, 1976.

Dimond SJ: Tactual and auditory vigilance in split brain man. *J. Neurol. Neurosurg. Psychiatry: 42,* 70 – 74, 1979a.

Dimond SJ: Performance by split brain humans on lateralized vigilance tasks. *Cortex: 15,* 43 – 50, 1979b.

Ellenberg L, Sperry RW: Capacity for holding sustained attention following commissurotomy. *Cortex: 15,* 421 – 438, 1979.

Eviatar Z, Zaidel E: The right hemisphere lexicon: Selective advantage for short emotional words. Unpublished manuscript, Department of Psychology, UCLA, 1988.

Eviatar Z, Menn L, Zaidel E: Right hemisphere contribution to lexical analysis. Manuscript submitted for publication, 1989.

Ferguson SM, Rayport M, Corrie WS: Neuropsychiatric observations on behavioral consequences of corpus callosum section for seizure control. In Reeves AG (Editor), *Epilepsy and the Corpus Callosum.* New York: Plenum, pp. 501 – 514, 1985.

Foldi NS, Cicone M, Gardner H: Pragmatic aspects of communication in brain-damaged patients. In Segalowitz SJ (Editor), *Language Functions and Brain Organization.* New York: Academic Press, pp. 51 – 66, 1983.

Foss DJ: Experimental psycholinguistics. *Annu. Rev. Psychol.: 39,* 301 – 348, 1988.

French LA, Johnson DR, Brown IA, Van-Bergen FB: Cerebral hemispherectomy for control of intractable convulsive seizures. *J. Neurosurg.: 12,* 154 – 164, 1955.

Gardner H, Brownell H: *Right Hemisphere Communication Battery.* Boston, MA: Psychology Service, VAMC, 1986.

Gardner H, Brownell HH, Wapner W, Michelow D: Missing the point: The role of the right hemisphere in the processing of complex linguistic material. In Perecman E (Editor), *Cognitive Processing in the Right Hemisphere.* New York: Academic Press, pp. 169 – 191, 1983.

Gazzaniga MS: *The Bisected Brain.* New York: Appleton-Century-Crofts, 1970.

Gazzaniga MS, Hillyard S: Language and speech capacity of the right hemisphere. *Neuropsychologia: 9,* 273 – 280, 1971.

Gazzaniga MS, Sperry R: Language after section of the cerebral commissures. *Brain: 90,* 131 – 148, 1967.

Goldberg E, Costa LD: Hemisphere differences in the acquisition and use of descriptive systems. *Brain Lang.: 14,* 144 – 173, 1981.

Goodglass H: Disorders of naming following brain injury. *Am. Sci.: 63,* 647 – 655, 1982.

Goodglass H, Berko-Gleason J, Hyde MR: Some dimensions of auditory language comprehension in aphasia. *J. Speech Hear. Res.: 13,* 124 – 143, 1970.

Gordon HW: Right hemisphere comprehension of verbs in patients with complete forebrain commissurotomy: Use of the dichotic method and manual performance. *Brain Lang.: 11,* 76 – 86, 1980.

Gordon HW, Carmon A: Transfer of dominance in speed of verbal response to visually presented stimuli from right to left hemisphere. *Percept. Motor Skills: 42,* 1091 – 1100, 1976.

Gott P: Language after dominant hemispherectomy. *J. Neurol. Neurosurg. Psychiatry: 36,* 1082 – 1088, 1973a.

Gott PS: Cognitive abilities following right and left

hemispherectomy. *Cortex: 9,* 266 – 274, 1973b.

Griffith H, Davidson M: Long-term changes in intellect and behaviour after hemispherectomy. *J. Neurol. Neurosurg. Psychiatry: 29,* 571 – 76, 1966.

Heeschen C, Reiches F: On the ability of brain-damaged patients to understand indirect speech acts. Unpublished manuscript, 1979.

Hillier NF: Case report: Total left cerebral hemispherectomy for malignant glioma. *Neurology: 4,* 718 – 721, 1954.

Hoffman HJ, Hendrick EB, Dennis M, Armstrong D: Hemispherectomy for Sturge-Weber syndrome. *Child's Brain: 5,* 233 – 248, 1979.

Hood P, Perlstein M: Infantile spastic hemiplegia: II. Laterality of involvement. *Am. J. Phys. Med: 34,* 457 – 466, 1955.

Johnson JP, Sommers RK, Weidner WE: Dichotic ear preference in aphasia. *J. Speech Hear. Res.: 20,* 116 – 129, 1977.

Johnson LE: Vocal responses to left visual field stimuli following forebrain commissurotomy. *Neuropsychologia: 22,* 153 – 166, 1984.

Kertesz A: *Aphasia and Associated disorders: Taxonomy, Localization and Recovery.* New York: Grune & Stratton, 1979.

Kohn B, Dennis M: Selective impairments of visuo-spatial abilities in infantile hemiplegics after right cerebral hemidecortication. *Neuropsychologia: 12,* 505 – 512, 1974.

Kutas M, Hillyard SA, Gazzaniga MS: Processing of semantic anomaly by right and left hemispheres of commissurotomy patients: evidence from event-related brain potentials. *Brain: 111,* 553 – 576, 1988.

Lambert AJ: Right hemisphere language ability: 1. Clinical evidence. *Curr. Psychol. Rev.: 2,* 77 – 94, 1982.

Landis T, Regard M, Serrat A: Iconic reading in a case of alexia without agraphia caused by a brain tumour: A tachistoscopic study. *Brain Lang.: 11,* 45 – 53, 1980.

Lecours AR: Myelogenetic correlates of the development of speech and language. In Lenneberg EH, Lenneberg E (Editors), *Foundations of Language Development: A Multidisciplinary Approach.* New York: Academic Press, Vol. 1, pp. 121 – 135, 1975.

Lenneberg EH: *Biological Foundations of Language.* New York: Wiley, 1967.

Levy J: Information processing and higher psychological functions in the disconnected hemispheres of human commissurotomy patients. Unpublished Doctoral Dissertation, Division of Biology, California Institute of Technology, 1969.

Levy J: Psychobiological implications of bilateral asymmetry. In Dimond SJ, Beaumont JG (Editors), *Hemisphere Functions in the Human Brain.* London: Elek, pp. 121 – 183, 1974.

Levy J, Trevarthen C: Perceptual, semantic and phonetic aspects of elementary language processes in split-brain patients. *Brain: 100,* 105 – 118, 1977.

Levy J, Nebes R, Sperry R: Expressive language in the surgically separated minor hemisphere. *Cortex: 7,* 49 – 58, 1971.

Levy J, Trevarthen C, Sperry RW: Perception of bilateral chimeric figures following hemispheric deconnexion. *Brain: 95,* 61 – 78, 1982.

Lezak MD: *Neuropsychological Assessment,* second edition. New York: Oxford University Press, 1983.

Liberman AM: The specialization of the language hemisphere. In Schmitt FO, Worden FG (Editors), *The Neurosciences: Third Study Program.* Cambridge, MA: MIT Press, pp. 43 – 56, 1974.

McKeever WF, Sullivan KF, Ferguson SM, Rayport M: Typical cerebral hemisphere disconnection deficits following corpus callosum section despite sparing of the anterior commissure. *Neuropsychologia: 19,* 745 – 755, 1981.

McKeever WF, Sullivan KF, Ferguson SM, Rayport M: Right hemisphere speech development in the anterior commissure-spared commissurotomy patient: a second case. *Clin. Neuropsychol.: 4,* 17 – 22, 1982.

McKeever WF, Sullivan KF, Ferguson SM, Rayport M: Hemisphere disconnection in patients with corpus callosum section. In Reeves AG (Editor), *Epilepsy and the Corpus Callosum.* New York: Plenum, pp. 451 – 466, 1985.

Measso G, Zaidel E: Effect of response programming on hemispheric differences in lexical decision. *Neuropsychologia:* in press.

Milberg W, Blumstein SE: Lexical decision and aphasia: Evidence for semantic processing. *Brain Lang.: 14,* 371 – 385, 1981.

Milner B: Hemispheric specialization: Scope and limits. In Schmitt FO, Worden FG (Editors), *The Neurosciences: Third Study Program.* Cambridge, MA: MIT Press, pp. 698 – 717, 1974.

Molfese VJ, Molfese DL, Parsons C: Hemisphere processing of phonological information. In Segalowitz SJ (Editor), *Language Functions and Brain Organization.* New York: Academic Press, pp. 29 – 49, 1983.

Moscovitch M: Right hemisphere language. *Top. Lang. Disord.: 1,* 41 – 61, 1981.

Myers JJ: Right hemisphere language: Science or fiction? *Am. Psychol.: 39,* 315 – 320, 1984.

Myers JJ: Cognitive transfer from right to left hemisphere after section of the forebrain commissures. Unpublished Doctoral Dissertation. Pasadena: Division of Biology, California Institute of Technology, 1984.

Myers JJ, Sperry RW: Interhemispheric communication after section of the forebrain commissures. *Cortex: 21,* 249 – 260, 1985.

Nass RD, Gazzaniga MS: Cerebral lateralization and specialization in human central nervous system. In *Handbook of Physiology – the Nervous System, Vol. 5, Part 2.* Washington DC: American Society of Physiology, pp. 701 – 761, 1987.

Nebes RD: Investigations on lateralization of function in the disconnected hemispheres of man. Unpublished Doctoral Dissertation, Division of Biology, California Institute of Technology, 1971.

Nebes RD, Sperry RW: Hemispheric disconnection syndrome with cerebral birth injury in the dominant arm area. *Neuropsychologia: 9,* 247 – 259, 1971.

Nielsen J: *Agnosia, Apraxia, Aphasia: Their Value in Cerebal Localization.* New York: Hoeber, 1946.

Ogden JA: Language and memory functions after long recovery periods in left-hemispherectomized subjects. *Neuropsychologia: 26,* pp. 645 – 659, 1988.

Patterson K, Vargha-Khadem F, Polkey CE: Reading with one

hemisphere. *Brain: 112,* 39 – 63, 1989.

Patterson KE, Marsall JC, Coltheart M (Editors): *Surface Dyslexia.* London: Lawrence Erlbaum, 1985.

Rosenthal R, Hall JA, DiMatteo MR, Rogers PL, Archer D: *Sensitivity to Nonverbal Communications: The PONS Test.* Baltimore: Johns Hopkins University Press, 1979.

Ross ED: The aprosodias. *Arch. Neurol.: 38,* 561 – 569, 1981.

Sass JK: Dual-task methodology and corpus callosotomy: a new model and case study. Paper presented at the 15th Annual International Neuropsychology Society Meeting. Washington, DC, 1987.

Schweiger A, Zaidel E, Field T, Dobkin B: Right hemisphere contribution to lexical access in an aphasic with deep dyslexia. *Brain Lang.: 37,* 73 – 89, 1989.

Segalowitz SJ, Gruber FA: *Language Development and Neurological Theory.* New York: Academic Press, 1977.

Sidtis JJ, Volpe BT, Wilson DH, Rayport M, Gazzaniga MS: Variability in right hemisphere language functions: Evidence for a continuum of generative capacity. *J. Neurosci.: 1,* 323 – 331, 1981.

Smith A: Speech and other functions after left (dominant) hemispherectomy. *J. Neurol. Neurosurg. Psychiatry: 29,* 467 – 471, 1966.

Spencer SS, Spencer DD, Williamson PD, Sass K, Novelly RA, Mattson RH: Corpus callosotomy for epilepsy. II. Neuropsychological outcome. *Neurology: 38,* 24 – 28, 1988.

Sperry RW: Some effects of disconnecting the cerebral hemispheres. *Science: 217,* 1223 – 1226, 1982.

Sperry RW, Gazzaniga MS: Language following surgical disconnection of the hemispheres. In Darley FL (Editor), *Brain Mechanisms Underlying Speech and Language.* New York: Grune and Stratton, pp. 108 – 121, 1967.

Sperry RW, Zaidel E, Zaidel D: Self recognition and social awareness in the disconnected minor hemisphere. *Neuropsychologia: 17,* 153 – 166, 1979.

Strauss E, Verity C: Effects of hemispherectomy in infantile hemiplegics. *Brain Lang.: 20,* 1 – 11, 1983.

TenHouten WD, Hoppe KD, Bogen JE, Walter DO: Alexithymia: an experimental study of cerebral commissurotomy patients and normal control subjects. *Am. J. Psychiatry: 143,* 312 – 316, 1986.

Teng ET, Sperry RW: Interhemispheric interaction during simultaneous bilateral presentation of letters or digits in commissurotomized subjects. *Neuropsychologia: 11,* 131 – 140, 1973.

Trevarthen C: Hemispheric specialization. In *Handbook of Physiology – The Nervous System III.* Washington DC: American Society of Physiology, pp. 1129 – 1190, 1984.

Trevarthen C, Sperry RW: Perceptual unity of the ambient visual field in human commissurotomy patients. *Brain: 96,* 547 – 570, 1973.

Verity CM, Strauss EH, Moyes PD, Wada JA, Dunn HG, Lapointe JS: Long-term follow-up after cerebral hemispherectomy: neurophysiologic, radiologic, and psychological findings. *Neurology: 32,* 629 – 639, 1982.

Zaidel DW: Observations on right hemisphere language function. In Rose FC, Whurr R, Wyke MA (Editors), *Aphasia.* London: Whurr Publishers, pp. 170 – 187, 1988.

Zaidel D, Sperry RW: Memory impairment after commissurotomy in man. *Brain: 97,* 263 – 272, 1974.

Zaidel D, Sperry RW: Some long-term motor effects of cerebral commissurotomy in man. *Neuropsychologia: 15,* 193 – 204, 1977.

Zaidel E: Linguistic competence and related functions in the right cerebral hemisphere of man following commissurotomy and hemispherectomy (Doctoral dissertation, California Institute of Technology). Diss. Abs. Int., 34: 2350B (University Micro-films No. 73 – 26, 481), 1973.

Zaidel E: A technique for presenting lateralized visual input with prolonged exposure. *Vision Res.: 15,* 283 – 289, 1975.

Zaidel E: Language, dichotic listening, and the disconnected hemispheres. In Walter DO, Rogers L, Finzi-Fried JM (Editors), *Conference on Human Brain Function.* Los Angeles: University of California, Brain Information Service, BRI Publications Office, pp. 103 – 110, 1976a.

Zaidel E: Auditory vocabulary of the right hemisphere following brain bisection or hemidecortication. *Cortex: 12,* 191 – 211, 1976b.

Zaidel E: Unilateral auditory language comprehension on the Token Test following cerebral commissurotomy and hemispherectomy. *Neuropsychologia: 15,* 1 – 18, 1977.

Zaidel E: Auditory language comprehension in the right hemisphere following cerebral commissurotomy and hemispherectomy: a comparison with child language and aphasia. In Caramazza A, Zurif EB (Editors), *Language Acquisition and Language Breakdown: Parallels and Divergencies.* Baltimore: Johns Hopkins University Press, 229 – 275, 1978a.

Zaidel E: Lexical organization in the right hemisphere. In Buser PA, Rougeul-Buser A (Editors), *Cerebral Correlates of Conscious Experience.* Amsterdam: Elsevier, pp. 177 – 197, 1978b.

Zaidel E: Concepts of cerebral dominance in the split brain. In Buser PA, Rougeul-Buser A (Editors), *Cerebral Correlates of Conscious Experience.* Amsterdam: Elsevier, pp. 263 – 284, 1978c.

Zaidel E: On measuring hemispheric specialization in man. In Rybak B (Editor), *Advanced Technobiology.* Alphen aan den Rijn: Sijthoff & Noordhoff, pp. 365 – 404, 1979a.

Zaidel E: Long term stability of hemsipheric Token Test scores following brain bisection and hemidecortication. In Boller F, Dennis M (Editors), *Auditory Comprehension with the Token Test.* New York: Academic Press, pp. 135 – 159, 1979b.

Zaidel E: The split and half brains as models of congenital language disability. In Ludlow CL, Doran-Quine ME (Editors), *The Neurological Bases of Language Disorders in Children: Methods and Directions for Research.* NINCDS Monograph 22. Wahington, DC: U.S. Government Printing Office, pp. 55 – 89, 1979c.

Zaidel E: Hemispheric intelligence: the case of the Raven Progressive Matrices. In Friedman MP, Das JP, O'Connor N (Editors), *Intelligence and Learning.* New York: Plenum Press, pp. 531 – 552, 1981.

Zaidel E: Reading in the disconnected right hemisphere: An aphasiological perspective. In Zotterman Y (Editor), *Dyslexia: Neuronal, Cognitive and Linguistic Aspects.* Oxford: Pergamon Press, pp. 67 – 91, 1982.

Zaidel E: Disconnection syndrome as a model for laterality effects in the normal brain. In Hellige J (Editor), *Cerebral*

Hemisphere Asymmetry: Method, Theory and Application. New York: Praeger, pp. 95 – 151, 1983a.

Zaidel E: On multiple representations of the lexicon in the brain: the case of the two hemispheres. In Studdert-Kennedy M (Editor), *Psychobiology of Language.* Cambridge, Mass.: MIT Press, pp. 105 – 125, 1983b.

Zaidel E: Right hemisphere language. In Benson DF, Zaidel E (Editors), *The Dual Brain: Hemispheric Specialization in Humans.* The UCLA Medical Forum Series. New York: Guilford, pp. 205 – 231, 1985.

Zaidel E: Hemispheric monitoring. In Ottoson D (Editor), *Duality and Unity of the Brain.* Hampshire: Macmillan, pp. 247 – 281, 1987.

Zaidel E: Lexical decision and semantic facilitation in the split brain. Unpublished manuscript, Department of Psychology, UCLA, 1989a.

Zaidel E: Hemispheric independence and interaction in word recognition. In von Euler C, Lundberg I, Jennerstrand G (Editors), *Brain and Reading.* Hampshire: Macmillan, pp. 77 – 97, 1989b.

Zaidel E, Peters AM: Phonological encoding and ideographic reading by the disconnected right hemisphere: two case studies. *Brain Lang.: 14,* 205 – 234, 1981.

Zaidel E, Zaidel DW, Sperry RW: Left and right intelligence: case studies of Raven's Progressive Matrices following brain bisection and hemidecortication. *Cortex: 17,* 167 – 186, 1981.

Zaidel E, White H, Sakurai E, Banks W: Hemispheric locus of lexical congruity effects: neuropsychological reinterpretation of psycholinguistic results. In Chiarello C (Editor), *Right Hemisphere Contributions to Lexical Semantics.* New York: Springer, pp. 71 – 88, 1988.

Zollinger R: Removal of left cerebral hemisphere; report of a case. *Arch. Neurol. Psychiatry: 34,* 1055 – 1064, 1935.

© 1990 Elsevier Science Publishers B.V. (Biomedical Division)
Handbook of Neuropsychology, Vol. 4
F. Boller and J. Grafman (Eds)

CHAPTER 7

Memory and spatial cognition following commissurotomy

Dahlia W. Zaidel

Department of Psychology, UCLA, Los Angeles, CA, U.S.A.

There are two main parts to this chapter. The first deals with memory, the second with spatial cognition. The first part reviews the most significant papers that report memory testing of commissurotomy patients. Then, the data are summarized with a focus on six issues that must be considered in evaluating the effects of partial or complete hemispheric disconnection on memory functions. In the second part, we first describe the historical background, from a neurological perspective, to hemispheric specialization of spatial cognition. Next, we review the main results on lateralized tests of spatial perception and comprehension. Finally, the pitfalls involved in reaching conclusions on spatial cognition from commissurotomy patients versus patients with unilateral lesions are briefly discussed.

Memory

Memory is clearly a complex function, more basic than hemispheric specialization, and understanding the functions of the forebrain commissures will not necessarily hold the key to knowing the mechanisms subserving memory. At the same time, students of the memory process must reckon with these tracts of fibers. We know that they serve as communication channels between the two hemispheres, and, that the two halves of the human brain are specialized for different yet complementary functions (e.g., Sperry, 1974), including different storage/retrieval processes in long-term semantic memory (Zaidel, 1987). In animal work, for example, split-brain monkeys trained to respond to certain stimuli with one hemisphere required nearly as much time to relearn the same task with the second hemisphere (Sperry and Stamm, 1957). In other words, knowledge and thus memory of the task were established only on one side. The main question to be asked, then, is 'what is the role of the interhemispheric commissures in memory functions?' The answer may be gleaned from studies reviewed below.

The role of the interhemispheric commissures in memory

The first study to address this issue systematically, and, to date, the study with the largest group of patients, was reported by D. Zaidel and Sperry in 1974. This investigation was undertaken to verify family reports of persistent mild to moderate difficulty with memory following the operation. Since then, several other studies of commissurotomy patients have reported conflicting results.

The following is not an exhaustive review of the literature. A brief description of each of the major studies in which memory assessment was attempted is provided below. Although indentical memory measures were not administered by all investigators, some, fortunately, have used similar tests and the majority have used at least one, the

TABLE 1

Summary of cases described in the studies reviewed in this chapter

Study	Patients total	Surgery				Etiology	Handedness	Pre-op data	Age range at testing	Post-op follow-up period
		commissurotomy		callosotomy						
		complete	partial	complete	partial					
Zaidel and Sperry, 1974	10	8: cc, ac, hc	2: 2/3 cc, ac, hc	–	–	epilepsy	R	no	20 – 41	3 – 8 years
Ledoux et al., 1977	1			1		epilepsy	R	yes	15	6 – 10 weeks
Geffen et al., 1980	2				2 ant. trunk	3rd vent. cyst	R	no	22 – 69	?
Trope et al., 1983	4			4		epilepsy	3R; 1L	yes	20 – 24	6 – 24 months
Bentin et al., 1984	6				6: 3 ant. trunk 1 mid. trunk 2 post. trunk	cyst; tumor	R	1 yes 5 no	12 – 40	6 – 24 months
Novelly and Lifrak, 1985	4			3 2 2-stage	1: 2/3 cc	epilepsy	3R; 1L	yes	20 – 39	3 weeks – 1 year

cc = corpus callosum; ac = anterior commissure; hc = hippocampal commissure; 2/3 cc = anterior 2/3 corpus callosum.

Wechsler Memory Scale (Wechsler, 1945). For this reason, the emphasis in reviewing each study is on the standardized tests common to all or most studies. Table 1 provides a general summary of the patient populations.

Zaidel, D. and Sperry, 1974

Of the 10 patients studied, two had a partial section, while 8 had a complete section of the forebrain commissures. In the partial commissurotomy patients, the anterior two-thirds of the corpus callosum (CC) was transected along with complete section of the hippocampal and anterior commissures. In the complete commisurotomy patients, the CC, hippocampal and anterior commissures were all sectioned. Whenever the massa intermedia was visualized it, too, was sectioned. The surgery was performed in a single stage. In addition, because of the surgical approach it is assumed that columnar fornix fibers have been partially interrupted on one side in a few cases. It is unlikely that there was any bilateral fornix damage. Extra-callosal cortical damage associated with the surgery or the epilepsy is probably present in all cases but it was not considered to be extensive or concentrated in hippocampal structures.

Unfortunately, no pre-operative scores on memory tests are available. The standardized memory tests administered post-operatively were The Wechsler Memory Scale (WMS), Benton's Revised Visual Retention Test (BVRT) (Benton, 1963), Memory for Objects (Wells and Ruesch, 1945), Visual Sequential Memory (VSM), a subtest of the Illinois Test of Psycholinguistic Abilities (ITPA) (Kirk et al., 1968), Knox Cubes Test (Arthur, 1947), and Memory for Designs (MFD) (Graham and Kendall, 1960). The results can be summarized as follows. (1) All patients, regardless of extent of surgery, showed memory performance substantially below their IQs (WAIS Intelligence Quotient), as judged by the IQ – MQ (Wechsler Memory Quotient) difference. (2) Complete commissurotomy patients were particularly poor in performing the non-verbal, visual task of the WMS. (3) Compared to the normal population, both partial and complete commissurotomy patients obtained particularly low scores on the 'hard' versus 'easy' word associations subtest of the WMS. (4) Partial commissurotomy patients obtained low scores on the short story passages of the WMS.

A subsequent study by Huppert (1981) on three of the same complete commissurotomy patients confirmed the presence of a memory deficit by showing that two patients, N.G. and R.Y., required 8 times the exposure duration of pictorial stimuli required by normal subjects in order to subsequently remember them. On the other hand, one patient, L.B., required normal acquisition exposure durations. This is consistent with LB's normal scores on 4 of the tests administered by Zaidel and Sperry (1974). Huppert's study also found that retention of pictorial information even one week after initial training was within a normal range in all three patients. The conclusion reached by this author is that 'interhemispheric co-operation is relatively unimportant for normal retention although co-operation may be necessary for normal learning' (p. 310).

Ledoux et al., 1977

This study reported the pre- and post-operative results of a single case, D.H., on three standardized memory tests, in addition to four other laboratory tests. Here, too, the surgery was undertaken in order to relieve intractable epilepsy (which developed around age 10) and consisted of complete section of the CC in a single stage. The patient was 15 years old at the time the surgery was performed and when both pre- and post-operative tests were administered. There was substantial extra-callosal damage in the right temporal lobe suffered at age 10 and the surgical report (Wilson et al., 1982) indicates right hemisphere atrophy. The standardized tests administered were the WMS, VSM and MFD. The authors concluded that there were no post-operative deficits in memory.

Specifically, on the majority of tests and subtests D.H. not only improved following surgery but his scores were generally higher than those obtained by the patients in the Caltech series. At the same time, there are two striking similarities to the two partial commissurotomy patients, N.F. and D.M., in that series: D.H.'s performance was virtually the same as these two patients' on the MFD and on the story passages in the WMS. It is particularly noteworthy that memory for story passages is the only measure on which there was some post-operative decline in D.H. N.F. and D.M., for whom there are only post-operative scores, performed poorly on this subtest as well, especially when compared to the complete commissurotomy patients. Thus, the commonality in performance pattern suggests that the mnestic skills required for remembering short narratives are particularly sensitive to callosal damage, even if partial. (This issue of memory for story passages is discussed later on in the chapter.)

Geffen et al., 1980

Two patients, aged 22 and 69, underwent partial callosotomy for the removal of colloid cysts in the third ventricle. Part of the trunk of the CC, sparing the splenium and the genu, was sectioned in both cases. In addition, patient W.F. had damage in both fornices while patient G.O. had only some interruption of columnar fibers in the right fornix. There was minimal extra-callosal cortical damage. Two standardized tests of memory functions were administered postoperatively, the WMS and BVRT.

Compared to the normal population, there was no impairment postoperatively in one patient, G.O., but a clear impairment was present in the other patient, W.F., who had a subnormal MQ. The IQ – MQ difference for W.F. was similar to those in the Caltech study, that is, his memory performance was far worse than would have been predicted from his IQ score. Furthermore, W.F. performed poorly on the story passages and associative learning subtests of the WMS and obtained scores within the range of those obtained by the Caltech cases. On the other hand, his scores on the visual reproduction subtest score were far higher than theirs. At the same time, his 'number correct' score on the BVRT, was, again, within the mean range found in the Zaidel and Sperry study. The two partial commissurotomy patients (N.F. and D.M.) on the Caltech group obtained higher scores than did either W.F. or G.O. Could this inconsistency be merely a reflection of individual differences with the 'better able' obtaining higher scores than the 'less able'?

The authors' conclusion was that callosal lesions per se are not responsible for the observed memory deficits but that bilateral fornix damage in conjunction with such lesions may have detrimental effects on memory. This was inferred from the observation that G.O. had only unilateral fornix damage while W.F. suffered bilateral (anterior) fornix damage. They bolstered their argument for fornix involvment in their patients' deficit by citing fornix damage in the Caltech patients. However, in comparison, the Caltech patients suffered only minimal unilateral fornix damage, on either the right or the left side, and only in six of the patients reported in the memory study. Given that, on the whole, the Caltech patients obtained lower scores than W.F., it is unlikely that bilateral fornix damage is the principal cause of the memory deficit seen in that patient. (This point is discussed further in a subsequent section.)

Trop et al., 1983

Four patients underwent a complete corpus callosotomy in a single stage (sparing the anterior and, reportedly, the hippocampal commissures) in order to alleviate intractable epilepsy. Several memory tests were administered before and after surgery and performance was reduced on all tests after the surgery. Only one test, the WMS, was common to the studies described previously. In three patients the MQ diminished after surgery and the IQ – MQ difference was substantial. At the same time, the authors found no significant change in IQ. Scores on the associate learning subtest of the WMS were particularly low and were attributed to the 'hard' word associations. This is consistent with previous reports (Zaidel and

Sperry, 1974; Ledoux et al., 1977). The conclusion reached by the investigators from both the clinical and behavioral data as well as from the reports of family members is that reduced memory function is a consequence of the commissurotomy.

Bentin et al., 1984
Six patients suffering from intraventricular cysts or mid-brain tumors underwent a surgical procedure which severed small sections of the trunk of the corpus callosum. The sections varied between patients: in four cases (with intraventricular cysts) only the anterior part of the callosal trunk was sectioned, while in two other patients (with tumors in the pineal region) only the posterior callosal trunk (presumably sparing the splenium) was incised. In addition to the WMS (administered pre- and post-operatively in one patient) all patients were studied on laboratory tactile tests which involved a strong memory component.

The results showed a clear memory impairment in three patients with lesions in the posterior or anterior portion of the trunk of the CC. The IQ – MQ difference was substantial post-operatively in all three. In addition, however, one other patient had only a mild IQ – MQ difference; in another patient the MQ was slightly higher than the IQ, while in another there was essentially no difference. Moreover, in some of the laboratory tests reported, poor performance in all patients was attributed to the memory component.

The authors concluded that since memory impairment was present in three patients with lesions in different callosal regions, the impairment is not related to the site on the trunk where the lesion is located. This is consistent with an earlier study by Dimond et al. (1977) which reported memory impairment in a patient with a section in the posterior portion of the trunk of the corpus callosum. They pointed out that their laboratory tests consisting of complex tactile tests were particularly sensitive to interhemispheric transfer deficits in those patients with lesions in the anterior part of the trunk of the callosum, posterior to the foramen of Monro, especially if the task involved a memory component. They stated their view as being consistent with Geffen et al.'s (1980) position that the deficit is probably not due to callosal damage per se but rather to damage to the fornix and, they added, to damage caused by intraventricular lesions (damage to the fornix in their patients' case could have occurred during the surgical approach or could be due to the tumor itself).

Novelly and Lifrak, 1985; Sass et al., 1987
Although 24 patients were studied on a variety of cognitive and memory measures, thus far details relevant to memory are available on only four patients (Novelly and Lifrak, 1985). Results on Russell's revised WMS are available for a pre- and post-operative comparison. The verbal memory and pictorial memory subtests were administered. Three patients underwent a complete callosotomy, while a fourth had only the anterior two-thirds of the callosum sectioned. The anterior commissure was spared in all. However, two of the complete callosotomy patients had a two-stage surgery.

Compared to the pre-operative performance, the results showed reduced scores on the verbal memory subtest to varying degrees from 'substantial' in patients S.F., M.D. and P.D. to 'practically none' in D.M. at follow-up periods ranging from 3 weeks to 1 year after surgery. Post-operative scores on the memory for pictures subtest showed mild improvement, no change, or slight reduction. The issue of memory deficits following surgery was not emphasized in discussion of the cases.

Ferguson et al., 1982
It is important to briefly review an additional report although results of standardized memory tests are not covered there (Ferguson et al., 1982). Six patients who underwent a two-stage, complete section of the CC as well as of the hippocampal commissure were studied both before and after surgery. The authors' summary table shows that in four patients, the 'factor' of attention-memory-sequencing was impaired, in another one there was no change (for the remaining patient no data were available).

The following is a description of one of these patients: "P.O.V. (age 27) is said by her parents to be forgetful to the point that she cannot be depended on to keep track of her medication. Appointments also are often missed. For example, preparing to keep an appointment with the dentist, she may call her mother the night before to arrange transportation for the next day. The following morning, the patient is completely unaware of the arrangement" (Ferguson et al., 1982, pp. 511 – 512). McKeever (1987, personal communication) observed that after repeated administrations of the word association subtest of the WMS, as late as 4 years following surgery, P.O.V.'s performance was well below normal. Yet, following operation, seizures were reduced and no changes in personality or in speech production were observed.

Another patient, R.E.D., is described as follows: "Preoperatively, R.E.D. could be depended upon to follow instructions for retrieving an item from the freezer, taking a note to the workshop supervisor, or finding her way daily to the bus. Since operation she may carry out instructions incorrectly or may become lost at the workshop" (Ferguson et al., 1982, p. 512). This patient, too, had a reduction in seizure frequency. Her personality improved in both assertiveness and awareness and no impairment in language function was noted.

Do the forebrain commissures play a role in memory functions?

A review of the commissural section literature strongly suggests that the forebrain commissures do play a role, particularly in the acquisition stage. Fig. 1 illustrates the frequency of impairment, as compared to no change or improvement, even in patients with small sections of the forebrain commissures. Fig. 2 focuses on those cases where it was possible to compare pre- to post-operative scores on the WMS. This figure shows a bigger loss of memory relative to intelligence post-operatively.

However, the present picture is muddied by a

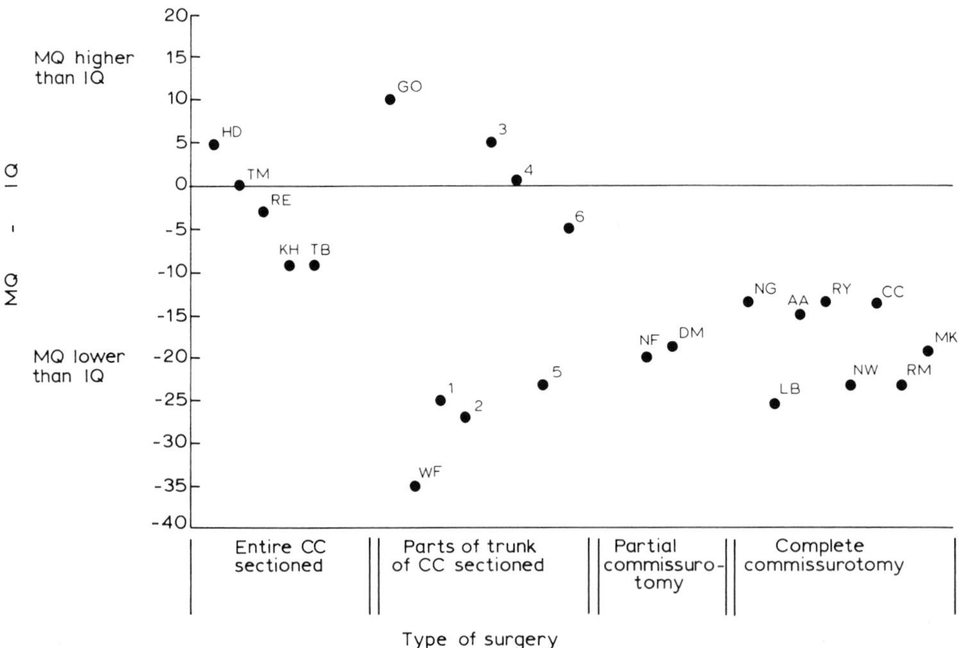

Fig. 1. Scatter diagram of post-operative MQ – IQ scores. A score of 100 for either MQ (Memory Quotient) or IQ (Intelligence Quotient) indicates normal memory or intelligence. The zero line indicates no difference between MQ and IQ. Points above it represent higher IQ than MQ, while points below it indicate lower MQ than IQ.

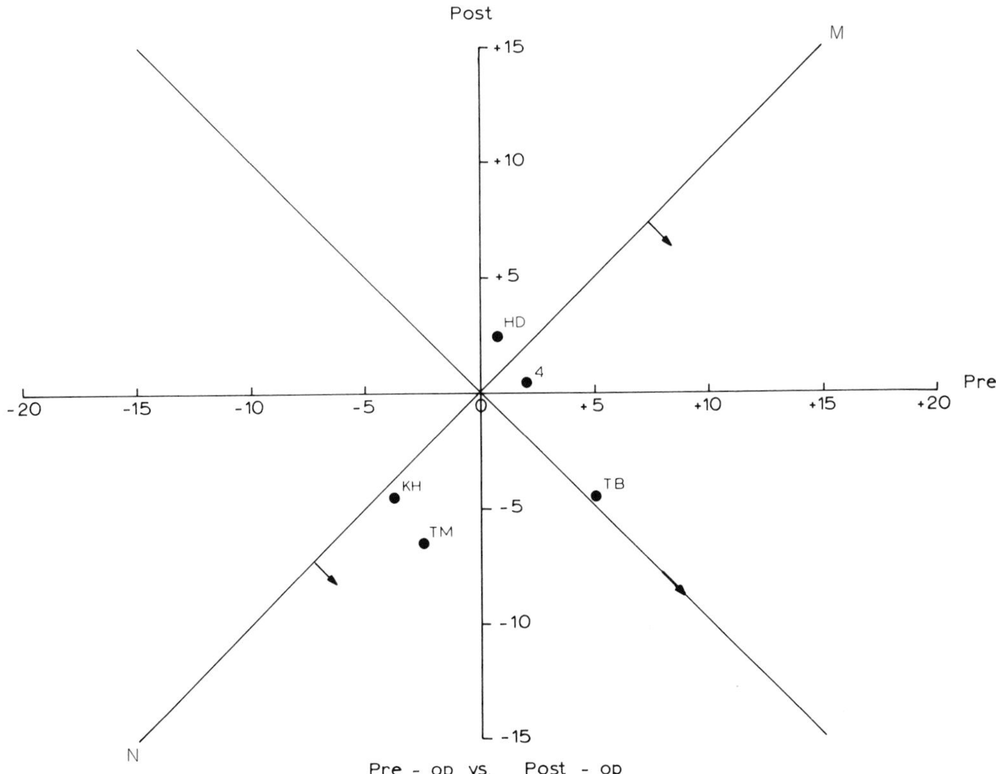

Fig. 2. Pre- (x axis) and post- (y axis) operative MQ – IQ differential. Positive scores denote higher MQ than IQ. The diagonal line MN represents equal pre- and post-operative differentials. Points below it represent a higher pre-operative differential, i.e., a bigger loss of memory relative to intelligence post-operatively.

number of confounding factors: age at symptom onset, age at time of surgery, etiology, presence versus absence of the disconnection syndrome, extent of commissural section, single versus two-stage surgery, number and kind of memory tests administered, number of patients studied, length of post-operative follow-up, individual variability in memory ability per se, and so on. All of these could affect the results. Thus, in the absence of uniformity among cases, the assessment of commissural involvement is somewhat difficult.

Even so, three observations are worth pointing out. (1) Some decrement, varying from mild to substantial in severity, is often present following section of the CC alone, or with only one small lesioned region. This strongly suggests a functional role for the CC in memory. (2) Single, as opposed to serial, section does not appear to affect occurrence of memory impairment. (3) The word association and story passage subtests of the WMS appear to be more sensitive than other standardized tasks to partial or complete forebrain commissurotomy.

Speculations on significant issues

Subcortical extra-callosal damage

Given both the particular surgical approach in many cases and the anatomical juxtaposition of certain limbic system structures, direct or indirect extra-callosal damage to sub-cortical neural systems involved in memory (i.e. the fornix and hippocampus) is highly likely. The hippocampal commissure located under and adhering to the corpus callosum is the part of this neural system most likely to be lesioned. Anatomically, this commissure is part of the hippocampus, in particular the rostral portion, the uncal hippocampus (Pandya and Rosene, 1982). Damage to each of these limbic system structures is implicated in memory deficits as adduced from patient or animal studies (see Squire, 1987, for review). A good case in point is that of H.M., a man who has suffered anterograde amnesia following bilateral removal of the hippocampus (Scoville and Milner, 1957). Damage to the fornix, a neural tract that connects the hippocampal system to other limbic structures, has been implicated in memory deficits in laboratory animals (Bachevlier et al., 1985). In humans (not undergoing commissurotomy) there is one report (Heilman and Sypert, 1977) of a case with lesions localized there (as well as in the hippocampus) resulting in memory deficits. As described earlier, during commissurotomy, interruption of columnar fibers in the fornix is somewhat common, though not obligatory. Unfortunately, data on lesions in the fornix and on the effects such lesions may have on memory in humans are sparse (Parkin, 1987) and, according to one view, 'the functional link usually presumed to exist between the hippocampus and the mammillary nuclei has been overstated' (Squire, 1987, p. 196). In any case, there is no agreement on the effects of fornix lesions alone on memory. However, in view of the evidence reviewed above, possible extra-callosal damage to the limbic system incurred during the operation should not be ignored in assessing the effects on memory.

With the foregoing in mind, it is reasonable to ask if the memory deficit in commissurotomized patients is due in part to damage to the hippocampal-fornix system. In certain cases, everything else being equal, the extent of the damage may determine presence versus absence of memory decrement. Thus, we may speculate that in cases where there is an improvement or no change after the surgery, the hippocampal commissure may not have been damaged or was only affected minimally during the procedure. On the other hand, what about cases where only anterior regions of the CC were sectioned, surgically 'distant' from the hippocampal commissure? In other words, there is no need to assume damage to this commissure in all cases of surgical callosal lesions.

The fornix and commissurotomy It is important to focus the discussion on the fornix since, as described above, a few reports have concluded that lesions there could be the major contributing cause for the memory impairment in commissurotomy patients, rather than the surgical lesions in the callosum itself. Such speculations are based on a very small number of cases, lacking uniformity in lesion size. The role of the fornix in memory functions in such cases could be resolved by looking at a large, relatively homogeneous group. That opportunity is provided in the Caltech patients. A summary of the status of the fornix in these patients (compiled by J.E. Bogen, 1970) is as follows. No damage is assumed for M.K., R.M., A.A. and R.Y. (If any damage did occur in R.Y.'s case it would have been slight and on the right.) Damage on the right is assumed for N.G. and L.B. (In the case of N.G. the fornix was reportedly divided, and in L.B. a little damage from the retractor may have occurred.) Damage on the left is assumed to be present for N.W., C.C., D.M. and N.F. In the case of D.M., the fornix was divided. In N.W.'s case, it was only partially transected.

To illustrate the point above, let us focus further on patient L.B. in the Caltech series. Briefly, he underwent complete commissurotomy at an early age and obtained scores within the normal range on four of the standardized memory tests administered. At the same time, his IQ – MQ difference was the largest in the group. Considering that the right fornix incurred only minor damage from the retractor it seems unlikely that fornix damage played a significant role in his memory impairment.

Etiology

Functional compensation may be more extensive in some patients than in others. The effect of commissurotomy or callosotomy on memory functions is clearly complicated by lack of uniformity in damage to neuronal tissue. Not only do some of these patients have either partial or complete section but also, due to etiology, there may be additional extra-callosal damage. Some patients, for instance, have had epilepsy since early childhood while in others seizures started in their teens or adulthood as a result of trauma. Yet others were supposedly normal until a tumor occurred. However, some tumors develop slowly, creating changes that possibly allow functional reorganization, much as serial brain lesions do. Thus, although the tumor may have been discovered at age 12, the damaging process and its concomitant compensatory mechanism may have started earlier.

Relative hemispheric independence in memory functions

The following possibility is suggested: in those cases where no impairment was reported, or the surgery led to improvement, sectioning part or all of the forebrain commissures may have promoted hemispheric independence so that only one hemisphere carried the memory load. That is, the surgery eliminated or minimized the usual dependence on 'sharing', as in 'communication' between the two hemispheres. Alternatively, sectioning removed unhealthy inhibition of the diseased over the healthy tissue thereby permitting adequate memory functioning. This may be particularly true when intelligence level (as measured by the WAIS IQ) is above normal. In other words, when memory impairment is seen, it may be complicated by poorly functioning general cognitive processes. The performance of two patients, L.B. (Zaidel and Sperry, 1974) and H.D. described by Ledoux et al. (1978), may serve as illustrations of this point: L.B. did have a reduced MQ and the IQ – MQ difference was substantial but, at the same time, he performed within the normal range on four other standardized memory tests. His Full Scale IQ was 106 (post-operative). Patient H.D.'s IQ was 103 (post-operative) and his performance on all three standardized tests administered was normal. Given that he suffers from right hemisphere atrophy (possibly only in the temporal lobe region) and that the post-operative performance was reported improved over the pre-operative one, it is reasonable to suggest that one hemisphere (the left?) was mainly performing the tasks. Similarly, patient L.B.'s performance may have reflected a well functioning single hemisphere. This implies that following disconnection "the basic mechanism for engram formation may not be impaired, only the associated processes which involve interhemispheric co-operation . . . " (Zaidel and Sperry, 1974).

Advantages and disadvantages in pre-operative testing

These epileptic patients usually take heavy doses of medication in order to alleviate their seizures. Thus, preoperative memory scores could be affected both by the high seizure activity as well as by the medication. Thus, even though availability of pre-operative scores appears crucial from a scientific perspective, how can we be sure that they reflect the 'true' abilities of a person with an intact brain? After all, following surgery, both medication levels and seizure activity are reduced substantially. Patients who have shown no decrement, or even improvement, after, as compared to before, surgery may not have obtained higher scores than before surgery if it weren't for the heavy medication and brain metabolic imbalance caused by seizure activity existing preoperatively. Ideally, improvement after surgery should be reflected in both IQ and MQ measures. A valid approach to test this issue would be to record memory level well before surgery is indicated, and before the patient's condition has deteriorated so as to require surgery, and then to compare it to scores after surgery.

A comment

In reading the reports of the studies reviewed above, the reader may get the impression that the emphasis is on results that show improvement or no change in memory following surgery. Put differently, the authors seem to down-play the presence of memory impairments, even if mild. However, close scrutiny of the results reveals the presence of consistent deficits across studies and possibly of individual anomalous cases. That variable memory impairment is present is illustrated in the summary of post-operative MQ – IQ differences plotted in Fig. 1 and in the summary of pre- versus post-operative MQ – IQ differences (admittedly, a very small number of cases) in Fig. 2. Perusal of both of these figures clearly shows post-operative memory deficit, as measured on one standardized memory test, albeit to varying degrees. Thus, in spite of a possible bias against reporting memory deficits, the data do suggest a consistent impairment, varying from mild to substantial, even with partial section of forebrain commissural fibers.

Conclusion: left versus right hemisphere memory

The number of studies in which memory tests were administered to each hemisphere separately in commissurotomy patients is small indeed. Those that could be considered meaningful were with patients who underwent complete commissurotomy (the Caltech series). These studies are reviewed briefly below. Additional relevant tests are described in the next section.

Using the tactile modality, Milner and Taylor (1968) found that the right hemisphere was superior to the left in remembering individual nonsense shapes. Subsequently, Zaidel and Sperry (1973b) showed that when either common objects or nonsense shapes had to be remembered in a temporal sequential order, the left hemisphere had the better memory. Thus, hemispheric superiority was shown to be determined by task demands rather than by stimulus material (process dominance versus material specificity).

In vision, E. Zaidel (1979) found that the left hemisphere was superior to the right in remembering sequences of nonsense figures (visual sequential subtest of the ITPA) presented all at once. Subsequently, however, when the same test was administered tactually (using metal etched patterns), performance dropped appreciably in the left hemisphere and no laterality effects were observed.

The overall conclusion for all of these studies is that memory levels in each disconnected hemisphere are lower than in normal control subjects or in patients with unilateral brain damage (Milner and Taylor, 1972). This conclusion could be seen as consistent with the hypothesis that the forebrain commissures are important in memory formation, but it is not yet clear at which stage – acquisition, storage or retrieval – they play the most significant role.

Spatial cognition

As early as 1876 Hughlings Jackson prophetically ascribed a dominant role to the posterior right hemisphere in spatial perception, 'visual ideation' as he called it. But in spite of recurring case histories inferring involvement of the right parieto-occipital region in spatial perception and construction, the prevailing view in the first half of the twentieth century was that the left hemisphere in right-handers was dominant for all higher mental functions, verbal as well as nonverbal. It remained to modern neuropsychologists beginning in the 1940s and 1950s to demonstrate conclusively using case studies with well verified lesion localization that the right hemisphere is specialized for spatial perception. But the full impact of that point of view was brought home dramatically with the evidence from the Caltech series of patients with complete cerebral commissurotomy in the 1960s.

The commissurotomy data are, however, only partly consistent with the modern clinical neurological view. When the same tests that had shown selective deficit with right-sided lesions were administered to commissurotomy patients (e.g., Mooney Faces), using a special contact lens method for prolonged lateralized presentations, discrepant results were often obtained (E. Zaidel, personal communication). Moreover, commissurotomy data confirmed right hemisphere specialization for certain aspects of spatial perception, but provided little or no evidence for right hemisphere specialization in spatial constructions. Only one aspect of constructional apraxia, i.e., copying (Bogen and Gazzaniga, 1965; Bogen, 1969; Zaidel and Sperry, 1977), has been shown to be present in the left hemisphere following disconnection. While the specialization of the disconnected right hemisphere for spatial perception was confirmed by several workers (reviewed by Nebes, 1974), the tests used to determine this were not standard because of methodological limitation in stimulus presentation.

The following sections review the main studies that have shed light on spatial cognition following commissurotomy. The emphasis is largely on investigations of the complete commissurotomy cases in the Caltech group because they demonstrate the disconnection syndrome across all modalities, ensuring thereby lateralization of the input to one hemisphere. In other groups of commissurotomy patients not all cases have shown the disconnection syndrome and where the syndrome was present, this was not true for all modalities.

An extensive review of hemispheric specialization based on findings with the Caltech cases was published in 1974 by Nebes. Consequently, only some of the important studies up until that year are covered here. Later, there were fewer studies by comparison but some are reviewed. They all extended the earlier findings.

Visuo-constructive abilities

The first evidence confirming asymmetry in visuospatial functions was reported by Bogen and Gazzaniga in 1965. They found that two patients, N.G. and W.J., were able to copy a cube in free vision with the left hand better than with the right. Similarly, patient W.J. constructed Kohs blocks designs better with the left hand than with the right. At the same time, these investigators found in preliminary tests that this patient using his sense of touch, could pick out the correct design in an array consisting of several designs better with his right than with his left hand. These results, Bogen and Gazzaniga have suggested, 'may show the presence of a visuoperceptive capacity within the left hemisphere adequate for yes or no answers but insufficient to direct a complex voluntary act'.

In a later study (Ledoux et al., 1978), the above basic findings were partially confirmed by the performance of a corpus callosotomy patient (a complete section of the CC) on the block design test. When the patterns were flashed to either visual half field, performance was better with left visual field exposures than with right visual field exposures. As in the previous study, under free vision conditions, both hands were able to construct the patterns but the left hand was more efficient.

Spatial perception

In 1968 Levy-Agresti and Sperry reported the first important study of spatial functions in these patients while using a modified version of a psychological test (Spatial Perception subtest of the Differential Aptitude Tests). Levy separately tested the ability of each hemisphere to visualize two-dimensional representations of three-dimensional shapes (Levy, 1974). The test was administered tactilely and consisted of blindly palpating wooden geometrical figures and selecting with the homolateral hand the one choice (out of three) that represented the unfolded version of the target figure. The results showed a left hand – right hemisphere superiority over the right hand – left hemisphere. These findings were replicated on a larger number of patients in a later study conducted by Kumar (1976). Moreover, Levy's data analysis suggested qualitative asymmetries, namely, that those trials which required synthetic or 'gestalt' thinking strategies were predominantly solved by the right hemisphere, whereas trials in which the solution required an analytic or piece-meal problem-solving approach were better performed by the left hemisphere. Although postulated earlier from the performance of unilateral brain-damaged patients (Paterson and Zangwill, 1944), the notion of different thinking strategies for each hemisphere became well known following publication of Levy's study.

Further support for this interpretation was obtained in additional studies. Nebes (1971) administered a tactile test in which the task was to match a specific arc with its parent circle, and conversely. Several different sizes of arcs and circles were used. The task was cross-modal in nature: one part of the task was always presented tactilely and another was always shown in free vision. Results showed a left hand superiority over the right. The conclusion was that the right hemisphere is specialized for global, holistic perception. Later, Hatta (1978) confirmed Nebes' results in normal subjects through the use of lateralized tachistoscopic presentation of the arcs and circles.

Evidence that each hemisphere uses different strategies for solving non-verbal problems was further obtained in the performance of commissurotomy patients on a cross-modal, tactile version of the Raven Coloured Progressive Matrices Test (Zaidel and Sperry, 1973a). The task was to choose the metal etched pattern which would best fit a missing section in the target pattern. The choices were presented tactually (and blindly) and the target in free vision. All patients consistently showed a left over right hand superiority on a selected sample of problems. However, when the entire test was administered the difference between the hands became non-significant. There were, however qualitative differences between the two hands. With their right hands, the patients were slow and tended to verbally describe the details, while with their left hands they were quick and silent. This provides further evidence for the hypothesis advanced by Levy-Agresti and Sperry (1968). Observations on performance speed for the two hands confirmed these findings (Franco and Sperry, 1977). In a subsequent study (Zaidel et al., 1979), the superiority of the right hemisphere on the Raven test was confirmed when the test was presented visually. Two patients wearing a special scleral contact lens were tested on the entire test. Again, the difference between the two hemispheres was quantitatively small but performance strategies were clearly different in each hemisphere: the left hemisphere appeared to be sensitive to item difficulty, and improvement was observed when error correction was encouraged. By contrast, there was no sensitivity to item difficulty nor improvement with error correction in the right hemisphere.

That the right hemisphere specializes in global strategies in the processing of patterns was further demonstrated by Nebes (1973). Dot arrays were briefly exposed in each visual half field and the task was to decide whether or not the dots were aggregated so as to form vertical or horizontal lines. The performance in the left visual half field was found to be superior to that in the right visual field, regardless of which hand was used to signal the answer. Thus, perception of the global relationship of the dots to one another was superior in the right hemisphere.

In an effort to find out which geometrical aspects may be involved in hemispheric specialization for spatial relations, Franco and Sperry (1977) administered a cross-modal tactile test. The task was to determine which tactilely felt shape matched visually presented patterns. The shapes and the patterns were constructed according to specific rules which defined Euclidean, affine, projective and topological geometry. The findings showed relatively uniform performance across the different types of geometrical shapes with the left hand and graded performance with the right hand. With the right hand, Euclidean structures were well matched but performance declined until topological ones were matched at chance level. The authors proposed that when many defining features were involved, as in the Euclidean structures, the analytic strategies of the left hemisphere were most effective, but when there were hardly any defining features, as in topological structures, the global thinking strategies of the right hemisphere were best suited for the task.

Imagery and the right hemisphere

It is commonly agreed that imagery is an important component in performing spatial perception tasks. Right hemisphere specialization in spatial cognition has long been considered to be the result of specialization in mental imagery. However, there have been conflicting reports about deficits in imagery following left or right hemisphere brain damage (see review by Ehrlichman and Barrett, 1983) or even about exclusive right hemisphere superiority in spatial tasks. Recently, Farah (1984) proposed that some imagery components may be specialized in the left hemisphere, those generated from long-term memory, for instance. Studying the performance of one callosotomy patient, J.W., Farah et al. (1985) reported that image generation of lower-case letters from their upper-case version was superior in the right visual half field. The left hemisphere imagery component in some imagery or spatial cognition tasks, then, may be partly responsible for the conflicting results in the literature.

The question of imagery in the right hemisphere was investigated further by Corballis and Sergent (1988) in one complete commissurotomy patient, L.B. (Caltech series). The image-generation task of lower-case letters was administered and the results confirmed those with callosotomy patient J.W. On the other hand, when a mental rotation task was introduced, L.B.'s right hemisphere was consistently better than the left. Since previous evidence based on results obtained with patients suffering from posterior damage in the right hemisphere has indicated poor performance in determining sidedness of inverted human figures (Ratcliff, 1979) and since in most of the studies described in earlier sections of this chapter superior mental visualization in the right hemisphere was assumed, L.B.'s performance on mental rotation tasks is not surprising. Nevertheless, this was the first study to address that question directly in commissurotomy patients and the results obtained were in the predicted direction.

Memory for hard-to-verbalize patterns

Two separate studies have demonstrated the superiority of the left hand – right hemisphere in remembering spatial configurations. Milner and Taylor (1972) presented meaningless specially constructed wire figures to complete commissurotomy patients in order to determine which hand would better match them at varying delay intervals. In this matching-to-sample test five out of seven patients performed the task better with their left than with their right hand when the delay in matching was set at zero. With longer delays, hand performance was variable. Kumar (1977) designed a tactile version of the Memory For Designs Test to determine hemispheric memory for the patterns. The patterns were etched on metal plates and subjects felt them blindly with each hand separately. The task was to draw the designs in both free vision and out of sight with the palpating hand after the target pattern had been removed. Kumar found that the left hand was superior to the right in all four patients with complete commissurotomy.

In the visual modality, E. Zaidel (1978) administered a memory test in which hard-to-verbalize patterns were used. Two patients wearing the special scleral lens were tested. Benton's Visual Retention Test – Multiple Choice version was administered. After the target pattern had been scanned unilaterally, a multiple-choice array was presented at varying delay intervals. The right hemisphere was found to have a memory score superior to that of the left hemisphere when the delay was 15 seconds, but with longer delays, up to 60 seconds, this advantage disappeared.

Performance on the tasks described above, however, cannot by itself be taken as evidence for right hemisphere specialization in spatial cognition without parallel tests in which spatial configurations characteristic of ordinary, easy-to-verbalize objects are used. The latter are just as 'spatial' as the wire figures or metal etched designs described above. Ideally, the left hand would continue to be superior to the right. In sum, only with additional tests in which the memory component is stressed and in which ordinary objects are used would we be able to conclude that apprehension of spatial configuration is superior in the right hemisphere following commissurotomy.

Extra-personal space

Left-sided hemi-inattention or spatial neglect is commonly observed in patients with right-sided lesions in posterior regions, usually parietal (Weinstein and Friedland, 1977). Neurologists have reasonably surmised that the right hemisphere specializes in the internal representation of the external world, especially of the left half of space. The implication is that in such patients the intact left hemisphere lacks the ability to compensate by attending to the left half of space or the body. One would think that following disconnection from the right hemisphere, the left hemisphere would suffer from left hemi-inattention. However, this does not seem to have occurred, even in the period right after surgery (see copied figures in Bogen and Gazzaniga, 1965).

This question was first addressed directly in data analysis of tests presented visually with the scleral lens technique. Responses in both the Illinois Test of Psycholinguistic Abilities and the Raven's Coloured Progressive Matrices Test were analysed specifically to determine preferences for one side of space or for response positions (E. Zaidel, 1978; Zaidel et al., 1981). The findings for both tests can best be summarized as follows. "In general, there is no consistent and significant neglect of ipsilateral visual space in unilateral presentations, i.e., there is no preference for response alternatives on the side of the page which is contralateral to the working hemisphere" (E. Zaidel, 1981, p. 175).

A subsequent study (Plourde and Sperry, 1982) was specifically designed to determine whether hemi-inattention or spatial neglect is present following commissurotomy. Using a common neurological measure, three complete commissurotomy patients were administered several tests that measured presence of hemi-spatial neglect of extra-personal or of personal space. One of those was a test where subjects were instructed to bisect lines with each hand separately. The results indicated no unilateral neglect of either half of space. In addition, "results for the left hemisphere revealed substantial awareness for the left side of the body and also for extrapersonal space, far greater than suggested by the unilateral lesion data" (Plourde and Sperry, 1982, p. 95).

These results "highlight again the difference between the functional competence of a disconnected or isolated hemisphere and that of a patient with a circumscribed lesion in the contralateral hemisphere: unilateral cognitive competence following cerebral commissurotomy . . . is free of some of the focal deficits, such as unilateral neglect of contralateral space following right-brain damage, which are common in free performance with hemispheric lesions" (Zaidel et al., 1981, p. 175).

Final remarks

It is apparent from the survey of the literature that the evidence for right hemisphere superiority for spatial cognition is supported by the performance of commissurotomy patients. The results obtained with these patients have refined, sharpened and strengthened early notions of right hemisphere specialization. This and the dramatic nature of the surgery and findings have most probably helped put the right hemisphere on the 'map' of human cognition. Moreover, the study of this area of cognition has provided clues about brain mechanisms which could not have been discovered earlier from the study of unilateral brain-damaged patients alone. The case of hemi-neglect or inattention discussed above can serve as good illustration of this point: left hemi-inattention in patients with posterior right hemisphere damage has suggested a unique specialization in the right hemisphere for the contralateral half of space, yet neither of the disconnected hemispheres in complete commissurotomy patients has been found to specialize in the contralateral half of space only. (Similarly, to the best of my knowledge, there is no evidence from left hemispherectomy cases for unilateral neglect of space on the left side). Another example is the clinical symptom of prosopagnosia, the acquired inability to recognize people by their faces alone. While some consider that the anatomical basis for the disorder is bilateral posterior damage (Damasio, 1985), others consider that it is the damage in the right hemisphere which gives rise to this condition. Yet neither the disconnected left nor the right hemisphere of commissurotomy patients has ever been found to suffer from prosopagnosia (see, Sperry et al., 1979). In short, the dynamics of brain organization following disconnection are such that they may resemble the normal brain rather than the brain organization inferred from localized hemispheric damage.

Acknowledgements

The preparation of this chapter was supported by NINCDS grant NS-18973 to DWZ. I thank Charles Hamilton, Eran Zaidel and Robert Nebes for their helpful suggestions, and Kathleen Frederick for preparation of the graphs.

References

Arthur G: *A Point Scale of Performance Tests, Revised Form II.* New York: The Psychological Corporation, 1947.

Bachvalier J, Saunders R, Mishkin M: Visual recognition in monkeys: effects of transection of fornix. *Exp. Brain Res.: 57,* 547 – 553, 1985.

Bentin S, Sahar A, Moscovitch M: Interhemispheric information transfer in patients with lesions in the trunk of the corpus callosum. *Neuropsychologia: 22,* 601 – 611, 1984.

Benton AL: *The Revised Visual Retention Test.* New York: The Psychological Corporation, 1963.

Bogen JE: The other side of the brain. I: Dysgraphia and dyscopia following cerebral commissurotomy. *Bull. Los Ang. Neurol. Soc.: 34,* 73 – 105.

Bogen JE, Gazzaniga MS: Cerebral commissurotomy in man: minor hemisphere dominance for certain visuospatial functions. *J. Neurosurg.: 23,* 394 – 399, 1965.

Corballis MC, Sergent J: Imagery in a commissurotomized patient. *Neuropsychologia: 26,* 13 – 26, 1988.

Critchley M: *The Partiel Lobes.* London: Arnold, 1953.

Damasio AR. Prosopagnosia. *Trends Neurosci: 8,* 132 – 135, 1985.

DeRenzi E, Spinnler H: Visual recognition in patients with unilateral cerebral disease. *J. Nerv. Ment. Dis.: 142,* 513 – 525, 1966a.

DeRenzi E, Spinnler H: Facial recognition in brain damage patients. An experimental approach. *Neurology: 16,* 145 – 152, 1966b.

Dimond SJ, Scannell RE, Brouwers EYM: Functions of the centre (trunk) of the corpus callosum in man. *Brain: 100,* 543 – 562, 1977.

Ehrlichman H, Barrett J: Right hemisphere specialization for mental imagery: a review of the evidence. *Brain Cognition: 2,* 55 – 76, 1983.

Ettliner G: The description and interpretation of pictures in cases of brain damage. *J. Ment. Sci.: 106,* 1337 – 1346, 1960.

Farah MJ: The neurological basis of mental imagery: a componential analysis. *Cognition: 18,* 145 – 272, 1984.

Farah MJ, Gazzaniga MS, Holtzman JD, Kosslyn SM: A left hemisphere basis for visual mental imagery? *Neuropsychologia: 23,* 115 – 118, 1985.

Ferguson SM, Rayport M, Corrie SW: Neuropsychiatric observation on behavioral consequences of corpus callosum section for seizure control. In Reeves AG (Editor), *Epilepsy and the Corpus Callosum.* New York: Plenum, 1985.

Franco L, Sperry RW: Hemisphere lateralization for cognitive processing of geometry. *Neuropsychologia: 15,* 107 – 114, 1977.

Geffen G, Walsh A, Simpson D, Jeeves M: Comparison of the effects of transcortical and transcallosal removal of intraventricular tumours. *Brain: 103,* 773 – 788, 1980.

Graham FK, Kendall BS: Memory-for-design-test: Revised general manual. *Perception and Motor Skills: 11,* 147 – 188 (Monograph Supplement 2 – VII), 1960.

Hatta T. Functional hemispheric asymetries in an inferential thought task. *Psychologia: 20,* 145 – 50, 1977.

Hecaen H, Angelergues R: Agnosia for faces. *Arch. Neurol.: 7,* 92 – 100, 1962.

Heilman KM, Sypert GW: Korsakoff's syndrome resulting from bilateral fornix lesions. *Neurology: 27,* 490 – 493, 1977.

Huppert FA: Memory in split-brain patients: a comparison with organic amnesic syndromes. *Cortex: 17,* 303 – 312, 1981.

Jackson JH: *Selected Writings, 2,* Taylor J (Editor). London: Hodder and Stoughton, 1932.

Kimura D: Right temporal-lobe damage. *Arch. Neurol.: 8,* 264 – 271, 1963.

Kirk SA, McCarthy JJ, Kirk WD: *Illinois Test of Psycholinguistic Abilities: Examiner's Manual.* University of Illinois Press, 1968.

Kumar S: Cognition of figural transformation after commissurotomy. *Percept. Motor Skills: 43,* 350, 1976.

Kumar S: Short term memory for nonverbal tactual task after cerebral commissurotomy. *Cortex: 23,* 55 – 61, 1977.

Lansdell H: Relation of extent of temporal removals to closure and visuomotor factors. *Percept. Motor Skills: 31,* 491 – 498, 1970.

Ledoux JE, Risse GL, Springer SP, Wilson DH, Gazzaniga MS: Cognition and commissurotomy. *Brain: 100,* 87 – 104, 1977.

Ledoux JE, Wilson DH, Gazzaniga MS: Block design performance following callosal sectioning: observations on functional recovery. *Arch. Neurol.: 35,* 506 – 508, 1978.

Levy-Agresti J, Sperry RW: Differential perceptual capacities in the major and minor hemispheres. *Proc. Natl. Acad. Sci. USA: 61,* 1161, 1968.

Levy J: Psychological implications of bilateral asymmetry. In Dimond SJ, Beaumont JG (Editors), *Hemispheric Function in the Human Brain.* London: Elek Science, 1974.

McFie J, Piercy MF: Intellectual impairment with localized cerebral lesions. *Brain: 75,* 292 – 311, 1952.

Meier MJ, French LA: Lateralized eficits in complex visual discrimination and bilateral transfer of reminiscences following unilateral temporal lobectomy. *Neuropsychologia: 3,* 261 – 272, 1965.

Milner B: Visual recognition and recall after right temporal lobe excision in man. *Neuropsychologia: 6,* 191 – 209, 1968.

Milner B, Taylor L: Right hemisphere superiority in tactile pattern recognition after commissurotomy: evidence for nonverbal memory. *Neuropsychologia: 10,* 1 – 15, 1972.

Nebes RD: Superiority of the minor hemisphere in commissurotomized man for the perception of part-whole relations. *Cortex: 11,* 333 – 349, 1971.

Nebes RD: Perception of dot patterns by the disconnected right and left hemisphere in man. *Neuropsychologia: 11,* 285 – 290, 1973.

Nebes RD: Hemispheric specialization in commissurotomized man. *Psychological Bulletin: 81,* 1 – 14, 1974.

Novelly RA, Lifrak MD: Forebrain commissurotomy reinstates effects of preexisting hemisphere lesions; an examination of the hypothesis. In Reeves AG (Editor), *Epilepsy and the Corpus Callosum.* New York: Plenum, 1985.

Parkin A: *Memory and Amnesia: An Introduction.* Oxford: Blackwell, 1987.

Paterson A, Zangwill OL: Disorders of visual space perception associated with lesions of the right cerebral hemisphere. *Brain: 67,* 331 – 358, 1944.

Plourde G, Sperry RW: Left hemisphere involvement in left spatial neglect from right-sided lesions: a commissurotomy study. *Brain: 107,* 95 – 106, 1982.

Pandya DN, Rosene DL: Some observations on trajectories and topography of commissural fibers. In Reeves AG (Editor), *Epilepsy and the Corpus Callosum.* New York: Plenum, 1985.

Ratcliff G: Spatial thought, mental rotation, and the right cerebral hemisphere. *Neuropsychologia: 17,* 49 – 54, 1979.

Sass KJ, Novelly RA, Spencer DD: Memory and callosotomy: Series 1. Prodeedings of the Annual International Neuropsychology Society Meeting, Washington DC, 1987.

Scoville WB, Milner B: Loss of recent memory after bilateral hippocampal lesions. *J. Neurol. Neurosurg. Psychiatry: 20,* 11 – 21, 1957.

Sperry RW: Lateral specialization of cerebral function in the surgically separated hemispheres. In McGuigan FJ, Schoonover RA (Editors), *Psychophysiology of Thinking.* New York: Academic Press.

Sperry RW, Stamm JS: Function of corpus callosum in contralateral transfer of somesthetic discrimination in cats. *J. Comp. Physiol. Psychol.: 50,* 138 – 143, 1957.

Sperry RW, Zaidel E, Zaidel D: Self recognition and social awareness in the deconnected minor hemisphere. *Neuropsychologia: 17,* 153 – 166, 1979.

Squire LR: *Memory and Brain.* Oxford: Oxford University Press, 1987.

Trope IH, Gur RE, Sussman NM, Saykin A, Gur RC: Memory impairment before and after callosotomy. Proceedings of the International Neuropsychological Society Meeting, Mexico City, 1983.

Warrington EK, James M: An experimental investigation of facial recognition in patients with unilateral cerebral lesions. *Cortex: 3,* 317 – 326, 1967.

Wechsler D: A standardized memory scale for clinical use. *J. Psychol.: 19,* 87 – 95, 1945.

Weinstein EA, Friedland RP: *Hemi-inattention and Hemisphere Specialization.* New York: Raven Press, 1977.

Wells FL, Ruesch J: *Mental Examiner's Handbook.* New York: The Psychological Corporation, 1945.

Wilson DH, Reeves AG, Gazzaniga MS: 'Central' commissurotomy for intractable generalized epilepsy: Series two. *Neurology: 32,* 687 – 697, 1982.

Zaidel DW: Hemispheric asymmetry in long-term semantic relationships. *Cognitive Neuropsychol.: 4,* 321 – 332, 1987.

Zaidel D, Sperry RW: Performance on the Raven's Coloured Progressive Matrices Test by subjects with cerebral commissurotomy. *Cortex: 9,* 34 – 39, 1973a.

Zaidel D, Sperry RW: Lateralized tests for temporal sequential order in the left and the right hemispheres of man. *Biol. Annu. Rep.* (Caltech): p. 54, 1973b.

Zaidel DW, Sperry RW: Memory impairment after commissurotomy in man. *Brain: 97,* 263 – 272, 1974.

Zaidel D, Sperry RW: Some long-term motor effects following commissurotomy in man. *Neuropsychologia: 15,* 193 – 204, 1977.

Zaidel E: Concepts of cerebral dominance in the split brain. In Buser PA, Rougeul Busser A (Editors), *Cerebral Correlates of Conscious Experience.* Amsterdam: Elsevier, pp. 263 – 284, 1978.

Zaidel E: Performance on the ITPA following cerebral commissurotomy and hemispherectomy. *Neuropsychologia: 17,* 259 – 280, 1979.

Zaidel E, Zaidel DW, Sperry RW: Left and right intelligence: case studies of Raven's Progressive Matrices following brain bisection and hemidecortication. *Cortex: 17,* 167 – 186, 1981.

Section 8

(Part 1)

Aging and Dementia

editor

S. Corkin

© 1990 Elsevier Science Publishers B.V. (Biomedical Division)
Handbook of Neuropsychology, Vol. 4
F. Boller and J. Grafman (Eds)

CHAPTER 8

Animal models of age-related cognitive decline

C.A. Barnes

Department of Psychology, University of Colorado, Boulder, CO 80309, U.S.A.

Introduction

The argument has often been raised that if one desires to understand the aging process in humans, and to discover how to manipulate this process, then one should study the species of direct interest. Indeed, the proof of the effectiveness of any animal model of human aging must be a test of its relevance to the human condition. If the findings from that species aid in the understanding of human deficits, then explication of their underlying mechanisms may result in the discovery of a potential therapeutic reversal of such cognitive defects, which after all is one principal goal of such an experimental approach. While it is difficult to simulate pathological conditions that seem to be uniquely acquired by humans, considerable insight into the behavioral manifestation of conditions such as Alzheimer's disease has been gained through animal model approaches. Much more direct comparisons can be made between animals and humans if the process of normal aging is studied. All mammals undergo ontogenetic alterations that involve processes of growth, sexual maturity, reproductive senescence, and death. The most striking species difference in this process involves the amount of time ensuing between birth and death – or the maximum life span. The study of the aging process in species with shorter life spans than humans can actually be used to experimental advantage, as will be discussed below. The premise of this chapter is that the use of animal models to understand human aging can be an appropriate and productive approach. However, the advantages and disadvantages must be fully appreciated before realistic interpretations of the use of different animal models can be made. The rationale and underlying assumptions of such an experimental endeavor will therefore be made explicit, as far as possible, throughout this chapter.

There are at least two primary reasons that investigators choose to study animal models of cognitive changes that occur with advanced age, rather than directly studying humans. The first includes variables relating to experimental control of genotype, knowledge of past experience, diet, possible contact with environmental toxins, and social interactions. If the goal is to understand cognitive change that results from the normal aging process, baseline performance levels must be measured with as many of these variables constrained as possible. It is simply not possible to achieve this level of control in humans as compared to other animals. Another primary rationale for using animals comes from the increased ability to use invasive approaches to understand the cognitive change from a neurobiological perspective. The assumption here is that the fundamentals of biological aging that lead to cognitive change can be understood by examining any number of mammalian species, or even perhaps by studying organisms in other phyla. The search for the underlying brain changes responsible for the behavioral alterations found in animals has been motivated by basic scientific and therapeutic reasons. The hypothesis is that through the study of how neuronal information processing changes with age an insight will be gained into the critical underlying mechanisms responsible for adaptive behavior throughout ontogeny. Furthermore, if such a level of understanding can be reached, then interventive procedures can be designed intelligently. The ultimate goal is to improve the life quality of the elderly human by attenuating such age-associated cognitive decline.

The most ideal approach that an investigator might take to study normal aging in an animal would be to go to the psychogerontological literature first to find the primary difficulties that exist in human cognition in healthy elderly people. The investigator could then attempt to design a task for the species of choice which could show whether there were corresponding deficits in that animal with old age. Similarly, the investigator could examine the human literature on brain damage or pathological conditions and could then develop tasks for the species of interest which are sensitive to the malfunction of the brain structure damaged by surgery, accident, or disease in humans. If old animals are impaired on such tasks, or if damage to the same structures in young animals produces a similar syndrome, then a clue to the underlying brain structure involved in the deficit may have been discovered. A combination of these approaches would naturally be the most powerful, since deficits on behavioral tasks designed to be sensitive to normal aging and to the functioning of a particular brain area would potentially facilitate predictions about treatment strategies.

Although the approaches discussed above are a logical beginning, in practice, the human gerontological literature has often been ignored where choices of animal behavioral tasks are concerned. It might be argued that investigators studying humans have not developed language-independent tests that would lend themselves easily to adaptation for animals. While this may have been true some decades ago, this is simply not the case at present. The lack of attempts at such correspondence must find explanation elsewhere, and to some extent might be attributable to a quite valid interest in age-related cognitive changes in the species of study. In this case a sensitive test for the animal in question might not as yet find a human analogue, but may be very good at describing a deficit in that animal. This is not to say that many investigators studying learning and memory processes in old animals make no attempt to bridge their findings to human deficits; however, the exact relationship is not always clear for the reasons mentioned above. Because of this, the findings from the animal studies discussed here will be grouped in broad categories relevant to the general approaches used for testing. Other reviews of this literature have organized the materials differently (e.g., Arenberg and Robertson-Tchabo, 1977; Bartus et al., 1983b; Bartus, 1988; Bartus and Dean, 1987; Botwinick, 1973; Elias, 1979; Elias and Elias, 1975, 1976, 1977; Elias et al., 1975; Goodrick, 1980; Ingram, 1983, 1985; Jakubczak, 1973; Jensen et al., 1980; Jerome, 1959; Kubanis and Zornetzer, 1981; Martinez et al., 1988; Sarter, 1987; Sprott, 1980; Sprott and Stavnes, 1975; Zornetzer and Rogers, 1983).

Animal models in current use

Most of the mammals used for studies of cognitive change with age have been rodents (primarily rats and mice, although gerbils have been suggested as a potentially useful model; Cheal, 1986). There are a number of advantages in using such animals, including their rich behavioral repertoire, control over genetic and other experimental variables, and their relatively short life spans. Cross-sectional and longitudinal designs can be effectively implemented with rodents without the possible confounding factors of cohort effects faced in human studies using the former approach, or subject and experimenter attrition and testing improvements faced in human studies using the latter approach. The advantages of genetic control are particularly salient in the case of mice, where breeding has been carefully planned and controlled for many generations and animals are available with different maximum life spans, behavioral traits or disease susceptibilities (Sprott, 1980). Vendor availability is not a trivial issue in research on aging. The National Institute on Aging of the U.S. Public Health Service has made a substantial contribution to subsidizing and making available a wide variety of barrier-reared strains of rats and mice. However, if the investigator is interested in using guinea pigs, rabbits, cats, fish, etc. in aging studies, these animals are not yet supported by the Institute, and therefore are likely to be costly or difficult to obtain with sufficient birth and health records. Although other animals, such as birds and molluscs, have been used in aging studies, they too have been less frequently used than rats and mice.

Nonhuman primates obviously provide the closest model to normal human aging that is possible. The data from these animals are both particularly valuable and particularly difficult to obtain compared with other mammals. First of all, the life span of certain monkeys is nearly half that of humans (Davis and Leathers, 1985), and the expense of proper primate facilities allows only a limited number of laboratories to have access to such animals. With the recent improvements in animal care and maintenance procedures nonhuman primates may even survive to older ages (Davis, 1985; Tigges et al., 1988). Certainly the life span of mice and rats has been lengthened in the recent past by such husbandry improvements (Myers, 1978), leading some investigators to believe that it is only possible to know the true 'biological age' of the organism by actual behavioral and neural tests (a point elaborated in the next section). Nevertheless there are a number of primate centers around the world, as well as that of the National Institute on Aging, that have made possible experiments on old monkeys through the stable support of primate colonies. Some of the main problems with the primate subject population include uncertainty of age (although this should be less problematic in the future), and partially unknown and/or very elaborate training histories. The latter may pose a problem in that behavior measured from an aging 'expert' versus the behavior of aging nonexperts may result in disparate profiles. As will be discussed below, however, a number of very important studies have been completed that have circumvented such difficulties and provide important insights into memory deficits experienced by aging nonhuman primates.

Separation of learning and memory deficits from artifacts of the behavioral testing situation

There are a number of issues which are important to address concerning potential artifacts or confounds that might arise unequally for different age groups in behavioral testing situations. All of these issues also apply to studies of human aging and are not necessarily resolved in that literature either. The following includes a discussion of certain of the more difficult variables to control which are often not overtly addressed, but which apply in differing degrees to most of the work in the area.

The question of biological or functional age

One of the first issues that must be considered in any study of aging organisms is the question of what ages of animals to compare or what constitutes an old animal in the species of interest. While this might seem to be a trivial point, a good deal of effort has been expended by gerontologists in the attempt to define aging and to reach a conceptual agreement on what constitutes the best index of old age (Borkan and Norris, 1980; Costa and McCrae, 1980; Dyundikova et al., 1981; Ingram, 1983; Ingram et al., 1982a; Ludwig and Smoke, 1980; Shock, 1981; Short et al., 1987; Skalicky et al., 1980; Tobin, 1981). The difficulty of this problem can be appreciated by considering the extent of individual differences in behavior of older humans (e.g. Shock, 1981) or other animals (e.g., Bayne, 1985; Goodrick, 1980; Ingram, 1985). The fact that even genetically and environmentally similar organisms do not always 'age' at the same rate raises problems for simple models of the aging process (Deerberg et al., 1980;

Schlettwein-Gsell, 1970). Different organ systems can age at different rates, and these do not necessarily correspond between individuals. This variability in older organisms can actually be useful experimentally if the amount of change in some brain process can be correlated with the extent of a behavioral change observed within the individual. However, because chronological age may not be the best indicator of the age state of an organism, a more objective 'biological or functional age' has been suggested as an alternative to the simple index of the passage of time (e.g. Bourliere, 1970). Such a view emphasizes the importance of addressing age using multiple levels of analysis, recognizing that linear models may not describe the process adequately (e.g., Costa and McCrae, 1980). Unfortunately there remains controversy as to the best statistical predictors of aging in both the behavioral and physiological domains. This has led some to conclude that chronological age is still the best predictor available to judge the aging process (Costa and McCrae, 1980), although it does not by any means account for all of the variance in behavior (Ingram, 1983). This is not to say that the elegant approaches such as the one Ingram (1983), for example, has used to correlate chronological age with motor performance over the life span of the mouse, or that Sprott (1980) has used to examine learning of a task over the life span across strains of mice, will not prove to be the most rigorous in defining the appropriate age of an organism. The point is that, at present, it is impractical to expect that the majority of investigators can handle the number of animals necessary to do thorough behavioral and neural test batteries across the life span in the animal or strains of interest.

Because this kind of work is beyond the scope of many scientists interested in aging, the next best method is to choose three or more age groups of animals in any given strain that span a significant portion of the known life span. Using more than two age groups will guard against mistaken inferences due to nonmonotonic functions of the variables of interest. Furthermore, the 50% mortality point of the species (basically the LD_{50} of life) can be used as an approximate guide to judge that the animal is senescent (Mos and Hollander, 1987). Multiple stocks or strains should also be used (Elias, 1979) to test the generality of any behavioral change observed. However, as will be shown below, a comparison of two age groups is probably the most common approach utilized, and very few studies include a comparison of different strains. Again, the reasons for this tend to be financial and practical rather than a clear choice to ignore the best possible approaches to experimental design. However, the limitations on interpretation of data produced by these constraints must be recognized.

The other issue subsumed under the question of the biological age of the organism is the extent to which disease contributes to the process. Should aging be considered as only the processes that occur in all of the species during their life span? Or should all possible lesions which may not be shared by all in the population, but which certainly lead to mortality, be included in the definition? This issue revolves around the distinction between normal and pathological aging (e.g., Howell, 1949; Ludwig and Smoke, 1980; Wisniewski and Terry, 1976). In the case of mice and rats, the details of the histopathological characteristics of a variety of strains are known quite well as long as the animals are kept in pathogen-free barrier environments (e.g., Coleman et al., 1977; Storer, 1966). Under these circumstances a strong case for the pattern of deteriorative change experienced by the majority of the population can be documented and any deviation therefrom can be operationally defined as abnormal. The main problem with this distinction between normal and pathological is that, in practice, most investigators take animals from these barrier facilities and bring them into their own laboratories, which are not pathogen free. This makes it even more imperative that routine pathological tests are performed on the animals after testing so that any changes observed in behavior can be attributed to normal rather than unusual health conditions in the species studied.

Potential noncognitive variables influencing performance on behavioral tasks

A separation of 'pure' age-related learning and memory changes from sensory, motor, emotional or motivational alterations that might occur with age may at first appear arbitrary because these factors might normally contribute to the deficits observed in older animals and humans. However, the goal in many experiments using animals has been to gain control of these variables so that they might be manipulated and examined separately to provide a framework for an evaluation of their influence on the learning process. This could be particularly valuable, from a theoretical perspective, in situations where it might be unethical to use such control procedures in humans. Also, from a practical standpoint, it simply may not be very interesting to obtain deficits in older animals on visual discrimination problems if the animals had cataracts or were lame rather than if they exhibited this deficit because of information-processing difficulties. Some investigators have been extraordinarily careful to consider and control for these variables and some have not. It is therefore important to keep in mind the possible confounding factors that may arise if these aspects are ignored when evaluating the work in this field.

It has been recognized for some time that it is important to control for possible sensory changes that could occur between age groups and might interfere with the learning process (e.g., Goetsch and Isaac, 1982; Yerkes, 1909). It is critical to ensure that the old animals can see, hear, smell or feel the stimuli that are important for good performance of the task. This can be done either by using very salient stimuli for both ages, or by determining whether increasing the salience of the stimuli will improve the performance of the old animals. In shock-motivated tasks, where old animals may be larger and have more resistant skins, shock intensity could prove to be a very important variable. Sprott and Stavnes (1975), for example, found that while raising the shock intensity was effective in improving the avoidance performance of older animals of one mouse strain, in another strain such an increase was not effective in changing the behavior of the older animals. This experiment underscores the importance of directly determining the appropriate sensory conditions for the species and strain of interest because these variables may not be generalizable. Another method that can be used to assess the contribution of sensory loss to cognitive change in animals is to determine whether there is a strong relationship between these factors. Davis (1985), for example, was able to construct a rather strong case against factors such as sensory loss and organ pathology being the primary cause of the cognitive impairments in the monkeys he examined, as there was a very low and nonsignificant correlation between these variables and the behavior of the primates on various cognitive tasks sensitive to the aging process.

Another important factor to consider in studies of cognition and aging is whether the task places demands on the animal in terms of motor coordination, dexterity, speed or strength. Ingram (1983; Ingram et al., 1983a), for example, has assessed motor performance over the life span of the C57BL/6J mouse. The test battery he used consisted of measures of the animals' forearm grip strength, a tightrope that measured upper body strength as well as traction and muscular coordination, a rotorod that measured coordination and balance, behavior in terms of exploratory locomotion in a runway, and general running in an activity-wheel cage. The results showed profound changes in motor behavior occurring over the life span of these animals, with some of the tasks discriminating between age groups better than others. There are also certain aspects of motor activity that change in the old rats as well (Campbell et al., 1980; Janicke et al., 1983; Marshall and Berrios, 1979; Shirley, 1928; Wallace et al., 1980b). Therefore it is not unreasonable to expect that there may be similar behavioral changes in other strains and species. If these kinds of behaviors are necessary for the performance of the cognitive task of interest, then these motor deficits could significantly contribute to the behavioral outcome of the test. Because such motor and cognitive deficits of old animals can be modified by exercise and complexity of their home environments (Goodrick, 1984; Samorajski et al., 1985; Warren et al., 1982), housing conditions will also contribute to the experimental results. Some consideration of these factors is needed in the appropriate design of experiments. Similar precautions have been taken in the design of human experiments in terms of acknowledging that the demands of timed or paced tasks often bias against the good performance of elderly adults (e.g., Salthouse, 1985; Welford, 1977). The accuracy of performance is often considered the relevant variable, rather than the speed with which the older individual makes the choice or decision. Tasks that allow the animals to self-regulate the pace have also been developed for primates (e.g., Bartus et al., 1978), and speed-independent measures have been emphasized in a variety of tasks used to test old rodents (e.g., Barnes, 1979; Rapp et al., 1987).

Determining whether emotional, motivational or attentional variables are equivalent between age groups is not a simple problem. However, there have been a number of successful approaches to this issue. The method of 'differential deprivation' has therefore been employed in some instances, so that on appetitive tasks the old animals would be made more hungry than the young animals (e.g., Corke, 1964; Goodrick, 1968; Margolin and Bunch, 1940; Stone, 1929a,b). Thus if the behavior of the old animals was not as good as that of the young animals, it would probably not be attributable to lower motivation. Other examples of this include using equivalent amounts of water deprivation between age groups, which is more stringent on old animals because of impairments in hydrostatic mechanisms (Cahn and Borzeix, 1984; Elias and Elias, 1977; Ingram, 1985; Jakubczak, 1970). The idea, then, is to compare results of studies using different motivational levels in old animals trained on a particular task to determine whether this manipulation reduces the age deficit. If it does not, then the case for some other variable being responsible for the behavioral deficit is strengthened. Even more convincing arguments can be built for an information-processing deficit with tasks that are designed to use different motivators or that have differing attentional demands. If the age difference continues to converge towards the same results, then again the investigator can be more confident that the age difference is not due to motivational factors.

The issue of attentional differences between age groups has also been problematic to control as a potential contributor to age-related cognitive deficits. Some reasonably convincing arguments have included observations that, for example, monkeys in the older age groups appear to be even more attentive and deliberate on certain behavioral tasks than are the younger animals (Presty et al., 1987). While this does not rigorously rule out attentional factors, it does serve to remind investigators that careful scrutiny of their animals can aid in the realistic generation of hypotheses concerning the processes responsible for age-related behavioral change (and see Bayne, 1985).

The behavioral impact of a number of other variables on animals used in an age comparison of performance should also be considered, including experimental design factors, circadian variables (Ingram et al., 1982b), and other lifetime experiences of the animals. Doty, for example, has shown that 20 consecutive days of picking up rats and placing them into a container for three minutes can profoundly influence avoidance and open field behavior of animals, especially very young (less than one month) or older (between 1.5 and 2 years) rats. The effect of this type of handling on the old rats was to improve their performance on the avoidance task and to increase their activity and decrease their defecation scores in the open field situation (Doty, 1968; Doty and Doty, 1967). The mechanism responsible for this effect is unclear, although it may not be due simply to sympathetic-adrenal medullary system activation, since it has been shown that the mild stress of handling elevates blood plasma levels of epinephrine and norepinephrine to the same extent in rats from 4 to 24 months of age (McCarty, 1981). The type and extent of handling, however, may be critical to the results observed, as Goodrick (1971a) did not find a difference in open field behavior of old rats that had been 'gentled' before testing (brushed for 5 minutes per day for 10 consecutive days). The relevant controlling factors remain to be determined; however, it is clear that handling procedures need to be specifically stated as part of the methods, so that true replication of experiments is possible. Another interesting but potentially confounding factor is the breeding history of the animals used in age comparisons of cognitive variables. Ingram et al. (1983b) have shown, for example, that old virgin animals perform better than old retired breeders in some situations, and suggest that appropriate age comparisons should be made either between retired breeders or between virgin animals to avoid this confound.

What does the behavioral task measure?

One fundamental issue here involves whether the particular task used biases either against or in favor of a particular age group. While some tasks require a relatively precise performance strategy for optimal solution, many behavioral situations can be solved using a number of alternative strategies. Barnes et al. (1980), for example, demonstrated this in a two-choice discrimination problem. Young and old rats solve this task equally well, so that by the ordinary measure of number of trials to criterion, no age difference could be detected. After the animals had learned the problem well, however, subsequent tests were made to determine how individual animals actually solved the problem. When this analysis was made it was found that the old and young animals tended to use different strategies for performance (the younger animals used a spatial strategy a significantly greater proportion of the time). Thus, an equivalent rate of learning does not always ensure that the animals are performing equivalently.

From a slightly different perspective, Rigter et al. (1980) were able to eliminate an age difference in an active avoidance task by moving the escape platform to the side of the apparatus rather than having it in its normal position in the middle of the apparatus. Because the older rats responded by running along the side, older animals were given a relative response advantage over young animals. Goodrick was also able to construct a situation that benefited older animals to a greater degree than young animals, possibly because the older animals learned the forced response sequences more easily because there were fewer competing strategies (Goodrick, 1975c). Another variable to consider is the extent to which animals of different ages are willing to venture a response. This issue has had a lively history in the human gerontological literature, and Davis (1978) suggests that the old monkeys he has tested perform with greater caution than do the younger monkeys. It is clear, therefore, that the behavioral differences obtained between age groups involve complicated interaction between approaches to problem solving and changes in the ability to learn and to remember. It is up to the investigator to consider whether there are multiple ways in which a task may be solved and whether the demands of the task favor a particular group, before firm conclusions about age differences can be drawn from the experiment.

Another point of confusion in the literature on old animal learning and memory is the ambiguity often present in the exact definition of these constructs. These issues have been debated since the inception of psychology, and it is therefore not surprising for them to appear in the relatively new field of gerontology. The answer is not going to be resolved here; however, a number of guidelines might be used to structure the interpretation of the data discussed below. The initial acquisition of a particular problem is often taken as 'learning'. However, it must be recognized that, for example, if training trials are given once per day, slower acquisition of a problem could be a result of an inability to learn, a faster rate of forgetting of the problem from day to day, or a combination of these factors and others. 'Memory' for a learned problem, on the other hand, is often divided into shorter-term (minutes or hours) or longer-term (days or weeks) forms of information storage (see Kubanis and Zornetzer, 1981). It remains a matter of debate whether the neurobiological process of information storage can be exactly separated on the basis of these time scales, but this distinction has often been useful in animal experiments in terms of whether the memory demand is restricted to a single trial situation, or whether the memory for the problem must be maintained from day to day (Honig, 1978). One way to develop a case for a pure memory deficit would be to make certain that the same performance levels are reached in all age groups before testing for rate of forgetting. An even stronger test would include training to different levels of performance and measuring forgetting rates over multiple levels of learning strength. Another variable that must be considered is whether the older animal has actually learned the problem, but simply cannot bring to mind the relevant information. This situation is typically described as a problem of retrieval, and it is often difficult to separate the contributions that access failures might make to forgetting. Arguments can be developed against a retrieval deficit, for example, by demonstrating that in some behavioral situations old animals can use information normally, but the relative contributions remain to be clarified in both the human and the animal literature. A reasonable interpretation of the results of various learning and memory experiments will be presented below. The caveats just discussed, however, should be kept in mind throughout.

General activity and exploratory behaviors

There are, unfortunately, no studies that directly assess the activity levels of primates in situations where they are unrestrained and free to explore the test environment, although a general slowing of response speed has been noted in old rhesus monkeys (Davis, 1978; Davis and Ruggiero, 1973) as well as dexterity and agility changes (Fletcher and Mowbray, 1962), much as has been noted in elderly humans. The activity level of mice and rats has been measured across the life span of a number of strains. One of the most common methods used to test the exploratory behavior of these animals is to use one of a number of versions of the 'open field' task. In general, animals are placed into an arena of various sizes and shapes, and are allowed to move about the space in lighted or dim illuminaton conditions, or a combination of these. Either the movement is recorded (as square crossings or photo beam interruptions) for a set amount of time, or the amount of time spent engaged in 'exploratory' activity is estimated (often by the amount of time spent in the lighted rather than dim portion of the apparatus). In agreement with initial observations (Munn, 1950; Slonaker, 1907, 1912), most investigators have found a decrease in general activity at the older ages which has been interpreted as a decline in exploratory activity on a number of forms of the open field task (Brennan et al., 1982; Doty and Doty, 1967; Elias et al., 1975; Forbes and Macrides, 1984; Furchtgott et al., 1961; Goodrick, 1965, 1966, 1967a, 1971a,b, 1975a; Ingram, 1983; Ingram et al., 1983a; Parsons et al., 1973; Sprott and Eleftheriou, 1974; Vasquez et al., 1983; Werboff and Havlena, 1962; Willig et al., 1987). Although the majority of studies have found a decline, not all experiments report an age difference (Ingram et al., 1987; Janicke et al., 1983). This points to the importance of considering genotype, sex and housing conditions of the animals under study, as they may lead to different patterns of results on exploration (Sprott, 1980). In general, however, Goodrick's (1971a) summary of exploration over the life span of rodents appears to hold: there are two peak periods of exploratory activity, one just after weaning and one just after sexual maturity is attained (Goodrick, 1967a). Animals between these stages and those which are sexually mature show less exploratory activity, with the oldest animals showing the least amount of this behavior.

Another way in which to monitor general activity characteristics of animals across their life span is with the use of an activity wheel. In general there is an overall decline in the amount of 'voluntary' running of rodents in a wheel apparatus with age (Desroches et al., 1964; Goodrick, 1975a; Ingram, 1983; Ingram et al., 1983a; Jakubczak, 1970; Jones et al., 1953; Ordy and Schjeide, 1973; Wax, 1977; Wax and Goodrick, 1978) and in total bar-press activity in voluntary activity-rest periods (Wax and Goodrick, 1975), although this is not necessarily the case for all species (Ingram et al., 1987). Because general psychomotor functioning may affect certain of the cognitive tests discussed below, it is important to know how the different strains of rats and mice compare across age. Thus, information concerning the details of the changes in motor patterns across genotype and sex has been very valuable in assessing what impact these factors may have on cognitive variables of interest (Dean et al., 1981; Gage et al., 1984a; Gibson et al., 1981; Ingram, 1983; Ingram et al., 1983a, 1987; Janicke et al., 1983; Marshall and Berrios, 1979; Miquel and Blasco, 1978; Wallace et al., 1980b).

An alternative method of evaluating the significance of a decline in exploratory or locomotor behaviors in animals is to examine the pattern of responses over time, rather than simply the total amount of activity. The results from experiments using old rodents have indicated that these animals show habituation impairments in behaviors ranging from activity in novel environments to hole-board nose-poke tasks (Brennan et al., 1981, 1982, 1984; Fraley and Springer, 1981a,b), and complementary results have been found in Aplysia, where old animals show deficits in habituation and sensitization of the siphon withdrawal reflex (Bailey et al., 1983). The common factor in these experiments appears to be the older animals' inability to retain the habituation or sensitization experience across time or sessions. Such a deficit might adversely influence the learning of other more complicated environmental problems where the discrimination between meaningful and irrelevant stimuli is important, which underscores the potential importance to the organism of these simple forms of learning.

Appetitively motivated behaviors

Operant tasks

Rodents of different ages have been compared on their ability to perform relatively simple operant tasks for reward in a number of studies. Goodrick, for example, found that the total amount of bar pressing was similar in young and old AJ and C57BL/6J mice (1975a) and Wistar albino rats (1975b; and see Desroches et al., 1964). Age differences have been detected, however, using other procedures and contingencies as measures of performance, although some of the differences may be strain-dependent (Goodrick, 1975a) or linked to motor strategies of the older animals (Stephens et al., 1985). The old rats used in the Stephens et al. experiment were impaired overall relative to young animals in the acquisition and reversal of a continuously reinforced bar-pressing response for food. However, the deficit appeared to be almost completely attributable to learning the actual bar-press response itself, as old animals were capable of very good levels of responding after more extensive training on this aspect of the procedure. Age differences have also been noted between young and old squirrel monkeys, where the older animals show lower levels, but more consistent rates of responding, through a session for light reinforcement (Lorig and Isaac, 1983) and greater disruption of fixed-interval responding with the presentation of novel auditory stimuli (Harrison and Isaac, 1984). These observations emphasize the importance of minimizing potentially confounding non-cognitive performance factors which bias against the good performance of old animals.

Campbell and Haroutunian (1981) detected no age differences in acquisition of a fixed interval schedule (FI 60); however, the old animals (26 months) did not retain this problem over 16 days as well as did the younger rats (6 and 12 months). Wallace et al. (1980a) trained animals on a bar-press task where the food was delivered after either auditory or visual signals. If the two signals were the same, a bar press would result in reward. If they were different, no reward would be delivered.

Six- and 23-month-old Fischer 344 rats performed similarly over delay intervals up to 5 seconds. In another experiment, old rats (24 months) performed more poorly than young animals (7 months) on a task in which the rats were reinforced for responding when the stimulus presented was different from the previous trial's stimulus (Pontecorvo et al., 1988). As the intertrial interval increased, the old animals' accuracy became proportionately worse. In contrast, if young and old animals were overtrained on a schedule that reinforced low rates of responding (DRL), older rats showed very stable memory for this task for at least 3 weeks (Hamm et al., 1984). It is likely that the level of training is an important variable to consider in these types of task when retention is measured between age groups.

Solyom and Miller (1965) observed a difference in acquisition using a variable-interval schedule of responding between 5- and 20-month-old rats, and old rats also appear to learn the DRL schedule more slowly than do young animals (Hamm et al., 1983). Additional evidence for changes in the ability of old animals to discriminate temporal relations between stimuli come from the studies of Meck and Church (1985) and Meck et al. (1986), who found that, as animals aged, their behavior was much more variable on a peak-interval timing task, with the maximal response rates also shifting with age. Furthermore, older animals do not perform as well as younger rats on a three-lever chain task that requires animals to press three bars in the correct order before receiving reward (Corke, 1964). The difficulty the old animals had in performing this sequence correctly occurred even though they actually showed somewhat higher rates of overall responding in this experiment (Corke, 1964). It appears, therefore, that acquisition and retention deficits on operant tasks can be obtained over the life span of mice and rats independent of general activity level declines in the old animals. Whether one obtains a deficit in acquisition appears to be task- and strain-dependent, whereas deficits in retention tend to be detected if the animals have not been overtrained on the problem.

Two-choice discrimination problems

Fields (1953) trained 1- and 15-month-old Sprague-Dawley rats to discriminate between visual patterns and to jump to the cue that would be rewarded. He found performance differences between these two age groups, even though the oldest group was not near the 50% mortality for that strain of rat. The most likely explanation for this result is a combination of animal illness and motor skill problems (jumping with greater body mass) rather than a true learning deficit in the older rats. Most other experiments using old rats or mice have not supported the view that there is a substantial cognitive change on simple visual discrimination problems where motor demands were not difficult for the older animal (Barnes et al., 1980; Botwinick et al., 1962, 1963; Corwin et al., 1982; Dean et al., 1981; Harrison, 1981; Kay and Sime, 1962; Lowy et al., 1985; Sarter and Markowitsch, 1983; Stephens et al., 1985; Winocur, 1984), although old gerbils may exhibit more difficulty on a pattern discrimination problem in a T-maze than young gerbils (Greenberg, 1978).

While the acquisition of these discrimination problems has been shown to be similar between age groups in the studies cited above, many of these experiments either detected changes in the way in which the different groups solved the problem or could create situations where the older animals showed poorer performance. For example, Harrison (1981) concluded that the small difference detected between age groups in an auditory location discrimination problem was most probably due to hearing loss in the older rats. While there were no age differences in acquisition or reversal of a two-choice Y-maze problem in the Sarter and Markowitsch (1983) study, the older animals appeared to extinguish faster than the younger rats. Winocur (1984) could disrupt the recall of a visual pattern discrimination in old rats if he produced a situation where there was a high degree of interference, and much the same result has been found for memory of the spatial location of a visual stimulus in old monkeys (Bartus and Dean,

1979). Likewise, Dean et al. (1981) could only obtain an age difference in a T-maze brightness discrimination task (motivated by shock) if they trained the mice to their non-preferred arm. They obtained no age difference if the training was to the preferred brightness, suggesting age differences in the strength of prior sensory preferences. In a similar fashion, Stephens et al. (1985) obtained a reversal deficit on a brightness discrimination only if the old animals had not been trained and reversed on a two-choice position task. If the old animals had previous experience in task reversal, their performance on the brightness reversal was eqüivalent to that of the young animals.

Sime and Kay (1962) found that 6-month-old rats were better at learning a shape discrimination than 16-month animals, but that the older rats were actually better at learning a height discrimination problem. They hypothesized that deficiencies in selective perceptual mechanisms or memory processes might be the cause of the age deficit. While their oldest age group was not senescent, their results emphasize the importance of using multiple tasks or the same task under different conditions for fully evaluating cognitive impairments with age. Barnes et al. (1980), for example, found that young and old Long Evans rats learned a two-choice discrimination problem at the same rate. When they tested the animals with 'probe trials' to determine how the animals actually solved the task (e.g., cue, response or spatial strategies), a very different result emerged. The older animals almost never solved the task by remembering where the goal was in the environment (spatial strategy), while the younger animals used such a strategy a significant proportion of the time. This suggests that there may be a strategy preference shift with age, possibly due to an inability of the older animals to use spatial information effectively. Lowy et al. (1985) also used the same apparatus to test old rats' ability to solve different discrimination problems. While there was no difference between 9- and 24-month ACI rats in their ability to solve a brightness discrimination in a T-maze, the older rats showed impairments in three other conditions in the T-maze. One involved longer-term reference memory of a spatial discrimination in the maze, the second involved shorter-term working memory of a response alternation in the maze, and the third involved reversal of these problems. The cognitive processes involved in each of these versions of the T-maze task were affected similarly by age: older rats made more errors than did the younger animals. Again, this suggests that the type of memory or information-processing required by the task may be the critical feature in obtaining the age deficits. It is not necessarily possible to predict whether there will be a deficit found in a two-choice situation unless the way in which the animals solve the problem is known. Furthermore, these kinds of data argue against the notion that age-related memory impairments are a simple function of task complexity (Goodrick, 1972), since all the T-maze problems were rather easy.

Aged non-human primates do not tend to show behavioral deficits on visual discrimination problems involving color or pattern discrimination (Bartus et al., 1979; Davis, 1978; Harris, 1979; Johnson and Davis, 1973; Riopelle and Rogers, 1965). On tasks involving object recognition or position discriminations, particularly when delays are imposed between the stimulus presentations and the required response, old monkeys do tend to show deficits (Arnstein and Goldman-Rakic, 1985; Bartus, 1979a,b; Bartus et al., 1978, 1980a, 1982a; 1983a; Borkus et al., 1971; Flicker et al., 1985; Marriott and Abelson, 1980; Moss et al., 1988; Presty et al., 1987; Riopelle and Rogers, 1965; Walker et al., 1988). Because the monkeys are not generally impaired on standard visual discrimination problems, the impairment, which is particularly severe on short-term spatial memory tasks, is not likely to be due to a variety of nonspecific factors. For example, in the subject-paced delayed-response task developed by Bartus and his colleagues (the Automated General Experimental Device, or AGED), Bartus et al. (1978) were able to control for possible confounding factors in their testing procedures due to attention, motivation, visual acuity and psychomotor coordination. The 18 – 21-year-old rhesus monkeys were worse at remembering where flashes of light had occurred on the 3 × 3 matrix panel than the 3 – 4-year-old animals at delay intervals greater than zero, suggesting true cognitive changes for selective aspects of aging primate behavior. Because Bartus and his colleagues have tended to use the procedure that allows young and old animals to 'self-pace' themselves to learn the basics of task performance, it is only possible to directly compare the memory components for the animals. The form of the learning curves for acquisition of such delayed-response tasks remains equivocal, both because acquisition measures are difficult to compare on self-paced tasks, and because of conflicting results in studies examining acquisition of delayed non-matching to sample visual-recognition memory tasks. With regard to the latter point, one group of investigators did not find clear evidence for an acquisition deficit in old monkeys (Presty et al., 1987), while another group did (Moss et al., 1988). This discrepancy may be due to the fact that the shortest delay interval used by Presty et al. (1987) was 10 seconds, as compared to 30 seconds used by Moss et al. (1988). It will be important to determine the contribution made by accelerated processes of forgetting during the delay interval to poor acquisition of these tasks.

As was found in experiments using rats, it does not appear that task difficulty per se can completely account for the age impairments noted in primates. The acquisition of color or pattern discrimination problems of increasing complexity did not result in retention deficits in older monkeys (Bartus et al., 1979) nor did an increase in difficulty of a delayed non-matching to sample visual recognition task result in an interaction between the degree of performance deficit obtained between age groups and the memory demand (Moss et al., 1988; Presty et al., 1987). Even in tasks where the initial learning of discrimination problems has been equivalent, faster forgetting of the problem has often been noted in old primates (Davis et al., 1982; Medin, 1969; Medin and Davis, 1974; Medin et al., 1973; Struble et al., 1985). While reversal of certain discrimination problems has been found to result in special difficulties for older rhesus monkeys (Bartus et al., 1979; Davis, 1978), reversals of other types of problem do not always result in such deficits in older primates (Bernstein, 1961). This argues against the notion that older animals exhibit rigidity or inflexibility across all behaviors. Furthermore the behavioral changes in primates appear to be task-dependent (as are the changes for old rodents) and very much influenced by imposed delay intervals.

Multiple-unit T-mazes and radial mazes

Stone examined learning and memory capacities over 2 years of the rat's life span using a behavioral test battery which ranged in complexity from visual discrimination and escape learning to a 14-unit T-maze and a 17-unit Carr maze. The general findings from his classic set of monographs describing the results of these tests (Stone, 1929a,b) were that the older animals did not show striking cognitive impairments compared with his younger rats. Although it has remained a matter of debate whether Stone's data can be interpreted as providing evidence *for* age-related learning *impairments* (Arenberg and Robertson-Tchabo, 1977; Jerome, 1959; Botwinick, 1973) or *for* total *preservation* of the cognitive function of rats with age (Munn, 1950), a small proportion of his oldest animals did appear to show some deficits. Part of the reason for the remarkably good performance of his 2-year-old rats may have been the particular strain of rat that he used. The rats were rather long-lived, having an average life span of 3 rather than 2 years, which is more typical of the strains used today (Goodrick, 1980). Therefore, his findings probably reflect the behavior of rodents through late maturity but not through senescence. Furthermore, recent studies employing similar mazes have consistently found age-related deficits in shorter-lived strains of rats.

Verzar-McDougall (1957) used a 13-unit multiple T-maze to test rats in five age groups ranging from 2 to 30 months. Good performance in this task requires that the animals choose the most efficient route to travel from the starting point to the goal box, with a minimum of entries into blocked alleyways. In this study the rats' performance scores became worse with advancing age, both in the acquisition of the task and in its retention. After about 20 months of age the variability in performance of the rats increased dramatically, with some of the animals in the oldest groups showing severe impairments. Verzar-McDougall stressed the importance of considering individual differences in the interpretation of the age comparisons, although not enough information was provided to be certain that the health of the animals was not the primary factor influencing the variability. Following this report a number of other laboratories demonstrated reliable differences between age groups, even after using a variety of rigorous control procedures on the multiple-unit T-maze problem (Goldman et al., 1987; Goodrick, 1968, 1972, 1973a,b, 1975; Ingram, 1988; Klein, 1983; Klein and Michel, 1977; Skalicky et al., 1984). Goodrick (1968) used a differential deprivation procedure, where the older animals were restricted in food intake to 75% of their normal free feeding weight, while the young animals were restricted to 80% of free feeding weight. Even though the old rats were highly motivated to perform the task under these conditions, they did not perform as accurately as did the younger rats. Furthermore, Ingram (1985) has shown that an age-related deficit in performance is still evident in old rats on this maze using shock motivation, and Jordan and Sokoloff (1959) found age-related deficits using a 14-choice water maze. Although the old animals made more errors overall on the 14-unit T-maze, the pattern of errors was the same in the different age groups (Goodrick, 1973b): the first part of the maze was the most difficult, while the fewest errors were made in the area of the maze nearest the goal. Although it is difficult to give a precise interpretation of results concerning extinction of a response if the groups did not learn the problem equally well, the old animals did show more overall responding in the extinction trials than the younger animals (Goodrick, 1968).

In T-mazes with four choices or fewer, the error rates were shown to be the same in the different age groups (Goodrick, 1972). Goodrick interpreted these findings as consistent with the notion that dimension of difficulty is the variable responsible for the age deficit. However, a more plausible interpretation in view of more recent data (e.g., Barnes et al., 1980; Bartus et al., 1979; Lowy et al., 1985; Presty et al., 1987; Rapp et al., 1987) is that the strategies or memory systems engaged in the 14-choice problem might differ from those in the 1- or 4-choice situations. The systems operational in the 1- and 4-choice problems may be relatively more intact in older animals. Another reason to suspect that the older and younger animals are learning the 14-choice problem differently is the fact that the two age groups benefit differently from massed versus distributed trials on the problem (Goodrick, 1968, 1973a). That is, the older animals learned the problem better with massed trials (4 per day) whereas the younger animals learned better if the trials were given once per day. It may be that memory for the task decays more quickly from day to day in the older rats and that more practice per day retards this forgetting in that age group. Old animals also benefit more from receiving 20 trials of forced correct response practice on the 14-unit maze, whereas in comparison this training actually impaired the younger rats' performance on this problem. If, as some investigators have suggested (Barnes et al., 1980; Rapp et al., 1987), old animals do not tend to use spatial strategies for task solution, then this may imply that old rats are using response strategies which benefit from the forced procedures, whereas the young rats may have competing spatial strategies which, under these conditions, would lead to relatively worse performance. Overall, there is clear agreement that older animals have difficulty acquiring and retaining the 14-unit multiple T-maze problem.

Another type of task that has consistently shown age deficits in rats is the radial maze, which is considered a test primarily of spatial working memory

(Olton and Samuelson, 1976). Perfect performance of this task involves entering each arm of the maze once to obtain food or water reward, without re-entering any of the arms where reward has previously been obtained. In its most typical configuration there are eight arms. With one exception, all studies comparing rodents on this task have found that old animals take more trials to reach a given criterion of performance than do young animals (Barnes et al., 1980; Beatty et al., 1985, 1987; Bierley et al., 1986; Campbell et al., 1980; Davis et al., 1983; de Toledo-Morrell and Morrell, 1985; de Toledo et al., 1981, 1984a,b; Gallagher et al., 1985; Geinisman et al., 1986a,b; Ingram et al., 1981; Van Gool et al., 1985; Wallace et al., 1980a; Willig et al., 1987). The one exception is also the only study in which young (8 months) and old (28 months) mice were compared (Bernstein et al., 1985). Thus, there may be a difference, at least between C57BL/6J mice and many strains of rats, in terms of changes in spatial cognition with age, or in their ability to solve the task using response patterns. In fact, it has been noted that mice appear to solve the problem differently from rats (Mizumori et al., 1982). It remains to be determined how many other strains of mice show the same preservation of this behavior.

Several lines of evidence suggest that the older rats' impairment on the radial maze is a cognitive one. For example, Van Gool et al. (1985) used brown Norway rats of 8 and 33 months of age and recorded visual evoked potentials as well as behavior on the radial 8-arm maze. Overall, the old rats performed more poorly than the young rats, but there was no correlation between performance on the maze and the visual evoked potentials. Thus, a change in visual sensitivity cannot easily explain the impaired performance of the older rats. Furthermore, Gallagher et al. (1985) were able to show that the behavioral deficits seen in old Long Evans hooded rats were not likely to be attributable to problems of learning the motor requirements of the task. They accomplished this by first training the animals in one room and then comparing their performance on learning the same maze in a second room. The old animals eventually reached the same level of accuracy in room 1 as did the young animals; however, when they were transferred to room 2, they were slower than the young animals to reach peak performance levels, presumably due to their inability to use the new spatial information as effectively as the young animals. In support of this general conclusion Barnes et al. (1987) have shown that old animals perform just as well as young animals on a nonspatial version of a working memory task on the radial maze, implying that spatial information processing is particularly compromised in old rats. Other arguments that tend to speak against noncognitive factors being primarily responsible for the age differences seen on the radial maze include the observations that improvements can be made in old animals' spatial behavior after certain drug treatments (de Toledo-Morrell et al., 1984b; Gallagher et al., 1985) or if animals are given extensive training on the task sometime before testing in old age (Beatty et al., 1985; Bierley et al., 1986).

Aversively motivated behaviors

By far the most commonly used method to provide animals with incentive to perform in aversively motivated tasks is electrical shock. There are, however, a number of other non-appetitive methods that can be used to ensure that the animals will perform reliably, including avoidance of bright lights, escape from pools of water, and ingestion of substances that later make the animal ill.

Circular platform

The circular platform is a spatial reference memory task first developed for age comparisons of spatial memory, which utilizes the fact that rodents naturally prefer dark enclosed spaces to brightly illuminated open spaces. The problem involves finding which one of 18 holes (lining the periphery of the platform) leads to a dark escape chamber underneath the brightly illuminated circular surface, always in the same location with respect to the distal cues in the environment. The most effective strategy for solving the task is spatial, because motor patterns and odor trails cannot be used. The general results are that the old animals are worse at remembering the spatial location of the escape chamber from day to day than are the younger rats (Barnes, 1979; Barnes et al., 1980, 1989; Rigter et al., 1984) and forget the location over a 2 month retention interval more quickly than the younger animals (Barnes and McNaughton, 1985).

Water escape tasks

The Morris water task (Morris, 1981) is conceptually similar to the circular platform spatial reference memory problem, using water to motivate the animal to find a hidden escape platform in a large pool. In the spatial version of this task, the old animals rather consistently show poorer retention of where the hidden platform is from day to day than do younger animals (Beigon et al., 1986; Clarke et al., 1986; Decker et al., 1988; Gage and Bjorklund, 1986; Gage et al., 1984a,b; Gallagher and Pelleymounter, 1988; Ghirardi et al., 1989; Meaney et al., 1988; Pelleymounter et al., 1987; Rapp et al., 1987). If the escape platform is raised above the surface of the water so that the task is now a visual discrimination problem rather than a spatial navigation problem, old Long Evans rats' performance is just as good as the younger rats' (Rapp et al., 1987). Furthermore, Rapp et al. (1987) were able to provide direct additional support for the interpretation that the strategies that the old rats use to obtain equivalent performance levels may differ from those of young rats, especially if they are given the choice. In one experiment they used an ambiguous version of the visual discrimination problem, where the platform was always left in the same location over trials. The rats could therefore use either a cue or place strategy for accurate performance. When the platform was removed during 'probe' trials, the young animals had acquired a significant spatial bias for the location of the cued platform as shown by their search pattern, while the old rats exhibited no such bias. This, again, suggests that spatial information processing poses particular problems for the older animals. There is one report that did not find a deficit in acquisition of this task in old Long Evans rats (Lindner and Schallert, 1988), although probe trials were not given in this experiment to evaluate spatial searching patterns. These authors argue that the Long Evans strain may be particularly resistant to age-related behavioral deficits; however, the bulk of the studies using aged rats of this strain or other pigmented-eyed long-lived strains (Brown Norway) *have* found spatial behavior deficits (Barnes, 1979; Decker et al., 1988; Gallagher et al., 1985; Gallagher and Pelleymounter, 1988; Meaney et al., 1988; Pelleymounter et al., 1987; Rapp et al., 1987; Van Gool et al., 1985).

Birren and Kay (1958) and Kay and Birren (1958) first noted that old rats were slower and became fatigued sooner than young rats, although with practice they improved their swimming performance. For this reason, it was critical for the studies using the Morris water task to demonstrate that the total path-length measure (see Hubbard, 1915) was longer for the older animals as well as the overall latency scores, as the latter could have been a reflection of motor deficiencies (Write et al., 1971). Birren (1962) later showed that young and old rats learned a two-choice discrimination in a water maze equally well, which is reminiscent of most of the two-choice appetitively motivated tasks discussed above. Goodrick (1967b), however, did find a difference between old and young Wistar rats in the number of errors made on an 8-choice water task, and Jordan and Sokoloff (1959) found that old rats made many more errors in a 14-choice water maze. Furthermore, Rigter et al. (1980) and Vasquez et al. (1983) both found that old male rats were slower to learn the place of a pole in a water pool where they could escape. Because only latency measures were reported, it is difficult to be confident that this effect was a cognitive one.

Classical conditioning

Classical conditioning of the nictitating membrane or eyelid response in rabbits, cats and humans has revealed a change in the ability to condition such responses in older organisms (Graves and Solomon, 1985; Harrison and Buchwald, 1983; Powell et al., 1981, 1984; Woodruff-Pak and Thompson, 1985; Woodruff-Pak et al., 1987), and particularly striking correspondences are found across the lifespan of aging rabbits and humans (Solomon et al., 1988; Woodruff-Pak, 1988). Because of the recent progress made in understanding the neural circuits that underlie these behaviors, it has been possible to relate the behavioral changes to neural alterations in aged animals. Although different investigators have obtained somewhat different results concerning the performance of aging rabbits on delay versus trace conditioning paradigms, the reasons for these apparent discrepancies are likely to be a function of differences in task parameters such as using shock or airpuff unconditioned stimuli or different lengths of inter-stimulus intervals (e.g. Buchanan and Powell, 1988). Overall the data suggest a large deficit in acquisition of the conditioned response in old animals, especially in paradigms involving delays. The conditioned emotional response has also been studied in old animals (Campbell et al., 1980, 1984; Solyom and Miller, 1965). This procedure measures suppression of a behavior (such as bar pressing) during the presentation of a conditioned stimulus which had previously been paired with an inescapable shock. Solyom and Miller (1965) reported that younger rats tended to suppress a higher proportion of their responses than did older rats. However, a very weak shock was used in their experiment and this could have been responsible for the age difference. Campbell and his colleagues did not find age differences in conditioned emotional responses. Taste aversion learning also appears to remain intact across the life span of rats, mice and Japanese quail (Guanowsky and Misanin, 1983; Ingram and Peacock, 1980; Martinez and Rigter, 1983; Meinecke, 1974; Springer and Fraley, 1981). In this sort of task the animals learn to avoid eating or drinking something previously paired with a noxious event. While there is no evidence for acquisition deficits, Ingram and Peacock (1980) showed that, compared to 4-month rats, 12- and 24-month rats tended to show a stronger resistance to extinction. Furthermore, retention of this experience remained strong following a 1-month interval for all age groups tested (Guanowsky and Misanin, 1983). Therefore, it is apparent that this associative mechanism remains intact in older animals.

Shock-motivated tasks

A very large number of experiments have been performed using shock as the incentive for performance in examining learning and memory across the life span of rats and mice. There are a variety of behaviors that can be tested using this form of motivation, including the following: training the animal to remain stationary to avoid shock; training the animal to move, turn a wheel or press a bar to avoid shock; and training an animal to discriminate a place, light or tone to avoid shock. Acquisition, retention and extinction deficits have been found in old animals compared with young animals in nearly all of the situations just listed above (Bartus et al., 1980b; Brizzee and Ordy, 1979; Dean et al., 1981; Doty, 1966, 1968; Doty and Doty, 1964; Freund and Walker, 1971; Fuchs et al., 1986; Golczewski et al., 1982; Gold and McGaugh, 1975; Gold et al., 1981; Hamm, 1981; Jensen et al., 1980; Kubanis et al., 1982; Lippa et al., 1980; Martinez and Rigter, 1983; McNamara et al., 1977; Oliverio and Bovet, 1966; Ordy et al., 1978; Ordy and Schjeide, 1973; Ray and Barrett, 1973; Rigter et al., 1980; Ruthrich et al., 1982; Sprott, 1972; Vasquez et al., 1983; Yerkes, 1909; Zornetzer et al., 1982). On the other hand, a number of other experiments have not shown age-related deficits in either acquisition, retention, or both, on the same sorts of tasks, particularly if certain 'special conditions' were implemented (Brizzee and Ordy, 1979; Davis et al., 1981; Doty, 1966, 1968, 1972; Doty and Doty, 1964, 1966; Hamm, 1981; Rigter et al., 1980; Ruthrich et al., 1982; Sprott, 1972; Stavnes and Sprott, 1975; Vasquez et al., 1983; Zornetzer et al., 1982). There are many reasons for these inconsistencies, not the least of which being the age groups of animals compared and the genotype. Sprott (1978) has provided an example of this difficulty by demonstrating that there is a wide range of performance differences in a passive avoidance situation even between senescent C57Bl/6J and DBA/2J mice when compared to hybrid mice of the same age: the latter showed an acquisition deficit, the former did not. Because confusion often arises concerning the exact reason for the observed deficits, it has been suggested that avoidance-learning tests might be related more to age differences in emotionality or some other variable than to age differences in learning ability (Goodrick, 1980). At the very least, the avoidance procedures have not always allowed for control of all the variables one would theoretically demand of a study of the effects of aging on cognition (Sprott and Stavnes, 1975).

On the other hand, there are a number of experiments that attempt to address certain of the potential confounding variables in shock experiments, and there are a number of reproducible effects worth emphasizing. First of all, careful examination of the shock intensity used across ages should produce more confidence in the results of experiments that do find age differences in acquisition. Hamm (1981), for example, was able to eliminate age differences in the acquisition of a passive avoidance problem in his Sprague-Dawley rats by increasing shock duration. McCarty established that plasma levels of norepinephrine (1981), mean arterial blood pressure and heart rate (1985) after routine handling were the same across the life span of the Fischer 344 rat. However, after footshock, norepinephrine rose less and there was less tachycardia in older animals than in the younger animals. It is not exactly clear how this might influence performance, but it should be considered when interpreting the results of such studies. Sprott and Symons (1976) measured the threshold to elicit the jaw-jerk reflex following electrical stimulation in two strains of mice. There were no changes in threshold across the life span in these mice. Sprott and Symons, therefore, argued that such centrally mediated reflexes are not compromised with age and thus are not likely to contribute to the avoidance deficits. Spangler and Ingram (1986) exposed young and old mice to inescapable shock and then examined their performance in a T-maze swimming task to test for possible cognitive effects of the shock treatment. They found no evidence of differential impairment across age, and thus no evidence for a greater vulnerability to stress in this situation for the old animals. Furthermore, in experiments designed to compare forgetting rates of young and old rats using shock-motivated tasks, a very reliable case has been built that old animals of a number of species show more rapid forgetting of these problems (Dean et al., 1981; Gold and McGaugh, 1975; Gold et al., 1981; Martinez and Rigter, 1983; Rigter et al., 1980; Zornetzer et al., 1982).

Attempts to ameliorate age-related cognitive declines

With the rather large background of behavioral data from which to design animal experiments, a parallel line of research has emerged which has emphasized the testing of various drugs or the examining of neurotransmitter and hormone systems that might be involved in the production of age-related cognitive declines (Aldinio et al., 1985; Aporti et al., 1986; Barnes et al., 1989; Bartus et al., 1980a, 1981, 1982b; Bickford-Wimer et al., 1987; Brett et al., 1986; Calderini et al., 1985a,b; Cooper et al., 1980; Corwin et al., 1985; Davis et al., 1983; Deyo et al., 1989; Drago et al., 1981, 1988; Ennaceur and Delacour, 1987; Fitten et al., 1987, 1988; Flood and Cherkin, 1986, 1988; Flood et al., 1981, 1983; Gallagher et al., 1985; Ghirardi et al., 1989; Gibson and Peterson, 1980; Giurgea et al., 1983; Gold et al., 1977; Harman et al., 1976; Ingram and McDaniel, 1980; Kessler et al., 1986; Komiskey et al., 1981; Lal et al., 1973; Landfield et al., 1981; le Poncin-Lafitte et al., 1984b; Leathwood et al., 1982; Leslie et al., 1985; Lippa et al., 1980; Mervis et al., 1985; Messing et al., 1982; Mizumori et al., 1985; Porsolt et al., 1987; Ruthrich et al., 1983; Schumacher, 1968; Sternberg et al., 1985; Strong et al., 1980; Welsh and Gold, 1984; Wenk et al., 1987). The focus, for example, on improving cholinergic system function in old organisms with drug treatment has met with modest or mixed success (e.g., Bartus et al., 1982b) especially in clinical trials with humans (e.g., Growdon et al., 1986; Haroutunian et al., 1985a). Part of the problem in some experiments is the choice of patients for the drug trials, some of them having such extensive brain damage that it would be remarkable if the chemical supplements could overcome the loss of circuitry of the cholinergic and other neurochemical systems (e.g. Walker and Olton, 1987). Other substances that induce a wider variety of changes in membrane function of neuronal cells, such as phosphatidylserine, have been used successfully to ameliorate deficits in retention of passive avoidance performance in old animals (Aporti et al., 1986; Calderini et al., 1985a,b; Corwin et al., 1985). These results need to be thoroughly verified in human experiments. While there have been successes and failures among the agents tested, probably the most salient aspect of these data is the diversity of substances that can actually benefit the older animal. This emphasizes the necessity for the consideration of the contribution of multiple neurohumoral systems to the observed behavioral changes in both normal aging and in pathological conditions (e.g., Altman and Normile, 1988; Zornetzer, 1986; Gibson and Peterson, 1986).

Other approaches to the question of the underlying neurobiological mechanisms involved in the cognitive changes seen with age have included attempts to mimic this deficit by the development of specific genetic lines of animals (Miyamoto et al., 1986), by producing lesions with reversible brain cooling methods (Alexander, 1982), and by inducing chemical, electrolytic or ischemic-induced lesions of specific brain areas (e.g., Altman et al., 1985; Bartus et al., 1985; Bresnahan et al., 1988; Friedman et al., 1983; Haroutunian et al., 1985b; Helper et al., 1983; Kesner et al., 1987; le Poncin-Lafitte et al., 1984a; Murphy and Boast, 1985; Murray and Fibiger, 1985; Olton and Wenk, 1987; Ordy et al., 1988; Petit et al., 1980; Wenk and Olton, 1984; Wenk et al., 1987). Complementary approaches include the brain grafting or cell growth stimulation methods, which attempt to restore youthful brain function by implantation of fetal cells (Gage and Bjorklund, 1986), or by infusion of nerve cell growth factors (Fischer et al., 1987). Some of these methods are proving to be successful for models of normal aging and others for models of dementia. Clearly it is only when we have control over both our behavioral methods and their neurobiological underpinnings that we will be able to develop the most useful therapeutic strategies.

Summary of cognitive changes in senescent animals and future directions

The first point that should be emphasized is the fact that cognitive declines, if they are detected in old animals, are rather subtle. A normal healthy old animal is not comparable to an animal with massive brain damage, or even to an animal that has had a particular brain structure completely removed. Rather, aged animals appear to have selective deficits in information processing which probably reflect changes in neuronal function at many brain sites. Although these alterations lead to a clear set of behavioral changes, the pattern of change is far from that of amnestic humans who have experienced stroke, accidental brain injury or Alzheimer's disease. Part of the reason that this point is important is that normal elderly humans also show these subtle forms of behavioral alteration (e.g., Albert, 1988; Craik, 1984; Crook et al., 1986; Poon, 1985). In this sense the animals that have been used to date provide a good model for human aging.

After consideration of the literature on learning and memory in animals, another clear theme that emerges is the need to understand more thoroughly what kinds of information processing our behavioral tasks are measuring, since the age deficits are often task-dependent. With regard to 'learning', there is a clear need for a more rigorous examination of the acquisition process in old animals. Researchers, often in an attempt to overcome the problems involved in equating performance factors between age groups, are not always able to produce appropriate learning-curve comparisons between groups. It will be very important in the future to design experiments that allow direct comparisons of both learning and forgetting if the influence of age on mnemonic processes is to be fully appreciated. Overall the deficits in old animals tend to support the notion that 'memory' is not a unitary phenomenon. Not surprisingly, current concepts of memory typically acknowledge at least two or more types of process that can exist in temporally limited or more extended forms. One of the best reasons to believe that this is the case comes from the evidence that these systems appear to be represented by anatomically distinct brain regions. Selective damage may alter one but leave other capacities intact. From the foregoing review it is clear that certain learning and memory systems may be relatively spared by the aging process, while others may be more susceptible to change. It is interesting, for example, that in both primates and rodents tasks that have a strong spatial component tend to give old animals particular difficulty. This offers an interesting point of convergence between the human and animal literature, as aged humans also have difficulty with certain spatial problems (Evans et al., 1984; Light and Zelinski, 1983; Ohata and Kirasic, 1983; Walsh et al., 1981; Weber et al., 1978; Zelinski and Light, 1988). Examination of the brain structures involved in processing this type of information may reveal the kinds of underlying neurological change that result in such behavioral change. Another notable point from the literature is that in a number of strains and species and over both appetitively and aversively motivated tasks, old animals very often show faster forgetting of the to-be-remembered information. This provides an excellent point of focus for future experiments that aim to investigate treatments for age-related cognitive decline.

Acknowledgements

I am grateful to E.J. Green, B. Leonard, B.L. McNaughton, S.J.Y. Mizumori and P.R. Rapp for their comments on the manuscript, and to B. Peterson and C. Elkins for assistance with manuscript preparation. Preparation of this manuscript was supported by PHS grant K04-AG00243.

References

Albert MS: Cognitive function. In Albert MS, Moss MB (Editors), *Geriatric Neuropsychology.* New York: Guilford Press, pp. 33 – 53, 1988.

Aldinio C, Aporti F, Calderini G, Mazzari S, Zanotti A, Toffano G: Experimental models of aging and quinolinic acid. *Methods Findings Exp. Clin. Pharmacol.: 7,* 563 – 568, 1985.

Alexander GE: Functional development of frontal association cortex in monkeys: Behavioral and electrophysiological studies. *Neurosci. Res. Prog. Bull.: 20,* 471 – 479, 1982.

Altman HJ, Normile HJ: What is the nature of the role of the serotonergic nervous system in learning and memory: Prospects for development of an effective treatment strategy for senile dementia. *Neurobiol. Aging: 9,* 627 – 638, 1988.

Altman HJ, Croslan RD, Jenden DF, Berman RF: Further characterizations of the nature of the behavioral and neurochemical effects of lesions to the nucleus basalis of Meynert in the rat. *Neurobiol. Aging: 6,* 125 – 130, 1985.

Aporti F, Borsato R, Calderini G, Rubini T, Toffano G, Zanotti A, Valzelli L, Goldstein L: Age-dependent spontaneous EEG bursts in rats: effects of brain phosphatidylserine. *Neurobiol. Aging: 7,* 115 – 120, 1986.

Arenberg D, Robertson-Tchabo EA: Learning and aging. In Birren JE, Schaie KW (Editors), *Handbook of the Psychology of Aging.* New York: Van Nostrand Reinhold, pp. 421 – 449, 1977.

Arnsten AFT, Goldman-Rakic PS: Alpha 2-adrenergic mechanisms in prefrontal cortex associated with cognitive decline in aged nonhuman primates. *Science: 230,* 1273 – 1276, 1985.

Bailey CH, Castellucci VF, Hoister J, Chen M: Behavioral changes in aging Aplysia: a model system for studying the cellular basis of age-impaired learning, memory, and arousal. *Behav. Neural Biol.: 38,* 70 – 81, 1983.

Barnes CA: Memory deficits associated with senescence: A neurophysiological and behavioral study in the rat. *J. Comp. Physiol. Psychol.: 93,* 74 – 104, 1979.

Barnes CA, McNaughton BL: An age comparison of the rates of acquisition and forgetting of spatial information in relation to long-term enhancement of hippocampal synapses. *Behav. Neurosci.: 99,* 1040 – 1048, 1985.

Barnes CA, Nadel L, Honig WK: Spatial memory deficit in senescent rats. *Can. J. Psychol.: 34,* 29 – 39, 1980.

Barnes CA, Green EJ, Baldwin J, Johnson WE: Behavioral and neurophysiological examples of functional sparing in senescent rat. *Can. J. Psychol.: 41,* 131 – 140, 1987.

Barnes CA, Eppich C, Rao G: Selective improvement of aged rat short-term spatial memory by 3,4-diaminopyridine. *Neurobiol. Aging: 10,* 337 – 341, 1989.

Bartus RT: Effects of aging on visual memory, sensory processing and discrimination learning in the non-human primate. In Ordy JM, Brizzee K (Editors), *Aging 10: Sensory Systems and Communication in the Elderly.* New York: Raven Press, pp. 85 – 114, 1979a.

Bartus RT: Four stimulants of the central nervous system: Effects on short-term memory in young versus aged monkeys. *J. Am. Geriatr. Soc.: 27,* 289 – 297, 1979b.

Bartus RT: The need for common perspectives in the development and use of animal models for age-related cognitive and neurodegenerative disorders. *Neurobiol. Aging: 9,* 445 – 451, 1988.

Bartus RT, Dean RL: Recent memory in aged non-human primates: hypersensitivity to visual interference during retention. *Exp. Aging Res.: 5,* 385 – 400, 1979.

Bartus RT, Dean RL: Animal models for age-related memory disturbances. In Coyle L (Editor), *Animal Models of Dementia: A Synaptic Neurochemical Perspective.* New York: Alan R. Liss, pp. 69 – 79, 1987.

Bartus RT, Fleming D, Johnson HR: Aging in the rhesus monkey: debilitating effects on short-term memory. *J. Gerontol.: 33,* 858 – 871, 1978.

Bartus RT, Dean RL, Fleming DL: Aging in the rhesus monkey: effects on visual discrimination learning and reversal learning. *J. Gerontol.: 34,* 209 – 219, 1979.

Bartus RT, Dean RL, Beer B: Memory deficits in aged cebus monkeys and facilitation with central cholinomimetics. *Neurobiol. Aging: 1,* 145 – 152, 1980a.

Bartus RT, Dean RL, Goas JA, Lippa AS: Age-related changes in passive avoidance retention: modulation with dietary choline. *Science: 209,* 301 – 303, 1980b.

Bartus RT, Dean RL, Sherman KA, Friedman E, Beer B: Profound effects of combining choline and piracetam on memory enhancement and cholinergic function in aged rats. *Neurobiol. Aging: 2,* 105 – 111, 1981.

Bartus RT, Dean RL, Beer B: Neuropeptide effects on memory in aged monkeys. *Neurobiol. Aging: 3,* 61 – 68, 1982a.

Bartus RT, Dean RL, Beer B, Lippa AS: The cholinergic hypothesis of geriatric memory dysfunction. *Science: 217,* 408 – 417, 1982b.

Bartus RT, Dean RL, Beer B: An evaluation of drugs for improving memory in aged monkeys: implications for clinical trials in humans. *Psychopharmacol. Bull.: 19,* 168 – 184, 1983a.

Bartus RT, Flicker C, Dean RL: Logical principles for the development of animal models of age-related memory impairments. In Crook T, Ferris S, Bartus R (Editors), *Assessment in Geriatric Psychopharmacology.* Connecticut: Mark Pawley Assoc., pp. 263 – 299, 1983b.

Bartus RT, Flicker C, Dean RL, Pontecorvo M, Figueiredo JC, Fisher SK: Selective memory loss following nucleus basalis lesions: long term behavioral recovery despite persistent cholinergic deficiencies. *Pharmacol. Biochem. Behav.: 23,* 125 – 135, 1985.

Bayne, KAL: Qualitative observations of idiosyncratic behavior in old monkeys. In Davis RT, Leathers CW (Editors), *Behavior and Pathology of Aging in Rhesus Monkeys.* New York: Alan R. Liss, pp. 201 – 221, 1985.

Beatty WW, Bierley RA, Boyd JG: Preservation of accurate spatial memory in aged rats. *Neurobiol. Aging: 6,* 219 – 225, 1985.

Beatty WW, Clouse BA, Bierley RA: Effects of long-term restricted feeding on radial maze performance by aged rats. *Neurobiol. Aging: 8,* 325 – 327, 1987.

Bernstein IS: Response variability and rigidity in the adult chimpanzee. *J. Gerontol.: 16,* 381 – 386, 1961.

Bernstein D, Olton DS, Ingram DK, Waller SB, Reynolds MA: Radial maze performance in young and aged mice: neurochemical correlates. *Pharmacol. Biochem. Behav.: 22,* 301 – 307, 1985.

Bickford-Wimer PC, Parfitt K, Hoffer BJ, Freedman R: Desipramine and noradrenergic neurotransmission in aging: failure to respond in aged laboratory animals. *Neuropharmacology: 26,* 597 – 605, 1987.

Biegon A, Greenberger V, Segal M: Quantitative histochemistry of brain acetylcholinesterase and learning rate in the aged rat. *Neurobiol. Aging: 7,* 215 – 217, 1986.

Bierley RA, Rixen GJ, Troster AI, Beatty WW: Preserved spatial memory in old rats survives 10 months without training. *Behav. Neural Biol.: 45,* 223 – 229, 1986.

Birren JE: Age differences in learning a two-choice water maze by rats. *J. Gerontol.: 17,* 207 – 213, 1962.

Birren JE, Kay H: Swimming speed of the albino rat. I. Age and sex differences. *J. Gerontol.: 13,* 374 – 377, 1958.

Borkan GA, Norris AH: Assessment of biological age using a profile of physical parameters. *J. Gerontol.: 35,* 177 – 184, 1980.

Borkus ML, Davis RT, Medin DL: Confusion errors in monkey short-term memory. *J. Comp. Physiol. Psychol.: 77,* 206 – 211, 1971.

Botwinick J: *Aging and Behavior.* New York: Springer, 1973.

Botwinick J, Brinley JF, Robbin JS: Learning a position discrimination and position reversals by Sprague-Dawley rats of different ages. *J. Gerontol.: 17,* 315 – 319, 1962.

Botwinick J, Brinley JF, Robbin JS: Learning and reversing a four-choice multiple Y-maze by rats of three ages. *J. Gerontol.: 18,* 279 – 282, 1963.

Bourliere F: *The Assessment of Biological Age in Man.* Geneva: World Health Organization, No. 37, pp. 1 – 67, 1970.

Brennan MJ, Allen D, Aleman D, Azmitia EC, Quartermain D: Age differences in within-session habituation of exploratory behavior: effects of stimulus complexity. *Behav. Neural Biol.: 42,* 61 – 72, 1984.

Brennan MJ, Blizard DA, Quartermain D: Amelioration of an

age-related deficit in exploratory behavior by preexposure to the test environment. *Behav. Neural Biol.: 34,* 55 – 62, 1982.

Brennan MJ, Dallob A, Freidman E: Involvement of hippocampal serotonergic activity in age-related-changes in exploratory-behavior. *Neurobiol. Aging: 2,* 199 – 203, 1981.

Bresnahan E, Kametani E, Spangler M, Chachich M, Wiser P, Ingram D: Fimbria-fornix lesions impair acquisition performance in a 14-unit T maze similar to prior observed performance deficits in aged rats. *Psychobiology: 16,* 243 – 250, 1988.

Brett LP, Levine R, Levine S: Bidirectional responsiveness of the pituitary-adrenal system in old and young male and female rats. *Neurobiol. Aging: 7,* 153 – 159, 1986.

Brizzee KR, Ordy JM: Age pigments, cell loss and hippocampal function. *Mech. Ageing Dev.: 9,* 143 – 162, 1979.

Bruce PR, Herman JF: Spatial knowledge of young and elderly adults: Scene recognition from familiar and novel perspectives. *Exp. Aging Res.: 9,* 169 – 173, 1983.

Buchanan SL, Powell DA: Age-related changes in associative learning: Studies in rabbits and rats. *Neurobiol. Aging: 9,* 523 – 534, 1988.

Cahn J, Borzeix MG: Water, electrolytes contents of the brain and cerebral function in aged rats. *Monogr. Neural Sci.: 11,* 85 – 92, 1984.

Calderini G, Aporti F, Bellini F, Bonetti AC, Teolato S, Zanotti A, Toffano G: Pharmacological effect of phosphatidylserine on age-dependent memory dysfunction. *Ann. N. Y. Acad. Sci.: 444,* 504 – 506, 1985a.

Calderini G, Aporti F, Bonetti AC, Zanotti A, Toffano G: Serine phospholipids and aging brain. In Lal H, Labella F, Lane F (Editors), *Endocoids.* New York: Alan R. Liss, pp. 383 – 386, 1985b.

Campbell BA, Haroutunian V: Effects of age on long-term memory: retention of fixed interval responding. *J. Gerontol.: 36,* 338 – 341, 1981.

Campbell BA, Krauter EE, Wallace JE: Animal models of aging: sensory-motor and cognitive function in the aged rat. In Stein DG (Editor), *Psychobiology of Aging.* New York: Elsevier/North-Holland, pp. 201 – 226, 1980.

Campbell BA, Sananes CB, Gaddy JR: Animal models of infantile amnesia, benign senescent forgetfulness, and senile dementia. *Neurobehav. Toxicol. Teratol.: 6,* 467 – 471, 1984.

Cheal ML: The gerbil: a unique model for research on aging. *Exp. Aging Res.: 12,* 3 – 21, 1986.

Clarke DJ, Gage FH, Nilsson OG, Bjorklund A: Grafted septal neurons form cholinergic synaptic connections in the dentate gyrus of behaviorally impaired aged rats. *J. Comp. Neurol.: 252,* 483 – 492, 1986.

Coleman GL, Barthold SW, Osbaldiston GW, Foster SJ, Jonas AM: Pathological changes during aging in barrier-reared Fischer 344 male rats. *J. Gerontol.: 32,* 258 – 278, 1977.

Cooper RL, McNamara MC, Thompson WG: Vasopressin and conditioned flavor aversion in aged rats. *Neurobiol. Aging: 1,* 53 – 57, 1980.

Corke PP: Complex behavior in 'old' and 'young' rats. *Psychol. Rep.: 15,* 371 – 376, 1964.

Corwin J, Vicedomini JP, Nonneman AJ, Valetino L: Serial lesion effect in rat medial frontal cortex as a function of age. *Neurobiol. Aging: 3,* 69 – 76, 1982.

Corwin J, Dean RL, Bartus RT, Rotrosen J, Watkins DL: Behavioral effects of phosphatidylserine in the aged Fischer 344 rat: amelioration of passive avoidance deficits without changes in psychomotor task performance. *Neurobiol. Aging: 6,* 11 – 15, 1985.

Costa PT Jr, McCrae RR: Functional age: a conceptual and empirical critique. In Haynes SG, Feinleib M. (Editors), *Epidemiology of Aging.* Washington: U.S. Government Printing Office, NIH Publication No. 80 – 969: 23 – 46, 1980.

Craik FIM: Age difference in remembering. In Squire LR, Butters N (Editors), *Neuropsychology of Memory.* New York: Guilford Press, pp. 3 – 12, 1984.

Crook T, Bartus RT, Ferris SH, Whitehouse P, Cohen GD, Gershon S: Age-associated memory impairment: Proposed diagnostic criteria and measures of clinical change. Report of a National Institute of Mental Health Work Group. *Dev. Neuropsychol.: 2,* 261 – 276, 1986.

Davis HP, Rosenzweig MR, Kinkade PT, Bennett EL: Effects of anisomycin on retention of the passive-avoidance habit as a function of age. *Exp. Aging Res.: 7,* 33 – 44, 1981.

Davis HP, Idowu A, Gibson GE: Improvement of 8-arm maze performance in aged Fischer 344 rats with 3,4-diaminopyridine. *Exp. Aging Res.: 9,* 211 – 214, 1983.

Davis RT: Old monkey behavior. *Exp. Gerontol.: 13,* 237 – 250, 1978.

Davis RT: The effects of aging on the behavior of rhesus monkeys. In Davis RT, Leathers CW (Editors), *Behavior and Pathology of Aging Rhesus Monkeys.* New York: Alan R. Liss, 1985, pp 57 – 82.

Davis RT, Leathers CW (Editors): *Behavior and Pathology of Aging Rhesus Monkeys,* New York: Alan R. Liss, Inc., 1985.

Davis RT, Ruggiero FT: Memory in monkeys as a function of preparatory interval and pattern complexity of matrix displays. *Am. J. Physiol. Anthropol.: 38,* 573 – 578, 1973.

Davis RT, Bennett CL, Weisenburger WP: Repeated measurements of forgetting by rhesus monkeys (*Macaca mulatta).* Percept. Motor Skills: 55: 703 – 709, 1982.

de Toledo-Morrell L, Morrell F: Electrophysiological markers of aging and memory loss in rats. *Ann. N. Y. Acad. Sci.: 444,* 296 – 311, 1985.

de Toledo-Morrell L, Morrell F, Kessler ES, Fleming S: Spatial memory and hippocampal kindling are impaired as a function of aging. *Neurology (Ny): 31,* 101, 1981.

de Toledo-Morrell L, Morrell F, Fleming S: Age-dependent deficits in spatial memory are related to impaired hippocampal kindling. *Behav. Neurosci.: 98,* 902 – 907, 1984a.

de Toledo-Morrell L, Morrell F, Fleming S, Cohen MM: Pentoxifylline reverses age-related deficits in spatial memory. *Behav. Neural Biol.: 42,* 1 – 8, 1984b.

Dean RL, Scozzafava J, Goas JA, Regan B, Beer B, Bartus RT: Age-related differences in behavior across the life span of the C57BL/6J mouse. *Exp. Aging Res.: 7,* 427 – 451, 1981.

Decker MW, Pelleymounter MA, Gallagher M: Effects of training on a spatial memory task on high affinity choline uptake in hippocampus and cortex in young adult and aged rats. *J. Neurosci.: 8,* 90 – 99, 1988.

Deerberg F, Rapp K, Rehm S, Pittermann W: Genetic and environmental influences on life span and diseases in Han:Wistar rats. *Mech. Ageing Dev.: 14,* 333 – 343, 1980.

Desroches HF, Kimbrell GM, Allison JT: Effect of age and experience of bar pressing and activity in the rat. *J. Gerontol.: 19,* 168 – 172, 1964.

Deyo RA, Straube KT, Disterhoft JF: Nimodipine facilitates associative learning in aging rabbits. *Science: 243,* 809 – 811, 1989.

Doty BA: Age and avoidance conditioning in rats. *J. Gerontol.: 21,* 287 – 290, 1966.

Doty BA: Effects of handling on learning of young and aged rats. *J. Gerontol.: 23,* 142 – 144, 1968.

Doty BA: The effects of cage environment upon avoidance responding of aged rats. *J. Gerontol.: 27,* 358 – 360, 1972.

Doty BA, Doty LA: Effect of age and chlorpromazine on memory consolidation. *J. Comp. Physiol. Psychol.: 57,* 331 – 334, 1964.

Doty BA, Doty LA: Facilitative effects of amphetamine on avoidance conditioning in relation to age and problem difficulty. *Psychopharmacologia (Berlin): 9,* 234 – 241, 1966.

Doty BA, Doty LA: Effects of handling at various ages on later openfield behaviour. *Can. J. Psychol.: 21,* 463 – 470, 1967.

Drago F, Canonico PL, Scapagnini U: Behavioral effects of phosphatidylserine in aged rats. *Neurobiol. Aging: 2,* 209 – 213, 1981.

Drago F, Valerio C, D'Agata V, Lauria N, Scapagnini U: Dihydroergocryptine improves behavioral deficits of aged male rats. *Neurobiol. Aging: 9,* 285 – 290, 1988.

Dyundikova VA, Silvon ZK, Dubina TL: Biological age and its estimation. I. Studies of some physiological parameters in albino rats and their validity as biological age tests. *Exp. Gerontol.: 16,* 13 – 24, 1981.

Elias MF: Aging studies of behavior with Fischer 344, Sprague-Dawley, and Long-Evans rats. In Gibson DC, Adelman RC, Finch C (Editors), *Development of the Rodent as a Model System of Aging.* Washington, DC: U.S. Government Printing Office, DHEW Publication No. (NIH) 79 – 161: 253 – 297, 1979.

Elias PK, Elias MF: Effects of age on learning ability: contributions from the animal literature. *Exp. Aging Res.: 2,* 165 – 186, 1976.

Elias PK, Elias MF: Motivation and activity. In Birren IE, Schaie, KW (Editors), *Handbook of the Psychology of Aging.* New York: Van Nostrand Reinhold, pp. 357 – 383, 1977.

Elias PK, Elias MF, Eleftheriou BE: Emotionality, exploratory behavior, and locomotion in aging inbred strains of mice. *Gerontologia: 21,* 46 – 55, 1975.

Ennaceur A, Delacour J: Effect of combined or separate administration of piracetam and choline on learning and memory in the rat. *Psychopharmacology: 92,* 58 – 67, 1987.

Evans G, Brennan P, Skorpanich MA, Held D: Cognitive mapping and elderly adults: verbal and location memory for urban landmarks. *J. Gerontol.: 39,* 452 – 457, 1984.

Fields PE: The age factor in multiple-discrimination learning by white rats. *J. Comp. Physiol. Psychol.: 46,* 387 – 389, 1953.

Fischer W, Wictorin K, Bjorklund A, Williams LR, Varon S, Gage FH: Amelioration of cholinergic neurons atrophy and spatial memory impairment in aged rats by nerve growth factor. *Nature: 329,* 65 – 68, 1987.

Fitten LJ, Flood JF, Baxter CF, Tachiki KH, Perryman K: Long-term oral administration of memory-enhancing doses of tacrine in mice: a study of potential toxicity and side effects. *J. Gerontol.: 42,* 681 – 685, 1987.

Fitten LJ, Perryman K, Tachiki K, Kling A: Oral tacrine administration in middle-aged monkeys: effects on discrimination learning. *Neurobiol. Aging: 9,* 221 – 224, 1988.

Fletcher HJ, Mowbray JB: Note on learning in an aged monkey. *Psychol. Rep.: 10,* 11 – 13, 1962.

Flicker C, Dean RL, Watkins DL, Fisher SK, Bartus RT: Behavioral and neurochemical effects following neurotoxic lesions of a major cholinergic input to the cerebral cortex in the rat. *Pharmacol. Biochem. Behav.: 18,* 973 – 982, 1983.

Flicker C, Dean R, Bartus RT, Ferris SH, Crook T: Animal and human memory dysfunctions associated with aging, cholinergic lesions, and senile dementia. *Ann. N. Y. Acad. Sci.: 444,* 515 – 517, 1985.

Flood JF, Cherkin A: Scopolamine effects on memory retention in mice: a model of dementia? *Behav. Neural Biol.: 45,* 169 – 184, 1986.

Flood JF, Cherkin A: Effect of acute arecoline, tacrine and arecoline + tacrine post-training administration on retention in old mice. *Neurobiol. Aging: 9,* 5 – 8, 1988.

Flood JF, Landry DW, Jarvik ME: Cholinergic receptor interactions and their effects on long-term memory processing. *Brain Res.: 215,* 177 – 185, 1981.

Flood JF, Smith GE, Cherkin A: Memory retention: potentiation of cholinergic drug combinations in mice. *Neurobiol. Aging: 4,* 37 – 43, 1983.

Forbes WB, Macrides F: Temporal matching of sensory-motor behavior and limbic theta rhythm deteriorates in aging rats. *Neurobiol Aging: 5,* 7 – 17, 1984.

Fraley SM, Springer AD: Duration of exposure to a novel environment affects retention in aging mice. *Behav. Neural Biol.: 33,* 293 – 302, 1981a.

Fraley SM, Springer AD: Memory of simple learning in young, middle-aged, and aged C57/BL6 mice. *Behav. Neural Biol.: 31,* 1 – 7, 1981b.

Freund G, Walker DW: The effect of aging on acquisition and retention of shuttle box avoidance in mice. *Life Sci.: 10,* 1343 – 1349, 1971.

Friedman E, Lerer B, Kuster J: Loss of cholinergic neurons in the rat neocortex produces deficits in passive avoidance learning. *Pharmacol. Biochem. Behav.: 19,* 309 – 312, 1983.

Fuchs A, Martin JR, Bender R, Harting J: Avoidance acquisition in adult and senescent rats. *Gerontology: 32,* 91 – 97, 1986.

Furchtgott E, Wechkin S, Dees JW: Open-field exploration as a function of age. *J. Comp. Physiol. Psychol.: 54,* 386 – 388, 1961.

Gage FH, Bjorklund A: Cholinergic septal grafts into the hippocampal formation improve spatial learning and memory in aged rats by an atropine-sensitive mechanism. *J. Neurosci.: 6,* 2837 – 2847, 1986.

Gage FH, Dunnett SB, Bjorklund A: Spatial learning and motor deficits in aged rats. *Neurobiol. Aging: 5,* 43 – 48, 1984a.

Gage FH, Kelly PA, Bjorklund A: Regional changes in brain glucose metabolism reflect cognitive impairments in aged rats. *J. Neurosci.: 4,* 2856 – 2865, 1984b.

Gallagher M, Pelleymounter MA: Spatial learning deficits in old rats: a model for memory decline in the aged. *Neurobiol. Aging: 9,* 549 – 556, 1988.

Gallagher M, Bostock E, King R: Effects of opiate antagonists on spatial memory in young and aged rats. *Behav. Neural Biol.: 44,* 374 – 385, 1985.

Geinisman Y, de Toledo-Morrell L, Morrell F: Loss of perforated synapses in the dentate gyrus: Morphological substrate of memory deficit in aged rats. *Proc. Nat. Acad. Sci. USA: 83,* 3027 – 3031, 1986a.

Geinisman Y, de Toledo-Morrell L, Morrell F: Aged rats need a preserved complement of perforated axospinous synapses per hippocampal neuron to maintain good spatial memory. *Brain Res.: 398,* 266 – 275, 1986b.

Ghirardi O, Milano S, Ramacci MT, Angelucci L: Acetyl-l-carnitine and spatial learning in senescent rats. *Prog. Neuro-Psychopharmacol. Biol. Psychiatry:* in press, 1989.

Gibson G, Peterson C: Acetylcholine metabolism in senescent mice. *Age: 3,* 116, 1980.

Gibson G, Peterson C: Consideration of neurotransmitters and calcium metabolism in therapeutic design. In Crook C, Bartus RT, Ferris S, Gershon S (Editors), *Treatment Development Strategies for Alzheimer's Disease.* Connecticut: Mark Powley Associates, pp. 499 – 517, 1986.

Gibson GE, Peterson C, Jenden D: Brain acetylcholine synthesis declines with senescence. *Science: 213,* 674 – 676, 1981.

Giurgea CE, Greindl M-G, Preat S: Nootropic drugs and aging. *Acta Psychiatr. Belg.: 83,* 349 – 358, 1983.

Goetsch VL, Isaac W: Age and visual sensitivity in the rat. *Physiol. Psychol.: 10,* 199 – 201, 1982.

Golczewski JA, Hiramoto RN, Ghanta VK: Enhancement of maze learning in old C57BL/6 mice by dietary lecithin. *Neurobiol. Aging: 3,* 223 – 226, 1982.

Gold PE, McGaugh JL: Changes in learning and memory during aging. In Ordy JM, Prizzee KR (Editors), *Advances in Behavioral Biology.* New York: Plenum Press, 16: 145 – 158, 1975.

Gold PE, van Buskirk R, Haycock JW: Effects of post-training epinephrine injections on retention of avoidance training in mice. *Behav. Biol.: 20,* 197 – 204, 1977.

Gold PE, McGaugh JL, Hankins LL, Rose RP, Vasquez BJ: Age dependent changes in retention in rats. *Exp. Aging Res.: 8,* 53 – 58, 1981.

Goldman H, Berman RF, Gershon S, Murphy SL, Altman HJ: Correlation of behavioral and cerebrovascular functions in the aging rat. *Neurobiol. Aging: 8,* 409 – 416, 1987.

Goodrick CL: Social interactions and exploration of young, mature, and senescent male albino rats. *J. Gerontol.: 20,* 215 – 218, 1965.

Goodrick CL: Activity and exploration as a function of age and deprivation. *J. Genet. Psychol.: 108,* 239 – 252, 1966.

Goodrick CL: Exploration of nondeprived male Sprague-Dawley rats as a function of age. *Psychol. Rep.: 20,* 159 – 163, 1967a.

Goodrick CL: Behavioral characteristics of young and senescent inbred female mice of the C57BL/6J strain. *J. Gerontol.: 22,* 459 – 464, 1967b.

Goodrick CL: Learning, retention, and extinction of a complex maze habit for mature-young and senescent Wistar albino rats. *J. Gerontol.: 23,* 298 – 304, 1968.

Goodrick CL: Variables affecting free exploration responses of male and female Wistar rats as a function of age. *Dev. Psychol.: 4,* 440 – 446, 1971a.

Goodrick CL: Free exploration and adaptation within an open field as a function of trials and between-trial-interval for mature-young, mature-old, and senescent Wistar rats. *J. Gerontol.: 26,* 58 – 62, 1971b.

Goodrick CL: Learning by mature-young and aged Wistar albino rats as a function of test complexity. *J. Gerontol.: 27,* 353 – 357, 1972.

Goodrick CL: Maze learning of mature-young and aged rats as a function of distribution of practice. *J. Exp. Psychol.: 98,* 344 – 349, 1973a.

Goodrick CL: Error goal-gradients of mature-young and aged rats during training in a 14-unit spatial maze. *Psychol. Rep.: 32,* 359 – 362, 1973b.

Goodrick CL: Behavioral differences in young and aged mice: strain differences for activity measures, operant learning, sensory discrimination, and alcohol preference. *Exp. Aging Res.: 1,* 191 – 207, 1975a.

Goodrick CL: Adaptation to novel environments by the rat: effects of age, stimulus intensity, group testing, and temperature. *Dev. Psychobiol.: 8,* 287 – 296, 1975b.

Goodrick CL: Behavioral rigidity as a mechanism for facilitation of problem solving for aged rats. *J. Gerontol.: 30,* 181 – 184, 1975c.

Goodrick CL: Problem solving and age: a critique of rodent research. In Sprott RL, (Editor), *Age, Learning Ability and Intelligence.* New York: Van Nostrand Reinhold, pp. 5 – 25, 1980.

Goodrick CL: Effects of lifelong restricted feeding on complex maze performance in rats. *Age: 7,* 1 – 2, 1984.

Graves CA, Solomon PR: Age-related disruption of trace but not delay classical conditioning of the rabbit's nictitating membrane response. *Behav. Neurosci.: 99,* 88 – 96, 1985.

Greenberg G: Failure to observe visual discrimination in old gerbils: replication report. *J. Gen. Psychol.: 99,* 169 – 171, 1978.

Growdon JH, Corkin S, Hugg FJ, Rosen TJ: Piracetam combined with lecithin in the treatment of Alzheimer's disease. *Neurobiol. Aging: 7,* 269 – 276, 1986.

Guanowsky V, Misanin JR: Retention of conditioned taste aversion in weanling, adult, and old-age rats. *Behav. Neural Biol.: 37,* 173 – 178, 1983.

Hamm RJ: Hypothermia-induced retrograde amnesia in mature and aged rats. *Dev. Psychobiol.: 14,* 357 – 364, 1981.

Hamm RJ, Knisely JS, Dixon CE: An animal model of age changes in short-term memory: the DRL schedule. *Exp. Aging Res.: 9,* 23 – 25, 1983.

Hamm RJ, Dixon CE, Knisely JS: Long-term memory of a DRL task in mature and aged rats. *Exp. Aging Res.: 10,* 39 – 42, 1984.

Harman D, Hendricks S, Eddy DE, Seibold J: Free radical theory of aging: Effect of dietary fat on central nervous system function. *J. Am. Geriatr. Soc.: 24,* 301 – 307, 1976.

Haroutunian V, Davis KL, Davis BM, Horvath TB, Johns CA, Mohs RC: The study of cholinomimetics in Alzheimer's disease and animal models. In Iversen SD (Editor), *Psychopharmacology: Recent Advances and Future Prospects.* London: Oxford Publishing, pp. 170 – 181, 1985a.

Haroutunian V, Kanof P, Davis KL: Pharmacological alleviation of cholinergic lesion induced memory deficits in rats. *Life Sci.: 37,* 945 – 952, 1985b.

Harris AV: Backward and forward masking in *Macaca mulatta.*

Folia Primatol.: 32, 43 – 46, 1979.

Harrison DW, Isaac W: Disruption and habituation of stable fixed-interval behavior in younger and older monkeys. *Physiol. Behav.: 32,* 341 – 344, 1983.

Harrison JM: Effects of age on acquisition and maintenance of a location discrimination in rats. *Exp. Aging Res.: 7,* 467 – 476, 1981.

Harrison J, Buchwald J: Eyeblink conditioning deficits in the old cat. *Neurobiol. Aging: 4,* 45 – 51, 1983.

Helper DJ, Olton DS, Wenk GL, Coyle JT: Lesions in nucleus basalis magnocellularis and medial septal area of rats produce qualitatively similar memory impairments. *J. Neurosci.: 5,* 866 – 876, 1985.

Honig WK: Studies of working memory in the pigeon. In Hulse SH, Fowler H, Honig SH (Editors), *Cognitive Process in Animal Behavior.* Hillsdale, NJ: Lawrence Erlbaum, pp. 211 – 248, 1978.

Howell T: Old age. *Geriatrics: 4,* 281 – 292, 1949.

Hubbard H: The effect of age on habit formation in the albino rat. *Behav. Monogr.: 2,* 1 – 55, 1915.

Ingram DK: Toward the behavioral assessment of biological aging in the laboratory mouse: Concepts, terminology, and objectives. *Exp. Aging Res.: 9,* 225 – 238, 1983.

Ingram DK: Analysis of age-related impairments in learning and memory in rodent models. *Ann. N. Y. Acad. Sci.: 444,* 312 – 331, 1985.

Ingram DK: Complex maze learning in rodents as a model of age-related memory impairment. *Neurobiol. Aging: 9,* 475 – 485: 1988.

Ingram DK, McDaniel WF: Failure of B6 deficiency to affect performance of aging rats in a passive avoidance task. *Exp. Aging Res.: 6,* 61 – 67, 1980.

Ingram DK, Peacock LJ: Conditioned taste aversion as a function of age in mature male rats. *Exp. Aging Res.: 6,* 113 – 123, 1980.

Ingram DK, London ED, Goodrick CL: Age and neurochemical correlates of radial maze performance in rats. *Neurobiol. Aging: 2,* 41 – 47, 1981.

Ingram DK, Archer JR, Harrison DE, Reynolds MA: Physiological and behavioral correlates of life span in aged C57BL/6J mice. *Exp. Gerontol.: 17,* 295 – 303, 1982a.

Ingram DK, London ED, Reynolds MA: Circadian rhythmicity and sleep: effects of aging in laboratory animals. *Neurobiol. Aging: 3,* 287 – 297, 1982b.

Ingram DK, London E, Waller SB, Reynolds MA: Age-dependent correlation of motor performance with neurotransmitter synthetic enzyme activities in mice. *Behav. Neural Biol.: 39,* 284 – 298, 1983a.

Ingram DK, Spangler EL, Vincent GP: Behavioral comparison of aged virgin and retired breeder mice. *Exp. Aging Res.: 9,* 111 – 113, 1983b.

Ingram DK, Weindruch R, Spangler EL, Freeman JR, Walford RL: Dietary restriction benefits learning and motor performance of aged mice. *J. Gerontol.: 42,* 78 – 81, 1987.

Jakubczak LF: Age differences in the effects of water deprivation on activity, water loss and survival of rats. *Life Sci.: 9,* 771 – 780, 1970.

Jakubczak LF: Age and animal behavior. In Eisdorfer C, Lawton MP (Editors), *The Psychology of Adult Development and Aging.* Washington, DC: American Psychological Association, pp. 98 – 111, 1973.

Janicke B, Schulze G, Coper H: Motor activity with aging. In Cervos-Navarro J, Sarkander J-I (Editors), *Brain Aging: Neuropathology and Neuropharmacology.* New York: Raven Press, pp. 275 – 288, 1983.

Jensen RA, Martinez JL, McGaugh JL, Messing RB, Vasquez BJ: The psychobiology of aging. In Maletta GJ, Pirozzolo FJ (Editors), *The Aging Nervous System.* New York: Praeger, pp. 110 – 125, 1980.

Jerome EA: Age and learning – experimental studies. In Birren J (Editor), *Handbook of Aging and the Individual.* University of Chicago Press, pp. 655 – 699, 1959.

Jones DC, Kimeldorf J, Rubadeau DO, Castanera TJ: Relationships between volitional activity and age in the male rat. *Am. J. Psychol.: 172,* 109 – 114, 1953.

Johnson CK, Davis RT: Seven-year retention of oddity learning set in monkeys. *Percept. Motor Skills: 37,* 920 – 922, 1973.

Jordon J, Sokoloff B: Air ionization, age, and maze learning of rats. *J. Gerontol.: 14,* 344 – 348, 1959.

Kay H, Birren JE: Swimming speed of the albino rat. II. Fatigue, practice and drug effects on age and sex differences. *J. Gerontol.: 13,* 378 – 385, 1958.

Kay H, Sime ME: Discrimination learning with old and young rats. *J. Gerontol.: 17,* 75 – 80, 1962.

Kesner RP, Adelstein T, Crutcher KA: Rats with nucleus basalis magnocellularis lesions mimic mnemonic symptomatology observed in patients with dementia of the Alzheimer's type. *Behav. Neurosci.: 101,* 451 – 456, 1987.

Kessler AR, Kessler B, Yehuda S: In vivo modulation of brain cholesterol level and learning performance by a novel plant lipid: Indications for interactions between hippocampal-cortical cholesterol and learning. *Life Sci.: 38,* 1185 – 1192, 1986.

Klein AW: Synaptic density correlated with maze performance in young and aged rats. A preliminary study. *Mech. Ageing Dev. 21,* 245 – 255, 1983.

Klein AW, Michel ME: A morphometric study of the neocortex of young adult and old maze-differentiated rats. *Mech. Ageing Dev.: 6,* 441 – 452, 1977.

Komiskey HL, Cook TM, Lin C-F, Hayton WL: Impairment of learning or memory in the mature and old rat by diazepam. *Psychopharmacology: 73,* 304 – 305, 1981.

Kubanis P, Zornetzer SF: Age-related behavioral and neurobiological changes: a review with an emphasis on memory. *Behav. Neural Biol.: 31,* 115 – 172, 1981.

Kubanis P, Zornetzer SF, Freund G: Memory and postsynaptic cholinergic receptors in aging mice. *Pharmacol. Biochem. Behav.: 17,* 313 – 322, 1982.

Lal H, Pogacar S, Daly PR, Puri SK: Behavioral and neuropathological manifestations of nutritionally induced central nervous system 'aging' in the rat. *Prog. Brain Res.: 40,* 128 – 140, 1973.

Landfield PW, Baskin RK, Pitler TA: Brain aging correlates: retardation by hormonal-pharmacological treatments. *Science: 214,* 581 – 584, 1981.

Le Poncin-Lafitte M, Grosdemouge C, Duterte D, Rapin JR: Simultaneous study of haemodynamic, metabolic and behavioral sequelae in a model of cerebral ischaemia in aged rats: effects of nicergoline. *Gerontology: 30,* 109 – 119, 1984a.

Le Poncin-Lafitte M, Lamproglou Y, Duterte D, Rapin JR: Simultaneous study of learning, cerebral hemodynamics, and metabolism in aged rats: effects of a dopaminergic agonist. *Monogr. Neural Sci.: 11,* 68 – 77, 1984b.

Leathwood PD, Heck E, Mauron J: Phosphatidyl choline and avoidance performance in 17 month-old SEC/1ReJ mice. *Life Sci.: 30,* 1065 – 1071, 1982.

Leslie FM, Loughlin SE, Sternberg DB, McGaugh JL, Young LE, Zornetzer SF: Noradrenergic changes and memory loss in aged mice. *Brain Res.: 359,* 292 – 299, 1985.

Light LL, Zelinski EM: Memory for spatial information in young and old adults. *Dev. Psychol.: 19,* 901 – 906, 1983.

Lindner MD, Schallert T: Aging and atropine effects on spatial navigation in the Morris water task. *Behav. Neurosci.: 102,* 621 – 634, 1988.

Lippa AS, Pelham RW, Beer B, Critchett DJ, Dean RL, Bartus RT: Brain cholinergic dysfunction and memory in aged rats. *Neurobiol. Aging: 1,* 13 – 19, 1980.

Lorig TS, Isaac W: The effects of light reinforcement and noise on young and old squirrel monkeys (*Saimiri sciureus*). *Exp. Aging Res.: 9,* 97 – 100, 1983.

Lowy AM, Ingram DK, Olton DS, Waller SB, Reynolds MA, London ED: Discrimination learning requiring different memory components in rats: Age and neurochemical comparisons. *Behav. Neurosci.: 99,* 638 – 651, 1985.

Ludwig FC, Smoke ME: The measurement of biological age. *Exp. Aging Res.: 6,* 497 – 522, 1980.

Margolin SE, Bunch ME: The relationship between age and the strength of hunger motivation. *Comp. Psychol. Monogr.: 16,* 1 – 34, 1940.

Marriott JG, Abelson JS: Age differences in short-term memory of test-sophisticated rhesus monkeys. *Age: 3,* 7 – 9, 1980.

Marshall JF, Berrios N: Movement disorders of aged rats: reversal by dopamine receptor stimulation. *Science: 206,* 477 – 479, 1979.

Martinez JL, Jr, Rigter H: Assessment of retention capacities in old rats. *Behav. Neural Biol.: 39,* 181 – 191, 1983.

Martinez JL, Jr, Schulteis G, Janak PH, Weinberger SB: Behavioral assessment of forgetting in aged rodents and its relationship to peripheral sympathetic function. *Neurobiol. Aging: 9,* 697 – 708, 1988.

McCarty R: Aged rats: diminished sympathetic-adrenal medullary responses to acute stress. *Behav. Neural Biol.: 33,* 204 – 212, 1981.

McCarty R: Cardiovascular responses to acute footshock stress in adult and aged Fischer 344 male rats. *Neurobiol. Aging: 6,* 47 – 50, 1985.

McNamara MC, Benignus G, Benignus VA, Miller AT Jr: Active and passive avoidance in rats as a function of age. *Exp. Aging Res.: 3,* 3 – 16, 1977.

Meaney MJ, Aitken DH, Burkel C, Bhatnager S, Sapolski RM: Effect of neonatal handling on age-related impairments associated with the hippocampus. *Science: 239,* 76 – 78, 1988.

Meck WH, Church RM: Arginine vasopressin inoculates against age-related changes in temporal memory. *Ann. N. Y. Acad. Sci.: 444,* 453 – 456, 1985.

Meck WH, Church RM, Wenk GL: Arginine vasopressin inoculates against age-related increases in sodium-dependent high affinity choline uptake and discrepancies in the content of temporal memory. *Eur. J. Pharmacol.: 130,* 327 – 331, 1986.

Medin DL: Form perception and pattern reproduction by monkeys. *J. Comp. Physiol. Psychol.: 68,* 412 – 419, 1969.

Medin DL, Davis RT: Memory. In Schrier AL, Stollnitz F (Editors), *Behavior of Nonhuman Primates.* New York: Academic Press, 5: 1 – 47, 1974.

Medin DL, O'Neil P, Smeltz E, Davis RT: Age differences in retention of concurrent discrimination problems in monkeys. *J. Gerontol.: 28,* 63 – 67, 1973.

Meinecke RO: Retention of one-trial learning in neonate, young adult, and aged Japanese quail. *J. Gerontol.: 29,* 172 – 176, 1974.

Mervis R, Horrocks L, Demediuk P, Wallace L, Meyer DR, Beall S, Caris K, Naber E: Neurobehavioral effects of chronic choline-containing diets on the adult and aging C57BL/6NNIA mouse brain. *Ann. N. Y. Acad. Sci.: 444,* 469 – 470, 1985.

Messing RB, Rigter H, Nickolson VJ: Memory consolidation in senescence: effects of CO_2, amphetamine and morphine. *Neurobiol. Aging: 3,* 133 – 139, 1982.

Miquel J, Blasco MA: A simple technique for evaluation of vitality loss in aging mice, by testing their muscular coordination and vigor. *Exp. Gerontol.: 13,* 389 – 396, 1978.

Miyamoto M, Kiyota Y, Yamazaki N, Nagaoka A, Matsuo T, Nagawa Y, Takeda T: Age-related changes in learning and memory in the senescence-accelerated mouse (SAM). *Physiol. Behav.: 38,* 399 – 406, 1986.

Mizumori SJY, Patterson TA, Sternberg H, Rosenzweig MR, Bennett EL, Timiras PS: Effects of dietary choline on memory and brain chemistry in aged mice. *Neurobiol. Aging: 6,* 51 – 56, 1985.

Mizumori SJY, Rosenzweig MR, Kermisch MG: Failure of mice to demonstrate spatial memory in the radial maze. *Behav. Neural Biol.: 35,* 33 – 45, 1982.

Morris RGM: Spatial localization does not require the presence of local cues. *Learn. Motiv.: 12,* 239 – 260, 1981.

Mos J, Hollander CF: Analysis of survival data on aging rat cohorts: Pitfalls and some practical considerations. *Mech. Ageing Dev.: 38,* 89 – 105, 1987.

Moss MB, Rosene DL, Peters A: Effects of aging on visual recognition memory in the rhesus monkey. *Neurobiol. Aging: 9,* 495 – 502, 1988.

Munn NL: *Handbook of Psychological Research on the Rat.* Boston: Houghton Mifflin Co., 1950.

Murphy DE, Boast CA: Searching for models of Alzheimer's disease: a comparison of four amnestic treatments in two behavioral tasks. *Ann. N. Y. Acad. Sci.: 444,* 450 – 452, 1985.

Murray CL, Fibiger HC: Learning and memory deficit after lesions of the nucleus basalis magnocellularis: reversal by physostigmine. *Neuroscience: 14,* 1025 – 1032, 1985.

Myers DD: Review of disease patterns and life span in aging mice: genetic and environmental interactions. In *National Foundation – March of Dimes Genetic Effects on Aging.* New York: Alan R. Liss, 14: 41 – 53, 1978.

Ohata RJ, Kirasic KC: The investigation of environmental learning in the elderly. In Rowles GD, Ohata RJ (Editors), *Aging and Milieu.* New York: Academic Press, pp. 83 – 95, 1983.

Oliverio A, Bovet D: Effects of age on maze learning and avoidance conditioning of mice. *Life Sci.: 5,* 1317 – 1324, 1966.

Olton DS, Samuelson RJ: Remembrance of places passed: Spatial memory in rats. *J. Exp. Psychol. Anim. Behav. Processes: 2,* 97 – 116, 1976.

Olton DS, Wenk G: Dementia: animal models of the cognitive impairments produced by degeneration of the basal forebrain cholinergic system. In Meltzer HY (Editor), *Psychopharmacology: The Third Generation of Progress.* New York: Raven Press, pp. 941 – 953, 1987.

Ordy JM, Schjeide OA: Univariate and multivariate models for evaluating long-term changes in neurobiological development, maturity and aging. *Prog. Brain Res.: 40,* 25 – 51, 1973.

Ordy JM, Brizzee KR, Kaack B, Hansche J: Age differences in short-term memory and cell loss in the cortex of the rat. *Gerontology: 24,* 276 – 285, 1978.

Ordy JM, Thomas GJ, Volpe BT, Dunlap WP, Colombo PM: An animal model of human-type memory loss based on aging, lesion, forebrain ischemia, and drug studies with the rat. *Neurobiol. Aging: 9,* 667 – 683, 1988.

Parsons PJ, Fagan T, Spear NE: Short-term retention of habituation in the rat: a developmental study from infancy to old age. *J. Comp. Physiol. Psychol.: 84,* 545 – 553, 1973.

Pelleymounter MA, Smith MY, Gallagher M: Spatial learning impairments in aged rats trained with a salient configuration of stimuli. *Psychobiology: 15,* 248 – 254, 1987.

Petit TL, Biederman GB, McMullen PA: Neurofibrillary degeneration, dendritic dying back, and learning-memory deficits after aluminum administration: Implications for brain aging. *Exp. Neurol.: 67,* 152 – 162, 1980.

Pontecorvo M, Clissold DB, Conti LH: Automated repeated measures tests for age related cognitive impairments. *Neurobiol. Aging: 9,* 617 – 625, 1988.

Poon LW: Differences in human memory with aging: nature, causes, and clinical implications. In Birren JE, Schaie KW (Editors), *The Handbook of the Psychology of Aging.* New York: Van Nostrand Reinhold, pp. 427 – 462, 1985.

Porsolt RD, Lenegre A, Avril I, Steru L, Doumont G: The effect of exifone, a new agent for senile memory disorder, on two models of memory in the mouse. *Pharmacol. Biochem. Behav.: 27,* 253 – 256, 1987.

Powell DA, Buchanan SL, Hernandez LL: Age-related changes in classical (Pavlovian) conditioning in the New Zealand albino rabbit. *Exp. Aging Res.: 7,* 453 – 465, 1981.

Powell DA, Buchanan SL, Hernandez LL: Age-related changes in Pavlovian conditioning: Central nervous system correlates. *Physiol. Behav.: 32,* 609 – 616, 1984.

Presty SK, Bachevalier J, Walker LC, Struble RG, Price DL, Mishkin M, Cork LC: Age differences in recognition memory of the rhesus monkey (*Macaca mulatta). Neurobiol. Aging: 8,* 435 – 440, 1987.

Rapp PR, Rosenberg RA, Gallagher M: An evaluation of spatial information processing in aged rats. *Behav. Neurosci.: 101,* 3 – 12, 1987.

Ray OS, Barrett RJ: Interaction of learning and memory with age in the rat. *Adv. Behav. Biol.: 6,* 17 – 39, 1973.

Rigter H, Martinez JL, Crabbe JC Jr: Forgetting and other behavioral manifestations of aging. In Stein DG (Editor), *The Psychobiology of Aging: Problems and Perspectives.* New York: Elsevier North-Holland, 161 – 175, 1980.

Rigter H, Veldhuis HD, de Kloet ER: Spatial learning and the hippocampal corticosterone receptor system of old rats: effects of the ACTH4 – 9 analogue ORG2766. *Brain Res.: 309,* 393 – 398, 1984.

Riopelle AJ, Rogers CM: Age changes in chimpanzees. In Schrier AM, Harlow HF, Stollnitz F (Editors), *Behavior in Nonhuman Primates.* New York: Academic Press, pp. 449 – 462, 1965.

Ruthrich H-L, Wetzel W, Matthies H: Acquisition and retention of different learning tasks in old rats. *Behav. Neural Biol.: 35,* 139 – 146, 1982.

Ruthrich H-L, Wetzel W, Matthies H: Memory retention in old rats: improvement by orotic acid. *Psychopharmacology: 79,* 348 – 351, 1983.

Salthouse TA: Speed of behavior and its implications for cognition. In Birren JE, Schaie KW (Editors), *Handbook of the Psychology of Aging.* New York: Van Nostrand Reinhold, pp. 400 – 426, 1985.

Samorajski T, Delaney C, Durham L: Effect of exercise on longevity, body weight, locomotor performance, and passive-avoidance memory of C57BL/6J mice. *Neurobiol. Aging: 6,* 17 – 24, 1985.

Sarter M: Measurement of cognitive abilities in senescent animals. *Int. J. Neurosci.: 32,* 765 – 774, 1987.

Sarter M, Markowitsch HJ: Reduced resistance to progressive extinction in senescent rats: a neuroanatomical and behavioral study. *Neurobiol. Aging: 4,* 203 – 215, 1983.

Schlettwein-Gsell D: Survival curves of an old age rat colony. *Gerontologia: 16,* 111 – 115, 1970.

Schumacher SS: Age-related physiological and behavioral changes as a function of active thyroglobulin immunity. *Diss. Abstr.: 29(1-B),* 396, 1968.

Shirley M: Studies in activity. II. Activity rhythms, age, and activity: activity after rest. *J. Comp. Psychol.: 8,* 159 – 186, 1928.

Shock NW: Indices of functional age. In Danon D, Shock NW, Marois M (Editors), *Aging: A Challenge to Science and Society.* Oxford: Oxford University Press, pp. 270 – 286, 1981.

Short R, Williams DD, Bowden DM: Cross-sectional evaluation of potential biological markers of aging in pigtailed macaques: effects of age, sex, and diet. *J. Gerontol.: 42,* 644 – 654, 1987.

Sime ME, Kay H: Inter-problem interference and age. *J. Gerontol.: 17,* 81 – 87, 1962.

Skalicky M, Hofecker G, Sment A, Niedermuller H: Models of the biological age of the rat. II. Multiple regression models in the study on influencing aging. *Mech. Ageing Dev.: 14,* 361 – 377, 1980.

Skalicky M, Bubna-Littitz H, Hofecker G: The influence of persistent crowding on the age changes of behavioral parameters and survival characteristics of rats. *Mech. Ageing Dev.: 28,* 325 – 336, 1984.

Slonaker JR: The normal activity of the white rat at different ages. *J. Comp. Neurol. Psychol.: 17,* 342 – 359, 1907.

Slonaker JR: Normal activity of the albino rat from birth to natural death, rate of growth, and duration of life. *J. Anim. Behav.: 2,* 20 – 42, 1912.

Smith G: Animal models of Alzheimer's disease: experimental cholinergic denervation. *Brain Res. Rev.: 13,* 103 – 118, 1988.

Solomon PR, Beal MF, Pendlebury WW: Age-related disruption of classical conditioning: A model systems approach to memory disorders. *Neurobiol. Aging: 9,* 535 – 546, 1988.

Solyom L, Miller S: The effect of age differences on the acquisition of operant and classical conditioned responses in rats. *J. Gerontol.: 20,* 311 – 314, 1965.

Spangler EL, Ingram DK: Effects of inescapable shock on maze performance as a function of age in mice. *Exp. Aging Res.: 12,* 39 – 42, 1986.

Springer AD, Fraley SM: Extinction of a conditioned taste aversion in young, mid-aged, and aged C57/BL6 mice. *Behav. Neural Biol.: 32,* 282 – 294, 1981.

Sprott RL: Passive-avoidance conditioning in inbred mice: effects of shock intensity, age, and genotype. *J. Comp. Physiol. Psychol.: 80,* 327 – 334, 1972.

Sprott RL: The interaction of genotype and environment in the determination of avoidance behavior of aging inbred mice. In *The National Foundation – March of Dimes Genetic Effects on Aging.* New York: Alan R. Liss, 14: 109 – 120, 1978.

Sprott RL: Senescence and learning, behavior in mice. In Sprott RL (Editor), *Age, Learning Ability and Intelligence,* New York: Van Nostrand Reinhold Co., pp. 26 – 40, 1980.

Sprott RL, Eleftheriou BE: Open-field behavior in aging inbred mice. *Gerontologia: 20,* 155 – 162, 1974.

Sprott RL, Stavnes K: Avoidance learning behavior genetics, and aging: a critical review and comment on methodology. *Exp. Aging Res.: 1,* 145 – 168, 1975.

Sprott RL, Symons JP: The effects of age and genotype upon the jaw-jerk reflex in inbred mice. *J. Gerontol.: 31,* 660 – 662, 1976.

Stavnes K, Sprott RL: Effects of age and genotype on acquisition of an active avoidance response in mice. *Dev. Psychobiol.: 8,* 437 – 445, 1975.

Stephens DN, Weidmann R, Quartermain D, Sarter M: Reversal learning in senescent rats. *Behav. Brain Res.: 17,* 193 – 202, 1985.

Sternberg DB, Martinez JL, Gold PE, McGaugh JL: Age-related memory deficits in rats and mice: enhancement with peripheral injections of epinephrine. *Behav. Neural Biol.: 44,* 213 – 220, 1985.

Stone CP: The age factor in animal learning: I. Rats in the problem box and the maze. *Genet. Psychol. Monogr.: 5,* 1 – 130, 1929a.

Stone CP: The age factor in animal learning: II. Rats on a multiple light discrimination box and a difficult maze. *Genet. Psychol. Monogr.: 6,* 125 – 201, 1929b.

Storer JB: Longevity and gross pathology at death in 22 inbred mouse strains. *J. Gerontol.: 21,* 404 – 409, 1966.

Strong R, Hicks P, Hsu L, Bartus RT, Enna SJ: Age-related alterations in the rodent brain cholinergic system and behavior. *Neurobiol. Aging: 1,* 59 – 63, 1980.

Struble RG, Price DL, Jr, Cork LC, Price DL: Senile plaques in cortex of aged normal monkeys. *Brain Res.: 361,* 267 – 275, 1985.

Tigges J, Gordon TP, McClure HM, Hall EC, Peters A: Survival rate and life span of rhesus monkeys at the Yerkes Regional Primate Research Center. *Am. J. Primatol.: 15,* 263 – 273, 1988.

Tobin JD: Physiological indices of aging. In Danon D, Shock NW, Marois M (Editors), *Aging: A Challenge to Science and Society.* Oxford: Oxford University Press, pp. 286 – 295, 1981.

van Gool WA, Mirmiran M, van Haaren F: Spatial memory and visual evoked potentials in young and old rats after housing in an enriched environment. *Behav. Neural Biol.: 44,* 454 – 469, 1985.

Vasquez BJ, Martinez JL, Jensen RA, Messing RB, Rigter J, McGaugh JL: Learning and memory in young and aged Fischer 344 rats. *Arch. Gerontol. Geriatr.: 2,* 279 – 291, 1983.

Verzar-McDougall EJ: Studies in learning and memory in ageing rats. *Gerontologia: 1,* 65 – 85, 1957.

Walker LC, Olton DS: Neurotransmitters and memory: role of cholinergic, serotonergic, and noradrenergic systems. *Behav. Neurosci.: 101,* 325 – 332, 1987.

Walker LC, Kitt CA, Struble RG, Wagster MV, Price DL, Cork LC: The neural basis of memory decline in aged monkeys. *Neurobiol. Aging: 9,* 657 – 666, 1988.

Wallace JE, Krauter EE, Campbell BA: Animal models of declining memory in the aged: short-term and spatial memory in the aged rat. *J. Gerontol.: 35,* 355 – 363, 1980a.

Wallace JE, Krauter EE, Campbell BA: Motor and reflexive behavior in the aging rat. *J. Gerontol.: 35,* 364 – 370, 1980b.

Walsh D, Krauss I, Regnier V: Spatial ability, environmental knowledge and environmental use. In Liben L, Patterson AH and Newcombe N (Editors), *Spatial Representation and Behavior Across the Life Span.* New York: Academic Press, pp. 321 – 357, 1981.

Warren JM, Zerweck C, Anthony A: Effects of environmental enrichment on old mice. *Dev. Psychobiol.: 15,* 13 – 18, 1982.

Wax TM: Affects of age, strain, and illumination intensity on activity and self-selection of light-dark schedules in mice. *J. Comp. Physiol. Psychol.: 91,* 51 – 62, 1977.

Wax TM, Goodrick CL: Voluntary exposure to light by young and aged albino and pigmented inbred mice as a function of light intensity. *Dev. Psychobiol.: 8,* 297 – 303, 1975.

Wax TM, Goodrick CL: Nearness to death and wheel running behavior in mice. *Exp. Gerontol.: 13,* 233 – 236, 1978.

Weber R, Brown L, Weldon J: Cognitive maps of environmental knowledge and preference in nursing home patients. *Exp. Aging Res.: 4,* 157 – 174, 1978.

Welford AT: Motor performance. In Birren JE, Schaie KW (Editors), *Handbook of the Psychology of Aging.* New York: Van Nostrand Reinhold, pp. 450 – 496, 1977.

Welsh KA, Gold PE: Age-related changes in brain catecholamine responses to a single footshock. *Neurobiol. Aging: 5,* 55 – 59, 1984.

Wenk GL, Olton DS: Recovery of neocortical choline acetyltransferase activity following ibotenic acid injection into the nucleus basalis of Meynert in rats. *Brain Res.: 293,* 184 – 186, 1984.

Wenk G, Hughey D, Boundy V, Kim A, Walker L, Olton D: Neurotransmitters and memory: role of cholinergic, serotonergic, and noradrenergic systems. *Behav. Neurosci.: 100,* 325 – 332, 1987.

Werboff J, Havlena J: Effects of aging on openfield behavior. *Psychol. Rep.: 10,* 395 – 398, 1962.

Willig F, Palacios A, Monmaur P, M'Harzi M, Laurent J, Delacour J: Short-term memory, exploration and locomotor activity in aged rats. *Neurobiol. Aging: 8,* 393 – 402, 1987.

Winocur G: The effects of retroactive and proactive interference on learning and memory in old and young rats. *Dev. Psychobiol.: 17,* 537 – 545, 1984.

Wisniewski HM, Terry RD: Neuropathology of the aging brain. In Terry RD, Gershon S (Editors), *Neurobiology of Aging.* New York: Raven Press, pp. 265 – 280, 1976.

Woodruff-Pak DS: Aging and classical conditioning: parallel studies in rabbits and humans. *Neurobiol. Aging: 9,* 511 – 522, 1988.

Woodruff-Pak DS, Thompson RF: Classical conditioning of the eyelid response in rabbits as a model system for the study of brain mechanisms of learning and memory in aging. *Exp. Aging Res.: 11,* 109 – 122, 1985.

Woodruff-Pak DS, Lavond DG, Logan CG, Thompson RF: Classical conditioning in 3-, 30-, and 45-month-old rabbits: behavioral learning and hippocampal unit activity. *Neurobiol. Aging: 8,* 101 – 108, 1987.

Write WE, Werboff J, Haggett BN: Aging and water submersion in C57BL/6J mice: initial performance and retest as a function of recovery and water temperature. *Dev. Psychobiol.: 4,* 363 – 373, 1971.

Yerkes RM: Modifiability of behavior in its relations to the age and sex of the dancing mouse. *J. Comp. Neurol. Psychol.: 19,* 237 – 271, 1909.

Zelinski EM, Light LL: Young and older adults' use of context in spatial memory. *Psychol. Aging: 3,* 99 – 101: 1988.

Zornetzer SF: The noradrenergic locus coeruleus and senescent memory dysfunction. In Crook C, Bartus RT, Ferris S, Gershon S (Editors), *Treatment Development Strategies for Alzheimer's Disease.* Connecticut: Mark Powley Associates, pp. 337 – 359, 1986.

Zornetzer SF, Rogers J: Animal models for assessment of geriatric mnemonic deficits. In Crook T, Ferris S, Bartus RT (Editors), *Assessment in Geriatric Psychopharmacology.* Connecticut: Mark Powley Associates, pp. 301 – 322, 1983.

Zornetzer SF, Thompson R, Rogers J: Rapid forgetting in aged rats. *Behav. Neural Biol.: 36,* 49 – 60, 1982.

Handbook of Neuropsychology, Vol. 4
F. Boller and J. Grafman (Eds)

CHAPTER 9

Brain imaging and cerebral metabolism

Robert P. Friedland

Brain Aging and Dementia Section, Laboratory of Neurosciences, National Institute on Aging, National Institutes of Health, Bethesda, 20892, U.S.A.

'These facts seem to us to indicate the existence of an automatic mechanism by which the blood-supply of any part of the cerebral tissue is varied in accordance with the activity of the chemical changes which underlie the functional action of that part. Bearing in mind that strong evidence exists of localization of function in the brain, we are of opinion that an automatic mechanism, of the kind just referred to, is well fitted to provide for a local variation of the blood-supply in accordance with local variations of the functional activity.'

C.S. Roy and C.S. Sherrington, 1890 (p. 105)

'To locate the damage which destroys speech and to locate speech are two different things.'

J.H. Jackson, 1874 (p. 130)

Introduction to imaging approaches to brain-behavior relationships

Roy and Sherrington proposed the existence of an automatic mechanism to adjust regional cerebral blood flow (rCBF) to varying local metabolic rates. Their conclusions have proven to be a very accurate description of the intricate relationship which exists between regional cerebral blood flow and regional levels of neuronal activity. The basic work of the brain is the maintenance of neuronal membrane potentials, a process which requires the constant use of energy. Thus the brain needs a nearly continuous supply of glucose and oxygen because (1) it is not able to store sufficient energy to supply the brain's needs for periods longer than a few minutes; (2) it is not able to effectively use circulating energy sources other than glucose (except during infancy or during starvation); and (3) it cannot effectively obtain energy from glucose in the absence of oxygen. Because of this need of the brain for a continuous oxygen and nutrient supply there is a precise coupling both between rCBF and regional cerebral metabolism, and between local cerebral metabolic rates and local brain activity. Evidence for coupling of neuronal activity, CBF and metabolism can be found in studies of rats following vibrissal stimulation where the spatial distribution of activation of flow and metabolism is nearly identical, limited to columns with diameters of 375 to 500 micrometers (Greenberg et al., 1979). Local CBF may increase as soon as 1 second following activation of neurons, and may be spatially restricted to within 250 micrometers of the site of increased neuronal activity (Silver, 1978). This coupling of flow to metabolism to neuronal activity is not, however, present for all varieties of cerebral activity. Fox and Raichle and colleagues have recently shown that vibratory stimulation of the fingers causes focal CBF and glucose use increases which are apparently not matched by equivalent increases of oxygen or glucose utilization (Fox and Raichle, 1986; Raichle et al., 1987; Fox et al., 1988). The biochemical basis of this metabolic uncoupling is unclear. Also, flow-metabolism coupling is not preserved in acute stroke, and has not been quantitatively tested in most pathological conditions. While the existence of flow-metabolism coupling was first suggested by Roy and Sherrington in 1890, its physiological mechanism remains unknown (Lou et al., 1987). Despite our incomplete knowledge at present, a wide range of studies have been performed in man, in health and disease, which demonstrate the power of this functional coupling of flow, metabolism and neuronal activity for studies of cerebral function. Techniques are now available for the precise noninvasive identification of brain anatomy in vivo, and new approaches have also been developed for noninvasive quantitative assessment in three dimensions of aspects of cerebral physiology. This chapter will review these new technologies in their application to brain-behavior issues in the aging brain.

Methods for neuroimaging investigations

Structural imaging: x-ray computed tomography (CT) and magnetic resonance imaging (MRI)

X-ray computed tomography (CT) is a radiological technique which provides for the three-dimensional reconstruction of the relative densities of regions of the human brain. Density, or mean atomic weight, determines the relative attenuation of x-rays passing through the tissue. This physical parameter is represented in the image as the relative intensity of brightness of a volume element (or voxel) on a grey scale from white (high density, high attenuation of x-rays) to black (low density, low attenuation of x-rays). Because of the relative density variations of cerebral structures, we are able to visualize the cerebral cortex, white matter, deep nuclei and ventricular system using CT. However, the precise quantification of density (or CT number) is not performed reliably with CT (Albert et al., 1984a). There is considerable blurring of the image of the underlying cerebral cortex, particularly in the floor of the middle cranial fossa, adjacent to the petrous pyramids of the temporal bone, because of an artefact (beam hardening) induced by the very high density of the skull (Gado et al., 1975).

Magnetic resonance imaging (MRI) is related to an older technique (nuclear magnetic resonance) which has been adapted only recently for use in imaging studies. MRI is based on the presence in atomic nuclei of nuclear spins which behave like small magnets. The most common magnetic nucleus in the body is that of hydrogen (a proton), whose distribution is similar to the distribution of water (Budinger and Lautebur, 1984). When a static magnetic field is applied to the body the protons become aligned with the external field, producing a net magnetization. A coil near the subject is then used to apply a rapidly alternating magnetic field at an appropriate radiofrequency to change the direction of the nuclear spins relative to the direction of the stronger static magnetic field. The magnetized nuclei return to the equilibrium state when the alternating field is turned off and emit energy in the process. The time variation in the amplitude of the emitted radiofrequency is affected by the physical-chemical properties of the tissue and the molecular environment of the nuclei (Budinger and Lautebur, 1984). This can be used to provide images in three dimensions which reflect aspects of tissue composition. Because the differences in water density in various brain structures are greater than the differences in relative x-ray attenuation values, MRI provides better contrast than CT for brain studies. In particular, MRI provides excellent definition of the grey-white boundary and outstanding information concerning white matter structures throughout the brain. There is very little MRI signal from bone, so structures such as the temporal lobe, which are subject to beam hardening artefact with CT, are well visualized with MRI. MRI also has the advantage of requiring no exposure of the subject to ionizing radiation. Present information indicates that MRI is safe for repeated use (Budinger and Lautebur, 1984). Certain limitations apply to MRI studies. Patients with metallic implants cannot be studied and cooperation with the imaging procedure is more demanding for MRI than for CT, because of the tighter confines of the patient bed.

CT and MRI methods are sensitive to an artefact called the partial volume effect, as are all tomographic reconstruction techniques. If the size of an object of interest approaches the magnitude of the slice thickness of the tomograph (usually in the range of 10 mm), visualization of the object depends in large part on whether or not it happens to be centered in the slice, or whether it is present equally on two adjacent slices. Because of this effect there may be considerable variability in the appearance of smaller structures (e.g., temporal horn, tail of the caudate nucleus). Thus relatively small lesions may be missed with any tomographic imaging technique. For example, in one study of stroke, 43% of infarctions were missed on CT, and 16% missed on MRI in scans performed within the first week following onset of the lesion (Kertesz et al., 1987). The clinical use of these anatomical imaging techniques relies upon visual inspection of the images, which has obvious shortcomings for research studies. This can be ameliorated in some situations by the quantitative assessment of anatomical features using computer-based volumetric techniques (Luxenberg et al., 1987).

Functional imaging: positron emission tomography (PET) and single photon emission computed tomography (SPECT)

PET is the in vivo equivalent of autoradiography – it provides quantitative data about the spatial distribution of injected radiopharmaceuticals (Brownell and Budinger, 1982). The time course in the body of the injected compounds can also be studied with PET, along with collection of data on the time course of the injected compound in the arterial blood. The labeled compounds used for PET have been extensively studied in animals to determine the physico-chemical significance of their uptake in terms of mathematical models. These tracer kinetic models can then be applied to PET data to produce physiologically important information. The following parameters can be measured with PET: rCBF; regional cerebral glucose utilization rates (rCMRglc); regional cerebral oxygen utilization rates (rCMRO_2); regional cerebral blood volume (rCBV); regional radioreceptor ligand binding densities and affinities (e.g., opiates, dopamine, serotonin and norepinephrine); bidirectional blood-brain transport of glucose; neurotransmitter precursor uptake (e.g., labeled L-dopa); neurotransmitter-degrading enzymes (for catecholamines); tissue pH; cerebral pharmacokinetics of labeled drugs; and blood-brain barrier integrity (clearance constants for Rb-82 and Ga-68 EDTA). It should be stressed that many of these physiological variables studied with PET cannot be measured with any other technique, either before or after death. The spatial resolution of the latest generation of PET tomographs is excellent (full width at half maximum of 2.5 mm to 5 mm). The reader is referred to several excellent reviews of PET for further details (Reivich and Alavi, 1985; Sokoloff et al., 1985; Lammertsma, 1985; Jameison et al., 1988).

Physiological imaging with PET is limited by the high cost of the procedure and by the requirement, in most cases, for cyclotron-produced radioisotopes. SPECT is an emission tomographic technique which does not require a local cyclotron for production of radioisotopes. Both greater availability and lower cost make it a technique of potentially great clinical utility. However, the quantitative potential of SPECT is less than that provided by PET and the spatial resolution is also lower (12 mm full width at half maximum). SPECT studies of rCBF and relative radioreceptor ligand binding (e.g., acetylcholine, dopamine) have been performed (Winchell et al., 1980; Fazio et al., 1984; Budinger, 1985; Coleman et al., 1986) and show promise for both clinical and research use.

Neuroimaging studies of healthy aging

Changes in the structure of the brain accompanying aging in normal individuals are well documented. Post-mortem studies have revealed atrophy of the cerebral hemispheres, shrinkage of the cortical ribbon, enlargement of the lateral ventricles and a loss of large neurons in the cortex (Tomlinson et al., 1968; Davis and Wright, 1977; Katzman and Terry, 1983). The occurrence of these changes is quite variable. The post-mortem observation of ventricular enlargement and cortical atrophy in an elderly individual is not a reliable indicator of dementia; conversely, demented subjects may have no evidence of pathology on gross examination of the brain. These gross findings have been extensively confirmed in studies using CT and MRI in healthy aged subjects (Soininen et al., 1982; Schwartz et al., 1985). Both ventricular enlargement and cortical atrophy are frequently seen with CT and MRI imaging in healthy aged subjects (Glydensted, 1977; Jacoby et al., 1980a; Gado et al., 1983; Barron et al., 1976; Yamamura et al., 1980). Although both CT and MRI studies demonstrate a variable loss of brain structure with age in healthy people, it is not possible at present to define the precise tissue type which is lost in this process, although it is assumed to be primarily a loss in grey matter (Creasey et al., 1986). The literature on the relationships between cortical atrophy and ventricular enlargement and behavior in healthy aged subjects is inconsistent; in general, in individuals who are free of dementing disease there is no relationship between brain atrophy, as documented by CT, and cognitive function (Creasey et al., 1986). In vivo imaging has three advantages over post-mortem studies for the assessment of atrophy: (1) ventricular structures are observed in the living state, unobscured by fixation artifact; (2) repeat studies can be done at various points in a subject's life or during the course of an illness; and (3) quantitative measures can be applied to the computer-stored data.

White matter changes have also been documented on CT and MRI in healthy elderly subjects. Diminished attenuation of periventricular white matter is occasionally observed in CT studies, particularly in the frontal lobes (Zatz et al., 1982; Rezek et al., 1986; Zimmerman et al., 1986; Steingart et al., 1987a,b; Lotz et al., 1986). Periventricular patches of intense signal have been a frequent observation in T_2 weighted MRI studies in otherwise healthy aged subjects. They appear to be more common in older patients, and in individuals with hypertension, but do not have a direct relationship with impaired cognitive function (Brant-Zawadski et al., 1985; Roberts and Caird, 1976; Awad et al., 1986a,b).

Studies of healthy human aging have also been conducted with positron emission tomography using (fluorine-18) 2-fluoro-2-deoxy-D-glucose (FDG). These studies are based on early work by Kety and Sokoloff and colleagues on global cerebral blood flow and metabolism in healthy aging (Kety, 1956; Frackowiak, 1987). Recent studies of healthy aging in man have reported either a decrement (Kuhl et al., 1982; Yoshii et al., 1987) or the lack of any change (Duara et al., 1984) in glucose utilization rates. As pointed out by Rapoport and colleagues (1983), methodological factors may account for these differences. The studies showing no change in rCMRglc were performed in the eyes-closed and ears-occluded state, whereas the investigations showing an age-associated decrement in rCMRglc were performed without sensory deprivation. In the latter situation the loss of sensory input associated with healthy aging (e.g., cataracts, conductive hearing loss) may have contributed to the observed decline in metabolism. There are also important differences in the health criteria required for entry into healthy groups between these studies. The definition of what constitutes the proper selection criteria for inclusion into a healthy aging study has been a crucial issue since the early days of this work. Clearly, 'normality' in the sense of the dictionary definition, 'conforming to the regular or more usual pattern' (Critchley, 1985), is not what is of interest here. The more usual pattern in the aged is an assortment of chronic medical illnessess and consumption of medication; this situation is quite removed from the question of 'healthy' aging, which is of primary interest but is certainly not the usual or 'normal' pattern.

Neuroimaging studies of age-related neurological disease

Alzheimer's disease (AD)

The loss of brain substance found in AD is

reflected during life by enlargement in the third and lateral ventricles and cortical sulci (Tomlinson et al., 1970; Blessed et al., 1986) as detected by CT and MRI. As in healthy aging, this cerebral atrophy is quite variable, and the anatomical imaging appearance of the brain cannot be used to determine the presence or absence of dementia, or to establish the diagnosis of AD. The size of the lateral and third ventricles can be quantitated using CT or MRI with volumetric techniques (Albert et al., 1984b; Arai et al., 1983; Brinkman et al., 1984; Luxenberg et al., 1986). In general, measures of ventricular enlargement are not consistently related to features of cognitive impairment in AD (Bird, 1982). In a longitudinal study, Luxenberg and colleagues (1987) found the rate of change of ventricular size in AD to be correlated with the rate of behavioral decline. Rates of third and lateral ventricular decline were calculated using CT scans performed with a mean interscan interval of 1.3 years (n = 18) (Luxenberg et al., 1987). There was no overlap between rates of enlargement of the lateral ventricles in male AD patients (13.33 ± 2.00 (SE) cm^3/year in 12 male patients), as compared to 12 male controls (−0.51 ± 0.35 (SE) cm^3/year).

MRI is expected to become a particularly valuable technique for measurement of brain volume and chemical composition changes in dementia, because of the absence of the beam hardening artefact and the excellent contrast between grey and white matter with this technique. Quantitative studies of brain using MRI are in the early stages at present. MRI studies have shown the occasional appearance of diffuse and patchy periventricular and deep areas of intense signal in AD patients, especially on T2 weighted images (Friedland et al., 1984b; Erkinjuntti et al., 1984; Johnson et al., 1986; McGeer et al., 1986a,b; Erkinjuntti et al., 1987). However, these changes are also found in healthy older patients (Gerard and Weisberg, 1986; Sze et al., 1986), as noted above, and their pathophysiological significance remains to be determined. In AD patchy intense white matter lesions on MRI are related to periventricular hypodensity seen on CT imaging (Steingart et al., 1987). These lesions are found in up to one-third of AD patients, and should not cause the diagnosis to be made suspect unless present to a severe degree. White matter changes in imaging studies of AD patients may be related to selective incomplete white matter infarction (Englund et al., 1988).

PET studies of rCMRglc have been performed in AD subjects by many laboratories (Foster et al., 1983, 1984; Friedland et al., 1983, 1985a,b, in press; Reivich et al., 1983; Kuhl et al., 1985; Duara et al., 1986; McGeer et al., 1986a,b).

This physiological imaging approach has been shown to be valuable for the differential diagnosis of dementia. Also, PET studies have revealed important relationships between metabolism and behavior.

In subjects with probable AD, defined according to ADRDA-NINCDS criteria (McKhann et al., 1984), low rates of rCMRglc are found throughout neocortex, with the greatest decrements found in the temporal and parietal regions, with sparing of the primary sensory and motor cortices (Fig. 1) (Friedland et al., 1983, 1984a,b; Foster et al., 1983, 1984; Benson et al., 1983; McGeer et al., 1986). These metabolic abnormalities are found in the early phases of the disease (Friedland et al., 1985a; Haxby et al., 1986b) and are stable over time (Haxby et al., 1985; Grady et al., 1988). Similar findings of temporal and parietal accentuation of the physiological abnormalities in AD have also been noted in studies of rCBF (Gustafson et al., 1974, 1984; Barclay et al., 1984; Risberg 1985; Prohovnik et al., 1989) and regional cerebral metabolic rate for oxygen (Frackowiak et al., 1981). Little overlap is found between measures of regional temporal-parietal rCMRglc reduction in AD and healthy age-matched subjects (Friedland et al., 1983, 1985a,b, in press).

In addition to temporal-parietal hypometabolism, PET studies in AD have documented significant left-right asymmetries of rCMRglc in association cortices that are not found in healthy subjects. The distribution of areas of

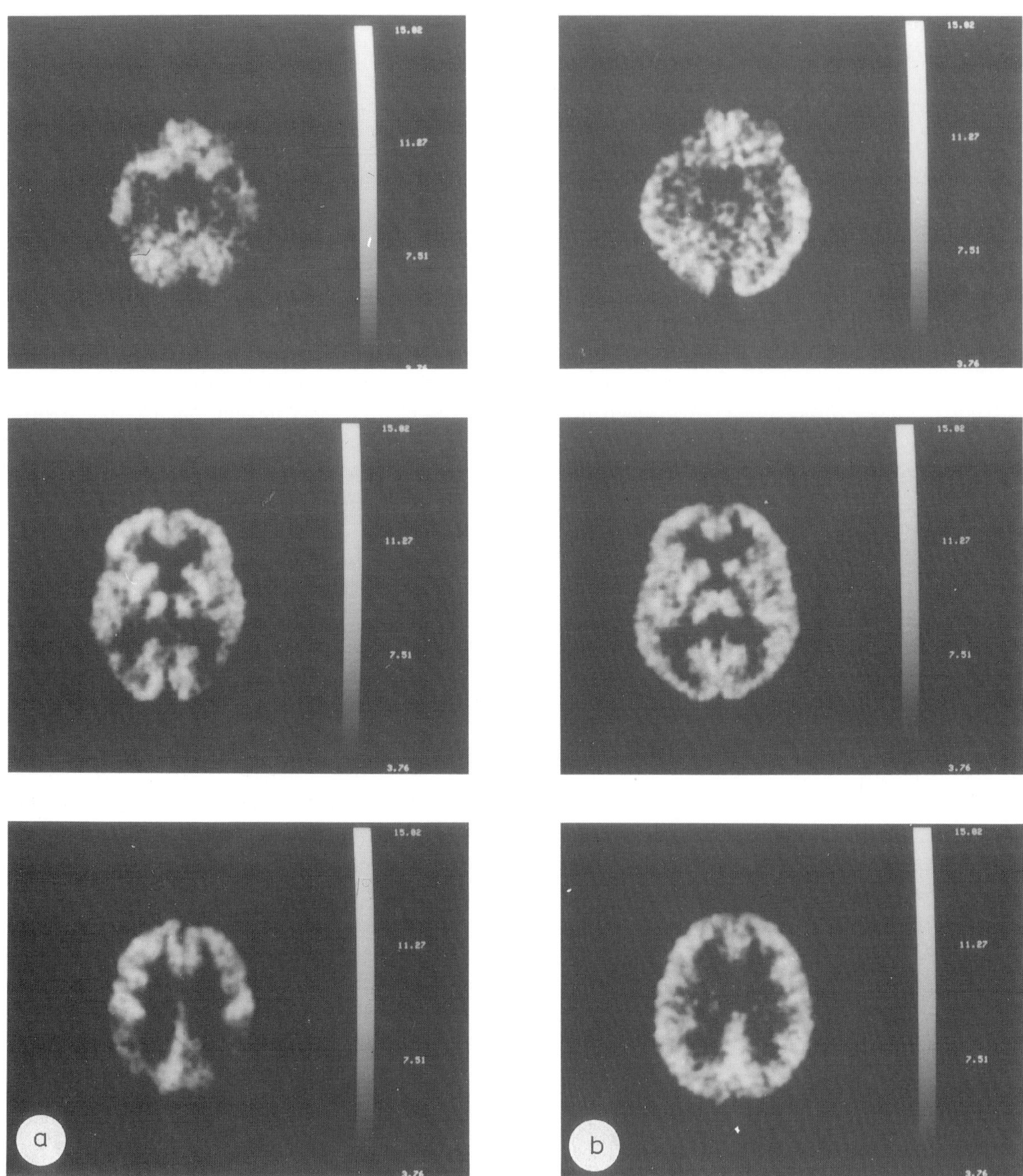

Fig. 1. PET images of glucose metabolism in an AD patient (a) and a healthy control subject (b). Bilateral temporal-parietal hypometabolism is seen in the AD patient, with relative sparing of the deep nuclei and primary frontal and occipital sensory-motor cortices. The scales on the right refer to units of glucose utilization (mg/100 g of brain/min). In the AD patient the decrease in glucose use in temporal and parietal cortex is greater on the right than on the left hemisphere. The right side of the patient's head is on the right side of the image.

hypometabolism throughout the brain is often asymmetrical. These asymmetries are not uniformly distributed throughout the population of AD subjects; some patients have greater right-sided impairment while others have greater left-sided impairment (Friedland et al., 1985a; Haxby et al., 1985). Longitudinal studies have shown that these asymmetries are maintained over time in individual patients (Grady et al., 1988; Haxby et al., 1986b). A study by Koss and colleagues (1985) has reported that older patients with AD are more likely to have left frontal hypometabolism, while presenile AD patients are more likely to have right temporal-parietal hypometabolism. These findings were related to relatively greater visuospatial dysfunction in the presenile group, and relatively greater verbal fluency impairment in the senile patients. These observations were only partially confirmed in a report from Grady and colleagues (Grady et al., 1987).

Abnormalities in regional glucose utilization rates found in AD are very closely related to the nature of the behavioral-cognitive deficits found in individual patients. Right temporal and parietal hypometabolism is related to visuospatial impairment, and left temporal and parietal hypometabolism is related to features of disturbed language performance (Friedland et al., 1983, 1985a; Haxby et al., 1985; Foster et al., 1983; Grady et al., 1988). Metabolic alterations in the disease are also related to the course of the behavioral symptomatology, as patients with predominant right hemispheric metabolic impairment are more likely to have more rapid progression in visuospatial dysfunction (Friedland et al., 1985a,b; Grady et al., 1988; Haxby et al., 1986b). Thus, it is apparent that the marked behavioral heterogeneity in AD is related, as least in part, to unequal degrees of disease severity in different regions of the brain. The marked degree of individual variation in the regional expression of AD in the brain, and the relations of this variability to behavior, were not appreciated prior to the use of PET. This work provides an excellent example of the value of the physiological imaging approach to studies of brain-behavior relationships.

SPECT studies of AD patients have yielded results similar to those obtained with PET. Decreased rCBF in temporal and parietal cortex has been found in several laboratories (Gemmell et al., 1984; Bonte et al., 1986; Cohen et al., 1986; Jagust et al., 1987; Johnson et al., 1987). Overlap of regional measures between AD and control groups is small (Mueller et al., 1986; Jagust et al., 1987). These findings are in keeping with the coupling of flow and metabolism in AD, as reported by Frackowiak and colleagues (1981). Using SPECT Jagust and associates (1987) reported an association between a measure of relative temporal-parietal cortex flow reduction and disease severity, as measured by the Mini-Mental State Examination.

Other dementing illnesses

The predilection for the metabolic alterations in AD to affect mainly temporal-parietal cortex is not generally shared by other dementing illnesses. Multi-infarct dementia produces diffuse lesions throughout the brain (Kuhl et al., 1983). PET-FDG studies at UCLA and elsewhere have shown the occurrence in multi-infarct dementia of multiple lesions in cortex, deep nuclei, subcortical white matter and cerebellum (Kuhl et al., 1983). More lesions are found with PET-FDG studies in multi-infarct dementia than with CT. Patchy whole brain reductions in rCBF have been found in SPECT studies of patients with multi-infarct dementia (Komitani et al., 1988). In a study of a subject with subcortical arteriosclerotic encephalopathy (Binswanger's disease), PET-FDG images showed multiple cortical defects without the focal cortical accentuation found in AD (Friedland et al., 1986). In normal pressure hydrocephalus diffuse hypometabolism has been reported, again without focal accentuation in any lobe of the cerebrum (Jagust et al., 1985). However, bilateral reductions in glucose use similar to that found in AD have also been reported in 'normal' pressure hydrocephalus (Friedland, 1989). Diffuse hypometabolism with marked asymmetry and accentuation in frontal and anterior temporal regions was found in two autopsy-verified cases of Pick's disease (Friedland et al., 1986; Kamo et al., 1987). Bilateral superior frontal cortex hypometabolism has been reported in PET studies of subjects with progressive supranuclear palsy (Foster et al., 1986). In a study of one patient with Creutzfeldt-Jakob disease asymmetrical temporal-parietal hypometabolism, similar to that found in AD, was observed (Friedland, 1984a). Overall, there have been relatively few PET studies of non-Alzheimer dementia.

Parkinson's disease

PET studies of rCBF and glucose utilization in Parkinson's disease have produced conflicting results. Cerebral blood flow in the basal ganglia is reported to be essentially unchanged (Perlmutter and Raichle, 1985; Monastruc et al., 1987) or increased (Leenders et al., 1985; Globus et al., 1985; Wolfson et al., 1985) in the disease. Reduced rCBF and glucose use has also been found in cortex in the disease (Kuhl et al., 1984; Globus et al., 1985; Perlmutter and Raichle, 1985). In Parkinson's disease patients increased (Martin et al., 1984), unchanged (Rougemont et al., 1983) and decreased (Kuhl et al., 1984; Henriksen and Boas, 1985) glucose use in the basal ganglia has been detected. Pallidal rCBF asymmetries have been related to laterality of motor impairment by Perlmutter and Raichle (1985). Levodopa treatment has been reported to increase rCBF in Parkinson's disease (Bes et al., 1983; Raichle et al., 1984; Monastruc et al., 1987), in what is thought to be primarily a vascular effect (Leenders et al., 1985). On the other hand, Melamed and colleagues (1978) and Perlmutter and Raichle (1985) have reported the lack of an effect of levodopa treatment on rCBF in the disease. In studies of Parkinson's disease patients with dementia cortical alterations similar to those seen in AD have been detected, with accentuation of hypometabolism in parietal cortex (Kuhl et al., 1985). This could be a reflection of concurrent AD in these Parkinson's disease patients. The lack of consensus of PET studies of flow and metabolism in Parkinson's disease could be due to differences in overall disease severity, as well as other methodological factors.

PET studies of dopaminergic function in Parkinson's disease using the catecholamine reuptake blocker nomfensine labeled with carbon-11 have demonstrated reduced dopamine reuptake sites in the putamen contralateral to the most involved extremity (Tedroff et al., 1988). Reduced F-18 6-fluoro-L-dopa uptake in the contralateral putamen has also been observed (Nahmias et al., 1985; Leenders et al., 1986).

Problems and prospects for neuroimaging approaches to brain-behavior relationships

The use of neuroimaging techniques in the study of aging and age-related disorders holds great promise. There are many methodological features which are important to keep in mind when reviewing this work, and when considering the potential for future studies.

First, it is crucial to have an extensively validated model, in order to verify that the parameter under study is the correct one, and to determine that the quantitative nature of the experiment is accurate and reliable. The deoxyglucose method used in PET-FDG studies is a thoroughly validated quantitative model. However, SPECT studies have generally poor quantitation, due to inherent physical limitations. It is also important for PET or SPECT studies of radioreceptor binding, or other parameters of brain function studied, to include validation that the parameter under study is not primarily a reflection of flow, which may affect the distribution of all injected compounds. This issue can also be related to the original study by Roy and Sherrington (1890), referred to earlier. In that study the dependent variable was most likely regional brain volume, and not rCBF, as the experimenters were recording the pressure exerted by the exposed brain on a drum applied to its surface. The direct relationships which exist between brain volume, regional cerebral blood volume and rCBF most probably allowed the prescient conclusions of Roy and Sherrington to be made (they did, however, fail to note the autoregulation of the cerebral circulation with changes in the arterial blood pressure). This issue of definition of the parameter(s) under study can also be raised in reference to MRI, where the nature of some of the observed 'abnormalities' remains completely unknown.

Second, problems are found in the definition of patient populations in neuroimaging studies. This is particularly true in studies of AD, which remains a diagnosis which can be made definite only with biopsy or autopsy. Clearly, post-mortem follow-up studies are crucial in this regard. Also, data on the study of the early and late stages of AD are limited at present, and there is relatively little experience with the other important causes of dementia. Furthermore, neuroimaging studies have not yet been performed using random populations, but rather only on highly selected groups of patients whose medical health is otherwise outstanding. Epidemiologically based studies will be difficult to achieve with PET because of the high cost, but may be possible with CT, MRI or SPECT. Cohort effects are also important to consider, particularly in studies of age effects on brain structure and metabolism. Young and old subject groups matched for excellent health, education, economic and social status, occupation, geographical location and gender may still differ in other ways. Older subjects may be less likely than younger subjects to spontaneously process information which is available to them, and older subjects may be more distractable than younger subjects (Hulicka and Grossman, 1967; Craik and Simon, 1980). Nutritional effects on early brain development may also be partly responsible for cohort differences in aging studies of brain structure and metabolism.

Third, the behavioral state under which physiological imaging studies are performed may also have important influences on the metabolic or flow patterns observed. Some AD PET studies are performed in the eyes- and ears-occluded state, while others are performed with eyes and ears open. The only study so far which has addressed this issue suggests that these parameters are not crucial. In studies performed during stage II sleep induced by intravenous diazepam, Foster and colleagues (1987) found persistent temporal-parietal hypometabolism in AD, on a background of globally depressed rCMRglc. Studies on the use of behavioral activation paradigms in PET investigations of dementia are currently under way. There are a number of important considerations in these studies, as reviewed in Table 1. These variables can influence the results in PET or SPECT activation studies, and all require careful attention. The eyes- and ears-occluded state may predispose subjects to fall asleep, which is difficult to determine or to prevent in a subject who cannot be stimulated. Anxiety, emotional state and motivation have been documented to affect rCBF (Gur et al., 1987). Attentional differences can be a source of confounding in nearly all studies of human performance. Activation studies must control for varied sensory stimulation and motor responses called for in the paradigm. If cognitive processing is being studied it is necessary to demonstrate that the subjects have sufficient memory to recall the task instructions. Performance quality is obviously variable in the dementias. The loss of observed metabolic or flow responses might therefore be an indication of the inability of the patient to perform the task,

TABLE 1

Variables involved in functional activation

1. Arousal
2. Anxiety
3. Emotion
4. Attention
5. Motivation
6. Sensory stimulation
7. Motor response
8. Memory processes
9. Cognitive processes
10. Performance quality
11. Circadian and other rhythms

rather than a physiological change in the brain making the tissue resistant to activation. Although circadian rhythms have been shown to affect rCMRglc in animals, control of PET studies for time of day is difficult because of the complexities of tomograph and cyclotron scheduling in most institutions.

The meaning of activation or lack of activation in studies of diseased subjects is unclear. As stated by John Hughlings Jackson in 1874, the localization of dysfunction is not the same as the localization of function. This is particularly true for studies in conditions such as AD, where the pathology, although focally concentrated in some regions, is widespread throughout the forebrain. Moreover, metabolic abnormalities in hippocampus or amygdala cannot currently be determined, because of their small volumes and the limited resolution of current tomographs. It is also likely that individual differences in functional activation may be due, in part, to differences in individual strategies of task performance, or to differences in the relative mental effort required; will two subjects have different degrees of cortical activation if despite similar overall scores on the task, one finds the task easy, and the other finds it stressful, and requiring a great output of mental effort? Functional imaging studies of brain function in dementing illnesses must take these factors into account. Studies of cerebral activation which deal with these variables may produce results which are relevant to the organization of the brain, and to brain-behavior relationships in the disease state under study. However the generalizability for findings of such studies to brain function in general remains speculative. The use of activation paradigms with PET in healthy subjects is a powerful approach to the study of brain function, as demonstrated by the studies of Raichle and colleagues (Raichle et al., 1987; Fox and Raichle, 1986).

Summary and future directions

Anatomical and physiological imaging techniques are valuable approaches to the study of human brain aging and age-related disease during life. CT and MRI are useful in detecting intracranial pathology such as multi-infarct dementia, tumor, subdural hematoma and obstructive hydrocephalus. CT and MRI are also useful in delineating the volumes of the cerebrospinal fluid spaces in the brain. MRI is potentially more useful for clinical and research studies in aging and dementia because of the inherently greater contrast for cerebral structures imaged with MRI. Future studies with MRI should allow for quantitative assessment of cortical atrophy and temporal horn enlargement in dementing illnesses, as well as measurement of atrophy of amygdala and hippocampus in AD.

Physiological imaging studies of glucose utilization and rCBF have shown specific findings in AD which help distinguish the disease from other dementing illnesses. These studies have also revealed previously unknown physiological asymmetries in the disease which provide an explanation for the behavioral heterogeneity of the disease. Studies with receptor ligands and related compounds may help to expand further our knowledge and understanding of the pathophysiology of dementing diseases (Greenamyre et al., 1985). Studies using functional activation in aging and dementia may also be valuable in understanding brain-behavior relationships in aging and dementia, but must be performed with precise definition of study parameters and performance characteristics.

Acknowledgements

The author is grateful to C. Grady, J. Haxby, B. Horwitz, S.I. Rapoport, J. Luxenberg, W. Theodore, W. Jagust and E. Koss for their helpful comments and support.

References

Albert M, Naeser MA, Levin HL, Garvey AJ: CT density numbers in patients with senile dementia of the Alzheimer's type. *Arch. Neurol.: 40,* 1264–1269, 1984a.

Albert M, Naeser MA, Levine HL, Garvey AJ: Ventricular size in patients with presenile dementia of the Alzheimer's type.

Arch. Neurol.: 4, 1258 – 1263, 1984b.

Arai H, Kobayaskhi K, Ikeda K, Nagao Y, Ogihara R, Kosaka K: A computed tomography study of Alzheimer's disease. *J. Neurol.: 229,* 69 – 77, 1983.

Awad IA, Spetzler RF, Hodak JA, Awad CA, Carey R: Incidental subcortical lesions identified on magnetic resonance imaging in the elderly. I. Correlation with age and cerebrovascular risk factors. *Stroke: 17,* 1084 – 1089, 1986a.

Awad IA, Johnson PC, Spetzler RF, Hodak JA: Incidental subcortical lesions identified on magnetic resonance imaging in the elderly. II. Postmortem pathological correlations. *Stroke: 17,* 1090 – 1097, 1986b.

Barclay L, Zemcov A, Blass JP, McDowell FH: Rapid rate of decline of cerebral blood flow in progressive dementias. *Monogr. Neural Sci.: 11,* 107 – 110, 1984.

Barron SA, Jacobs L, Kinkel WR: Changes in the size of normal lateral ventricles during aging determined by computerized tomography. *Neurology: 26,* 1011, 1976.

Benson DF, Kuhl DE, Hawkins RA, Phelps ME, Cummings JL, Tsai SY: The fluorodeoxyglucose ^{18}F Scan in Alzheimer's disease and multi-infarct dementia. *Arch. Neurol.: 40,* 711 – 714, 1983.

Bes A, Guell A, Fabre N, Arne-Bes MC, Geraud G: Effects of dopaminergic agents (piribedil and bromocriptine) on cerebral blood flow in parkinsonism. *J. Cereb. Blood Flow Metab.: 3,* S490 – 491, 1983.

Bird JM: Computerized tomography, atrophy and dementia: a review. *Prog. Neurobiol.: 19,* 91 – 115, 1982.

Blessed G, Tomlinson BE, Roth M: The association between quantitative measures of dementia and of senile change in the cerebral grey matter of elderly subjects. *Br. J. Psychiatry: 4,* 797 – 811, 1986.

Bonte JF, Ross ED, Chehabi HH, Devous MD: SPECT study of regional cerebral blood flow in Alzheimer's disease. *J. Comput. Assist. Tomogr.: 10,* 579 – 583, 1986.

Bradley Jr. WG, Waluch V, Brant-Zawadzki M, Yadley RA, Wycoff RR: Patchy, periventricular white matter lesions in the elderly: a common observation during NMR imaging. *Noninvasive Med. Imaging: 1,* 35 – 41, 1984.

Brant-Zawadzki M, Fein G, Van Dyke C, Kiernan R, Davenport L, De Groot J: MR imaging of the aging brain: patchy white-matter lesions and dementia. *Am. J. Neuroradiol.: 6,* 675 – 682, 1985.

Brinkman SD, Largen Jr JW: Changes in brain ventricular size with repeated CT scans in suspected Alzheimer's disease. *Am. J. Psychiatry: 141,* 81 – 83, 1984.

Brinkman SD, Sarwar M, Levin HS, Morris III HH: Qualitative indexes of computed tomography in dementia and normal aging. *Radio: 138,* 89 – 92, 1981.

Brownell GL, Budinger TF, Lauterbur PC, McGeer PL: Positron tomography and nuclear magnetic resonance imaging. *Science: 215,* 619 – 626, 1982.

Budinger TF: Quantitative single photon emission tomography for cerebral flow and receptor distribution imaging. In Reivich M, Alavi A (Editors), *Positron Emission Tomography.* New York: Alan R. Liss, pp. 227 – 240, 1985.

Budinger TF, Lauterbur PC: NMR technology for medical studies. *Science: 226,* 288 – 298, 1984.

Cohen MB, Graham LS, Lake R, Metter EJ, Fitten J, Kullkarni MK, Sevrin R, Yamada L, Chang CC, Woodruff N, King AS: Diagnosis of Alzheimer's disease and multiple infarct dementia by tomographic imaging of iodine-123 IMP. *J. Nuclear Med.: 27,* 744 – 769, 1986.

Coleman RE, Blinder RA, Jaszczak RJ: Single photon emission computed tomography part II: clinical applications. *Invest. Radiol.: 21,* 1 – 11, 1986.

Costa DC, Ell PJ, Burns A, Philpot M, Levy M: CBF tomogram with ^{99m}Tc-HM-PAO in patients with dementia (Alzheimer type and HIV) and Parkinson's disease – initial results. *J. Cereb. Blood Flow Metab.: 8,* S109 – S115, 1988.

Craik FIM, Simon E: Age differences in memory: The roles of attention and depth of processing. In Poon LW, Fozard JL, Cermak LS, Arenberg D, Thompson LW (Editors), *New Directions in Memory and Aging.* Hillsdale, NJ: Lawrence Erlbaum, 1980.

Creasey H, Schwartz M, Frederickson H, Haxby J, Rapoport SI: Quantitative computed tomography in dementia of the Alzheimer type. *Neurology: 36,* 1563 – 1568, 1986.

Critchley M: *Butterworth's Medical Dictionary,* Second Edition. London: Butterworth's, pp. 1164, 1978.

Davis PJM, Wright EA: A new method for measuring cranial cavity volume and its application to the assessment of cerebral atrophy at autopsy. *Neuropathol. Appl. Neurobiol.: 3,* 341, 1977.

Drayer B, Burger P, Darwin R, Riederer S, Herfkens R, Johnson GA: Magnetic resonance imaging of brain iron. *Am. J. Neuroradiol.: 7,* 373 – 80, 1986.

Duara R, Margolin RA, Robertson-Tchabo EA, London ED, Schwartz M, Renfrew JW, Koziarz BJ, Sundaram M, Grady C, Moore AM, Ingvar DH, Sokoloff L, Weingartner H, Kessler RM, Manning RG, Channing MA, Cutler NR, Rapoport SI: Cerebral glucose utilization, as measured with positron emission tomography in 21 resting healthy men between the ages of 21 and 83 years. *Brain: 106,* 761 – 775, 1983.

Duara R, Grady C, Haxby J, Ingvar D, Sokoloff L, Margolin RA, Manning RG, Cutler NR, Rapoport SI: Human brain glucose utilization and cognitive function in relation to age. *Neurology: 16,* 702 – 713, 1984.

Duara R, Grady C, Haxby J, Sundaram M, Cutler NR, Heston L, Moore A, Schlageter N, Larson S, Rapoport SI: Positron emission tomography in Alzheimer's disease. *Neurology: 36,* 879 – 887, 1986.

Englund E, Brun A, Alling C: White matter changes in dementia of Alzheimer's type. Biochemical and neuropathological correlates. *Brain: 111,* 1425 – 1439, 1988.

Erkinjuntti T, Sipponen JT, Iivananinen M, Ketonen L, Sulkava R, Sepponen RE: Cerebral NMR and CT imaging in dementia. *J. Comput. Assist. Tomogr: 8,* 614 – 618, 1984.

Erkinjuntti T, Ketonen L, Sulkava R, Sipponen J, Vuorialho M, Iivanainen M: Do white matter changes on MRI and CT differentiate vascular dementia from Alzheimer's disease? *J. Neurol. Neurosurg. Psychiatry: 50,* 37 – 42, 1987.

Eyldenssed: Measurements of the normal ventricular system and hemispheric sulci of 100 adults with computed tomography. *Neuroradiology: 14,* 183, 1977.

Fazio F, Lenzi GL, Gerundni P, Collice M, Gilardi MC, Colombo R, Taddei G, Del Maschio A, Piacentini M, Kung HF, Blau M: Tomographic assessment of regional cerebral perfusion using intravenous I-123 HIPDM and a rotating gamma camera. *J. Comput. Assist. Tomogr.: 8,* 911 – 921, 1984.

Foster NL, Chase TN, Fedio P, Patronas NJ, Brooks R, Di Chiro G: Alzheimer's disease: focal cortical changes shown by positron emission tomography. *Neurology: 33,* 961 – 965, 1983.

Foster NL, Chase TN, Mansi L, Brooks R, Fedio P, Patronas NJ, Di Chiro G: Cortical abnormalities in Alzheimer's disease. *Ann. Neurol.: 16,* 649 – 654, 1984.

Foster NL, Gilman S, Berent S, Hichwa RD: Distinctive patterns of cerebral glucose metabolism in progressive supranuclear palsy and Alzheimer's disease studied with positron emission tomography. *Neurology: 36 (Suppl 1),* 338, 1986.

Fox PT, Raichle ME: Focal physiological uncoupling of cerebral blood flow and oxidative metabolism during somatosensory stimulation in human subjects. *Proc. Natl. Acad. Sci. USA: 83,* 1140 – 1144, 1986.

Fox PT, Raichle ME, Mintun MA, Dense C: Nonoxidative glucose consumption during focal physiologic neural activity. *Science: 241,* 462 – 464, 1988.

Frackowiak RSJ, Pozzilli C, Legg NJ, Du Boulay GH, Marshall J, Lenzi GL, Jones T: Regional cerebral oxygen supply and utilization in dementia. A clinical and physiological study with oxygen-15 and positron tomography. *Brain: 104,* 753 – 778, 1981.

Friedland RP: 'Normal' pressure hydrocephalus and the saga of the treatable dementias. *J. Am. Med. Assoc.: 262,* 2577 – 2581, 1989.

Friedland RP, Budinger TF, Ganz E, et al: Regional cerebral metabolic alterations in dementia of the Alzheimer type: positron emission tomography with [^{18}F]fluorodeoxyglucose. *J. Comput. Assist. Tomogr.: 7,* 590 – 598, 1983.

Friedland RP, Prusiner S, Jagust W, Budinger TF: Bitemporal hypometabolism in Creutzfeldt-Jakob disease: positron emission tomography with [^{18}F]-fluorodeoxyglucose. *J. Comput. Assist. Tomogr.: 8,* 978 – 981, 1984a.

Friedland RP, Budinger TF, Brant-Zawadzki MN, Jagust WJ: The diagnosis of Alzheimer-type dementia: a preliminary comparison of PET and proton NMR imaging. *J. Am. Med. Assoc.: 252,* 2750 – 2752, 1984b.

Friedland RP, Budinger TF, Koss E, Ober BA: Alzheimer's disease: anterior-posterior and lateral hemispheric alterations in cortical glucose utilization. *Neurosci. Lett.: 53,* 235 – 240, 1985a.

Friedland RP, Koss E, Jagust WJ: Lateral hemispheric asymmetries of glucose use in Alzheimer's disease: relationships to behavior, age of onset and prognosis. *J. Cereb. Blood Flow Metab.: 5 (Suppl 1),* S123 – 124, 1985b.

Friedland RP, Jagust WJ, Ober BA, Dronkers NF, Koss E, Simpson GV, Ellis WG, Budinger TF: The pathophysiology of Pick's disease: a comprehensive case study. *Neurology: 36 (Suppl 1), 268,* 1986 (Abstract).

Friedland RP, Jagust WJ, Huesman, Koss E, Knittel B, Mathis CA, Ober BA, Mazoyer BM, Budinger TF: Regional cerebral glucose transport and utilization in Alzheimer's disease. *Neurology:* in press.

Friedland RP, Horwitz B, Grady C, DeCarli C, Schapiro MB, Kumar A, Rapoport SI: An ROC analysis of the diagnostic accuracy of PET with FDG and X-ray computed tomography in Alzheimer's disease. *J. Cereb. Blood Flow Metabol.: 9 (Suppl 1),* S566, 1989.

Gado M, Phelps M: The peripheral zone of increased density in cranial computed tomography. *Radiology: 11,* 71 – 74, 1975.

Gado M, Hughes CP, Danziger W, Chi D, Jost G, Berg L: Volumetric measurements of the cerebrospinal fluid spaces in demented subjects and controls. *Radiology: 144,* 535 – 538, 1982.

Gado M, Hughes CP, Danziger W, Chi D: Aging, dementia, and brain atrophy: a longitudinal computed tomographic study. *Am. J. Neuroradiol.: 4,* 699 – 702, 1983.

Gemmell HG, Sharp EF, Evans NTS, Beeson JAO, Lyall D, Smith FW: Single photon emission tomography with I-123 isopropylamphetamine in Alzheimer's disease and multi-infarct dementia. *Lancet: 2,* 1348, 1984.

Gerard G, Weisberg LA: MRI periventricular lesions in adults. *Neurology: 36,* 998 – 1001, 1986.

Globus M, Mildworf B, Melamed E: Cerebral blood flow and cognitive impairment in Parkinson's disease. *Neurology: 35,* 1135 – 1139, 1985.

Grady CL, Haxby JV, Schlageter NL, Berg G, Rapoport SI: Stability of metabolic and neuropsychological asymmetries in dementia of the Alzheimer's type. *Neurology: 36,* 1390 – 1392, 1986.

Grady CL, Haxby JV, Horwitz B, Berg G, Rapoport SI: Neuropsychological and cerebral metabolic function in early vs. late onset dementia of the Alzheimer type. *Neuropsychologia: 25,* 807 – 816, 1987.

Grady CL, Haxby JV, Horwitz B, Sundaram M, Berg G, Schapiro M, Friedland RP, Rapoport SI: A longitudinal study of the early neuropsychological and cerebral metabolic changes in dementia of the Alzheimer type. *J. Clin. Exp. Neuropsychol.: 10,* 576 – 596, 1988.

Greenamyre JT, Penney JB, Young AB, D'Amato CJ, Hicks SP, Shoulson I: Alterations in L-glutamate binding in Alzheimer's and Huntington's Disease. *Science: 227,* 1496 – 1498, 1985.

Greenberg J, Hand P, Sylvestro A, Reivich M: Localized metabolic-flow couple during functional activity. *Acta Neurol. Scand.: 60 (Suppl. 72),* 12 – 13, 1979.

Gur RC, Gur RE, Resnick SM, Skolnick BE, Alavi A, Reivich M: The effect of anxiety on cortical cerebral blood flow and metabolism. *J. Cereb. Blood Flow Metab.: 7,* 173 – 177, 1987.

Gustafson L, Risberg J: rCBF related to psychiatric symptoms in dementia with onset in the presenile period. *Acta Psych. Scand.: 50,* 516 – 538, 1974.

Gustafson L, Risberg J, Johanson M, Brun A: Evaluation of organic dementia by regional cerebral blood flow measurements and clinical and psychometric methods. *Monogr. Neural Sci.: 11,* 111 – 117, 1984.

Haxby JV, Duara R, Grady CL, Cutler NR, Rapoport SI: Relations between neuropsychological and cerebral metabolic asymmetries in early Alzheimer's disease. *J. Cereb. Blood Flow: 5,* 193 – 200, 1985.

Haxby JV, Grady CL, Ranjan J, Robertson-Tchabo EA, Koziarz B, Cutler NR, Rapoport SI: Relations among age, visual memory, and resting cerebral metabolism in 40 healthy men. *Brain Cognition: 5,* 412 – 417, 1986a.

Haxby JV, Grady CL, Duara R, Schlageter N, Berg G, Rapoport SI: Neocortical metabolic abnormalities precede nonmemory cognitive defects in early Alzheimer's-type dementia. *Arch. Neurol.: 43,* 882–885, 1986b.

Henrikson L, Boas J: Regional cerebral blood flow in hemiparkinsonian patients. Emission computed tomography of inhaled xenon-133 before and after levodopa. *Acta Neurol. Scand.: 71,* 257–266, 1985.

Hulicka IM, Grossman JL: Age-group comparisons for the use of mediators in paired-associate learning. *J. Gerontol.: 22,* 46–51, 1967.

Inzitari D, Diaz F, Fox A, Hachinski VC, Steingart A, Lau C, Donald A, Wade J, Mulic H, Merskey H: Vascular risk factors and leuko-araiosis. *Arch. Neurol.: 44,* 42–46, 1987.

Jacoby R, Levy R: Computed Tomography in the elderly: 2. senile dementia: diagnosis and functional impairment. *Br. J. Psychiatry: 136,* 256–269, 1980b.

Jacoby RJ, Levy R, Dawson JM: Computed tomography in the elderly: 1. the normal population. *Br. J. Psychiatry: 136,* 249–255, 1980a.

Jackson JH: On the nature of the duality of the brain. *Medical Press Circular: i,* 19, 41, 63 (1874). Reprinted in Taylor J. (Editor), *The Selected Writings of John Hughlings Jackson, Vol. 2,* New York: Basic Books, pp 130, 1958.

Jagust WJ, Friedland RP, Budinger TF: Positron emission tomography differentiates normal pressure hydrocephalus from Alzheimer's disease. *J. Neurol. Neurosurg. Psychiatry: 48,* 1091–1096, 1985.

Jagust WJ, Budinger TF, Huesman RH, Friedland RP, Mazoyer BM, Knittel BL: Methodological factors affecting PET measurements of cerebral glucose metabolism. *J. Nuclear Med.: 27,* 1358–1361, 1986.

Jagust WJ, Budinger TF, Reed BR: The diagnosis of dementia with single photon emission computed tomography. *Arch. Neurol.: 44,* 258–262, 1987.

Jamieson D, Alavi A, Jolles P, Chawluk J, Reivich M: Positron emission tomography in the investigation of central nervous system disorders. *Radiol. Clin. North Am.: 26,* 1075–1088, 1988.

Johnson K, Buonanno F, Davis K, Growdon JH, Rosen TJ, Corkin S: Comparison of MR and X-ray CT in dementia. *Neurology: 36 (Suppl. 1),* 265, 1986 (Abstract).

Johnson KA, Mueller ST, Walshe TM, English RJ, Holman BL: Cerebral perfusion imaging in Alzheimer's disease: use of single photon emission CT and lofetamine hydrochloride I 123. *Arch. Neurol.: 44,* 165–168, 1987.

Kamo H, McGeer PL, Harrop R, McGeer EG, Calne DB, Martin WR, Pate BD: Positron emission tomography and histopathology in Pick's disease. *Neurology: 37,* 439–45, 1987.

Katzman R, Terry R: Normal aging of the nervous system. In *The Neurology of Aging.* Philadelphia: F.A. Davis, pp. 15–50, 1983.

Kertesz A, Black SE, Nicholson L, Carr T: The sensitivity and specificity of MRI in stroke. *Neurology: 37,* 1580–85, 1987.

Kety SS: Human cerebral blood flow and oxygen consumption related to aging. *Assoc. Res. Nerv. Mental Dis. Proc.: 35,* 31–45, 1956.

Komatani A, Yamaguchi K, Sugai Y, Takanashi T, Kera M, Shihohara M, Kawakatsu S: Assessment of demented patients by dynamic SPECT of inhaled xenon-133. *J. Nuclear Med.: 29,* 1621–1626, 1988.

Koss E, Friedland RP, Ober BA, Jagust WJ: Differences in lateral hemispheric asymmetries of glucose utilization between early and late-onset Alzheimer-type dementia. *Am. J. Psychiatry: 142,* 638–640, 1985.

Kuhl DE, Barrio JR, Huang SC, Selin C, Ackermann RF, Lear JL, Wu JL, Lin TH, Phelps ME: Quantifying local cerebral blood flow by *n*-isopropyl-*p*-^{123}I-iodoamphetamine (IMP) tomography. *J. Nuclear Med.: 23,* 196–203, 1982.

Kuhl DE, Metter EJ, Riege WH, Hawkins RA, Mazziotta JC, Phelps ME, Kling AS: Local cerebral glucose utilization in elderly patients with depression, multiple infarct dementia, and Alzheimer's disease. *J. Cereb. Blood Flow Metab.: (3 Suppl. 1),* S494–495, 1983.

Kuhl DE, Metter EJ, Riege WH: Patterns of local cerebral glucose utilization determined in Parkinson's disease by the [^{18}F]fluorodeoxyglucose method. *Ann. Neurol.: 15,* 419–424, 1984.

Kuhl DE, Metter EJ, Benson DF, Ashford JW, Riege WH, Fujikawa DG, Morkhom CH, Mazziotta JC, Maltese A, Dorsey DA: Similarities of cerebral glucose metabolism in Alzheimer's and Parkinsonian dementia. *J. Cereb. Blood Flow Metab.: (Suppl. 1),* S168–170, 1985.

Lammertsma AA, Frackowiak RS: Positron emission tomography. *Crit. Rev. Biomed. Eng.: 13,* 125–169, 1985.

Leenders KL, Wolfson LI, Gibbs JM, et al: The effects of L-DOPA on regional cerebral blood flow and oxygen metabolism in patients with Parkinson's disease. *Brain: 108,* 171–191, 1985.

Leenders KL, Palmer AJ, Quinn N, Clark JC, Firnau G, Garnett ES, Nahmias C, Jones T, Marsden CD: Brain dopamine metabolism in patients with Parkinson's disease measured with positron emission tomography. *J. Neurol. Neurosurg. Psychiatry: 49,* 853–860, 1986.

Lotz PR, Ballinger WE, Guisling RG: Subcortical arteriosclerotic encephalopathy: CT spectrum and pathologic correlation. *Am. J. Radiol.: 7,* 817–822, 1986.

Lou HC, Edvinsson L, MacKenzie E: The concept of coupling of cerebral blood flow to brain function: revision required? *Ann. Neurol.: 22,* 289–297, 1987.

Luxenberg J, Friedland RP, Rapoport SI: Quantitative -ray computed tomography (CT) in dementia of the Alzheimer type (DAT). *Can. J. Neurol. Sci.: 13,* 570–572, 1986.

Luxenberg JS, Haxby JV, Creasey H, Sundaram M, Rapoport SI: Rate of ventricular enlargement in dementia of the Alzheimer type correlates with rate of neuropsychological deterioration. *Neurology: 37,* 1135–1140, 1987.

McGeer PL, Kamo H, Harrop R: Comparison of PET, MRI, and CT with pathology in a proven case of Alzheimer's disease. *Neurology: 36,* 1569–1574, 1986a.

McGeer PL, Kamo H, Harrop R, Li DKB, Tuokko H, McGeer EG, Adam MJ, Ammann W: Positron emission tomography in patients with clinically diagnosed Alzheimer's disease. *J. Can. Med. Assoc.: 134,* 597–607, 1986b.

McKhann G, Drachman D, Folstein M, Katzman R, Price D, Stadlan EM: Clinical Diagnosis of Alzheimer's Disease: report of the NINCDS-ADRDA Work Group under the auspices of DHHS task force on Alzheimer's disease. *Neurology: 34,* 939–944, 1984.

Martin WRW, Beckman JH, Calne DB, Adam MJ, Harrop R, Rogers JG, Ruth TJ, Sayre CI, Pate BD: Cerebral glucose metabolism in Parkinson's disease. *Can. J. Neurol. Sci.: 11,*

169 – 173, 1984.

Melamed E, Lavy S, Cooper G, Bentin S: Regional cerebral blood flow in Parkinsonism. Measurement before and after levodopa. *J. Neurol. Sci.: 38,* 391 – 397, 1978.

Montastruc JL, Celsis P, Agniel A, Demonet JF, Doyon B, Puel M, Marc-Vergnes JC, Rascol A: Levodopa-induced regional cerebral blood flow changes in normal volunteers and patients with Parkinson's disease. Lack of correlation with clinical or neuropsychological improvements. *Movement Disorders: 2,* 279 – 289, 1987.

Mueller SP, Johnson KA, Hamil D, English RJ, Nagel SJ, Ichise M, Holman BL: Assessment of I-123 IMP SPECT in mild/moderate and severe Alzheimer's disease. *J. Nuclear Med.: 27,* 889, 1986 (Abstract).

Nahmias C, Garnett ES, Firnau G, Lang A: Striatal dopamine distribution in parkinsonian patients during life. *J. Neurol. Sci.: 69,* 223 – 230, 1985.

Neirinckx RD, Nowotnik DP, Canning L, Harrison RC, Pickett RD, Volkert WA, Troutner D, Chaplin S: Development of the first routinely-available Tc-99m labelled agent for the measurement of rCBF by SPECT. *J. Nuclear Med.: 27,* 905, 1986 (Abstract).

Perlmutter JS, Raichle ME: Regional blood flow in hemiparkinsonism. *Neurology: 35,* 1127 – 1134, 1985.

Pizzolato G, Dam M, Borsato N, Saitta B, Da Col C, Perlotto N, Zanco P, Ferlin G, Battistin L: [^{99m}Tc]-HM-PAO SPECT in Parkinson's disease. *J. Cereb. Blood Flow Metab.: 8,* S101 – S108, 1988.

Prohovnik I, Smith G, Sackeim HA, Mayeux R, Stern Y: Gray-matter degeneration in presenile Alzheimer's disease. *Ann. Neurol.: 25,* 117 – 124, 1989.

Raichle MC, Fox PT, Mintun MA, Dense C: Cerebral blood flow and oxidative glycolysis are uncoupled by neuronal activity. *J. Cereb. Blood Flow Metab.: 7 (Suppl. 1),* S300, 1987.

Raichle ME, Perlmutter JS, Fox PT: Parkinson's disease: metabolic and pharmacological approaches with positron emission tomography. *Ann. Neurol.: 15,* S131 – 132, 1984.

Rapoport SI, Duara R, London ED, Margolin RA, Schwartz M, Cutler NR, Partanen M, Shinowara NL: Glucose metabolism of the aging nervous system. In Samuel D (Editor), *Aging of the Brain.* New York: Raven, pp. 111 – 121, 1983.

Reivich M, Alavi A: *Positron Emission Tomography.* New York: Alan R. Liss, 1985.

Reivich M, Alavi A, Ferris S, Christman D, Fowler J, MacGregor R, Farkas T, Greenberg J, Dann R, Wolf A: Assessment of regional glucose metabolism in aging brain and dementia with positron emission tomography. *Aging: 23,* 385 – 394, 1983.

Rezek DL, Morris JC, Fulling KJ, Gado MH: Periventricular white matter lucencies in SDAT and healthy aging. *Neurology: 36 (Suppl. 1),* 263, 1986 (Abstract).

Risberg J: Cerebral blood flow in dementias. *Dan. Med. Bull.: 32,* 48 – 51, 1985.

Roberts MA, Caird FI: Computerized tomography and intellectual impairment in the elderly. *J. Neurol. Neurosurg. Psychiatry: 39,* 986 – 989, 1976.

Rougemont D, Baron JC, Collard P, Bustany P, Comar D, Agid Y: Local cerebral metabolic rate of glucose (lCMRglc) in treated and untreated patients with Parkinson's disease. *J. Cereb. Blood Flow Metab.: 3 (Suppl.),* S504 – 505, 1983.

Roy CS, Sherrington CS: On the regulation of the blood-supply of the brain. *J. Physiol. (Lond.): 11,* 85 – 108, 1890.

Schwartz M, Creasey J, Grady CL, Deleo JM, Frederickson HA, Cutler MN, Rapoport SI: Computed tomographic analysis of brain morphometries in 30 healthy men, aged 21 to 81 years. *Ann. Neurol.: 17,* 146 – 157, 1985.

Sharp P, Gemmell H, Cherryman G, Besson J, Crawford J, Smith F: Application of Iodine-123-labeled isopropylamphetamine imaging to the study of dementia. *J. Nuclear Med.: 27,* 761 – 768, 1986.

Silver IA: Cellular microenvironment in relation to local blood flow. In Elliot K, O'Connor M (Editors), *Cerebral Vascular Smooth Muscle and its Control,* Ciba Foundation Symposium 56. New York: Elsevier, pp. 49 – 61, 1978.

Smith FW, Besson JAO, Gemmell HG, Sharp PF: The use of technetium-99m-HM-PAO in the assessment of patients with dementia and other neuropsychiatric conditions. *J. Cereb. Blood Flow Metab.: 8,* S116 – S122, 1988.

Soininen H, Puranen M, Riekkinen PJ: Computed tomography findings in senile dementia and normal aging. *J. Neurol. Neurosurg. Psychiatry: 45,* 50 – 54, 1982.

Sokoloff L: *Brain Imaging and Brain Function.* Research publications, Vol. 63: Association for research in nervous and mental disease. New York: Raven Press, 1985.

Steingart A, Hachinski VC, Lau C, Fox AJ, Fox H, Lee D, Inzitari D, Merskey H: Cognitive and neurological findings in demented patients with diffuse white matter lucencies on computed tomographic scan (leuko-araiosis). *Arch. Neurol.: 44,* 36 – 39, 1987a.

Steingart A, Hachinski VC, Lau C, Fox AJ, Diaz F, Cape R, Lee D, Inzitari D, Merskey H: Cognitive and neurological findings in subjects with diffuse white matter lucencies on computed tomographic scan (leuko-araiosis). *Arch. Neurol.: 44,* 32 – 35, 1987b.

Sze G, De Armond SJ, Brant-Zawadzki M, Davis RL, Norman D, Newton TH: Foci of MRI signal (pseudo lesions) anterior to the frontal horns: histologic correlations of a normal finding. *Am. J. Radiol.: 147,* 331 – 337, 1986.

Tedroff J, Aquilonious S-M, Hartvig P, Lundqvist H, Gee AG, Uhlin J, Langstrom B: Monoamine re-uptake sites in the human brain evaluated in vivo by means of ^{11}C-nomfensine and positron emission tomography: the effects of age and Parkinson's disease. *Acta Neurol. Scand.: 77,* 192 – 201, 1988.

Tomlinson BE, Blessed G, Roth M: Observations on the brains of non-demented old people. *J. Neurol. Sci.: 7,* 7331 – 7356, 1968.

Tomlinson BE, Blessed G, Roth M: Observations on the brains of demented old people. *J. Neurol. Sci.: 11,* 205 – 242, 1970.

Winchell HS, Horst WD, Braun L, Oldendorf WH, Hattner R, Parker H: *N*-Isopropyl-[^{123}I]*p*-iodoamphetamine: single pass uptake and washout; binding to brain synaptosomes; and localization in dog and monkey brain. *J. Nuclear Med.: 21,* 947 – 952, 1980.

Wolfson LI, Leenders KL, Brown LL, Jones T: Alterations of cerebral blood flow and oxygen metabolism in parkinson's disease. *Neurology: 35,* 1399 – 1405, 1985.

Yamamura H, Ito M, Kubota K, Matsuzawa T: Brain atrophy

during aging: a quantitative study with computed tomography. *J. Gerontol.: 35,* 492, 1980.

Yoshii F, Barker WW, Chang JY, Glusberg MD, Apicella A, Duara R: Sensitivity of CMRglc to gender, age and cerebrovascular risk factors. *J. Cereb. Blood Flow Metab.: 7 (Suppl. 1),* 549, 1987.

Zatz Jr LM, Jernigan TL, Ahumada AJ: White matter changes in cerebral computed tomography with aging. *J. Comput. Assist. Tomogr.: 6,* 19–23, 1982.

Zimmerman RD, Fleming CA, Lee BCP, Saint-Louis, LA, Deck MDF: Periventricular hyperintensity as seen by magnetic resonance: prevalence and significance. *Am. J. Radiol.: 146,* 443–450, 1986.

Handbook of Neuropsychology, Vol. 4
F. Boller and J. Grafman (Eds)

CHAPTER 10

Olfaction

Richard L. Doty

Smell and Taste Center, Department of Otorhinolaryngology and Human Communication, and Department of Physiology, School of Medicine, University of Pennsylvania, Philadelphia, PA 19104, U.S.A.

Introduction

The sense of smell has been sorely neglected by the neuropsychological community, despite its importance in determining the flavor of foods and beverages and in protecting the organism from environmental hazards such as fire, leaking gas, spoiled food and polluted air. Thus, a perusal of widely used contemporary neuropsychology text books finds that olfaction receives either extremely scant attention (e.g., Heilman and Valenstein, 1979) or is not mentioned at all (e.g., Beaumont, 1983). Typical is the sole reference to olfaction (p. 48) in Lezak's (1983) monograph, 'Another prominent mass lying within each of the cerebral hemispheres is the amygdala, which has direct connections with the primitive centers involving the sense of smell.'

There are several reasons for this neglect: first, olfactory dysfunction, compared to dysfunction of vision, hearing, balance or tactile sensation, is less obvious and rarely influences such everyday activities as locomotion and social interaction; second, as alluded to in Lezak's quotation, this sensory system is assumed by many to be 'primitive' and not of great concern to humans; third, until recently, easy-to-use quantitative tests of olfactory function have not been generally available; and fourth, the benefits derived from olfactory sensation are typically taken for granted. Indeed, it is often only after smell loss or distortion has occurred that its importance becomes evident.

The present chapter challenges the assumption that the sense of smell is of little clinical importance to man and presents evidence that disorders of this sense are not only debilitating to the patient, but may reflect the early stages of a number of degenerative neurological disorders. To aquaint the non-specialist with fundamental aspects of this complex sense, a brief discussion of the anatomy and function of the peripheral and central olfactory pathways is first presented, followed by an analysis of the olfactory deficits observed in the elderly and in some common age-related disorders.

Basic anatomy and physiology

Olfactory epithelium and olfactory bulb

Air-borne odorant molecules, drawn into the nose during inhalation, penetrate the highest recesses of the nasal chambers, pass through a thin (< 50 μm) layer of mucus, and bind to cilia of bipolar receptor cells located on a $2-4$ cm^2 patch of specialized epithelium (Fig. 1). This epithelium contains approximately 6 million of these receptor cells (which collectively constitute Cranial Nerve I), along with a complement of microvillar and supporting cells. The bipolar receptor cells are unique neural elements, as they periodically reconstitute themselves (Graziadei and Monti-Graziadei, 1978; Hinds et al., 1984). The number of cilia per cell ranges from 10 to 30 (Moran et al., 1982). Unlike the cilia of the respiratory epithelium, mature olfactory cilia lack the biochemical machinery necessary for intrinsic motility and are comparatively long (i.e., often > 30 μm). The mucus of the olfactory region is largely derived from the sustentacular cells and the acinar cells of Bowman's glands (Getchell et al., 1984).

The unmyelinated axons of the receptor cells collect into small fasciculi at the base of the epithelium and enter the brain cavity through the foramina of the cribriform plate. These fasciculi then terminate within the olfactory bulbs in spherical masses of neuropile termed glomeruli, where they divide into bundles of 25 to 100 axons and synapse with dendrites of second-order neurons (Fig. 2). Convergence of the order of 1000 to 1 occurs between the receptor cells and the second-order cells. The axons of the largest second-order cells (mitral and tufted cells) comprise the medial and lateral olfactory tracts and have primary projections to the basal medial regions of the cerebral cortex, including the prepyriform cortex, the entorhinal cortex and the periamygdaloid region. Some projections terminate in the anterior olfactory nucleus, from which connections are made to the opposite olfactory bulb through the anterior commissure.

Much of the neural activity within the olfactory bulb involves complex local feedback circuits. Glomeruli contain, in addition to processes from receptor, mitral and tufted cells, projections from short-range horizontal neurons which interconnect neighboring glomeruli and presumably contribute to the enhancement of contrast among adjacent channels. Furthermore, axonal collaterals from mitral and tufted cells synapse with granule cells (the most numerous cell type in the olfactory bulb) which send, in turn, inhibitory output back to the bulbar regions containing the primary and secondary dendrites of the mitral and tufted cells

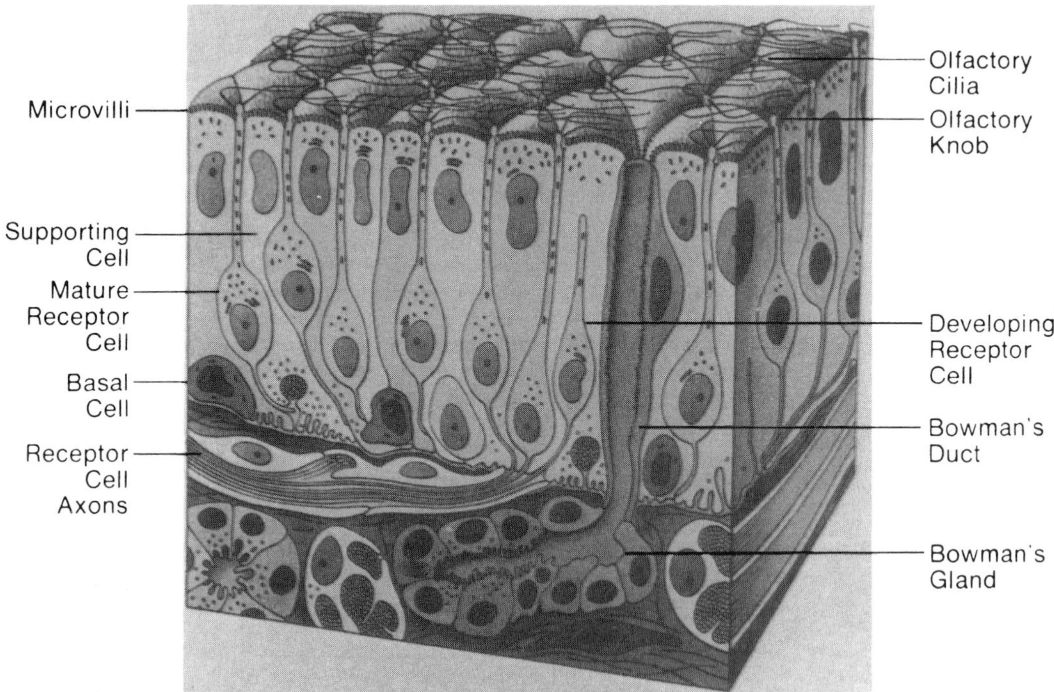

Fig. 1. The cellular organization of the vertebrate olfactory epithelium. From Warwick R, Williams PL: *Gray's Anatomy*. Philadelphia: Saunders, 1973. Used with permission.

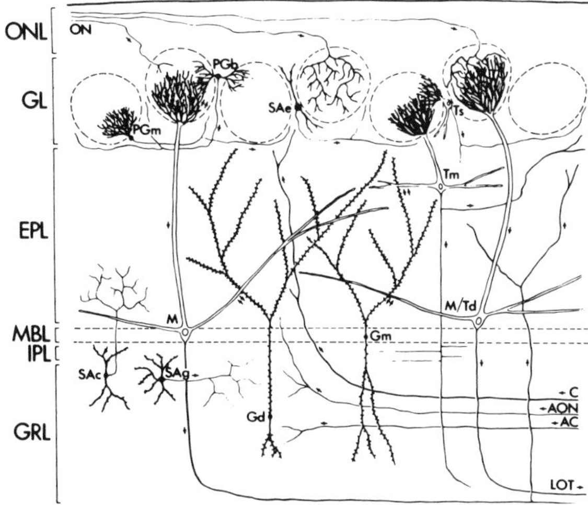

Fig. 2. Diagram of main layers and types of olfactory bulb neurons in the mammalian olfactory bulb as based upon Golgi stained material. Main layers are indicated on left as follows: ONL, olfactory nerve layer; GL, glomerular layer; EPL, external plexiform layer; MBL, mitral body layer; IPL, internal plexiform layer; and GRL, granule cell layer. ON, olfactory nerves; PGb, periglomerular cells with biglomerular dendrites; PGm, periglomerular cell with monoglomerular dendrites; SAe, short-axon cell with extraglomerular dendrites; M, mitral cell; M/Td, displaced mitral cell or deep tufted cell; Tm, middle tufted cell; Ts, superficial tufted cell; Gm, granule cell with cell body in mitral body layer; Gd, granule cell with cell body in deep layers; SAc, short-axon cell of Cajal; SAg, short-axon cell of Golgi; C, centrifugal fibers; AON, fibers from anterior olfactory nucleus; AC, fibers from anterior commissure; LOT, lateral olfactory tract. From Shepherd GM: Synaptic organization of the mammalian olfactory bulb. *Physiol. Rev.: 52,* 864–917, 1972. Used with permission.

themselves (Fig. 2). This 'inhibitory' feedback loop results not only in reciprocal inhibition among neighboring mitral or tufted cells (thereby resulting in enhanced contrast among adjacent cells analogous to that initiated by the short-range horizontal neurons), but also in self-inhibition of mitral or tufted cell output (thereby limiting the firing frequency and making the output to some degree independent of the input). In addition to this negative feedback loop, a 'positive' feedback loop exists in which mitral and tufted cell axon collaterals project directly back into the bulbar regions containing the primary and secondary dendrites of the mitral and tufted cells, thereby bypassing the granule cells. This latter arrangement appears to provide a means for spreading excitation at very low levels of stimulation when the inhibitory feedback system lacks too little input to be activated (MacLeod, 1971).

It is important to note that the olfactory bulb also contains many efferent (i.e., centrifugal) projections from higher brain regions which somehow modulate or alter the incoming signals (Heimer, 1968; Powell and Cowan, 1963). For example, projections are present (mainly to granule cells) from sectors of the olfactory cortex, the nucleus of the horizontal limb of the diagonal band, the locus coeruleus, the dorsal raphe nucleus and regions of the hypothalamus. Furthermore, fibers from the pars externa of the anterior olfactory nucleus project through the anterior commissure in a well-organized topographic manner to the contralateral bulb, possibly providing coordination between related parts of the olfactory bulbs on the two sides (Schonfeld and Macrides, 1984).

Central connections and projections

The olfactory tract flattens posteriorly and divides into two fiber bundles termed the lateral and medial striae. The medial stria becomes continuous with the subcallosal area and the paraterminal gyrus. Some of these fibers reach the olfactory tubercle and the anterior perforated substance. The fibers of the lateral olfactory tract pass along the lateral edge of the external olfactory peduncle and spread over the whole prepiriform lobe, including the periamygdaloid complex, making ipsilateral connections with the anterior olfactory nucleus, the olfactory tubercle, the prepiriform cortex, the periamygdaloid cortex, the lateral entorhinal cortex and the corticomedial amygdaloid nuclei – structures which are collectively termed the 'olfactory cortex' (Price, 1987). In man, the periamygdaloid and the prepiriform regions are found in barely visible gyri near the uncus (the semilunaris and ambiens gyri, respectively). The entorhinal area (Brodmann's area 28) is comparatively large in humans, occupying a significant portion of the anterior hippocampal gyrus (Brodal, 1981). This region is the origin of a major afferent input into the hippocampus.

The olfactory bulb fibers terminate in the most superficial of the layers of the olfactory cortex (layer Ia; Price, 1973), whose thickness decreases progressively as a function of distance from the lateral olfactory tract (reflecting, in part, decreases in the number of olfactory bulb axons which are present; Price, 1987). There appears to be no well-defined topographic organization in these projections, in that small areas of the bulb can project to large areas of the olfactory cortex and small areas of the cortex can receive fibers from large areas of the olfactory bulb (Haberly and Price, 1977). However, mitral and tufted cells are differentially represented in the olfactory cortex, with mitral cells projecting to all parts of the olfactory cortex and tufted cells projecting mainly to the anterior part of the olfactory cortex near the lateral olfactory tract (i.e., the lateral olfactory tubercle; Haberly and Price, 1977).

The different components of the olfactory cortex are connected in a broad and overlapping manner via an associational fiber system which has a well-defined laminar pattern of termination in the deep part of cortical layer I (layer Ib) and deeper cortical layers (primarily layer III) (Price, 1987). Some degree of topographical organization is apparent at this level, in that associational areas near the lateral olfactory tract evidence the heaviest projections to cortical areas near the tract, whereas such regions lateral or caudal to the tract project most heavily to caudal, medial or lateral cortical areas. Other corticocortical projections are also found in smaller areas of the olfactory cortex, including ones from the nucleus of the lateral olfactory tract, the anterior cortical amygdaloid nucleus and the periamygdaloid cortex. With the exception of the anterior cortical nucleus projections (which end throughout layer I), most of these projections terminate in cortical layer II below the association fiber system (Price, 1987).

Numerous brain regions receive projections from the olfactory cortex, including the orbital neocortex, the dorsomedial and submedial thalamic nuclei, the lateral hypothalamus, the amygdala and the hippocampus (Price, 1987). It is noteworthy that the hypothalamus receives not only fibers from the olfactory cortex, but also projections from the olfactory bulb. These projections, along with those between the hypothalamus and the corticomedial amygdaloid nuclei, are of significance to a number of activities, since these brain regions play important roles in the modulation or initiation of eating, reproduction and emotional behaviors.

Influence of aging on smell function

In addition to smoking and gender, age has been shown to be significantly correlated with the ability to smell. Indeed, when the relative influences of a number of subject variables are examined statistically, age invariably accounts for the greatest proportion of variance (e.g., Doty et al., 1984). However, it is not known to what extent such sensory changes represent aging processes, per se, or alterations in the sensory system brought about by factors correlated with age (e.g., cumulative viral insults, repeated exposures to air pollutants, etc.). Whatever their basis, age-related alterations are found in a variety of olfactory tasks, as indicated below.

Odor identification

It is now well established that, on average, older people have difficulty in identifying or recognizing odorants (e.g., Murphy, 1985; Schemper et al., 1981; Schiffman, 1977). As the result of the development of an easy-to-use quantitative microencapsulated test of olfactory function (the University of Pennsylvania Smell Identification Test or UPSIT (commercially termed the Smell Identification Test^{TM}, Sensonics, Inc., Haddonfield, NJ)), the odor-identification ability of thousands of subjects has now been evaluated and the function relating olfactory identification performance to age has been established (Doty et al.,

1984a,b). In general, (a) peak performance occurs during the third to fifth decades of life and markedly declines after the seventh decade, (b) smokers perform worse than nonsmokers, and (c) men perform worse than women, particularly in the later years (Fig. 3). More than half the subjects between the ages of 65 and 80 years show considerable impairment, whereas more than three-quarters of those over the age of 80 years do so. The poor scores in the older age range are unlikely to be due to losses in memory, per se, since (a) the memory load on the UPSIT probably does not exceed the span of immediate attention and (b) UPSIT scores of elderly subjects do not significantly correlate with scores on the Wechsler Memory Scale (Doty et al., 1984a). Interestingly, the sex difference appears to occur in a number of cultural groups and is probably universal (Doty et al., 1985).

Odor detection

As in the case of odor identification, impairment in the ability to detect low concentrations of odorants is generally found in the later years and may well be a primary basis for the marked decrease in the ability to identify odors (e.g., Chalke et al., 1958; Fordyce, 1961; Kimbrell and Furtchgott, 1963; Murphy, 1983; Schiffman et al., 1976; Venstrom and Amoore, 1968). Although the data are limited, the decline in olfactory sensitivity appears to follow a function similar to that observed for odor identification, as shown in Fig. 4 for the rose-like odorant phenyl ethyl alcohol, and is composed of both linear and quadratic components (Deems and Doty, 1987). Note that the sensitivity decreases at an earlier age in men than in women.

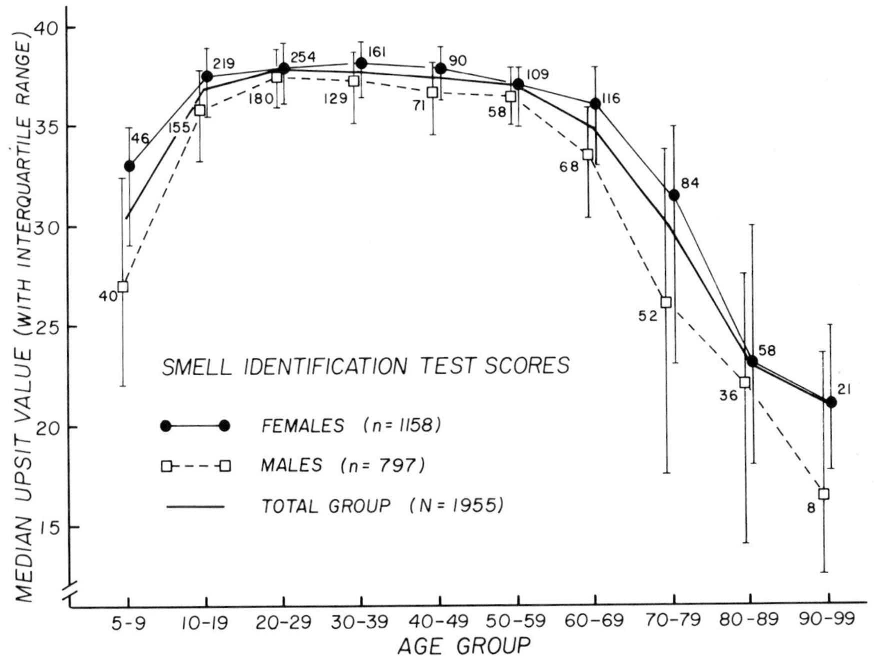

Fig. 3. University of Pennsylvania Smell Identification Test (UPSIT) scores as a function of age in a large heterogeneous group of subjects. Numbers by data points indicate sample sizes. From Doty et al.: Smell identification ability: changes with age. *Science: 226,* 1441 – 1443, 1984. Used with permission.

Suprathreshold odor intensity perception

Suprathreshold odor intensity perception is also altered in elderly compared to young subjects. Stevens et al. (1982), for example, asked 20 young (18 to 25 yrs) and 20 elderly (65 to 83 yrs) subjects to provide intensity magnitude estimates for concentrations of isoamyl butyrate (a relatively non-irritating odorant) and carbon dioxide (a trigeminal stimulus with minimal or no odor qualities), as well as to a low-pitched noise. The estimates of noise (presented in the same test session as the odorants) allowed for the normalization of the subjects' scales of measurement (under the assumption that subjects perceive the auditory stimulus in a similar manner; see Stevens and Marks, 1980). These investigators found that the standardized magnitude estimation functions of the young and the old for each odorant were nearly parallel. However, the function of the older subjects for both odorants was displaced downward (i.e., with a lower y-intercept), suggesting that older people have a proportional loss of smell function across a broad range of stimulus concentrations. A similar finding was reported by Stevens and Cain (1985), with sodium chloride as the non-olfactory matching stimulus and iso-amyl butyrate, benzaldehyde, d-limonene, pyridine, ethanol, iso-amyl alcohol as odorants.

Age-related decrements in suprathreshold smell perception have also been reported for odorants presented to the olfactory receptors from inside the oral cavity, as during chewing and swallowing (retronasal olfaction) (Stevens and Cain, 1986). Since the intensity of retronasally perceived odor is largely dependent upon mouth movements (such as those which occur normally during deglutition; cf. Burdach and Doty, 1987), some age-related alterations in retronasal odor perception may be caused by alterations of pressure/flow relationships within the nasopharynx which result from changes in such behaviors as the speed and amount of chewing and swallowing.

Odor discrimination

The ability to distinguish qualitatively between odorants is impaired in many elderly people, as exemplified by multidimensional scaling studies (which represent relative perceptual differences among stimuli as distances in spatial coordinates). Thus, Schiffman and Pasternak (1979) had sixteen 19 – 25-year-olds and sixteen 72 – 78-year-olds rate 91 pairs of 14 commercial food flavors on a 5-inch 'same-different' rating scale. The multidimensional scaling procedure yielded a two-dimensional solution in which two main clusters emerged (simulated fruit flavors and simulated meat flavors). Analysis of the spaces of individual subjects suggested that some of the elderly subjects could not discriminate between many of the odorants, since a number of stimuli normally

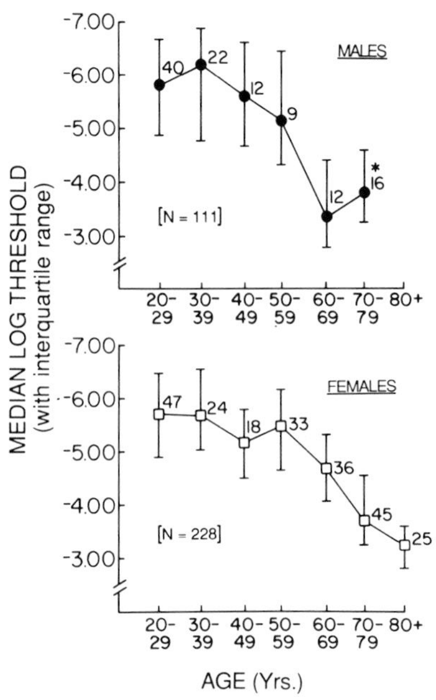

Fig. 4. Mean log phenyl ethyl alcohol detection threshold values as a function of age (decade) and gender in non-smoking men and women. Numbers by data points indicate sample sizes. From Deems and Doty: Age-related changes in the phenyl ethyl alcohol odor detection threshold. *Trans. PA Acad. Opthalmol. Otolaryngol.: 39,* 646 – 650, 1987. Used with permission.

found in disparate sectors of the multidimensional space were located near one another.

Odor hedonicity

Odors are frequently described using hedonic descriptors (e.g., 'good', 'bad', 'pleasant', 'unpleasant'; cf. Harper et al., 1968; Schiffman, 1974). When the similarity judgements of subjects are subjected to multidimensional scaling analysis, the primary dimension observed in the multidimensional space appears to be one of pleasantness/unpleasantness (Schiffman, 1974). Although the basis of this phenomenon is unknown, it presumably reflects the hedonic role that odors play in the monitoring of foodstuffs, the avoidance of polluted environments, and, at least in the case of most non-human mammals, sexual behavior (cf. Doty, 1974, 1986). Although alterations in the perceived pleasantness of an odor can be theoretically independent of alterations in its perceived intensity, there is often an association between these two dimensions. For instance, certain odorants judged pleasant at low concentrations are judged even more pleasant at high concentrations, and some odorants judged unpleasant at low concentrations are typically judged more unpleasant at high concentrations. However, a given individual's basic odor preference can be idiosyncratic, and strict monotonicity is rarely the rule. For example, subjects who dislike low concentrations of the odor of licorice (anethole) report it to be even more unpleasant at higher concentrations, whereas subjects who like this odor find it more pleasant at higher concentrations (Doty, 1975).

If an odorant is perceived as less intense by an elderly person than by a younger one, then its perceived pleasantness or unpleasantness would also be expected to be correspondingly altered, depending upon the form of the intensity/pleasantness relationship for the odorant in question. It is therefore not surprising that Murphy (1983) found that increases in menthol concentration produced much larger increments in estimates of odor pleasantness by young than by elderly subjects. Similarly, the observations by Springer and Dietzmann (see Engen, 1977) that diesel fumes are less offensive to older than to younger persons conceivably reflects age-related decreased nasal chemosensitivity.

Medical problems and diseases commonly affecting smell function in middle to late life

Upper respiratory viral infections

Upper respiratory infections are probably the most common basis for permanent decreased smell perception in people of 50 or more years of age (Deems et al., 1989). Whether this reflects some age-related lack of resistance to viral insult or simply a culmination of repeated insults to the olfactory epithelium (or both) is unknown. Autopsy and biopsy studies indicate that the integrity of the olfactory epithelium decreases with age, metaplasia occurs from respiratory epithelium, and scar tissue blocks the transit of olfactory receptor cell axons through the cribriform plate of the olfactory bulb (Douek et al., 1975; Nakashima et al., 1984).

Nasal sinus disease

Nasal sinus disease, including allergic rhinitis, polyposis, bacterial rhinitis, and sinusitis, can lead to decreased olfactory function in elderly persons. Although it is generally believed that the severity of allergic nasal symptoms decreases with aging, the frequency of nasal polyposis reportedly increases with advancing years (Settipane and Chaffee, 1977). Unlike most age-related olfactory disorders, however, those which are a direct result of nasal sinus disease have a reasonable prognosis, since restoration of a patent airway through pharmacological or surgical intervention is possible in some cases and can enhance access of odorants to the receptors.

Head trauma

Of the variety of head injuries that can influence olfactory function, those which involve rapid acceleration/deceleration of the brain are most commonly associated with smell loss. For example, coup and contrecoup contusions, in which the brain is significantly displaced for a moment within the confines of the skull, can result in the shearing or tearing of the olfactory filaments at the level of the cribriform plate. Contusions or bruises of the frontal or temporal cortices, as well as ischemia, can also result in injury to regions associated with olfactory perception. Although the frequency of head injury is higher in younger than in older people (presumably as a result of greater participation in active sports and more carelessness or inexperience in vehicle operation and other activities), the magnitude of the olfactory dysfunction appears to be equivalent in young and old accident victims (Deems et al., 1989). It is of interest to note that from 5% to 10% of serious head injury cases show olfactory dysfunction, although this statistic has yet to be calculated separately for young and old cases (for reviews, see Costanzo and Becker, 1986, and Sumner, 1976).

Alzheimer's disease

A number of well-controlled studies have noted olfactory dysfunction in patients with Alzheimer's disease (AD). In the case of odor identification, uniformity of findings exists; namely, all such studies note that the ability to identify odors is greatly impaired in this disease (Doty et al., 1987; Koss et al., 1987; Knupfer and Spiegel, 1986; Rezek, 1987; Serby et al., 1985; Warner et al., 1986). In the case of threshold-level olfactory sensitivity, all reports but one (Koss et al., 1987) indicate decreased odor sensitivity for at least some odorants (e.g., Doty et al., 1987; Knupfer and Spiegel, 1986; Murphy and Nerison, 1987; Rezek, 1987; Schiffman, personal communication). Close inspection of the data of the one exception (Koss et al., 1987) reveals, however, that of the 8 probable and 2 possible AD patients tested, one was anosmic and two evidenced threshold values within the hyposmic range. Thus, even the data of this study suggest that AD is associated with an olfactory sensitivity deficit.

A recent report suggests that AD patients show marked impairment on an odor recognition memory task, but not on a suprathreshold odor discrimination task (although the data from the latter task are not presented; Moberg et al., 1987). The deficit on the odor memory task was more marked than deficits on analogous visual and verbal recognition memory tests. Unfortunately, the olfactory, visual and verbal tasks were not equated for initial familiarity or difficulty, making the cross-modal comparisons problematic. Not surprisingly, there was a tendency for patients with less severe dementia (scores ≥ 24 on the Mini-

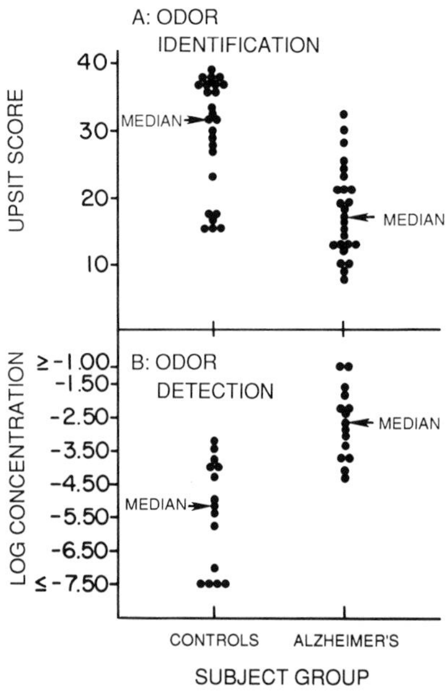

Fig. 5. (A) University of Pennsylvania Smell Identification Test (UPSIT) scores for patients with Alzheimer's disease and for age-, gender- and race-matched controls. (B) Detection threshold values for phenyl ethyl alcohol for patients with Alzheimer's disease and for matched controls. Each dot signifies an individual subject's data point. From Doty et al.: Presence of both odor identification and detection deficits in Alzheimer's disease. *Brain Res. Bull.: 18,* 597 – 600, 1987. Used with permission.

Mental State Exam or MMSE; Folstein et al., 1975) to score higher on the odor memory task than those with more severe dementia (< 24 on the MMSE).

Data from our laboratory which illustrate the odor identification and detection deficits of Alzheimer's disease are presented in Fig. 5. To measure identification, the UPSIT was administered to 25 patients who satisfied stringent criteria for the clinical diagnosis of probable AD and who scored above 35 on the Picture Identification Test (PIT; a test identical in content and format to the UPSIT except that pictures rather than odors are presented; Vollmecke and Doty, 1985). To measure detection, a single-staircase forced-choice odor detection threshold test using the rose-like odorant phenyl ethyl alcohol was administered to 15 AD patients and matched controls. Although some overlap appears between the AD and the control subject data, very few AD patients performed better than their individually matched controls. No statistically significant difference was present between the test scores of patients at Stage I and Stage II of the disease, suggesting that the olfactory deficit may occur early in the disease process and remain relatively constant thereafter.

The aforementioned olfactory deficits are presumably related to structural alterations that have been recently described in the olfactory pathways of patients with AD, although cause-and-effect relationships have yet to be determined. There is now evidence that neurofibrillary tangles and neuritic plaques are disproportionately found within limbic structures associated with olfactory function (Esiri and Wilcock, 1984; Esiri et al., 1986; Hooper and Vogel, 1976; Pearson et al., 1985; Reyes et al., 1987). Pearson et al. (1985) summarize the olfactory involvement as follows: 'The invariable finding of severe and even maximal involvement of the olfactory regions in Alzheimer's disease is in striking contrast to the minimal pathology in the visual and sensorimotor areas of the neocortex and cannot be without significance. In the olfactory system, the sites that are affected – the anterior olfactory nucleus, the uncus, and the medial group of amygdaloid nuclei – all receive fibers directly from the olfactory bulb. These observations at least raise the possibility that the olfactory pathway is the site of initial involvement of the disease' (p. 4534). Such findings gain even more significance in the context of theories that some dementia-related diseases may be related to environmental toxins or viruses (cf. Esiri, 1982), and evidence that (a) the olfactory system can be a major conduit of materials from the nasal cavity into the central nervous system (Shipley, 1985; Stroop et al., 1984; Tomlinson and Esiri, 1983; Monath et al., 1983) and (b) inoculation of rodents with some viruses results in necrosis of the olfactory neuroepithelium, the olfactory bulbs and tracts, and the prepyriform cortex (e.g., Goto et al., 1977; Reinacher et al., 1983).

Parkinson's disease

Although it was generally believed until the 1960s that Parkinson's disease was associated with dysfunction limited to motor symptoms (Proctor et al., 1964), it is now clear that most patients with this disease have a number of sensory and cognitive deficits, including difficulty in detecting, recognizing and identifying odorants (for a general review of non-olfactory cognitive aspects of parkinsonism, see Growden and Corkin, 1986).

The first study to demonstrate olfactory dysfunction in parkinsonism was that of Anasari and Johnson (1975). This study found amyl acetate detection thresholds of 22 PD patients to be significantly higher than the thresholds of 37 controls. This decrease in sensitivity to amyl acetate was confirmed by Ward et al. (1983) and Quinn et al. (1987).

In an extensive study, Ward et al. (1983) demonstrated suprathreshold olfactory deficits in PD patients, in addition to threshold deficits. For example, 28 PD patients were required to select, from a set of three test tubes, the one which contained a neat concentration of phenyl ethyl methyl ethyl carbinol. This task was repeated three times and a score ranging from 0 to 3 (i.e., no correct responses to correct responses on all three trials) was assigned to each subject. The mean score of the PD patients was 1.5 (SEM = 0.2), whereas that of controls was 2.7 (SEM = 0.1). These workers also tested identical twins and found no evidence that the olfactory alterations are inherited.

Recently we administered the UPSIT and PIT to 93 parkinsonians who had symptoms ranging in duration from 3 months to 55 years (Doty et al., 1988). Ratings of 11 neurological symptoms (3 bilateral) were obtained at the time of testing. Since 12 of the patients scored below 35 on the PIT, the study group was reduced to 81 patients and their matched controls. The number of patients at each of the Hoehn and Yahr (1967) stages were as follows: I = 22; II = 21; III = 25; IV = 11, and V = 2. Of this group, 38 patients and 38 controls were also administered the PEA odor-detection threshold test, and odor identification was retested in 24 patients after intervals ranging from 5 months to three years.

The data of this study revealed that the PD patients had a marked decrement in the ability both to identify and to detect odorants (Fig. 6). The olfactory deficit appeared to be relatively stable, since (a) no statistically meaningful relationship was present between the olfactory test scores and the time since the onset of symptoms (Figs. 7 and 8) and (b) longitudinal changes did not occur in the test scores.

Since the PD test scores were similar to those of the AD patients tested earlier (Doty et al., 1987), we statistically compared the olfactory test scores of these two groups of patients. To achieve this assessment, we first matched each AD patient to a PD patient on the basis of ethnic background, age,

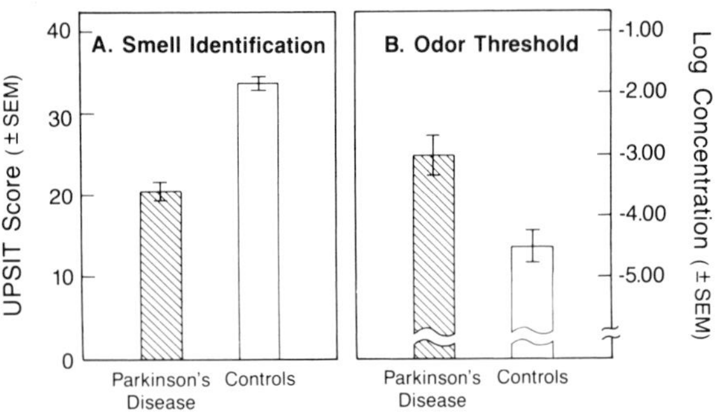

Fig. 6. (A) University of Pennsylvania Smell Identification Test (UPSIT) scores of Parkinson's disease patients and matched normal controls. (B) Phenyl ethyl alcohol (PEA) odor-detection threshold values of PD patients and matched normal controls. From Doty et al.: Olfactory dysfunction in Parkinson's disease: a general deficit unrelated to neurologic signs, disease stage, or disease duration. *Neurology: 38,* 1237–1244, 1988. Used with permission.

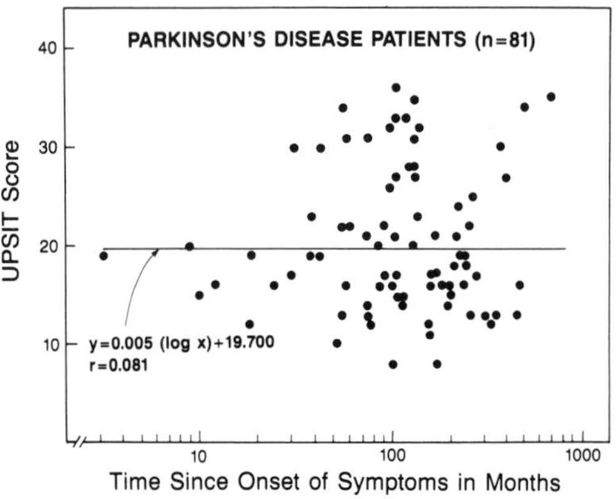

Fig. 7. University of Pennsylvania Smell Identification Test (UPSIT) scores of Parkinson's disease patients as a function of disease duration. From Doty et al.: Olfactory dysfunction in Parkinson's disease: a general deficit unrelated to neurologic signs, disease stage, or disease duration. *Neurology: 38,* 1237–1244, 1988. Used with permission.

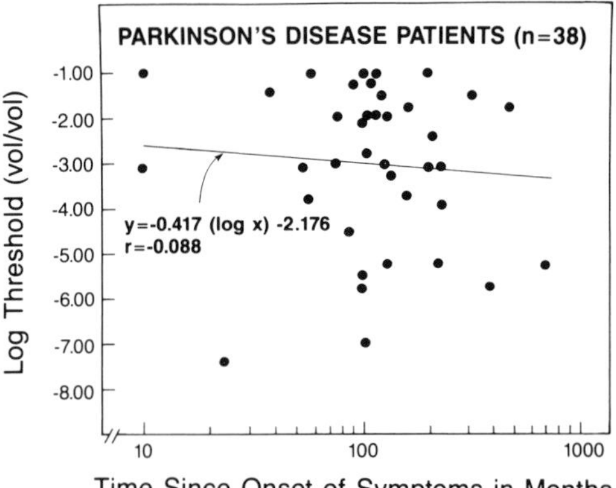

Fig. 8. Phenyl ethyl alcohol (PEA) odor-detection threshold values of Parkinson's disease patients as a function of disease duration. From Doty et al.: Olfactory dysfunction in Parkinson's disease: a general deficit unrelated to neurologic signs, disease stage, or disease duration. *Neurology: 38,* 1237–1244, 1988. Used with permission.

gender and smoking habits, and then subjected the UPSIT and PEA threshold scores to separate analyses of covariance with disease type as a factor and PIT score as a covariate (Doty et al., 1988). The covariate was important because many of the PIT scores of the AD patients fell below those of the PD patients within the 35 to 40 PIT score range, making it impossible to directly match all of the subjects on this cognitive variable.

No significant difference between the UPSIT test scores of the PD and AD patients was found, although the PIT covariate was highly significant, indicating that – even within the PIT range from 35 to 40 – the AD patients performed more poorly than did the PD patients on the PIT. A similar result was found for the detection threshold data, although the covariate did not reach significance at the 0.05 probability level (probably because of the smaller sample size).

Recently, we performed a factor analysis on data obtained from 53 patients to whom a number of cognitive and perceptual motor tests, in addition to the PIT, had been given (Doty et al., 1989). Included in the test battery was the Randt memory test (Randt et al., 1980), a number cancellation test, a reaction time test, a finger-tapping test, and selected verbal and performance subscales of the Wechsler Adult Intelligence Scale – Revised (WAIS-R; Wechsler, 1981). For this analysis, we combined the WAIS-R Information, Digit Span, Vocabulary and Similarities subtests into a single verbal score ('WAIS-Verbal') and the Picture Completion, Block Design and Digit Symbol subtests into a single performance score ('WAIS-Performance'). Similarly, we combined the Randt General Information, Five Items, Paired Words, Short Story and Picture Recognition modules into a 'Randt Memory Score'.

As seen in Table 1, six easily interpretable factors were extracted which accounted for 73.6% of the total variance. Factor 1 was clearly a cognitive/memory factor, loading most heavily (i.e., loadings > 0.50) with the Randt Memory, PIT, Number Cancellation and WAIS-R Verbal and Performance measures. Interestingly, this factor also had factor loadings > 0.50 from the neurological measures of bradykinesia and masking. Factor 2 was a gross motor factor, having factor loading > 0.50 for the neurological ratings of rigidity, alternating movements and masking, and factor loadings between 0.40 and 0.50 for left and right hand reaction times. Factor 3 appeared to be an oral motor factor, loading heavily on the speech, voice and swallow neurological ratings. Interestingly, this factor also received strong loadings from the variables of (a) disease duration, (b) thalamic surgery and (c) balance, gait and turning. Factor 4 was a fine motor factor, having strong loadings from the left and right hand finger-tapping and reaction time tests. Factor 5 was clearly an olfactory function factor, having meaningful loadings only from the UPSIT and the PEA odor-detection threshold test. Factor 6 proved to be a tremor factor, loading primarily with the neurological ratings of left and right tremor.

The aforementioned findings suggest that the olfactory dysfunction of PD is relatively independent of cognitive and motor symptoms. Further exploration of these data has shown no pattern of smell loss to the various items on the UPSIT for either the Alzheimer's or Parkinson's disease patients, implying that the odor-identification problem is unlikely to be specific to any given set of odorants. Interestingly, of 25 Parkinson's disease patients asked to answer whether or not some type of odor was noticed after sniffing each odorant item of the UPSIT, only seven responded 'no' to any odorant of the test. Of these seven, only three responded 'no' to more than one odorant, and the number of odorants responded to by even these three individuals was small (2, 3 and 6 items, respectively). These observations, along with the fact that only a few of the PD patients evidenced anosmia on the PEA detection threshold test, support the notion that the olfactory disorder of PD is rarely one of total smell loss.

Huntington's disease

The first symptoms of Huntington's disease are

TABLE 1

Varimax-rotated factor matrix for olfactory, neuropsychological and motor measurement variables. Loadings > 0.50 are printed in bold face for emphasis (R = right; L = left). See text for details. From Doty et al.: The olfactory and cognitive deficits of Parkinson's disease are independent. *Ann. Neurol.: 25,* 166–171, 1989, with permission

Variable	Factor I: cognitive/ memory	Factor II: gross motor	Factor III: oral motor	Factor IV: fine motor	Factor V: olfactory	Factor VI: tremor
Randt Memory	**.880**	–.077	–.157	.024	–.086	.225
WAIS-R [Perf]	**.810**	–.204	–.147	–.088	.001	–.108
WAIS-R [Verb]	**.780**	–.165	–.039	–.078	–.052	–.132
PIT	**.763**	–.191	.158	–.141	.014	.161
Cancellation	**.753**	–.045	–.368	–.246	.108	–.027
Bradykinesia	**–.527**	.433	.355	.400	.309	.184
Rigidity [L]	.050	**.883**	–.062	.066	–.018	.097
Rigidity [R]	–.074	**.858**	.014	.086	.050	–.017
Altern Move [L]	–.392	**.792**	.186	.033	–.025	–.022
Altern Move [R]	–.378	**.748**	.222	–.057	.041	–.026
Masking	–.499	**.564**	.407	.221	.186	.210
React Time [R]	–.298	.491	–0.22	.437	.265	–.395
Speech	–.064	–.021	**.839**	.059	–.040	–.212
Disease Duration	.036	.114	**.789**	.135	–.097	.140
Voice	–.313	.035	**.786**	–.043	–.053	–.019
Thalamic Surgery	.022	.012	**.682**	–.092	.193	.159
Bal Gait Turn	–.425	.342	**.639**	.160	.227	.121
Disease Stage	–.426	.458	**.601**	.201	.233	.201
Swallow	–.010	.001	**.523**	.232	–.454	–.004
Tapping [L]	.041	–.068	–.075	**–.870**	.097	–.089
Tapping [R]	.189	–.101	–.132	**–.818**	.133	.001
React Time [L]	–.294	.409	–.109	**.546**	.271	–.314
Smell Threshold	.142	.091	.102	.056	**.888**	–.152
UPSIT	.344	–.028	.024	.205	**–.617**	.202
Tremor [L]	.050	–.104	.167	.082	–.042	**.828**
Tremor [R]	–.079	.205	–.057	–.050	–.219	**.581**

typically recognized in middle age, and this disease serves as a classic example of gene action late in life with autosomal dominant transmission (McClearn and Foch, 1985). Recently, Mobert et al. (1987) reported, in a study of 38 HD patients and 38 controls, that HD patients evidence a marked deficit in an odor-recognition memory task and, furthermore, that such dysfunction is present in early-affected patients with minimal chorea or cognitive deficits and with normal verbal and visual recognition memory performance. The early HD and late HD patients reportedly performed normally on a '3-stage odor discrimination task', although data for this latter task were not presented. This pioneering study suggests that a genetically determined dementia-related disorder can be accompanied by smell dysfunction at the time of its phenotypic expression.

General issues and summary

The studies reviewed in this chapter indicate that the sense of smell is dramatically altered in older age and in a number of age-related diseases. The deficits appear to be widespread and detectable by various olfactory tests, including tests of detection threshold, odor identification and odor memory. However, considerable interindividual variability exists and the physiological basis of these changes is not clear. In many healthy elderly people smell loss appears to occur as a result of one or more causes, including viral insult, cumulated exposure to toxic fumes, head trauma and calcification of the cribriform plate.

While a number of workers have hypothesized that some environmental factor, such as an air-borne virus or metallic element, could be responsible for the olfactory dysfunction of Alzheimer's disease (and perhaps other dementia-related diseases), only circumstantial data are available to support this point. Since the genetically determined dementia-related disorder of Huntington's chorea appears to be predictably associated with alterations in smell function, it is possible that the olfactory system is particularly vulnerable to destruction from a number of degenerative neurological disorders and that environmental agents, per se, need not be the basis for the sensory problem. However, more data are needed before one can rule out the possibility that such agents, either alone or in conjunction with a genetic substrate, play some etiological role even in these disorders.

Although it is tempting to assume, as have authors such as Koss et al. (1987), that alterations in threshold function reflect 'peripheral' olfactory dysfunction and that alterations in odor identification and other more demanding tasks reflect 'central' olfactory dysfunction, there is little empirical support at present for such a simple dichotomy. Despite the fact that a peripheral/central distinction is useful in clinical audiology (where threshold loss is commonly associated with CN VIII pathology), an evaluation of the usefulness of this distinction in olfaction requires further research. The limited data suggest that both identification and detection deficits commonly arise from damage to the olfactory epithelium, even though identification deficits unassociated with detection deficits can occur in central brain disorders (see Eichenbaum et al., 1983; Mair et al., 1986).

There is controversy as to whether the olfactory deficits observed in dementia-related diseases are due to the dementia, per se. Because non-sensory aspects of performance on olfactory tests are probably influenced in a monotonic manner by the degree of dementia, one would expect to find statistically significant negative correlations between ratings of dementia and olfactory test scores, particularly when patients with moderate dementia are included in the subject population (e.g., Jensen and Murphy, 1988). However, it is difficult to untangle the sensory and performance factors in such groups. The fact that considerable olfactory deficits are present in parkinsonian patients with minimal or non-existent dementia (and in AD patients with very mild dementia) suggests that the olfactory dysfunction, per se, is not dependent upon the underlying dementia. This notion is supported by (a) the factor analysis study of Doty et al. (1988b) in which the olfactory test scores loaded strongly on a factor which received no significant loadings from neuropsychological cognitive measures and (b) anecdotal reports from a few AD and PD patients and/or their spouses that alterations in smell sensitivity appeared to have preceded the onset of the motor or cognitive problems. On the other hand, one can envisage instances – particularly in the later stages of the disease processes – where both the olfactory system and cortical regions associated with dementia become progressively coinvolved in a way that makes it impossible to determine the degree to which cognitive and sensory factors contribute to the sensory disturbances.

It is apparent from the studies reviewed in this chapter that significant recent progress has been made in elucidating the nature and prevalence of olfactory disturbances in elderly patients and in patients with dementia-related diseases. Further advances in this area will be facilitated by the administration of a broader range of standardized olfactory tests (including ones of odor memory) to such people, as well as detailed postmortem neurochemical and structural studies of their olfactory pathways. Furthermore, studies of patients with other dementia-related diseases (e.g., Down's syndrome and Pick's disease) will provide a better understanding of the factors which underlie the sensory disorders. A big challenge for the next decade will be to determine the pathophysiological bases of these sensory disturbances and whether therapeutic strategems can be developed to reverse, halt or mitigate their progression.

Acknowledgements

This work was supported by Grant NS 16365 from the National Institute of Neurological and Communicative Disorders and Stroke and Grant AG 08148 from the National Institute on Aging.

References

Anasari KA, Johnson A: Olfactory function in patients with Parkinson's disease. *J. Chron. Dis.: 28,* 493 – 497, 1975.

Beaumont JG: *Introduction to Neuropsychology.* New York: Guilford Press, 1983.

Brodal A: *Neurological Anatomy in Relation to Clinical Medicine,* 3rd Edition. New York: Oxford University Press, 1981.

Burdach KJ, Doty RL: The effects of mouth movements, swallowing and spitting on retronasal odor perception. *Physiol. Behav.: 41,* 353 – 356, 1987.

Chalke HD, Dewhurst JR, Ward CW: Loss of sense of smell in old people. *Public Health (Lond.): 72,* 223 – 230, 1958.

Costanzo RM, Becker DP: Smell and taste disorders in head injury and neurosurgery. In Meiselman HL, Rivlin RS (Editors), *Clinical Measurement of Taste and Smell.* New York: MacMillan Publishing Company, pp. 565 – 578, 1986.

Deems DA, Doty RL: Age-related changes in the phenyl ethyl alcohol odor detection threshold. *Trans. PA Acad. Opthalmol. Otolaryngol.: 39,* 646 – 650, 1987.

Deems DA, Doty RL, Settle RG, Snow JB Jr, Moore-Gillon V, Shaman P, Mester AF, Kimmelman CP, Brightman VJ: Smell and taste disorders: analysis of patient data from the University of Pennsylvania Smell and Taste Center. Submitted.

Doty RL: A cry for the liberation of the female rodent. *Psychol. Bull.: 81,* 159 – 172, 1974.

Doty RL: An examination of relationships between the pleasantness, intensity and concentration of 10 odorous stimuli. *Percept. Psychophys.: 17,* 492 – 496, 1975.

Doty RL, Shaman P, Dann M: Development of the University of Pennsylvania Smell Identification Test: a standardized microencapsulated test of olfactory function. *Physiol. Behav. (Monogr.): 32,* 489 – 502, 1984a.

Doty RL, Shaman P, Applebaum SL, Giberson R, Sikorski L, Rosenberg L: Smell identification ability: changes with age. *Science: 226,* 1441 – 1443, 1984b.

Doty RL, Applebaum SL, Zusho H, Settle RG: A cross-cultural study of sex differences in odor identification ability. *Neuropsychologia: 23,* 667 – 672, 1985.

Doty RL: Odor-guided behavior in mammals. *Experientia: 42,* 257 – 271, 1986.

Doty RL, Reyes PF, Gregor T: Presence of both odor identification and detection deficits in Alzheimer's disease. *Brain Res. Bull.: 18,* 597 – 600, 1987.

Doty RL, Deems D, Stellar S: Olfactory dysfunction in Parkinson's disease: a general deficit unrelated to neurologic signs, disease stage, or disease duration. *Neurology: 38,* 1237 – 1244, 1988.

Doty RL, Riklan M, Deems DA, Reynolds C, Stellar S: The olfactory and cognitive deficits of Parkinson's disease: evidence for independence. *Ann. Neurol.: 25,* 166 – 171, 1989.

Douek E, Bannister DH, Dodson HC: Recent advances in the pathology of olfaction. *Proc. R. Soc. Med.: 68,* 467 – 470, 1975.

Eichenbaum H, Morton TH, Potter H, Corkin S: Selective olfactory deficits in case H.M. *Brain: 106,* 459 – 472, 1983.

Engen T: Taste and smell. In Birren JE, Schaie KW (Editors), *Handbook of the Psychology of Aging.* New York: Van Nostrand Reinhold, pp. 554 – 561, 1977.

Esiri MM: Viruses and Alzheimer's disease. *J. Neurol. Neurosurg. Psychiatry: 45,* 759 – 760, 1982.

Esiri MM, Wilcock PK: The olfactory bulb in Alzheimer's disease. *J. Neurol. Neurosurg. Psychiatry: 47,* 56 – 60, 1984.

Esiri MM, Pearson RCA, Powell, TPS: The cortex of the primary auditory area in Alzheimer's disease. *Brain Res.: 366,* 385 – 387, 1986.

Folstein M, Folstein S, McHugh PR: Mini-Mental State: a practical method for grading the cognitive stage of patients for the clinician. *J. Psychiatr. Res.: 12,* 189 – 198, 1975.

Fordyce ID: Olfactory tests. *Br. J. Ind. Med.: 18,* 213 – 215, 1961.

Getchell TV, Margolis FL, Getchell ML: Perireceptor and receptor events in vertebrate olfaction. *Prog. Neurobiol.: 23,* 317 – 345, 1984.

Goto N, Hirano N, Aiuchi M, Hayashi T, Fujiwara K: Nasoencephalopathy of mice infected intranasally with a mouse hepatitis virus, JHM strain. *Jap. J. Exp. Med.: 47,* 59 – 70, 1977.

Graziadei PPC, Monti-Graziadei GA: The olfactory system: a model for the study of neurogenesis and axon regeneration in mammals. In Cotman CW (Editor), *Neuronal Plasticity.* New York: Raven Press, pp. 131 – 153, 1978.

Growdon JH, Corkin S: Cognitive impairments in Parkinson's disease. *Adv. Neurol.: 45,* 383 – 392, 1986.

Haberly LB, Price JL: The axonal projection patterns of the mitral and tufted cells of the olfactory bulb in the rat. *Brain Res.: 129,* 152 – 157, 1977.

Harper R, Bate-Smith EC, Land DG: *Odour Description and Odour Classification.* New York: American Elsevier, 1968.

Harrison PJ: Pathogenesis of Alzheimer's disease – beyond the cholinergic hypothesis: discussion paper. *J. R. Soc. Med.: 79,* 347 – 352, 1986.

Heilman KM, Valenstein E: *Clinical Neuropsychology.* New York: Oxford University Press, 1979.

Heimer L: Synaptic distribution of centripetal and centrifugal nerve fibres in the olfactory system of the rat. An experimental study. *J. Anat. (Lond.): 103,* 413 – 432, 1968.

Hinds JW, Hinds PL, McNelly NA: An autoradiographic study of the mouse olfactory epithelium: evidence of long lived receptors. *Anat. Rec.: 210,* 375 – 383, 1984.

Hoehn MM, Yahr MD: Parkinsonism: onset, progression and mortality. *Neurology: 17,* 427 – 442, 1967.

Hooper MW, Vogel FS: The limbic system in Alzheimer's

disease. *Am. J. Pathol.: 85,* 1 – 13, 1976.

Jensen MM, Murphy C: Olfactory thresholds in Alzheimer's disease are correlated with neuropsychological assessment of dementia. Abstract 127; AChemS-X; Tenth Annual Meeting of the Association for Chemoreception Sciences. Sarasota: Hyatt Sarasota, April 27 – May 1, 1988.

Kimbrell GM, Furchtott E: The effect of aging on olfactory threshold. *J. Gerontol.: 18,* 364 – 365, 1963.

Knupfer L, Spiegel R: Differences in olfactory test performance between normal aged, Alzheimer and vascular type dementia individuals. *Int. J. Geriatr. Psychiatry: 1,* 3 – 14, 1986.

Koss E, Weiffenbach JM, Haxby JV, Friedland RP: Olfactory detection and recognition in Alzheimer's disease. *Lancet: i,* 622, 1987.

Lezak MD: *Neuropsychological Assessment.* New York: Oxford University Press, 1983.

MacLeod P: Structure and function of higher olfactory centers. In Beidler LM (Editor): *Handbook of Sensory Physiology, Vol. 4. Olfaction.* New York: Springer-Verlag, 1971.

Mair RG, Doty RL, Kelly KM, Wilson CS, Langlais PJ, McEntee WJ, Vollmecke TA: Multimodal sensory discrimination deficits in Korsakoff's psychosis. *Neuropsychologia: 24,* 831 – 839, 1986.

McClearn G, Foch TT: Behavioral genetics. In Birren JE, Schaie KW (Editors), *Handbook of the Psychology of Aging.* New York: Van Nostrand Reinhold, pp. 113 – 143, 1985.

McKhann G, Drachman D, Folstein M, Katzman R, Price D, Stadlan EM: Clinical diagnosis of Alzheimer's disease. Report of the NINCDS-ADRDA work group under the auspices of the Department of Health and Human Services task force on Alzheimer's disease. *Neurology: 34,* 939 – 944, 1984.

Moberg PJ, Pearlson GD, Speedie LJ, Lipsey JR, Folstein SE: Olfactory recognition: differential impairments in early and late Huntington's and Alzheimer's disease. *J. Clin. Exp. Neurpsychol.: 9,* 650 – 664, 1987.

Monath TP, Croop CB, Harrision AK: Mode of entry of a neurotropic arbovirus into the central nervous system: reinvestigation of an old controversy. *Lab. Invest.: 48,* 339 – 410, 1983.

Moran DT, Rowley III JC, Jafek BW, Lovell MA: The fine structure of the olfactory mucosa in man. *J. Neurocytol.: 11,* 721 – 746, 1982.

Murphy C: Age-related effects on the threshold, psychophysical function and pleasantness of menthol. *J. Gerontol.: 38,* 217 – 222, 1983.

Murphy C: Cognitive and chemosensory influences on age-related changes in the ability to identify blended foods. *J. Gerontol.: 40,* 47 – 52, 1985.

Murphy C, Nerison R: Olfactory decrements in Alzheimer's disease. *Chem. Senses: 12,* 686, 1987 (Abstr.).

Nakashima T, Kimmelman CP, Snow JB Jr: 1984, Structure of human fetal and adult olfactory neuroepithelium. *Arch. Otolaryngol.: 110,* 641 – 646, 1984.

Pearson RCA, Esiri MM, Hiorns RW, Wilcock GK, Powell TPS: Anatomical correlates of the distribution of the pathological changes in the neocortex in Alzheimer disease. *Proc. Natl. Acad. Sci. USA: 82,* 4531 – 4534, 1985.

Proctor F, Riklan M, Cooper IS, Teuber H-L: Judgment of visual and postural vertical by parkinsonian patients. Neurology: 14, 287 – 293, 1964.

Powell TBS, Cowan WM: Centrifugal fibres in the lateral olfactory tract. *Nature: 199,* 1296 – 1297, 1963.

Powell TBS, Cowan WM, Raisman G: The central olfactory connections. *J. Anat.: 99,* 791 – 813, 1965.

Price JL: An autoradiographic study of complementary laminar patterns of termination of afferent fibers to the olfactory cortex. *J. Comp. Neurol.: 150,* 87 – 108, 1973.

Price JL: The central olfactory and accessory olfactory systems. In Finger TE, Silver WL (Editors), *Neurobiology of Taste and Smell.* New York: John Wiley & Sons, pp. 179 – 203, 1987.

Proctor F, Riklan M, Cooper IS, Teuber H-L: Judgment of visual and postural vertical by parkinsonian patients. *Neurology: 14,* 287 – 293, 1964.

Quinn NP, Rossor MN, Marsden CD: Olfactory threshold in Parkinson's disease. *J. Neurol. Neurosurg. Psychiatry: 50,* 88 – 89, 1987.

Randt CT, Brown ER, Osborne D: A memory test for longitudinal measurement of mild to moderate deficits. *Clin. Neuropsychol.: 2,* 184 – 194, 1980.

Reinacher M, Bonin J, Narayan O, Scholtissek C: Pathogenesis of neurovirulent influenza A virus infection in mice: route of entry of virus into brain determines infection of different populations of cells. *Lab. Invest.: 49,* 686 – 692, 1983.

Reyes PR, Golden GT, Fagel PL, Zalewska M, Fariello RG, Katz L, Carner E: The prepiriform cortex in dementia of the Alzheimer type. *Arch. Neurol.: 44,* 644 – 645.

Rezek DL: Olfactory deficits as a neurologic sign in dementia of the Alzheimer type. *Arch. Neurol.: 44,* 1030 – 1032, 1987.

Schemper T, Voss S, Cain WS: Odor identification in young and elderly persons: sensory and cognitive limitations. *J. Gerontol.: 36,* 446 – 452, 1981.

Schiffman S: Physicochemical correlates of olfactory quality. *Science: 185,* 112 – 117, 1974.

Schiffman S: Food recognition by the elderly. *J. Gerontol.: 32,* 586 – 592, 1977.

Schiffman S, Pasternak M: Decreased discrimination of food odors in the elderly. *J. Gerontol.: 34,* 73 – 79, 1979.

Schiffman SS, Moss J, Erickson RP: Thresholds of food odors in the elderly. *Exp. Aging Res.: 2,* 389 – 398, 1976.

Schoenfeld TA, Macrides F: Topographic organization of connections between the main olfactory bulb and pars externa of the anterior olfactory nucleus in the hamster. *J. Comp. Neurol.: 227,* 121 – 135, 1984.

Settipane GA, Chaffee F: Nasal polyps in asthma and rhinitis. *J. Allergy Clin. Immunol.: 59,* 17 – 21, 1977.

Serby M, Corwin J, Conrad P, Rotrosen J: Olfactory dysfunction in Alzheimer's disease and Parkinson's disease (Letter). *Am. J. Psychiatry: 142,* 781 – 782, 1985.

Shipley MT: Transport of molecules from nose to brain: Transneuronal anterograde and retrograde labeling in the rat olfactory system by wheat germ agglutin-horseradish peroxidase applied to the nasal epithelium. *Brain Res. Bull.: 15,* 129 – 142, 1985.

Stevens JC, Cain WS: Age-related deficiency in the perceived strength of six odorants. *Chem. Senses: 10,* 517 – 529, 1985.

Stevens JC, Cain WS: Smelling via the mouth: effect of aging. *Percept. Psychophys.: 40,* 142 – 146, 1986.

Stevens JC, Marks LE: Cross-modal matching functions

generated by magnitude estimation. *Percept. Psychophys.: 27,* 379 – 389, 1980.

Stevens JC, Plantinga A, Cain HS: Reduction of odor and nasal pungency associated with aging. *Neurobiol. Aging: 3,* 125 – 132, 1982.

Stroop WG, Rock DL, Fraser NW: Localization of herpes simplex virus in the trigeminal and olfactory systems of the mouse central nervous system during acute and latent infections by in situ hybridization. *Lab. Invest.: 51,* 27 – 38, 1984.

Sumner D: Post-traumatic anosmia. *Brain: 87,* 107 – 120, 1964.

Tomlinson AH, Esiri MM: Herpes simplex encephaltitis: immunohistological demonstration of spread of virus via olfactory pathways in mice. *J. Neurol. Sci.: 60,* 473 – 484, 1983.

Venstrom D, Amoore JE: Olfactory threshold in relation to age, sex or smoking. *J. Food Sci.: 33,* 264 – 265, 1968.

Vollmecke T, Doty RL: Development of the Picture Identification Test (PIT): a research companion to the University of Pennsylvania Smell Identification Test. *Chem. Senses: 10,* 413 – 414, 1985 (Abstr.).

Ward CD, Hess WA, Calne DB: Olfactory impairment in Parkinson's disease. *Neurology: 33,* 943 – 946, 1983.

Warner MD, Peabody CA, Flattery JJ, Tinklenberg JR: Olfactory deficits and Alzheimer's disease. *Biol. Psychiatry: 21,* 116 – 118, 1986.

Wechsler D: *WAIS-R Manual.* New York: The Psychological Corporation, 1981.

Handbook of Neuropsychology, Vol. 4
F. Boller and J. Grafman (Eds)

CHAPTER 11

Vision and aging

Cynthia Owsley[1] and Michael E. Sloane[2]

[1] *Department of Ophthalmology, School of Medicine/Eye Foundation Hospital and* [2] *Department of Psychology, University of Alabama at Birmingham, Birmingham, Al 35294 U.S.A.*

Introduction

This chapter is designed to provide an overview of how the aging process affects various aspects of human visual function. Since many neuropsychological tests and evaluation procedures are administered visually, it is important to understand what kinds of visual deficits an older adult can face. In addition, many of the visual functions described in this chapter are often incorporated into assessment batteries that can assist clinicians in the differential diagnosis of disorders which affect the visual system. Furthermore, it is important to recognize the types of visual dysfunction older adults experience since many of their performance problems may be inappropriately attributed to cognitive deficits, when in fact vision impairment may be the primary causative factor.

The research literature on aging and vision is quite extensive and, in the interest of space limitations, we have chosen to cover only those studies which highlight our major points. For additional coverage of this diverse topic, the reader is referred to other review chapters and volumes (e.g., Weale, 1963, 1982; Sekuler et al., 1982; Kline and Schieber, 1985; Owsley et al., 1986).

What is 'normal' aging?

The focus of the research described in this chapter is on older adults who are free from ocular disease and who would be considered by most eye care specialists to be in good ocular health. Despite a 'clean bill' of eye health, these older adults often experience significant visual problems that interfere with their routine daily activities (Kosnik et al., 1988). Admittedly, there is an arbitrary line between what is considered good eye health in the elderly vs. the early stages of pathological or sight-threatening conditions (see Ludwig and Smoke, 1980; Johnson, 1985; Johnson and Choy, 1987). There are many anatomical and physiological changes in the visual system in later adulthood, as described below. These changes in their minor forms are considered 'normal' accompaniments to growing old, but in their more advanced stages, they can cause serious vision impairment and are consequently designated as 'disease'. For example, the crystalline lens in an older adult undergoes some degree of increased density and opacification. When this increased density progresses to where it causes significant functional problems, it is generally termed 'cataract'. A similar point can be made for the macular changes that typify virtually all older retinae, such as pigmentary mottling and the appearance of drusen. When these changes become more serious and co-occur with decreased acuity, a diagnosis of age-related macular degeneration (AMD) is usually made. Thus, since these anatomical changes lie on a continuum rather than fall into dichotomous categories, the criteria for defining 'normal eye health' in older adults are not easy to specify.

What complicates matters further is that there

are no widely used and validated scales for clinically evaluating anatomical structures of the eye. For example, what one clinician calls 'early' AMD, may be a more advanced case to another; what one clinician calls a '2 + ' nuclear sclerotic cataract may be a 'trace' cataract to another. Because of these problems, it is difficult to compare results across studies. The solution lies, at least in part, with specifying as clearly as possible the eye health criteria by which older adults are selected for the study sample, and also in developing criteria and evaluation techniques which are valid, reliable and widely available. There have been some recent advances in this area regarding the evaluation of the lens and the retina (e.g., West et al., 1988; Hyman et al., and AMD Risk Factors Study Group, 1988).

Despite these problems in defining normal aging, the study of visual function in adults who are free from identifiable ocular disease is worthwhile. First, many older adults never fall victim to ocular disease, yet they still experience significant visual difficulties that hamper the quality of their daily lives. Much of the research on vision and aging has the goal of understanding the origins of these visual problems so that they can be remedied. Second, ophthalmological tests of functional vision require age-matched norms. If an older adult's performance is compared to norms generated from young adults, that older adult will often fall out of the normal range and be viewed as 'failing' the test. Third, it is important to study aging per se because many of the aging-related deficits in visual function can mimic the effects of ocular disease, and it is important to differentiate between the two whenever possible.

As the reader will note below, research has demonstrated that many aspects of visual function tend to decline in later adulthood, even when an individual is free from ocular pathology. Despite these average trends, however, it is important to point out that there is a wide variability in the visual capacities of older adults, with some older adults performing well within the normal range of young adults and others showing clearcut deficits. In other words, simply because a person is old does not automatically mean this individual has a visual sensitivity loss.

Although this chapter centers on older adults free from significant eye disease, it is important to provide some balance to this introduction by pointing out that ocular disease and vision loss are more prevalent in older adults than in the younger population. The four leading causes of serious vision impairment in older adults in the US, as estimated by the Framingham Eye Study, are age-related macular degeneration, cataract, glaucoma and diabetic retinopathy (Leibowitz et al., 1980). For example, the Framingham Study found that approximately 19% of adults between age 65 and 74 have at least one of these diseases; the prevalence increases with increasing age, reaching almost 50% in the 75 + age group. When uncorrectable vision impairment progresses to the point where it significantly interferes with daily life, the individual is said to have 'low vision' (see Faye, 1984). The elderly are disproportionately represented in this group, with one estimate suggesting that they comprise about 70% of the low vision population (Kirchner and Peterson, 1979).

Optical changes

There are several changes in the older eye which affect its optical properties. Because vision depends upon the imaging ability of the eye's optics, age-related changes in the optics can have significant effects on older adults' ability to see. One major change in the older eye is that there is increased light absorption by ocular structures along the visual axis, which reduces the absolute light level reaching the photoreceptors. These structures include the crystalline lens (Said and Weale, 1959; Pokorny et al., 1987), and to a minimal extent the cornea and the vitreous (Boettner and Wolter, 1962). This increased absorption in later adulthood interacts with wavelength, with much greater absorption occurring at the short wavelength end of the spectrum (Said and Weale, 1959; van Norren and Vos, 1974). Another feature of the old eye which reduces retinal illuminance is 'senile miosis', which refers to the tendency of the older adult's pupil to be smaller than that of younger adults. This miosis is most pronounced at lower light levels where a younger adult's pupil would increase in diameter, whereas an older adult's would remain at a relatively small size (Loewenfeld, 1979). The main negative effect of senile miosis is that it reduces the amount of light reaching the retina, thereby decreasing acuity and contrast sensitivity. However, a small pupil also has some beneficial effects on vision in that it minimizes optical aberration and increases depth-of-focus.

Another major change in the optics of the eye in later life is increased intraocular light scatter, which is presumably due to the increased opacity of the lens and other parts of the optical media (Wolf, 1960; Allen and Vos, 1967; Block and Rosenblum, 1987). This accentuated light scatter in older adults is believed to reduce the contrast of the retinal image (Wolf and Gardiner, 1965; Paulsson and Sjostrand, 1980; Hemenger, 1984), thereby lowering older adults' contrast sensitivity. It is thought to be responsible for older adults' heightened sensitivity to disability glare (Wolf, 1960; Fisher and Christie, 1965; Wolf and Gardiner, 1965; Reading, 1968; Pulling et al., 1980).

The amplitude of accommodation of the lens (i.e., the lens's ability to focus) decreases throughout adulthood, a condition called presbyopia (see Hofstetter, 1965). By the 60s and 70s very little accommodative ability remains, and most older adults require corrective lenses to see optimally at near distances. This point is important to researchers from a practical standpoint when comparing younger and older adults' performance, especially when targets are presented at near distances. While most young adults can naturally accommodate so that they are correctly focused on the target, older adults' presbyopia requires that they be provided with plus lenses to eliminate their refractive error. The axis of astigmatism also tends to change during adulthood, shifting to 'against the rule' in later life (Weale, 1963). A more general point is that researchers cannot assume that a participant's 'walk-in' (habitual) optical correction is the best in terms of correction of refractive error. Owsley et al. (1983) found that adults' acuity could often be improved by several lines on a letter chart by modifying their walk-in optical correction.

It is interesting to note that not all optical properties of the eye change during adulthood. The macular pigment is a yellow carotenoid pigment located in the central five degrees around the fovea and has a filtering effect on the light reaching the photoreceptors. Its main absorption band is in the short wavelength end of the spectrum (peak at 460 nm). Although there are wide individual differences in macular pigment density, this range of variability does not change during adulthood (Werner et al., 1987). Another optical property that does not change during adulthood is the chromatic aberration of the eye (Howarth et al., 1988).

Neural changes

There have been a few reports of aging-related changes in the neural aspects of the visual pathway. However, it is still unknown what degree of influence these neural changes actually have on visual function in the elderly. A loss of rods and cones in the human retina reportedly occurs in later adulthood (Marshall et al., 1980; Marshall and Laties, 1985; Yuodelis and Hendrickson, 1986; Marshall, 1987). A decrease in cone density in later life has also been noted for the rhesus monkey, a common animal model in the study of the human visual system (Ordy et al., 1980). It is interesting to note that data reported by Curcio (1986) have not supported the hypothesis of aging-related cone loss in humans. Whereas earlier studies estimated density from a very small number of donor retinae, Curcio's study (1986) has involved estimations based on retina from several younger and older donors, and has reported that cone density estimates from older retina fell well within the range of densities from younger retina. This finding underscores the importance of large sample sizes in studying aging and also encourages us to re-evaluate the earlier work on aging and retinal anatomy.

The density of human cone photopigment reportedly declines with age (Kilbride et al., 1986), although other studies have suggested that this age-related change may be relatively minor or nonexistent (van Norren and van Meel, 1985; Elsner et al., 1988). Marshall et al. (1980) further found that the outer segments of photoreceptors lose their normal stacked-disk appearance as groups of lamellae are bent and distorted. Psychophysical data also imply that there may be disturbances in photoreceptor architecture in that older adults display abnormal Stiles-Crawford effects (Smith et al., 1988), suggesting photoreceptor misalignment in the older retina or possibly swelling of remaining photoreceptors after receptor loss.

Other studies on the aging retina include a report that in the older retina, cell bodies from the outer nuclear layer are displaced into the outer plexiform layer and the photoreceptor layer (Gartner and Henkind, 1981). Optic nerve fibers apparently decrease in number in later life, although there is considerable variability (Balaszi et al., 1984). Other optic nerve changes include swelling and sinuous-like pathways in both dendrites and axons (Vrabec, 1965a; Dolman et al., 1980). Cortical and higher pathway alterations in later life have also been described. There have been reports of substantial cell loss associated with aging in the visual cortex (see Brody, 1955, 1973; Wisniewski and Terry, 1976; Strehler, 1976; Devaney and Johnson, 1980). Also reported are neurofibrillary degeneration, shrinkage of dendritic arbors, loss of dendritic spines and a decrease in extracellular space (see Scheibel and Scheibel, 1975; Wisniewski and Terry, 1976; Strehler, 1976). It is interesting to note that although these changes could be observed in visual cortex, they were much more severe in other areas of cortex, such as the prefrontal and superior temporal areas. There are also some reports of changes in the function of neurotransmitters in the visual cortex (McGeer and McGeer, 1976; Samorajaski, 1977).

In summary, there are a variety of optical and neural changes in the visual system during the aging process, which could conceivably contribute to visual dysfunction. In the rest of this chapter we describe a number of aging-related changes in visual function and discuss the mechanisms believed to underlie these deficits.

Age-related changes in visual function

Acuity

The measurement of visual acuity, the smallest spatial detail which can be resolved, is the standard way of evaluating pattern vision in a clinical exam. Acuity is typically assessed by having the patient read high-contrast, high-luminance letter charts, a test which is easy to administer and to perform. There have been many studies which have examined how acuity changes during adulthood, and several of these studies have been summarized in Fig. 1 (adopted from Pitts, 1982). All studies agree that acuity declines during adulthood, but the actual rate of the decline, the decade of onset and other features of the acuity-age relationship are not widely agreed upon because of methodological differences among the studies. Variables which could affect this age trend and which were not typically controlled in the early work include refractive error and the presence of ocular pathology, which we have already pointed out is much more prevalent in the older adult population. Recent studies have attempted to control these factors and have found that even when older adults are refracted for the test distance and have good eye health, they still exhibit decreased resolution (Frisen and Frisen, 1981; Owsley et al., 1983). Weale (1975, 1987) has argued that a large portion of this acuity loss is due to neural deterioration along the visual pathway during the aging process, although this claim has not yet been empirically verified.

Often ignored in analysing the problem of aging and acuity loss are crucial stimulus features of the letter chart. For example, charts having low luminance and/or low contrast exacerbate older adults' acuity problems, in many cases more so than they would for younger adults (Richards, 1977; Adams et al., 1988). In addition, the spacing of the letters on a chart can influence the degree of older adults' acuity problems. Older adults tend to experience contour interaction effects ('crowding') over a larger spatial extent than do younger adults, which hampers their acuity (Sloane et al., 1987).

Spatial contrast sensitivity

Spatial contrast sensitivity testing determines how much contrast an individual requires to detect a pattern of a given size (see Bodis-Wollner and Camisa, 1980, for overview). Size is typically specified in terms of the spatial frequency of a vertical bar grating having a sinusoidal luminance profile. Contrast is defined as the difference between maximum and minimum luminance on the bar grating, divided by their sum. When contrast sensitivity is measured for stationary gratings presented in central vision, older adults, even those in good ocular health, tend to exhibit a loss in sensitivity at higher spatial frequencies (Derefeldt et al., 1979; Owsley et al., 1983). The magnitude of older adults' contrast sensitivity loss increases with increasing spatial frequency. Fig. 2 illustrates this finding. In addition, this loss increases in magnitude with decreasing ambient light level (Sloane et al., 1988), as illustrated in Fig. 2. Although the underlying basis of this loss has not been completely defined, several points are clear from research to date: Older adults' contrast sensitivity loss is not attributable to refractive error (Owsley et al., 1983), senile miosis of the pupil (Sloane et al., 1988), or cognitive factors associated with decision-making in setting a sensory threshold (Morrison and Reilly, 1986; Higgins et al., 1988). Furthermore, neural changes in the aging visual system apparently have some role in this

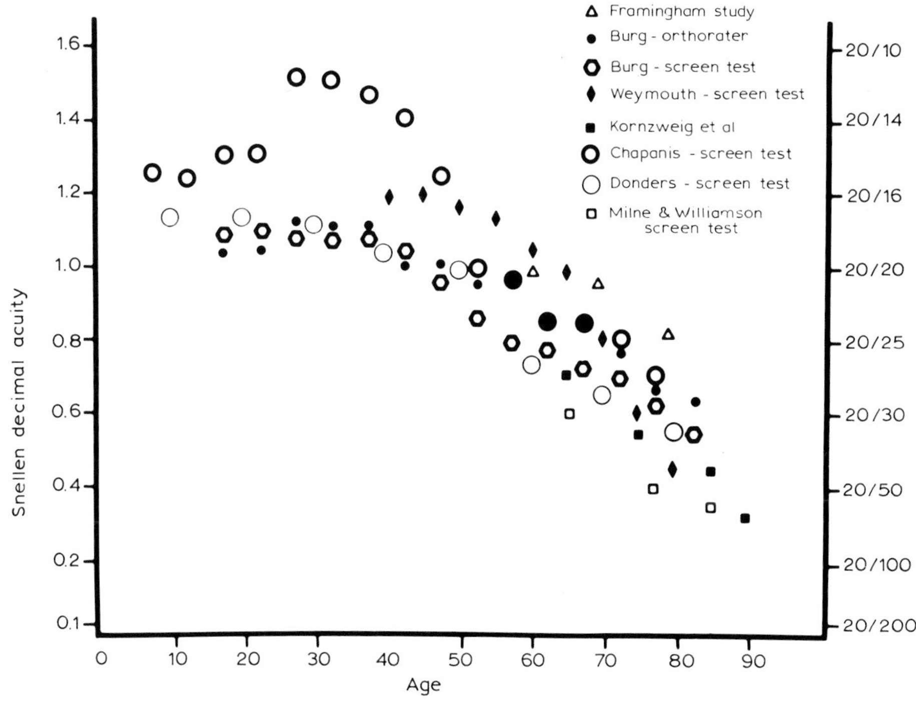

Fig. 1. Mean letter acuity as a function of age as reported in several studies. From Pitts (1982).

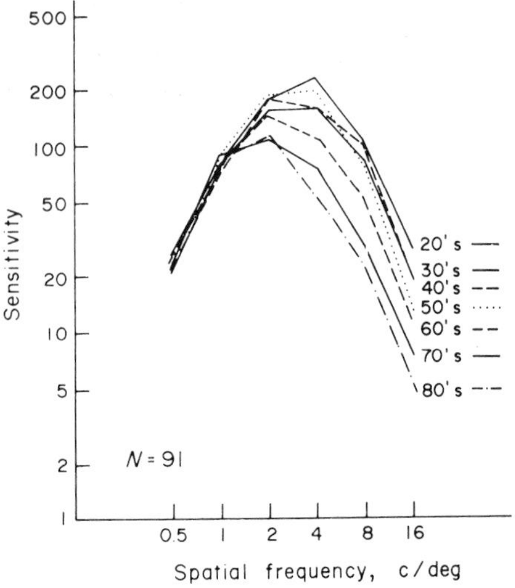

Fig. 2. Mean spatial contrast sensitivity for different decades of age during adulthood. From Owsley et al. (1983).

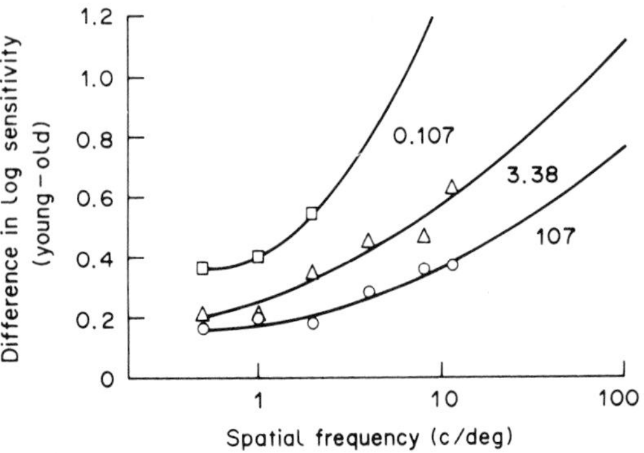

Fig. 3. Mean vision loss in older adults (relative to young adults) for spatial contrast sensitivity measured at three light levels spanning a three log unit range. From Sloane et al. (1988).

sensitivity loss in the elderly, since the function relating contrast sensitivity and target luminance as measured in older adults has a steeper slope than that of younger adults (Sloane et al., 1988).

To evaluate the neural contribution to spatial contrast sensitivity, researchers have developed a technique based on laser interferometry which bypasses the optics of the eye (e.g., Arnulf and Dupuy, 1960; Campbell and Green, 1965). Studies applying this test to the elderly population have generated mixed results. Two studies found no change in neural sensitivity with age (Dressler and Rassow, 1981; Kayazawa et al., 1981), whereas two others have found that older adults have significant decreases in neural sensitivity at higher spatial frequencies (Morrison and McGrath, 1985; Elliott, 1987). Optical factors which most likely contribute to older adults' contrast sensitivity loss, but whose roles have not yet been empirically quantified, include intraocular light scatter and reduced retinal illuminance in the older eye.

Temporal sensitivity

A common way in which the temporal resolving ability of the visual system is evaluated is by measuring critical flicker fusion (CFF), the temporal frequency at which a light appears to be fused or non-flashing. Older adults tend to have lower CFFs than do younger adults, suggesting that the temporal resolution of the visual system decreases with increasing age during adulthood (Misiak, 1947; Coppinger, 1955; McFarland et al., 1958; Huntington and Simonsen, 1965). This loss is thought to be neurally-based (e.g., Kline and Schieber, 1985), but no empirical study has systematically examined how optical and neural variables contribute to older adults' reduced CFF.

Analogous to spatial contrast sensitivity testing, temporal contrast sensitivity can also be assessed by measuring the amount of contrast that is necessary to detect whether a homogeneous target is flickering (see Kelly, 1972, for overview). The temporal contrast sensitivity function is often called the de Lange function (see de Lange, 1958). The luminance of the target is sinusoidally modulated around a time-averaged luminance level, and the depth of modulation is known as the 'contrast'. The frequency of the modulation can also be varied, and thus a temporal contrast sensitivity function can be measured. Earlier studies which measured temporal contrast sensitivity in older adults reported that this function was unaffected by aging (Tyler, 1981; Tyler et al., 1984). However, more detailed work has revealed that older adults have reduced temporal contrast sensitivity, particularly at intermediate and high temporal frequencies (Wright and Drasdo, 1985; Mayer et al., 1988; Kuyk and Wesson, 1989). This vision loss cannot be entirely attributed to reduced retinal illuminance in the older eye or refractive error, although not all agree (Wright and Drasdo, 1985). Mayer et al. (1988) have argued on the basis of a sub-sample of preliminary data that aging brings about a decreased visual sensitivity, but not a change in the temporal characteristics of the visual response, whereas Tyler (1989) has presented evidence that the decrease in temporal contrast sensitivity during aging is related to a change in the time constant of the neural response.

Older adults also tend to have a decreased ability to discriminate one direction of motion from another highly similar one (Ball and Sekuler, 1986) and have decreased contrast sensitivity for moving targets (Sekuler et al., 1980; Owsley et al., 1983). These aging-related deficits cannot be explained by optical factors, such as refractive error and reduced retinal illuminance, or by cognitive factors, implying that they have a neural basis.

Color vision

Age-related changes in color vision fall into the category of 'acquired color deficiencies' (see Birch et al., 1979 for overview) which manifest themselves by a loss in color discrimination, especially along the blue – yellow axis, i.e., they mimic the relatively rare tritan color deficiency. These tritan-like errors are indicative of deficiencies in short wavelength sensitive (SWS) cones ('blue cones') or possibly increased short wavelength absorption by the aging lens (e.g., Eisner, 1986). Acquired color deficiencies can be assessed using arrangement tests such as the Farnsworth Dichotomous Test for Color Blindness (Panel D-15) which was designed to select for those with more severe color discrimination losses (Verriest, 1963; Adams et al., 1982). The Farnsworth-Munsell 100 Hue Test (FM 100), although more time consuming than the D-15, is a very sensitive measure for detecting acquired color deficiencies since it was designed to test hue discrimination in a normal population as well as to yield a quantitative assessment of the degree and area of color confusion in observers with color deficiencies. A recent study (Knoblauch et al., 1987) has confirmed in a quantitative fashion the results of earlier reports (Ohta, 1961; Verriest, 1963; Krill and Schneidermanm 1964; Verriest et al., 1982; Smith et al., 1985), finding an increase in the number of errors on the FM 100 with age. These errors were not randomly distributed about the hue circle but became progressively more bipolar-oriented, mostly along the tritan axis.

Age-related changes in color vision can also be measured using a color matching technique used in an anomaloscope, an optical instrument in which the patient matches the colors seen in each half of a small bipartite field. Anomaloscopes using the Pickford-Lakowski match (yellowish white to be matched by some mixture of yellow and blue; see Pickford and Lakowski, 1960) are much more sensitive to acquired color deficiencies than those using the Rayleigh match which involves wavelengths at the long end of the spectrum. With increasing age, normal trichromats will accept a wider range of color matches indicative of decreased sensitivity in the SWS cone pathway (Lakowski, 1958; Ohta and Kato, 1976).

Spectral sensitivity measurements, which quantify how much energy of a given wavelength is needed for threshold detection of a target, have also pointed to deficiencies in the SWS cone pathway (Jaffe et al., 1982; Eisner et al., 1987; Haegerstrom-Portnoy et al., 1989; Johnson et al., 1988). By choosing appropriate chromatic, spatial, and temporal parameters for the target and its background, one can effectively isolate chromatic mechanisms dominated by either SWS, middle wavelength sensitive (MWS) or long wavelength sensitive (LWS) cones. Haegerstrom-Portnoy (1988) found that the loss of SWS cone sensitivity was greater in non-foveal areas than in the fovea, suggesting that the macular pigment may provide some protection for the fovea from damage incurred from light exposure over the course of a lifetime.

The finding of reduced sensitivity of SWS cones in studies isolating the three chromatic mechanisms does not rule out the contribution of the preretinal, optical factors discussed previously. Recent studies have utilized estimates of the spectral absorption of the ocular media, determined separately for each subject, in measuring spectral sensitivity of the three chromatic mechanisms. Individual correction for preretinal absorption is important in obtaining accurate measurements of retinal sensitivity since, even within a given age group, there are substantial individual differences in the optical density of the lens and the macular pigment (Sample et al., 1988; Werner et al., 1987). Werner and Steele (1988) found that spectral sensitivity for a 440 nm target fell off at a rate of 0.15 log units per decade and at a rate of 0.08 following correction for media absorption. Johnson et al. (1988) offer similar values of 0.13 and 0.09 log units per decade for uncorrected and corrected values, respectively. Thus, even when media absorption is factored out, there remains a significant age-related decline in spectral sensitivity in the SWS cone mechanism. Another important point made by Werner and Steele's data (1988) is that the age-correlated decline in spectral sensitivity for MWS and LWS cone mechanisms, specified at the retinal level, is similar in magnitude to the age-associated decline in the SWS cone mechanism. It is not known whether the origins of these deficits are receptoral or postreceptoral. A parallel loss in spectral sensitivity in all three cone mechanisms mimics a reduction in retinal illuminance. Knoblauch et al. (1987) found that the error distributions of their older subjects on the FM 100 could be mimicked by younger adults performing the test under lower illumination. Both Knoblauch et al. (1987) and Werner and Steele (1988) have pointed out that the tritan-like performance of elderly subjects in color assessment tests may result from the Bezold-Brucke hue shift which refers to the change in perceived hue with changing intensity. At low intensities the reddish-greenish components of a stimulus predominate over bluish and yellowish, producing a change in color appearance.

In summary, older adults exhibit a more tritan-like performance in color vision tasks. There is no doubt that the nonuniform spectral absorption characteristics of the aging ocular media contribute to older adults' tritan-like performance in color vision assessment. When pre-retinal effects are factored out, there remains an age-related decline in sensitivity which Werner and Steele (1988) claim affects all three chromatic mechanisms. Others have argued that there is a differential loss in the SWS cone mechanism due to its vulnerability to the effects of aging. It has been shown that ocular disease decreases the sensitivity of the SWS cone pathway disproportionately, although the reason for this vulnerability is not well understood. SWS cones are reportedly more susceptible to metabolic and light damage (Sperling et al., 1980; de Monasterio et al., 1981). It is not clear whether the vulnerability is located in the cone receptor itself or in postreceptoral mechanisms (Hood and Greenstein, 1988).

Dark adaptation

Dark adaptation refers to a time-dependent visual process during which the perceiver is initially exposed to a bright light level, which is then followed by darkness. Visual threshold is measured over time during the adaptation to darkness; it is initially high, but gradually drops to an asymptotic level. The dark adaptation process reveals fundamental properties about cone and rod function (see Barlow, 1972, for overview). This laboratory situation can be likened to the visual conditions we encounter when walking into a dark movie theater after being out in the bright outdoors. The numerous studies on aging and dark adaptation (see Pitts, 1982; Weale, 1982, for overview) have indicated that older adults have elevated thresholds throughout the entire time-course of adaptation to darkness, including both the cone and rod portions of the function (Robertson and Yudkin, 1944; Steven, 1946; Birren et al., 1948; Birren and

Shock, 1950; McFarland and Fisher, 1955; McFarland et al., 1960; Luria, 1960; Domey and McFarland, 1961). Figure 4 illustrates this effect. The rate of recovery of sensitivity apparently does not change (Birren and Shock, 1950; Eisner et al., 1987). The specific magnitude of the age effect varies across studies, most likely due to methodological differences among the studies. Factors which would heavily influence older adults' sensitivity include the wavelength of the test target (e.g., shorter wavelengths will elevate their thresholds due to lens filtering effects) and the ocular health of older subjects (e.g., individuals with AMD and/or cataract will have higher thresholds). Unfortunately no investigator has systematically evaluated various stimulus and eye health variables within the context of a single study so that the relative effects of these variables can be teased out. As a result, there is little agreement about what mechanisms underlie older adults' difficulties in dark adaptation. Some researchers have suggested that lenticular changes and senile miosis can largely account for the threshold elevation (Robertson and Yudkin, 1944; Weale, 1982), while others have argued that neural and metabolic factors also play a significant role (McFarland et al., 1960; Pitt, 1982).

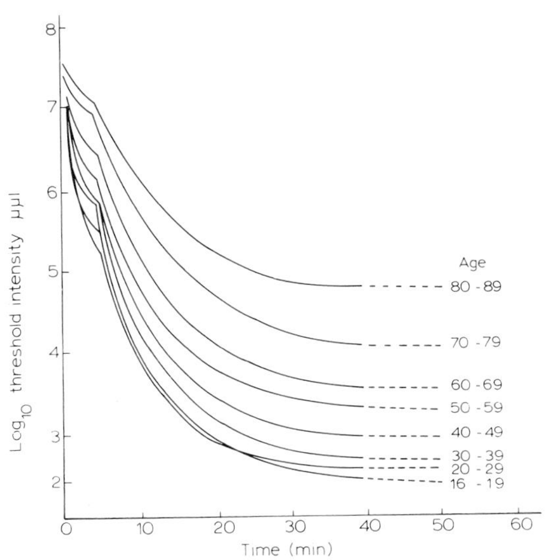

Fig. 4. Mean dark adaptation for different age groups. From McFarland et al. (1960).

Oculomotor function

The ability to maintain an image on the fovea appears to be unaffected by age (Warabi et al., 1984; Kosnik et al., 1986, 1987). The Kosnik et al. (1986, 1987) study used a dual Purkinje-image tracking system to monitor fixation stability in older adults and found it to be as stable as that found in young adults. Fixation stability across trials and its maintenance throughout the testing session were also equivalent for both age groups. It is not known whether the fixation stability of young and old observers would be differentially affected by the presence of static or dynamic distractor stimuli. Nevertheless, it appears that in the case of maintaining fixation on a small luminous target against a dark background, aging does not appear to affect mechanisms subserving this ability. There is anatomical support for this finding in that the small extraocular muscle fibers considered to be most involved in the tonic control of eye position are less affected by aging than are fibers involved in the dynamic control of eye position (Miller, 1975).

Age-related deficits in dynamic oculomotor control have been reported. With regard to saccadic eye movements, whose aim is to bring a peripherally presented target onto the fovea, there is a consistent finding that older adults show an increased latency of saccadic onset (Spooner et al., 1980; Abel et al., 1983; Warabi et al., 1984). There is less agreement about the magnitude of an age-related deficit in saccadic velocity and saccadic duration. Abel et al. (1983) found only slight reductions in both parameters with age which were shadowed by large individual variability within both age groups. Warabi et al. (1984) and Spooner et al. (1980) found significant age-related deficits in saccadic velocities especially for large amplitude saccades (above 20°). While Warabi et al. (1984) showed that older people took longer to locate a target (due to increased latency and reduced saccadic velocity), they also point out that the saccadic slowing was accompanied by an increase in saccadic duration. The preservation of this inverse relationship suggests that the feedback mechanisms responsible for altering saccade duration inherent in the neural control of saccade size are preserved in the elderly. It should also be pointed out that saccade accuracy, in terms of the directional components and success in bringing a target onto the fovea, is not affected by age. This again suggests that critical components in the neural control of oculomotor activity are immune to aging.

Older observers, when using smooth pursuit eye movements to track a moving target, exhibit significantly slower pursuit velocities for target velocities greater than 10° per s (Sharpe and Sylvester, 1978). Sharpe and Sylvester (1978) also reported increased latencies in the initiation of smooth pursuit eye movements in the older group. Spooner et al. (1980) reported substantial deficits in smooth pursuit even though the age ranges of their 'young' and 'old' groups overlapped. The age-related losses they reported may be exaggerated by having used laboratory personnel who had served as normal, young controls in previous studies.

Given the reported age-related deficits in pursuit eye movements, one might expect that older peoples' ability to resolve detail in relative motion, either observer- or target-induced, might be impaired. With increasing target velocity, dynamic visual acuity (DVA) decreases, presumably due to inadequate gain of the smooth pursuit system with resultant smearing of the retinal image (Murphy, 1978). Burg (1967, 1968, 1971) in his large-scale study of driving accidents assessed DVA using a moving checkerboard acuity stimulus, and found that DVA declined with age. Reading (1972), and a more recent study by Scialfa et al. (1988), has also reported data indicative of age-related decline in DVA. Scialfa et al. (1988) and Burg (1966) have suggested that age-related declines in DVA are larger than for static visual acuity measures.

Another finding in the oculomotor and aging literature includes a restriction in upward gaze. Chamberlain (1971) found a progressive symmetric limitation of upward gaze with increasing age. There is little or no anatomical evidence for cell loss in the oculomotor nuclei or more specific age-related lesions in the third nerve nucleus which might produce this symptom. Chamberlain suggested a 'non-use' hypothesis for the deficit and gave some support to the claim by showing normal upward gaze in elderly patients with kyphosis.

Binocular vision

Psychophysical assessment of binocular vision allows direct examination of a visual function mediated by neurons of the visual cortex, thus facilitating accurate localization of any age-related deficit that might exist. Despite such advantages, there have been very few studies which address the issue of aging-related deficits in binocular vision.

There are three psychophysical measures which have been used to index the degree of normal binocular function in human observers: interocular transfer, binocular summation and stereopsis. In the interocular transfer paradigm, an observer monocularly adapts to a high contrast stimulus for a few minutes and then the threshold contrast for that stimulus is measured separately in the adapted and unadapted eye. The extent to which an adaptation aftereffect (threshold elevation) can be measured in the previously unadapted eye is an indication of the existence of binocularly innervated mechanisms in visual cortex (Movshon et al., 1972). There has been no systematic study of how aging affects interocular transfer.

Binocular summation refers to superior performance on a visual task when it is carried out binocularly rather than monocularly. This superiority is greater than that predicted on a statistical basis (probability summation) and must therefore be attributed to some form of facilitative neural interaction at the level of binocular combination in the visual cortex (see Blake and Fox, 1973; Blake et al., 1981, for reviews). Again there has been no direct study of binocular summation in the elderly. Even studies which do measure sensitivity in both eyes separately and together often fail to evaluate the magnitude of binocular summation (e.g., Ross et al., 1985). Our own analysis of Ross et al.'s (1985) group data indicates that their younger observers showed substantial summation (41 – 129%), while summation in the older group was much lower (11 – 27%) and was most likely attributable to probability summation alone.

Stereopsis refers to the ability to judge relative depth on the basis of binocular disparity, the difference in the monocular images as computed by disparity-sensitive neurons in the visual cortex. It is a potent binocular cue for depth perception, but there are also many monocular depth cues (e.g., texture gradients, motion parallax), which also underlie our ability to judge depth and distance of objects in the environment. Since older adults have an increased frequency of falls and postural instability, it makes sense to look for possible deficits in their depth perception. However, there have been few studies of how aging affects stereoacuity, i.e., the smallest amount of binocular disparity which can be accurately detected. At first glance, the literature would indicate little change in stereoacuity up until the fourth decade with significant declines thereafter (Hoffman, 1959; Jani, 1966; Bell et al., 1972; Hofstetter and Bertsch, 1976). Hoffman et al. (1959) reported that older adults were less accurate in aligning two rods in depth in a Howard-Dolman apparatus than were young adults. Older subjects were only screened for 'brain damage' and the lack of eye health data constrains any firm conclusions. Jani (1966) in a large sample study at a state fair used a Diastereo test of stereopsis and found that the percentage failing the test rose in an accelerating fashion from about 50 years of age onward. Since only one magnitude of disparity was tested, the pass/fail nature of this measure reveals little about the limits of stereoacuity. The Diastereo test also lends itself to confounding motion parallax information. Furthermore, it is not unreasonable to expect that more of the older participants had acuities closer to the 20/40 acuity criterion for inclusion, and therefore an accurate assessment of stereopsis may have been compromised. Bell et al. (1972) claim that the most dramatic change in stereoacuity coincides with age-related changes in the dioptric media during the early 40s. No information is given about eye health criteria for subject participation.

In summary, the conclusions of the studies examining the effects of aging on stereoacuity must be viewed as tentative since none of the studies discussed above (1) were rigorous about the visual health and optical correction of participants, (2) yielded direct measures of stereoacuity or (3) used tests of stereoacuity which convincingly isolated the cue of binocular disparity.

Visual fields

Visual sensitivity throughout the field of view is adversely affected by the aging process. Although the amount of reduction associated with aging is less profound than that found in pathological processes, aging-related change in the visual field is nevertheless significant. Studies using kinetic perimetry have indicated that the borders, or isopters, of the visual field are constricted in older adults (Drance et al., 1967; Wolf, 1967; Burg, 1968; Williams, 1983). More recently, a number of studies using automated, static-type perimetry have found that older adults exhibit a generalized

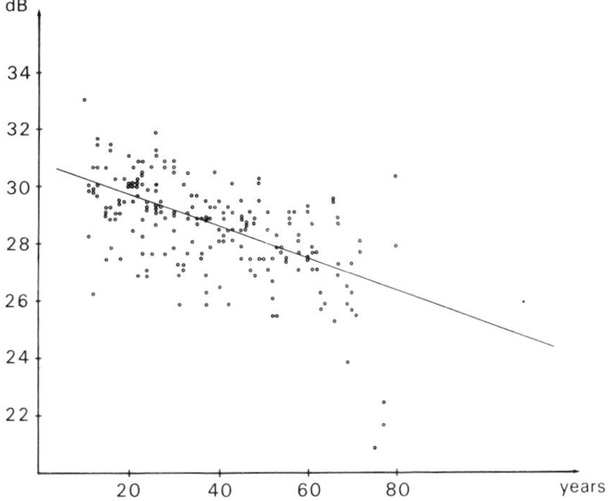

Fig. 5. Scatter plot of sensitivity of the central 30 degrees of the visual field as a function of age. From Haas et al. (1986).

loss in sensitivity throughout the central 30 degrees of the field (as illustrated in Fig. 5) with some studies suggesting a slightly greater sensitivity reduction in more peripheral areas (Haas et al., 1986; Jaffe et al., 1986; Brenton and Phelps, 1986). These age-related changes in visual field cannot be accounted for by changes in the optics of the older eye, such as increased lens density and senile miosis (Johnson et al., 1989), implying a neural basis for field changes.

Another approach to examining the visual field is to assess the 'functional' or 'useful' field of view, which involves the localization and identification of complex visual stimuli in the periphery (Sanders, 1970; Verriest et al., 1983). While standard visual field testing as described above seeks to minimize environmental factors typical of everyday situations, assessment of the useful field of view includes features designed to mimic everyday visual activities, such as complex visual scenes with distracting stimuli and the simultaneous use of both central and peripheral vision. The limits of the useful field of view are affected by many factors such as the presence of a secondary task and background distractor stimuli, and the similarity of target and distractor stimuli (Leibowitz and Appelle, 1969; Ikeda and Takeuchi, 1975; Williams, 1982; Sekuler and Ball, 1986; Ball et al., 1988; Engel, 1971; Treisman and Gelade, 1980). The impact of these variables is much greater for older adults in that aging is associated with a restricted field of view (Rabbitt, 1965; Plude and Hoyer, 1985; Sekuler and Ball, 1986; Scialfa et al., 1987). An older adult's field of view can be up to three times smaller than for younger adults (Ball et al., 1988). Furthermore, tests assessing the useful field of view are better predictors of older adults' reported problems in peripheral vision than is clinical perimetry, suggesting that traditional field tests underestimate the extent of older adults' functional visual problems (Ball et al., 1990).

Visual electrophysiology

The visually evoked potential (VEP) is a gross electrical signal generated by the occipital cortex in response to a visual stimulus. It reflects, in part, the integrity of the visual system from the retina to the visual cortex (see Regan, 1972; Sokol, 1976, for overview). Because its measurement does not rely on the patient making subjective threshold judgments, it is considered to be a relatively objective assessment of the primary visual pathway. Properties of the VEP will vary according to many factors, such as stimulus type (e.g., flash, pattern reversal), intensity, flicker rate, size and retinal location, as well as patient variables such as pupil diameter, refractive error and level of light adaptation. Since space limitations do not permit us to review how each of these factors interacts with the aging process, we will limit our remarks to the pattern-reversal VEP.

It is generally agreed that the peak latency of the first positive component (P_1) of the pattern reversal VEP increases during adulthood, as illustrated in Fig. 6. Most studies suggest that during early and middle adulthood this latency increase is rather small or non-existent, but later in adulthood, after age 60 or so, latency increases more noticeably (Celesia and Daly, 1977; Stockard et al., 1979; Shaw and Cant, 1980; Sokol et al., 1981; Snyder et al., 1981; Wright et al., 1985). Older adults' increased latency appears to be more severe with smaller check-sizes (Sokol et al., 1981; Wright et al., 1985) and with lower target luminance (Shaw and Cant, 1980; Coben, 1977).

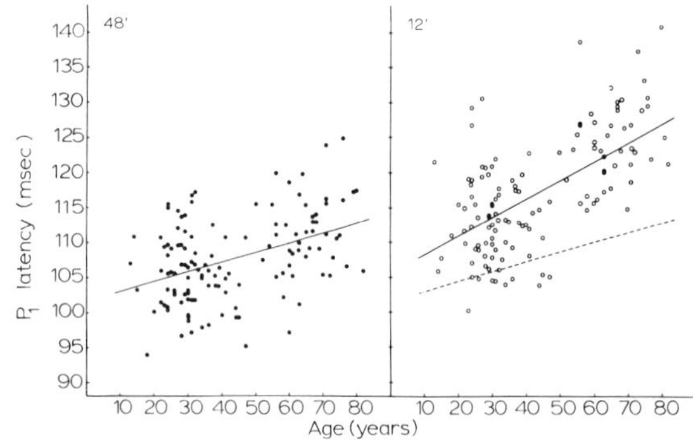

Fig. 6. Scatter plot of latency of the first postive component (P_1) of the pattern-reversal VEP, for two check sizes. From Sokol et al. (1981).

In contrast to the significant changes in P_1 latency during adulthood, the P_1 amplitude apparently remains unchanged after the 20s (Celesia and Daly, 1977; Snyder et al., 1981; Wright et al., 1985). How later components of the pattern-reversal VEP are affected by aging has been less reported. There is some evidence that the latency of later waves decreases during the aging process (Kjaer, 1980; Shearer and Dustman, 1980); however, the opposite has also been reported, i.e., that the later waves increase in latency during aging (Cosi et al., 1982; Wright et al., 1985).

Some researchers argue that the age-related latency increases in the P_1 component are neurally based, and are related to reduced nerve conduction velocity (Sokol et al., 1981; Shaw and Cant, 1980; Celesia and Daly, 1977). Possible mechanisms underlying this age-related decrease are nerve demyelination, deterioration in the retina, LGN and cortex leading to poor synaptic transmission, and shrinkage of dendritic arbors, all of which are supported by anatomical evidence. However, one study has argued that increased latency in older adults can simply be attributed to the reduced retinal illuminance in the older eye due to senile miosis (Wright et al., 1985).

The electroretinogram (ERG) is another common electrophysiological test of the visual system (see Gouras, 1970; Berson, 1981, for overview). The ERG is a measure of the composite electrical activity of millions of retinal cells, including the photoreceptors, the cells of the outer and inner nuclear layers of the retina and its supportive tissue (e.g., Mueller cells), and the retinal pigment epithelium. It is currently believed that the ganglion cells and the optic nerve fiber layer do not contribute to the flash ERG. There have been a few studies that have examined how aging affects the ERG and, of those reported, most have utilized the flash, rather than the pattern, ERG.

It is difficult to obtain a coherent picture about how aging affects the flash, full-field ERG since studies have used different stimulus variables and recording set-ups. Nevertheless, we will attempt a few summary statements. The earlier work on this topic indicates that the amplitude of the B-wave in the dark-adapted ERG decreases in later adulthood (Karpe et al., 1950; Zeidler, 1959; Peterson, 1968). More recent work by Weleber (1981) also found a reduced B-wave amplitude, for both light-adapted cones and dark-adapted rods. Other work has indicated that there are increased implicit times of the A- and B-waves in the dark-adapted ERG, as well as a reduction in the amplitude of the B-wave (Wright et al., 1985; Martin and Heckenlively, 1982). For the photopic ERG (presumably cone-mediated), similar findings have been noted, with age-associated declines in the A- and B-wave amplitudes, and increases in the B-wave implicit time (Martin and Heckenlively, 1982) and perhaps in the A-wave implicit time as well (Wright et al., 1985). However, Weleber (1981) failed to find age-dependent effects for the implicit times of all positive wave peaks in cone- and rod-mediated ERGs. Focal ERGs are recorded when stimulation is localized to a specific retinal area. Birch and Fish (1988) have reported that the amplitude of the flash ERG is decreased for older adults when stimulation is limited to the fovea, but an age-dependent response was not obtained from the parafoveal area.

Systematic studies on aging and the pattern ERG have been rare. The pattern ERG is thought to reflect electrical activity in retinal ganglion cells, so is potentially a useful tool for teasing apart the underlying basis of older adults' visual dysfunction. One study has reported that the amplitude of the photopic pattern ERG is decreased in older adults, with the largest decrease occurring for larger check sizes (Trick et al., 1986). Celesia et al. (1987) have reported that for older adults there is also an increased latency for both the a- and b-waves of the pattern ERG.

Routine visual tasks

The studies described thus far in this chapter have primarily dealt with specific aspects of vision using laboratory-type targets and tasks. It is also quite useful to directly examine how older adults perform in visual tasks which are part of their routine, daily activities. Compared to the large literature described above, there have only been a handful of studies which have dealt directly with visual performance in situations which are part of everyday life.

Face perception is a valuable social skill, yet it appears that older adults operate at a disadvantage in this activity in a low contrast environment. Older individuals require about twice the contrast to detect and discriminate faces than younger adults, which cannot be explained by refractive error or cognitive factors related to decision-making in a threshold task (Owsley et al., 1981). This perceptual problem could not be strongly predicted from their letter acuity, which was 20/25 or better for all subjects; however, further work showed that the problem could be better predicted from their spatial contrast sensitivity (Owsley and Sloane, 1987).

Postural instability and falls are a significant problem for older adults. Although there are many factors underlying this problem, it is believed that declining vision in later life has some role (see Nickens, 1985; Cohn and Lasley, 1985), but thus far there have been no comprehensive studies examining this link. One study has provided some suggestion that visual abilities and falls are related in the elderly. Tobis et al. (1981) found that older adults who had problems with falling had significantly greater error scores in a task measuring the visual perception of verticality and horizontality, than patients with no or a minimal history of falling.

Older drivers have disproportionately more accidents and cited traffic violations (Planek, 1973; State of California Dept. of Motor Vehicles, 1982), and their accident profiles tend to include failures to heed signs, to yield the right of way and to turn safely and also include more frequent junction accidents (Campbell, 1966; Moore et al., 1982). Although impaired vision is believed to underlie at least part of older adults' driving problems, it has been difficult to establish a strong link between vision and driving performance, probably because there are a multitude of factors associated with safe driving. Burg (1967, 1968, 1971; see also Hills and Burg, 1977) carried out a large sample study of over 14 000 California drivers in order to examine the relationship between various visual abilities and driving record. He found that in drivers age 54 and older there was a significant relationship between DVA and increased risk of traffic accidents and convictions, but it is important to point out that this correlation, although statistically significant, was so weak that it was insignificant from a practical standpoint. He also reported weak correlations between driving record, and static acuity and glare recovery. Hofstetter (1976) classified drivers in a large sample (which included older adults) as having poor acuity (in the lower quartile of the sample) or good acuity (above the median). He found that the percentage of drivers with poor acuity who reported three or more accidents was approximately double the percentage of drivers with good acuity who reported three or more accidents. The only study that has found a link between visual field sensitivity and driving is by Johnson and Keltner (1986). In a large sample study (n = 10 000) they found that the small subset of drivers with severe binocular field loss (mostly older drivers) had accident and conviction rates twice as high as those with normal visual fields. No study to date, however, has established a link between the more subtle types of field loss and driving ability.

A few studies have looked at older adults' ability to see highway signs, although most of this work has been based on smaller samples than the studies just described. Sivak et al. (1981) found that for older adults, legibility distance for highway signs under nighttime driving conditions was 65 – 77% of those of young adults, even though older and younger subjects had similar high luminance acuity. They further found that this nighttime legibility problem in older adults was non-existent for older adults whose *low*-luminance acuity was similar to that of younger adults (Sivak and Olson, 1982). Furthermore, Evans and Ginsburg (1985) found that the distance at which older adults could discriminate two highway signs was significantly shorter than in young adults, and Owsley and Sloane (1987) found that older adults required more contrast to detect and identify highway signs than did younger adults. Both of these visual problems were significantly related to older adults' spatial contrast sensitivity.

Alzheimer's disease

Alzheimer's disease (AD) is a dementing disorder of unknown cause in which there is degeneration of neuronal subpopulations in the central nervous system (see earlier chapters for a detailed discussion of this disease). Recently there have been indications that the primary visual pathway may by involved in this disease. Hinton et al. (1986) have reported that there was widespread degeneration in the optic nerves of eight out of ten AD patients studied. Of the four retinae that were studied histologically, three had reduced numbers of ganglion cells and a reduced thickness of the nerve-fiber layer when compared to age-matched controls. However, other work has indicated that the primary visual cortex appears to be relatively spared from the types of degeneration (e.g., neuronal loss, neuritic plaques, neurofibrillary tangles) which characterize other parts of the Alzheimer brain such as the hippocampus and neocortical association areas (Kemper, 1984; Pearson et al., 1985).

Clinical case reports have suggested that AD patients can suffer from decreased acuity and spatial contrast sensitivity, abnormal eye movements and spatial disorientation (Cogan, 1985; Sadun et al., 1987}. However, there has been very little empirical work carried out to substantiate these clinical impressions. There have been two studies on spatial contrast sensitivity in AD patients but they have produced conflicting results. One study suggested that patients with AD exhibit decreased sensitivity over a wide range of spatial frequencies (Nissen et al., 1985). False-alarm rates were similar in the AD group and the age-matched normal group, suggesting that AD patients' decreased sensitivity was probably not due to a more conservative response criterion during the psychophysical test. On the other hand, another study found no difference in spatial contrast sensitivity between AD patients and age-matched controls (Schlotterer et al., 1983), although they did find that AD patients were more susceptible to visual backward masking.

It is difficult to reconcile the different findings in the two contrast sensitivity studies. Possible reasons for the disparate results include differing criteria for selecting AD patients in the two studies, failure to correct for refractive error in both older groups, and failure to screen patients thoroughly for ocular pathology. Large sample studies with more stringent control of these variables may be the only way to clarify this issue. Another concern is whether psychophysical measurements can be validly made on a patient suffering from AD. The setting of a sensory threshold is not a simple task, and many psychophysical procedures, especially forced-choice methods, can be difficult for the novice subject, even when cognitively normal. If decreased visual sensitivity is found in Alzheimer patients, it is rarely clear whether this visual deficit should be attributed to a sensory loss or a performance problem, or both. Therefore, rather than solely using traditional psychophysical techniques to study visual function in AD, it may be more fruitful to supplement these techniques with electrophysiological measures such as the ERG and the VEP and also behavioral measures such as those used to study vision in human infants and young children.

A few studies have already examined the VEP in AD. Regarding the flash VEP, there is general agreement that patients with AD typically exhibit increased latency in the later peaks, particularly P_2 (Wright et al., 1984; Visser et al., 1976; Orwin et al., 1986). In the pattern-reversal VEP, the latency of the P_1 peak appears to be unchanged, although the latency of later peaks are reportedly increased (Harding et al., 1985; Visser et al., 1985).

How AD affects the ERG has not been widely addressed to date. Trick et al. (in press) recently reported that the amplitude of the pattern ERG in AD patients (n = 13) was lower than age-matched normals for both the transient and steady-state response, but especially for the steady-state (fast flicker) response. They argued that these results support the notion of retinal ganglion cell dysfunction, particularly for larger ganglion cells, which is consistent with the anatomical data of Hinton et al. (1986) described earlier. The flash ERG appears to be normal in AD disease patients, indicating that the more distal retina may not be affected by this disease (Katz et al., in press).

Conclusion

In this chapter, we have outlined various ways in which visual function declines in later life, even for those individuals who are considered to be in good eye health according to standard clinical tests. Studies have repeatedly found that older adults have decreased visual sensitivity to many types of laboratory-type targets, yet it is rather remarkable that we still know relatively little about how these vision impairments actually affect older adults' daily lives. Therefore, during the next decade we hope to witness more research initiatives which utilize a human factors approach in studying the role of vision in older adults' performance in everyday tasks.

A second area which deserves concentrated study concerns the underlying causes of older adults' visual deficits. Research to date has been very successful in describing the types of deficits older adults face, but study of the underlying basis of their vision impairment is much more elusive. The optics of the eye change during adulthood in a complicated fashion and, although it is widely believed that the neuroanatomy and -physiology of the visual pathways change during aging, we actually know very little about the nature of these changes, their magnitude or their functional significance. The primary task of researchers is to untangle these optical and neural factors in order to evaluate their impact on visual function, and to further evaluate them in terms of the known changes in cognitive and motor abilities experienced in later life.

Acknowledgements

We thank Karlene Ball, Ph.D., Harold Skalka, M.D. and Tom Boll, Ph.D., for helpful comments on an earlier version of this chapter, and Toby Basan for editorial assistance. Preparation of this chapter was supported by National Institutes of Health grants AG04212, EY06390, and EY03039, and a Department Development grant from Research to Prevent Blindness to the UAB Department of Ophthalmology.

References

Abel LA, Troost BT, Dell'Osso LF: The effects of age on normal saccadic characteristics and their variability. *Vis. Res. 23*, 33–37, 1983.

Adams AJ, Rodic R, Husted R, Stamper R: Spectral sensitivity and color discrimination in glaucoma and glaucoma suspect patients. *Invest. Ophthalmol. Vis. Sci.: 23*, 516–524, 1982.

Adams AJ, Wang LS, Wong L, Gould B: Visual acuity changes with age: some new perspectives. *Am. J. Optom. Physiol. Optics: 65*, 403–406, 1988.

Allen MJ, Vos JJ: Ocular scattered light and visual performance as a function of age. *Am. J. Optom. Physiol. Optics: 44*, 717–727, 1967.

Arnulf A, Dupuy O: La transmission des contrastes par le systeme optique de l'oeil et les sevils de contrastes retimens. *Acad. Sci. (Paris): 250*, 2757–2759, 1960.

Balaszi AG, Rootmen J, Drance SM, Schulzer M, Douglas GR: The effect of age on the nerve fiber population of the human optic nerve. *Am. J. Ophthalmol.: 97*, 760–766, 1984.

Ball K, Beard BL, Roenker DL, Miller RL, Griggs DS: Age and visual search: expanding the useful field of view. *J. Optical Soc. Am. A: 5*, 2210–2219, 1990.

Ball K, Owsley C, Beard B: Clinical visual perimetry underestimates peripheral field problems in older adults. *Clin. Vis. Sci.*: in press, 1989.

Ball K, Sekuler R: Improving visual perception in older observers. *J. Gerontol.: 41*, 176–182, 1986.

Barlow HB: Dark and light adaptation: psychophysics. In Jameson D, Hurvich LM (Editors.) *Handbook of Sensory Physiology*. Berlin, Heidelberg, New York: Springer-Verlag, Ch. 1, pp. 1–28, 1972.

Bell MD, Wolf E, Bernholtz CD: Depth perception as a function of age. *Aging Hum. Dev.: 3*, 77–81, 1972.

Berson EL: Electrical phenomena in the retina. In Moses RA (Editor.) *Adler's Physiology of the Eye: Clinical Applica-*

tion. 7th Edition, St. Louis, Toronto, London: The CV Mosby Co., pp. 466 – 529, 1981.

Birch DG, Fish GE: Focal cone electrograms: aging and macular disease. *Doc. Opthalmol.: 69*, 211 – 220, 1988.

Birch J, Chisholm IA, Kinnear P, Marre M, Pinckers AJLG, Pokorny J, Smith VC, Verriest G: Acquired color vision defects. In Pokorny J, Smith VC, Verriest G., Pinckers AJLG (Editors.) *Congenital and Acquired Color Vision Defects*. New York: Grune & Stratton, Ch. 8, pp. 243 – 348, 1979.

Birren JE, Bick MW, Fox C: Age changes in the light threshold of the dark adapted eye. *J. Gerontol.: 3*, 267 – 271, 1948.

Birren JE, Shock NW: Age changes in rate and level of visual dark adaptation. *J. Appl. Physiol.: 2*, 407 – 411, 1950.

Blake R, Fox R: The psychophysical inquiry into binocular summation. *Percept. Psychophys.: 14*, 161 – 185, 1973.

Blake R, Sloane ME, Fox R: Further developments in binocular summation. *Percept. Psychophys.: 30*, 266 – 276, 1981.

Block MG, Rosenblum WM: MTF measurements on the human lens. *J. Optical Soc. Am. A: 4*, 7, 1987.

Bodis-Wollner I, Camisa JM: Contrast sensitivity measurement in clinical diagnosis. In Lessell S, van Dalen JTW (Editors.) *Neuro-ophthalmology*. Amsterdam, Oxford, Princeton: Excerpta Medica, Vol. 1, pp. 373 – 401, 1980.

Boettner EA, Wolter JR: Transmission of the ocular media. *Invest. Ophthalmol. Vis. Sci.: 1*, 776 – 783, 1962.

Brenton RS, Phelps CD: The normal visual field on the Humphrey field analyzer. *Opthalmologica: 193*, 56 – 74, 1986.

Brody H: Aging of the vertebrate brain. In Rockstein M, Sussman ML (Editors.) *Development of Aging in the Nervous System*. New York: Academic Press Inc., pp. 121 – 133, 1973.

Brody H: Organization of the cerebral cortex. III. A study of aging in the human cerebral cortex. *J. Comp. Neurol.: 102*, 511 – 566, 1955.

Burg A: Visual acuity as measured by dynamic and static tests: a comparative evaluation. *J. Appl. Psychol.: 50*, 460 – 466, 1966.

Burg A: The relationship between test scores and driving record: general findings. *Department of Engineering*, University of California, Los Angeles, Report No. 67 – 24, 1967.

Burg A: Lateral visual field as related to age and sex. *J. Appl. Psychol.: 52*, 10 – 15, 1968.

Burg A: Vision test scores and driving record: additional findings. *Department of Engineering*, University of California, Los Angeles, Report No. 68 – 27, 1968.

Burg A: Vision and driving: a report on research. *Hum. Fact.: 13*, 79 – 87, 1971.

Campbell BJ: Driver age and sex related to accident time and type. *Traffic Safety Res. Rev.: 10*, 36 – 44, 1966.

Campbell FW, Green DG: Optical and retinal factors affecting visual resolution. *J. Physiol.: 181*, 576 – 593, 1965.

Celesia GG, Kaufman D, Cone S: Effects of age and sex on pattern electroretinograms and visual evoked potentials. *Electroencephalogr. Clin. Neurophysiol.: 68*, 161 – 171, 1987.

Celesia GG, Daly RF: Effects of aging on visual evoked responses. *Arch. Neurol.: 34*, 403 – 407, 1977.

Chamberlain W: Restriction in upward gaze with advancing age. *Am. J. Ophthalmol.: 71*, 341 – 346, 1971.

Coben LA: The effect of aging and of dimming the stimulus upon the visual evoked response to reversing checks in man. *Electroencephalogr. Clin. Neurophysiol.: 43*, 559, 1977.

Cogan DG: Visual disturbances with focal progressive dementing disease. *Am. J. Ophthalmol.: 100*, 68 – 72, 1985.

Cohn TE, Lasley DJ: Visual depth illusion and falls in the elderly. *Clin. Geriatr. Med.: 1*, 601 – 619, 1985.

Coppinger NW: The relationship between critical flicker frequency and chronological age for varying levels of stimulus brightness. *J. Gerontol.: 10*, 48 – 52, 1955.

Cosi V, Vitelli E, Gozzoli L, Corona A, Ceroni M, Callieco R: Visual evoked potentials in aging of the brain. In Courjon J, Mauguiere F, Revol M (Editors.) *Clinical Applications of Evoked Potentials in Neurology*. New York: Raven Press, pp. 109 – 115, 1982.

Curcio CA: Aging and topography of human photoreceptors. *J. Optical Soc. Am. A: 3*, P59, 1986.

de Lange H: Research into the dynamic nature of the human fovea-cortex systems with intermittent and modulated light. I. Attenuation characteristics with white and colored light. *Optical Soc. Am.: 48*, 777 – 784, 1958.

deMonasterio FM, Schein SS, McCrane LP: Staining of blue-sensitive cones of the macaque retina by a fluorescent dye. *Science: 213*, 1278, 1981.

Derefeldt G, Lennerstrand G, Lundh B: Age variations in normal human contrast sensitivity. *Acta Ophthalmol.: 57*, 679 – 690, 1979.

Devaney KO, Johnson HA: Neuron loss in the aging visual cortex of man. *J. Gerontol.: 35*, 836 – 841, 1980.

Dolman CL, McCormick AQ, Drance SM: Aging of the optic nerve. *Arch. Ophthalmol.: 98*, 2053 – 2058, 1980.

Domey RG, McFarland RA: Dark adaptation as a function of age: individual prediction. *Am. J. Ophthalmol.: 51*, 1262 – 1268, 1961.

Drance SM, Berry V, Hughes A: Studies of the effects of age on the central and peripheral isopters of the visual field in normal subjects. *Am. J. Ophthalmol.: 63*, 1667 – 1672, 1967.

Dressler M, Rassow, B: Neural contrast sensitivity measurements with a laser interference system for clinical and screening application. *Invest. Ophthalmol. Vis. Sci.: 21*, 737 – 744, 1981.

Eisner A: D-15 test results in people aged sixty and older. Noninvasive assessment of the visual system. (Optical Society of America, Washington, D.C.) *Tech. Dig.: 86*, WA3 – 1, 1986.

Eisner A, Fleming SA, Klein ML, Mauldin M: Sensitivities in older eyes with good acuity: cross-sectional norms. *Invest. Ophthalmol. Vis. Sci.: 28*, 1824 – 1831, 1987.

Elsner AE, Berk L, Burns SA, Rosenberg PR: Aging and human cone photopigments. *J. Optical Soc. Am. A: 5*, 2106 – 2112, 1988.

Elliott DB: Contrast sensitivity decline with aging: a neural or optical phenomenon? *Ophthalmol. Physiol. Optics: 7*, 415 – 419, 1987.

Engel FL: Visual conspicuity, directed attention and retinal locus. *Vis. Res.: 11*, 563 – 576, 1971.

Evans DW, Ginsburg AP: Contrast sensitivity predicts age-related differences in highway sign discriminability. *Hum. Factors: 27*, 637 – 642, 1985.

Faye EE: *Clinical Low Vision*. Boston: Little, Brown & Co.,

1984.

Fisher AJ, Christie AW: A note on disability glare. *Vis. Res.: 5*, 565–571, 1965.

Frisen L, Frisen M: How good is normal acuity? A study of letter acuity thresholds as a function of age. *Graefes Arch. Ophthalmol.: 215*, 149–157, 1981.

Gartner S, Henkind P: Aging and degeneration of the human macula I. Outer nuclear layer and photoreceptors. *Br. J. Ophthalmol.: 65*, 23–28, 1981.

Gouras P: Electroretinology: some basic principles. *Invest. Ophthalmol. Vis. Sci.: 9*, 557–569, 1970.

Haas A, Flammer J, Schneider U: Influence of age on the visual fields of normal subjects. *Am. J. Ophthalmol.: 101*, 199–203, 1986.

Haegerstrom-Portnoy G: Short-wavelength-cone sensitivity loss with aging: a protective for role macular pigment? *J. Optical Soc. Am. A: 5*, 2140–2144, 1988.

Haegerstrom-Portnoy G, Hewlett SE, Barr SAN: S cone loss in aging. In Verriest G (Editor.) *Colour Vision Deficiencies IX*. Junk Publishers, The Hague, pp. 349–356, 1989.

Harding GFA, Wright CE, Orwin A: Primary presenile dementia: the use of the visual evoked potential as a diagnostic indicator. *Br. J. Psychiatry: 147*, 532, 1985.

Hemenger RP: Intraocular light scatter in normal vision loss with age. *Appl. Optics: 23*, 1972–1974, 1984.

Higgins KE, Jaffe MJ, Caruso RC, deMonasterio FM: Spatial contrast sensitivity: effects of age, test-retest, and psychophysical method. *J. Optical Soc. Am.: 5*, 2173–2180, 1988.

Hills BL, Burg A: A re-analysis of California driver vision data: general findings Report 768. Transport and Road Research Laboratory, Crowthorne. England, 1977.

Hinton DR, Sadun AA, Blanks JC, Miller CA: Optic-nerve degeneration in Alzheimer's disease. *N. Engl. J. Med.: 315*, 485–487, 1986.

Hoffman CS, Price AC, Garrett ES, Rothstein W: Effect of age and brain damage on depth perception. *Percept. Mot. Skills: 9*, 283–286, 1959.

Hofstetter HW: A longitudinal study of amplitude changes in presbyopia. *Am. J. Optom.: 42*, 3–8, 1965.

Hofstetter HW: Visual acuity and highway accidents. *J. Am. Optom. Assoc.: 47*, 887–893, 1976.

Hofstetter HW, Bertsch JD: Does stereopsis change with age? *Am. J. Optom. Physiol. Optics: 53*, 664–667, 1976.

Hood DC, Greenstein VC: Blue (s) cone vulnerability: a test of a fragile receptor hypothesis. *Appl. Optics: 27*, 1025–1029, 1988.

Howarth PA, Zhang XX, Bradley A, Still DL, Thibos LN: Does the chromatic aberration of the eye vary with age? *J. Optical Soc. Am. A: 5*, 2087–2092, 1988.

Huntington JM, Simonson E: Critical flicker fusion frequency as a function of exposure time in two different age groups. *J. Gerontol.: 20*, 527–529, 1965.

Hyman L, Schachat A, Ferris F, Schwartz P, Fine S, Phillips D, Zucherberg A, Jon T, Steiner S, Leske MC, AMD Risk Factor Study Group: Classification of age related macular degeneration. *Invest. Ophthalmol. Vis. Sci. (supplement): 29*, 120, 1988.

Ikeda M, Takeuchi T: Influence of foveal load on the functional visual field. *Percept. Psychophys.: 18*, 255–260, 1975.

Jaffe GJ, Alvarado JA, Juster RP: Age-related changes of the normal visual field. *Arch. Ophthalmol.: 104*, 1021–1025, 1986.

Jaffe MJ, deMonasterio FM, Podgor MJ: Retinal ageing and blue-sensitive cone function. *Invest. Ophthalmol. Vis. Sci. (supplement): 22*, 218, 1982.

Jani SN: The age factor in stereopsis screening. *Am. J. Optom.: 43*, 653–657, 1966.

Johnson CA, Adams AJ, Lewis RA: Evidence for a neural basis of age-related visual field loss in normal observers. *Invest. Ophthalmol. Vis. Sci.: 30,* 2056–2064, 1989.

Johnson CA, Adams AJ, Twelker JC, Quigg JM: Age-related changes of the central visual field for short-wavelength sensitive (SWS) pathways. *J. Optical Soc. Am. A: 5*, 2131–2139, 1988.

Johnson CA, Keltner JL: Incidence of visual field loss in 20,000 eyes and its relationship to driving performance. *Arch. Ophthalmol.: 101*, 371–375, 1986.

Johnson HA: Is aging physiological or pathological? In Johnson HA (Editor.) *Relations Between Normal Aging and Disease*. New York: Raven Press, 1985.

Johnson MA, Choy D: On the definition of age-related norms for visual function testing. *Appl. Optics: 26*, 1449–1454, 1987.

Karpe G, Rickenbach K, Thomasson S: The clinical electroretinogram. I. The normal electroretinogram above fifty years of age. *Acta Ophthalmol.: 28*, 301–305, 1950.

Katz B, Rimmer S, Iragui V, Katzman R: Abnormal pattern electroretinogram in Alzheimer's disease: evidence for retinal ganglion cell degeneration? *Ann. Neurol.: 26,* 221–225, 1989.

Kayazawa F, Yamamoto T, Itoi M: Clinical measurement of contrast sensitivity function using laser generated sinusoidal grating. *Japn. J. Ophthalmol.: 25*, 229–236, 1981.

Kelly DH: Flicker, In Jameson D, Hurvich LM (Editors.) *Handbook of Sensory Physiology*. New York: Springer-Verlag, Ch. 11, pp. 273–302, 1972.

Kemper T: Neuroanatomical and neuropathological changes in normal aging and dementia. In Albert ML (Editor.) *Clinical Neurology of Aging*. London: Oxford University Press, pp. 9–52, 1985.

Kilbride PE, Hutman LP, Fishman M, Read JS: Foveal cone pigment density differences in the aging human eye. *Vis. Res.: 26*, 321–325, 1986.

Kirchner C, Peterson R: The latest data on visual disability from NCHS. *J. Vis. Impairment Blindness 73*, 151–153, 1979.

Kjaer M: Visual evoked potential in normal subjects and patients with multiple sclerosis. *Acta Neurol. Scand.: 62*, 1–13, 1980.

Kline DW, Schieber F: Vision and aging. In Birren JE, Schaie KW (Editors.) *Handbook of the Psychology of Aging*. New York: Van Nostrand Reinhold Co., Ch. 12, pp. 296–331, 1985.

Knoblauch K, Saunders F, Kusuda M, Hynes R, Podgor M, Higgins KE, deMonasterio FM: Age and illuminance effects in the Farnsworth-Munsell 100-hue test. *Appl. Optics; 26*, 1441–1448, 1987.

Kosnik W, Fikre J, Sekuler R: Visual fixation stability in older adults. *Invest. Ophthalmol. Vis. Sci.: 27*, 1720 – 1725, 1986.

Kosnik W, Kline D, Fikre J, Sekuler R: Ocular fixation control as a function of age and exposure duration. *Psychol. Aging: 2*, 302 – 305, 1987.

Kosnik W, Winslow L, Kline D, Rasinski K, Sekuler R: Vision changes in daily life throughout adulthood. *J. Gerontol.: 43*, 63 – 70, 1988.

Krill AE, Schneiderman A: A hue discrimination defect in so-called normal corners of color vision defects. *Invest. Ophthalmol. Vis. Sci. 3*, 445 – 456, 1964.

Kuyk T, Wesson M: Changes in flicker sensitivity with age. *Invest. Ophthalmol. Vis. Sci. (supplement): 30*, 314, 1989.

Lakowski R: Age and color vision. *Adv. Sci.: 15*, 231 – 236, 1958.

Leibowitz HM, Krueger DE, Maunder LR, Milton RC, Kini MM, Kahn HA, Nickerson RJ, Pool J, Colton TL, Ganley JP, Loewenstein JI, Dawber TR: The Framington eye study monograph. *Surv. Ophthalmol. (supplement): 24*, 335 – 610, 1980.

Leibowitz HW, Appelle S: The effect of a central task on luminance thresholds for peripherally presented stimuli. *Hum. Factors: 11*, 387 – 392, 1969.

Loewenfeld IE: Pupillary changes related to age. In Thompson HS (Editor.) *Topics in Neuro-ophthalmology*. Baltimore: Williams & Wilkins, 1979.

Ludwig FC, Smoke ME: The measurement of biological aging. *Exp. Aging Res.: 6*, 497 – 521, 1980.

Luria SM: Absolute visual threshold and age. *J. Optical Soc. Am.: 50*, 86 – 87, 1960.

Marshall J: The ageing retina: physiology or pathology. *Eye: 1*, 282 – 295, 1987.

Marshall J, Grindle J, Ansell PL, Borwein B: Convolution in human rods: an aging process. *Br. J. Ophthalmol.: 63*, 181 – 187, 1980.

Marshall J, Laties A: The special pathology of the aging macula. In La Vail MM, Hollyfield JG, Anderson RE (Editors.) *Retinal Degeneration: Experimental and Clinical Studies*. New York: Liss, 1985.

Martin DA, Heckenlively JR: The normal electroretinogram. *Doc. Ophthalmol. Ser.: 31*, 135 – 144, 1982.

Mayer MJ, Kim CBY, Svingos A, Glucs A: Foveal flicker sensitivity in healthy aging eyes. I. Compensating for pupil variation. *J. Optical Soc. Am.: 5*, 2201 – 2209, 1988.

McGeer DL, McGeer P: Neurotransmitter metabolism in aging brain. In Terry RD, Gershan S (Editors.) Neurobiology of aging. New York: Raven Press, pp. 389 – 403, 1976.

McFarland RA, Domey RG, Warren AB, Ward DC: Dark adaptation as a function of age: I. A statistical analysis. *J. Gerontol.: 15*, 149 – 154, 1960.

McFarland RA, Fisher MB: Alterations in dark adaptation as a function of age. *J. Gerontol.: 10*, 424 – 428, 1955.

McFarland RA, Warren B, Karis C: Alterations in flicker frequency as a function of age and light: dark ratio. *J. Exp. Psychol.: 56*, 529 – 538, 1958.

Miller JE: Aging changes in extraocular muscles. In Lennerstrand G, Bach-Y-Rita P (Editors.) *Basic Mechanisms of Ocular Motility and Their Clinical Implications*. Oxford: Pughman Press, pp. 47 – 62, 1975.

Misiak H: Age and sex differences in critical flicker frequency. *J. Exp. Psychol.: 37*, 318 – 332, 1947.

Moore RL, Sedgely IP, Sabey BE: Ages of car drivers involved in accidents with special reference to junctions. *Transp. Road Res. Lab. HS-033: 142*, 1 – 30, 1982.

Morrison JD, McGrath C: Assessment of the optical contributions to the age-related deterioration in vision. *Q. J. Exp. Physiol.: 70*, 249 – 269, 1985.

Morrison JD, Reilly J: An assessment of decision-making as a possible factor in the age-related loss of contrast sensitivity. *Perception: 15*, 541 – 552, 1986.

Movshon JA, Chambers BEI, Blakemore C: Interocular transfer in normal humans and those who lack stereopsis. *Perception: 1*, 483 – 490, 1972.

Murphy BJ: Pattern thresholds for moving and stationary gratings during smooth eye movements. *Vis. Res.: 18*, 521 – 530, 1978.

Nickens H: Intrinsic factors in falling among the elderly. *Arch. Int. Med.: 145*, 1089 – 1093, 1985.

Nissen MJ, Corkin S, Buonanno FS, Growdon JH, Wray SH, Bauer J: Spatial vision in Alzheimer's disease. *Arch. Neurol.: 42*, 667 – 671, 1985.

Ohta Y: Study on the generalized color discrimination test report-1. *Acta Ophthalmol.: 65*, 512 – 519, 1961.

Ohta Y, Kato H: Colour perception changes with age. Test results by P-N anomaloscope. *Mod. Probl. Ophthalmol.: 17*, 345 – 352, 1976.

Ordy JM, Brizzee KR, Hansche J: Visual acuity and foveal cone density in the retina of the aged rhesus monkey. *Neurobiol. Aging: 1*, 133 – 140, 1980.

Orwin A, Wright CE, Harding GFA, Rowan DC, Rolfe EB: Serial visual evoked potential recordings in Alzheimer's disease. *Br. Med. J. 293*, 9 – 10, 1986.

Owsley C, Sekuler R, Boldt C: Aging and low-contrast vision: face perception. *Invest. Ophthalmol. Vis. Sci.: 21*, 362 – 364, 1981.

Owsley C, Sekuler R, Siemsen D: Contrast sensitivity throughout adulthood. *Vis. Res.: 23*, 689 – 699, 1983.

Owsley C, Kline DW, Werner JS, Greenstein V, Marshall J: Optical radiation effects on aging and visual perception. In Waxler M, Hitchins VM (Editors.) *Optical Radiation and Visual Health*. Boca Raton, Florida: CRC Press, Inc., Ch. 7, pp. 125 – 136, 1986.

Owsley C, Sloane ME: Contrast sensitivity, acuity, and the perception of 'real-world' targets. *Br. J. Ophthalmol.: 71*, 791 – 796, 1987.

Paulsson LE, Sjostrand J: Contrast sensitivity in the presence of a glare light. *Invest. Ophthalmol. Vis. Sci.: 19*, 401 – 406, 1980.

Pearson RCA, Esiri MM, Hiorns RW, Wilcock GK, Powell TPS: Anatomical correlates of the distribution of the pathological changes in the neocortex in Alzheimer's disease. *Proc. Natl. Acad. Sci. USA: 82*, 4531 – 4534, 1985.

Peterson H: The normal b-potential in the single-flash clinical electroretinogram. *Acta Ophthalmol. Suppl.: 99*, 5 – 60, 1968.

Pickford RW, Lakowski R: The Pickford-Nicolson anomaloscope for testing and measuring colour sensitivity and colour blindness, and other tests and experiments. *Br. J. Physiol. Optics: 17*, 131 – 150, 1960.

Pitts DG: The effects of aging on selected visual functions: dark adaptation, visual acuity, stereopsis, and brightness contrast.

In Sekuler R., Kline D, Dismukes K (Editors.) *Aging and Human Visual Function*. New York: Alan R. Liss, Inc., pp. 131 – 159, 1982.

Planek TW: The aging driver in today's traffic: a critical review. *Aging and Highway Safety: The Elderly in a Mobile Society 7*: 1973.

Plude DJ, Hoyer WJ: Attention and performance: identifying and localizing age deficits. In Charness N (Editor.) *Aging and Performance*. London: Wiley, pp. 47 – 99, 1985.

Pokorny J, Smith VC, Lutze M: Aging of the human lens. *Appl. Optics: 26*, 1437 – 1440, 1987.

Pulling NH, Wolf E, Sturgis SP, Vaillancourt DR, Dolliver JJ: Headlight glare resistance and driver age. *Hum. Factors: 22*, 103 – 112, 1980.

Rabbitt PMA: An age-decrement in the ability to ignore irrelevant formation. *J. Gerontol.: 20*, 233 – 238, 1965.

Regan D: Evoked potentials to changes in the chromatic contrast and luminance contrast of checkerboard stimulus patterns. In Arden GB (Editor.) *The visual system: neurophysiology, biophysics and their clinical application, Vol. 24, Advances in experimental medicine and biology*. New York: Plenum Press, pp. 171 – 187, 1972.

Reading VM: Visual resolution as measured by dynamic and static tests. *Pflüggers Arch.: 333*, 17 – 26, 1972.

Reading VM: Disability glare and age. *Vis. Res.: 8*, 207 – 214, 1968.

Richards OW: Effects of luminance and contrast on visual acuity, ages 16 – 90 years. *Am. J. Optom. Physiol. Optics: 54*, 178 – 184, 1977.

Robertson GW, Yukin, J: Effect of age upon dark adaptation. *J. Physiol.: 103*, 1 – 8, 1944.

Ross JE, Clarke DD, Bron AJ: Effect of age on contrast sensitivity function: uniocular and binocular findings. *Br. J. Ophthalmol.: 69*, 51 – 56, 1985.

Sadun AA, Borchert M, DeVita E, Hinton DR, Bassi CJ: Assessment of visual impairments in Alzheimer's disease. *Am. J. Ophthalmol.: 104*, 113 – 120, 1987.

Said FS, Weale RA: The variation with age of the spectral transmissivity of the living human crystalline lens. *Gerontologia: 3*, 213 – 231, 1959.

Samorajski T: Central neurotransmitter substances and aging: a review. *J. Am. Geriatr. Soc. 25*, 337 – 347, 1977.

Sample PA, Esterson FD, Weinreb RN, Boynton RM: The aging lens: in vivo assessment of light absorption in 84 human eyes. *Invest. Ophthalmol. Vis. Sci.: 29*, 1306 – 1311, 1988.

Sanders AF: Some aspects of the selective process in the functional field of view. *Ergonomics: 13*, 101 – 117, 1970.

Scheibel ME, Scheibel AB: Structural changes in the aging brain. In Brody H, Harmon D, Ordy JM (Editors.) *Aging*: New York: Raven Press, pp. 11 – 37, 1975.

Schlotterer G, Moscovitch M, Crapper-McLachlan D: Visual processing deficits as assessed by spatial and backward masking in normal aging and Alzheimer's disease. *Brain: 107*, 309 – 325, 1983.

Scialfa CT, Garvey PM, Gish KW, Deering LM, Leibowitz HW, Goebel CG: Relationships among measures of static and dynamic visual sensitivity. *Hum. Factors: 30*, 677 – 687, 1988.

Scialfa LCT, Kline DW, Lyman BJ: Age differences in target identification as function of retinal location and noise level: examination of the useful field of view. *Psychol. Aging: 2*, 14 – 19, 1987.

Sekuler R, Ball K: Visual localization: age and practice. *J. Optical Soc. Am. A: 3*, 864 – 867, 1986.

Sekuler R, Hutman LP, Owsley C: Human aging and spatial vision. *Science; 209*, 1255 – 1256, 1980.

Sekuler R, Kline D, Dismukes K: *Aging and Human Visual Function*. New York: Alan R. Liss, Inc., 1982.

Sharpe JA, Sylvester TO: Effect of aging on horizontal smooth pursuit. *Invest. Ophthalmol. Vis. Sci.: 17*, 465 – 468, 1978.

Shaw NA, Cant BR: Age-dependent changes in the latency of the patterned visual evoked potential. *Electroencephalogr. Clin. Neurophysiol.: 48*, 237 – 241, 1980.

Shearer DE, Dustman RE: The pattern reversal evoked potential: the need for laboratory norms. *Am. J. Electroencephalogr. Technol.: 20*, 185 – 200, 1980.

Sivak M, Olson PL: Nighttime legibility of traffic signs: conditions eliminating the effects of driver age and disability glare. *Accid. Anal. Prev.: 14*, 87 – 93, 1982.

Sivak M, Olson PL, Pastalan LA: Effect of driver's age on nighttime legibility of highway signs. *Hum. Factors: 23*, 59 – 64, 1981.

Sloane ME, Owsley C, Alvarez SL: Aging, senile miosis and spatial contrast sensitivity at low luminance. *Vis. Res.: 28*, 1235 – 1246, 1988.

Sloane ME, Owsley C, Jackson C: Aging and luminance adaptation effects in spatial contrast sensitivity. *J. Optical Soc. Am. A: 5*, 2181 – 2190, 1988.

Sloane ME, Owsley C, Nash R, Helms H: Acuity and contour interaction in older adults. *Gerontologist: 27*, 132A, 1987.

Smith VC, Pokorny J, Diddie KR: Color matching and Stiles-Crawford effect in observers with early age-related macular changes. *J. Optical Soc. Am. A: 5*, 2113 – 2121, 1988.

Smith VC, Pokorny J, Pass AS: Color axis determination in the Farnsworth-Munsell 100-hue test. *Am. J. Ophthalmol.: 100*, 176, 1985.

Snyder EW, Dustman RE, Shearer DE: Pattern reversal evoked potential amplitudes: life span changes. *Electroencephalogr. Clin. Neurophysiol.: 52*, 429 – 434, 1981.

Sokol S: Visually evoked potentials: theory, techniques and clinical applications. *Surv. Ophthalmol.: 21*, 19 – 43, 1976.

Sokol S, Moskowitz A, Towle VL: Age related changes in the latency of the visual evoked potential: influence of check size. *Electroencephalogr. Clin. Neurophysiol.: 51*, 559 – 562, 1981.

Sperling HG, Johnson C, Harwerth RS: Differential spectral photic damage to primate cones. *Vis. Res.: 20*, 1117, 1980.

Spooner JW, Sakala SM, Baloh RW: Effect of aging on eye tracking. *Arch. Neurol.: 37*, 575 – 576, 1980.

State of California Department of Motor Vehicles: *Senior Facts*. Sacramento, California: 1982.

Steven DM: Relation between dark adaptation and age. *Nature; 157*, 376 – 377, 1946.

Stockard JJ, Hughes JF, Sharborough FW: Visually evoked potentials to electronic pattern reversal: latency variations with gender age and technical factors. *Am. J. Electroencephalogr. Technol.: 19*, 171 – 204, 1979.

Strehler BL: Aging and the human brain. In Terry RD, Gershon S (Editors.) *Neurobiology of Aging*. New York: Raven Press, pp. 1 – 22, 1976.

Tobis JS, Nayak L, Hoehler F: Visual perception of vertically and horizontal among elderly fallers. *Arch. Med. Rehab.: 62*, 619–662, 1981.

Treisman AM, Gelade G: A feature-integration theory of attention. *Cognitive Psychol.: 12*, 97–136, 1980.

Trick GL, Barris MC, Bickler-Bluth M: Abnormal pattern electroretinograms in patients with senile dementia of the Alzheimer's type. *Ann. Neurol.: 26,* 226–231, 1989.

Trick GL, Trick LR, Haywood KM: Altered pattern evoked retinal and cortical potentials with human senescence. *Curr. Eye Res.: 5*, 717–724, 1986.

Tyler CW: Specific deficits of flicker sensitivity in glaucoma and ocular hypertension. *Invest. Ophthalmol. Vis. Sci.: 20*, 204–212, 1981.

Tyler CW: Two processes control variations in flicker sensitivity over the lifespan. *J. Optical Soc. Am. A: 6,* 481–490, 1989.

Tyler CW, Ryu S, Stamper R: The relation between visual sensitivity and intraocular pressure in normal eyes. *Invest. Ophthalmol. Vis. Sci.: 25*, 103–105, 1984.

van Norren D, van Meel GJ: Density of human cone photopigments as a function of age. *Invest. Ophthalmol. Vis. Sci.: 26*, 1014–1016, 1985.

van Norren D, Vos JJ: Spectral transmission of the human ocular media. *Vis. Res.: 14*, 1237–1244, 1974.

Verriest G: Further studies on acquired deficiency of color discrimination. *J. Optical Soc. Am.: 53*, 185–195, 1963.

Verriest G, Barca L, Dobois-Poulsen A, Houtmans MJM, Inditsky B, Johnson C, Overington I, Ronchi L, Villani S: The occupational visual field: I. Theoretical aspects: the normal functional visual field. In Greve EL, Heijl A (Editors.) *Fifth International Visual Field Symposium*. The Hague: Dr. W. Junk Publishers, pp. 165–185, 1983.

Verriest G, Van Loethm J, Uvijls A: A new assessment of the normal ranges of the Farnsworth-Munsell 100-hue test scores. *Am. J. Ophthalmol.: 93*, 635–642, 1982.

Visser SL, Stam FC, Van Tilburg W, Op Den Velde W, Blom JL, De Rijke W: Visual evoked response in senile and presenile dementia. *Electroencephalogr. Clin. Neurophysiol.: 40*, 385–392, 1976.

Visser SL, Van Tilburg W, Hooijer C, Jonker C, Rijke W: Visual evoked potentials (VEPs) in senile dementia (Alzheimer's type) and in non-organic behavioral disorders in the elderly; comparison with EEG parameters. *Electroencephalogr. Clin. Neurophysiol.: 60*, 115–121, 1985.

Vrabec F: Spherical swelling of retinal axons in the aged. *Br. J. Ophthalmol.: 49*, 113–119, 1965.

Vrabec F: Senile changes in the ganglion cells of the human retina. *Br. J. Ophthalmol.: 49*, 561–572, 1965.

Warabi T, Kase M, Kato T: Effect of aging on the accuracy of visually guided saccadic eye movement. *Ann. Neurol.: 16*, 449–454, 1964.

Weale RA: *The Aging Eye*. London: HK Lewis & Co., 1963.

Weale RA: Senile changes in visual acuity. *Trans. Ophthalmol. Soc. U. K.: 95*, 36–38, 1975.

Weale RA: *A Biography of the Eye*. London: HK Lewis & Co., 1982.

Weale RA: Senile ocular changes, cell death, and vision. In Sekuler R, Kline D, Dismukes K (Editors.) *Aging and Human Visual Function*. New York: Alan R. Liss, Inc., pp. 161–171, 1982.

Weale RA: Senescent vision: is it all the fault of the lens? *Eye: 1*, 217–221, 1987.

Weleber RG: The effect of age on human cone and rod ganzfeld electroretinograms. *Invest. Ophthalmol. Vis. Sci.: 20*, 392–399, 1981.

Werner JS, Donnelly SK, Kliegl R: Aging and human macular pigment density. *Vis. Res.: 27*, 257–268, 1987.

Werner JS, Steele VG: Sensitivity of human foveal color mechanisms throughout the lifespan. *J. Optical Soc. Am. A: 5*, 2122–2130, 1988.

West SK, Rosenthal F, Newland HS, Taylor HR: Use of photographic techniques to grade nuclear cataracts. *Invest. Ophthalmol. Vis. Sci.: 29*, 73–77, 1988.

Williams LJ: Cognitive load and the functional field of view. *Hum. Factors: 24*, 683–692, 1982.

Williams TD: Aging and central visual area. *Am. J. Optom. Physiol. Optics: 60*, 888–891, 1983.

Wisniewski HM, Terry RD: Neuropathology of aging brain. In Terry RD, Gershon S (Editors.) *Neurobiology of Aging*. New York: Raven Press, 265–280, 1976.

Wolf E: Glare and age. *Arch. Opthalmol.: 64*, 502–514, 1960.

Wolf E: Studies on the shrinkage of the visual field with age. *Highway Res. Rec.: 167*, 1–7, 1967.

Wolf E, Gardiner JS: Studies on the scatter of light in the dioptric media of the eye as a basis of visual glare. *Arch. Ophthalmol.: 74*, 338–345, 1965.

Wright CE, Drasdo N: The influence of age on the spatial and temporal contrast sensitivity function. *Doc. Ophthalmol.: 59*, 385–395, 1985.

Wright CE, Harding GFA, Orwin A: Presenile dementia: the use of the flash and pattern VEP in diagnosis. *Electroencephalogr. Clin. Neurophysiol.: 57*, 405–415, 1984.

Wright CE, Williams DE, Drasdo N, Harding GFA: The influence of age on the electroretinogram and visual evoked potential. *Doc. Ophthalmol.: 59*, 365–384, 1985.

Yuodelis C, Hendrickson A: A qualitative and quantitative analysis of the human fovea during development. *Vis. Res.: 26*, 847–855, 1986.

Zeidler I: The clinical electroretinogram. Value of the b-potential in different age groups and its differences in men and women. *Acta Ophthalmol.: 37*, 294–301, 1959.

Handbook of Neuropsychology, Vol. 4
F. Boller and J. Grafman (Eds)

CHAPTER 12

Language in normal aging and age-related neurological diseases

F. Jacob Huff

Alzheimer's Disease Research Center, University of Pittsburgh, Pittsburgh, PA, U.S.A.

Introduction

This chapter will first review changes in language ability that occur during normal aging, and will then consider the language disorders associated with a number of neurological diseases which affect older people. The main focus of the chapter will be on Alzheimer's disease, both because it is the most prevalent dementing disorder in the geriatric population and because disruption of language ability is a prominent clinical feature of the disease.

Studies of language in normal aging

The systematic study of changes in language ability during normal aging was initiated in conjunction with the development of standardized neuropsychological test batteries such as the Wechsler Adult Intelligence Scale (WAIS; Wechsler, 1958). On the vocabulary subtest of the WAIS, 40- and 70-year-olds do not differ in their ability to define words or to recognize the correct definition among several alternatives (Fox, 1947), although older individuals tend to produce longer definitions, involving multiword explanations and descriptions (Botwinick et al., 1975). Longitudinal examination suggests that vocabulary abilities actually improve between early adulthood and middle age (Owens, 1953), and indicate that preservation of verbal abilities into later life may be underestimated in cross-sectional studies because of the confounding of age-related changes with educational and cultural differences between successive age cohorts (Schaie and Parham, 1977).

This point is illustrated in the original normative data for the Boston Naming Test (BNT; Borod et al., 1980), which requires the subject to name objects depicted in line drawings. Borod et al. reported lower scores on the BNT in older subjects, but this observation may have been an artifact of the lower education levels among the older subjects in their sample. Subsequent studies with the same test have shown either a much smaller age effect (Van Gorp et al., 1986) or no age effect (LaBarge et al., 1986) in individuals ranging from 60 to 85 years with equivalent level of education. Aging thus does not appear to substantially alter word-finding ability as measured by the Boston Naming Test.

In contrast, verbal fluency tests, which also reflect word-finding ability, do show an age-related decline which is detected even when potential cohort effects are eliminated through a longitudinal study design (Schaie and Parham, 1977; McCrae et al., 1987). Verbal fluency tests require the subject to produce multiple exemplars of a semantic category (e.g., animals), or words beginning with a particular letter, within a limited interval of time. In addition to word-finding ability, these tests also reflect capacity for sustained attention, speed of cognitive processing and speech production (or writing, in some versions of the task), and ability to suppress the dominant responses in order to produce additional responses on the task (Perret, 1974). It is not clear to what extent the age-related decline in verbal fluency performance may be determined by changes in these other cognitive abilities rather than by a decline in lexical retrieval ability.

A possible explanation for the contrast between the degree of age effect observed in fluency and that in confrontation naming tasks may lie in the fact that in fluency tasks the subject is given minimal guidance in retrieving words from lexical-semantic memory, whereas in confrontation naming a picture cue prompts retrieval of each word. Studies of semantic priming, in which lexical-semantic information is elicited automatically without the subject's conscious effort or awareness, indicate no decline with advancing age (Nebes et al., 1986; Light et al., 1986; Light and Burke, in press). This observation suggests the hypothesis that to the extent that a word retrieval task involves implicit or automatic lexical-semantic processing, no decline with aging will be observed, whereas to the extent that explicit or effortful lexical semantic processing is involved, an age-related decrement will be found. This distinction may explain the greater age effect in fluency tests than in confrontation naming tests. Another test of word-finding ability which probably lies between these two tests along the dimension of automatic versus effortful processing is naming in response to a verbal definition. An age-related decrement has been observed on this task (Bowles and Poon, 1984) which appears to be intermediate in degree between those observed for verbal fluency and for confrontation naming. The distinction between automatically and effortful processing which arose in cognitive psychology (Hasher and Zacks, 1979), thus may be important in discriminating lexical-semantic language functions that deteriorate during normal aging from those which are preserved. A similar distinction was suggested by Goodglass (1980) on the basis of studies of abnormal naming in patients with focal brain lesions (see Chapter 13, Vol. 1 of this series), and we will see later in this chapter that the distinction is also useful in describing the lexical-semantic impairment in patients with the diffuse brain pathology of Alzheimer's disease.

Production of discourse involves effortful lexical-semantic processing, and also requires elaboration of syntactic and thematic organization. Obler (1980) reported that the written discourse of elderly adults was characterized by fewer sentences with more words than that of middle-aged adults, suggesting that the older subjects' discourse was syntactically and thematically more elaborate. In contrast, on a test measuring the information content in spoken descriptions of common objects, Bayles et al. (1985a) observed a decline in performance among 70-year-old subjects followed longitudinally, and also in comparison with 50- and 60-year-old subjects. North et al. (1986) also reported poorer performance on discourse measures in older than in middle-aged subjects, which correlated with poorer performance on cognitive tests. Older individuals thus appear to be less efficient in the effortful cognitive process of encoding information into discourse. A possible compensatory response to this change may be to produce longer sentences, which nevertheless do not contain greater information content than those of younger adults performing the same task.

Sentence length is not necessarily related to syntactic complexity, however, and several investigators have suggested that older adults have difficulty processing more complex syntactic structures, particularly on tasks requiring effortful processing, such as drawing inferences in comprehension of individual sentences or narrative discourse (Cohen, 1979; Till and Walsh, 1980; Emery, 1985; North et al., 1986). On the other hand, automatic syntactic processing of sentences appears to be preserved, as manifested in facilitation of the perception of target words preceded by meaningfully related sentences (Cohen and Faulkner, 1983; Nebes et al., 1986). Ability to recognize and correct syntactically aberrant sentences is also preserved (Bayles et al., 1985), a task which probably involves less effortful processing than drawing inferences from sentences. These results again suggest that the distinction between automatic and effortful processing may be useful in describing the pattern of preservation and decline in language function during normal aging. In reaching this conclusion, however, an interaction between age and the automatic-effortful dimension has been inferred from studies using different language materials to test automatic and effortful processing. Investigations controlling this and other possible confounding variables will be necessary in order to support the hypothesis that automatic language processing is preserved, whereas effortful, deliberate processing declines with age.

The language disorder in Alzheimer's disease

Diagnostic issues

Seglas (Obler and Albert, 1985) in 1892 described the language phenomena commonly observed in demented patients with various etiologies, and a disorder of language expression and comprehension was recognized by Alzheimer in his description of the clinical presentation of the disease to which his name is now applied eponymically (Alzheimer, 1907). Although the consistent association of language disorder with Alzheimer's disease (AD) has long been recognized (Sjogren, 1952), systematic efforts to characterize this disorder have emerged only in the last several decades. These efforts have been hampered by the difficulty of differentiating AD from other forms of dementia. The recent development of clinical diagnostic criteria (Mc Khann et al., 1984) that are widely accepted and validated by clinical (Huff et al, 1987) and pathological (Martin et al., 1987) studies has diminished this methodological problem, but it continues to be an important concern in interpreting contemporary studies of language function in AD.

A number of investigations have indicated that language is always impaired in patients with AD who survive to the middle stages of dementia severity (Appell et al., 1982; Cummings et al., 1985; Murdoch et al., 1987) and it may occur as the first symptom of dementia (Pogacar and Williams, 1984). Comparison of the relative prevalence of different cognitive deficits indicates that the disorder of lexical-semantic language is second after impairment of recent memory among the commonly occuring deficits in patients with AD (Huff et al., 1987). Some have suggested that presence of language impairment be made a criterion for clinical diagnosis of AD (Cummings et al., 1985; Murdoch et al., 1987), but this proposal is weakened by the fact that some patients have substantial non-linguistic deficits before they develop language symptoms (Martin et al., 1986; Huff and Growdon, 1986; Faber-Langendoen et al., 1988), and that some patients with gradually progressive aphasia may not have AD (Mesulam, 1982).

Comparison with aphasic syndromes associated with focal brain lesions

Because dementia involves cognitive as well as linguistic impairments, the appropriateness of applying the term 'aphasia' to the language disorder in dementia has been questioned (Bayles and Kaszniak, 1987). Nevertheless, there is general support for that terminology (Gonzalez-Rothi, 1988), and comparisons between the language disorders of focal and diffuse brain diseases have proved to be instructive in characterizing the latter disorders. Although many aspects of language are affected in advanced cases of AD-type dementia, lexical and semantic abilities appear to be particularly vulnerable early in the illness, whereas syntactic and phonological abilities are relatively preserved (Irigaray, 1973; Bayles, 1982). The typical pattern of impairments has been described as progressing from one resembling anomic aphasia, through patterns resembling transcortical sensory aphasia, to Wernicke's and global aphasia (Appell et al., 1982; Cummings et al., 1985; Murdoch et al., 1987). The language disorder of AD differs from these classical aphasic syndromes, for example, exhibiting greater fluency in the early stages than is typical in anomic aphasia (Appell et al., 1982), and showing less neologistic paraphasia (Cummings et al., 1985; Nicholas et al., 1985; Murdoch et al., 1987) and better auditory comprehension (Holland et al., 1986) in later stages than is typical in transcortical sensory aphasia. It has been suggested that preservation of automatic language skills in patients with AD may account for their relatively good performance on tasks such as sentence repetition (Holland et al., 1986), which is one of the defining features of transcortical sensory aphasia.

General features and progression of language impairment

In the early stages of dementia, language impairment may be manifested by word-finding pauses in conversational speech. Patients may have difficulty developing a chain of related ideas in discourse (Bayles, 1982). In formal language testing, these impairments in discourse may be manifested by a slower rate of speech and perseveration of phrases (Hier et al., 1985). Patients are also impaired on tests of verbal fluency, verbal description of objects, vocubulary, reading comprehension, verbal reasoning and linguistic disambiguation (Bayles and Kaszniak, 1987). Verbal fluency tests are particularly sensitive to deficits in the early stage of language impairment (Millner and Hague, 1975; Rosen, 1980), perhaps because they demand deliberate, effortful lexical-semantic processing (Jorm, 1986; Huff et al., 1986b). Verbal fluency is known to be affected by frontal lobe lesions (Perret, 1974), but the impairment in patients with AD probably reflects more widespread brain pathology affecting both attentional and semantic memory functions (Miller, 1984; Ober et al., 1986).

In the middle stage of language impairment, perseveration becomes a more prominent symptom, including both ideational repetition of phrases or themes (Bayles, 1982), and palilalia, the immediate repetition of a syllable or word (Hier et al., 1985). The perseverations probably result from multiple factors, including failure to self-monitor speech, poor recent memory, paucity of ideas and inability to change mental set (Shindler et al., 1984; Bayles et al., 1985b). At this stage of impairment, syntactic complexity is often maintained, as measured by the use of prepositional phrases, subordinate clauses and other complex grammatical constructions (Kempler et al., 1987), but paragrammatic errors emerge, as manifested by errors in the selection of semantically appropriate prepositions (Obler, 1983), and lexical content falls as more pronouns and semantically imprecise words are selected (Hier et al., 1985). At this stage it is common to observe deficits in auditory comprehension, reading comprehension and writing, but articulation of speech, including the ability to read aloud, is preserved (Schwartz et al., 1979; Appell et al., 1982; Cummings et al., 1986; Murdoch et al., 1987). Although automatic syntactic processes are relatively preserved, as evidenced by intact priming of word recognition by the content of stimulus sentences (Nebes et al., 1986) and intact ability to disambiguate homophones on the basis of syntactic context (Kempler et al., 1987), syntactic tasks that involve effortful processing, such as drawing logical inferences, are impaired at this stage in the language disorder of AD (de Ajuriaguerra and Tissot, 1975; Emery, 1985).

The most advanced stage is marked by profound impairments in language production and comprehension. Some patients become mute, echolalic, logoclonic or profoundly palilalic (Cummings and Benson, 1983), but others produce speech which is largely correct phonologically and syntactically, although the content is meaningless (Bayles and Kaszniak, 1987).

Association of language disorder with other clinical features

It has been suggested that language impairment may be more common in cases of AD that develop before age 65 (Seltzer and Sherwin, 1983; Chui et al., 1985). Such differences were not detected in a comparison of WAIS profiles in early-onset and late-onset cases (Loring and Largen, 1985), but the verbal subtests of the WAIS were designed to measure well-learned language skills and may be insensitive to deficits in effortful language processes that are impaired in AD. Another negative study (Sulkava and Amberla, 1982) examined language comprehension and expression separately, but grouped multiple measures within each category. More detailed studies of language abilities have also generally been negative (Selnes et al., 1988), but some have suggested that whereas lexical-semantic production abilities measured in naming and fluency tests are impaired to a similar degree in early-onset and late-onset cases, auditory comprehension and writing may be more affected in early-onset cases (Cummings et al., 1985; Filley et al., 1986; Becker et al., 1987). These results raise the possibility that early-onset cases may have more severe left posterior hemisphere involvement by the pathological process of AD (Filley et al., 1986), which may result in poorer performance on tasks that require syntactic processing, whereas the severity of lexical-semantic impairments is similar in early-onset and late-onset cases (Becker et al., 1987). These results are supported by a study comparing aphasic with non-aphasic patients with AD (Faber-Langendoen et al., 1988). In that study the mean age at onset of dementia was three years less among aphasic patients, who had prominent impairments in reading comprehension and written expression. With progression of dementia, aphasic patients developed disproportionately greater impairments in tasks requiring sentence repetition and comprehension, whereas the progression of lexical-semantic impairments was similar in aphasic and non-aphasic patients. These results suggest again that a prominent left hemisphere involvement is associated with earlier onset of AD and is associated with greater disruption of the syntactic aspects of both spoken and written language.

It has also been suggested that development of a language disorder early in the course of AD is associated with a more rapid progression of dementia (Kaszniak et al., 1978; Seltzer and Sherwin, 1983; Chui et al., 1985; Knesevich et al., 1986; Holland et al., 1986; Faber-Langendoen et al., 1988; Huff et al., in press). The fact that language impairment tends to enhance the apparent severity as measured by most standard instruments was not taken into account in most of these studies, but in several of them an attempt was made to avoid this effect by measuring severity with a behavioral rating scale thought to be relatively independent of the patient's language function (Knesevich et al., 1986; Faber-Langendoen et al., 1988; Huff et al., in press). Others have shown that the degree of naming impairment is strongly related to both behavioral and cognitive ratings of severity, and have suggested using a measure of anomia as an index of the severity of dementia in AD (Skelton-Robinson, 1984).

Another suggestion has been that language disorder is characteristic of a familial form of AD (Breitner and Folstein, 1984). Others have not confirmed this suggestion (Chui et al., 1985), or have observed a lower prevalence of aphasia among cases of confirmed familial AD (Cummings et al., 1985; Knesevich et al., 1985). These results must be viewed cautiously, however, because if few relatives have survived to the age of risk for developing AD, a negative family history does not disprove a genetic pathophysiology of AD in the proband. When such 'censoring' of secondary cases by age is taken into account, recent studies are consistent with an autosomal dominant genetic determination of AD in both early-onset and late-onset cases (Breitner et al., 1987; Huff et al., 1988a).

Cognitive mechanisms and anatomic basis

Although an association of left hemisphere involvement with the more prominent syntactic processing abnormality in early-onset cases has been suggested, clinical-anatomic correlations in support of that hypothesis have not yet been produced. An anatomic basis also remains to be established for the greater vulnerability of effortful over automatic language processing in AD (Jorm, 1986), but it has been proposed that automatic processing is performed by vertically oriented colums of cells in the cerebral cortex, whereas effortful processing relies on integration of such columns by horizontal dendritic branches, which appear to be more drastically reduced in AD than are vertical connections (Kempler et al., 1987). The anatomic basis for the lexical-semantic impairment in AD is also unknown, and the remainder of this section will be devoted to that topic and an interrelated discussion of possible cognitive mechanisms underlying the lexical-semantic aspect of the language disorder in AD.

The cognitive deficit that underlies the impairment in naming visually presented objects in AD has been a matter of controversy. Some have suggested that a deficit in visual perception accounts for this impairment (Rochford, 1971; Kirshner et al., 1984), but others have reported that errors in visual confrontation naming of objects are more often semantically than visually related to the target (Bayles and Tomoeda, 1983; Martin and Fedio, 1983; Shuttleworth and Huber, 1988; Smith et al., 1989), and that AD patients without visual deficits have impaired naming (Huff et al., 1986b; Martin et al., 1986), indicating that the anomia of AD is more strongly associated with a lexical-semantic impairment.

Patients with AD exhibit a more pronounced word frequency effect in object naming than do normal elderly subjects (Barker and Lawson, 1968; Kirshner et al., 1984), implying that less commonly used words become more difficult to retrieve. Many patients are unable to match even highly familiar words with their referents, however, and their errors indicate overextension of verbal labels to semantically related referents (Schwartz et al., 1979; Martin and Fedio, 1983; Huff et al., 1986b). Such patients are typically able to correctly assign more general category labels (e.g., vegetables, tools), demonstrating intact processing of more general semantic information (Warrington, 1975; Huff et al., 1986b; Smith et al., 1989). The confusion of objects within semantic categories can also be demonstrated with nonverbal tasks, such as picture sorting (Schwartz et al., 1979) and pantomime recognition (Kempler, 1988; Huff et al., 1988b), indicating that the impairment involves semantic cognition which is not limited to language. This confusion is most evident on recognition tests as incorrect selection of responses that are semantically related to the target (Huff et al., 1986b), and may not be evident when the incorrect responses presented are semantically unrelated to the correct responses (Nebes and Brady, 1988).

The strong correlation between impairment on semantic recognition tasks and impaired lexical retrieval on object naming and verbal fluency tasks (Martin and Fedio, 1983; Huff et al., 1986b) suggests that the retrieval deficit may at least in part be a result of the semantic impairment. This semantic impairment appears to involve disruption or loss of the specific information necessary to distinguish semantically related words or concepts, as evidenced by the inability of demented patients to correctly order the defining attributes of specified words (Grober et al., 1985). Because patients with AD consistently fail to name the same items on different occasions (Schwartz et al., 1979; Huff et al., 1986a, 1988b) and show impaired naming regardless of the mode of access into the lexicon (Hier et al., 1985), it has been suggested that their naming impairment results from loss of lexical-semantic information. This conclusion is supported by the finding that AD patients also consistently err on the same items in successive trials of a pantomime recognition test, a nonverbal measure of semantic knowledge of objects (Huff et al., 1988b). The observation that name retrieval is inferior to name recognition when both are tested using the same materials (Huff et al., 1988b), however, indicates that a deficit in retrieval from lexical-semantic memory also contributes to anomia in AD.

Some investigators have demonstrated normal semantic priming in AD patients using tasks that require a recognition response (Nebes et al., 1984, 1986), suggesting that automatic lexical-semantic processing is intact, at least early in the course of

AD. AD patients may actually have a heightened susceptibility to inhibitory priming mechanisms thought to be mediated by automatic semantic processing (Ober and Shenaut, 1988). Even on recognition tasks that involve attention-dependent processes, AD patients show intact semantic priming (Nebes et al., 1989). On such tasks, priming effects may be greater for items with 'degraded' semantic representations as determined by tests of semantic knowledge (Chertkow et al., 1989). In contrast, priming was found to be diminished in patients with AD on a task requiring lexical retrieval (Shimamura et al., 1987). In another study (Huff et al., 1988b), analysis of corresponding items in a recognition test and in priming of lexical retrieval indicated that priming of retrieval occurred in AD patients only for items about which they demonstrated recognition. This result is consistent with the hypothesis that information about items not recognized is lost and therefore retrieval cannot be initiated by any mechanism, including the relatively automatic mechanism of priming.

The lexical-semantic impairment in AD may thus be due to two mechanisms: (1) loss of semantic information; and (2) impairment in retrieval of lexical-semantic information. Patients with anomia due to left hemisphere stroke appear to have a greater retrieval deficit, whereas patients with AD appear to have more loss of information when both types of patient are studied with the same tests (Huff et al., 1988b). This result suggests that loss of lexical-semantic information may result from distributed lesions in the cortex of both cerebral hemispheres, as occurs in AD, whereas impaired retrieval may be associated with pathology in the left or language-dominant hemisphere. Schwartz et al. (1979) suggested that the syntactic and phonological operations necessary for language production are anatomically 'tightly wired' in the language-dominant left hemisphere, whereas lexical processes required in nominal reference involve a widespread neuronal network with a bilateral cerebral distribution. This model is consistent with the one described above to account for the lexical-semantic impairment in AD, if it is presumed that retrieval of lexical information for language production is a dominant or left hemisphere function. The model proposed by Schwartz and colleagues implies that the anatomically distributed lexical-semantic system is more vulnerable than the more compact syntactic and phonological systems to the distributed pathological process of AD. The occurrence of syntactic and phonological impairments later in the course of AD may be accounted for in this model by the eventual accumulation of a critical number of lesions in the dominant hemisphere language-processing areas.

The dissociability of the phonological representation of words from their meanings is indicated by a variety of evidence (see Chapter 16, Vol. 1), including the fact that patients with dementia can read words they no longer comprehend (Schwartz et al., 1979). Such observations suggest that the phonological lexicon may not have the same anatomic substrate as the concepts in semantic memory (Bayles and Kaszniak, 1987). This suggestion implies another variant of the model described above, in which the dominant hemisphere contains a phonological lexicon as well as the retrieval mechanism connecting that lexicon with the bilaterally distributed semantic memory system. Phonological repesentation of words may be stored in the non-dominant as well as the dominant hemisphere, however, and the extent to which this occurs may vary considerably among individuals (see Chapter 6 of this volume). Studies using positron emission tomography may be useful in evaluating these models (Posner et al., 1988). Cases of AD with prominent lexical-semantic impairments have lower glucose metabolism in the left than the right cerebral hemisphere (Martin et al., 1986; see Chapter 9 of this volume for discussion), but it is not clear whether this association reflects loss of lexical-semantic information or defective retrieval of that information.

A loss of neurons that use acetylcholine as a neurotransmitter has been documented to occur in AD brain, raising the possibility that this biochemical abnormality may be related to the cognitive deficits of AD patients, and such a relationship has been established with regard to the deficit in recent memory (Caine et al., 1981; Beatty et al., 1986). Administration of the cholinergic antagonist scopolamine has generally been found to impair verbal fluency at higher doses than are required to disrupt recent memory functions, but in one study the effect of scopolamine on verbal fluency was enhanced in AD patients compared to age-matched control subjects (Sunderland et al., 1987), suggesting that a cholinergic deficit may underlie the lexical-semantic impairment in AD. Another study indicated that the effect of scopolamine on verbal fluency may be mediated by disruption of attention rather than lexical-semantic processing, and found no effect of scopolamine on naming to definition, a more specific test of lexical-semantic ability (Huff et al., 1988c).

Some features of the language deterioration in AD follow the reverse sequence observed in language development, prompting the suggestion that AD involves greater vulnerability of language functions that develop later (Ajuriaguerra and Tissot, 1975; Warrington, 1975; Martin and Fedio, 1983; Emery, 1985). Although this hypothesis is attractive, exceptions to it have been documented (Schwartz et al., 1979; Cummings et al., 1986) and, as Obler (1983) has pointed out, given the complexity of human development, it is unlikely that language or other aspects of cognition deteriorate in precisely the reverse fashion to their development.

Language disorder in other dementias

Dementia associated with multiple cerebral infarctions

In patients with multiple-infarct dementia (MID), excluding those with infarctions in Wernicke's or Broca's areas and with gross aphasia, lexical-semantic abilities are better preserved than in patients with AD, but syntax and the motor aspects of speech are more impaired (Hier et al., 1985; Powell et al., 1988). The syntactic deficit is characterized by reduced complexity, manifested for example in less use of subordinate clauses, and more paragrammatisms, such as production of incomplete sentence fragments. The motor speech abnormalities include dysarthria, reduced rate, and disruption of melody and pitch. Late in the clinical course, the speech of patients with MID tends to become increasingly laconic, and takes on some of the characteristics of Broca's aphasia (Hier et al., 1985).

Although the abnormality of motor speech best distinguishes MID from AD, nearly all MID patients studied by Powell et al. (1988) manifested impaired language comprehension. Those authors speculated that because 83% of their patients had lesions involving subcortical structures, the shared features of their language disorders may reflect a common anatomic substrate. Patients with paramedian mesencephalic and diencephalic infarctions do not, however, consistently develop significant language impairment (Katz et al., 1987). It remains to be determined whether there is a specific anatomic basis for the language disorder in MID, or whether MID represents a heterogeneous collection of pathological and clinical syndromes which share a cerebrovascular etiology.

Pick's disease and related disorders

The frontal and anterior temporal lobar atrophy of Pick's disease, which in some cases predominantly involves the left cerebral hemisphere (Wechsler et al., 1982), commonly results in aphasia. The earliest language symptoms are commonly word-finding difficulty in conversational speech and anomia, with progression to excessive use of verbal stereotypes, echolalia, and mutism in the terminal stages of the illness (Cummings and Duchen, 1981). Language disorder typically occurs earlier in the clinical course of Pick's disease than in AD (Sjogren, 1952; Wechsler et al., 1982). A number of cases have been described which share neuropathological features of Pick's disease and AD, and are characterized by a prominent language disorder (Morris et al., 1984; Holland et al., 1985). A case of dementia with marked frontal atrophy, but in which microscopic examination did not confirm either Pick's disease or AD, was described by Whitaker (1976). This patient had no spontaneous speech, and gave no indication of preserved auditory comprehension, but in her echolalic repetition of utterances she corrected syntactic and phonological errors, although not semantic anomalies. This remarkable example of dissociation of language functions in dementia was influential historically in generating interest in the study of language in dementia patients.

Huntington's disease, Parkinson's disease and progressive supranuclear palsy

These dementing disorders primarily involve degeneration of subcortical structures, although the cerebral cortex is also affected. It has been suggested that they manifest less language impairment, but more motor abnormality in speech production, than AD and Pick's disease, in which pathological changes in the cerebral cortex are a prominent pathological feature (Obler and Albert, 1981). Some studies have failed to confirm such differences (Mayeux et al., 1983; Bayles and Kaszniak, 1987), however, and all of these studies suffer from the methodological difficulty of matching for severity of dementia between patients with qualitatively different dementing illnesses. For example, Mayeux et al. (1983) compared patients with AD, Huntington's disease (HD) and Parkinson's disease (PD) who had roughly comparable degrees of functional disability. They found that overall cognitive impairment was greater in AD than in either HD or PD, and that only in AD did language ability show a significant decline with increasing functional disability. They noted, however, that while all their AD patients were demented, only 60% with HD and 39% with PD met criteria for dementia. When subgroups with each disease were selected who were comparable in overall cognitive impairment, there were no differences between them in degree of language impairment or other cognitive deficits. Although a global language measure was used in that study, and the negative result thus leaves open the possibility that differences would be detected in more specific language abilities, this result nevertheless calls into question the notion that these degenerative dementing disorders produce qualitatively different syndromes of dementia and language disorder.

Leaving aside the comparative issue, there is disagreement over the extent to which language is affected in these disorders. In HD, impairment on verbal fluency tests has been attributed by some to a generalized retrieval problem affecting all aspects of memory (Butters et al., 1987), whereas preservation of the ability to correctly sort words into categories suggested that semantic memory is intact (Caine et al., 1977). The latter task is not very sensitive, however, and a recent study of semantic priming in HD indicates that even mildly demented patients have a lexical-semantic deficit (Smith et al., 1988). Similarly, one study suggested that language was relatively preserved during the early stages of dementia (Josiassen, 1983), but more comprehensive language evaluation has documented that patients have word-finding difficulty, make paraphasic errors, and suffer articulatory and syntactic impairments (Gordon and Illes, 1987). A study of speech timing in HD indicated that speech planning and initiation were normal but documented poor control over the duration of syllables, pauses and sentences (Ludlow et al., 1987).

Patients with PD also manifest poor control over the duration of speech events (Ludlow et al., 1987; Illes et al., 1988) and other mechanical aspects of speech, including articulation, loudness, pitch and melody, as well as having abnormal mechanics of writing (Cummings et al., 1988). In patients without overt dementia, these difficulties are accompanied by minimal impairments in language, some of which may represent adaptations to their motor speech deficits (Illes et al., 1988). An impairment in the prosodic aspect of language may be the chief exception to this generalization (Scott et al., 1984), although there is evidence that the disorder of prosody may relate to the deficit in motor control rather than to a loss of the linguistic knowledge required to make prosodic distinctions (Darkins et al., 1988). A mild confrontation naming deficit was suggested by one study in which performance on the Boston Naming Test was one standard deviation below the norms for age and education (Matison et al., 1982), but another study found normal performance on the same test in non-demented PD patients (Freedman et al., 1984). It is possible that prolonged response latency due to bradykinesia accounts for the former result: a time limit was imposed on naming responses, and another study found prolonged naming response latencies but no increase in errors or qualitative difference in error types in non-demented patients with PD compared to control subjects (Gamsu, 1986). Confrontation naming is generally normal in mildly demented patients with PD (Bayles and Tomoeda, 1983), and in overtly demented patients the naming impairment is milder than in AD patients with comparable overall severity of dementia (Bayles and Tomoeda, 1983; Cummings et al., 1988). Verbal fluency is reduced even in non-demented PD cases (Matison et al., 1982; Cummings et al., 1988), probably due to their motor deficit, but despite their motor speech impairment demented PD patients perform better than comparably demented AD patients on fluency tests and on ratings of the information content of spontaneous speech (Cummings et al., 1988). These results suggest that the lexical-semantic impairment in PD is milder than that in AD. Different patterns of memory and frontal lobe impairments are also observed in demented PD and AD patients (Pillon et al., 1986), supporting the suggestion that the dementia syndrome of PD may be unique. Concurrent AD may nonetheless produce or contribute to the dementia in some PD patients (Boller et al., 1980). Such cases may account for the failure to find differences between the language impairments in PD and AD in some studies (Mayeux et al., 1983; Bayles and Kaszniak, 1987). Studies involving PD patients with a broad range of intellectual impairments have variously reported no deficits in naming or vocabulary (Pirrozolo et al., 1982) and deficits in multiple language areas (Globus et al., 1985). Such discrepancies may result from differences in the proportions of demented and non-demented cases that were included. Subject selection may thus critically influence the results in studies of language in PD.

Albert et al. (1974) used progressive supranuclear palsy (PSP) as the prototypical disorder in characterizing subcortical dementia. In their five cases and 37 others in the literature, they noted no cases with the aphasia, agnosia and apraxia that characterize AD and Pick's disease, although dysarthric, hypophonic and monotone speech were commonly described. Naming latency was often prolonged, but patients demonstrated intact naming if sufficient time was allowed. Several patients were impaired in finding categorical similarities between items, however, suggesting that they had some degree of lexical-semantic deficit. Several cases of PSP with prominent naming impairment and expressive aphasia have subsequently been reported (Perkin et al., 1978), but systematic neuropsychological assessment of 25 patients (Maher et al., 1985) revealed only mild word-finding difficulties in seven, and no evidence of more severe dysphasia or comprehension difficulties. A comparison of patients with PSP and AD (Pillon et al., 1986) showed a trend toward greater naming impairment in the latter on a brief and somewhat insensitive naming test. These results generally support the original thesis of Albert et al. that the language disorder of PSP differs from those of AD and Pick's disease, although the distinction may be less complete than it was originally conceived to be.

Other disorders

Language impairment may occur in other neurological diseases that commonly affect older individuals. For example, patients with alcoholic Korsakoff's syndrome have a deficit in semantic memory that is evident in both word-retrieval (Cermak et al., 1978; Butters et al., 1987) and verbal judgement tasks (Kovner et al., 1981). Other disorders, such as stroke, tumors and head trauma, may also affect language abilities, depending on the locus of brain injury. The language symptoms associated with such lesions may in part be determined by the patient's age, as suggested by the fact that patients with Wernicke's aphasia tend to be older than those with Broca's aphasia (Obler and Albert, 1981).

Summary and future directions

A variety of language changes occur during normal aging and in age-related neurological diseases. These changes offer a wealth of opportunities to characterize the cognitive mechanisms associated with language capacities and to investigate their neuronal basis. It can be anticipated that theoretical and practical advances will result from exploration of such topics as the differentiation of automatic and effortful language processes, the possibility of defining subgroups of Alzheimer's disease with different language symptoms associated with specific clinical, anatomic, metabolic or genetic features, and studies comparing the language symptoms in different age-related neurological diseases.

Although the development of treatment strategies for most of these disorders is only beginning, measurements of lexical-semantic and other language abilities are likely to be valuable in evaluating proposed treatments (Huff et al., 1986a; Flicker et al., 1987). The preservation of semantic priming mechanisms in AD suggests the possibility of cognitive intervention strategies to enhance lexical-semantic processing. The fact that semanting priming is preserved not only for tasks involving automatic processing, but also for tasks involving effortful lexical-semantic processing (Nebes et al., 1989; Huff et al., 1988b), extends the potential application of such intervention strategies to a broad range of language functions. Another promising avenue for treatment is the use of medication known to be effective for the peripheral motor abnormalities of PD to treat the motor speech abnormalities in aphasia due to cerebral infarction (Albert et al., 1988). Language symptoms have not been measured extensively in the many trials of cholinergic treatments for AD, and when they have been examined the result has been negative (Brinkman and Gershon, 1983; Growdon et al., 1985). As the neurotransmitter systems involved in speech and language functions become better understood, other pharmacological treatments may be developed.

Acknowledgements

Mr. Jack Protetch and Ms. Debra Johnson provided valuable assistance in preparing this chapter. This work was supported by United States Public Health Service Grants AG03705, AG05133 and MH30915.

References

Albert ML, Bachman DL, Morgan A, Helm-Estabrooks N: Pharmacotherapy for aphasia. *Neurology: 38,* 877 – 879, 1988.

Albert ML, Feldman RG, Willis AL: The 'subcortical dementia' of progressive supranuclear palsy. *J. Neurol. Neurosurg. Psychiatry: 37,* 121 – 130, 1974.

Appell J, Kertesz A, Fismann M: A study of language functioning in Alzheimer patients. *Brain Lang.: 17,* 73 – 91, 1982.

Alzheimer A: On a peculiar disease of the cerebral cortex. (1907) Translated and discussed by Wilkins RH, Brady IA: Alzheimer's disease. *Arch. Neurol.: 21,* 109 – 110, 1969.

Barker MG, Lawson JS: Nominal aphasia in dementia. *Br. J. Psychiatry: 114,* 1351 – 1356, 1968.

Bayles KA: Language function in senile dementia. *Brain Lang.: 16,* 265 – 280, 1982.

Bayles KA, Kazniak AW: *Communication and Cognition in Normal Aging and Dementia.* Boston: Little, Brown and Company, 1987.

Bayles KA, Tomoeda CK: Confrontation naming impairment in dementia. *Brain Lang.: 19,* 98 – 114, 1983.

Bayles KA, Tomoeda CK, Boone DR: A view of age-related changes in language function. *Dev. Neuropsychol: 1,* 231 – 264, 1985a.

Bayles KA, Tomoeda CK, Kaszniak AW, Stern LZ, Eagans KK: Verbal perseveration of dementia patients. *Brain Lang.: 25,* 102 – 116, 1985b.

Beatty WW, Butters N, Janowsky DS: Patterns of memory failure after scopolamine treatment: implications for cholinergic hypotheses of dementia. *Behav. Neural Biol.: 45,*

196 – 211, 1986.

Becker JT, Huff FJ, Nebes RD, Holland A , Boller F: Neuropsychological function in Alzheimer's disease: patterns of impairment and rates of progression. *Arch. Neurol.: 45,* 263 – 268, 1988.

Boller F, Mizutani T, Roessman U, Gambetti P: Parkinson's disease, dementia, and Alzheimer disease: clinicopathological correlations. *Ann. Neurol.: 7,* 329 – 335, 1980.

Borod JD, Goodglass H, Kaplan E: Normative data on the Boston Diagnostic Aphasia Examination, Parietal Lobe Battery, and the Boston Naming Test. *J. Clin. Neuropsychol.: 2,* 209 – 215, 1980.

Botwinick J, West R, Strorandt M: Qualitative vocabulary responses and age. *J. Gerontol.: 30,* 574 – 577, 1975.

Bowles NL, Poon LW: Aging and retrieval of words in semantic memory. *J. Gerontol.: 40,* 71 – 77, 1985.

Breitner JCS, Folstein MF: Familial Alzheimer dementia: a prevalent disorder with specific clinical features. *Psychol. Med.: 14,* 63 – 80, 1984.

Breitner JCS, Silverman JM, Mohs RC, Davis KL: Familial aggregation in Alzheimer's disease: comparison of risk among relatives of early- and late-onset cases, and among male and female relatives in successive generations. *Neurology: 38,* 207 – 212, 1988.

Brinkman SD, Gershon S: Measurement of cholinergic drug effects on memory in Alzheimer's disease. *Neurobiol. Aging: 4,* 139 – 145, 1983.

Butters N, Ranholm E, Salmon DP, Grant I: Episodic and semantic memory: a comparison of amnesic and demented patients. *J. Clin. Exp. Neuropsychol.: 9,* 479 – 497, 1987.

Caine ED, Ebert MH, Weingartner H: An outline for the analysis of dementia. *Neurology: 27,* 1087 – 1092, 1977.

Caine ED, Weingartner H, Ludlow CL, Cudahy EA, Wehry S: Qualitative analysis of scopolamine-induced amnesia. *Psychopharmalogy: 74,* 74 – 80, 1981.

Cermak LS, Reale L, Baker E: Alcoholic Korsakoff patient's retrieval from semantic memory. *Brain Lang.: 5,* 215 – 226, 1978.

Chertkow H, Bub D, Seidenberg M: Priming and semantic memory loss in Alzheimer's disease. *Brain Lang.: 36,* 420 – 446, 1989

Chui HC, Teng EL, Henderson V, Moy AC: Clinical subtypes of dementia of the Alzheimer type. *Neurology: 35,* 1544 – 1550, 1985.

Cohen G: Language comprehension in old age. *Cognitive Psychol.: 11,* 412 – 429, 1979.

Cohen G, Faulkner D: Word recognition: age difference in contextual facilitation effects. *Br. J. Psychol.: 74,* 239 – 251, 1983.

Cummings JL, Benson DF: *Dementia: A Clinical Approach.* Boston: Butterworth Publishers, 1983.

Cummings JL, Duchen LW: Kluver-Bucy syndrome in Pick disease: clinical and pathologic correlations. *Neurology: 31,* 1415 – 1422, 1981.

Cummings JL, Benson DF, Hill, MA, Read, S: Aphasia in dementia of the Alzheimer type. *Neurology: 35,* 394 – 397, 1985.

Cummings JL, Houlihan JP, Hill MA: The pattern of reading deterioration in dementia of the Alzheimer type: observations and implications. *Brain Lang.: 29,* 315 – 323, 1986.

Cummings JL, Darkins A, Mendez M, Hill MA, Benson DF: Alzheimer's disease and Parkinson's disease: comparison of speech and language alterations. *Neurology: 38,* 680 – 684, 1988.

Darkins AW, Fromkin VA, Benson DF: A characterization of the prosodic loss in Parkinson's disease. *Brain Lang.: 34,* 315 – 327, 1988.

de Ajuriaguerra J, Tissot R: Some aspects of language in various forms of senile dementia (comparisons with language in childhood). *Foundations of Language Development.* New York: Academic Press, pp. 323 – 339, 1975.

Emery OB: Language and aging. *Exp. Aging Res.: 11,* 3 – 60, 1985.

Faber-Langendoen K, Morris JC, Knesevich JW, LaBarge E, Miller JP, Berg L: Aphasia in senile dementia of the Alzheimer type. *Ann. Neurol.: 23,* 365 – 370, 1988.

Filley CM, Kelly J, Heaton RK: Neuropsychologic features of early- and late-onset Alzheimer's disease. *Arch. Neurol.: 43,* 574 – 576, 1986.

Flicker C, Ferris SH, Crook T, Bartus RT: Implications of memory and language dysfunction in the naming deficit of senile dementia. *Brain Lang.: 31.* 187 – 200, 1987.

Fox C: Vocabulary ability in later maturity. *J. Educ. Psychol.: 38,* 482 – 492, 1947.

Freedman M, Rivoira P, Butters N, Sax DS, Feldman RG: Retrograde amnesia in Parkinson's disease. *Can. J. Neurol. Sci.: 11,* 297 – 301, 1984.

Gamsu CV: Confrontation naming in Parkinsonian patients: post-operative anomia revisited. *Neuropsychologia: 24,* 727 – 729, 1986.

Globus M, Mildworf B, Melamed E: Cerebral blood flow and cognitive impairment in Parkinson's disease. *Neurology: 35,* 1135 – 1139, 1985.

Gonzalez-Rothi L: Position paper read at the American Speech and Hearing Association annual meeting: 1988.

Goodglass H: Disorders of naming following brain injury. *Am. Sci.: 68,* 647 – 655, 1980.

Gordon WP, Illes J: Neurolinguistic characteristics of language production in Huntington's disease: a preliminary report. *Brain Lang.: 31,* 1 – 10, 1987.

Grober E, Buschke H, Kawas C, Fuld P: Impaired ranking of semantic attributes in dementia. *Brain Lang.: 26,* 276 – 286, 1985.

Growdon JH, Corkin S, Huff FJ, Rosen TJ: Piracetam combined with lecithin in the treatment of Alzheimer's disease. *Neurobiol. Aging: 7,* 269 – 270, 1986.

Hasher L, Zacks RT: Automatic and effortful processes in memory. J. Exp. Psychol.: 108: 356 – 388, 1979.

Hier B, Hagenlocker K, Shindler AG: Language disintegration in dementia: effects of etiology and severity. *Brain Lang.: 25,* 117 – 133, 1985.

Holland AL, Boller F, Bourgeois M: Repetition in Alzheimer's disease: a longitudinal study. *J. Neurolinguist.: 2,* 163 – 177, 1986.

Holland AL, McBurney DH, Moossy J, Reinmuth OM: The dissolution of language in Pick's disease with neurofibrillary tangles: a case study. *Brain Lang.: 24,* 36 – 58, 1985.

Huff FJ, Growdon JH: Neurological abnormalities associated with severity of dementia in Alzheimer's disease. *Can J. Neurol. Sci.: 13,* 403 – 405, 1986.

Huff FJ, Collins C, Corkin S, Rosen TJ: Equivalent forms of the Boston Naming Test. *J. Clin. Exp. Neuropsychol.: 8,* 556 – 562, 1986a.

Huff FJ, Corkin S, Growdon JH: Semantic impairment and anomia in Alzheimer's disease. *Brain Lang.: 28,* 235 – 249, 1986b.

Huff FJ, Becker JT, Belle SH, Nebes RD, Holland AL, Boller F: Cognitive deficits and clinical diagnosis of Alzheimer's disease. *Neurology: 37,* 1119 – 1124, 1987.

Huff FJ, Auerbach J, Chakravarti A, Boller F: Risk of dementia in relatives of patients with Alzheimer's disease. *Neurology: 38,* 786 – 790, 1988a.

Huff FJ, Mack L, Mahlmann J, Greenberg S: A comparison of lexical-semantic impairments in left hemisphere stroke and Alzheimer's disease. *Brain Lang.: 34,* 262 – 278, 1988b.

Huff FJ, Mickel SF, Corkin S, Growdon JH: Cognitive functions affected by scopolamine in Alzheimer's disease and normal aging. *Drug Dev. Res.: 12,* 271 – 278, 1988c.

Huff FJ, Belle SH, Shim YK, Ganguli M, Boller F: Prevalence and prognostic value of neurologic abnormalities in Alzheimer's disease. *Dementia:* in press.

Illes J, Metter EJ, Hanson WR, Iritani S: Language production in Parkinson's disease: acoustic and linguistic considerations. *Brain Lang.: 33,* 146 – 160, 1988.

Irigaray L: *Le Language des Dements.* The Hague: Mouton, 1973.

Jorm AF: Controlled and automatic information processing in senile dementia: a review. *Psychol. Med.: 16,* 77 – 88, 1986.

Josiassen RC, Curry IM, Mancall EL: Development of neuropsychological deficits in Huntington's disease. *Arch. Neurol.: 40,* 791 – 796, 1983.

Kaszniak AW, Fox J, Gandell DL, Garron DC, Huckman MA, Ramsey RG: Predicators of mortality in presenile and senile dementia. *Ann. Neurol.: 3,* 246 – 252, 1978.

Katz DI, Alexander MP, Mandell AM: Dementia following strokes in the mesencephalon and diencephalon. *Arch. Neurol.: 44,* 1127 – 1133, 1987.

Kempler D: Lexical and pantomine abilities in Alzheimer's disease. *Aphasiology: 2,* 147 – 159, 1988.

Kempler D, Curtiss S, Jackson C: Syntactic preservation in Alzheimer's disease. *J. Speech Hearing Res.: 30:* 343 – 350, 1987.

Kirshner HS, Webb WG, Kelly MP: The naming disorder of dementia. *Neuropsychologia: 22,* 23 – 30, 1984.

Knesevich JW, Toro FR, Morris JC, LaBarge E: Aphasia, family history, and the longitudinal course of senile dementia of the Alzheimer type. *Psychiatry Res.: 14,* 255 – 263, 1985.

Knesevich JW, LaBarge E, Edwards D: Predictive value of the Boston Naming Test in mild senile dementia of the Alzheimer type. *Psychiatry Res.: 19,* 155 – 161, 1986.

Kovner R, Mattis S, Gartner J, Goldmeier R: A verbal semantic deficit in the alcoholic Korsakoff syndrome. *Cortex: 17,* 419 – 426, 1981.

LaBarge E, Edwards D, Knesevich JW: Performance of normal elderly on the Boston Naming Test. *Brain Lang.: 27,* 380 – 384, 1986.

Light LL, Burke DM (Editors): Patterns of language and memory in old age. *Language, Memory and Aging.* Cambridge: Cambridge University Press, pp. 244 – 271, 1988.

Light LL, Singh A, Capps JL: Dissociation of memory and awareness in young and older adults. *J. Clin. Exp. Neuropsychol.: 8,* 62 – 74, 1986.

Loring DW, Largen JW: Neuropsychological patterns of presenile and senile dementia of the Alzheimer type. *Neuropsychologia: 23,* 351 – 357, 1985.

Ludlow CL, Connor NP, Bassich CJ: Speech timing in Parkinson's and Huntington's disease. *Brain Lang.: 32,* 195 – 214, 1987.

Maher E, Smith EM, Lees AJ: Cognitive deficits in the Steele-Richardson-Olszewski syndrome (progressive supranuclear palsy). *J. Neurol. Neurosurg. Psychiatry: 48,* 1234 – 1239, 1985.

Martin A, Fedio P: Word production and comprehension in Alzheimer's disease: the breakdown of semantic knowledge. *Brain Lang.: 19,* 124 – 141, 1983.

Martin A, Brouwers P, Lalonde F, Cox C, Teleska P, Fedio P: Towards a behavioral typology of Alzheimer's disease: *J. Clin. Exp. Neuropsychol.: 8,* 594 – 610, 1986.

Martin EM, Wilson RS, Penn RD, Fox JH, Clasen RA, Savoy SM: Cortical biopsy results in Alzheimer's disease: correlation with cognitive deficits. *Neurology: 37,* 1201 – 1204, 1987.

Matison R, Mayeux R, Rosen J, Fahn S: 'Tip-of-the-tongue' phenomenon in Parkinson Disease. *Neurology: 32,* 567 – 570, 1982.

Mayeux R, Stern Y, Rosen J, Benson DF: Is 'subcortical dementia' a recognizable clinical entity? *Ann. Neurol.: 14,* 278 – 283, 1983.

McCrae RR, Arenberg D, Costa PT: Decline in divergent thinking with age: cross-sectional, longitudinal and cross-sequential analyses. *Psychol. Aging: 2,* 130 – 132, 1987.

McKahn G, Drachman D, Folstein M, Katzman R, Price D, Stadlan EM: Clinical diagnosis of Alzheimer's disease: report of the NINCDS-ADRDA work group under the auspices of the Department of Health and Human Services task force on Alzheimer's disease. *Neurology: 34,* 934 – 944, 1984.

Mesulam MM: Slowly progressive aphasia without generalized dementia. *Ann. Neurol.: 11,* 592 – 598, 1982.

Miller E: Verbal fluency as a function of a measure of verbal intelligence and in relation to different types of cerebral pathology. *Br. J. Clin. Psychol.: 23,* 53 – 57, 1984.

Miller E, Hague F: Some characteristics of verbal behaviour in presenile dementia. *Psychol. Med.: 5,* 255 – 259, 1975.

Morris JC, Cole M, Banker BQ, Wright D: Hereditary dysphasic dementia and the Pick-Alzheimer spectrum. *Ann. Neurol.:16,* 455 – 466, 1984.

Murdoch BE, Chenery HJ, Wilks V, Boyle RS: Language disorders in dementia of the Alzheimer type. *Brain Lang.: 31,* 122 – 137, 1987.

Nebes R, Boller F, Holland A: Use of semantic context by patients with Alzheimer's disease. *Psychol. Aging: 1,* 261 – 269, 1986.

Nebes RD, Brady CB: Integrity of semantic fields in Alzheimer's disease. *Cortex: 24,* 291 – 299, 1988.

Nebes RD, Brady CB, Huff FJ: Automatic and attentional mechanisms of semantic priming in Alzheimer's disease. *J. Clin. Exp. Neuropsychol.: 11,* 219 – 230, 1989.

Nebes RD, Martin DC, Horn LC: Sparing of semantic memory in Alzheimer's disease. *J. Abnormal Psychol.: 93,* 321 – 330,

1984.

Nicholas M, Obler LK, Albert ML, Helm-Estabrooks N: Empty speech in Alzheimer's disease and fluent aphasia. *J. Speech Hearing Res.: 28,* 405 – 410, 1985.

North AJ, Ulatowska HK, Macaluso-Haynes S, Bell H: discourse performance in older adults. *Int. J. Aging Hum. Dev.: 23,* 267 – 283, 1986.

Ober BA, Shenaut GK: Lexical decision and priming in Alzheimer's disease. *Neurospychologia: 26,* 273 – 286, 1988.

Ober BA, Dronkers NF, Koss E, Delis DC, Friedland RP: Retrieval from semantic memory in Alzheimer-type dementia. *J. Clin. Exp. Neuropsychol.: 8,* 75 – 92, 1986

Obler LK: Narrative discourse style in the elderly. In Obler LK, Albert ML (Editors), *Language and Communication in the Elderly.* Lexington, MA: Heath, pp. 75 – 90, 1980.

Obler LK: Language and brain dysfunction in dementia. In Segalowitz S (Editor), *Language Functions and Brain Organization.* New York: Academic Press, pp. 267 – 282, 1983.

Obler LK, Albert ML: Language and aging: a neurobehavioral analysis. In Beasley DS, Davis GA (Editors), *Aging: Communication Process and Disorders.* New York: Grune & Stratton, 1981.

Obler LK, Albert ML: Historical note: Jules Seglas on language in dementia. *Brain Lang.: 2,* 214 – 325, 1985.

Owens WA: Age and mental abilities: a longitudinal study. *Genet. Psychol. Monogr.: 48 (Pts. 1 and 2),* 3 – 54, 1953.

Perkin GD, Lees AJ, Stern GM, Kocen RS: Problems in the diagnosis of progressive supranuclear palsy. *Can. J. Neurol. Sci.: 5,* 167 – 173, 1978.

Perret E : The left frontal lobe of man and the suppression of habitual responses in verbal categorical behavior. *Neuropsychologia: 12,* 323 – 330, 1974.

Pirozzolo FJ, Hansch EC, Mortimer JA, Webster DD, Kuskowski MA: Dementia in Parkisons's disease: a neuropsychological analysis. *Brain Cognition: 1,* 71 – 83, 1982.

Pogacar S, Williams RS: Alzheimer's disease presenting as slowly progressive aphasia. *R. I. Med. J.: 67,* 181 – 185, 1984.

Posner MI, Petersen SE, Fox PT, Raichle ME: Localization of cognitive operations in the human brain. *Science: 240,* 1627 – 1631, 1988.

Powell AL, Cummings JL, Hill MA, Benson DF: Speech and language alterations in multi-infarct dementia. *Neurology: 38,* 717 – 719, 1988.

Rochford G: A study of naming errors in dysphasic and in demented patients. *Neuropsychologia: 9,* 437 – 443, 1971

Rosen WG: Verbal fluency in aging and dementia. *J. Clin. Neuropsychol.: 2,* 135 – 146, 1980.

Schaie KW, Parham IA: Cohort-sequential analyses of adult intellectual development. *Dev. Psychol.: 13,* 649 – 653, 1977.

Schwartz MF, Marin OSM, Saffran EM: Dissociations of language function in dementia: a case study. *Brain Lang.: 7,* 277 – 306, 1979.

Scott S, Caird FI, Williams B: Evidence for an apparent sensory speech disorder in Parkinson's disease. *J. Neurol. Neurosurg. Psychiatry: 47,* 840 – 843, 1984.

Selnes OA, Carson K, Rovner B, Gordon MD: Language dysfunction in early- and late-onset possible Alzheimer's disease. *Neurology: 38,* 1053 – 1056, 1988.

Seltzer B, Sherwin I: A comparison of clinical features in early- and late-onset primary degenerative dementia. One entity or two? *Arch. Neurol.: 40,* 143 – 146, 1983.

Shimamura AP, Salmon DP, Squire LR, Butters N: Memory dysfunction and word priming in dementia and amnesia. *Behav. Neurosci.: 101,* 347 – 351, 1987.

Shindler AG, Caplan LR, Hier DB: Intrusions and perseverations. *Brain Lang.: 23,* 148 – 158, 1984.

Shuttleworth EC, Huber SJ: The naming disorder of dementia of Alzheimer type. *Brain Lang.: 34,* 222 – 234, 1988.

Sjogren H: Clinical analysis of morbus Alzheimer and morbus Pick. *Acta Psychiatr. Neurol. Scand.: 82 (Suppl.),* 68 – 115, 1952.

Skelton-Robinson M, Jones S: Nominal dysphasia and the severity of senile dementia. *Br. J. Psychiatry: 145,* 168 – 171, 1984.

Smith SR, Murdoch BE, Chenery HJ: Semantic abilities in dementia of the Alzheimer type. *Brain Lang.: 36,* 314 – 324, 1989.

Smith S, White R, Lyon L, Granholm E, Butters N: Priming semantic relations in patients with Huntington's disease. *Brain Lang.: 33,* 27 – 40, 1988.

Sulkava R, Amberla K: Alzheimer's disease and senile dementia of Alzheimer type. A neuropsychological study. *Acta Neurol. Scand.: 65,* 651 – 660, 1982.

Sunderland T, Tariot PN, Cohen RM, Weingartner H, Mueller EA, Murphy DL: Anticholinergic sensitivity in patients with dementia of the Alzheimer type and age-matched controls. *Arch. Gen. Psychiatry: 44,* 418 – 426, 1987.

Till RE, Walsh DA: Encoding and retrieval factors in adult memory for implicational sentences. *J. Verbal Learn. Verbal Behav.: 19,* 1 – 16, 1980.

Van Gorp WG, Satz P, Keirsch ME, Henry R: Normative data on the Boston Naming Test for a group of normal older adults. *J. Clin. Exp. Neuropsychol.: 8,* 702 – 705, 1986.

Warrington EK: The selective impairment of semantic memory. *Q. J. Exp. Psychol.: 27,* 635 – 657, 1975.

Wechsler AF, Verity MA, Rosenschein S, Fried I, Scheibel AB: Pick's Disease: a clinical, computed tomographic, and histologic study with Golgi impregnation observations. *Arch. Neurol.: 39,* 287 – 290, 1982

Wechsler D: *The Measurement and Appraisal of Adult Intelligence* (4th edn.). Baltimore: Williams and Wilkins, 1958.

Whitaker H: A case of the isolation of the language function. In Whitaker H, Whitaker H (Editors), *Studies in Neurolinguistics:* New York: Academic Press, pp. 1 – 58, 1976.

Handbook of Neuropsychology, Vol. 4
F. Boller and J. Grafman (Eds)

CHAPTER 13

Spatial abilities and deficits in aging and age-related disorders

Jenni A. Ogden

Department of Psychology, University of Auckland, Private Bag, Auckland, New Zealand

Introduction

The term 'spatial abilities' when applied to humans covers a wide range of functions from the relatively lower-level perceptual processes to the higher-level processes involved in spatial cognition. Examples of lower-level spatial processes are the perception of shape differences and line orientation, and examples of higher-level spatial processes are mental rotation and the mental transformation of shapes. Numerous other functions have a spatial component, such as right-left discrimination, orientation in space, and spatial memory. In addition, some spatial functions become evident only after brain damage. For example, the phenomenon of unilateral spatial neglect, which often follows damage to the right parietal lobe, provides a dramatic example of a deficit at a level of spatial awareness that is not apparent until the brain is damaged.

This chapter will not cover all of the spatial functions and dysfunctions that have been documented in humans. This is in part because of sparseness of the research on spatial abilities in aging and dementing populations, and in part because the specialist and complex nature of some of these spatial functions places them more appropriately within another neuropsychological framework. Thus, perceptual spatial abilities will be touched on only briefly, and spatial memory will be mentioned only where it appears relevant to other spatial abilities.

The spatial abilities and disorders that will be reviewed in the context of aging and age-related dementing disorders include exploration of space, spatial orientation, cognitive mapping, environmental knowledge, spatial cognition, and visuospatial constructional abilities.

This chapter first outlines the historical aspects of research into spatial abilities, and then defines the main categories of spatial ability and disorder that will be reviewed. The next two sections discuss the significance that hemispheric specialization and sex differences may have in relation to spatial deficits in the aging and dementing brain. Then some of the practical aspects of carrying out neuropsychological assessments in the elderly and demented will be described. One aim of this section is to point out the pitfalls of neuropsychological research in these clinical populations, and the consequent difficulties in obtaining 'clean' results. Studies of spatial abilities and dysfunctions in normal aging, and in the different dementias will then be reviewed. Finally, some conclusions will be drawn about our current knowledge of spatial functions in elderly and dementing people, and future research directions will be suggested.

A historical perspective on research into spatial deficits

In the mid- to late-nineteenth century, interest among neurologists in spatial deficits was overshadowed by the excitement generated by the discoveries of the relationship the aphasias had to damage of relatively localized lesions of the left hemisphere (Broca, 1865; Wernicke, 1874). Research into spatial disorders was probably also held back by the difficulty of defining the various functions that have a spatial component. While considerable progress has been made over the last 100 years, the area remains remarkably confused.

In 1876, John Hughlings Jackson documented a case study of a woman who tried to read by starting at the lower right-hand corner of the page and proceeding backwards, and had difficulty dressing and finding her way around. At autopsy she was found to have a glioma of the right posterior hemisphere. In 1888, Jules Badal published a study of a woman with a variety of spatial deficits, but this case was not noticed until years later (Benton and Myers, 1956). A report of topographical disorientation was published by Foerster in 1890, and since then there has been a steady output of single-case and group studies (Balint, 1909; Holmes, 1918; Kleist, 1934; Poppelreuter, 1917).

While a few neurologists observed that spatial disabilities appeared to follow right-hemispheric damage more often than left-hemispheric damage (Brain, 1941; Dide, 1938), it was Hecaen and his co-workers (Hecaen et al., 1951, 1956) and Zangwill and colleagues (Ettlinger et al., 1957; McFie et al., 1950; McFie and Zangwill, 1960) who, by studying groups of patients with lateralized lesions, were able to provide conclusive evidence that spatial dysfunctions were associated with right-hemispheric brain damage more frequently than with left brain damage.

The relatively recent influence of psychological thought on neurology has facilitated our understanding of spatial functions by using experimental methodology to tease apart the components of complex 'symptoms', and combining our knowledge of neurological deficits with studies of spatial processes in a non-neurological population. Today, our understanding of spatial functions and deficits in a young and middle-aged population is much greater than it was 100 years ago, and most of our knowledge of spatial disorders is based on studies of subjects with unilateral brain damage (see De Renzi, 1982, for a wide-ranging review). However, the influence that aging has on spatial abilities and the impairment of spatial functions caused by the more diffuse and wide-spread brain pathologies which mark the dementing diseases are areas that are only beginning to find a place in the research literature.

Categories of spatial deficit

Space exploration

Space exploration is an essential ingredient in human perception and behaviour. It not only pervades our every activity when we are relating to our external world, but it also plays an essential role in our perceptions of our own bodies. While all of our sense modalities are involved in the exploration of space, in humans the visual system plays a particularly important role. For example, we use our visual system to scan the environment, to focus on objects we wish to attend to, and to guide the movement of our bodies and limbs in order to interact with the object of attention. Other higher attentional functions are brought into play during these processes; for example in macaque monkeys there are various diverse groups of neurons in the parietal cortex that fire only when the animal looks at an interesting target (e.g. food within the monkey's reach), or if the contralateral arm satisfies some appetitive drive such as grooming, picking up food, or tripping a switch that brings a liquid reward (Lynch, 1980).

The neurological case reported by Balint (1909) provides a good example of a severe disorder of spatial exploration in a patient who had full visual fields, and was alert, cooperative, and had no other cognitive impairments. This patient had bilateral softenings of the parietal lobe. He was apparently able to attend to and perceive only one object at a time. He had a severe disorder of reaching, and if asked to grasp an object could only do so if he hit it by chance. The patients described by Holmes (1918) also had severe impairments of space exploration, but differed from Balint's case in that they also had disturbed ocular movements. They were unable to maintain fixation, follow a moving target, converge to an approaching object, or blink in response to a visual threat. This was not due to paralysis of the ocular muscles, but to a higher mechanism for ocular movements, probably caused by damage to the angular gyrus.

While these 'global' deficits of space exploration appear to follow bilateral damage, there is a more common disorder, unilateral spatial neglect, which results from a unilateral brain lesion. The patient with this disorder does not respond to stimuli in the side of space opposite to the brain lesion. The most severe neglect occurs following a lesion to the right parietal cortex, but neglect also occurs following lesions to the frontal cortex, the cingulate gyrus, the thalamus, and the basal ganglia (Heilman et al., 1985). Unilateral lesions in these areas in the left hemisphere also result in neglect, although the symptoms tend to be much milder and to resolve more quickly than after right-hemispheric lesions (Ogden, 1985). Mesulam (1983) has proposed that these different areas form a cortical network for directed attention and unilateral neglect, and that damage to a particular part of the network might result in one form of neglect, whereas damage to more than one area might result in a more severe clinical form of neglect. This suggests perhaps that it might be pertinent to look for neglect-like disorders of spatial exploration in patients with dementia, given that some dementias result in damage to more than one of these areas. The problem for clinical assessment is that neglect might be masked by other cognitive deficits also demonstrated by the dementing patient.

Orientation in space

There are two main aspects of orientation in space. The first aspect includes judgements of the relationships external objects have to one another (allocentric space). The second aspect includes relationships objects have to the perceiver's body (egocentric space). There is some evidence that these two classes of spatial orientation can be disturbed by lesions in different cortical areas. Semmes et al. (1963) were the first to produce data suggesting that in humans the anterior cortical areas (particularly the left) tended to impair concepts of egocentric space, and posterior lesions impaired concepts of allocentric space. While these findings have been partially supported by animal research (Butters et al., 1971; Milner et al., 1977; Pohl, 1973), other studies with animals have confused the area. For example, Brody and Pribram (1978) found that monkeys with frontal ablations were impaired on tasks involving allocentric as well as egocentric space. Further human research may help to clarify the matter.

Another class of disorders which are sometimes grouped with disorders of spatial orientation are those concerned with the localization, discrimination and awareness of body parts. However, it seems clear that these disorders of body schema do not play a critical role in disorders of extrapersonal disorientation, as the two types of disorder usually occur independently of each other (Benton, 1969). This is corroborated by the fact that the body schema disorders (left-right confusion, finger agnosia and autotopagnosia) occur following left-hemispheric lesions, whereas extrapersonal disorientation tends to follow right-hemispheric lesions.

Disorders of topographical memory may also cause spatial disorientation, but presumably because the patient has lost the ability to remember spatial configurations and relationships rather than being disoriented per se. Patients with topographical memory deficits have usually had bilateral lesions involving the occipital lobes (Dunn, 1895; Peters, 1896; Wilbrand, 1892), but there is also evidence for topographical amnesia after unilateral lesions resulting in a hemianopia (Meyer, 1900). The inability to find their way about suffered by some people with dementing diseases may be due to such an amnesia, rather than to spatial disorientation. The ability to compile, update and recall cognitive maps has been studied in animals (O'Keefe and Nadel, 1978) but not in humans. This function seems to be concerned with a context-dependent memory which continuously develops and updates objective spatial representations. In rats it can be disturbed by hippocampal lesions. Only future research will tell us whether a similar dysfunction can be found in those dementing diseases where there is neuronal loss in the hippocampus. Such a dysfunction may also explain a loss of environmental knowledge if this relies to some extent on the ability to update and recall maps of the environment.

A related phenomenon which is sometimes seen in dementing patients is that of reduplicative paramnesia. These patients relocate a familiar surrounding to a different location. For example, they may insist that the hospital they are in is situated in the town where they spent their childhood. Pick (1903) first described this in a patient with senile dementia. Reduplicative paramnesia can also include persons, time, events and body parts as well as space (Weinstein, 1969), and is best related to amnesic disorders rather than to disorders of topographical orientation.

Spatial cognition

When a task goes beyond localizing and perceiving simple stimuli, and involves the mental manipulation of spatial information, it falls into the category of 'spatial thinking.' Such tasks include identifying a pattern embedded in another pattern, imagining how objects would look if seen from a different angle, mentally rotating objects in one's imagination, imagining what a two-dimensional shape would look like if folded into a three-dimensional shape, and deducing rules from the spatial arrangements of objects. Thinking spatially takes time, and therefore the brain-behaviour relationships involved are not readily studied in an experimental situation with normal subjects in which, for example, information is briefly confined to one half of the brain. Therefore most of our knowledge on the brain systems that mediate spatial thought must come from studies of humans with brain damage. One exception to this can be found in a study of normal subjects in which EEG measures demonstrated laterality effects for an imagery task (Ornstein et al., 1980).

Another difficulty in this area of research is the complexity of spatial thought and the many different abilities and possible strategies that may be involved in the processes leading to the final solution. Even given that the experimenter ensures that the brain-damaged subject can perceive the spatial information and understands what the task is, there are presumably many different strategies which may be used from this point which may not be 'conscious' or verbalizable, and may be a reflection of the subject's premorbid learned skills, or a compensatory strategy made necessary by the brain damage. In a normal aging population, the deterioration of spatial thinking processes can be assessed, but it is difficult to see how any deficits might be related to specific brain systems, unless EEG measures or imaging techniques such as positron emission tomography (PET) are used. In a dementing population some correlations between spatial thinking processes and brain areas or systems might be made in cases where localized brain pathology can be clearly established.

Constructional apraxia

The disorder broadly labelled as 'constructional apraxia' has been a favourite of neurologists for many years. This is probably because it can easily be assessed at the bedside, and because it is believed to be a sensitive indicator of parietal damage. The construction of objects is a complex process. It involves the perception of the components of a model and the analysis of the spatial relationships between those components, and the execution of a motor plan designed to duplicate the model. Clearly the constructional ability involves spatial cognition, but because of its importance in neurological practice it will be considered separately here.

The belief that constructional apraxia is

associated with parietal damage is quite well supported in the literature (Critchley, 1953), but there is evidence that patients with lesions of the frontal lobes also demonstrate constructional apraxia (Benson and Barton, 1970). As Luria and Tsvetkova (1964) pointed out, the planning and controlling of successive steps when reproducing a structured pattern is an essential part of the constructional process, and these processes can be disrupted by frontal lobe damage.

Various early studies found that constructional apraxia was more frequent following right-hemispheric rather than left-hemispheric lesions (Piercy et al., 1960; Benton and Fogel, 1962; Arrigoni and De Renzi, 1964; De Renzi and Faglioni, 1967). However, later studies have shown an equal frequency following right- and left-hemispheric lesions (Benton, 1973; Colombo et al., 1976; Arena and Gainotti, 1978). This in part probably reflects the use of simpler constructional tests, thus allowing the inclusion of patients who have receptive language disorders and left-hemispheric damage.

The discovery that constructional apraxia may occur after lesions to either hemisphere has stimulated research into qualitative differences which might relate to hemispheric specialization. Apart from the common finding that right brain-damaged patients tend to fail to reproduce the left side of a figure as the result of unilateral spatial neglect (Gainotti and Tiacci, 1970), it has been claimed that right brain-damaged patients' constructions show generally disorganized spatial relationships and defective orientation in space, whereas left brain-damaged patient's constructions are oversimplified and have a reduced number of details (McFie and Zangwill, 1960). Whether or not these claims can be thoroughly substantiated, it is probably true that constructional disorders occurring following lesions to different areas of the brain are the result of quite different deficits. It may be necessary to identify the subcomponents of constructional apraxia via the study of patients with localized lesions before an attempt is made to assess the underlying deficits of constructional apraxia when it is demonstrated by a dementing person.

Hemispheric specialization

Most research on hemispheric specialization addresses language functions, and there is now extensive evidence that the left hemisphere is dominant for language in about 96% of right-handed adults and 70% of left-handed adults (Milner, 1975). Whether or not the right hemisphere has at birth the potential to take over language functions in an equivalent fashion to the left hemisphere is as yet unresolved (Bishop, 1983; Dennis and Kohn, 1975; Lenneberg, 1967; Ogden, 1988). However, assessments of subjects who have had hemispherectomies after early hemispheric damage show that the remaining hemisphere, whether right or left, develops language abilities to a normal or near-normal level (Ogden, 1988). One apparent result of this is that visuospatial abilities are impaired, possibly because one hemisphere cannot do everything, and 'right-hemispheric' functions are the ones that suffer (Bigler and Naugle, 1985; Ogden, 1989; Woods and Teuber, 1973; Verity et al., 1982).

In the intact brain, the right hemisphere has a firm claim to specialization in that it plays the predominant role in the processing of spatial and non-verbal information (De Renzi, 1982). The right hemisphere is more proficient than the left at processing melodic patterns and environmental sounds (Curry, 1967; Kimura, 1964), visual non-verbalizable patterns and unfamiliar faces (Marcel and Rajan, 1975; Witelson, 1977), non-verbal tactile spatial stimuli (Witelson, 1974) and braille (Harris et al., 1976). This specialization for spatial skills is only relative, however, as is evidenced by the difficulties many patients with left parietal lesions have with spatial concepts.

Given that visuospatial impairments are often amongst the earlier symptoms of dementing diseases of the Alzheimers type, it would be reasonable to look in these patients for areas of neuronal loss and damage in the posterior cortex, particularly in the right hemisphere. If visuospatial impairments occur earlier than verbal impairments in a normal aging population, then it might be hypothesized that the right hemisphere ages more rapidly or earlier than the left hemisphere.

Sex differences

Spatial abilities have also been related to sex differences, and a number of studies support a female superiority on some linguistic skills and a male superiority on skills that require the ability to think spatially. Harris (1978) reviews the extensive literature on gender and spatial abilities, and finds a male superiority on the recall and detection of shapes, mental rotation tasks, geometrical skills, sense of direction and map reading, and geographical knowledge. However, Caplan et al. (1985) identified a number of serious flaws in many of the studies that claimed to find a male superiority in the ability to perform spatial tasks. Their most serious criticism was that the construct 'spatial abilities' was ill-defined and therefore possibly illegitimate. This difficulty in defining spatial abilities has been noted earlier in this chapter, and Caplan et al.'s critique further highlights the problems of reviewing the literature on spatial deficits in elderly and dementing people, whatever their sex. If, as the folklore would have it, males are superior on spatial tasks, it will almost certainly turn out to be the result of complex interactions between genetic, hormonal and environmental factors. The main implication a possible sex difference has for research on spatial functioning in elderly and dementing groups of subjects is that it invalidates comparisons between the sexes when looking at the deterioration of spatial abilities.

Practical aspects of assessing elderly and dementing people

While some people in their seventies and eighties are alert and cooperative during neuropsychological testing, many will be slower and less interested in performing well than younger people. In addition, many old people have visual and auditory acuity problems, and are not as flexible and adaptable as they were when younger. These factors must therefore be taken into consideration when designing neuropsychological tests if spuriously low scores and incorrect conclusions about their mental capacities are to be avoided (Lezak, 1983). Timed tests are a particularly bad choice, as are tests involving fine motor coordination. Where possible tests should be constructed out of familiar materials such as playing cards, and, where the subject is required to read or see detail on a picture, the stimuli should be large and clear. Obviously, it is important to use the appropriate age norms when comparing the deficits of a dementing population with their healthy peers. Old people, and particularly those with dementing disorders, may tire easily and their ability to concentrate for any length of time may be poor. A common practice amongst clinicians when assessing elderly people is to use language that is so simple that it is demeaning to the subject. While to use language free of jargon is important whatever the age of the subject, the tendency to treat old people like small children (e.g. 'Let us try this one next') should be avoided (Lezak, 1983). Such a practice would seem to serve no good purpose even when communicating with a patient with advanced dementia.

Testing should take place when the subject is not tired, usually in the morning, and sessions are best kept fairly short. It is pointless to continue testing when the subject shows signs of fatigue, confusion, or becomes uncooperative for any reason. The test environment should be well lit and quiet, with no distractions. The tester should allow for considerable time before and between tests, as not only do elderly people require more rest than younger people between tests, but they also like to talk about their problems and life experiences with a sympathetic listener. The experienced neuropsychologist will encourage this for two reasons: first it helps to build and maintain rapport, and second it sometimes reveals useful qualitative data relevant to the subject's neuropsychological performance. While some patients who have a dementing disorder may be unaware and unconcerned about their poor performance on tests, it is a mistake to think that all patients with dementia lack insight. In the early stages of these diseases, probably before any reliable diagnosis can be made, elderly people are often exceptionally sensitive to deficits in their performance and only too aware of the prognosis should they have a dementing disease. Therefore it is very important to give positive feedback wherever possible, and to give a test the subject will probably be able to cope with after a difficult one. The tester should be prepared to stop testing if the subject is clearly unable to do the test and is becoming upset. Depression is quite common in the elderly population, especially in people in the very early stages of dementia. Where possible the depression should be treated before giving a neuropsychological assessment, especially if it is for research purposes.

Tests of spatial ability which can be used in the assessment of elderly and dementing populations include any tests that can be given untimed and that the individual can cope with given his or her particular sensory impairments. Tests such as the WAIS Block Design subtest can provide useful qualitative and quantitative data if given untimed, but the scores must of course be compared with untimed scores, or alternatively each subject can act as his or her own control if longitudinal assessments are carried out. Tests such as the WAIS Picture Arrangement subtest may be inappropriate if the subject has visual acuity problems. Generally speaking, complexity of detail is best avoided. Tests where the stimuli are presented on a computer screen can be useful as long as there is a way of stopping the test at any time if the subject becomes confused or tired. In addition, the speed of stimulus presentation should be adjustable to suit the information-processing capacity of the subject.

Studies of spatial abilities in normal aging

Epidemiologists estimate that between 5 and 20% of the population over 65 years of age suffer from mild to severe dementia (Gunner-Svensson and Jensen, 1976; Nielson, 1962) and most of the remaining members in this age group also show some degree of mental alteration. The boundary between mild dementia and normal aging (senescence) is not a clear one, and it has been suggested that all mental impairments seen in aged people are related to a lesser or greater degree to Alzheimer-type cortical neuropathological changes (Cummings and Benson, 1983, p. 275). Neurological changes that occur in senescence include a slowing of the background alpha rhythm (Drachman and Hughes, 1971), an increased latency in the late components of visual, auditory and somatosensory evoked responses (Goodin et al., 1978), and larger ventricles and widening cortical sulci on computerized tomography studies (Huckman et al., 1975).

A number of investigators have reported a more rapid decline with age on some WAIS Performance subtests (e.g. Picture Arrangement and Digit Symbol) than on Verbal subtests (e.g. Vocabulary and Information) (Berkowitz and Green, 1963; Doppelt and Wallace, 1955; Eisdorfer and Wilkie, 1973; Harwood and Naylor, 1971; Jarvik et al., 1962). These relatively greater declines with age on Performance subtests may be due to factors other than visuospatial deficits, however. Healthy elderly subjects have been found to perform normally on tests such as the Raven Matrices and the Block Design subtest of the WAIS (Katzman, 1982, cited by Cummings and Benson, 1983, p. 277) unless the tests are timed, although Doppelt and Wallace (1955) and Klodin (1975) found significant differences between the scores of elderly and young subjects on the timed and untimed versions of the Block Design subtest. Although the elderly subjects benefited more than the younger subjects with additional time, eliminating the time restriction did not eliminate differences between old and young. A study by Farver (1975, cited by Cummings and Benson, 1983, p. 278) found age-related deficits in block construction, memory for stick designs, the Hooper Visual Organization Test, and clock setting.

Elderly people also show more segmentation and perseveration on drawing tasks than young people (Veroff, 1980). Plude et al. (1986) found that elderly people (mean age = 67) were significantly poorer at drawing a cube to command than younger people (mean age = 21), and the older subjects were also less accurate than the younger subjects at discriminating between distorted and undistorted cubes. If, however, the subjects were provided with markers indicating the size of the lines, the elderly subjects performed as well as the younger subjects. This improvement in performance when external structure is provided may indicate that the decreased ability of elderly people to draw three-dimensional shapes is due to executive 'frontal-lobe' deficits rather than visuospatial deficits per se.

Eslinger and Benton (1983) found a gradual decline with age in the ability to perform tests of facial discrimination and judgement of line orientation. Cummings and Benson (1983, p. 278) point out that these impairments are usually due to frontal or parietal lobe dysfunction, and therefore may be manifestations of changes in these cortical areas in the aging brain.

Shelton et al. (1982) demonstrated that while there was an age-related decrement on a visuospatial paired-associate memory task, an age-related decrement was also found on a verbal paired-associate memory task. They concluded that while visuospatial abilities do decline with age, this is not necessarily an indication of a more rapid decline in right-hemispheric functions relative to left-hemispheric functions. In support of this, Hatta et al. (1984) found that while there was an age-related decline on a task of judging whether successively presented nonsense tactile stimuli to each hand were identical or not (presumed to be a right-hemispheric task), there was also an age-related decline (i.e. an overall decline in scores) on a left-hemispheric dichotic listening task using pairs of two-syllable meaningful words. Thus, there was no evidence to suggest any selective deterioration of right- or left- hemispheric functions. Nebes et al. (1983) measured the speed at which young and old subjects identified words and pictorial stimuli presented to either the right or left visual field. Both young and old subjects identified words faster when they were in the right visual field, and pictorial stimuli when they were in the left visual field. However, on a test of visual spatial learning which used the rationale of selective reminding and evaluated memory and learning of spatial positions of objects, performance declined with age more steeply than performance on an auditory verbal selective reminding task (Muramoto, 1984).

Adamowicz and Hudson (1978) found age-related decrements on a memory task where the stimuli were complex black and white matrices. The memory deficits were associated with stimulus complexity but not with response delay. Danziger and Salthouse (1978) found elderly people less effective at identifying incomplete figures, and concluded it was because older adults were unable to utilize stimulus information as effectively as younger adults in making perceptual decisions. Flicker et al. (1984) found a decline with age on a visuospatial recall task, and Moore et al. (1984) found significant differences in memory for location on the Tactual Performance Test across most of the age span. Pezdek (1983) and Light and Zelinski (1983) found that older people had more difficulty encoding and recalling spatial locations than young people. On real-world memory tasks where subjects were tested for location memory of urban landmarks (Evans et al., 1984) and recognition of environmental scenes from familiar and novel perspectives (Bruce and Herman, 1983), elderly people performed worse than younger people.

On tests of spatial cognition, Ludwig (1982) found an impairment in elderly people on a task of visualizing a complete pattern after viewing its component parts, and Berg et al. (1982) and Gaylord and Marsh (1975) found an age-related decrement on speed of mental rotation. Herman and Bruce (1983) found that older subjects were less accurate than younger subjects on the Shepard and Metzler (1971) mental rotation task, and men were better than women throughout adulthood. Herman and Coyne (1980) found no age difference on a task involving imagining an array of objects rotated relative to their current position, but found an age-related decrement when subjects were asked to determine the location of target objects from imagined locations.

In summary, current evidence suggests that spatial abilities do decline over the age of 65, but this may be more a consequence of the heavy load many spatial tasks put on the visual, perceptual and memory systems, and the speeded nature or response time measures used in some of these tests (Perret and Birri, 1982). There is little evidence for a significantly decreased ability in the elderly to *think* spatially, and the evidence to suggest that visuospatial right-hemispheric functions deteriorate with age relative to verbal left-hemispheric functions is also sparse. The main problem in this area of research is that of designing tests of spatial abilities which can be analysed independently of the sensory decrements and perceptual-motor slowing that accompany the normal aging process.

Studies of spatial dysfunctions in the dementias

Alzheimer's disease and Pick's disease

Pick's disease is 10 to 15 times rarer than Alzheimer's disease (AD). Neither is a diffuse or global disorder, in that areas of primary motor, somatosensory and visual cortex and subcortical structures are relatively spared until late in the clinical course after dementia is well established. In AD granulovacuolar degeneration occurs mainly in the hippocampus, and the neurofibrillary tangles and senile plaques are most apparent in the temporoparieto-occipital junction area, the temporolimbic regions and the posterior cingulate gyrus (Corsellis, 1976). In Pick's disease the brain atrophy tends to involve the temporal and/or frontal lobes, while a small number of patients have atrophy of the posterior hemispheric regions. The atrophy is bilateral in 30% of cases, left-sided in 50% and right-sided in 20% (Corsellis, 1976).

One of the difficulties in reviewing the research literature on spatial deficits in the different dementing disorders is that frequently the patient group includes patients with dementias of unspecified etiologies, or, if the etiologies are specified, the test results of the different dementia groups are analysed together.

In AD visuospatial skills are often impaired relatively early in the disease (Adams and Victor, 1977), although some of the apparent visuospatial deficits may be the result of other cognitive impairments such as perseveration and stimulus-bound responses (Moss and Albert, 1988). Patients with AD suffer from disorientation and are unable to copy three-dimensional figures accurately (Cummings and Benson, 1983, p. 39; Rosen and Mohs, 1982). On the WAIS they obtain their lowest scores on Block Design (Perez et al., 1975; Semple et al., 1982) and have difficulty copying the designs of the Benton visual retention test (Semple et al., 1982). In the middle stages of the disease, patients with AD also have difficulties with dressing (Hardeson and MacLachlan, 1930), and are impaired on body-part naming, visual memory for geometric forms and matching geometric forms (Rosen and Mohs, 1982). Grossi and Orsini (1978) found that patients with AD were unable to reproduce the spatial arrangement of eight crosses, and did not improve on a second trial.

Brouwers et al. (1984) compared the spatial abilities of groups of patients with AD and Huntington's disease (HD), and found a double dissociation. The patients with AD were impaired on tasks identified as involving extrapersonal perception and construction (Rey complex figure and a stylus maze test) but were not impaired on a task involving egocentric space (road-map test of direction). The patients with HD demonstrated the opposite pattern of scores. Brouwer et al. suggested that this may be consistent with the neuropathological changes in the two diseases; i.e., parietal atrophy in AD, and neuronal loss in the frontal cortex and in the caudate nucleus and putamen in HD.

In Muramoto's (1984) study in which normal elderly people and patients with AD were compared on two selective reminding tasks (an auditory verbal task and a visual spatial task), the AD group showed a severe impairment on the visual spatial task relative to the auditory verbal task. The degree of impairment correlated well with the degree of dementia.

In Pick's disease visuospatial skills are spared in the early stages and deteriorate only in the late stages (6 to 12 years) (Cummings and Benson, 1983). By this stage the patients are profoundly demented, thus making it extremely difficult to assess spatial abilities reliably. This, and the relative rarity of the disorder, probably explain the paucity of research studies on spatial deficits in Pick's disease.

In summary, there are definitely visuospatial impairments quite early on in AD, but in Pick's disease visuospatial deficits only appear in the late stages when it is almost impossible to differentiate them from the profound dementia. These differences correlate with the neuropathological changes in the two diseases; that is, patients with AD have neuronal degeneration in the temporoparietal areas, whereas the pathology of Pick's disease in usually concentrated in the temporal and/or frontal areas.

Huntington's disease and Parkinson's disease

Huntington's disease (HD), Parkinson's disease (PD) and progressive supranuclear palsy (PSP) have sometimes been termed the subcortical dementias. This term is inappropriate, however, as these diseases involve the frontal cortex or the frontal-subcortical connections as well as the basal ganglia. The basal ganglia, thalamus and prefrontal cortex form a frontal-subcortical system, and therefore pathology of any part of this system can result in the same dysfunctions (Nauta, 1979). There is a lack of research on spatial deficits in PSP, and therefore only research on spatial deficits in HD and PD will be reviewed here.

In HD, dysfunctions in language and memory are usually the first cognitive symptoms to appear. As the disease progresses, concentration and judgement become impaired, and frontal-like disorders become apparent. These include difficulties in initiating problem-solving behaviours, and organization, planning and sequential arrangement of information. Deficits on some spatial tasks become evident at this stage (Cummings and Benson, 1983, p. 75). Potegal (1971) reported an impairment on a task involving the manipulation of personal space, and on the same task patients with PD were not impaired. Brouwers et al. (1984) have also reported an impairment on spatial tasks involving egocentric space but not extrapersonal space for patients with HD.

There has been a recent upsurge of interest in specific cognitive deficits and dementia in PD. The issue of whether cognitive deficits demonstrated by patients with PD who are not demented are isolated deficits or simply an early stage of a progressive dementia is a controversial one. In the early stages, patients with PD demonstrate deficits similar to those seen as a result of frontal lobe lesions. For example, they are impaired on tasks that require shifting mental set (Bowen et al., 1972, 1975, 1976; Cools et al., 1984; Lees and Smith, 1983; Mayeux et al., 1981). Investigations defining the circuitry linking frontal regions and neurons within the striatum provide a possible anatomic basis for this (Alexander et al., 1986). Patients with PD but without dementia also demonstrate deficits on tests that require an integration of postural and visual information (Proctor et al., 1964), and on tests of spatial orientation (Bowen et al., 1972). They also demonstrate a significant impairment when copying a complex figure (Ogden et al., 1987). Sharpe et al. (1983) gave patients with PD and a control group tasks which involved making gestures that required (i) the symbolic representation of implement usage on verbal command and by imitation, and (ii) the imitation of non-symbolic hand positions (i.e. non-representational items). The PD group were poorer on both tasks, making significantly more spatial errors on the non-representational tasks than the controls.

In summary, patients with HD and PD demonstrate a different pattern of early cognitive deficits. Patients with HD tend to show language and memory deficits in the early stages, and patients with PD demonstrate impairments on tasks involving sequencing, motor planning, shifting set and visuospatial perception. Research in the area of spatial deficits in these disorders and PSP is either lacking or, as in the case of PD, has only recently begun to gain momentum. One of the problems to be overcome is that of assessing spatial disorders in a population with severe movement deficits.

Multi-infarct dementia

Multi-infarct dementia is caused by a series of infarcts resulting from vascular pathology. Spatial deficits will appear when infarcts occur in localized cortical or subcortical areas that mediate spatial functions. It is therefore not possible to make generalizations about patterns of cognitive deficit in this disorder.

Jakob-Creutzfeldt disease

Jakob-Creutzfeldt disease is a very rare and rapidly progressive viral disease, making research into specific spatial deficits virtually impossible. Within a few weeks of the initial symptoms of vague physical discomfort, fatigue and lowered concentration appearing, widespread hemispheric atrophy develops accompanied by a range of neurological and cognitive impairments. While spatial deficits are almost certainly present, any measurement of these would be hopelessly confounded by the global dementia.

Future directions

The term 'spatial abilities' covers a wide range of complex neuropsychological functions and, while many spatial disorders demonstrated by neurological patients have been documented for over a hundred years, careful qualitative analyses of spatial functions using methods developed by cognitive psychologists have gained momentum relatively recently. While there are many excellent studies on spatial abilities in normal human subjects, there are few on an aging population, and even fewer on an aging population with the additional complicating factor of dementia. Only in diseases such as PD, where the neuropathology in the early stages appears to be confined to relatively localized cerebral areas, can a substantial number of studies on specific spatial abilities be found.

With the development of sophisticated imaging technology there has been an increase in our knowledge of the neuropathology of the dementing diseases, and even this is overshadowed by the rapid advances in the identification of neurotransmitters and specific neuronal pathways. These recent advances provide hope that the normal aging brain and some of the dementing diseases will soon be better understood. As we learn more about the specific neuropathologies of the different dementias, it becomes more meaningful to study the patterns of neuropsychological deficit and sparing in these patients.

The other possibility is to analyse the functional and structural systems underlying spatial deficits via the study of younger people with relatively well-localized cerebral lesions, and then apply this knowledge to elderly and dementing populations. Thus, elderly or dementing patients who are found to have a particular spatial impairment may be hypothesized to have damage in a particular region of the brain or neuronal system, and imaging or neurophysiological techniques and assays of neurotransmitters could be used to test this.

It is also of value to document the neuropsychological deficits that appear in the progression of the different dementias. This can become a diagnostic aid as well as a guide to the management of patients with these diseases.

The potential for research in all these areas is great, and there is a need for well-controlled studies of aging and dementing populations which use the ingenious neuropsychological tests and methods that are the hallmark of good cognitive psychology. In a multidisciplinary framework, such neuropsychological studies can be related to neuroanatomical and physiological findings. Ultimately we may be able to define different spatial abilities and relate them to structural or biochemical systems in the brain, and in addition understand how spatial abilities are influenced by aging and the dementing diseases.

References

Adamowicz JK, Hudson BR: Visual short-term memory, response delay and age. *Percept. Motor Skills: 46,* 267 – 270, 1978.

Adams RD, Victor M: *Principles of Neurology,* 3rd Edition. New York: McGraw-Hill, 1977.

Alexander GE, Delong MR, Strick PL: Parallel organisation of functionally segregated circuits linking basal ganglia and cortex. *Ann. Rev. Neurosci.: 9,* 357 – 382, 1986.

Arena R, Gainotti G: Constructional apraxia and visuoperceptive disabilities in relation to laterality of cerebral lesions. *Cortex: 14,* 463 – 473, 1978.

Arrigoni G, De Renzi E: Constructional apraxia and hemispheric locus of lesion. *Cortex: 1,* 170 – 197, 1964.

Badal J: Contribution a l'etude des cecites psychiques. Alexie, agraphie, hemianopsie inferieure, trouble de sens de l'espace. *Arch. Ophtalmol.: 8,* 97 – 117, 1888.

Balint R: Seelenlahmung des 'Schauens', optische Ataxie, raumliche Storung der Aufmerkamseit. *Monatschr. Psychiatr. Neurol.: 25,* 51 – 81, 1909.

Benson D, Barton M: Disturbances in constructional ability. *Cortex: 6,* 19 – 46, 1970.

Benton AL: Disorders of spatial orientation. In Vinken PJ, Bruyn GW (Editors), *Handbook of Clinical Neurology, Vol. III,* Amsterdam: North-Holland Publishing Company, 1969.

Benton AL: Visuoconstructive disability in patients with cerebral disease: its relationship to side of lesion and aphasic disorder. *Doc. Ophthalmol.: 34,* 67 – 76, 1973.

Benton AL, Fogel ML: Three-dimensional constructional praxias. *Arch. Neurol.: 7,* 347 – 354, 1962.

Benton AL, Meyers R: An early description of the Gerstmann syndrome. *Neurology: 6,* 838 – 842, 1956.

Berg C, Hertzog C, Hunt EU: Age differences in the speed of mental rotation. *Dev. Psychol.: 18,* 95 – 107, 1982.

Berkowitz B, Green RF: Changes in intellect with age. 1. Longitudinal study of Wechsler-Bellevue scores. *J. Genet. Psychol.: 103,* 3 – 21, 1963.

Bigler ED, Naugle RI: Case studies in cerebral plasticity. *Int. J. Clin. Neuropsychol.: 7,* 12 – 23, 1985.

Bishop DVM: Linguistic impairment after left hemidecortication for infantile hemiplegia? A reappraisal. *Q. J. Exp. Psychol.: 35A,* 199 – 1207, 1983.

Bowen FP, Hoehn MM, Yahr MD: Alternations in spatial orientation as determined by a route-walking test. *Neuropsychologia: 10,* 355 – 361, 1972.

Bowen FP, Kamienny RS, Burns MM, Yahr MD: Parkinsonism: effects of levodopa on concept formation. *Neurology: 25,* 701 – 704, 1975.

Bowen FP, Burns MM, Brady E, Yahr MD: A note on alterations of personal orientation in Parkinsonism. *Neuropsychologia: 14,* 425 – 429, 1976.

Brain WR: Visual disorientation with special reference to lesions to the right cerebral hemisphere. *Brain: 64,* 244 – 272, 1941.

Broca P: Sur la siege de la faculte du langage articule. *Bull. Soc. Anthropol. 6,* 377 – 393, 1865.

Brody BA, Pribram, KH: The role of the frontal and parietal cortex in cognitive processing. *Brain: 101,* 607 – 633, 1978.

Brouwers P, Cox C, Martin A, Chase T, Fedio P: Differential perceptual-spatial impairment in Huntington's and Alzheimer's dementias. *Arch. Neurol.: 41,* 1073 – 1076, 1984.

Bruce PR, Herman JF: Adults' mental rotation of spatial information: effects of age, sex and cerebral laterality. *Exp. Aging Res.: 9,* 83 – 85, 1983.

Butters N, Pandya D, Sanders K, Dye P: Behavioural deficits in monkeys after selective lesions within the middle third of sulcus principalis. *J. Comp. Physiol. Psychol.: 76,* 8 – 14, 1971.

Caplan PJ, MacPherson GM, Tobin P: Do sex-related differences in spatial abilities exist? *Am. Psychol.: 40,* 786 – 799, 1985.

Colombo A, De Renzi E, Faglioni P: The occurrence of visual neglect in patients with unilateral cerebral disease. *Cortex: 12,* 257 – 263, 1976.

Cools AR, Van den Bercken JHL, Horstink MWI, Van Spaendonc KPM, Berger HJC: Cognitive and motor shifting attitude disorders in Parkinson's Disease. *J. Neurol. Neurosurg. Psychiatry: 47,* 443 – 453, 1984.

Corsellis J: Aging and the Dementias. In Blackwood W, Corsellis J (Editors), *Greenfields Neuropathology.* Chicago: Yearbook Medical Publishers, pp. 796 – 848, 1976.

Critchley M: *The Parietal Lobes.* London: Arnold, 1953.

Cummings JL, Benson DF: *Dementia: A Clinical Approach.* Boston: Butterworths, 1983.

Curry FKW: A comparison of left-handed and right-handed subjects on verbal and nonverbal dichotic listening tasks. *Cortex: 3,* 343 – 352, 1967.

Danziger WL, Salthouse TA: Age and the perception of incomplete figures. *Exp. Aging Res.: 4,* 67 – 80, 1978.

Dennis M, Kohn B: Comprehension of syntax in infantile hemiplegics after cerebral hemidecortication: left-hemisphere superiority. *Brain Lang.: 2,* 472 – 48, 1975.

De Renzi E: *Disorders of Space Exploration and Cognition.* London: John Wiley and Sons, 1982.

De Renzi E, Faglioni P: The relationship between visuospatial impairment and constructional apraxia. *Cortex: 3,* 327 – 342, 1967.

Dide M: Diagnostic anatomo-cliniques de desorientations temporo-spatiales. *Rev. Neurol.: 69,* 720 – 725, 1938.

Doppelt JE, Wallace WL: Standardization of the Wechsler Adult Intelligence Scale for older persons. *J. Abnorm. Soc. Psychol.: 51,* 312 – 330, 1955.

Drachman DA, Hughes TR: Memory and the hippocampal complexes. III. Aging and temporal EEG abnormalities. *Neurology: 21,* 1 – 6, 1971.

Dunn TD: Double hemiplegia with double hemianopsia and loss of a geographic center. *Trans. Coll. Physicians Phila.: 17,* 45 – 55, 1895.

Eisdorfer C, Wilkie F: Intellectual changes with advancing age. In Jarvik WM, Eisdorfer C, Blum JE (Editors), *Intellectual Functioning in Adults.* New York: Springer, pp. 21 – 29, 1973.

Eslinger PJ, Benton AL: Visuoperceptual performances in aging and dementia: clinical and theoretical implications. *J. Clin. Neuropsychol.: 5,* 213 – 220, 1983.

Ettlinger G, Warrington E, Zangwill OL: A further study of visuo-spatial agnosia. *Brain: 80,* 335 – 361, 1957.

Evans GW, Brennan PL, Skorpanich MA, Held D: Cognitive mapping and elderly adults: verbal and location memory for urban landmarks. *J. Gerontol.: 39,* 452 – 457, 1984.

Farver P: Performance of older adults on a test battery designed to measure parietal lobe functions. Boston University, College of Allied Health Professions, unpublished Masters degree thesis, 1975.

Flicker C, Bartus R, Crook TH, Ferris SH: Effects of aging and dementia upon recent visuospatial memory. *Neurobiol. Aging: 5,* 275 – 283, 1984.

Foerster O: Ueber Rindenblindheit. *Graefe's Arch. Ophthalmol.: 32,* 94 – 108, 1890.

Gaylord SA, Marsh GR: Age differences in the speed of a spatial cognitive process. *J. Gerontol.: 30,* 674 – 678, 1975.

Goodin DS, Squires KC, Starr A: Long latency event-related components of the auditory evoked potential in dementia. *Brain: 101,* 635 – 648, 1978.

Grossi D, Orsini A, de Michele G: The copying of geometric drawings in dementia. *Acta. Neurol.: 33,* 355 – 360, 1978.

Gunner-Svensson F, Jensen K: Frequency of mental disorders in old age. *Acta Psychiatr. Scand.: 53,* 283 – 297, 1976.

Hardeson DK, MacLachlan SH: Alzheimer's Disease. *J. Mental Sci.: 76,* 646 – 661, 1930.

Harris LI: Sex differences in spatial ability: possible environmental, genetic and neurological factors. In Kinsbourne M (Editor), *Asymmetric Function of the Brain.* New York: Cambridge University Press, 1978.

Harris LJ, Wagner NM, Wilkinson J: Cerebral hemispheric specialization in Braille discrimination: evidence from blind and sighted subjects. Paper presented at the XXI International Congress of Psychology, Paris, 1976.

Harwood E, Naylor GFK: Changes in the constitution of the WAIS intelligence pattern with advancing age. *Aust. J. Psychol.: 23,* 297 – 303, 1971.

Hatta T, Yamamoto M, Mito H: Functional hemisphere differences in auditory and tactile recognition in aged people. *Shinrigaku Kenkyu: 54,* 358 – 363, 1984.

Hecaen H, Ajuriaguerra de J, Massonet J: Les troubles visuoconstructifs par lesions parieto-occipitales droites. Role des perturbations vestibulaires. *Encephale: 1,* 122 – 179, 1951.

Hecaen H, Penfield W, Bertrand C, Malmo R: The syndrome of apractognosia due to lesions of the minor cerebral hemisphere. *Arch. Neurol. Psychiatr.: 75,* 400 – 434, 1956.

Heilman KM, Watson RT, Valenstein E: Neglect and related disorders. In Heilman KM, Valenstein E (Editors), *Clinical Neuropsychology,* 2nd Edition. Oxford: Oxford University Press, Ch.10, pp. 243 – 293, 1985.

Herman JF, Bruce PR: Adults' mental rotation of spatial information: effects of age, sex and cerebral laterality. *Exp. Aging Res.: 9(2),* 83 – 85, 1983.

Herman JF, Coyne AC: Mental manipulation of spatial information in young and elderly adults. *Dev. Psychol.: 16,* 537 – 538, 1980.

Holmes G: Disturbances of visual orientation. *Br. J. Ophthalmol.: 2,* 449 – 468 and 506 – 518, 1918.

Huckman MS, Fox JH, Topel JL: The validity of criteria for the evaluation of cerebral atrophy by computed tomography. *Radiology: 116,* 85 – 92, 1975.

Jackson JH: Case of large cerebral tumour without optic neuritis and with left hemiplegia and imperception. In Taylor J (Editor), *Selected Writings of John Hughlings Jackson.* London: Hodder and Stoughton, pp. 146 – 152, 1932.

Jarvik LF, Kallman FJ, Falek A: Intellectual changes in aged twins. *J. Gerontol.: 17,* 289 – 294, 1962.

Katzman R: Annual course, Neurology of Aging. Washington DC: American Academy of Neurology, April 26, 1982.

Kimura D: Left-right differences in the perception of melodies. *Q. J. Exp. Psychol.: 16,* 355 – 358, 1964.

Klodin VM: Verbal facilitation of perceptual-integrative performance in relation to age. Doctoral dissertation, Washington University, St.Louis, 1975.

Lees AJ, Smith E: Cognitive deficits in the early stages of Parkinson's Disease. *Brain: 106,* 257 – 270, 1983.

Lenneberg EH: *Biological Foundations of Language.* New York: John Wiley and Sons, 1967.

Lezak D: *Neuropsychological Assessment,* 2nd Edition. Oxford: Oxford University Press, 1982.

Light LL, Zelinski EM: Memory for spatial information in young and old adults. *Dev. Psychol.: 19,* 901 – 906, 1983.

Ludwig TE: Age differences in mental synthesis. *J. Gerontol.: 37,* 182 – 189, 1982.

Luria AR, Tsvetkova LS: The programming of constructive activity in local brain injuries. *Neuropsychologia: 2,* 95 – 108, 1964.

Lynch JC: The functional organization of posterior parietal association cortex. *Behav. Brain Sci.: 3,* 485 – 499, 1980.

McFie J, Zangwill OL: Visual-constructive disabilities associated with lesions of the left cerebral hemisphere. *Brain: 83,* 243 – 260, 1960

McFie J, Piercy MF, Zangwill OL: Visuo-spatial agnosia associated with lesions of the right cerebral hemisphere. *Brain: 73,* 167 – 190, 1950.

Marcel T, Rajan P: Lateral specialization for recognition of words and faces in good and poor readers. *Neuropsychologia: 13,* 489 – 497, 1975.

Mayeux R, Stern Y, Rosen J, Leventhal J: Depression, intellectual impairment and Parkinson's Disease. *Neurology: 31,* 645 – 650, 1981.

Mesulam MM: The functional anatomy and hemispheric specialization for directed attention. *Trends Neurosci.:* 384 – 387, 1983.

Meyer O: Ein-und doppelzeitige homonyme Hemianopsie mit Orientierungsstorungen. *Monatsschr. Psychiatr. Neurol.: 8,* 440 – 456, 1900.

Milner AD, Ockleford EM, Dewar W: Visuo-spatial performance following posterior parietal and lateral frontal lesions in stumptail Macaques. *Cortex: 13,* 350 – 360, 1977.

Milner B: Psychological aspects of focal epilepsy and its neurosurgical management. In Purpura DP, Penry JK, Walters RD (Editors), *Advances in Neurology, Vol. 8.* New York: Raven Press, Ch. 15 pp. 299 – 319, 1975.

Moore TE, Richards B, Hood J: Aging and the coding of spatial information. *J. Gerontol.: 39,* 210 – 212, 1984.

Moss MB, Albert MS: Alzheimer's disease and other dementing disorders. In Albert MS, Moss MB (Editors), *Geriatric*

Neuropsychology. New York: Guilford Press, pp. 145 – 178, 1988.

Muramoto O: Selective reminding in normal and demented aged people: auditory verbal versus visual spatial task. *Cortex: 20,* 461 – 478, 1984.

Nauta WJH: A proposed conceptual reorganisation of the basal ganglia and telencephalon. *Neuroscience: 4,* 1875 – 1881, 1979.

Nebes RD, Madden DJ, Berg WD: The effect of age on hemispheric asymmetry in visual and auditory identification. *Exp. Aging Res.: 9,* 87 – 91, 1983.

Nielson J: Geronto-psychiatric period-prevalence investigation in a geographically delimited population. *Acta Psychiatr. Scand.: 38,* 307 – 330, 1962.

Ogden JA: Antero-posterior interhemispheric differences in the loci of lesions producing visual hemineglect. *Brain Cognition: 4,* 59 – 75, 1985.

Ogden JA: Language and memory functions after long recovery periods in left-hemispherectomized subjects. *Neuropsychologia: 26,* 645 – 659, 1988.

Ogden JA: Visuospatial and other 'right-hemisphere' functions after long recovery periods in left-hemispherectomized subjects. *Neuropsychologia: 27,* 765 – 776, 1989.

Ogden JA, Growdon JH, Corkin S: Impaired ability of patients with Parkinson's Disease to shift conceptual set in visuospatial tasks. *Int. J. Neurosci.: 35,* 132, 1987.

O'Keefe J, Nadel L: *The Hippocampus as a Cognitive Map.* London: Oxford University Press, 1978.

Ornstein R, Johnstone J, Herron J, Swencionis C: Differential right hemisphere engagement in visuospatial tasks. *Neuropsychologia: 18,* 49 – 64, 1980.

Perez FL, Rivera VM, Meyer JS, Gay JRA, Taylor RL, Mather NT: Analysis of intellectual and cognitive performance in patient with multi-infarct dementia, vertebrobasilar insufficiency with dementia and Alzheimer's Disease. *J. Neurol. Neurosurg. Psychiatry: 38,* 533 – 540, 1975.

Perret E, Birri R: Aging, performance decrements, and differential cerebral involvement. In Corkin S, Davis KL, Growdon JH, Usdin E, Wurtman RJ (Editors), *Alzheimer's Disease: A Report of Progress (Aging, Vol. 19).* New York: Raven Press, pp. 133 – 139, 1982.

Peters A: Ueber die Beziehungen zwischen Orientierungstorungen und ein-und doppelseitiger Hemianopsie. *Arch. Augenheilk.: 32,* 175 – 187, 1896.

Pezdek K: Memory for items and their spatial locations by young and elderly adults. *Dev. Psychol.: 19,* 895 – 900, 1983.

Pick A: On reduplicative paramnesia. *Brain: 26,* 242 – 267, 1903.

Piercy M, Hecaen H, de Ajuriaguerra J: Constructional apraxia associated with unilateral cerebral lesions. Left and right sided cases compared. *Brain: 83,* 225 – 242, 1960.

Plude DJ, Milberg WP, Cerella J: Age differences in depicting and perceiving tridimensionality in simple line drawings. *Exp. Aging Res.: 12,* 221 – 225, 1986.

Pohl W: Dissociation of spatial discrimination deficits following frontal and parietal lesions in monkeys. *J. Comp. Physiol. Psychol.: 82* 227 – 239, 1973.

Potegal M: A note on spatial-motor deficits in patients with Huntington's disease: a test of a hypothesis. *Neuropsychologia: 9,* 233 – 235, 1971.

Proctor F, Riklan M, Cooper IS, Teuber H-L: Judgment of visual vertical and postural vertical by Parkinsonian patients. *Neurology: 14,* 287 – 293, 1964.

Rosen WG, Moks RC: Evolution of cognitive decline in dementia. In Corkin S, Davis KL, Growdon JH, Usdin E, Wurtman RJ (Editors), *Alzheimer's Disease: A Report of Progress (Aging, Vol. 19).* New York: Raven Press, pp. 133 – 139, 1982.

Semmes J, Weinstein S, Ghent L, Teuber HL: Correlates of impaired orientation in personal and extrapersonal space. *Brain: 86,* 747 – 772, 1963.

Semple SA, Smith CM, Swash M: The Alzheimer Disease Syndrome. In Corkin S, Davis KL, Growdon JH, Usdin E, Wurtman RJ (Editors), *Alzheimer's Disease: A Report of Progress (Aging, Vol. 19).* New York: Raven Press, pp. 93 – 107, 1982.

Sharpe MH, Cermak SA, Sax DS: Motor Planning in Parkinson patients. *Neuropsychologia: 21,* 455 – 462, 1983.

Shelton MD, Parsons OA, Leber WR: Verbal and visuospatial performance in male alcoholics: a test of the premature-aging hypothesis. *J. Consult. Clin. Psychol.: 52,* 200 – 206, April 1984.

Shepard RN, Metzler J: Mental rotation of three-dimensional objects. *Science: 171,* 701 – 703, 1971.

Verity CM, Strauss EH, Moyes PD, Wada JA, Dunn HG, Lapointe JS: Long-term follow-up after cerebral hemispherectomy: neurophysiologic, radiologic and psychological findings. *Neurology: 32,* 629 – 639, 1982.

Veroff A: The neuropsychology of aging. *Psychol. Res.: 41,* 259 – 268, 1980.

Weinstein EA: Reduplicative phenomena. In Vinken PJ, Bruyn GW (Editors), *Handbook of Neurology.* Amsterdam: North-Holland Publishing Company, Volume 3, 1969.

Wernicke C: *Der Aphasische Symptomencomplex.* Breslau: Cohn and Weigart, 1874.

Wilbrand H. Ein Fall von Seelenblindheit und Hemianopsie mit Sections-Befund. *Dtsch Z. Nervenheilk.: 2,* 361 – 387, 1892.

Witelson SF: Hemispheric specialization for linguistic and nonlinguistic tactual perception using a dichotomous stimulation technique. *Cortex: 10,* 3 – 17, 1974.

Witelson SF: Developmental dyslexia: two right hemispheres and none left. *Science: 195, 309 – 311,* 1977.

Woods BT, Teuber HL: Early onset of complementary specialization of cerebral hemispheres in man. *Trans. Am. Neurol. Assoc.: 98,* 113 – 115, 1973.

© 1990 Elsevier Science Publishers B.V. (Biomedical Division)
Handbook of Neuropsychology, Vol. 4
F. Boller and J. Grafman (Eds)

CHAPTER 14

Abstract thought in aging and age-related neurological disease

Alice Cronin-Golomb

Department of Psychology, Boston University, Boston, MA, U.S.A.

Introduction

Abstract thought, unlike memory, language or visuospatial function, has not benefitted from sufficiently strict theoretical, or even operational, definition to permit its systematic assessment in normal or neurological populations. Although neuropsychological examination often includes a test or two of 'abstract reasoning', this term is rarely defined, and the function is only imperfectly measured by tasks with high demands on memory, attention, perception or language skills. Moreover, even when individual tests are chosen carefully, the domain remains unexplored in any depth or breadth. This state of affairs is all the more surprising because clinicians are often readily able to recognize a deficit in abstract processes in their patients. Luria's bedside evaluations, for example, revealed in a short time at least as much about a patient's abstracting abilities as does many a standard, lengthy neuropsychological examination. The paradox inherent to our assessment of the neurologically impaired patient, then, consists of these two facts: we have not defined what it means to think abstractly, and we recognize a loss of this ability when we see it.

An explanation for the uncertainty in definition derives from the different historical treatments of abstract thought in philosophy and neurology (see Pikas, 1966, for a review). Beginning with Aristotle's concept of 'abstrahere', literally 'taking away', abstraction was defined as the process whereby the particulars of stimuli were disregarded and common features extracted. The first experimental studies by the philosopher-psychologists of the beginning of this century focussed on what we now call discrimination tasks. Methods of investigation ranged from introspection, in the early studies, to later behavioristic or associationistic techniques, as in C.L. Hull's investigations (1920). What united these otherwise disparate attempts to examine abstract processes was the common Aristotelian definition of abstraction.

The critical shift in the definition of abstract thought occurred with the works of the clinician Kurt Goldstein and his colleagues (e.g., Goldstein and Scheerer, 1941). Whereas previously the *process* of abstraction was the object of study, Goldstein placed emphasis on the nature of the *products* of the abstraction process. The less based on sensory experience, the more symbolic and representational the product, the more 'abstract' it was considered; by contrast, the more directly related the product was to sensory information, the more 'concrete' it was deemed. Goldstein thus proposed a dichotomy of 'attitude', abstract versus concrete, to describe the thought patterns of individuals in experimental as well as everyday situations, especially of individuals who had undergone neurological insult. Specifically, he noted that impairment of the 'abstract attitude' was especially clear in cases of lesions to the frontal lobes (Goldstein, 1963). Neuropsychologists continue to invoke Goldstein's dichotomy whenever they ask subjects to interpret familiar proverbs, then evaluate the responses along this abstract/concrete dimension.

As a consequence of these historical forces, there now exists a division of interest within psychological research on abstract thought; the recognition of the existence of this division may help to organize, if not unify, the field. On the one hand are workers who are mostly interested in the process of abstraction. Studies of categorization, including the child's development of basic-level categories (e.g., Rosch et al., 1976), fall into this area, as do many studies of problem-solving. On the other hand are investigators who examine the product of the abstraction process, or the hierarchy of the abstract: these workers, mostly neuropsychologists, examine concept formation and comprehension in terms of the quality of the concept formed. These two streams of research are not, of course, mutually exclusive. Categorization occurs not only at a basic level, emphasizing the process, but also at super- and subordinate levels, thus embedding the process within the abstract/concrete hierarchy. For concept formation, one wishes to know not only if the subject can use an abstract (as opposed to concrete) basis for forming a concept, but also whether or not the subject can control the process of abstraction by shifting from one way of organizing information to form a concept to another (abstract *or* concrete) way of organizing the same information to attain a different concept.

Because of the extensive crossing of the streams of research on abstract processes and products, it would appear forced and not terribly enlightening to attempt to organize the neuropsychological literature into the two camps as defined. A more fruitful strategy may be to view the large number of relevant studies in the context of a few broad topics that can accommodate both approaches. The topics I have chosen – concept formation, conceptual set-shifting, and problem-solving – emerged from a review of the rich literature on normal aging and abstract thought. What we feel it means to think abstractly – by whatever definition – is just what appears to be deficient in many normal elderly people, according to gerontological psychology. A main question posed by this literature is not 'What is abstract thought?', but rather the more empirically tractable, 'Is abstract thought dissociable from memory, attention, and other cognitive domains that are subject to change with age?'

Normal aging

A number of excellent articles have reviewed the literature on normal aging and abstract thought. Among the contributions of the past several years, chapters by the following authors are especially recommended: Arenberg (1982), Botwinick (1984a,b), Denney (1982), Giambra and Arenberg (1980), Kausler (1982a,b), Rabbitt (1977), Reese and Rodeheaver (1985) and Salthouse (1985).

Concept formation and shifting

Concept formation involves the ability to attain a new concept. Conceptual set-shifting describes the initiation of a new concept together with the suppression of a previously employed concept which is no longer appropriate to the task. There is much overlap between these two areas of study. By design, the most widely used neuropsychological measures of concept formation also assess the ability to shift conceptual set. In studies of normal aging, there has been some success in distinguishing between concept formation and shifting. Among the neurological disorders, only in Parkinson's disease have the two functions been distinguished behaviorally, as will be described in subsequent sections of this chapter.

Two types of test are commonly used to assess concept formation in normal aging and in neurological populations: sorting tasks and fluency measures. Sorting tasks are exemplified by the Wisconsin Card Sort Test (WCST) (Berg 1948; Grant and Berg 1948), in which the subject is required to sort cards according to color, shape or number, although the specific concept is not explicitly stated. The subject receives positive or negative feedback from the examiner with regard to the success of the sorting of each card according to the correct concept (e.g., size). At a designated point (unspecified to the subject), a new concept (e.g., color) becomes the basis for further sorting. The subject must infer the new concept from feedback as to the accuracy of the subsequent sorting. Continued success depends upon suppression of the initial concept, which is no longer reinforced (size), in favor of the new concept (color). Performance is measured in number of categories completed (i.e., number of different sorts, with one complete sort comprising a specific number of cards which form a common conceptual set) and in number of cards sorted. Examples of other categorization tasks include Weigl's sorting test (Weigl, 1941) and the Halstead Category Test (Halstead, 1947). In Weigl's test and its modifications, subjects sort numerous blocks of various sizes, colors, shapes and other dimensions in any one way they choose; thereafter, they are asked to sort the blocks again, along a dimension different from that used in the first sort. Both the ability to abstract information and the abstraction product itself are measured in this type of test, which further assesses the ability to shift conceptual set.

Verbal fluency measures are divided into tests of semantic (category) and symbolic (letter) fluency (e.g., Newcombe, 1969; Benton and Hamsher, 1976; respectively). Semantic and symbolic fluency involve, respectively, naming as many members of a given category (e.g., animals, vehicles) as possible in a prescribed period of time, or as many words as possible beginning with a given letter. Nonverbal or design fluency involves the construction of as many novel forms from a given number of elementary shapes or lines as possible within a time limit (Jones-Gotman and Milner, 1977). Fluency tests may additionally measure set-shifting whenever subjects are called upon to provide exemplars of more than one category; e.g., 'birds' followed by 'articles of clothing'. Perseverative errors, mainly in the form of intrusion from previously elicited categories, characterize deficits in the ability to shift set.

Several other neuropsychological tests measure different aspects of concept formation. The Picture Arrangement subtest of the Wechsler Adult Intelligence Scale – Revised (WAIS-R) (Wechsler, 1981) requires the arrangement in a logical order of a series of cartoon pictures so as to tell a story. The task thus requires the formation and maintenance of a reasonable story concept. The Concept Comprehension Test (CCT) (Cronin-Golomb, 1986a,b) involves the matching of pictures related on the basis of a specific concrete or abstract concept. The subject must understand the concept implied by the best possible match within a trial in order to eliminate from contention two other possible matches (Fig. 1). Somewhat similar to the CCT but using a verbal format is the WAIS-R Similarities subtest, in which the subject verbally describes how two words are related conceptually. Finally, various forms of a Proverbs Test (e.g., Gorham, 1956) assess the comprehension of common proverbs by requiring subjects to explain the proverbs in their own words, or to indicate from a choice ar-

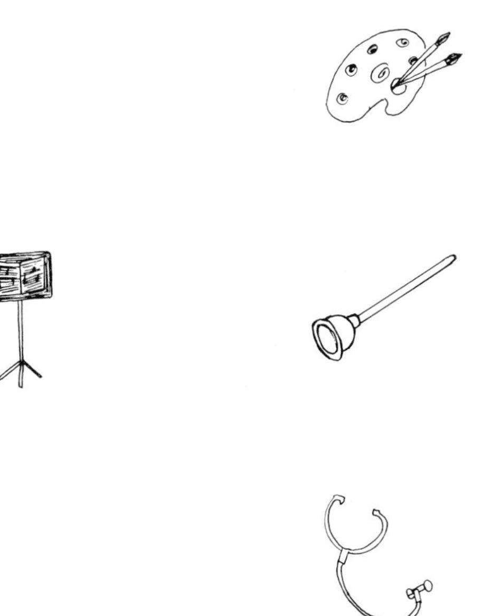

Fig. 1. A sample from the Concept Comprehension Test. The subject points to the member of the response array (right) that goes best with the target (left). Here, the music stand is related to the palette on the basis of 'art'.

ray the verbal interpretation that best captures the concept implied by the proverb.

Healthy elderly subjects appear to be impaired for some types of concept formation, and they may or may not have an additional deficit in set shifting performance relative to young adults. Old individuals showed limited concept attainment on such categorization tasks as Weigl's blocks (Thaler, 1956) and Halstead's Category Test (Mack and Carlson, 1978). Concept attainment was better when the sorting principle was provided by the examiner than when it was developed by the subject (Flicker et al., 1986). Elderly people were also impaired on non-sorting tests of concept formation, including the WAIS Picture Arrangement subtest (Eisdorfer and Cohen, 1961; Kausler, 1982b). In contrast to measures that use nonverbal stimuli, verbal tasks of concept attainment appear to be performed well with age. For example, it is generally agreed that verbal fluency is preserved in elderly individuals (Drachman and Leavitt, 1972; Kausler, 1982b; Schaie and Labouvie-Vief, 1974). A 'classic aging pattern' has been demonstrated repeatedly through use of multi-scale intelligence tests such as Primary Mental Abilities (Thurstone and Thurstone, 1962) or the WAIS: verbal ('crystallized') skills are maintained well with age relative to many nonverbal ('performance' or 'fluid') reasoning abilities (e.g., Birren, 1964; Botwinick, 1984a; Green, 1969; Kausler, 1982b; Schaie and Labouvie-Vief, 1974).

The question arises as to whether successful performance on a given task of concept formation may be predicted simply on the basis of the type of stimulus material employed – i.e., verbal or nonverbal – or, instead, whether different features of the task underlie the reported results. Findings of age effects for tasks involving verbal material suggest that the verbal – nonverbal distinction is too simplistic a basis for predicting performance on specific tasks at different ages: old people give more concrete verbal responses and are therefore less successful than young adults at proverb interpretation (Bromley, 1957), and performance by the aged is significantly worse than that of young adults on the verbal Similarities subtest of the WAIS (Doppelt and Wallace, 1955; Whelihan and Lesher, 1985). In inferring concepts from letter strings, old people were not worse overall, but did show error patterns different from those of young people (Wetherick, 1966). Cornelius (1984) has demonstrated that the nonverbal 'fluid' tasks are perceived by both young and old individuals as involving material that is less familiar and more difficult than in verbal, crystallized tasks. Along these lines, Mack and Carlson (1978) attributed the poor performance of healthy elderly subjects on Halstead's Category Test to task complexity, rather than to difficulty in understanding concepts.

With regard to conceptual set-shifting, findings are equivocal, with some researchers maintaining that the ability to shift set does not change with age (Boyarsky and Eisdorfer, 1972; Coppinger and Nehrke, 1972; Nehrke and Coppinger, 1971; Nehrke and Sutterer, 1978; Rogers et al., 1976), and others reporting that elderly subjects cling rigidly to inappropriate concepts that had been reinforced in earlier trials (Heglin, 1956; Offenbach, 1974; Wetherick, 1965; Witte, 1971). It has been noted that old people are less able than young to reverse ambiguous figures (Botwinick et al., 1959; Heath and Orbach, 1963), indicating that perceptual organization, and consequently shifts in such organization, may become less flexible with age (Rabbitt, 1977). Arenberg (1968) suggested that the difficulty in set-shifting sometimes experienced by old people may disappear when the memory load of the task is reduced. Rabbitt (1977) further postulated that shifts may handicap the performance of aged individuals only if the shifts incidentally increase task complexity. The latter point is well illustrated by a study in which performance of the Wisconsin Card Sort Test improved greatly when the elderly subjects were trained to verbalize the stimulus dimensions that had been reinforced (Crovitz, 1966). Haaland et al. (1987), assessing WCST performance in a group of well-educated, medically healthy adults ranging in age from 64 to 87, found a significant age effect for only 2 of the 6 performance measures (number of categories attained and total errors). Further, this effect occurred only for the oldest group (ages 80 – 87). None of the elderly groups in this study made more perseverative errors than did a group of young adults. On the WCST, then, there is some evidence for an age-related impairment in concept formation, but there is no direct support for a coincidental deficit in set-shifting.

In brief, the bulk of the evidence points to some impairment in concept formation with age, particularly when nonverbal materials are used in a task. In contrast, set-shifting is not always observed to be impaired and, where it is, the deficit may be attributable to factors such as perceptual organization, memory load or task complexity, rather than to diminished set-shifting ability in itself.

Problem-solving

Problem-solving, like abstract thought in general, refers to the macroscopic behavior of a multicomponential system. Information-processing models of human problem-solving are based on the assumptions that several different processes occur in the course of solving a problem, and that these processes can be studied independently of each other to some significant extent (e.g., Newell and Simon, 1972). Although these models differ in specifics, most incorporate the following processes: (1) perception of the nature of the problem (orientation; identification of the initial state); (2) retrieval of relevant information from long-term memory; storage in short-term memory (or working memory) as the information is applied to the current problem; and the generation and testing of hypotheses; (3) comparison of the generated solution with criteria for solution given at the outset of the problem, followed by (a) recognition of the correct solution, or (b) recognition that the problem remains unsolved, and subsequent generation of another strategy. Within this broadly conceived framework, problems may vary tremendously in their processing requirements.

In spite of the great variety of tasks employed and the lack of explicit organizing principles for them, the assessment of problem-solving in elderly individuals is unified by a result common to the majority of studies: the ability to solve problems diminishes with age. A sampling, by no means exhaustive, of the types of problem on which old subjects perform poorly relative to young adults includes examples of logical reasoning, such as syllogisms (Friend and Zubek, 1958; Wright, 1981) and the sequencing of actions toward a defined goal (Allamanno et al., 1987; Arenberg, 1974; Young, 1966); Piagetian conceptualization tasks (reviewed in Denney, 1982; Kausler, 1982a; Reese and Rodeheaver, 1985); ‘twenty questions’, in which hypotheses developed by elderly subjects do not effectively constrain the set of possible solutions (Denney and Denney, 1973, 1982); hypothesis-testing using abstract stimuli (Offenbach, 1974) or concrete stimuli (Arenberg, 1968; Hayslip and Sterns, 1979); and a variety of series-completion tasks (reviewed in Salthouse and Prill, 1987), including Raven's Progressive Matrices (reviewed in Kausler, 1982b) and the Hukok Logical Thinking Matrices Test (Cronin-Golomb et al., 1986, 1987b), for the latter of which the mean score of a healthy elderly group was substantially lower than scores taken from norms obtained (by Daryn, 1977) with young adults.

Old people appear to be handicapped especially at solving problems that include irrelevant (Hoyer et al., 1979) or redundant information (Arensberg, 1968; but see Wetherick, 1964, for a study in which the performance of elderly subjects was not affected deleteriously by non-informative or redundant information). Several researchers have reported that elderly individuals are more competent in dealing with ‘real-life’ situations and practical problems than with problems devised for the laboratory, although impairment relative to young people on all types of these tests may still be seen (Denney, 1982; Horn, 1982; Rabbit, 1977; Reese and Rodeheaver, 1985; see Cornelius and Caspi, 1987, for a study of everyday problem-solving in which performance did not decline with age).

Detailed studies of how an individual goes about solving a given problem in its intellectual, motivational and social context (Giambra and Arenberg, 1980; Greeno, 1989) may provide explanations for such differences in performance of various kinds of problem by elderly people.

There is general agreement that a variety of factors unrelated to age, or factors secondary to increasing age, probably account for some proportion of the impairments on specific problem-solving tasks that have been observed in old adults. Important variables include general health, level of education, visual acuity, memory, speed of motor response, motivation, and other extrinsic factors (e.g., Botwinick, 1984a,b; Giambra and Arenberg, 1980; Green, 1969; Jones, 1959; Rabbitt, 1977; Reese and Rodeheaver, 1985; Rowe and Kahn, 1987; Schaie and Labouvie-Vief, 1974; Wright, 1981). There do not appear to be significant sex differences with age for most tasks of problem-solving ability that have been studied (e.g., Reese and Rodeheaver, 1985). In terms of information-processing models, old people may be handicapped at each stage of processing. (1) Orientation to the problem will be affected by verbal and visuospatial demands of the task, and by the ability to ignore irrelevant information. (2) Application of stored knowledge to the generation and testing of hypotheses will depend on the speed and integrity of memory systems, and on the ability to discover task-appropriate heuristics. (3) Recognition of an incorrect solution followed by generation of a new strategy will be related to the ability to shift conceptual set. (For an information-processing analysis of numerous studies of problem-solving in aging, see Kausler, 1982b). It appears that old people can be trained in the use of strategies that improve performance on particular tasks (reviewed in Botwinick, 1984a,b; Denney, 1982; Giambra and Arenberg, 1980; Labouvie-Vief, 1985), although the extent to which the improvement may generalize to other tasks and the longevity of the training effects are for the most part yet to be established.

Neuroanatomical correlations and implications

Brain changes occur at many levels with age. Cortical atrophy presents as widening of sulci, narrowing of gyri, decreased brain weight (Brody, 1978; Terry, 1978a; Terry et al., 1987) and increased ventricular size (Jacobs et al., 1978). The number of cortical cells declines (Brody, 1978; Terry, 1978a), and the dendritic spines of brain neurons become less extensive (Nandy, 1978). Activity declines for several neurotransmitters and their associated enzymes, including the monoamines (acetylcholine, dopamine and norepinephrine) as well as other systems (e.g., GABA) (McGeer, 1978; Ordy et al., 1975; Terry, 1978a). At the cellular level, neuritic plaques and neurofibrillary tangles are frequently present (Brizzee et al., 1975; Terry, 1978b). Physiological changes include slowing on the EEG of the alpha rhythm and increased prevalence of the slower theta and delta waves (Busse, 1978). Bioelectric indices (e.g., evoked potentials) provide evidence for deficits in arousal mechanisms with age (Albert and Kaplan, 1980). Decreases in cerebral blood flow, oxygen consumption and glucose metabolism may also be observed (Butler, 1978; Sokoloff, 1978). Several of these and other age-related changes of the brain's anatomy and physiology have been documented in two useful collections of papers, edited by Brody et al. (1975) and Katzman et al. (1978). Coleman and Flood (1987) have provided an excellent recent review of brain anatomical changes with age.

Although most studies find age-related changes throughout the brain, some researchers have provided evidence linking anatomical or physiological alterations with specific regions. Brody (1978), for example, documented a narrowing of the gyri and widening of the sulci especially in the fronto-temporal cortex. A diminished number of cortical cells in elderly individuals, relative to young adults, was found to occur predominantly in the superior frontal, superior temporal and precentral gyri, and in visual cortex. No significant cell loss was seen in the postcentral or inferior temporal gyri. The loss of cells appeared to occur continuously with age, with a total drop of 40%, at least for the frontal and temporal areas, observed by the ninth decade. Using sensitive image-analysis apparatus, Terry et al. (1987) determined that the magnitude of neuronal loss with age is less than Brody's figures indicated. Rather than cell loss, this group found a shrinkage of large neurons with a consequent increase in numbers of small neurons with age. In agreement with Brody, these changes were found to be localized more strongly to the frontal and temporal lobes than to parietal cortex. Cortical thinning was observed by Terry et al. in the midfrontal and superior temporal regions, and the number of glia appeared to increase with age in these areas but not in the inferior parietal cortex. Structural changes have been documented in third-layer pyramidal cells in prefrontal and superior temporal cortex in aged brains, including swelling and lumpiness of the soma and proximal dendrites, and progressive loss of horizontal dendrite masses (Scheibel and Scheibel, 1975). Besides cerebral cortex, age-related cell loss has been documented as well for hippocampus, amygdala, cerebellum and certain subcortical structures (reviewed in Coleman and Flood, 1987), including the locus coeruleus (Brody, 1978) and the substantia nigra (McGeer, 1978).

It was noted by Busse (1978) that temporal lobe foci are often observed on the irregular (relative to young normal) EEG records of elderly groups. Bioelectric measures of the activity of the autonomic nervous system (average evoked potential) and the central nervous system (galvanic skin response) indicate deficits in arousal with age; by virtue of the connectivity of the frontal lobes with the tegmentum and the subthalamic region (Nauta, 1971), it has been inferred that the frontal system may be impaired in the normal elderly (reviewed in Albert and Kaplan, 1980).

Kral (1978) has proposed that normal age-related changes, if they spare the hippocampal-fornix-mamillary body system, may be responsible for what he has called benign senescent forgetfulness, a condition in which neuropathological changes and their behavioral correlates are quantitatively milder, if not necessarily qualitatively different from those in Alzheimer's disease.

The pattern of cell loss and physiological change described above can account only poorly for the pattern of abstract thought observed in healthy elderly subjects. At first glance, the frontal lobes appear to be especially vulnerable to the effects of aging. Associated with this area are cell loss and shrinkage, intracellular abnormalities and impairments in arousal, as cited above, as well as other specific behavioral deficits (Albert and Kaplan, 1980). In a cross-sectional study, increasing age was associated with decline in blood flow to the prefrontal cortex, among other cortical areas (Shaw et al., 1984). The frontal lobes have been implicated in the ability to form concepts and to shift set (e.g., Drewe, 1974; Milner, 1963; Nelson, 1976). Results from studies of the neuropathology of the frontal lobes in normal aging and of behavioral changes in patients with frontal-lobe damage, taken together, suggest an anatomical basis for changes in behavior with age. Surprisingly, however, the predicted changes in frontally mediated behaviors do not occur reliably in normal aging, as a review of the relevant literature in gerontological psychology will attest. In particular, set-shifting, the quintessential frontally mediated behavior, is not consistently observed to be impaired with age. With regard to problem-solving ability, which, by contrast with concept formation and set-shifting, almost certainly diminishes with age, little work has been done on subjects with focal neurological damage. Shallice (1982) reported that subjects with left anterior lesions were impaired on a problem-solving task involving the rule-governed movement of beads on sticks; it is not known whether healthy old people perform normally relative to young adults on similar tasks. As discussed earlier, problem-solving ability seems likely to involve multiple processing components and hence to engage multiple regions of the brain besides the frontal lobes, including the hippocampus (involved in memory) and the locus coeruleus (involved in general attention), both of which structures appear to suffer cell loss in normal aging.

Parkinson's disease

Parkinson's disease (PD), a disorder of the basal ganglia and some subcortical nuclei, has come in recent years to be associated with specific cognitive deficits in the non-demented patient (e.g. Growdon and Corkin, 1986; Sagar, 1987). Individuals with PD may show disorders of memory and visuospatial ability, although linguistic skills appear to be relatively normal. Impairment is observed consistently in the domain of abstract thought.

Concept formation and shifting

With regard to concept formation in PD, the results of several studies taken together are equivocal, with some finding evidence for a deficit and others reporting normal performance. Conceptual set-shifting, by contrast, appears almost unequivocally to be impaired in PD.

On the Halstead Category Test, in which the subject must find a series of correct principles for categorizing a large number of visual stimuli, patients with PD of short disease duration performed normally, but were impaired relative to normal when disease duration exceeded 6 years (Matthews and Haaland, 1979). Researchers consistently observe a deficit in performance by patients with PD on the Wisconsin Card Sorting Test (WCST), relative to normal subjects (Bowen et al., 1975; Corkin et al., 1982; Gotham et al., 1986; Kimura et al., 1987; Lees and Smith, 1983; Stern and Mayeux, 1986; Taylor et al., 1986; also Dubois et al., 1988, and Pillon et al., 1986, on a modified Card Sort Test). PD patients were also impaired on the WCST relative to subjects with Alzheimer's disease who were matched to the PD group for mild cognitive decline (Corkin et al., 1982). Most of these workers have attributed the impaired performance on the WCST to a diminished ability of the subject with PD to shift from one concept to another, rather than to a deficit in concept formation itself.

Bowen (1976; and Bowen et al., 1975), who reported that patients with PD both form fewer concepts than do normal subjects and show difficulty in shifting to new concepts, related that many subjects with PD can verbalize the correct concept without being able to use this information to sort consistently according to that same concept (Bowen et al., 1975). This dissociation between verbal awareness and task performance has been observed as well by Lees and Smith (1983), Flowers and Robertson (1985) and Taylor et al. (1986), and suggests that concept formation is intact in PD relative to implementation of knowledge of a concept in sorting tasks. Some investigators who have suggested that concept formation is normal in PD relative to the ability to shift conceptual set have also described an improvement in performance by patients with PD when the rules of concept formation were explicit, rather than implicit in the type of feedback given by the examiner as sorting occurs (Flowers and Robertson, 1985; Taylor et al., 1986).

There are suggestions from non-sorting, non-fluency tasks that concept formation, as well as shifting, may be impaired in PD. Ogden et al. (1987) reported that subjects with PD are impaired on the WAIS-R Picture Arrangement subtest, indicating a possible difficulty in forming an initial story concept. Alternatively, the observed deficit could reflect a problem in shifting from an initial cognitive plan, which had been formed on the basis of information derived from the first one or two pictures, to a new plan incorporating the new picture elements in some logically unified whole. Growdon et al. (1987), Ledesma et al., (1986), Loranger et al. (1972) and Sullivan et al. (1985) likewise found PD deficits on this task; Growdon et al.'s nondemented patient group displayed a significant decline in performance with disease severity, on both timed and untimed versions of the task. Initial performance on Picture Arrangement was poor for a group of patients with PD, whose overall Performance IQ score on the WAIS, presumably including the Picture Arrangement subscore, improved temporarily with levodopa treatment. Testing was untimed under both the initial and drug conditions for this study (Loranger et al., 1975). Donnelly and Chase (1973) also observed improved Picture Arrangement subscores with levodopa therapy, although the magnitude of change was so small as to be explainable in terms of a practice effect. Cronin-Golomb et al. (1987a,b) noted impaired performance by patients with PD relative to control subjects on the Concept Comprehension Test (CCT). The patients performed slightly deficiently on the CCT subtest that assesses comprehension of abstract concepts, contrasting with their normal performance on the subtest involving concrete concepts. The CCT does not involve shifting of conceptual set, suggesting again the possibility of a specific deficit in concept formation or comprehension in patients with PD.

Neither Picture Arrangement nor the CCT would appear to engage predominantly verbal or visuospatial abilities. These tests are not subject, therefore, to the admonition of Taylor et al. (1986), that performance on tasks which are strongly lateralized to the right or left cerebral hemisphere will be affected by the side of initial or predominant parkinsonian involvement. Indeed, the right and left hemispheres of commissurotomized patients perform similarly to each other on the CCT (Cronin-Golomb, 1986a). In contrast, the Similarities subtest of the WAIS is completely verbal in format; different proportions of right- and left hemiparkinsonian individuals in a mixed subject pool could conceivably account for the differing results reported for this test, including impaired (Ledesma et al., 1986; Pillon et al., 1986; Reitan and Boll, 1971), normal (Cools et al., 1984; Loranger et al., 1972; Ransmayr et al., 1986) or superior performance (Asso, 1969) relative to control subjects. This situation would also hold for other expressly verbal tasks. Boller (1980; and Boller et al., 1980) and Celesia and Wanamaker (1972) found that demented subjects with PD were impaired on such tests as Similarities/Differences and proverb interpretation. Boller's patient group had been compared to normal subjects and to nondemented patients. Celesia and Wanamaker further described their subjects as showing deficits in abstract thinking and concept formation, although the measures used for assessment of these functions were not described. Garron et al. (1972) reported that a subset of patients with PD performed poorly on a test of comprehension of semantic classes. Semantic retrieval was found to be depressed in PD (Matison et al., 1982), but the same subjects were normal on the WAIS Vocabulary subtest, suggesting the lack of a general verbal deficit and hence the unviability of any explanation based on initial or predominant dysfunction of the left hemisphere.

A number of investigators have found indications of specific impairment in conceptual set-shifting in PD, regardless of the integrity of concept formation in these patients. Flowers and Robertson (1985) described their results with the Odd Man Out test, in which the subject chooses which one of the three or four presented items does not fit the concept being exercised; a second concept periodically alternates with the first one. When subjects with PD erred on this test, they did not choose randomly from the three- or four-choice response array, but rather confused the two specific items related to the two concepts that were being used alternately. That is, they apparently had no difficulty in forming the two different concepts; the deficit seemed to lie instead in the suppression of one response set in favor of another. Inability to suppress a competing conceptual set has also been cited by Lees and Smith (1983) and Bowen et al. (1975) as contributing to the sorting deficit of PD. A similar interpretation may be applied to Talland's results (1962), which described an inability of patients with PD to suppress the shift between alternating configurations of a Necker cube. The observation has also been made by some investigators that patients with PD are impaired on the Stroop Word-Color Test (Stroop 1935), which requires the subject to suppress the perceived name of a color written in ink of a different color (e.g., the word 'blue,' written in red ink) and to read aloud the ink color only ('red') (Stern and Langston, 1985; but Cools et al., 1984, and Growdon et al., 1987, have reported normal Stroop performance in PD). In a careful study of medicated and unmedicated patients with PD, Downes et al. (in press) described deficient performance as occurring when the response set included exemplars from a previously irrelevant stimulus dimension (extra-dimensional shift), whereas the patients responded normally to novel exemplars of a previously relevant dimension (intra-dimensional shift).

The inability to suppress alternative responses associated with competing conceptual sets would appear to predict a significant presence of errors involving perseveration, i.e., responses appropriate to one conceptual set which appear, inappropriately, during the presentation of the alternative conceptual set. Such errors have been found in PD by Lees and Smith (1983) on the WCST and on a measure of symbolic verbal fluency, by Oyebode et al. (1986), also for symbolic fluency, by Flowers and Robertson (1985) on the Odd Man Out test, and by Sandson and Albert (1987) on Luria's test of alternating labels. Severe perseverative behavior on the WCST was observed by Kimura et al. (1987) for twin brothers with familial fatal parkinsonism. Celesia and Wanamaker (1972) reported 'graphic perseveration' in their demented patients. Other workers, however, have found no predominance of perseverative errors on sorting tasks (Bowen et al., 1975; Cools et al., 1984; Corkin et al., 1982; Taylor et al., 1986). Similarly, perseverative errors in patients with PD, with or without dementia, did not occur more frequently than normal on a tactile reversal learning task (Freedman and Oscar-Berman, 1987), or on a task that involved intra- and extra-dimensional shifting of relevant stimulus dimensions (Downes et al., in press).

The extent of perseveration was not reported for several studies that described fluency deficits in PD relative to normal subjects (Semantic fluency: Cools et al., 1984; Growdon et al., 1987; Matison et al., 1982; Stern and Langston, 1985; Symbolic fluency: Taylor et al., 1986; Semantic/symbolic [results not differentiated]: Dubois et al., 1988; Pillon et al., 1986; Ideational fluency: Wilson et al., 1987). The issue is further complicated by the fact that some investigators have found no deficit in PD on symbolic verbal fluency (Growdon et al., 1987; Matison et al., 1982; Taylor et al., 1986) or nonverbal fluency (Taylor et al., 1986); indeed, one report described a slight superiority of the PD group relative to healthy control subjects for symbolic fluency (Gainotti et al., 1980).

Taylor and colleagues (1986) have offered a possible explanation for the inconsistency in findings with regard to perseverative errors on the WCST in terms of the use of different criteria in the measurement of perseveration. When these workers applied common criteria (as per Milner, 1963) to their own results and to the results of Lees and Smith (1983), who had reported the presence of perseverative errors, no evidence of perseveration was seen for either study. It is not known whether this argument for the use of common scoring criteria could also reconcile with Taylor et al.'s position the findings of intrusion errors by Bowen et al. (1975) and Flowers and Robertson (1985). Sandson and Albert (1987) have suggested that set-shifting dysfunction ('stuck-in-set') may be considered to be in itself a type of perseverative behavior, distinguishable from the abnormal production of intrusion errors ('recurrent perseveration') and from abnormal prolongation of current behavior ('continuous perseveration'). These investigators have found that patients with PD are subject especially to 'stuck-in-set' relative to recurrent or continuous perseveration. Sandson and Albert's taxonomy of perseverative behavior, which associates each of the three behavioral categories with anatomical, neuropsychological and pharmacological factors, may prove useful in providing a framework for future investigations to address the unresolved issue of perseverative behavior in PD.

The second inconsistency in findings, with regard to normality of performance in PD on fluency tests, was also addressed by Taylor et al.

(1986). When their patients, who, as a group, appeared to be normal on a fluency task, were divided into subgroups of patients with initial or predominant right-sided and left-sided motor symptoms (indicating dysfunction of the contralateral cerebral hemisphere), the former group did show a fluency deficit. This result is not unexpected in the light of left hemisphere dominance for many verbal processes in the majority of right-handed people. Further, the literature includes several reports of differential performance on particular cognitive tasks by left and right hemiparkinsonian patients which may be explained in terms of normal hemispheric specialization (Bentin et al., 1981; Bowen et al., 1972a,b; Direnfeld et al., 1984; Proctor et al., 1964; Riklan and Levita, 1964). Taylor et al. (1986) suggested that the PD group tested by Lees and Smith (1983) may have included a disproportionate number of right hemiparkinsonians, accounting for the fluency deficit reflected in the total-group mean performance. Arguing against Taylor et al.'s interpretation are the results of Oyebode et al. (1986), who did not find differences in performance by left and right hemiparkinsonians on a variety of cognitive measures, including symbolic fluency.

The impairment in PD of conceptual set-shifting ability that has been demonstrated amply with sorting tests such as the WCST and, to a lesser extent, with fluency measures is further underscored by results of studies using a variety of non-sorting, non-fluency tasks. Cools et al. (1984) found that subjects with PD, relative to normal subjects, produced a smaller percentage of correct responses after a finger-pushing sequence had been changed from an initial sequence. Talland and Schwab (1964) observed a deficit relative to normal when patients with PD engaged in a letter-cancelling task according to changing criteria for cancellation. In copying the Rey-Osterrieth Complex Figure, patients with PD seemed unable to move beyond a piecemeal approach, and seemed unable to perceive the figure as a whole; Ogden et al. (1987) interpreted both this method of copying the figure and the similarly poor performance by the same patients on the WAIS-R Picture Arrangement subtest in terms of an inability to shift from an initial cognitive set to a set more appropriate to the particular task. On the Trail Making Test, which involves conceptual set-shifting and visual tracking, PD groups were found to be impaired relative to normal (Ledesma et al., 1986; Matthews and Haaland, 1979; Pirozzolo et al., 1982; but see Taylor et al., 1986, for a study that found no impairment in the PD group using the same task. The discrepancy in results could conceivably involve the visual tracking demands of the task, as described by Pirozzolo's group.) Tactile reversal learning was reported to be deficient in patients with PD and dementia, though not in nondemented individuals with PD, relative to healthy control subjects (Freedman and Oscar-Berman, 1987). Wilson et al. (1987) have also reported on set-shifting tasks performed normally by nondemented patients with PD, including the description of unconventional uses for common objects, and the grouping and regrouping of a set of words by different categories. These workers described a dissociation within executive function in PD, with set-shifting being normal, but ideational fluency being impaired. Exclusive of Freedman and Oscar-Berman's and Wilson et al.'s negative findings with nondemented subjects, the large majority of published studies report significant impairment in the ability of individuals with PD to shift conceptual set.

A note is appropriate at this point regarding the comparability of studies with PD groups. Where discrepancies in results on similar or identical tests have been observed, several explanations could account for the differences, e.g., different scoring criteria, as in the case of the WCST with regard to perseveration, or differential right-left hemispheric involvement in tasks performed by left- and right-sided parkinsonian patients, as in the case of Similarities and verbal fluency tasks. An as yet unmentioned source of variability in results is differences among patient groups studied; idiopathic versus other types of PD (postencephalitic, atherosclerotic), presence or absence of subcortical surgery; history of use of dopaminergic and/or anticholinergic medications; extent of dementia; age; education; severity and duration of illness, to name a few relevant characteristics. For many of the reports cited in this chapter, the investigators provided only minimal information about some or all of these patient characteristics, making problematic the comparison of results and their competing explanations from study to study. This issue will not be discussed in detail again in this chapter; it should, however, be kept in mind by the reader as a general problem in the interpretation and comparison of study results.

In sum, deficits in concept formation and comprehension are sometimes observed in PD, and deficits in conceptual set-shifting are reported consistently for this disorder. This composite picture of disability has been described as a failure of executive function (Stern and Mayeux, 1986; Taylor et al., 1986) or, in other terms, a central programming deficit (Cools et al., 1984; Talland and Schwab, 1964). Such an executive failure appears to affect intellectual as well as motor functions in PD, especially when external cues to behavior are absent.

Problem-solving

Studies that have directly addressed problem-solving in PD have featured different aspects of this capacity. Morris et al. (1988) presented to nondemented patients with PD a 'Tower of London' puzzle (Shallice, 1982), which consists of 3 beads on 3 sticks. The subject must move the beads on the sticks in order to finally copy the correct (examiner's) bead-stick pattern, which is always available for the subject's inspection. The movement of the beads is governed by specific rules (e.g., move only one bead at a time). Scoring reflects the number of moves made to solve each problem, and the number of problems solved. The PD group performed the task as accurately as did control subjects, although the patients were slower to execute their moves. The relatively lengthy execution times for the PD group seemed to be not entirely attributable to motoric slowing, which was also evaluated in this study. Alberoni et al. (1988) also tested nondemented patients with PD using the Tower of London. The mean score for the PD group was not significantly lower than for the control group; the authors considered the possibility that the test was not difficult enough to be sensitive to possible subtle group differences in performance. Consonant with Morris et al.'s and Alberoni et al.'s findings, Saint-Cyr et al. (1988) demonstrated that subjects with PD performed a 3-disk tower problem (the 'Tower of Toronto') with normal accuracy. Impaired performance by these subjects was observed only upon administration of a 4-disk problem. The investigators have interpreted the pattern of results to indicate normal problem-solving ability in PD along with a diminished capacity for procedural (skill) learning, the latter of which became apparent only upon introduction of the 4-disk problem.

The finding of Morris et al., Alberoni et al. and Saint-Cyr et al. that problem-solving performance (as distinguished from speed of performance or procedural learning) is intact in PD is consistent with results obtained by other investigators using quite different problem-solving tasks. Lees and Smith (1983) noted no differences in performance by patients with PD and control subjects on the Cognitive Estimates Test, a measure of the ability to use general knowledge in dealing with novel situations (e.g., How long is an average man's spine?). Using an adapted form of Arenberg's (1968) Poisoned Food Problems, Cronin-Golomb et al. (1988) found that, while medicated or never-medicated patients with PD performed worse than did control subjects matched for age and education, the patients' errors were characterized specifically by the inability to suppress responses that had been relevant to the immediately preceding problem or to previous steps within the same problem. These nondemented patients had no difficulty with irrelevant or redundant information; their responses indicated preserved logical deductive capacities of a high order in the face of a deficit in set-shifting (Fig. 2). Talland (1962), using a series-completion task that assessed the ability to discover the nature of an orderly arrangement of figures and blanks on sets of cards, reported that control subjects did not outperform patients with PD, whether or not the latter were on drug therapy and regardless of the duration of their illness. In another series-completion task, the Hukok Logical Thinking Matrices Test (Daryn, 1977), Cronin-Golomb et al. (1986 and 1987b) found that nondemented patients with PD performed as well as healthy control subjects. The Hukok Test requires the completion of a pattern matrix, as does the commonly used Raven's Progressive Matrices (RPM) (Raven, 1960, 1965). Unlike the RPM, however, the Hukok Matrices comprise perceptually simple, repeating colors and forms, and thus do not confound visuospatial skills with logical thinking ability to the extent that this may occur in the RPM.

It is perhaps worthwhile to examine the problem of the RPM in some detail, because several studies comparing PD and other normal or neurological groups have made use of this test. All have found impaired performance in PD relative to normal, but, whereas some investigators claim to use the RPM to measure 'logical intelligence' (Alberoni et al., 1988; Della Sala et al., 1986; Horn et al., 1974), or 'abstract reasoning' (Growdon et al., 1987), others propose that the RPM assesses visuospatial skills (Dubois et al., 1988; Huber et al., 1986; Pillon et al., 1986) (Gainotti et al., 1980, assessed PD performance relative to other neurological groups, but not relative to normal). Horne (1971) considered the RPM to be a measure of intelligence, but describes the deficient performance on the test by patients with PD in terms of 'perceptual impairment'. The dual nature of the RPM has been suggested by item analysis: Zaidel (1981) classified RPM problems into two groups, one of which appeared to be solvable through visual pattern completion and the other through, additionally, the coordination of two abstract rules. The widely reported impairment in PD on the RPM may thus be indicative of a disorder of pattern perception, or of a dysfunction of logical reasoning ability, or both. Analysis by item has not been performed for the results obtained in PD by any of the investigators cited above. The multicomponential aspect of the RPM becomes especially important when the test is used as a reference measure, as was done by Alberoni et al. (1988): aiming to exclude parkinsonian patients who were likely to be demented, these workers accepted for their study only those subjects who performed the RPM at a higher level than represented by a given cut-off score, thereby possibly excluding patients whose 'logical intelligence' was intact but whose visuospatial skills were deficient. The result would be a subject sample skewed away from a true representation of parkinsonians, many of whom appear to have visuospatial impairments (e.g. Boller et al., 1984; Oyebode et al., 1986; Sagar, 1987). The visuospatial character of the RPM is further emphasized by the low correlation ($r = +0.26$) that Alberoni et al. found between scores on the RPM and on the Tower of London test for patients with PD. Were the RPM purely a

Meal	Outcome	Possibly Poisoned
tea lamb corn	died	tea lamb corn
tea veal rice	lived	tea* lamb corn
milk beef rice	lived	tea* lamb corn
milk lamb corn	died	tea* lamb corn
coffee veal corn	lived	tea* lamb

*error

Fig. 2. Performance by a subject with Parkinson's disease on a Poisoned Food Problem. 'Tea' was the answer to the previous problem. Note that the subject does not eliminate 'tea' where appropriate in the current problem, which is otherwise correctly solved.

test of 'logical intelligence', then one would expect a stronger positive correlation between performance on the RPM and on the Tower of London, another nonverbal test of logical problem-solving ability. In general, use of the RPM with subject groups suspected of having impairments of both visuospatial abilities and logical reasoning, as in PD, will not resolve the question of whether these groups have one, or other, or both impairments. Investigators may wish instead to use alternative tests that measure more circumscribed cognitive functions.

In sum, most studies of problem-solving in PD report no performance deficit on a variety of tasks, including logical reasoning (Towers of London and Toronto), cognitive estimation and series completion (Hukok Matrices). In contrast to these negative findings, several studies show that subjects with PD are deficient in performing another series-completion task, the RPM. The RPM, however, appears to be sensitive to visuospatial dysfunction as well as to deficits in logical reasoning ability, and the results obtained with this test in PD may reflect merely the impairment of visuospatial skills that is commonly observed in this disorder. Likewise, PD patients appeared to be impaired on Poisoned Food Problems, but careful error analysis revealed that the deficit lay in an inability to shift set between and within problems. Set-shifting, like visuospatial function, may well be impaired in individuals with PD, and tests must therefore be designed to measure or circumvent the potentially confounding effects of these deficits on the interpretation of problem-solving ability.

Neuroanatomical correlations and implications

The impairments in PD that have been observed in many studies of concept formation and shifting are reminiscent of dysfunctions associated with injury to the frontal lobes. For example, patients with frontal-lobe damage perform poorly on the Wisconsin Card Sort Test, displaying difficulty in shifting of conceptual set (Drewe, 1974; Milner, 1963). Milner observed that these subjects are often able to verbalize the correct concept while being unable to demonstrate the concept by correctly performing the sorting task. This characteristic has also been observed in patients with PD (Bowen et al., 1975; Lees and Smith, 1983; Flowers and Robertson, 1985; Taylor et al., 1986). Non-sorting tests that are sensitive to frontal-lobe injury, including fluency measures (Benton, 1968; Milner, 1964; Perret, 1974), proverb interpretation (Benton, 1968) and the Stroop Word-Color Test (Perret, 1974), are also performed poorly by some subjects with PD.

Several researchers interpret the cognitive similarities between patients with frontal-lobe injury and patients with PD as an implication, first, of the dysfunction of the basal ganglia in PD. Stern and Langston (1985) showed that patients with MPTP-induced parkinsonism resemble individuals with idiopathic PD in their pattern of performance on several neuropsychological tests. This finding implies that the cognitive deficits observed for both disorders arise from a common hypodopaminergic condition, a result, in MPTP at least, of the selective destruction of neurons in the substantia nigra. Stern and Mayeux (1986) have suggested that the basal ganglia and prefrontal cortex are both part of an anatomical system which is involved in the planning and modulation of ongoing behavior. More specifically, Taylor et al. (1986) have described the prefrontal cortex as a focus of outflow from the basal ganglia. The sharing of function between brain regions that has been hypothesized by these investigators offers a reasonable explanation for the fact that patients with disorders of the basal ganglia resemble patients with frontal-lobe lesions in certain aspects of cognitive performance.

The similarities between patients with PD and those with frontal lesions are, of course, not complete. Frontal dysfunction as a result of abnormal basal ganglia input to the frontal lobe (i.e., functional deafferentation) may be less extensive than the disordering effects of a lesion to the frontal tissue itself. On some tests that predict impairment in individuals with frontal-lobe injury, such as

'Tower'-type problem-solving tests (Shallice, 1982), patients with PD obtain normal scores (Alberoni et al., 1988; Saint-Cyr et al., 1988). Further, performance by patients with frontal injury on sorting and fluency tasks is characterized by the presence of extensive perseveration (e.g., Drewe, 1974; Milner, 1963; Nelson, 1976), whereas perseveration in PD has not been observed consistently. Clinically, the behavior of patients with PD does not appear to be 'frontal'; that is, they do not seem to be disinhibited, to lack insight, or to show unconcern when performing tests. Patients with PD do not exhibit abnormally low glucose metabolism in the frontal cortex (Kuhl et al., 1984; Rougemont et al., 1984). Perlmutter and Raichle (1985) have found normal blood flow to the frontal cortex in hemiparkinsonian subjects; others have reported that blood flow in PD may be somewhat reduced to the frontal cortex specifically (Wolfson et al., 1985) or along with reductions in the cortex generally (Globus et al., 1985). In an autopsy study of twin brothers with familial fatal parkinsonism, who had shown 'frontal' cognitive deficits such as poor performance on the WCST with extensive perseveration, no significant pathology of the frontal cortex was observed (Kimura et al., 1987).

The existence of differences between frontal and PD groups on some behavioral, physiological and histological measures does not refute the hypothesis of functional integration of the basal ganglia and prefrontal cortex, but rather suggests that the integration is partial. By delineating which 'frontal' behaviors are disrupted in diseases of the frontal lobes, the basal ganglia, or both, researchers may be able in future to localize specific behavioral functions to neuroanatomical or neurochemical maps of the frontal lobes that describe precisely the input of the basal ganglia to the frontal cortex. Careful neuropsychological studies of individuals with disorders of the basal ganglia, such as PD, progressive supranuclear palsy and Huntington's disease, and of patients with disorders of specific regions of the frontal cortex (e.g., dorsolateral vs. orbitofrontal), can contribute to this effort. Increased use of sensitive imaging techniques in future will facilitate the further association of cognitive abnormalities with the pathology of specific brain areas.

Progressive supranuclear palsy

Progressive supranuclear palsy (PSP), also known as the Steele-Richardson-Olszewski syndrome, is associated with neuropathological changes in the basal ganglia (including substantia nigra, substantia innominata, pallidum and subthalmus) and subcortical nuclei such as the superior colliculus, locus coeruleus and red nucleus (Steele et al., 1964; see also Agid et al., 1986, for a recent review of affected brain structures). The cerebrum is considered to be relatively uninjured. Studies assessing the behavioral sequelae of PSP have provided evidence for mild dementia or several specific cognitive deficits that cannot be explained completely in terms of the impairment in visual scanning that is prominent in this disorder.

Concept formation and shifting

Patients with PSP are impaired on many of the same tests of abstract thought as are subjects with PD. In PD, investigators have attempted to tease out the differential effects of the disorder on concept formation and conceptual set-shifting. In PSP, however, no such attempt has been made to clarify the nature of the deficit. Dubois et al. (1988) and Pillon et al. (1986) observed that subjects with PSP were impaired on a modified version of the Wisconsin Card Sort Task, as were patients with PD. Percentage of perseverative errors was not reported in either study. Another sorting task, the Weigl test, was failed by the majority of patients with PSP tested by Maher et al. (1985). Of the two case reports provided from this sample of patients, one described perseveration on the first sorting of the Weigl shapes; no mention was made regarding perseveration for the other case. Verbal fluency has been evaluated in a number of PSP studies. Relative to normal subjects, individuals with PSP were impaired for symbolic (letter) fluency (Albert et al., 1974; Cambier et al., 1985; Maher et al., 1985). Evidence for impaired verbal fluency, with results undifferentiated with regard to the semantic (category) and symbolic subtests, was found for PSP, relative to control subjects and also to groups with PD (Dubois et al., 1988; Pillon et al., 1986) or with Alzheimer's disease (Pillon et al., 1986). Semantic fluency was reported to be depressed for Cambier et al.'s PSP group, although no control groups were tested for comparison. Perseverative behavior was not assessed for any of the fluency results cited. Cambier et al., however, mentioned perseveration as a general problem, in that the palilalia observed for their patients resulted in the clinical impression of ideational perseveration. In a case study, Smith (1988) reported that PSP was associated with depressed category and symbolic fluency, but that the semantic and orthographic knowledge necessary for performing the tests was preserved. Thus a deficit in the initiation of concept formation was a more likely explanation for the observed decrements in fluency than were language impairments in the semantic or orthographic domains. Smith did not observe abnormal perseverations in this patient.

Concept formation or conceptual set-shifting in PSP has been evaluated with several of the non-sorting, non-fluency tasks used to assess these functions in PD. The Picture Arrangement subtest yielded the lowest of all WAIS subscores attained by patients with PSP (Maher et al., 1985). Like Sullivan et al. (1985) with regard to PD, Maher's group interpreted this performance in terms of a temporal ordering deficit in PSP. Other plausible explanations for poor performance on this test would involve defective formation of an initial story concept, or impaired shifting from an initial to a new, more complete conceptual set (Ogden et al., 1987). Cambier et al. (1985) also described poor performance by patients with PSP on a test of sequential arrangement of pictures to create a story.

The WAIS Similarities subtest, a verbal measure of concept comprehension, was significantly impaired in PSP relative to normal (Cronin-Golomb et al., 1989; Pillon et al., 1986), or at least relative to the patients' scores on the WAIS Vocabulary subtest (Maher et al., 1985). Cambier et al. (1985) likewise reported that patients with PSP performed poorly on Similarities, although these investigators did not compare PSP performance on this test with that of normal control subjects or with the patients' own performance on other tests. Kimura et al. (1981) also administered the WAIS to patients with PSP, reporting significant impairment relative to groups with frontal or occipital lesions on the Performance but not the Verbal subscale; scores for individual Verbal scale subtests (except for Arithmetic) were not reported, nor were most scores for subtests on the Performance scale, including Picture Arrangement. Albert et al. (1974) did not specify whether or not they used WAIS Similarities to evaluate their patients with PSP, but did note that, for the one of their cases given any mention in this regard, 'the ability to find the categorical similarities between similar items was impaired'. Albert's group further noted that two of their cases exhibited 'poor abstracting ability', and another showed 'diminished ability to manipulate acquired knowledge'; what functions were actually assessed, and what measures were used, was not specified. Similarly, D'Antona et al. (1985) described patients with PSP as showing 'impaired judgment', 'loss of abstracting ability' and 'perseverations', without specifying the methods that were used to assess these behaviors.

Constantinidis et al. (1970) noted that, although their single patient with PSP was able to perform a Piagetian task involving the concept of conservation, as well as other logic-based tasks, this patient's reasoning was disjointed, fragmented and lethargic ('hachés, fragmentés, et ralentis'). In a study of two cases with PSP (Cronin-Golomb et al., 1989), concept comprehension was found to be impaired relative to age-matched normal subjects, as measured with the Concept Comprehension Test. The deficit applied to abstract concepts only, with comprehension of concrete concepts found to be normal. Albert's and Maher's groups observed that proverb interpretation was concrete for the three cases and one case, respectively, mentioned in this regard in their reports, as did Cronin-Golomb et al. (1989) for two cases. In the latter study, the majority of responses for the PSP patients were concrete or absurd, whereas such responses were rarely elicited from normal subjects or individuals with PD (Fig. 3). Cambier et al. (1985) reported that eight of nine patients tested gave incorrect interpretations of both proverbs presented; the nature of the errors was not described.

In sum, studies assessing concept formation, comprehension and shifting in PSP consistently report impairments, often at least as great as in PD, although the investigators have not differentiated between the specific conceptual functions affected in this disorder.

Problem-solving

Few studies have evaluated problem-solving in PSP. Pillon et al. (1986) proposed to assess 'intellectual function' in this disorder through use of Raven's Progressive Matrices (RPM), which they

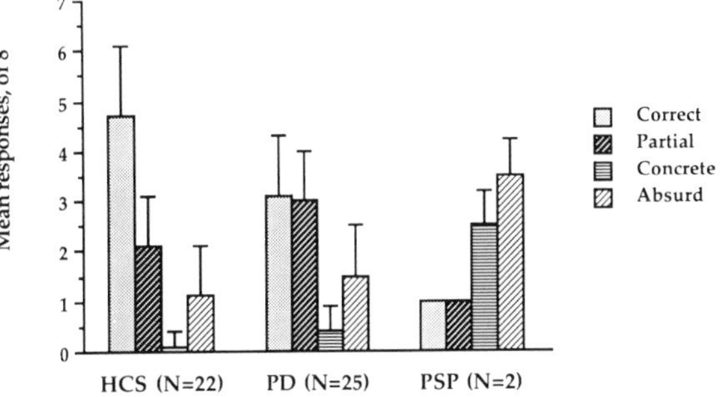

Fig. 3. Quality of responses to proverbs. Scoring: *correct* = 3, *partial* = 2, *concrete* = 1, *absurd* = 0. Total scores for the groups with Parkinson's disease (PD) and progressive supranuclear palsy (PSP) are significantly lower than for the healthy control subjects (HCS) matched for age and education. The majority of responses for the patients with PSP were concrete or absurd, whereas the HCS and PD groups rarely made these types of response.

also called a 'visuospatial task'. The PSP group was impaired on the RPM relative to control subjects, and their scores were not significantly different from those of patients with PD or Alzheimer's disease. Similarly, Dubois et al. (1988) reported that subjects with PSP were impaired on the RPM relative to normal subjects but were not different from PD patients on this 'visuospatial' measure. The problem of using the RPM with neurological groups in whom both logical reasoning and visuospatial skills may be impaired was mentioned in the previous section on PD. This caveat would appear to be especially relevant in the assessment of cognitive functions in patients with PSP, who are ophthalmoplegic on clinical evaluation (e.g., Steele et al., 1964) and show deficits in scanning or visuospatial function in their pattern of neuropsychological performance (Constantinidis et al., 1970; Kimura et al., 1981). On the Hukok Matrices, a series-completion task with fewer visuospatial demands than the RPM, two patients with PSP were found to be impaired relative to normal. Scanning deficits probably did not account for the poor performance on the Hukok Test, because these patients performed normally on another task (the Concrete subtest of the Concept Comprehension Test) which had scanning demands that seemed similar to those of the Hukok Matrices (Cronin-Golomb et al., 1989).

Verbal problem-solving was assessed by Cambier et al. (1985) in nine patients with PSP using the word problems devised by Luria (1980). No patient correctly completed more than three of the five problems, consistently failing the more difficult examples. Most of Cambier et al.'s patients also failed two problems of lineage (i.e., 'My father is John. His brother is Roger. What is my uncle's name?'). No comparison with control subjects was reported for this study. Of two nondemented patients with PSP tested by Cronin-Golomb et al. (1989), one failed four and the other failed five of ten Luria-type word problems. Both subjects also failed the two problems of lineage that were similar to those used by Cambier's group.

In short, although few studies have assessed problem-solving ability in PSP, the available evidence suggests that patients with this disease are impaired on both verbal and nonverbal measures. This performance is distinguishable from that of patients with PD, who solve many types of problem normally.

Neuroanatomical correlations and implications

The argument has been advanced by numerous researchers that patients with disease of the basal ganglia (specifically, PD) resemble behaviorally individuals with frontal-lobe dysfunction. The basis for this resemblance is that the basal ganglia project anatomically and neurochemically (i.e., via dopaminergic pathways) to the prefrontal cortex; the two brain regions hence form a functional unit. The evidence reviewed above indicates that individuals with another disorder of the basal ganglia, PSP, resemble patients with PD or with frontal injury in their neuropsychological test pattern. In PSP, the frontal cortex appears to be grossly normal (except for the presence of neurofibrillary tangles in some patients: e.g., Agid et al., 1986; Kish et al., 1985; Pillon et al., 1986; Ruberg et al., 1985; Steele, 1972; Steele et al., 1964). As in PD, there is likely to be a deafferentation or deactivation of the frontal cortex owing to the significant destruction of the basal ganglia in PSP (Cambier et al., 1985; Dubois et al., 1988; Pillon et al., 1986).

The functional consequences of frontal deafferentation are reflected in behavioral disorders, including the impairments in abstract thought described above as well as personality abnormalities characteristic of patients with frontal-lobe injury (Pillon et al., 1986). If the behavioral effects of PSP are more severe than those of PD, as, for example, Pillon, Dubois and their colleagues suggest, then the explanation may lie in the lesser destruction of the basal ganglia in PD than in PSP, which would result in less extensive frontal deafferentation in the former disease. In support of this view, glucose metabolism of patients with PD appears to be normal in the frontal cortex (Kuhl et al., 1984; Rougemont et al., 1984), whereas D'Antona et al. (1985) demonstrated frontal hypometabolism in PSP, as assessed with positron emission tomography (PET).

Although the PET findings and the neuroanatomical characteristics of PSP tempt one to conclude that frontal deafferentation does indeed occur in this disorder and fully explains the behavioral similarities between PSP and frontal groups, it should be kept in mind that the resemblance between these groups may in fact not be complete. For example, unlike in PD, researchers have not distinguished in PSP between a possible dysfunction of concept formation and a possible deficit in the ability to shift conceptual set. The issue of perseveration in PSP has been given only minimal consideration; the integrity of problem-solving ability in this group has also not been assessed in any depth. More thorough neuropsychological assessment in PSP is needed than has been accomplished to date, in order to permit meaningful evaluation of proposed neuroanatomical and neurophysiological explanations for the behavioral resemblance between PSP and frontal-lobe dysfunction. Because some subjects with PSP may show neuropathological changes of the frontal cortex (Agid et al., 1986), it would be important in evaluating a frontal deafferentation model to examine the relationship between 'frontal' behavior and pathology of the frontal lobes at autopsy in this disease. Also unexplored is the contribution to cognitive function of subcortical structures that may be lesioned or intact in individual patients with PSP (Agid et al., 1986).

Alzheimer's disease

Alzheimer's disease (AD) is the leading cause of dementia in elderly people. The disorder is characterized by cognitive impairments, predominantly of memory, but also in the domains of language and visuospatial function. The broad range of AD in terms of brain tissue and neurotransmitter systems involved and, correspondingly, cognitive functions affected presents a challenge to researchers: to demonstrate behavioral dissociations in subjects for whom few cognitive abilities are spared the ravages of the disease.

Concept formation and shifting

Although patients with AD are impaired on many tasks that also elicit deficient performance in patients with parkinsonian or other brain syndromes, the disorders are distinguishable behaviorally. Corkin et al. (1982) have reported that, while both AD and PD groups were deficient in performing the Wisconsin Card Sort Test (WCST) relative to age-matched healthy control subjects, the subjects with PD were in fact significantly worse on this test than were patients with AD who had been matched to the PD group for mild cognitive deficits. Impaired performance in AD on the WCST relative to healthy subjects has also been documented by Pillon et al. (1986). Presence or extent of perseverative behavior was not described in Pillon et al.'s study; Corkin et al. noted that subjects with AD had a greater percentage of perseverative errors than did patients with PD. Similarly, Freedman and Oscar-Berman (1987) reported that their AD group committed significantly more perseverative errors on a task of tactile reversal learning than did patients with PD, with or without dementia, or healthy control subjects.

Verbal fluency appears to be regularly impaired in AD. In studies that contrasted performance of AD and PD, nondemented subjects with PD consistently outperformed patients with AD for symbolic (Corkin et al., 1982; Gainotti et al., 1980) and semantic fluency (Corkin et al., 1982). Relative to healthy control subjects, AD groups were deficient for semantic fluency (Corkin et al., 1982; Huff et al., 1986; Martin and Fedio, 1983; Nebes et al., 1984; Pillon et al., 1986; Rosen, 1980) and for symbolic fluency (Becker et al., 1988; Botwinick et al., 1986; Corkin et al., 1982; Gainotti et al., 1980; Miller, 1984; Miller and Hague, 1975; Pillon et al., 1986; Rosen, 1980). Eslinger et al. (1985) also reported impairments in symbolic fluency in their demented patient group, which included individuals with AD, multi-infarct dementia (MID) and mixed dementia (AD and MID). Rosen (1980) noted that, in patients with mild AD, the symbolic task was performed more poorly than the semantic task, and that this differential performance was not present in the patients with moderate to severe dementia. Storandt et al. (1984) further found that performance on symbolic fluency in combination with the Trail Making Test (part A) and with specific subtests of the Wechsler Memory Scale correctly classified 98% of 42 patients with mild AD who were being compared with healthy control subjects. Becker (1988) has included the presence of deficits in symbolic fluency in his characterization of a dysexecutive component of memory loss in AD. These several studies of verbal fluency in AD, like some of the WCST results for this population, are not informative with regard to presence of perseverative errors. It is therefore not possible to characterize specifically the nature of the deficit in terms of concept formation as distinct from the ability to shift conceptual set. It has been noted by Fuld et al. (1982) that intrusion errors (non-immediate perseverative responses) occur commonly in AD; their presence is associated with cholinergic deficiency and neuropathological changes.

Attempts made in recent years to describe carefully the nature of the impairments seen in AD for semantic fluency have broader implications for the status of categorization abilities in this disorder. Martin and Fedio (1983) reported that their AD group showed diminished fluency when instructed to name different items that could be found in a supermarket. The patients not only produced fewer words than did healthy control subjects, but they also produced fewer specific items, relative to more general category names. Performance correlated negatively with disease duration. Huff et al. (1986) demonstrated that patients with AD were impaired at semantic fluency, and at rejecting incorrect names of target items (words or pictures) when the incorrect name referred to an item belonging to the same category as the target. Huff et al. and Martin and Fedio suggested on the basis of these results that patients with AD can distinguish between major categories of objects, but that specific semantic information of a kind required to distinguish between members of a single category either has been lost or cannot be accessed. Relatedly, Sherman et al. (1987) have reported that misnaming in AD often involves the commission of within-category substitutions (e.g., 'comb' for 'brush'). On a nonverbal categorization task, Flicker et al. (1986) found that patients with AD were deficient at object sorting when the principle for categorization was provided by the examiner, and were even more markedly impaired when they themselves were required to supply the principle. The results of these studies suggest that categorization is impaired in AD.

An explanation for deficient categorization as illustrated with the above tasks has been suggested by Grober et al. (1985), who found that demented patients, including those with AD, were close to normal at *recognizing* semantic associates of a given concept, but were impaired at *ranking* their importance to understanding the concept. For example, patients understood that 'fly', 'luggage' and 'radar' were related to the concept 'airplane', but were unable to judge the relative importance of these three associates to understanding the concept. Grober and colleagues interpreted their findings to mean that although specific semantic associates were not lost in AD, the retained information was not organized along normal lines; individual associates were not 'weighted' normally with respect to each other . Contrasting with these results with semantic associates are findings of normal organization of category knowledge in AD. AD patients showed a robust effect of typicality in judging whether or not a word belonged to a designated category (e.g., 'animal'); that is, they were faster to judge high-typical words ('cat') than low-typical words ('elk') (Cronin-Golomb et al., 1989; Nebes et al., 1986). In the study by Cronin-Golomb et al., speed in judging low- (but not high-) typical exemplars correlated with dementia severity. Impaired access to, rather than loss of, low-typical category information was suggested by the observation that the AD patients were correct, if slow, in their judgements. In the same study, AD patients were normal at ranking category exemplars on the basis of typicality, further indicating that organization is normal.

Difficulty in assessing the relative importance of semantic associates or in accessing specific classes of information, i.e., problems of categorization, reverberate in tests of concept comprehension: impairment is defined partly in terms of excessive concreteness of response for trials on which abstract concepts are deemed more appropriate. Thus, patients with AD performed deficiently on the WAIS Similarities subtest relative to normal subjects (Martin and Fedio, 1983; Pillon et al., 1986) and relative to subjects with MID (Perez et al., 1975). Crookes (1974) also found poor performance on Similarities in early dementia; the type of dementia was unspecified. In this context it may be important to note effects of stimulus materials (verbal versus nonverbal): the word-finding deficit characteristic of AD is more severe for abstract than for concrete words (Rissenberg and Glazer, 1987), and patients with AD tend to interpret proverbs and idioms, incorrectly, in a concrete fashion (Kempler et al., 1988). On the nonverbal Concept Comprehension Test (CCT), although subjects with AD were impaired as a group relative to healthy control subjects, with performance on the Concrete subtest being significantly better than on the Abstract subtest, many mildly to moderately demented subjects attained CCT scores in the normal range (Cronin-Golomb et al., 1987b). These patients were often correct in their pointing response on trials for which their accompanying verbal explanations were either excessively concrete or quite irrelevant. In this regard, patients with AD resemble subjects with complete commissurotomy, whose right hemispheres are capable of abstract association, as measured by the CCT, but who are unable to provide adequate verbal explanations of the basis for the same associations (Cronin-Golomb, 1986a).

Taken together with Grober et al.'s (1985) finding that the semantic information relating associates to concepts is not lost in AD, the results with the CCT suggest that the ability to recognize even abstract relationships between words or objects may be preserved in AD, although the ability to gain access to this information verbally may be restricted. Support for this hypothesis is provided by Huff et al.'s (1986) observation that categorization of pictures tended to be performed more efficiently in AD than was categorization of words. It has been suggested (Potter and Faulconer, 1975) that pictures can be categorized without first being named, implying the existence of a semantic network in which information is distributed across both cerebral hemispheres (Cronin-Golomb, 1986b; Huff et al., 1988; Schwartz et al., 1979) and hence can be accessed through either verbal or nonverbal stimulation. The existence of quasi-independent verbal and nonverbal stores would suggest that impaired retrieval or loss of information from one store need not preclude successful retrieval from the other. Access to abstract knowledge by the relatively nonverbal right hemisphere has been demonstrated repeatedly in human commissurotomy studies (e.g., Cronin-Golomb 1986a,b).

In examining the nature of verbal access to semantic knowledge in AD, Martin and Fedio (1983), using a test in which subjects were to match a word with a symbol referent (e.g., 'water' may be represented by parallel wavy horizontal lines), found that the patients were impaired relative to healthy subjects when the word referred to an object, an action or a modifier, but were normal when the word referred to an emotion. This difference between types of words with regard to successful responses suggests that impaired verbal access to the semantic network in AD may not be an all-or-nothing phenomenon. Similarly, Kempler et al. (1988) have reported that patients with AD performed more poorly in matching idiomatic phrases than novel, non-idiomatic phrases to pictures, implying that the abstract meanings associated with proverbs or idioms are less accessible than are meanings based on literal interpretation. Further work on semantic knowledge in AD using purely verbal, purely nonverbal and mixed verbal-nonverbal test designs is needed to elucidate the basis of concept formation and comprehension and its evolution over the course of AD.

With regard to non-sorting, non-fluency measures of set-shifting, Perez et al. (1975) found that performance on the WAIS Picture Arrangement subtest was deficient in AD relative to MID. As described in previous sections on PD and PSP, Picture Arrangement can be considered to be a measure of concept formation, conceptual set-shifting or temporal sequencing.

In short, unlike in PD, in which set-shifting but not concept formation is impaired consistently, work to date in AD does not distinguish the causes of deficits seen on both sorting and non-sorting tasks of categorization and fluency.

Problem-solving

Problem-solving involves attention and working memory, in addition to the skills necessary for solving the specific problem itself. Attention and memory are consistently impaired in AD. Word problems demand verbal comprehension and production, which are often abnormal in this disorder. Nonverbal problems, such as Raven's Progressive Matrices (RPM), may engage visuospatial abilities, which, like verbal skills, are often impaired in AD. The RPM has been used to assess 'visuospatial function' (Pillon et al., 1986), and 'visuospatial intelligence' in AD (Gainotti et al., 1980). LeDoux et al. (1983) also used the RPM with patients with AD; these investigators did not describe the function they were attempting to assess with the test. All three groups of researchers found that the patients with AD performed deficiently on the RPM, relative to healthy control subjects (Pillon et al.), to established norms (LeDoux et al.) and to subjects with MID or PD (Gainotti et al.). None of these studies invoked the possibility that patients with AD might be impaired at problem-solving rather than visuospatial function.

The Hukok Matrices appear to involve visuospatial skills to a lesser extent than does the RPM. As with the RPM, verbal abilities and memory are also not integral to successful performance on this test. Nevertheless, it has been found that patients with AD are impaired on the Hukok Matrices relative to healthy control subjects, suggesting that the logical reasoning skills that are basic to problem-solving are affected by the disease (Cronin-Golomb et al., 1986, 1987b). This study reported further that individuals with AD may perform poorly on the Hukok Test even while they are considered mildly impaired or normal on the basis of standard dementia ratings and other neuropsychological tests, including the Concept Comprehension Test. It appears that logical reasoning skills may be lost early in the course of AD, at a time when other cognitive functions, including the ability to understand concrete and abstract relationships and concepts, are still largely intact.

The integrity of verbal problem-solving ability in AD has not been examined. It is certainly possible that known impairments in verbal behavior in AD may preclude meaningful interpretation of results on standard tests of word problems in terms of problem-solving ability. The hint provided by the results with the Hukok Test, that logical reasoning skills may be impaired in AD before other cognitive functions, gives impetus to thorough investigation in future of problem-solving skills in AD, using carefully constructed tests that control for factors relating to memory, language, attention and visuospatial function.

Neuroanatomical correlations and implications

Because neuropathological and neurochemical changes in AD occur throughout the entire cerebral cortex, it is difficult to localize specific functions that are impaired in the disorder to specific cortical regions. Localization of functions affected in AD is effected primarily through information on the loci of those same functions provided by studies of other neurological patient groups. Hence, concept formation or shifting as well as verbal and nonverbal fluency may involve the frontal lobes, the activity of which appears to be disrupted in PD and especially in PSP. Fluency and sorting deficits can also be demonstrated in patients with lesions (Benton, 1968; Nelson, 1976; Perret, 1974) or excisions (Milner, 1963, 1964) of the frontal lobes.

The fact that behavioral deficits attributed to general frontal dysfunction occur in AD, PD and PSP as well as in subjects with frontal lesions does not necessarily imply that these deficits derive from identical malfunctions of the frontal lobes for all of these subject groups. Miller (1984), for example, cited the strong correlations in healthy subjects between performance on a symbolic fluency test and scores reflecting 'verbal IQ' (which comprised the combined scores of the WAIS Comprehension, Similarities and Vocabulary subtests) as evidence that poor verbal fluency in AD could be accounted for by these patients' general deficit in verbal intelligence. In contrast, the fluency deficit observed in subjects with frontal lesions appears to be a more specific phenomenon, because the verbal IQ of these individuals is relatively preserved. Further, patients with AD outperformed subjects with PD on the Wisconsin Card Sort Test but, for the same patients, the opposite pattern of performance (PD better than AD) held for symbolic and semantic fluency (Corkin et al., 1982). The patient groups had been matched for mild cognitive deficits. Gainotti et al. (1980) also found that patients with PD were better than those with AD on symbolic fluency. The most parsimonious explanation for these results is that fluency and sorting functions probably involve different areas of the frontal lobes, and that these areas are differentially affected in AD and PD. Indirect support for this view may be derived from the observation that in neither disorder is the frontal cortex homogeneously diseased or deactivated: In PD, glucose metabolism appears to be normal (Kuhl et al., 1984; Rougemont et al., 1984) and, in AD, neuropathological (Brun and Englund, 1981) and metabolic changes (Chase et al., 1984) affect the parietal and temporal lobes to a greater extent than the frontal lobes.

The temporal lobes may be involved in some non-fluency, non-sorting tasks of concept comprehension and problem-solving. In a study of war veterans with left, right or bilateral penetrating head injury, subjects with temporal lobe injury performed deficiently on the CCT but were normal on the Hukok Test (Cronin-Golomb et al., 1987c). Veterans with penetrating injury to the frontal, parietal or occipital lobes were normal on both tests. Small sample sizes precluded analysis of the results by side of lesion, but neither of these tests has been found to involve superior performance by one or other hemisphere of subjects with complete forebrain commissurotomy (CCT: Cronin-Golomb, 1986a; Hukok: Cronin-Golomb et al., 1986). Thus, the impairment on the CCT that has been observed for patients with AD may reflect the diseased state of the temporal cortex in this disorder (Brun and Englund, 1981.) In order to pursue meaningfully the question of localization of these and other aspects of concept comprehension and problem-solving, large samples of subjects with focal head injury, especially injury restricted to single lobes of the cerebrum, will need to be tested with a wide variety of tasks that measure concept comprehension and logical reasoning abilities.

Multi-infarct dementia

Multi-infarct dementia (MID) is associated with hypertension and derives its name from the presence in the cerebrum of multiple infarcts or lacunae. MID but not AD is described by abrupt onset, stepwise deterioration, fluctuating course, history of hypertension or strokes, and focal neurological signs or symptoms (Hachinski et al., 1975). Modern imaging techniques, especially magnetic resonance imaging, have revealed white-matter changes in normal elderly as well as demented individuals, prompting a re-evaluation of what is meant by a diagnosis of MID (see Roman, 1987, for a review).

Concept formation and shifting

MID and AD groups have been shown to perform equally poorly on symbolic fluency, with both groups being outperformed by subjects with PD (Gainotti et al., 1980). Healthy control subjects were not tested for comparison with the neurological groups in this study, and presence or extent of perseverative errors was not reported. Results on sorting tasks, such as the Wisconsin Card Sort Test (WCST), have not been reported for MID. Patients with MID have been shown to be superior in performance to patients with AD on WAIS Similarities and Picture Arrangement (Perez et al., 1975). Perez et al. supported the finding of MID superiority relative to AD on Picture Arrangement in a second study, in which subjects with MID received higher scores than did patients with AD on a shortened WAIS Performance IQ test, comprising the Picture Arrangement, Picture Completion and Block Design subtests. The MID and AD groups were equivalent for scores on the full WAIS (Verbal and Performance subscores) (Perez et al., 1976). No data were reported by Perez et al. in their two studies with regard to the performance of healthy control subjects compared to that of the neurological groups tested.

In brief, then, the little information available suggests that subjects with MID resemble those with AD for impoverished verbal fluency, but that MID involves less impairment of concept formation and perhaps set-shifting than AD, as measured by performance on Similarities and Picture Arrangement. Shifting of conceptual set has not been examined in MID as a function that may be distinguishable from concept formation. Documentation of the possible presence and extent of perseverative behavior on tests such as the WCST and verbal fluency is needed for this group.

Problem-solving

The arguments against the use of Raven's Progressive Matrices in populations in whom visuospatial function and problem-solving ability are not known to be normal should be familiar from previous sections. However, results with the RPM represent the only assessment to date of ostensible problem-solving skills in MID. Gainotti et al. (1980) reported that patients with MID resembled subjects with PD for performance on the RPM ('visuospatial intelligence'), and that both groups were more able on this test than were subjects with AD. Data from healthy control subjects were not reported. In a study of patients with cardiac disease or with AD, both groups attained scores on the RPM that placed them in the lowest quartile (LeDoux et al., 1983). Although these authors did not describe the cardiac patients in terms of MID, it seems possible that the observed cognitive difficulties were secondary to hypertension and arteriosclerosis, which are associated with both cardiac disease and MID. The scores of the cardiac and AD groups were not compared, apart from the reference to their common position in the lowest quartile of normal subjects; therefore it is not known whether LeDoux et al.'s results mirror Gainotti et al.'s findings of superior performance on the RPM by patients with MID relative to AD.

Neuroanatomical correlations and implications

The neuropsychological profile of MID is incomplete; attempts to associate behavior with specific anatomical and physiological characteristics of the brain in this disorder are hampered accordingly. This situation is attributable in part to the difficulty in diagnosing MID differentially from AD or even from normal aging. Although MID is ostensibly characterized by abrupt onset and stepwise progression of dementia, this pattern is seen occasionally in AD as well, either because an individual patient's history was reported inaccurately (i.e., an 'abrupt' onset had in fact occurred gradually), or because vascular episodes and AD can coexist, producing what is known clinically as a 'mixed' dementia. The area of disease in MID is variable and usually not sufficiently specific to permit meaningful correlations with observed patterns of abstract thought. A study of cerebral blood flow (CBF) changes in normal aging and in MID noted a bilateral decline in resting blood flow to the cerebral cortex in the diseased state (Shaw et al., 1984). In subjects matched for age and degree of mental deterioration, MID was associated with a significant decrease in several CBF variables relative to AD (Hachinski, 1978).

Other age-related dementias: Pick's disease, frontal-lobe dementia

Pick's disease is characterized by a progressive dementia with focal signs such as aphasia, apraxia and agnosia. Personality changes are observed frequently. Pathological status of the brain includes gross cortical atrophy, especially of the anterior regions, and intracellular inclusions known as Pick bodies. The integrity of abstract thought has not been described for patients with Pick's disease. The disorder is rare, the course of dementia often rapid, and the differential diagnosis of Pick's as opposed to , for example, AD is difficult. Based on the largely frontal involvement of the disease, it may be predicted that individuals with Pick's would show some impairment of concept formation and pronounced deficits in conceptual set-shifting. Problem-solving would be made difficult by the presence of aphasia and agnosia, as well as the emotional changes (apathy or mild euphoria) characteristic of the disease, although memory is said to be relatively preserved. On clinical examination, as described by Jervis (1971), patients with Pick's disease 'show some difficulty in thinking and concentration, are easily fatigued and distractible, and reveal a peculiar inability to elaborate new mental material, to deal with unaccustomed problems, or to adapt themselves to new situations'.

There has been increased interest in subjects who present with a clinical picture suggestive of progressive damage to the frontal lobes specifically. The pathology of such patients does not include the characteristic changes of AD, and also may not include classic Pick bodies. In a recent brain imaging study using single photon emission tomography, it was found that subjects with 'dementia of the frontal-lobe type' had selective reductions in the uptake of tracer in the anterior cerebral hemispheres. Besides showing abnormal changes in personality and attention, these same subjects performed poorly on tasks which are sensitive to frontal-lobe dysfunction, including semantic and symbolic fluency, design fluency and the modified Wisconsin Card Sort Test. For the latter test, a large proportion of errors were perseverative. Problem-solving was not addressed (Neary et al., 1988).

Summary

Normal aging Healthy elderly subjects have difficulty with some types of concept formation, especially on tasks that use nonverbal materials. Conceptual set-shifting is not impaired consistently, and observed deficits may be attributable to factors that are independent of or secondary to the aging process. Problem-solving ability diminishes with age. Although there are many brain changes associated with normal aging, specific changes account only poorly for the observed pattern of abstract thought in normal elderly individuals.

Parkinson's disease Deficits in concept formation are sometimes observed in PD. Set-shifting is impaired consistently, and may or may not involve perseverative behavior. Problem-solving performance appears to be normal, unless the task coincidentally involves speeded motor response, visuospatial skill, set-shifting ability or other functions known to be impaired in PD. The overall pattern of abstract thought in PD resembles in part that of individuals with lesions of the frontal lobes. An explanation for this behavioral similarity invokes the dissolution in PD of the normal functional integration of the basal ganglia and the frontal cortex.

Progressive supranuclear palsy Although little effort has been made to distinguish between concept formation and set-shifting with regard to performance on conceptual tests in PSP, all related tasks appear to be performed poorly by this group, and to an extent at least as great as in PD. Unlike in PD, all aspects of problem-solving ability that have been examined are impaired in PSP. Like PD, PSP seems to involve frontal-lobe deafferentation, although some PSP patients may also have direct frontal pathology.

Alzheimer's disease Conceptual skills, again not specified in terms of concept formation as distinct from set-shifting, appear to be impaired in AD. Patients are particularly incapable of assessing the relative importance of various associates of a concept. Problem-solving has not been assessed widely, especially for verbal material. Known difficulties in memory and language for these subjects would make results from such studies difficult to interpret. Dysfunctions of both the frontal and the temporal lobes may account for the observed pattern of performance.

Multi-infarct dementia The little information available suggests that patients with MID resemble those with AD for impoverished verbal fluency, but that MID involves sparing, relative to AD, of concept formation and possibly also set-shifting. Problem-solving has been examined only to a negligible extent in MID. The area of disease is variable and insufficiently specific to permit correlations with observed patterns of abstract thought.

Other age-related dementias Subjects with frontal-lobe dementia, as determined from brain imaging and clinical examination, are impaired for concept formation and set-shifting. Problem-solving has not been assessed. To date, attempts have not been made to relate diseased brain areas to patterns of abstract thought for Pick's disease.

Conclusions and future directions

Abstract thought includes the process of abstraction, and the products of that process as they fall along the abstract-concrete dimension. Various aspects of abstract thought appear to be impaired in normal aging and in several age-releated neurological diseases. In some cases, these impairments are dissociable from deficits in other cognitive domains. Insights into specific processes of abstract thought in well-studied neurological groups (e.g., set-shifting in Parkinson's disease) are provided by the association of neuroanatomy, physiology and chemistry with these cognitive processes. In the light of such findings, more thorough study of relatively neglected subject populations (e.g., Alzheimer's and other dementias) and behavioral topics (e.g., problem-solving) is clearly warranted. Further research on age-related neurological disease will undoubtedly inform our concepts of what happens to the brain, and consequently to specific behaviors, including aspects of abstract thought, in normal aging.

Researchers wishing to probe the depth and extent of intact abstract thought in the neurologically impaired patient must confront several challenges to accurate assessment. We need to be rigorous in reducing confounding factors arising from the pre- or postmorbid state of the individual; for example, by controlling for educational level and extent of dementia severity, respectively. Further, we must be willing to select or design tests that are appropriate for each patient group, taking into consideration known impairments in language, visuospatial function, memory or other domains. Finally, and critically, we must formulate theoretical or at least operational definitions of the abstract processes that we presume to study. Through these measures, the neuropsychologist may eventually catch up with the insightful clinician in describing a most valued and important aspect of human behavior.

Acknowledgements

I would like to thank Suzanne Corkin, Jordan Grafman, Jody Green, John Growdon and Jenni Ogden for their valuable comments on earlier versions of this manuscript. This work was supported by grant 1 F32 AGO5391 from the National Institute on Aging.

References

Agid Y, Javoy-Agid F, Ruberg M, Pillon B, Dubois B, Duykaerts C, Hauw J-J, Baron J-C, Scatton B: Progressive supranuclear palsy: anatomoclinical and biochemical considerations. In Yahr MD, Bergmann KJ (Editors), *Advances in Neurology, Vol. 45.* New York: Raven Press, pp. 191 – 206, 1986.

Alberoni M, Della Sala S, Pasetti C, Spinnler H: Problem solving ability of parkinsonians. *Ital. J. Neurol. Sci.: 9,* 35 – 40, 1988.

Albert ML, Feldman RG, Willis AL: The 'subcortical dementia' of progressive supranuclear palsy. *J. Neurol. Neurosurg. Psychiatry: 37,* 121 – 130, 1974.

Albert MS, Kaplan E: Organic implications of neuropsychological deficits in the elderly. In Poon LW, Fozard JL, Cermak LS, Arenberg D, Thompson LW (Editors), *New Directions in Memory and Aging. Proceedings of the George A. Talland Memorial Conference.* Hillsdale, NJ: Lawrence Erlbaum, pp. 403 – 432, 1980.

Allamanno N, Della Sala S, Laiacona M, Pasetti C, Spinnler H: Problem solving ability in aging and dementia: normative data on a non-verbal test. *Ital. J. Neurol. Sci.: 8,* 111 – 120, 1987.

Arenberg D: Concept problem solving in young and old adults. *J. Gerontol.: 23,* 279 – 282, 1968.

Arenberg D: A longitudinal study of problem solving in adults. *J. Gerontol.: 29,* 650 – 658, 1974.

Arenberg D: Changes with age in problem solving. In Craik FIM, Trehut S (Editors), *Aging and Cognitive Processes (Advances in the Study of Communication and Affect, Vol. 8).* New York: Plenum Press, Ch. 13, pp. 221 – 235, 1982.

Asso D: WAIS scores in a group of Parkinson patients. *Br. J. Psychiatry: 115,* 555 – 556, 1969.

Becker JT: Working memory and secondary memory deficits in Alzheimer's disease. *J. Clin. Exp. Neuropsychol.: 10,* 739 – 753, 1988.

Bentin S, Silverberg R, Gordon HW: Asymmetrical cognitive deterioration in demented and Parkinson patients. *Cortex: 17,* 533 – 544, 1981.

Benton AL: Differential behavioral effects in frontal lobe disease. *Neuropsychologia: 6,* 53 – 60, 1986.

Benton AL, Hamsher K deS: *Multilingual Aphasia Examination.* Iowa City: University of Iowa, 1976.

Berg EA: A simple objective technique for measuring flexibility in thinking. *J. Gen. Psychol.: 39,* 15 – 22, 1948.

Birren JE: *The Psychology of Aging.* Englewood Cliffs, NJ: Prentice-Hall, Ch. 8, pp. 171 – 197, 1964.

Boller F: Mental status of patients with Parkinson disease. *J. Clin. Neuropsychol.: 2,* 157 – 172, 1980.

Boller F, Mizutani T, Roessmann U, Gambetti P: Parkinson's disease, dementia, and Alzheimer's disease: clinicopathological correlations. *Ann. Neurol.: 7,* 329 – 335, 1980.

Boller F, Passafiume D, Keefe NC, Rogers K, Morrow L, Kim

Y: Visuospatial impairment in Parkinson's disease: role of perceptual and motor factors. *Arch. Neurol.: 41,* 485–490, 1984.

Botwinick J: *Aging and Behavior* (3rd edition). New York: Springer Publishing Company, Ch. 14, pp. 249–273, 1984a.

Botwinick J: *Aging and Behavior* (3rd edition). New York: Springer Publishing Company, Ch. 15, pp. 274–293, 1984b.

Botwinick J, Robbin JS, Brinley JF. Reorganization of perceptions with age. *J. Gerontol.: 14,* 85–88, 1959.

Botwinick J, Storandt M, Berg L: A longitudinal, behavioral study of senile dementia of the Alzheimer type. *Arch. Neurol.: 43,* 1124–1127, 1986.

Bowen FP: Behavioral alterations in patients with basal ganglia lesions. In Yahr MD (Editor), *The Basal Ganglia.* New York: Raven Press, pp. 169–180, 1976.

Bowen FP, Hoehn MM, Yahr MD: Cerebral dominance in relation to tapping and tracking behavior in patients with parkinsonism. *Neurology: 22,* 32–40, 1972a.

Bowen FP, Hoehn MM, Yahr MD: Parkinsonism: alterations in spatial orientation as determined by a route-walking test. *Neuropsychologia: 10,* 355–361, 1972b.

Bowen FP, Kamienny RS, Burns MM, Yahr MD: Parkinsonism: effects of levodopa treatment on concept formation. *Neurology: 25,* 701–704, 1975.

Boyarsky RE, Eisdorfer C: Forgetting in older persons. *J. Gerontol.: 27,* 254–258, 1972.

Brizzee KR, Harkin JC, Ordy JM, Kaack B: Accumulation and distribution of lipofuscin, amyloid, and senile plaques in the aging nervous system. In Brody H, Harman D, Ordy JM (Editors), *Clinical, Morphologic, and Neurochemical Aspects in the Aging Central Nervous System (Aging, Vol. 1).* New York: Raven Press, pp. 39–78, 1975.

Brody H: Cell counts in cerebral cortex and brainstem. In Katzman R, Terry RD, Bick KL (Editors), *Alzheimer's Disease: Senile Dementia and Related Disorders (Aging, Vol. 7).* New York: Raven Press, pp. 345–351, 1978.

Brody H, Harman D, Ordy JM (Editors): *Clinical, Morphologic, and Neurochemical Aspects in the Aging Central Nervous System (Aging, Vol. 1).* New York: Raven Press, 1975.

Bromley DB: Some effects of age on the quality of intellectual output. *J. Gerontol.: 12,* 318–323, 1957.

Brun A, Englund E: Regional pattern of degeneration in Alzheimer's disease: neuronal loss and histopathological grading. *Histopathology: 5,* 549–564, 1981.

Busse EW: Duke Longitudinal Study I: Senescence and senility. In Katzman R, Terry RD, Bick KL (Editors), *Alzheimer's Disease: Senile Dementia and Related Disorders (Aging, Vol. 7).* New York, Raven Press, pp. 59–68, 1978.

Butler RN: The National Institutes of Mental Health Study. In Katzman R, Terry RD, Bick KL (Editors), *Alzheimer's Disease: Senile Dementia and Related Disorders (Aging, Vol. 7).* New York: Raven Press, pp. 53–58, 1978.

Cambier J, Masson M, Viader F, Limodin J, Strube A: Le syndrome frontal de la paralysie supranucléaire progressive. *Rev. Neurol.: 141,* 528–536, 1985.

Celesia GG, Wanamaker WM: Psychiatric disturbances in Parkinson's disease. *Dis. the Nerv. System: 33,* 577–583, 1972.

Chase TN, Foster NL, Fedio P, Brooks R, Mansi L, Di Chiro G: Regional cortical dysfunction in Alzheimer's disease as determined by positron emission tomography. *Ann. Neurol. (Suppl.): 15,* S170–S174, 1984.

Coleman PD, Flood DG: Neuron numbers and dendritic extent in normal aging and Alzheimer's disease. *Neurobiol. Aging: 8,* 521–545, 1987.

Constantinidis J, Tissot R, de Ajuriaguerra J: Dystonie oculo-facio-cervicale ou paralysie progressive supranucléaire de Steele-Richardson-Olszewski. *Rev. Neurol.: 122,* 249–262, 1970.

Cools AR, Van den Bercken JHL, Horstink MWI, Van Spaendonck KPM, Berger HJC: Cognitive and motor shifting aptitude disorder in Parkinson's disease. *J. Neurol. Neurosurg. Psychiatry: 47,* 443–453, 1984.

Coppinger NW, Nehrke MF: Discrimination learning and transfer of training in the aged. *J. Genet. Psychol.: 120,* 93–102, 1972.

Corkin S, Growdon JH, Nissen MJ: Comparison of the dementias in Parkinson's disease and Alzheimer's disease. Presented at the VIIth International Symposium on Parkinson's disease, Frankfurt a.M., 1982.

Cornelius SW: Classic pattern of intellectual aging: Test familiarity, difficulty, and performance. *J. Gerontol.: 39,* 201–206, 1984.

Cornelius SW, Caspi A: Everyday problem solving in adulthood and old age. *Psychol. Aging: 2,* 144–153, 1987.

Cronin-Golomb A: Comprehension of abstract concepts in right and left hemispheres of complete commissurotomy subjects. *Neuropsychologia: 24,* 881–887, 1986a.

Cronin-Golomb A: Subcortical transfer of cognitive information in subjects with complete forebrain commissurotomy. *Cortex: 22,* 499–519, 1986b.

Cronin-Golomb A, Corkin S, Growdon JH: Early decline of logical reasoning skills in Alzheimer's disease. *Abstr. Soc. Neurosci.: 12,* 1163, 1986.

Cronin-Golomb A, Corkin S, Growdon JH: Relational ability in Alzheimer's disease and Parkinson's disease. *Clin. Neuropsychol.: 1,* 298, 1987a.

Cronin-Golomb A, Rho WA, Corkin S, Growdon JH: Abstract reasoning in age-related neurological disease. *J. Neural Transm. (Suppl): 24,* 79–83, 1987b.

Cronin-Golomb A, Rho WA, Corkin S: Dissociation of abstract reasoning abilities by locus of head injury. *Abstr. Soc. Neurosci.: 13,* 652, 1987c.

Cronin-Golomb A, Corkin S, Growdon JH: Impaired problem solving in Parkinson's disease: influence of set-shifting deficit. *Abstr. Soc. Neurosci.: 14,* 218, 1988.

Cronin-Golomb A, Corkin S, Growdon JH: Impaired problem solving in progressive supranuclear palsy. *Proc. Abstr. East. Psychol. Assoc.: 60,* 60, 1989.

Cronin-Golomb A, Keane MM, Corkin S, Growdon JH: Category typically effects in Alzheimer's disease. *Abstr. Soc. Neurosci.: 15,* 481, 1989.

Crookes TG: Indices of early dementia on WAIS. *Psychol. Rep.: 34,* 734, 1974.

Crovitz E: Reversing a learning deficit in the aged. *J. Gerontol.: 21,* 236–238, 1966.

D'Antona R, Baron JC, Samson Y, Serdaru M, Viader F, Agid Y, Cambier J: Subcortical dementia: frontal cortex hypometabolism detected by positron tomography in patients with progressive supranuclear palsy. *Brain: 108,* 785 – 799, 1985.

Daryn E: *The Hukok Logical Thinking Matrices Test.* Tel Aviv: Eked, 1977.

Della Sala S, Di Lorenzo G, Giordano A, Spinnler H: Is there a specific visuo-spatial impairment in Parkinsonians? *J. Neurol. Neurosurg. Psychiatry: 49,* 1258 – 1265, 1986.

Denney DR, Denney NW: The use of classification for problem solving: A comparison of middle and old age. *Dev. Psychol.: 9,* 275 – 278, 1973.

Denney NW: Aging and cognitive changes. In Wolman BB (Editor), *Handbook of Developmental Psychology.* Englewood Cliffs, NJ: Prentice-Hall, Ch. 45, pp. 807 – 827, 1982.

Denney NW, Denney DR: The relationship between classification and questioning strategies among adults. *J. Gerontol.: 37,* 190 – 196, 1982.

Direnfeld LK, Albert ML, Volicer L, Langlais PJ, Marquis J, Kaplan E: Parkinson's disease: the possible relationship of laterality to dementia and neurochemical findings. *Arch. Neurol.: 41,* 935 – 941, 1984.

Donnelly EF, Chase TN: Intellectual and memory function in parkinsonian and non-parkinsonian patients treated with L-dopa. *Dis. Nerv. System: 34,* 119 – 123, 1973.

Doppelt JE, Wallace WL: Standardization of the Wechsler Adult Intelligence Scale for older persons. *J. Abnorm. Soc. Psychol.: 51,* 312 – 330, 1955.

Downes JJ, Roberts AC, Sahakian BJ, Evenden JL, Robbins TW: Impaired extra-dimensional shift performance in medicated and unmedicated Parkinson's disease: evidence for a specific attentional dysfuction. *Neuropsychologia:* in press.

Drachman DA, Leavitt J: Memory impairment in the aged: storage versus retrieval deficit. *J. Exp. Psychol.: 93,* 302 – 308, 1972.

Drewe EA: The effect of type and area of brain lesion on Wisconsin Card Sorting Test performance. *Cortex: 10,* 159 – 170, 1974.

Dubois B, Pillon B, Legault F, Agid Y, Lhermitte F: Slowing of cognitive processing in progressive supranuclear palsy: a comparison with Parkinson's disease. *Arch. Neurol.: 45,* 1194 – 1199, 1988.

Eisdorfer C, Cohen LD: The generality of the WAIS standardization for the aged. *J. Abnorm. Soc. Psychol.: 62,* 520 – 527, 1961.

Eslinger PJ, Damasio AR, Benton AL, Van Allen M: Neuropsychologic detection of abnormal mental decline in older persons. *J. Am. Med. Assoc.: 253,* 670 – 674, 1985.

Flicker C, Ferris SH, Crook T, Bartus RT: The effects of aging and dementia on concept formation as measured on an object-sorting task. *Dev. Neuropsychol.: 2,* 65 – 72, 1986.

Flowers KA, Robertson C: The effect of Parkinson's disease on the ability to maintain a mental set. *J. Neurol. Neurosurg. Psychiatry: 48,* 517 – 529, 1985.

Freedman M, Oscar-Berman M: Tactile discrimination learning deficits in Alzheimer's and Parkinson's diseases. *Arch. Neurol.: 44,* 394 – 398, 1987.

Friend CM, Zubek JP: The effects of age on critical thinking ability. *J. Gerontol.: 13,* 407 – 413, 1958.

Fuld, PA, Katzman R, Davies P, Terry RD: Intrusions as a sign of Alzheimer dementia: chemical and pathological verification. *Ann. Neurol.: 11,* 155 – 159, 1982.

Gainotti G, Caltagirone C, Masullo C, Miceli G: Patterns of neuropsychologic impairment in various diagnostic groups of dementia. In Amaducci L, Davison AN, Antuono P (Editors), *Aging of the Brain and Dementia (Aging, Vol. 13).* New York: Raven Press, pp. 245 – 250, 1980.

Garron DC, Klawans HL, Narin F: Intellectual functioning of persons with idiopathic parkinsonism. *J. Nerv. Mental Dis.: 154,* 445 – 452, 1972.

Giambra LM, Arenberg D: Problem solving, concept learning, and aging. In Poon L (Editor), *Aging in the 1980s.* Washington, DC: American Psychological Association, Ch. 18, pp. 253 – 259, 1980.

Globus M, Mildworf B, Melamed E: Cerebral blood flow and cognitive impairment in Parkinson's disease. *Neurology: 35,* 1135 – 1139, 1985.

Goldstein K: *Human Nature in the Light of Psychopathology.* New York: Schocken Books, 1963.

Goldstein K, Scheerer M: Abstract and concrete behavior. An experimental study with special tests. *Psychol. Monogr.: 53,* 1941.

Gorham DR: A proverbs test for clinical and experimental use. *Psychol. Rep.: 1,* 1 – 12, 1956.

Gotham A-M, Brown RG, Marsden CD: Levodopa treatment may benefit or impair 'frontal' function in Parkinson's disease. *Lancet: 2,* 970 – 971, 1986.

Grant DA, Berg EA: A behavioral analysis of degree of reinforcement and ease of shifting to new responses in a Weigl-type card-sorting problem. *J. Exp. Psychol.: 38,* 404 – 411, 1948.

Green RF: Age-intelligence relationship between ages sixteen and sixty-four: a rising trend. *Dev. Psychol.: 1,* 618 – 627, 1969.

Greeno JG: A perspective on thinking. *Am. Psychol.: 44,* 134 – 141, 1989.

Grober E, Buschke H, Kawas C, Fuld P: Impaired ranking of semantic attributes in dementia. *Brain Lang.: 26,* 276 – 286, 1985.

Growdon JH, Corkin S: Cognitive impairment in Parkinson's disease. In Yahr MD, Bergmann KJ (Editors), *Advances in Neurology, Vol. 45: Parkinson's Disease.* New York: Raven Press, pp. 383 – 392, 1987.

Growdon JH, Corkin S, Desclos G, Rosen TJ: Hoehn and Yahr stage predicts the extent of cognitive deficit in Parkinson's disease (PD). Presented at the American Academy of Neurology, New York, NY, 1987.

Haaland KY, Vranes LF, Goodwin JS, Garry PJ: Wisconsin Card Sort Test performance in a healthy elderly population. *J. Gerontol.: 42,* 345 – 346, 1987.

Hachinski V: Cerebral blood flow: differentiation of Alzheimer's disease from multi-infarct dementia. In Katzman R, Terry RD, Bick KL (Editors), *Alzheimer's Disease: Senile Dementia and Related Disorders (Aging, Vol. 7).* New York: Raven Press, pp. 97 – 103, 1978.

Hachinski VC, Iliff L, DuBoulay GH, McAllister VL, Marshall J, Russel RWR, Symon L: Cerebral blood flow in dementia. *Arch. Neurol.: 32,* 632 – 637, 1975.

Halstead WC: *Brain and Intelligence.* Chicago: University of Chicago Press, 1947.

Hayslip B, Sterns HL: Age differences in relationships between crystallized and fluid intelligences and problem solving. *J. Gerontol.: 34,* 404–414, 1979.

Heath HA, Orbach J: Reversibility of the Necker-cube: IV. Responses of elderly people. *Percept. Motor Skills: 17,* 625–626, 1963.

Heglin HJ: Problem solving set in different age groups. *J. Gerontol.: 11,* 310–317, 1956.

Horn JL: The aging of human abilities. In Wolman BB (Editor), *Handbook of Developmental Psychology.* Englewood Cliffs, NJ: Prentice-Hall, Ch. 47, pp. 847–870, 1982.

Horn S: Some psychological factors in parkinsonism. *J. Neurol. Neurosurg. Psychiatry: 37,* 27–31, 1974.

Horne DJ: Performance on delayed response tasks by patients with parkinsonism. *J. Neurol. Neurosurg. Psychiatry: 34,* 192–194, 1971.

Hoyer WJ, Rebok GW, Sved SM: Effects of varying irrelevant information on adult age differences in problem solving. *J. Gerontol.: 34,* 553–560, 1979.

Huber SJ, Shuttleworth EC, Paulson GW: Dementia in Parkinson's disease. *Arch. Neurol.: 43,* 987–990, 1986.

Huff FJ, Corkin S, Growdon JH: Semantic impairment and anomia in Alzheimer's Disease. *Brain Lang.: 28,* 235–249, 1986.

Huff FJ, Mack L, Mahlmann J, Greenberg S: A comparison of lexical-semantic impairments in left hemisphere stroke and Alzheimer's disease. *Brain Lang.: 34,* 262–278, 1988.

Hull CL: Quantitative aspects of the evolution of concepts. *Psychol. Monogr.: 28,* 1920.

Jacobs L, Kinkel WR, Painter F, Murawski J, Heffner RR: Computerized tomography in dementia with special reference to changes in size of normal ventricles during aging and normal pressure hydrocephalus. In Katzman R, Terry RD, Bick KL (Editors), *Alzheimer's disease: Senile Dementia and Related Disorders (Aging, Vol. 7).* New York: Raven Press, pp. 241–260, 1978.

Jervis GA: Pick's disease. In Minckler J (Editor), *Pathology of the Nervous System, Vol. 2.* New York, McGraw-Hill, Ch. 101, pp. 1395–1404, 1971.

Jones HE: Intelligence and problem-solving. In Birren JE (Editor), *Handbook of Aging and the Individual.* Chicago: University of Chicago Press, Ch. 20, pp. 700–738, 1959.

Jones-Gotman M, Milner B: Design fluency: The invention of nonsense drawings after focal cortical lesions. *Neuropsychologia: 15,* 653–674, 1977.

Katzman R, Terry RD, Bick KL (Editors): *Alzheimer's Disease: Senile Dementia and Related Disorders (Aging, Vol. 7).* New York: Raven Press, 1978.

Kausler DH: *Experimental Psychology and Human Aging.* New York: John Wiley and Sons, Ch. 11, pp. 567–635, 1982a.

Kausler DH: *Experimental Psychology and Human Aging.* New York: John Wiley and Sons, Ch. 10, pp. 494–565, 1982b.

Kempler D, Van Lancker D, Read S: Proverb and idiom comprehension in Alzheimer disease. *Alzheimer Dis. Assoc. Disord.: 2,* 38–49, 1988.

Kimura D, Barnett HJM, Burkhart G: The psychological test pattern in progressive supranuclear palsy. *Neuropsychologia: 19,* 301–306, 1981.

Kimura D, Hahn A, Barnett HJM: Attentional and perseverative impairment in two cases of familial fatal parkinsonism with cortical sparing. *Can. J. Neurol. Sci.: 14,* 597–599, 1987.

Kish SJ, Chang LJ, Mirchandani L, Shannak K, Hornykiewicz O: Progressive supranuclear palsy: relationship between extrapyramidal disturbances, dementia, and brain neurotransmitter markers. *Ann. Neurol.: 18,* 530–536, 1985.

Kral, VA: Benign senescent forgetfulness. In Katzman R, Terry RD, Bick KL (Editors), *Alzheimer's Disease: Senile Dementia and Related Disorders (Aging, Vol. 7).* New York: Raven Press, pp. 47–51, 1978.

Kuhl DE, Metter EJ, Riege WH: Patterns of local cerebral glucose utilization determined in Parkinson's disease by the [^{18}F]fluorodeoxyglucose method. *Ann. Neurol.: 15,* 419–424, 1984.

Labouvie-Vief G: Intelligence and cognition. In Birren JE, Schaie KW (Editors), *Handbook of the Psychology of Aging* (2nd edition). New York: Van Nostrand Reinhold, Ch. 19, pp. 500–530, 1985.

Ledesma LK, Nicdao ST, Dantes MB, Perez MC: Neuropsychological profile of primary parkinsonism among Filipinos. In Yahr MD, Bergmann KJ (Editors), *Advances in Neurology (Vol. 45): Parkinson's Disease.* New York: Raven Press, pp. 421–424, 1986.

LeDoux JF, Blum C, Hirst W: Inferential processing of context: studies of cognitively impaired subjects. *Brain Lang.: 19,* 216–224, 1983.

Lees AJ, Smith E: Cognitive deficits in the early stages of Parkinson's disease. *Brain: 106,* 257–270, 1983.

Loranger AW, Goodell H, McDowell FH, Lee JE, Sweet RD: Intellectual impairment in Parkinson's syndrome. *Brain: 95,* 405–412, 1972.

Loranger A, Sweet RD, Goodell H, McDowell F: Parkinsonism, levodopa, and intelligence. *Int. J. Neurol.: 10,* 276–279, 1975.

Luria AR: *Higher Cortical Functions in Man* (2nd edition). New York: Basic Books, Ch. 12, pp. 562–585, 1980.

Mack JL, Carlson NJ: Conceptual deficits and aging: The Category Test. *Percept. Motor Skills: 46,* 123–128, 1978.

Maher ER, Smith EM, Lees AJ: Cognitive deficits in the Steele-Richardson-Olszewski syndrome (progressive supranuclear palsy). *J. Neurol. Neurosurg. Psychiatry: 48,* 1234–1239, 1985.

Martin A, Fedio P: Word production and comprehension in Alzheimer's disease: the breakdown of semantic knowledge. *Brain Lang.: 19,* 124–141, 1983.

Matison R, Mayeux R, Rosen J, Fahn S: 'Tip-of-the-tongue' phenomenon in Parkinson disease. *Neurology: 32,* 567–570, 1982.

Matthews CG, Haaland KY: The effect of symptom duration on cognitive and motor performance in parkinsonism. *Neurology: 29,* 951–956, 1979.

McGeer EG: Aging and neurotransmitter metabolism in the human brain. In Katzman R, Terry RD, Bick KL (Editors), *Alzheimer's Disease: Senile Dementia and Related Disorders (Aging, Vol. 7).* New York: Raven Press, pp. 427–440, 1978.

Miller E: Verbal fluency as a function of a measure of verbal intelligence and in relation to different types of cerebral pathology. *Br. J. Clin. Psychol.: 23,* 53–57, 1984.

Miller E, Hague F: Some characteristics of verbal behaviour in presenile dementia. *Psychol. Med.: 5,* 255 – 259, 1975.

Milner B: Effects of different brain lesions on card sorting. *Arch. Neurol.: 9,* 90 – 100, 1963.

Milner B: Some effects of frontal lobectomy in man. In Warren JM, Akert K (Editors), *The Frontal Granular Cortex and Behavior.* New York: McGraw-Hill, Ch. 15, pp. 313 – 334, 1964.

Morris RG, Downes JJ, Sahakian BJ, Evenden JL, Heald A, Robbins TW: Planning and spatial working memory in Parkinson's disease. *J. Neurol. Neurosurg. Psychiatry: 51,* 757 – 766, 1988.

Nandy K: Brain-reactive antibodies in aging and senile dementia. In Katzman R, Terry RD, Bick KL (Editors), *Alzheimer's Disease: Senile Dementia and Related Disorders (Aging, Vol. 7).* New York: Raven Press, pp. 503 – 512, 1978.

Nauta WJH: The problem of the frontal lobe: a reinterpretation. *J. Psychiatr. Res.: 8,* 167 – 187, 1971.

Neary D, Snowden JS, Northen B, Goulding P: Dementia of frontal lobe type. *J. Neurol. Neurosurg. Psychiatry: 51,* 353 – 361, 1988.

Nebes RD, Martin DC, Horn LC: Sparing of semantic memory in Alzheimer's disease. *J. Abnorm. Psychol.: 93,* 321 – 330, 1984.

Nebes RD, Boller F, Holland A: Use of semantic context by patients with Alzheimer's disease. *Psychol. Aging: 1,* 261 – 269, 1986.

Nehrke MF, Coppinger NW: The effect of task dimensionality on discrimination learning and transfer of training in the aged. *J. Gerontol.: 26,* 151 – 156, 1971.

Nehrke MF, Sutterer JR: The effects of overtraining on mediational processes in elderly males. *Exp. Aging Res.: 4,* 207 – 221, 1978.

Nelson HE: A modified card sorting test sensitive to frontal lobe defects. *Cortex: 12,* 313 – 324, 1976.

Newcombe F: *Missile Wounds of the Brain.* London: Oxford University Press, 1969.

Newell A, Simon HA: *Human Problem Solving.* Englewood Cliffs, NJ: Prentice-Hall, 1972.

Offenbach SI: A developmental study of hypothesis testing and cue selection strategies. *Dev. Psychol.: 10,* 484 – 490, 1974.

Ogden JA, Growdon JH, Corkin S: Impaired ability of patients with Parkinson's disease to shift conceptual set in visuospatial tasks. *Int. J. Neurosci.: 35,* 132, 1987.

Ordy JM, Kaack B, Brizzee KR: Life-span neurochemical changes in the human and nonhuman primate brain. In Brody H, Harman D, Ordy JM (Editors), *Clinical, Morphologic, and Neurochemical Aspects in the Aging Central Nervouw System (Aging, Vol. 1).* New York: Raven Press, pp. 133 – 189, 1975.

Oyebode JR, Barker WA, Blessed G, Dick DJ, Britton PG: Cognitive functioning in Parkinson's disease. In relation to prevalence of dementia and psychiatric diagnoses. *Br. J. Psychiatry: 149,* 720 – 725, 1986.

Perez FI, Rivera VM, Meyer JS, Gay JRA, Taylor RL, Mathew NT: Analysis of intellectual and cognitive performance in patients with multi-infarct dementia, vertebrobasilar insufficiency with dementia, and Alzheimer's disease. *J. Neurol. Neurosurg. Psychiatry: 38,* 533 – 540, 1975.

Perez FI, Stump DA, Gay JRA, Hart VR: Intellectual performance in multi-infarct dementia and Alzheimer's disease, a replication study. *Can. J. Neurol. Sci.: 3,* 181 – 187, 1976.

Perlmutter JS, Raichle ME: Regional blood flow in hemiparkinsonism. *Neurology: 35,* 1127 – 1134, 1985.

Perret E: The left frontal lobe of man and the suppression of habitual responses in verbal categorical behavior. *Neuropsychologia: 12,* 323 – 330, 1974.

Pikas A: *Abstraction and Concept Formation.* Cambridge, MA: Harvard University Press, 1966.

Pillon B, Dubois B, Lhermitte F, Agid Y: Heterogeneity of cognitive impairment in progressive supranuclear palsy, Parkinson's disease, and Alzheimer's disease. *Neurology: 36,* 1179 – 1185, 1986.

Pirozzolo FJ, Hansch EC, Mortimer JA, Webster DD, Kuskowski MA: Dementia in Parkinson disease: a neuropsychological analysis. *Brain Cognition: 1,* 71 – 83, 1982.

Potter MC, Faulconer BA: Time to understand pictures and words. *Nature: 253,* 437 – 438, 1975.

Proctor F, Riklan M, Cooper IS, Teuber H-L: Judgment of visual and postural vertical by parkinsonian patients. *Neurology: 14,* 287 – 293, 1964.

Rabbitt P: Changes in problem solving ability in old age. In Birren JE, Schaie K (Editors), *Handbook of the Psychology of Aging.* New York: Van Nostrand Reinhold, Ch. 25, pp. 606 – 625, 1977.

Ransmayr G, Poewe W, Ploerer S, Birbamer G, Gerstenbrand F: Psychometric findings in clinical subtypes of Parkinson's disease. In Yahr MD, Bergmann KJ (Editors), *Advances in Neurology, Vol. 45: Parkinson's Disease.* New York: Raven Press, pp. 409 – 411, 1986.

Raven JC: *Guide to the Standard Progressive Matrices.* London: HK Lewis, 1960.

Raven JC: *Guide to using the Coloured Progressive Matrices.* London: HK Lewis, 1965.

Reese HW, Rodeheaver D: Problem solving and complex decision making. In Birren JE, Schaie KW (Editors), *Handbook of the Psychology of Aging* (2nd edition). New York: Van Nostrand Reinhold, Ch. 18, pp. 474 – 499. 1985.

Reitan RM, Boll TJ: Intellectual and cognitive functions in Parkinson's disease. *J. Consult. Clin. Psychol.: 37,* 364 – 369, 1971.

Riklan M, Levita E: Psychological effects of lateralized basal ganglia lesions: a factorial study. *J. Nerv. Ment. Dis.: 138,* 233 – 240, 1964.

Rissenberg M, Glanzer M: Free recall and word finding ability in normal aging and senile dementia of the Alzheimer's type: the effect of item concreteness. *J. Gerontol.: 42,* 318 – 322, 1987.

Rogers CJ, Keyes BJ, Fuller BJ: Solution shift performance in the elderly. *J. Gerontol.: 31,* 670 – 675, 1976.

Roman GC: Senile dementia of the Binswanger type: a vascular form of dementia in the elderly. *J. Am. Med. Assoc.: 258,* 1782 – 1788, 1987.

Rosch E, Mervis CB, Gray WD, Johnson DM, Boyes-Braem P: Basic objects in natural categories. *Cognitive Psychol.: 8,* 382 – 439, 1976.

Rosen WG: Verbal fluency in aging and dementia. *J. Clin. Neuropsychol.: 2,* 135 – 146, 1980.

Rougemont D, Baron JC, Collard P, Bustany P, Comar D, Agid Y: Local cerebral glucose utilisation in treated and untreated patients with Parkinson's disease. *J. Neurol.*

Neurosurg. Psychiatry: 47, 824 – 830, 1984.
Rowe JW, Kahn RL: Human aging: usual and successful. *Science: 237,* 143 – 149, 1987.
Ruberg M, Javoy-Agid F, Hirsch E, Scatton B, L'Heureux R, Hauw J-J, Duyckaerts C, Gray F, Morel-Maroger A, Rascol A, Serdaru M, Agid Y: Dopaminergic and cholinergic lesions in progressive supranuclear palsy. *Ann. Neurol.: 18,* 523 – 529, 1985.
Sagar HJ: Clinical similarities and differences between Alzheimer's disease and Parkinson's disease. *J. Neural Transm. (Suppl.): 24,* 87 – 99, 1987.
Saint-Cyr JA, Taylor AE, Lang AE: Procedural learning and neostriatal dysfunction in man. *Brain: 111,* 941 – 959, 1988.
Salthouse TA: *A Theory of Cognitive Aging.* Amsterdam: North-Holland, Ch. 13, pp. 361 – 370, 1985.
Salthouse TA, Prill KA: Inferences about age impairments in inferential reasoning. *Psychol. Aging: 2,* 43 – 51, 1987.
Sandson J, Albert ML: Perseveration in behavioral neurology. *Neurology: 37,* 1736 – 1741, 1987.
Schaie KW, Labouvie-Vief G: Generational versus ontogenetic components of change in adult cognitive behavior: a fourteen-year cross-sequential study. *Dev. Psychol.: 10,* 305 – 320, 1974.
Scheibel ME, Scheibel AB: Structural changes in the aging brain. In Brody H, Harman D, Ordy JM (Editors), *Clinical, Morphologic, and Neurochemical Aspects in the Aging Central Nervous System (Aging, Vol. 1).* New York: Raven Press, pp. 11 – 37, 1975.
Schwartz MF, Marin OSM, Saffran EM: Dissociations of language function in dementia: a case study. *Brain Lang.: 7,* 277 – 306, 1979.
Shallice T: Specific impairments in planning. *Phil. Trans. R. Soc. Lond.: B298:* 199 – 209, 1982.
Shaw TG, Mortel KF, Meyer JS, Rogers RL, Hardenberg J, Cutaia MM: Cerebral blood flow changes in benign aging and cerebrovascular disease. *Neurology: 34,* 855 – 862, 1984.
Sherman J, Schweickert J, Garrett M, Growdon J, Corkin S: The nature of naming errors in Alzheimer's disease. Proceedings, Massachusetts Alzheimer's Disease Research Center, annual scientific session, Boston, 1987.
Smith ST: Verbal fluency in progressive supranuclear palsy. *Abstr. Soc. Neurosci.: 14,* 1047, 1988.
Sokoloff L: Cerebral blood flow and metabolism in the differentiation of dementias: general considerations. In Katzman R, Terry RD, Bick KL (Editors), *Alzheimer's Disease: Senile Dementia and Related Disorders (Aging, Vol. 7).* New York: Raven Press, pp. 197 – 202, 1978.
Steele JC: Progressive supranuclear palsy. *Brain: 95,* 693 – 704, 1972.
Steele JC, Richardson JC, Olszewski J: Progressive supranuclear palsy. *Arch. Neurol.: 10,* 333 – 359, 1964.
Stern Y, Langston JW: Intellectual changes in patients with MPTP-induced parkinsonism. *Neurology: 35,* 1506 – 1509, 1985.
Stern Y, Mayeux R: Intellectual impairment in Parkinson's disease. In Yahr MD, Bergmann KJ (Editors), *Advances in Neurology, Vol. 45: Parkinson's Disease.* New York: Raven Press, pp. 405 – 408, 1986.
Storandt M, Botwinick J, Danziger WL, Berg L, Hughes CP: Psychometric differentiation of mild senile dementia of the Alzheimer type. *Arch. of Neurol.: 41,* 497 – 499, 1984.
Stroop JR: Studies of interference in serial verbal reactions. *J. Exp. Psychol.: 18,* 643 – 662, 1935.
Sullivan EV, Sagar HJ, Gabrieli JDE, Corkin S, Growdon JH: Sequencing deficits in Parkinson's disease. *J. Clin. Exp. Neuropsychol.: 7,* 160, 1985.
Talland GA: Cognitive function in Parkinson's disease. *J. Nerv. Ment. Dis.: 135,* 196 – 205, 1962.
Talland GA, Schwab RS: Performance with multiple sets in Parkinson's disease. *Neuropsychologia: 2,* 45 – 53, 1964.
Taylor AE, Saint-Cyr JA, Lang AE: Frontal lobe dysfunction in Parkinson's disease: the cortical focus of neostriatal outflow. *Brain: 109,* 845 – 883, 1986.
Terry RD: Aging, senile dementia, and Alzheimer's disease. In Katzman R, Terry RD, Bick KL (Editors), *Alzheimer's Disease: Senile Dementia and Related Disorders (Aging, Vol.7).* New York: Raven Press, pp. 11 – 14, 1987a.
Terry RD, Ultrastructural alterations in senile dementia. In Katzman R, Terry RD, Bick KL (Editors), *Alzheimer's Disease: Senile Dementia and Related Disorders (Aging, Vol. 7).* New York: Raven Press, pp. 375 – 382, 1987b.
Terry RD, DeTeresa R, Hansen LA: Neocortical cell counts in normal human adult aging. *Ann. Neurol.: 21,* 530 – 539, 1987.
Thaler M: Relationships among Wechsler, Weigl, Rorschach, EEG findings, and abstract-concrete behavior in a group of normal aged subjects. *J. Gerontol.: 11,* 404 – 409, 1956.
Thurstone LL, Thurstone TG: *Primary Mental Abilities.* Chicago: Science Research Associates, 1962.
Wechsler D: *Wechsler Adult Intelligence Scale-Revised.* New York: Psychological Corporation, 1981.
Weigl E: On the psychology of so-called processes of abstraction. *J. Abnorm. Soc. Psychol.: 36,* 3 – 33, 1941.
Wetherick NE: A Comparison of the problem-solving ability of young, middle-aged and old subjects. *Gerontologia: 9,* 164 – 178, 1964.
Wetherick NE: Changing an established concept: a comparison of the ability of young, middle-aged and old subjects. *Gerontologia: 11,* 82 – 95, 1965.
Wetherick NE: The inferential basis of concept attainment. *Br. J. Psychol.: 57,* 61 – 69, 1966.
Whelihan WM, Lesher EL: Neuropsychological changes in frontal functions with aging. *Dev. Neuropsychol.: 1,* 371 – 380, 1985.
Wilson RS, Gilley DW, Tanner CM, Goetz CG, Rapp DT, Gans SL: Ideational fluency in Parkinson's disease. *Clin. Neuropsychol.: 1,* 284, 1987.
Witte KL: Optional shift behavior in children and young and elderly adults. *Psychonomic Sci.: 25,* 329 – 330, 1971.
Wolfson LI, Leenders KL, Brown LL, Jones T: Alterations of regional cerebral blood flow and oxygen metabolism in Parkinson's disease. *Neurology: 35,* 1399 – 1405, 1985.
Wright RE: Aging, divided attention, and processing capacity. *J. Gerontol.: 36,* 605 – 614, 1981.
Young ML: Problem-solving performance in two age groups. *J. Gerontol.: 21,* 505 – 509, 1966.
Zaidel E: Hemispheric intelligence: The case of the Raven Progressive Matrices. In Friendman MP, Das JP, O'Connor N (Editors), *Intelligence and Learning. Proceedings of the NATO Conference, York, England, 16 – 20 July 1979.* New York: Plenum Press, pp. 531 – 552, 1981.

© 1990 Elsevier Science Publishers B.V. (Biomedical Division)
Handbook of Neuropsychology, Vol. 4
F. Boller and J. Grafman (Eds)

CHAPTER 15

Aging and age-related neurological disease: remote memory

Harvey J. Sagar

Department of Neurology, Royal Hallamshire Hospital, Sheffield S10 2JF, U.K.

Introduction

Clinical observations of remote memory capacity in normal aging and age-related dementias have suggested poorer performance for events from the recent time periods, more distant events being relatively spared. Memory for all classes of information is usually considered to be lost equally, although some preservation of memory for more salient past events is assumed. Rigorous behavioural studies have examined these observations in normal aging and dementia using tests of autobiographical memory and memory for past public events.

Normal aging

Autobiographical memory

Pioneer studies on autobiographical memory were conducted by Galton (1879) using a technique in which personal recollections were produced in response to common cue words. From tests on himself in middle age, Galton concluded that the majority of autobiographical memories were drawn from the early part of life.

A more specific version of this method was administered by Crovitz and Schiffman (1974) to 98 college undergraduates, who were required to estimate the date of each autobiographical episode recalled. The resultant 1745 memories were plotted as a frequency distribution against the age of the memories. In this age group, the relationship between the frequency of memories recalled and the age of the episode was monotonic when plotted on log coordinates, recent memories being recalled more readily than distant ones. Crovitz and Schiffman concluded that autobiographical memory follows a simple retention function, analogous to that observed in laboratory experiments of new learning and recall. Robinson (1976), reanalysed by Rubin (1982), obtained parallel results using a similar method, and Rubin (1982) showed that the monotonic relationship between recall and age of episode was present in a free-recall paradigm and was thus independent of the cued-recall procedure. Assuming that people encode autobiographical memories at an equal rate across their lifetime (except for childhood amnesia), these results suggest that recall of autobiographical memories in young people is influenced largely by the time that has elapsed since encoding.

In the aging population, autobiographical recall is influenced by factors additional to those of a simple retention function. For subjects aged over 40 years, the frequency plot of number of memories against age of episode shows, in addition to the recency peak, a second peak corresponding to the period 20 – 40 years ago (reviewed by Rubin et al., 1986). The precise position of this secondary peak in the frequency plot depends upon the age of the subject; the older the subject, the more this secondary peak is shifted into the remote time periods (Franklin and Holding, 1977; Fitzgerald and Lawrence, 1984; Rubin et al., 1986) (Fig. 1). Comparison of the data from subjects of different ages shows that the age of memories that comprise this secondary peak can best be explained in terms of the age of the subject. Thus, subjects aged over 40 years tend to draw memories from the period when they were 10 to 30 years of age, as well as the most recent time periods. These results cannot be due to the salience of particular calendar years, such as war-time, which are independent of the age of the subject. The findings favour the development of 'reminiscence' with aging, whereby frequent life-review leads to strengthening of memories related to an individual's particular age (Rubin et al., 1986).

McCormack (1979) used Crovitz and Schiffman's (1974) technique on a group of particularly elderly subjects (range 66 – 97 years). The frequency of memories related declined steadily for events from the first to the third quarter of life and then showed some recovery for the last quarter. Although the general shape of this frequency distribution was equivalent to that of other studies using younger age groups, the proportion of memories drawn from the early time period was much greater in the older subjects.

Several authors have examined the influence of the stimulus cue on the response time and age of memories related using the word prompt technique. Robinson (1976) showed that college students generated memories to nouns and verbs more quickly than to affective prompts (feeling states) and that affective prompts generated memories from more recent time periods than did the other cues. Fitzgerald (1980, 1981), however, using similar methods, showed that response time and event age were not influenced by prompt type in young adolescent subjects; Franklin and Holding (1977) claimed that response time to cue words was independent of the age of adult subjects, although the effect of different prompts was not investigated. Rubin (1980) showed that high-imagery

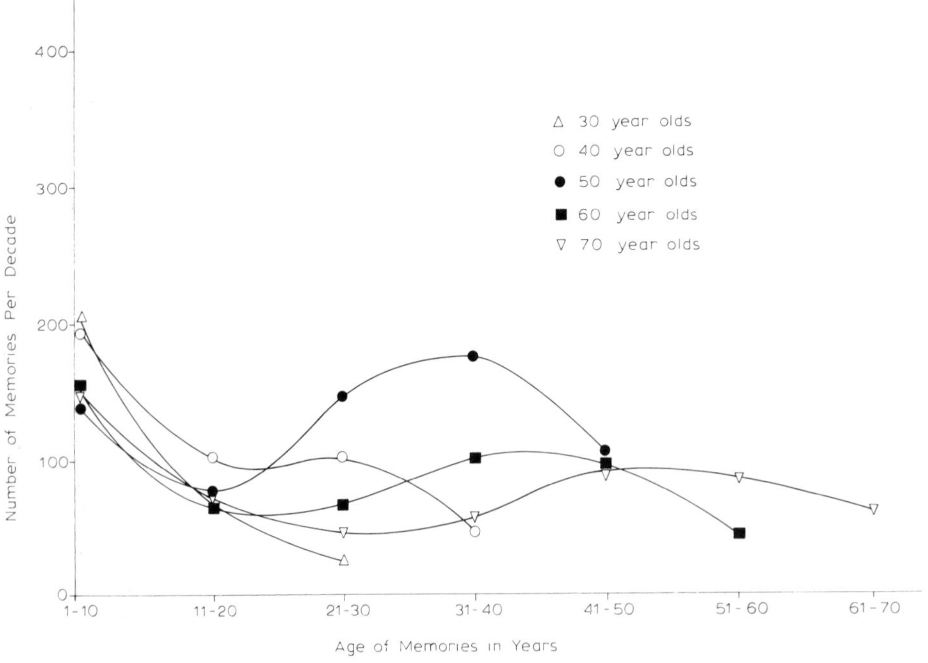

Fig. 1. Frequency distribution of autobiographical memories plotted against the age of the memory for subjects in five different age groups. Reproduced with permission from Franklin and Holding (1977).

words tended to evoke older memories in college students. Fitzgerald and Lawrence (1984) supported the findings of stable response time during adulthood. Words of high imagery rating were associated with short response times in all age groups; these words evoked older memories in college students and older adults (aged 60 – 75) but not in junior high school or middle-aged subjects. Taken together, these data suggest that differences between young and old subjects in the age of memories related are not clearly due to differential effects resulting from certain properties of the cue words. The use of different cue words may, however, contribute to the lack of consistency in results from different studies.

The study of the age distribution of autobiographical memories has certain pitfalls. Firstly, subjects must relate specific episodes and not generic memories representing the accumulation of multiple, similar experiences. Certain epochs of life may show a preponderance of such repetitive events and lead to an over-representation of this time period in a frequency distribution plot, if specific episodes are not selected. Although specificity is implied in most studies, it is rarely emphasized. The report of Franklin and Holding (1977), by contrast, states that 31% of the subjects' responses were 'recurrent events' and other studies may also include generic memories. Secondly, it is often very difficult to establish that subjects are recalling genuine events. Although some studies have attempted to obtain corroboration from relatives, such an approach assumes that the relative will have shared all past experiences with the subject and will have recall that is at least as good. The further along the life-span, the less likely are these conditions to apply, so that corroboration of memories is particularly difficult when the Galton technique is used in the aging population. Some studies have estimated the reliability of memories by examining consistency of recall between two test sessions one or more days apart (McCormack, 1979; Baddeley and Wilson, 1986; Sagar et al., 1985, 1988a). Inconsistent recall is often attributed to confabulation (Baddeley and Wilson, 1986) although the method does not allow evaluation of inconsistent retrieval of genuine memories. Sagar et al. (1988a) examined the age distribution of autobiographical memories related by a group of normal subjects (mean age 60 years) selecting highly specific memories that were consistently recalled on two successive days. The results confirmed earlier observations (reviewed by Rubin et al., 1986): most memories were drawn from the most recent decade but a cluster of memories were also drawn from the period 35 – 40 years ago, when the subject was aged 20 – 25 years (Fig. 2).

Memory for historical events

Warrington and Silberstein (1970) investigated

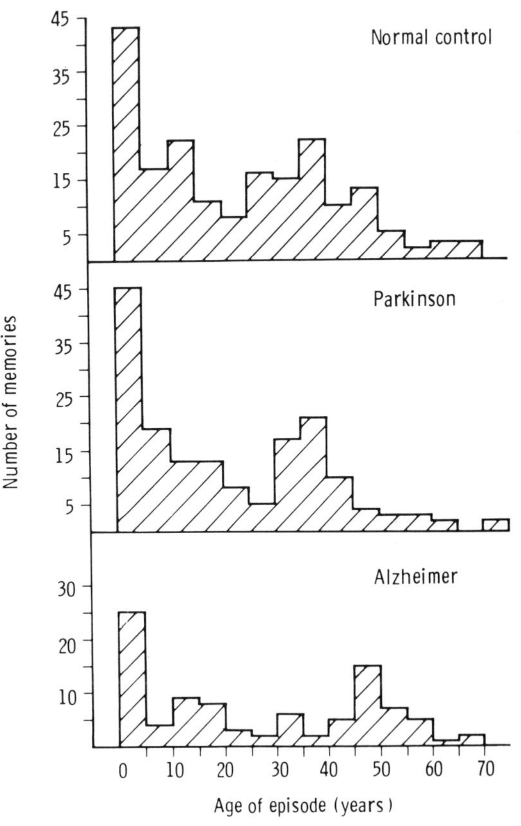

Fig. 2. Frequency distribution of autobiographical memories plotted against the age of the memory for normal elderly subjects, patients with PD and patients with AD. From Sagar et al. (1988a).

remote memory function in different age groups of normal subjects, using 40-item questionnaires concerning events of 1966 and 1967. Although statistical analyses were not reported, the results showed a decrease in recall scores in all age groups with increasing time intervals since the event; overall performance tended to decline with age. Recognition was superior to recall and showed less influence of age or time since the event, in keeping with other observations that recall tasks differentiate performance of young and old subjects better than do recognition tasks.

Warrington and Sanders (1971) assessed memory for famous faces and past historical events in normal subjects of different ages. Recall and recognition declined with increasing remoteness of the stimuli but there was no decade by age interaction to support the clinical impression that elderly subjects recall remote events better than recent ones. A group of 16-year-old subjects showed memory comparable to the other age groups for events and faces that had been prominent during their lifetime, but had poorer knowledge of more remote information. The performance of young subjects was similar even when highly educated individuals were selected (Squire, 1974) (Fig. 3). Squire et al. (1975) compared adult subjects, aged

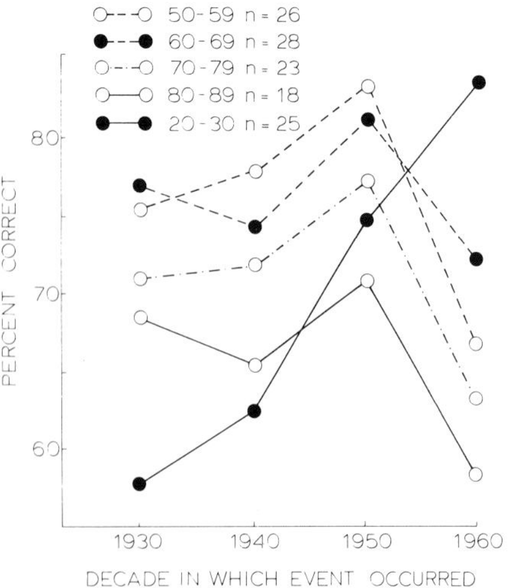

Fig. 3. Performance on a recognition test of famous events by subjects in different age groups. Reproduced with permission from Squire (1974).

24 – 70 years, with students, aged 11 – 13 years, on their test of one-season television programmes (Squire and Slater, 1975). The students recognized the content and temporal order of recently broadcast programmes as well or better than the adults but did significantly worse than the adults for the time period 1961 – 1967, when the students were less than 6 years of age. These studies show that individuals learn little about past historical events if they have not lived through the relevant time period, and remember little of the first 6 years of life; secondary acquisition of knowledge, from books and other historical sources, is less efficient than learning at the time the event occurred.

Poon et al. (1979) gave a questionnaire of past historical events to subjects in five approximately equal age groups from 30 to 'greater than 67' years. In all groups, recognition of recent events was superior to that of remote events, in keeping with the forgetting functions within remote memory described by Warrington and Silberstein (1970) and Squire (1974). The 30-year-old subjects performed significantly worse in recognition of events from the 1910s to the 1930s but there was no difference between the age groups for the remaining decades. The poor performance of 30-year-olds for the three earliest decades can be attributed to their not having been born at the time that these events occurred (Warrington and Sanders, 1971; Squire, 1974). In another study (Poon and Fozard, 1978), speed of retrieval from long-term memory, as assessed by a confrontation naming task, was faster in older subjects for unique dated objects but was faster in younger subjects for unique contemporary ones. This study supports the notion that retrieval from remote memory depends upon familiarity of the memoranda as well as the age of the subject.

Other studies have shown peak recall of past events to relate more to the age of the subject at the time the event occurred and to differ according to the nature of the recalled information and the sex of the subject (Botwinick and Storandt, 1974; Storandt et al., 1978). For historical items, recall by people aged 40 – 50 years was better than that of younger or older subjects, and optimal recall related to the period when subjects were 10 – 20 years of age; men performed better than women. For entertainment items, performance was closely linked to the age of the subject at the time of the event, but no sex differences were observed. These findings can be attributed to sex differences in exposure to different classes of information and underline the influence of social factors in memory for remote material.

Botwinick and Storandt (1980) investigated the effect of type of memory test, recall or recognition, on memory for remote socio-historical information or knowledge of the world of entertainment. In general, remote memory performance was better for the recent decades than for the more remote decades and recognition was superior to recall; in males, socio-historic information was recalled better than entertainment information. Overall best performance was provided by subjects aged 50 – 60 years. Older subjects recalled older information better than did younger subjects but, for recent information, the older subjects performed worse than the younger ones. Although the authors interpreted these findings as indicating that advancing age does not produce impairment in memory for very old items, the study was complicated by the fact that only the older age group was alive at the time of the most distant events. If the groups are compared only for those decades during which all subjects were alive, the older subjects performed consistently worse than the younger subjects.

Moscovitch (1982) gave the Famous Faces Test of Albert et al. (1979) to normal subjects aged over 65 years and compared the results with those of a group of undergraduate control subjects (Fig. 4). Performance by the aging group was best for faces from the 1920s and declined steadily for items from more recent decades. Performance of the younger group, however, was best for faces from the most recent decade and declined steadily across the more remote time periods. Although performance in the elderly group was superior to that of the young group for the more remote decades, the younger group performed consistently better than the older group for the time periods during which both groups were alive.

Perlmutter et al. (1980) compared young subjects (mean age 20 years) with older subjects (mean age 64 years) in their ability to recall the dates of past historical events or to make recency judgements about them. Dating capacity and recency discrimination were superior in females. No significant age differences emerged on either measure although younger adults tended to perform better than older adults for recent events. In both groups, dating capacity was poorer for remote events than for recent events. The sex differences are in contrast to those reported by Botwinick and Storandt (1974) and Storandt et al. (1978). Perlmutter et al. (1980), however, used university students as subjects and attributed the sex differences in performance to some elitism in the college-educated females. The relationship between performance and age of the event supports other studies that show decay in memory for past events with time. The finding that older subjects tended to show particular difficulty in dating recent events supports the hypothesis that aging involves selective preservation of more remote memories, even though dating capacity may in-

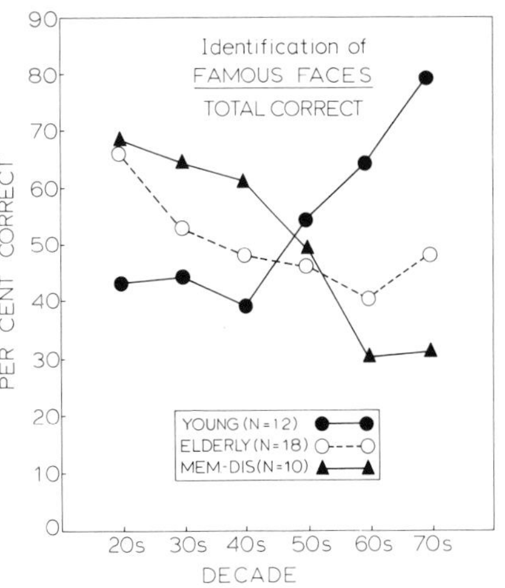

Fig. 4. Cued recall of famous faces by young and elderly normal subjects and patients with memory disorders (9 out of 10 with AD). Reproduced with permission from Moscovitch (1982).

volve cognitive processes that are not slavishly linked to memory for event-related information (Sagar et al., 1988a).

Hamsher and Roberts (1985) examined the capacity of subjects of different ages to recall the names of the most recent six United States Presidents and to place them in temporal order of office. A parallel task required identification and temporal sequencing of the same Presidents presented as photographs. The authors found no effect of age on the ability to name Presidents from photographs or to place the Presidents in temporal order of office. In free recall of the President's names, however, performance declined with age in subjects with 12 or fewer years of education, but not in a subgroup with 13 or more years of education. The different patterns of performance in the different tasks may be due partly to a task complexity effect, because performance by the control group showed free recall of President's names to be the most difficult task of all. Temporal sequencing was, however, dissociable from recall or identification of President's names, suggesting that sequencing performance may be independent of age whilst memory of the President's names is age-dependent.

Yarmey and Bull (1978) examined memory for contextual factors surrounding the death of President John Kennedy. Subjects of different ages recalled what they were doing at the time they learnt of President Kennedy's assassination and rated the clarity of their recollection on a 5-point scale. Memory of detailed contextual factors was then examined specifically by questions relating to time of day and location when they heard the news. Finally, the authors examined the subjects' memory for events that occurred between one and 24 hours before and after the learning of the assassination. Subjects aged over 65 years claimed poor recollection of activities compared with the other groups, but there was no difference between groups in recall of detailed contextual factors. Memory for activities before and after the assassination was poorest in the oldest age group. These results support a deterioration of recall with age, and the lower confidence rating in the elderly suggests that metamemory may decline concomitantly with recall. The lack of age differences in recall of contextual factors, however, suggests that contextual memory is independent of age.

Conclusion

Most studies to date suggest that aging impairs memory for past, public events. The ability to recall autobiographical episodes is less easy to assess because autobiographical memory tests sample only a small proportion of the available memoranda. For public events, memory for recent events is better than memory for remote events but performance differs according to the nature of the test. Public events which took place during an individual's life time are recalled and recognized better than those for which information has been gained from secondary sources. For personal events, preferential recall is partly from time periods corresponding to personal age 15 – 25 years, which may be due to effects of reminiscence and life review (Butler, 1964; Costa and Kasenbaum, 1967; Havighurst and Glasser, 1972; Mergler and Goldstein, 1983; Romaniuk, 1981; Salaman, 1970). The particular recall of autobiographical episodes from certain life periods may, however, also be due to the salience of events such as marriage, school graduation and birth of children, which are common to individuals and frequent in these time periods. The salience factors may influence encoding as well as later elaboration and retrieval. Finally, aging may spare some aspects of contextual memory and sequencing capacity; these observations are compatible with the notion that aging affects effortful memory processes and spares incidental or automatic memory processes.

Age-related neurological disease

Studies of remote memory function in the amnesic syndrome (reviewed by Squire and Cohen, 1984) have shown qualitatively different patterns of deficit depending upon the site and nature of the cerebral pathology. Although controversial (Sanders and Warrington, 1971, 1975; Weiskrantz, 1985), distinctions have been drawn between temporally limited deficits, in which more remote memories are spared (e.g. patient H.M.), and temporally extensive deficits, in which all remote time periods are affected (e.g. Korsakoff's syndrome). Temporally extensive deficits usually show a gradient of impairment in which more remote memories, although impaired, are spared relative to recent ones. Only recently has remote memory function been examined in patients with more widespread cognitive impairment.

Albert et al. (1981a) investigated remote memory function in Huntington's disease and Korsakoff's syndrome (KS), using a facial identification task (Albert et al., 1979). Unlike the Korsakoff group, which showed a temporally extensive deficit with gradient, the patients with Huntington's disease (HD) were impaired approximately equally for all decades examined (1930s to 1970s). A later study showed a qualitatively similar pattern of results in HD of recent onset (Albert et al., 1981b).

Few studies have reported remote memory performance in age-related neurological disease and only Alzheimer's disease (AD) and Parkinson's disease (PD) have been systematically examined. Wilson et al. (1981) gave the remote memory battery of Albert et al. (1979) to patients with AD; the battery consists of a facial identification task and recall and recognition tests of public events and famous people from the 1920s to the 1970s. The impairment in AD affected all decades approximately equally, a pattern similar to that of HD. Performance for the two most recent decades was slightly worse, a finding which was interpreted as an anterograde deficit due to insidiously advancing disease. Moscovitch (1982) also administered the Famous Faces Test of Albert et al. (1979) to 10 patients with AD, all but one of whom were in the early stages of the disease (Fig. 4). The patients were impaired only in identification of faces from the 1970s. Moscovitch reported the cued performance (using semantic and phonemic cues) but not the uncued performance. Thus, Moscovitch may have failed to find a more extensive deficit in the AD group because a relatively easy task was given to patients with only mild memory disorders.

Sagar et al. (1988a) examined remote memory function in patients with mild to moderate AD, using recall and recognition tests of personal and public events. The autobiographical memory test was a modification of the method of Crovitz and Schiffman (1974). The public-events tests consisted of a Famous Scenes Test in which recall and recognition of famous events were examined using news photographs drawn from the 1940s to the 1980s, and a verbal multiple-choice recognition test of public events from the 1940s to the 1970s (Squire and Cohen, 1982). Performance was compared with that of elderly normal subjects and patients with PD. Information related to content and date of past events was assessed separately. On the autobiographical memory test, patients with AD and the demented patients with PD recalled episodes preferentially from more remote time periods than did normal subjects (Fig. 2). The proportion of memories drawn from distant time periods was related to severity of dementia in both groups. In the recall of content of past public events, both groups showed a gradient of deficit in which remote events were affected less than recent ones (Fig. 5); for both groups, the magnitude and temporal extent of the retrograde loss were related to severity of dementia. On recognition testing, patients with PD performed normally but patients with AD continued to show deficits. The impairment was temporally extensive but, unlike performance on the recall test, showed no evidence of a temporal gradient; the impairment was approximately equal across all remote time periods (Fig. 6).

The temporal gradient of remote memory impairment in KS has been attributed to a gradually worsening anterograde amnesia that occurs over the years of alcohol abuse, before the onset of KS (Squire and Cohen, 1982; Butters and Albert, 1982). Insidious anterograde amnesia is an unlikely explanation of the temporal gradient in AD because the gradient extends back over many decades prior to the onset of clinical disease; the temporal extent of this deficit is related to severity of dementia at the time of testing and the gradient is evident on recall but not recognition tests. Moreover, even in KS, this hypothesis has lost support in the finding that the patient P.Z. developed an acute retrograde amnesia with gradient when tested with material from his own autobiography, written a few years before the onset of his KS (Butters and Cermak, 1986). In AD and PD, the temporal gradient on recall may be due to a strengthening of more distant memories with new experience. An increase in associative links with new memories may lead to a richness of interrelated retrieval cues which allows preferential retrieval of old memories when mediated through recall procedures. The relationship of temporal extent of retrograde loss to severity of dementia may explain the findings of Moscovitch (1982) in which mildly demented patients with AD showed a deficit in cued recall of events from the 1970s but not from earlier decades.

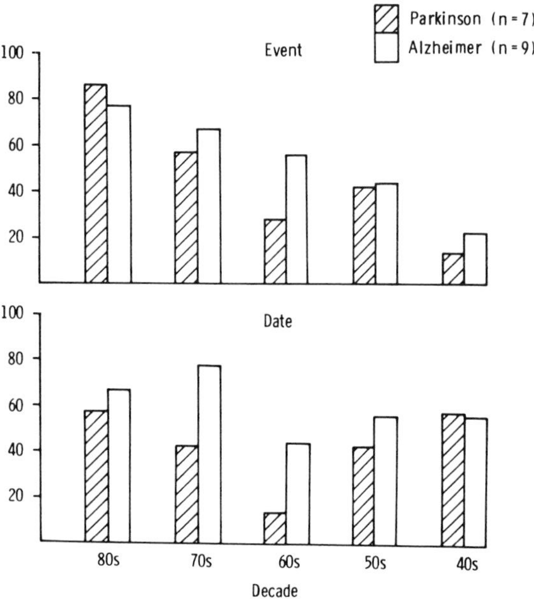

Fig. 5. Recall of event-related and dating information on the Famous Scenes Test in AD and PD. Results are expressed as the percentage of subjects who score below the normal range for events of each decade. From Sagar et al. (1988a).

Two other studies have confirmed the findings of Sagar et al. (1988) of a temporal gradient of remote memory capacity in AD. Beatty et al. (1988) compared performance of patients with AD and patients with HD on an updated version of the remote memory battery of Albert et al. (1979). When performance was expressed as the proportion of correctly recalled items that stemmed from

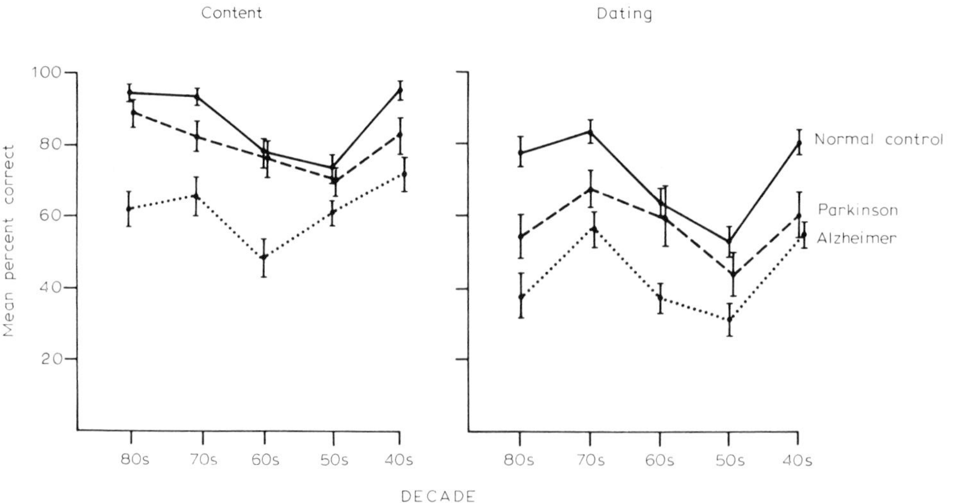

Fig. 6. Recognition of content and date in the Famous Scenes Test by normal elderly subjects and patients with PD or AD. From Sagar et al. (1988a).

each decade, the AD patients showed a gradient of deficit, not seen in the HD group, in which remote items were recalled better than recent ones. Kopelman (1989) examined remote memory for personal and public events in AD and KS, using a British version of the Famous Scenes Test of Sagar et al. (1985, 1988a), a famous names yes/no recognition test and recall tests of autobiographical facts and events. Both patient groups showed a gradient of deficit on all tests, in that memory for remote items was better than memory for recent ones. The finding of a temporal gradient on a purported test of semantic memory (personal facts) is surprising and seemingly argues against Cermak's (1984) hypothesis that the temporal gradient arises because remote memories are semantically represented, and robust, whereas recent memories are episodic, and friable. Kopelman's test, however, included personal 'facts', such as place and time of marriage, first job and a journey within the last year, which may involve episodic components. Thus, the pattern of recall of purely semantic information across decades remains inconclusive.

In the study by Sagar et al. (1988a), gradient effects were evident in recall of event content but not in recall of date. Moreover, in public and personal events tests, the PD group showed a relative impairment in dating capacity, compared with memory for the content of events, which was independent of severity of dementia. These results suggest that memory for date is served by cognitive processes independent of memory for event content, and that those processes underlying dating capacity are selectively disrupted in PD.

The lack of a direct correlation between event memory and dating capacity argues against any direct-access model of dating capacity in which dating is judged directly from properties of the content trace; such models include organization of events in memory in time order or deduction of temporal information from decaying memory trace strength. Rather, the dissociation suggests that dating is performed by indirect access, in which the date is reconstructed from fragments of memory of the event which are related to 'landmark' personal events of high salience and memorability for which the date is known as a fact (Loftus and Marburger, 1983; Friedman and Wilkins, 1985). This capacity to relate one memory trace to another may involve some manipulative system, such as the cognitive mediational system (Warrington and Weiskrantz, 1982; Warrington, 1985) or the higher-order 'executor' (Shallice, 1982; Baddeley and Wilson, 1986). Both of these systems are considered to be based upon the frontal lobes. In a later study of recency discrimination and item recognition in new learning, PD patients were disproportionately and selectively impaired in recency discrimination compared with AD patients who were impaired on both tasks (Sagar et al., 1988b). Recency discrimination is also known to be dependent upon frontal-lobe function (Milner, 1971, 1974; Corsi, 1972) and may be involved in dating capacity.

In a study of remote memory function in AD and KS, Kopelman (1989) also compared remote memory for events with aspects of temporal context memory, including dating capacity and recency discrimination of pictorial material. Both groups showed poor dating capacity and poor anterograde temporal context memory. In KS, patients with and without frontal atrophy on CT scan did not differ from each other in performance on tests of temporal context memory. In all groups, context memory scores, notably on dating and orientation, correlated with performance on some, but not all, tests sensitive to frontal-lobe dysfunction. Similar correlations were found between temporal context memory scores and memory quotient. Kopelman concluded that deficits in temporal context memory are unlikely to be related to frontal dysfunction in KS. Taken together with findings from other studies, however, the results suggest that memory for temporal context is based on a heterogeneous set of processes, including fact memory, recency discrimination and reconstruction, which are served by a number of different brain regions or neural systems. The relative involvement of each of these processes will differ according to the nature of the task provided, and the way in which the processes are disrupted will depend on the site and nature of the cerebral pathology. In evaluating temporal context memory, it is thus essential to take account of the patient group and the nature of the task. Even in a single but multifaceted disease such as AD, a deficit on a particular task may result from disruption of many different processes, which, in turn, are based on different brain regions or systems.

Freedman et al. (1984) gave the Famous Faces Test of Albert et al. (1979) to patients with PD. The results showed a temporally extensive pattern of deficit with no gradient in demented patients; nondemented patients scored normally. Only the cued results, however, were analysed. Huber et al. (1986) gave recall and recognition tests to two groups of patients with PD, one demented by clinical criteria and the other nondemented. Only the demented group showed impairment on this task. Recall and recognition showed temporally extensive deficits, affecting all decades approximately equally. The authors concluded that the remote memory test was useful to distinguish demented from nondemented PD patients. Neither Freedman et al. (1984) nor Huber et al. (1986) provided further breakdown of the groups to allow evaluation of the relationship between remote memory test performance and severity of dementia. The study by Sagar et al. (1988a) specifically examined recall performance in PD; the temporal extent of the retrograde deficit was related to scores on the Blessed Dementia Scale (Blessed et al., 1968). The finding of poor recall but normal recognition in PD is in keeping with the hypothesis that PD affects effortful memory processes selectively (Weingartner et al., 1984).

Brain-behaviour relationships in remote memory disorders

Evidence linking remote memory deficits with other aspects of memory loss is meagre and the relationship between patterns of remote memory impairment and underlying brain lesions is even more scanty. Some evidence indicates that remote memory function is served by processes distinct from those required for learning or for recall of recent events. Firstly, rare cases have been described of severe retrograde amnesia with preserved or only mildly impaired anterograde memory. Thus, Roman-Campos et al. (1980) reported a case of isolated retrograde amnesia of 5 years duration that occurred during recovery from transient global amnesia. Based on EEG findings, the main pathology was localized to the left temporal lobe. Goldberg et al. (1981, 1982) described dense retrograde amnesia of 20 years duration, with only mild anterograde amnesia, in a patient recovering from closed head injury. CT scan examinations showed lesions in both temporal lobes and the mesencephalic tegmentum. The retrograde amnesia was attributed to interruption of projections between the reticular nuclei, the mammillary bodies and the hippocampi. Secondly, patients with KS show correlations between remote memory impairment and anterograde amnesia for the 1960s and 1970s but not for more remote time periods (Shimamura and Squire, 1986). The correlation for the recent time periods can be explained by the development of anterograde amnesia during the recent years of alcohol abuse. The lack of correlation for more remote time periods, however, suggests that retrograde amnesia and anterograde amnesia involve different cognitive processes.

Studies of amnesic syndromes have attempted to discover an anatomical basis for the different patterns of remote memory impairment. Temporally limited patterns of remote memory deficit have been associated with medial temporal-lobe disease, whereas temporally extensive patterns have been linked to diencephalic lesions (reviewed by Squire and Cohen, 1984). A patient with bilateral thalamic infarction (Winocur et al., 1982), however, did not show a temporally extensive patterns of impairment. Others have suggested that involvement of the frontal lobes (Squire and Cohen, 1982; Moscovitch, 1982) or the basal forebrain nuclei (Damasio et al., 1985a,b) is necessary for the development of the temporally extensive loss, possibly in combination with a diencephalic or medial temporal-lobe lesion. In AD, any of these anatomical areas may be involved because the pathology is typically widespread through the frontal and temporal lobes, the hippocampi and the basal forebrain nuclei.

Cermak (1984) has suggested that recently acquired information is episodic in nature but that, with the passage of time, it loses temporal and spatial reference and becomes part of semantic memory (Tulving, 1972; Kinsbourne and Wood, 1975, 1982). Temporally extensive remote memory impairments with gradient are thus assumed to reflect a greater involvement of episodic memory than semantic memory. Applied to AD, the hypothesis may be inadequate because deficits in semantic memory as well as episodic memory have been reported (Weingartner et al., 1981, 1983). However, it remains possible that developing dementia in AD first involves episodic memory, producing a temporally extensive remote memory deficit with gradient. As the condition advances, semantic memory deficits become more prominent and result in increasing deficits for more remote time periods with, ultimately, equal involvement of all remote time periods (Sagar et al., 1988a). Weingartner et al. (1983) have suggested that episodic memory is served by the limbic diencephalic system whilst semantic memory is based upon the association cortex. Evidence that basal ganglia lesions alone can produce retrograde memory impairment has been shown in experimental animals by electrical stimulation of the caudate nucleus (Peeke and Herz, 1971; Thompson, 1958; Wyers et al., 1968, 1973) or substantia nigra (Fibiger and Phillips, 1976; Routtenberg and Holzman, 1973; Staubli and Huston, 1978) and by injection of substance P into the substantia nigra (Huston and Staubli, 1978). These findings may be relevant to the remote memory deficits of PD.

Behavioural similarities between PD and AD may be due to common pathology (reviewed by Sagar, 1985; 1987; Growdon and Corkin, 1986; Sagar and Sullivan, 1988). Cognitive features that distinguish PD from AD, such as the selective impairment in dating capacity and recency discrimination (Sagar et al., 1988a,b), are presumably based on pathological differences (Sagar, 1987; Sagar and Sullivan, 1988). In PD, these specific cognitive deficits may be due to pathology in the frontal lobes or their connections. Thus, several studies have provided evidence of frontal-lobe dysfunction in PD, behaviourally (Lees and Smith, 1983; Taylor et al., 1986; Pillon et al., 1986; Sagar and Sullivan, 1988) and neurophysiologically (Bes et al., 1982; Wolfson et al., 1985). PD differs from AD notably in the disruption of subcortical projection systems between the basal ganglia and the frontal lobes (Alexander et al., 1986). Moreover, PD involves loss of dopaminergic mesocorticolimbic projections (Thierry et al., 1978; Javoy-Agid and Agid, 1980), loss of cholinergic projection from the nucleus basalis to the frontal lobes (Perry et al., 1985) and loss of noradrenergic cells of the locus coeruleus, which also project to the frontal lobes (Hornykiewicz, 1982). Differential involvement of the subcortical-cortical neurotransmitter systems in AD and PD may account for disproportionately severe frontal-lobe deficits in PD. Although definitive evidence is lacking, a role of dopamine in temporal judgement is suggested by observations that the speed of the 'internal clock' in rats may be altered by manipulation of dopamine activity in the nervous system (Maricq and Church, 1983).

Summary and future directions

Performance on remote memory tasks in age-related neurological disease differs according to the age of the memory, nature of the recalled information, the type of task used and the underlying pathology. Thus, relative preservation of remote events, compared with recent ones, has been shown for recall but not recognition in AD and PD in one study; other studies, using different tests, find no qualitative difference between recall and recognition. Dating capacity did not show such a temporal gradient of deficit in either condition. The ability to recall or recognize past public events, and the temporal extent of the retrograde loss, are probably related to severity of dementia. Gradient effects have not, however, been demonstrated in HD. Few studies have examined performance according to the nature of the recalled information but PD may show selective deficits in dating capacity.

The cognitive processes that underlie these deficits remain unclear. However, the available data suggest dissociations between recall and recognition and between memories for event-related information and temporal context. Different patterns of performance across patient groups strongly suggest that these dissociations are linked to the site and nature of the cerebral pathology. Further studies are required to examine in detail the brain-behaviour relationships of remote memory function in age-related neurological disease. Within disease groups, studies are required which examine remote memory for different aspects of information, using recall and recognition tests; performance should be related to other cognitive functions and to the site of pathology, using neuro-imaging procedures. Across disease groups, comparisons are required which compare performance on similar tests. Remote memory function in diseases such as progressive supranuclear palsy, multi-infarct dementia, Pick's disease and other age-related dementias is largely unknown. Metamemory, memory for contextual information and sequencing capacity for remote information has been largely unexplored in age-related neurological disease and seldom has remote memory function been related to anterograde memory capacities. In diseases such as AD and PD in which neurochemical deficits are recognized, studies employing pharmacological manipulation in conjunction with detailed assessment of remote memory capacity may shed valuable light on brain-behaviour relationships in the disorders. The study of remote memory processes in age-related neurological disease remains in its infancy but the research field provides extensive scope for evaluation of neural and neurochemical processes involved in memory for past events.

References

Albert MS, Butters N, Levin J: Temporal gradients in the retrograde amnesia of patients with alcoholic Korsakoff's disease. *Arch. Neurol.: 36,* 211 – 216, 1979.

Albert MS, Butters N, Brandt J: Patterns of remote memory in amnesic and demented patients. *Arch. Neurol.: 38,* 495 – 500, 1981a.

Albert MS, Butters N, Brandt J: Development of remote memory loss in patients with Huntington's Disease. *J. Clin. Neuropsychol.: 3,* 1 – 12, 1981b.

Alexander GE, DeLong MR, Strick PL: Parallel organization of functionally segregated circuits linking basal ganglia and cortex. *Annu. Rev. Neurosci.: 9,* 357 – 381, 1986.

Baddeley A, Wilson B: Amnesia, autobiographical memory and confabulation. In Rubin D (Editor), *Autobiographical Memory,* Cambridge: Cambridge University Press, pp. 225 – 252, 1986.

Beatty WW, Salmon DP, Butters N, Heindel WC, Granholm EL: Retrograde amnesia in patients with Alzheimer's disease or Huntington's disease. *Neurobiol. Aging: 9:* 181 – 186, 1988.

Bes A, Guell A, Fabre N, Dupui PH, Victor G, Geraud G: Cerebral blood flow studied by Xe-133 inhalation technique: loss of hyperfrontal pattern. *J. Cereb. Blood Flow Metab.: 3,* 33 – 37, 1982.

Blessed G, Tomlinson BE, Roth M: The association between quantitative measures of dementia and of senile change in the cerebral grey matter of elderly subjects. *Br. J. Psychiatry: 114,* 797 – 811, 1968.

Botwinick J, Storandt M: *Memory Related Functions and Age.* Springfield, IL: Charles C. Thomas, 1974.

Botwinick J, Storandt M: Recall and recognition of old information in relation to age and sex. *J. Gerontol.: 35,* 70 – 76, 1980.

Butler RN: The life review: an interpretation of reminiscence in the aged. In Kastenbaum R (Editor), *New Thoughts on Old Age.* New York: Springer, pp. 265 – 280, 1964.

Butters N, Albert MS: Processes underlying failures to recall remote events. In Cermak LS (Editor), *Human Memory and Amnesia.* Hillsdale, NJ: Erlbaum, pp. 257 – 274, 1982.

Butters N, Cermak LS: A case study of the forgetting of autobiographical knowledge: implications for the study of retrograde amnesia. In Rubin D (Editor), *Autobiographical Memory.* Cambridge: Cambridge University Press, p. 253, 1986.

Cermak LS: The episodic/semantic distinction in amnesia. In Butters N, Squire LR (Editors), *The Neuropsychology of Memory.* New York: Guildford Press, pp. 55 – 62, 1984.

Corsi P: Human memory and the medial temporal region of the brain. Unpublished doctoral thesis, McGill University, 1972.

Costa P, Kastenbaum R: Some aspects of memories and ambitions in centenarians. *J. Genet. Psychol.: 110,* 3 – 16, 1967.

Crovitz HF, Schiffman H: Frequency of episodic memories as

a function of their age. *Bull. Psychonomic Soc.: 4,* 517 – 518, 1974.

Damasio AR, Graff-Radford NR, Eslinger PJ, Damasio H, Kassell N: Amnesia following basal forebrain lesions. *Arch. Neurol.: 42,* 263 – 271, 1985a.

Damasio AR, Eslinger PJ, Damasio H, et al: Multimodal amnesic syndrome following bilateral temporal and basal forebrain damage. *Arch. Neurol.: 42,* 252 – 259, 1985b.

Fibiger HC, Phillips AG: Retrograde amnesia after electrical stimulation of the substantia nigra: mediation by the dopaminergic nigro-neostriatal bundle. *Brain Res.: 116,* 23 – 33, 1976.

Fitzgerald JM: Sampling autobiographical memory reports in adolescents. *Dev. Psychol.: 16,* 675 – 676, 1980.

Fitzgerald JM: Autobiographical memory reports in adolescence. *Can. J. Psychol.: 35,* 69 – 73, 1981.

Fitzgerald JM, Lawrence R: Autobiographical memory across the life-span. *J. Gerontol.: 9,* 692 – 698, 1984.

Franklin HC, Holding DH: Personal memories at different ages. *Q. J. Exp. Psychol.: 29,* 527 – 532, 1977.

Freedman M, Rivoira P, Butters N, Sax DS, Feldman RG: Retrograde amnesia in Parkinson's disease. *Can. J. Neurol. Sci.: 11,* 297 – 301, 1984.

Friedman WJ, Wilkins AJ: Scale effects in memory for the time of events. *Memory Cognition: 13,* 168 – 175, 1985.

Galton F: Psychometric experiments. *Brain: 2,* 149 – 162, 1879.

Goldberg E, Antin SP, Bilder RM, Gerstman LJ, Hughes JEO, Mattis S: Retrograde amnesia: possible role of mesencephalic reticular activation in long-term memory. *Science: 213,* 1392 – 1394, 1981.

Goldberg E, Hughes JEO, Mattis S, Antin SP: Isolated retrograde amnesia: different etiologies, same mechanisms? *Cortex: 18,* 459 – 462, 1982.

Growdon JH, Corkin S: Cognitive impairments in Parkinson's disease. In: Yahr MD, Duvoisin RC (Editors), *Parkinson's Disease* (*Advances in Neurology* series). New York: Raven Press, 1986.

Hamsher KdeS, Roberts RJ: Memory for recent U.S. Presidents in patients with cerebral disease. *J. Clin. Exp. Neuropsychol.: 7,* 1 – 13, 1985.

Havighurst RJ, Glasser R: An exploratory study of reminiscence. *J. Gerontol.: 27,* 245 – 253, 1972.

Hornykiewicz O: Brain neurotransmitter changes in Parkinson's disease. In: Marsden CD, Fahn S (Editors), *Movement Disorders.* London: Butterworth Scientific, pp. 41 – 58, 1982.

Huber SJ, Shuttleworth EC, Paulson GW: Dementia in Parkinson's disease. *Arch. Neurol.: 43,* 987 – 990, 1986.

Huston JP, Staubli U: Retrograde amnesia produced by post-trial injection of substance P into substantia nigra. *Brain Res.: 159,* 468 – 472, 1978.

Javoy-Agid F, Agid Y: Is the mesocortical dopaminergic system involved in Parkinson's disease? *Neurology: 30,* 1326 – 1330, 1980.

Kinsbourne M, Wood F: Short-term memory processes and the amnesic syndrome. In Deutsch D, Deutsch JA (Editors), *Short-term Memory.* New York: Academic Press, pp. 258 – 291, 1975.

Kinsbourne M, Wood F: Theoretical considerations regarding the episodic-semantic distinction. In Cermak LS (Editor), *Human Memory and Amnesia.* Hillsdale, NJ: Erlbaum, pp. 195 – 217, 1982.

Kopelman MD: Remote and autobiographical memory, temporal context memory and frontal atrophy in Korsakoff and Alzheimer patients. *Neuropsychologia: 27,* 437 – 460, 1989.

Lees AJ, Smith E: Cognitive deficits in the early stages of Parkinson's disease. *Brain: 106,* 257 – 270, 1983.

Loftus EF, Marburger W: Since the eruption of Mt. St. Helens, has anyone beaten you up? Improving the accuracy of retrospective reports with landmark events. *Memory Cognition: 11,* 114 – 120, 1983.

Maricq AV, Church RM: The differential effects of haloperidol and methamphetamine on time estimation in the rat. *Psychopharmacology: 79,* 10 – 15, 1983.

McCormack PD: Autobiographical memory in the aged. *Can. J. Psychol.: 33,* 118 – 124, 1979.

Mergler NL, Goldstein MD: Why are there old people? Senescence as biological and cultural preparedness for the transmission of information. *Hum. Dev.: 26,* 72 – 90, 1983.

Milner B: Interhemispheric differences in the localisation of psychological processes in man. *Br. Med. Bull.: 2,* 272 – 277, 1971.

Milner B: Hemispheric specialization: scope and limits. In Milner B (Editor), *Hemispheric Specialization and Interaction.* Cambridge, MA: MIT Press, pp. 75 – 89, 1974.

Moscovitch M: A neuropsychological approach to perception and memory in normal and pathological aging. In Craik FIM, Trehub S (Editors), *Aging and Cognitive Processes.* New York: Plenum, pp. 55 – 78, 1982.

Peeke HVS, Herz MJ: Caudate nucleus stimulation retroactively impairs complex maze learning in the rat. *Science: 173,* 80 – 82, 1971.

Perlmutter M, Metzger R, Miller K, Nezworski T: Memory of historical events. *Exp. Aging Res.: 6,* 47 – 60, 1980.

Perry EK, Curtis M, Dick DJ, Candy JM, Atack JR, Bloxham CA, Blessed G, Fairbairn A, Tomlinson BE, Perry RH: Cholinergic correlates of cognitive impairment in Parkinson's disease: comparisons with Alzheimer's disease. *J. Neurol. Neurosurg. Psychiatry: 48,* 413 – 421, 1985.

Pillon B, Dubois B, Lhermitte F, Agid Y: Heterogeneity of cognitive impairment in progressive supranuclear palsy, Parkinson's disease and Alzheimer's disease. *Neurology: 36,* 1179 – 1185, 1986.

Poon LW, Fozard LJ: Speed of retrieval from long-term memory in relation to age, familiarity and datedness of information. *J. Gerontol.: 33,* 711 – 717, 1978.

Poon LW, Fozard JL, Paulshock DR, Thomas JC: A questionnaire assessment of age differences in retention of recent and remote events. *Exp. Aging Res.: 5,* 401 – 411, 1979.

Robinson JA: Sampling autobiographical memory. *Cognitive Psychol.: 8,* 578 – 595, 1976.

Roman-Campos G, Poser CM, Wood FB: Persistent retrograde memory deficit after transient global amnesia. *Cortex: 16,* 509 – 518, 1980.

Romaniuk M: Reminiscence and the second half of life. *Exp. Aging Res.: 7,* 315 – 336, 1981.

Routtenberg A, Holzman N: Memory disruption by electrical stimulation of the substrantia nigra, pars compacta. *Science: 181,* 83 – 86, 1973.

Rubin DC: 51 properties of 125 words: a unit analysis of verbal behavior. *J. Verbal Learn. Verbal Behav.: 19,* 736 – 755, 1980.

Rubin DC: On the retention function for autobiographical memory. *J. Verbal Learn. Verbal Behav.: 21,* 21 – 38, 1982.

Rubin DC: Wetzler SE, Nebes RD: Autobiographical memory across the lifespan. In Rubin DC (Editor), *Autobiographical Memory.* Cambridge: Cambridge University Press, pp. 202 – 221, 1986.

Sagar HJ: Brain-behavior relationships in amnesia and dementia. In Hutton JT, Kenny AD (Editors), *Senile Dementia of the Alzheimer type. Neurology and Neurobiology,* Vol. 18. New York: Alan R. Liss, pp. 87 – 104, 1985.

Sagar HJ: Clinical similarities and differences between Alzheimer's disease and Parkinson's disease. *J. Neural Transm.: Suppl. 24,* 87 – 99, 1987.

Sagar HJ, Sullivan EV: Patterns of cognitive impairment in dementia. In Kennard C (Editor), *Recent Advances in Clinical Neurology. Vol. 5.* Churchill Livingstone, pp. 47 – 86, 1988.

Sagar HJ, Cohen NJ, Corkin S, Growdon JH: Dissociations among processes in remote memory. *Ann. N. Y. Acad. Sci.: 444,* 533 – 535, 1985.

Sagar HJ, Cohen NJ, Sullivan EV, Corkin S, Growdon JH: Remote memory function in Alzheimer's disease and Parkinson's disease. *Brain:* 185 – 206, 1988a.

Sagar HJ, Sullivan EV, Gabrieli JDE, Corkin S, Growdon JH: Temporal ordering and short-term memory deficits in Parkinson's disease. *Brain:* 525 – 539, 1988b.

Salaman E: *A Collection of Moments. A Study of Involuntary Memories.* New York, St. Martin's Press, 1970.

Sanders HI, Warrington EK: Memory for remote events in amnesic patients. *Brain: 94,* 661 – 668, 1971.

Sanders HI, Warrington EK: Retrograde amnesia in organic amnesic patients. *Cortex: 11,* 397 – 400, 1975.

Shallice T: Specific impairments of planning. *Phil. Trans. R. Soc. Lond. B: 298,* 199 – 209, 1982.

Shimamura AP, Squire LR: Korsakoff's syndrome: a study of the relation between anterograde amnesia and remote memory impairment. *Behav. Neurosci.: 100,* 165 – 170, 1986.

Squire LR: Remote memory as affected by aging. *Neuropsychologia: 12,* 429 – 435, 1974.

Squire LR, Cohen NJ: Remote memory, retrograde amnesia, and the neuropsychology of memory. In Cermak LS (Editor), *Human Memory and Amnesia.* Hillsdale, NJ: Erlbaum, pp. 275 – 303, 1982.

Squire LR, Cohen NJ: Human memory and amnesia. In Lynch G, McGaugh JL, Weinberger NM (Editors), *Neurobiology of Learning and Memory.* New York: Guildford Press, pp. 3 – 64, 1984.

Squire LR, Slater PC: Forgetting in very long-term memory as assessed by an improved questionnaire technique. *J. Exp. Psychol. Hum. Learn. Memory: 104,* 50 – 54, 1975.

Squire LR, Slater PC, Chace PM: Retrograde amnesia: temporal gradient in very long-term memory following electroconvulsive therapy. *Science: 187,* 77 – 79, 1975.

Storandt M, Grant EA, Gordon BC: Remote memory as a function of age and sex. *Exp. Aging Res.: 4,* 365 – 375, 1978.

Taylor AE, Saint-Cyr JA, Lang AE: Frontal lobe dysfunction in Parkinson's disease. The cortical focus of neostriatal outflow. *Brain: 109,* 845 – 883, 1986.

Thierry AM, Tassin JP, Blanc G, Glowinski J: Studies on mesocortical dopamine systems. *Adv. Biochem. Psychopharmacol.: 19,* 205 – 216, 1978.

Thompson R: The effect of intracranial stimulation on memory in cats. *J. Comp. Physiol. Psychol.: 51,* 431 – 426, 1958.

Tulving E: Episodic and semantic memory. In: Tulving E, Donaldson W (Editors), *Organization of Memory.* New York: Academic Press, 1972.

Warrington EK: A disconnection analysis of amnesia. *Ann. N. Y. Acad. Sci.: 444,* 72 – 77, 1985.

Warrington EK, Sanders HI: The fate of old memories. *Q. J. Exp. Psychol.: 23,* 432 – 442, 1971.

Warrington EK, Silberstein M: A questionnaire technique for investigating very long term memory. *Q. J. Exp. Psychol.: 22,* 508 – 512, 1970.

Warrington EK, Weiskrantz L: Amnesia: a disconnection syndrome? *Neuropsychologia: 20,* 233 – 248, 1982.

Weingartner H, Kaye W, Smallberg SA, Ebert MH, Gillin JC, Sitaram N: Memory failures in progressive idiopathic dementia. *J. Abnorm. Psychol.: 90,* 187 – 196, 1981.

Weingartner H, Grafman J, Boutelle W, Kaye W, Martin PR: Forms of memory failure. *Science: 221,* 380 – 382, 1983.

Weingartner H, Burns S, Diebel R, LeWitt PA: Cognitive impairments in Parkinson's disease: distinguishing between effort-demanding and automatic cognitive processes. *Psychiatry Res.: 11,* 223 – 235, 1984.

Weiskrantz L: On issues and theories of the human amnesic syndrome. In Weinberger NM, McGaugh JL, Lynch G (Editors), *Memory Systems of the Brain.* New York: Guilford Press, pp. 380 – 415, 1985.

Wilson RS, Kaszniak AW, Fox JH: Remote memory in senile dementia. *Cortex: 17,* 41 – 48, 1981.

Winocur G, Oxbury S, Roberts R, Agnetti V, Davis C: Amnesia in a patient with bilateral lesions to the thalamus. *Neuropsychologia: 22,* 123 – 143, 1984.

Wolfson LI, Leenders KL, Brown LL, Jones T: Alterations of regional cerebral blood flow and oxygen metabolism in Parkinson's disease. *Neurology: 35,* 1399 – 1405, 1985.

Wyers EJ, Peeke HVS, Williston JS, Herz MJ: Retroactive impairment of passive avoidance learning by stimulation of the caudate nucleus. *Exp. Neurol.: 22,* 350 – 366, 1968.

Wyers EJ, Deadwyler SA, Hirasuna N, Montgomery D: Passive avoidance retention and retroactive caudate stimulation. *Physiol. Behav.: 11,* 809 – 819, 1973.

Yarmey AD, Bull MP: Where were you when President Kennedy was assassinated? *Bull. Psychonomic Soc.: 11,* 133 – 135, 1978.

Handbook of Neuropsychology, Vol. 4
F. Boller and J. Grafman (Eds)

CHAPTER 16

Psychiatric symptoms in dementia: interaction of affect and cognition

Carolyn C. Hoch and Charles F. Reynolds III

Western Psychiatric Institute and Clinic, University of Pittsburgh, School of Medicine, 3811 O'Hara Street, Pittsburgh, PA 15213, U.S.A.

Introduction

Complex interactions between aging, mood and cognition produce considerable overlap in the symptoms of dementing and depressive disorders in the elderly. Patients with developing dementia are vulnerable to affective decompensation. Similarly, a depressive illness in a fragile aging person can produce cognitive impairment. It would be ideal to see dementia and depression as 'pure elements' at a clinical level. In reality, however, elderly patients with simultaneous symptoms of both depression and dementia are common and frequently present diagnostic uncertainties, with several different clinical patterns of mixed dementia-depression (Riefler et al., 1982; Lazarus et al., 1987; Folstein and McHugh, 1978; McAllister, 1983; Feinberg and Goodman, 1984).

Clinically, the most important issue is to address the question, 'are demented patients who manifest depressive symptoms actually depressed?' The central question of experimental interest is whether the dementia syndrome of depression ('depressive pseudodementia') has the same pathogenesis as depression in the aged. Progress has been made over the past three decades in identification of depressive disorders which coexist with Alzheimer's disease (AD) (Reifler et al., 1982), depressive pseudodementia (Kiloh, 1961; Wells, 1979; McAllister and Price, 1982; Caine, 1981; McHugh and Folstein, 1979), and depression mimicked by dementia of the Alzheimer's type (Fineberg and Goodman, 1984). Clinical samples indicate that depressive symptoms are present in 20 – 40% of cognitively impaired patients (Reifler et al., 1982; Lazarus et al., 1987; Kensevich et al., 1983; Rabins, 1981, 1983); conversely, cognitive impairment in depressed elderly patients occurs in 10 – 50% of cases (Roth, 1976; Kay et al., 1955).

Patients with mixed symptoms of depression and dementia are a heterogeneous group. Differences occur in clinical manifestations, laboratory findings, family history, treatment response for depressive symptomatology (chemotherapy or electroconvulsive therapy) and long-term course. These patients are frequently diagnosed retrospectively based upon the reversibility of cognitive impairment following adequate treatment of their depression. Some elderly depressives with cognitive impairment may, in fact, be in the early stages of AD (or have other types of dementia), but cognitive impairment does not become clinically evident until depression supervenes. The accurate distinction of late-life depression and dementia has obvious importance in terms of treatment and prognosis.

Attempts to distinguish between depression and dementia have relied on specific symptoms, psychiatric history, onset and cause of illness, response to treatment and long-term outcome.

However, no definitive clinical or diagnostic profile has emerged for patients with mixed symptoms. Considerable debate continues regarding the type and significance of symptoms (Kiloh, 1961; Wells, 1979; Folstein and McHugh, 1978; McAllister, 1983) and prognosis (Folstein and McHugh, 1978; Rabins et al., 1984; Post, 1975; Reynolds et al., 1986).

The purposes of this chapter are to compare signs and symptoms in both illnesses through clinical approaches to differential diagnosis, to examine treatment, and to explore stability of diagnosis and course of illness.

Differential diagnosis of depression and dementia

The primary objective in differential diagnosis is the identification of treatable diseases. Clinical diagnosis includes the history, clinical phenomenology and neurological examination. In addition, there are recent pertinent clinical laboratory approaches, as well as experimental approaches using EEG sleep measures.

History

The foundation of differential diagnosis is the history, particularly in cases of more severe illnesses with an onset of less than six months. The developmental course of a depressive illness can often be distinguished from that of progressive brain failure by ascertaining whether symptoms of disturbed cognition or of disturbed mood and affect occurred first. Post (1975) states that with an affective disorder, the memory disorder becomes a problem only after the depression has become well established, whereas in cerebral deteriorations of late life, symptoms of depression, anxiety and paranoid behaviors have been foreshadowed by events such as failures at work and episodes of disorientation. Wells (1979), in a comprehensive review of 'pseudodementia', emphasized rapid progression of symptoms in pseudodementia versus a slower progression of symptoms in dementia. In addition to these symptoms, a history of depression also suggests a depression-related reversible dementia, but does not necessarily rule out the occurrence of a superimposed irreversible dementiform illness. A family history in first-degree relatives of either depression or dementia may also provide useful diagnostic clues. Finally, clinical experience suggests that a dementia of recent onset is more likely to be reversible (Roth, 1976).

Clinical phenomenology

Studies of the clinical phenomenology of coexistent depression and dementia have provided conflicting information about the clinical characteristics. Many data have been derived from brief cognitive and affective tests, such as the Folstein Mini-Mental State (Folstein et al., 1975), the Blessed Dementia Rating Scale (Blessed et al., 1968), the Clinical Dementia Rating Scale (Hughes et al., 1982) and the Hamilton Depression Scale (Hamilton, 1967), which are administered at the bedside and are useful tools for clinical diagnosis. Wells (1979) reports some consensus among geriatricians that 'near-miss' answers are more likely to be associated with organic mental disorders of an irreversible type, while 'don't know' answers are more characteristic of the negativistic and possibly depressed patient.

Folstein et al. (1975, 1978) found that patients with reversible dementia of depression frequently scored 22 or 23 out of a possible 30 points on the Mini-Mental State, while those patients with established dementia typically scored less than 22. Similarly, Rabins et al. (1984), in a study of depressed elderly patients with cognitive impairment, suggested that reversible dementia related to depression is distinguished by a high frequency of previous depression, current depressed mood, delusions and higher Mini-Mental State scores than in demented controls. Raskin and Gershon (1980), in a study of elderly patients with mixed clinical presentations, reported that depressed demented patients showed particular difficulties in

TABLE 1

Differential presentation and course of depression and dementia

	Major depressive disorder with cognitive impairment	Primary degenerative dementia with depressive features
History	Rapid onset, progressive deterioration over 6 to 12 months Earliest symptoms affective Past history of depression common	Insidious and indeterminate onset Earliest symptoms cognitive Negative history of depression
Clinical phenomenology	'Don't know' responses to questions Folstein Mini-Mental State Score ≥ 22 'Subcortical' cognitive deficits Higher depression ratings and symptomatology (e.g., Hamilton ≥ 21)	'Near-miss' responses; attempts to cover up inaccuracies Folstein Mini-Mental State Scores < 22 'Cortical' cognitive deficits Depression ratings inconclusive (Hamilton ratings usually less than 21)
Neurological examination	Non-focal abnormalities	Early stages non-focal; later stages specific abnormalities
Clinical laboratory approaches	EEG and CT scan normal	EEG and CT scan normal in early stages
Polysomnography	Short REM latencies Decreased sleep efficiency Poor sleep maintenance Early morning awakenings Increased REM percent	Normal to long REM latency Indeterminate NREM (Stage N) sleep Decreased slow-wave sleep Decreased REM percent Decreased REM density
Response to one night of total sleep deprivation	Decrease in symptoms of depression	No changes or worsening in symptoms of depression
Response to anti-depressant treatment	Decrease in symptoms of depression; improved cognitive performance	Decrease in depressive symptoms; little improvement in cognition
Life events	Increased rates of death from suicide; no increase in rate of dementia	Increased rates of institutionalization, adjudication of incompetence, and death from inanition

attending to and concentrating on the Mini-Mental State.

Caine's (1981) review of studies with these patients suggested that the cognitive deficits seen in depressed elderly are characterized by impairment in attention, orientation and memory ('subcortical' dementia), in contrast to the 'cortical' deficits of dyspraxia and dysphasia attributable to AD and other organic dementias. Gianotti et al. (1980) compared patients with AD, multi-infarct dementia, normal pressure hydrocephalus, Parkinson's disease (PD), Huntington's disease (HD) and depression on eight neuropsychological measures. The AD patients did consistently worse than other patients, with greater impairment on tests of memory and constructional praxis than the other groups.

A retrospective chart study by Reifler et al. (1986) reported a 31% occurrence of major affective disorder in 131 patients with dementia of the Alzheimer's type. Of these mixed-symptom patients, 85% showed improvement in mood and activities of daily living with antidepressant treatment. However, the authors found that dementia symptoms did not improve with treatment.

Lazarus and associates (Lazarus et al., 1987) investigated depressive symptoms in patients with primary degenerative dementia. They noted significantly higher scores on items which assess intra-psychic symptoms of depression such as anxiety, feelings of helplessness, hopelessness and worthlessness rather than neurovegetative symptoms. The subjects in this study did not score significantly higher than healthy controls on items measuring sleep disturbance or weight loss. In a naturalistic follow-up study of elderly patients with mixed clinical features of both depression and cognitive impairment, Reynolds and colleagues (1986) reported favorable outcome at two years associated with initial greater depressive symptomatology (17-item Hamilton rating of 21 or more), more intact cognitive function (Mini-Mental State of 21 or more) and neurovegetative changes of depression, especially those associated with sleep disturbance.

Merriam and colleagues (1988) assessed the prevalence and nature of psychiatric pathology in 175 community-residing AD patients. The author reported that 85% of their sample met criteria for diagnosis of a major depressive episode at the time of interview. They suggest that the depressive symptoms in AD may be due to structural rather than neurochemical brain changes.

Rovner et al. (1989) examined 144 AD patients for depression. A 17% prevalence rate of major depression was noted. The depressed AD patients had greater cognitive impairment than the nondepressed demented patients.

Burke et al. (in press) reported that depression-like symptoms (changes in psychomotor activity, interest, concentration and energy) are common in AD patients. However, according to these authors, the development of a major depression is rare in AD patients who were not depressed at or before the time of dementia diagnosis.

Finally, Reynolds and associates (1988a) performed a multivariate analysis of clinical phenomenological measures in elderly patients with depressive pseudodementia versus those having primary degenerative dementia with depressive features. Group assignment was made on the basis of demonstrated reversal of cognitive impairment as well as follow-up examinations to ascertain the presence or absence of progressive dementia. Clinical phenomenology was measured by the Folstein Mini-Mental State, the Blessed Dementia Rating Scale and the Hamilton Depression Rating Scale. Univariate contrasts of individual item scores indicated that the patient group with depressive pseudodementia (n = 14) showed significantly greater delayed insomnia (early morning awakening), higher ratings of psychological anxiety and more severe impairment of libido. The patients having primary degenerative dementia with depressive symptoms (n = 28) showed significantly more disorientation to time, greater difficulty finding their way about familiar streets and indoors, and more significant impairment with dressing. Discriminant function analysis, using these seven items, correctly identified 90.5% of the sample. While these results are promising for diagnosis, they require cross-validation in an independent sample.

Neurological examination

Patients with reversible dementia of depression usually show non-focal abnormalities on neurological examination. The same findings may be true of individuals in the early stages of AD. As the AD progresses to the more advanced stages, patients show more specific neurological abnormalities, particularly of gait, posture or reflexes, with such signs as rigidity or abnormal movements (e.g., tremors) as well as myoclonus or seizures (Paulson, 1977).

Clinical laboratory approaches

Depressive pseudodementia is usually associated with a normal electroencephalogram (EEG) and CT scan. Since the same findings are often true of early AD patients, refinements of these laboratory tests seem desireable. A more quantitative assessment of EEG activity in different frequency ranges was produced by adding power spectral analysis to the routine clinical electroencephalography. For example, Brenner and associates (1986) reported that in healthy elderly control subjects (representing 'normal' aging) there was a progressive increase of power in the theta band. In the case of elderly patients with probable AD, there was a greater shift of power into theta and delta ranges, while in elderly depressed patients power density may remain above 9 or 10 Hz. Such quantitative analysis may offer a means of differential diagnosis in patients with both depression and cognitive impairment. Stockard and colleagues (1980) provide some evidence that differences may exist between demented patients and the normal aged in the amplitude and latency of components of event-related potentials (ERP). Prolongation of the latency of components occurring during the first 10 milliseconds may be indicative of organic involvement. There are, however, no published studies of EEG power spectral analysis or ERP in retrospectively proven cases of the dementia syndrome of depression.

Many patients with dementia do not have evidence of cerebral atrophy on routine CT examination. Conversely, some patients with definite cerebral atrophy show no signs of dementia. Methods to refine this diagnostic tool are needed. Naeser et al. (1980) have suggested comparing a patient's cognitive functioning with the 'CT number', a measure related to the coefficient of attenuation of the brain tissue in a given location. They presented preliminary evidence of higher CT scan numbers in non-demented patients than in demented patients. This study included two depressed patients who showed higher CT numbers. The investigators suggested that the technique of CT numbers could be of use in the differential diagnosis of depression and dementia. George and colleagues (1981) found that measures of grey/white matter discriminability are significantly correlated with estimates of cognitive functioning in patients with AD. It must be pointed out that normative data are still needed with both these techniques in order to further define and, perhaps, reduce the overlap between the CT images of demented and non-demented individuals.

Cerebral blood flow has been demonstrated to be reduced in dementia, and this reduction correlates with the severity of cognitive impairment (Sokoloff, 1961). In early AD, a reduction in cerebral blood flow occurs in the frontal and temporal areas. Similarly, cerebral blood flow may be decreased, particularly in the left hemisphere (Mathew et al., 1980). While these data hold promise as a way of differentially diagnosing depression and dementia, more work is needed in order to elucidate differential blood flow patterns in patients with different types of depression (e.g., endogenous vs. non-endogenous), during acute phases of illness, during remission to determine state-trait markers, and using specific pharmacological probes.

Finally, the use of several laboratory examinations in differential diagnosis and prediction of treatment response has been proposed by Grunhaus and colleagues (1983), who propose a profile for the diagnosis of patients with depressive pseudodementia using clinical elements to measure mood and cognitive changes as well as CT scan and the dexamethasone suppression test (DST). They hypothesize the existence of three groups of patients who will show a pattern of differential response to somatic antidepressant therapy. The first is the 'true' pseudodementia group (dysphoric mood, dementia symptoms, abnormal DST and normal CT), whose symptoms of depression and cognitive impairment should improve with adequate antidepressant therapy (either a tricyclic antidepressant trial with therapeutic blood levels for at least three weeks or six or more ECT treatments). In a second group of patients with both depression and dementia of the Alzheimer's type (abnormal DST and abnormal CT), antidepressant treatment should be associated with normalization of the mood disorder and possible partial recovery of cognitive deficits. Finally, a third group of patients having a predominantly dementiform picture and few depressive symptoms (normal DST, abnormal CT) will show little response to antidepressant treatment and also may have enhanced vulnerability to the psychotoxic effects of such treatment. Given the modest sample size and the questionable relationship of the specificity of the DST to depression, the diagnostic approaches suggested in this article should be viewed as preliminary.

Approaches using EEG sleep data

Sleep disturbances are among the most frequent and disturbing features of depressed and demented elderly individuals. Sleep continuity disturbance and early morning awakening contribute to the severity of sleep fragmentation and are highly correlated with the overall severity of depression, as well as with increasing age.

Reynolds et al. (1985) reported that sleep physiological alterations are different in elderly depressed patients from those with probable AD. Depressed elderly patients, as compared to normal elderly controls and AD patients, have lower sleep efficiency, longer first REM periods, greater density of phasic rapid eye movements, and shorter first NREM sleep period (i.e., shorter REM latency). In AD patients, as the disease progresses in severity, the normal circadian rhythm of sleep/wake activity is disrupted and replaced by an arrhythmic polyphasic pattern of multiple episodes of sleeping and waking (Prinz et al., 1982). AD patients also show a gradual but progressive loss of phasic activity, both of rapid eye movements in dream sleep and of spindles and K-complexes in NREM sleep. In addition, the amount of slow-wave sleep and number of delta waves gradually diminished in dementia, while (by contrast) a temporal redistribution of delta activity occurs in depression, as evidenced by shifting of EEG slow waves from the short first NREM sleep period to the longer second NREM period (Reynolds et al., 1985). Finally, AD patients demonstrated significantly higher rates of sleep apnea activity (40 – 45%) than do elderly depressives (10 – 20%) (Hoch et al., 1986, 1989a).

Reynolds and associates (1988b) reported discriminant function analyses of sleep alterations in diagnostically 'pure' nondemented depressed and nondepressed demented patient groups. They attempted to determine which sleep measures could correctly classify and thus diagnostically separate patients. Overall, 80% of the diagnostically 'pure' patients were correctly identified. The four measures which contributed most to the successful separation of depressed and demented patients were REM latency (lower in depressives), REM percent (higher in depressives), 'indeterminate' REM sleep percent (higher in demented patients, reflecting greater loss of spindles and K-complexes), and early morning awakening (more marked in depressives). This discriminate function classification was successfully cross-validated in independent subsamples of diagnostically 'pure' depressed and 'pure' demented patients.

In a further study of EEG sleep in patients with mixed symptoms of depression and cognitive impairment, serial clinical ratings and sleep EEGs before and after one night of sleep deprivation were examined (Buysse et al., 1988). Subjects had three undisturbed baseline sleep nights, one night of total sleep deprivation (night 4), and two recovery nights. Patients with depressive pseudodementia (n = 8) were compared to patients having primary degenerative dementia with depressive features (n = 18). Patients with depressive pseudodementia had less service cognitive impairment at baseline and showed significant improvement in Hamilton Depression ratings after sleep deprivation. By contrast, patients having dementia with secondary depression showed no change or worsening in Hamilton Depression ratings (κ = 0.63, $p < 0.001$). In this same experiment, where sleep deprivation was used as a clinical and physiological probe, baseline sleep measures demonstrated significantly higher REM percent and phasic REM activity/intensity in pseudodemented compared with demented patients. While both groups had increases in sleep efficiency, sleep maintenance and slow-wave sleep following sleep deprivation, recovery night 2 was characterized by greater first REM period duration in depressive pseudo-dementia than in dementia (F = 7.60, $p < 0.002$). These differences in REM sleep rebound (using a REMP 1 cutoff of ≥ 25 minutes) permitted correct identification of 88.5% of patients (κ = 0.72, $p < 0.001$). As Carroll has pointed out (Carroll, in press), these findings illustrate the principle in biological psychiatry that functional laboratory measures will be more informative than baseline biological measures. Because functional measures are those which follow perturbation or challenge (in this case, sleep deprivation), they are designed 'to reveal the response capacity and regulatory integrity of a neurobiologic system (and hence) to reveal stronger evidence of dysregulation.'

EEG sleep variables have been studied as predictors of a two-year mortality in a group of 26 elderly patients with mixed symptoms of depression and cognitive impairment (Hoch et al., 1989b). In performing two-year follow-up for ascertainment of course and diagnosis, a 35% mortality rate (9/26) was observed among these patients, representing a standardized mortality ratio of 450%. In other words, the expected number of deaths over two years would have been 2/26, based upon age-, sex- and race-adjusted death rates (DHHS, 1988). The median time to mortality from polysomnographic evaluation was seven months, with a mean of 13.2 ± 12.6 months. Patients who had died by two-year follow-up did not differ significantly from survivors at baseline in age, sex or global severity of depression and cognitive impairment. However, nonsurvivors did score higher on the anergia item of the Hamilton depression scale ($p < 0.05$) and on the diminished emotional responsiveness item of the Blessed dementia rating scale (Fisher's exact probability = 0.05). There were no differences in survivors versus nonsurvivors with respect to rates of systemic medical illness requiring medication, rate of ECG abnormalities or rate of EEG abnormalities. The proportion of abnormal CT scan results was 50% in nonsurvivors versus 7% in survivors (Fisher's exact probability = 0.03).

With respect to EEG sleep measures, survivors and nonsurvivors did not differ in baseline sleep continuity measures or in NREM sleep architecture. However, REM sleep latency was lower in survivors than in survivors: 16.8 versus 44.1 minutes, respectively, ($p < 0.02$). Similarly, first REM period duration was longer in survivors than in nonsurvivors: 17.9 versus 11.1, respectively ($p < 0.02$). Apnea-hypopnea index (AHI) distributions also differed, with six of nine nonsurvivors having an AHI of ≥ 3 versus only three of seventeen survivors (Fisher's exact probability = 0.02).

A logistic regression analysis was used to model the relationship between EEG sleep predictors and survival status at two years. When REM latency, REM percent, first REM period duration, apnea-hypopnea index and CT scan results were used as predictor variables, the model retained REM latency and AHI. These two variables together accurately predicted survival status in 77% of patients. Patients with REM latency of more than 40 minutes and an apnea-hypopnea index of more than 3 were assigned a relative mortality risk of 3.7 ($p < 0.05$).

Sleep variables were also examined as predictors of time to mortality. The analysis indicated that time to mortality was significantly correlated with baseline REM sleep time (Spearman $\varrho = 0.78, p < 0.02$), REM sleep percent (Spearman $\varrho = 0.73, p < 0.03$) and duration of first REM period (Spearman $\varrho = 0.75, p < 0.02$).

Sleep continuity and NREM sleep architecture measures in the two recovery nights after sleep deprivation showed no differences between survivors and non-survivors. However, REM sleep time was higher on the second recovery night in survivors than in nonsurvivors: 81.7 versus 55.2 minutes, $p < 0.05$. This reflected a mean increase in REM time of 41% in survivors versus 21% in nonsurvivors.

In essence, it appears that nonsurviving mixed-symptom elderly patients were characterized by diminished response capacity both during wakefulness (i.e., greater anergia and blunting of emotional responsivity) and during sleep (i.e., blunted capacity for REM sleep generation and REM sleep rebound after total sleep deprivation).

Treatment

Given the prevailing conceptualization that depressive pseudodementia is a retrospective diagnosis based upon reversal of cognitive and affective symptoms through treatment of depression, it is useful to review the parameters of adequate antidepressant treatment for this group. Only limited data on the treatment response of elderly patients with mixed symptoms of depression and cognitive impairment have been published.

Reynolds and coworkers (1987) reported a study of open-trial antidepressant response in 16 patients with mixed symptoms of depression and cognitive impairment compared to a group of 16 depressed elderly without cognitive impairment. Criteria for adequate treatment specified a steady-state plasma nortriptyline level of 50 to 150 ng/ml for four consecutive weeks or a minimum of six electroconvulsive therapy (ECT) treatments. Ten of the mixed-symptom patients showed a 50% drop in Hamilton depression ratings as well as a significant decline in Blessed dementia rating. Improvement in Blessed dementia ratings was significantly correlated with improvement in Hamilton ratings (r = 0.65, $p < 0.01$). In cognitively intact depressed elders, the mean percent change in Hamilton rating was 72%. The authors suggested that elderly patients with mixed depression and cognitive impairment are treatable, and that treatment similar to that used with the cognitively intact depressed elderly produces significant relief of symptoms.

Diagnostic stability

No unanimity exists regarding the prognosis and clinical course of elderly patients with mixed depressive symptoms and cognitive impairment. Several investigators have reported that most depressed-demented patients do not recover cognitively (Kral, 1983; Wells, 1979; McAllister and Price, 1982; Shraberg, 1978). Others have concluded that co-existing cognitive impairment and major depression do not usually predict progressive dementing illness (Rabins et al., 1984).

In an eight-year follow-up study of 22 patients with 'depressive pseudodementia', Kral (1983) reported that 20 of 22 became permanently demented on follow-up. Rabins and colleagues (1984) reported that patients with a history of affective disorder, self-reports of depressed mood, self-blaming, hopelessness and somatic delusions, appetite disturbance and a sub-acute onset identify patients suffering from dementia caused by depression. Reynolds et al. (1986) studied 16 patients with mixed symptoms of depression and cognitive impairment for two years. Eight subjects showed clinical improvement and eight showed deterioration. Improvement at two years was associated with several baseline measures: a Folstein Mini-Mental State score of 21 or higher, a Hamilton Depression score of 21 or higher, and a sleep efficiency of less than 75%. Life events (i.e., appointment of a guardian, institutionalization, development of additional medical disorders, death and final diagnoses) were also noted for the sample during the longitudinal study period. None of the patients with clinical improvement had a guardian appointed, had been institutionalized or had died. By contrast, of the eight patients who showed deterioration, two had been judged incompetent, three had been institutionalized and three had died.

Elderly patients with mixed symptoms of depression and dementia represent a heterogenous group. A more favorable outcome may be associated with initially greater depressive symptomatology, higher cognitive function and, perhaps, neurovegetative changes of depression, such as early morning awakening.

Summary and future directions

The most salient issue facing clinicians who deal with elderly depressed and demented patients is to recognize the delicate and complex interaction which exists between aging, mood and cognition. Since an estimated 10% of the depressed elderly have reversible cognitive impairment of sufficient severity to mimic a dementiform illness and an additional 40% have a milder cognitive impairment, it is essential to distinguish the dementia syndrome of depression from depressive features associated with AD. The history, clinical presentation, mental status, neurological examination and routine laboratory tests may be useful for diagnosis. However, the only conclusive diagnostic test at present is whether the patient has resolution of affective and cognitive impairment with adequate antidepressant therapy. This method may be problematic because of the time it requires to establish adequate antidepressant treatment and because of the limited ability of the depressed elderly to tolerate antidepressant drugs (a patient may develop peripheral or central toxicity to medication).

The need for research to establish multidimensional correlates (neuropsychological, neuropharmacological, metabolic and chronobiological) of late-life depression and dementia is evident. This should enhance the ability to determine similarities in the pathogenesis of depressive pseudodementia and that of depressive symptoms in primary degenerative dementia.

Acknowledgements

Supported in part by National Institute of Mental Health grants 37869, 30915 and 00295, and by a grant from the John D. and Catherine T. MacArthur Foundation Research Network for the Psychobiology of Depression.

References

Blessed G, Tomlinson BE, Roth M: The association between quantitative measures of dementia and senile change in the cerebral gray matter of elderly subjects. *Br. J. Psychiatry: 114,* 797 – 811, 1968.

Brenner RP, Ulrich R, Spiker DG, Sclabassi R, Reynolds CF, Marin RS, Ballen F: Computerized EEG spectral analysis in elderly normal, demented, and depressed subjects. *Electroencephalogr. Clin. Neurophysiol.: 64,* 483 – 492, 1986.

Burke WJ, Rubin EH, Morris J, Berg L: Symptoms of 'depression' in senile dementia of the Alzheimer type. *Alzheimer's Dis. Assoc. Disord.:* in press.

Buysse DJ, Reynolds CF, Kupfer DJ, Houck PR, Hoch CC, Stack JA, Berman SR: Electroencephalographic sleep in depressive pseudodementia. *Arch. Gen. Psychiatry: 45,* 568 – 575, 1988.

Caine ED: Pseudodementia current concepts and future direction. *Archives of General Psychiatry: 38,* 1359 – 1364, 1981.

Carroll BJ: Diagnostic validity and laboratory studies: rules of the game. In Robin LN (Editor), *Validity of Psychiatric Diagnoses: Proceedings of the 78th Annual Meeting, American Psychopathological Association.* New York: Raven Press, in press.

Folstein MF, Folstein SE, McHugh RR: 'Mini-Mental Sate' – a practical method for grading the cognitive state of patients for the clinician. *J. Psychiatr. Res.: 12,* 189 – 198, 1975.

Feinberg T, Goodman B: Affective illness, dementia and pseudodementia. *J. Clin. Psychiatry: 45,* 99 – 103, 1984.

Folstein MF, McHugh, RP: Dementia syndrome of depression. In Katzman R, Terry RD, Beck KL, (Editors), *Aging, (Vol. 7), Alzheimer's Disease: Senile Dementia and Related Disorders.* New York: Raven Press, pp. 87 – 93, 1978.

Gainotti G, Caltagirone C, Masullo C, Miceli G: Patterns of neuropsychologic impairment in various diagnostic groups of dementia. In Amaducci L, Davison A, Antuono P (Editors), *Aging of the Brain and Dementia.* New York: Raven Press, pp. 245 – 250, 1980.

George AE, deLeon MJ, Fervis SH, Kricheff II: Parenchymal CT correlates of senile dementia (Alzheimer Disease): loss of gray-white matter discriminability. *Am. J. Neurol. Res.: 2,* 205 – 213, 1981.

Grunhaus L, Dilsaver S, Greden JT, Carroll BJ: Depressive pseudodementia. *Biol. Psychiatry: 18,* 215 – 225, 1983.

Hamilton M: Development of a rating scale for primary depressive illness. *Br. J. Soc. Clin. Psychol.: 6,* 278 – 296, 1967.

Hoch CC, Reynolds CF, Kupfer DJ, Houck PR, Berman SR, Stack JA: Sleep disordered breathing in normal and pathologic aging. *J. Clin. Psychiatry: 47,* 499 – 503, 1986.

Hoch CC, Reynolds CF, Nebes R, Berman SR, Campbell D, Kupfer DJ: Clinical significance of sleep-disordered breathing (SDB) in Alzheimer's disease: preliminary data. *J. Am. Geriatr. Soc.: 145,* 1099 – 1103, 1989a.

Hoch CC, Reynolds CF, Houck PR, Hall F, Berman SR, Buysse DJ, Dahl R, Kupfer DJ: Predicting mortality in mixed depression and dementia using EEG sleep variables. *J. Neuropsychiatry Clin. Neurosci.: 1,* 366 – 371, 1989b.

Hughes CP, Berg L, Danzeger WL, Coben LA, Martin RL: A new clinical scale for the staging of dementia. *Br. J. Psychiatry: 140,* 566 – 572, 1982.

Kay DE, Roth M, Hopkins B: Affective disorders arising in the Senium: I. Their association with cerebral degeneration. *J. Ment Sci.: 101,* 301 – 316, 1955.

Kiloh LG: Pseudo-dementia. *Acta Psychiatr. Scand.: 37,* 366 – 370, 1961.

Knesevich JW, Martin RL, Berg L, Danziger W: Preliminary report on affective symptoms in the early stages of senile dementia of the Alzheimer type. *Am. J. Psychiatry: 140,* 233 – 235, 1983.

Kral VA: The relationship between senile dementia (Alzheimer type) and depression. *Can. J. Psychiatry: 28,* 304 – 306, 1983.

Lazarus LW, Newton N, Cohler B, Lesser J, Schweon C: Frequency and presentation of depressive symptoms in patients with primary degenerative dementia. *Am. J. Psychiatry: 144,* 41 – 45, 1987.

Mathew RJ, Meyers JS, Francis DJ, Semchuk KM, Mortel K, Claghorn JL: Cerebral blood flow in depression. *Am. J. Psychiatry: 137,* 1449 – 1450, 1980.

McAllister TW: Overview: pseudodementia. *Am. J. Psychiatry: 140,* 528–533, 1983.

McAllister TW, Price TR: Severe depressive pseudodementia with and without dementia. *Am. J. Psychiatry: 139,* 626–629, 1982.

McHugh PR, Folstein MF: Psychopathology of dementia: implications for neuropathology: *Res. Publ. Assoc. Res. Nerv. Ment. Dis.: 57,* 17–30, 1979.

Merriam AE, Aronson MK, Gaston P, Wey SL, Katz I: The psychiatric symptoms of Alzheimer's disease. *J. Am. Geriatr. Soc.: 36,* 7–12, 1988.

Naeser MA, Gebhardt C, Levine HL: Decreased computerized tomography numbers in patients with presenile dementia. *Arch. Neurol.: 37,* 401–409, 1980.

Paulson GW: The neurological examination in dementia. In Wells CE (Editor), *Dementia.* Philadelphia: Davis, pp. 169–188, 1977.

Post F: Dementia, depression, and pseudodementia. In Benson DF, Blumer D (Editors), *Psychiatric Aspects of Neurologic Disease.* New York: Grune and Stratton, pp. 99–120, 1975.

Prinz PN, Peskind ER, Vitaliano PP, Raskind MA, Eisdorfer C: Changes in the sleep and waking EEGs of nondemented and demented elderly subjects. *J. Am. Geriatr. Soc.: 30,* 86–93, 1982.

Rabins PV: The prevalence of reversible dementia in a psychiatric hospital. *Hosp. Community Psychiatry: 32,* 490–492, 1981.

Rabins PV: Reversible dementia and the misdiagnosis of dementia. *Hosp. Community Psychiatry: 34,* 830–835, 1983.

Rabins PV, Merchant A, Nestadt G: Criterian for diagnosing reversible dementia caused by depression: validation by two-year followup. *Br. J. Psychiatry: 144,* 488–492, 1984.

Raskin A, Gershon S: Diagnosis and treatment of senile organic brain states of mild to moderate degree. *Psychopharmacol. Bull.: 16,* 23–25, 1980.

Reifler BV, Larson E, Hanley R: Coexistence of cognitive impairment and depression in geriatric outpatients. *Am. J. Psychiatry: 139,* 623–626, 1982.

Reifler B, Larson E, Teri L, Poulson M: Dementia of the Alzheimer's type and depression. *J. Am. Geriatr. Soc.: 34,* 855–859, 1986.

Reynolds CF, Kupfer DJ, Taska LS, Hoch CC, Spiker DG, Sewitch DE, Zimmer B, Marin RS, Nelson P, Martin D, Morycz R: EEG sleep in healthy elderly, depressed and demented subjects. *Biol. Psychiatry: 20,* 431–442, 1985.

Reynolds CF, Kupfer DJ, Hoch CC, Stack JA, Houch PR, Sewitch DE: Two-year follow up of elderly patients with mixed depression and dementia: clinical and electroencephalographic sleep findings. *J. Am. Geriatr. Soc.: 34,* 793–799, 1986.

Reynolds CF, Perel JM, Kupfer DJ, Zimmer B, Stack JA, Hoch CC: Open-trial response to antidepressant treatment in elderly patients with mixed depression and cognitive impairment. *Psychiatry Res.: 21,* 111–122, 1987.

Reynolds CF, Hoch CC, Kupfer DJ, Buysse DJ, Houck PR, Stack JA, Campbell DW: Bedside differentiation of depressive pseudodementia from dementia. *Am. J. Psychiatry: 145,* 1099–1103, 1988a.

Reynolds CF, Kupfer DJ, Houck PR, Hoch CC, Stack JA, Berman SR, Zimmer B: Reliable discrimination of elderly depressed and demented patients by EEG sleep data. *Arch. Gen. Psychiatry: 45,* 258–264, 1988b.

Roth M: The psychiatric disorders of later life. *Psychiatr. Ann.: 6,* 417, 1976.

Rovner BW, Broadhead J, Spencer M, Carson K, Folstein M: Depression and Alzheimer's disease. *Am. J. Psychiatry: 146,* 350–353, 1989.

Shraberg D: The myth of pseudodementia and the aging brain. *Am. J. Psychiatry: 135,* 601–603, 1978.

Sokoloff L: Cerebral circulation and metabolism changes associated with aging. *Res. Publ. Assoc. Nerv. Ment. Dis.: 41,* 237–254, 1961.

Stockard JJ, Stockard JE, Sharbrough FW: Brainstem auditory evoked potentials in neurology: Methodology, interpretation, clinical application. In Amenoff M (Editor), *Electrodiagnosis in Clinical Neurology.* New York: Churchill Livingstone, 1980.

U.S. Department of Health and Human Services: *Health United States, 1987* (Publication DHSS 88–1232). Hyattsville, MD: National Center for Health Services, pp. 56–57, 1988.

Wells CE: Pseudodementia. *Am. J. Psychiatry: 136,* 895–900, 1979.

Handbook of Neuropsychology, Vol. 4
F. Boller and J. Grafman (Eds)

CHAPTER 17

Sleep in the dementing disorders

Patricia Prinz, J. Steven Poceta and Michael V. Vitiello

Sleep and Aging Research Program, American Lake VA Medical Center, Clinical Research Centre, University Hospital, Psychiatry and Behavioral Sciences, RP-10, University of Washington, Seattle, WA 98195, U.S.A.

Introduction

Many aged individuals have difficulty sleeping and have a high frequency of sleep-related complaints. In 1977 alone, 25 million prescriptions for sedative-hypnotic agents were written to treat sleep complaints in the U.S.A. Forty percent of these were for elderly patients. The high frequency of sleep complaints reported by the aged probably derives from two distinct factors: (1) specific non-pathological sleep changes which accompany the aging process, and (2) the increased prevalence in the aged of various pathologies which may cause secondary sleep disorders.

Modern measurements of sleep and wakefulness patterns are based on all-night polygraphic recordings of the electrical signals generated by brain, postural muscle and eye movement activities. Additional physiological parameters, such as electrocardiogram, respiration, temperature and airflow, are often monitored in the sleep laboratory depending on the experimental and clinical questions to be answered.

Normal sleep is divided into two main categories comprising a total of five stages. Non-rapid eye movement (NREM) sleep includes stages 1, 2, 3 and 4. Rapid eye movement (REM) sleep is the fifth stage (also called dream, active or paradoxical sleep because the EEG recording is similar in appearance to the awake state).

In NREM sleep, the EEG slows relative to the waking state and muscle tonus is moderately reduced from the waking levels. In stage 1 sleep there is an absence of REMs and the EEG pattern is of low-amplitude, irregular, high-frequency activity. In stage 2 sleep, synchronous waves of 12 to 16 Hz (spindles) occur against a background of mixed-frequency EEG activity. In stage 3 sleep, high-amplitude (75 μV or more) slow (0.5 – 3 Hz) 'delta' waves become more frequent than in stage 2, comprising 20 – 49% of the EEG record. When these delta waves compose 50% or more of the EEG record, stage 4 sleep is reached. REM sleep is characterized by bursts of rapid eye movements (REMs), great reduction of muscle tonus and by low-amplitude, high-frequency EEG activity similar to that during wakefulness.

Sleep changes accompanying 'normal' aging have been quantitated in a number of studies. Common findings include increased fragmentation of nighttime sleep due to intrusions of wakefulness, decreased amounts of the deeper stages of NREM sleep (stages 3 and 4) and more modest decreases in REM sleep in older adults (Feinberg, 1968; Prinz, 1976; Roffwarg, 1966; Williams et al., 1974).

In the presence of pathologies affecting sleep, these normal age changes can become much more pronounced. The more common factors that impair sleep in older adults are listed below (excerpted from ASDC Nosology of Sleep Disorders, 1979).

Nocturnal respiratory dysfunction (sleep apnea)
This sleep disorder is characterized by a repeated cessation of breathing (apnea) for 10 seconds or longer, resulting in multiple nighttime awakenings and daytime sleepiness. Apnea episodes are more common in males than females and more common in older populations. Often the older patient will deny any sleep disturbance, but complain of excessive daytime sleepiness. The high prevalence of apnea episodes in the elderly population (30 to 50% of 'normal' older men experience 25 or more episodes per night) (Smallwood et al., 1984) is of particular concern when one considers that depressant drugs and alcohol can greatly worsen existing sleep apnea activity.

Nocturnal myoclonus
Nocturnal myoclonus describes two sleep-related neuro-muscular dysfunctions: Restless Leg Syndrome, a very strong pre-sleep urge to move one's legs repeatedly which results in sleep-onset insomnia, and Periodic Movements During Sleep, a rapid periodic and stereotypical flexion of the leg and foot which may awaken the patient repeatedly during the night. The incidence of nocturnal myoclonus appears to increase with age. Additionally, it often occurs in conjunction with sleep apnea.

Sleep disturbance secondary to physical illness or toxic metabolic states
A variety of medical problems may impair normal sleep. Common examples include arthritic and other pain syndromes, major medical conditions such as respiratory or cardiac disease, and diabetes mellitus. Nocturnal dyspnea and nocturia often disturb sleep in patients with congestive heart failure.

Sleep disturbances secondary to psychiatric illness
Psychiatric illnesses or emotional reactions to physical illnesses are common causes of disturbed sleep in the elderly patient. Depression is common in the older population, and disturbed sleep with early morning insomnia is often a cardinal manifestation of this illness.

Sleep disturbance associated with drug and alcohol use
Just as the likelihood of illness increases with age, so does the probability of employing multiple medications for its treatment. These drugs can produce secondary sleep disturbances. Chronic use of sleeping medications or alcohol is known to induce a drug-related insomnia. In addition to drug-induced insomnia, daytime effects of chronic hypnotic use include hypersomnolence, impaired cognition and impaired psychomotor functioning.

Sleep disturbances related to circadian rhythm changes
The amplitudes of the rest/activity and temperature rhythms are both diminished by advancing age in animals and man (Vitiello et al., 1986). It is conceivable that age-related impairment in sleep may be related to reductions in daytime activity level with associated damping or disorganization of rest/activity and other circadian rhythms.

Other sleep disorders
The sleep disorders discussed above are generally more prevalent in older than in young adult populations. Other sleep disorders exist which are less age-sensitive; these include (1) psychophysiological insomnia, in which tension and anxiety interfere with sleep, sometimes in conjunction with negative expectations about sleeping or the sleeping environment; (2) narcolepsy, in which neural control of sleep appears to be impaired; and (3) parasomnias, in which behaviors related to sleep are the source of distress, e.g., bruxism, enuresis, sleep walking.

Sleep disturbance secondary to dementing conditions
Dementing conditions are those which result in cognitive deficits. It is now recognized that Alzheimer's disease (AD) accounts for the largest proportion of cases of irreversible progressive

dementia (Terry and Katzman, 1983). Nevertheless, a substantial number of cases involve other disorders, such as multi-infarct dementia (or other cerebrovascular disorders), Parkinson's disease (PD) and alcohol-related encephalopathy. Less common causes of progressive dementia include anoxic and post traumatic encephalopathies, and Pick's, Huntington's and Jakob-Creutzfeldt diseases. Other conditions such as progressive supranuclear palsy or spinocerebrellar degeneration may also underlie progressive dementing disorders. Conditions producing dementing symptomatology which are potentially reversible include toxic drug or metabolic states and depression (as reviewed in Larson et al., 1986). Sleep disturbances caused by toxic and metabolic states are well-recognized and constitute an important part of the nosology of Sleep and Arousal Disorders (ASDC, 1979). Our review here will be restricted to those disorders resulting in an irreversible progressive dementia, with emphasis on studies that utilized diagnostic screening in order to obtain more homogeneous diagnostic study groups.

Brain structure and sleep-wake function

As the list of sleep disorders above indicates, impaired sleep is a common occurrence in a variety of abnormalities affecting brain function. Brain mechanisms governing sleep/wakefulness are both anatomically widespread and highly interactive (Jones, 1989; Siegel, 1989; Carlson, 1986). Sleep mechanisms are distributed in brain stem (raphe and tractus solitarius) as well as basal forebrain, preoptic, rostral hypothalamic, thalamic and cortical regions. Sleep systems are sensitive to a variety of neurotransmitters, including cholinergic, nonadrenergic, serotonergic, histaminergic and neuropeptide systems. Sleep systems are inhibited by sensory inputs and/or activated arousal systems. Arousal mechanisms include the mesencephalic reticular acting system and the locus coeruleus systems. Arousal systems are also sensitive to a variety of neurotransmitters, particularly adrenergic, cholinergic and neuropeptide ones. Arousal systems are facilitated by hormonally mediated stress states and by sensory inputs, and are highly interactive with sleep-generating systems. Experimental manipulations of sleep- or wakefulness-generating systems generally impair rather than improve physiological sleep, i.e., sleep with normal patterns of sleep stages followed by normal patterns of alertness (Jones, 1989; Siegel and Rogawski, 1988). This indicates that optimal sleep/wake functioning may depend on the overall integrity of widespread, interacting brain mechanisms. As we shall review below, this view is supported by nature's own experiments, the dementing disorders. Our review will describe the impaired sleep/wake functioning that is a striking, common feature to all the dementing disorders, even though each is characterized by a distinct pattern of neuronal degeneration.

Sleep change associated with AD

AD is a disorder of memory and cognition caused by a progressive neuronal degeneration of unknown etiology. It is estimated that 2 – 10% of the 22 million individuals in the United States over age 65 suffer from clinically significant dementing illness (Mortimer and Hutton, 1985). AD accounts for more than half of these cases of dementia (Terry and Katzman, 1983). Impairment of sleep-wake function is a common clinical observation in Alzheimer's dementia; nighttime insomnia and wandering often becomes a factor in a family's decision to institutionalize their demented relative, particularly when symptoms of delusions (sundown syndrome) are also present.

Polygraphic studies of all-night sleep patterns have validated the clinical observation of increased nighttime wakefulness (Prinz, 1982a,b; Loewenstein et al., 1982; Reynolds et al., 1985a). Some studies have documented an increase in daytime napping (Prinz et al., 1982a) and all but one (Reynolds et al., 1985c) have observed a decrease in nighttime slow-wave sleep and REM sleep in AD patients in varying stages of this progressive dementing disorder. Correlations between AD severity (assessed using cognitive function scores) and sleep impairment were noted in several of these studies.

Effect of severity of AD

Sleep/wakefulness patterns undergo progressive change that parallels AD severity. Fig. 1 summarizes a number of studies based on AD patients in varying stages, ranging from institutionalized late-stage probable AD patients (Prinz et al., 1982a) through community-dwelling mild or moderate stages (Prinz et al., 1982b, 1987a) to early-stage (Vitiello and Prinz, 1987) possible or probable AD patients. These research groups were highly screened to minimize confounding disorders. We employed DSMIII, NINCDS (McKhann et al., 1984) and laboratory research diagnostic criteria (Prinz et al., 1982b) for possible and probable AD. These diagnostic criteria have been confirmed histologically at autopsy in 15 of the 17 probable AD patients (88%) who have died as of this date. Studies were based on drug-free AD subjects and age-, sex- and education-matched control subjects. All subjects were screened for minimal health problems, minimal Hachinski (1974, 1975) scores, minimal depression and minimal evidence of sleep disorders such as apnea or myoclonus (Prinz et al., 1987b). All of the results described were based on testing done during a 72-hour stay by each subject on a clinical research center ward.

Figs. 1 – 5 show selected sleep measures declining in parallel with the decline in cognitive function that characterizes the progression of this disease. Cognitive decline (Fig. 1) is illustrated using the Mini Mental State examination (Folstein et al., 1975). The AD effect on sleep was significant even in the earliest stage AD group (Table 1): increased numbers of awakenings, increased WASO (Wake After Sleep Onset) and decreased percent of stage 3 – 4 sleep (of Time in Bed) were observed compared with control subjects (Vitiello and Prinz, 1987; Vitiello et al., 1989). Figs. 2 – 5 illustrate continued disruption of sleep/wake measures with increasing severity of AD. Periods spent in stage 3 – 4 sleep (Fig. 2) and in REM sleep (Fig. 3) as percentages of time in bed both show declines which closely parallel declines in cognitive function. Conversely, time spent awake (Fig. 4) and frequency of nighttime awakenings from sleep (Fig. 5) show increases with increasing AD severity.

Other sleep measures failed to differ reliably

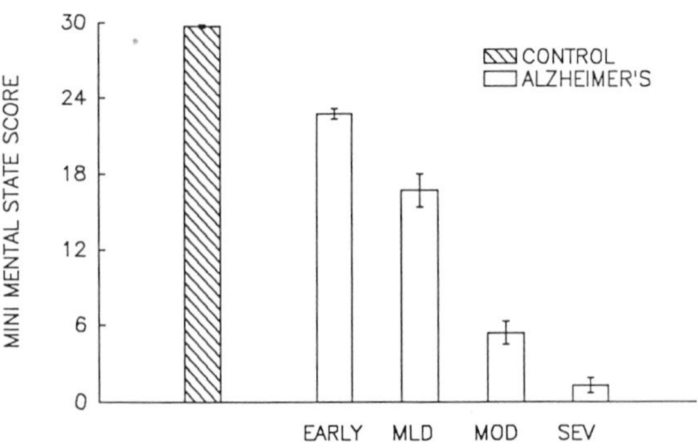

Fig. 1. Mean Mini Mental State scores ± standard error of the mean for control and early-stage AD groups (Vitiello et al., 1989), and from mild, moderate and severe AD groups (Prinz et al., 1982a,b) (n = 18, 16 and 10, respectively).

TABLE 1

Selected demographic, cognitive and sleep/wake measures for the control and early AD groups (mean ± standard deviation)

	Control	AD
n	46	44
Sex (% male)	43	45
Age (years)[a]	67.0 ± 6.6	70.7 ± 7.5*
Education (years)	14.3 ± 3.5	13.8 ± 3.1
MMS	29.7 ± 0.6	22.7 ± 2.9***
Hamilton dep. scale	8.3 ± 5.3	8.1 ± 3.8
Number of wakes	7.9 ± 3.4	10.4 ± 6.4*
WASO	50.3 ± 39.5	76.7 ± 46.3**
Percent wake	14.2 ± 8.7	18.4 ± 9.7
Percent 3 and 4	9.6 ± 4.6	7.4 ± 3.8**
Percent REM	19.2 ± 5.0	18.0 ± 6.0

* $p < 0.05$, ANOVA.
** $p < 0.01$, ANOVA.
*** $p < 0.001$, ANOVA.
[a] Age was covaried in examining sleep variables using ANCOVAs. However, as there was no significant age effect for any variable statistical differences are reported for ANOVAs.

from control levels in AD patients across a range of AD severities. This category included stage 1 and 2 sleep, time in bed at night, latency to sleep onset (Prinz et al., 1982) and REM latency (minutes of sleep between sleep onset and the first REM period) (Vitiello et al., 1984a; Reynolds et al., 1985a).

There is some theoretical basis for believing that impaired sleep may indicate neuronal degeneration in AD. Brainstem regions and neurohormonal pathways that regulate sleep undergo degenerative change in AD, as do cortical tissues that generate slow-wave EEG activity during sleep (reviewed in Prinz et al., 1982b). Impaired sleep in AD may thus result from loss of neuronal pathways that initiate and maintain sleep. This theoretical possibility led us to test whether sleep changes might serve as a biological marker for AD in its earliest, initial stages.

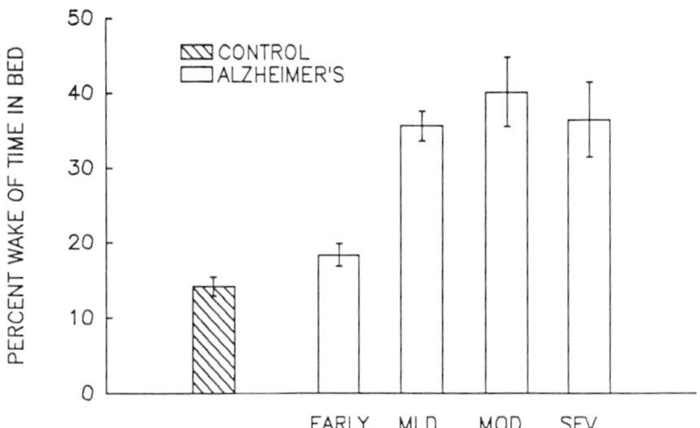

Fig. 4. Mean percent waketime of ± standard errors of the mean for control and early-stage AD groups from the current study (Vitiello et al., 1989), and from mild, moderate and severe AD groups (Prinz et al., 1982a,b) (n = 18, 16 and 10, respectively).

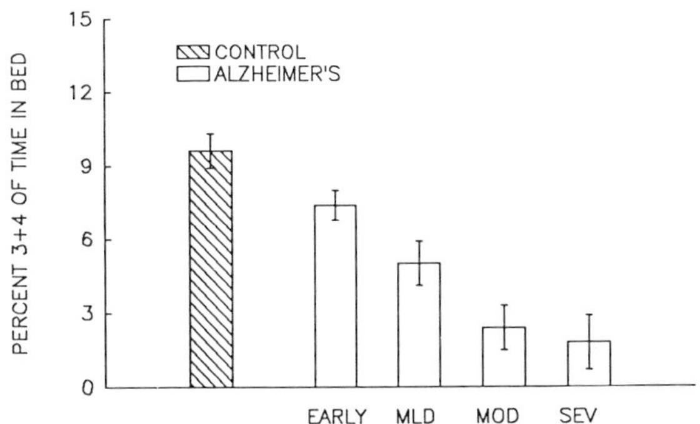

Fig. 2. Mean percent stages 3 and 4 of time in bed ± standard errors of the mean for control and early-stage AD groups (Vitiello et al., 1989), and from mild, moderate and severe AD groups (Prinz et al., 1982a,b) (n = 18, 16 and 10, respectively).

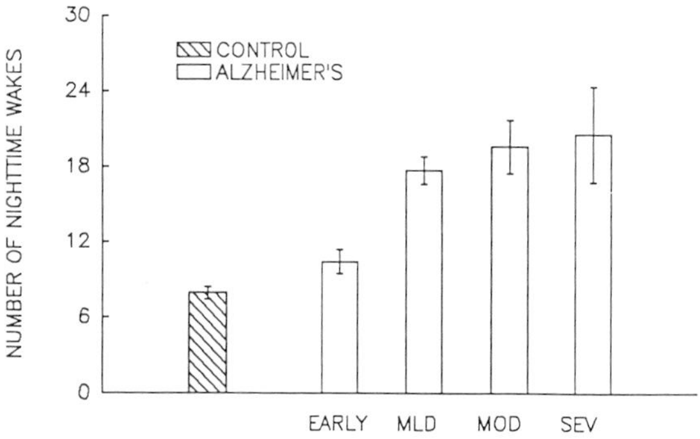

Fig. 5. Mean number of nighttime awakenings ⩾ minute in duration ± standard errors of the mean for control and early-stage AD groups (Vitiello et al., 1989), and from mild, moderate and severe AD groups (Prinz et al., 1982a,b) (n = 18, 16 and 10, respectively).

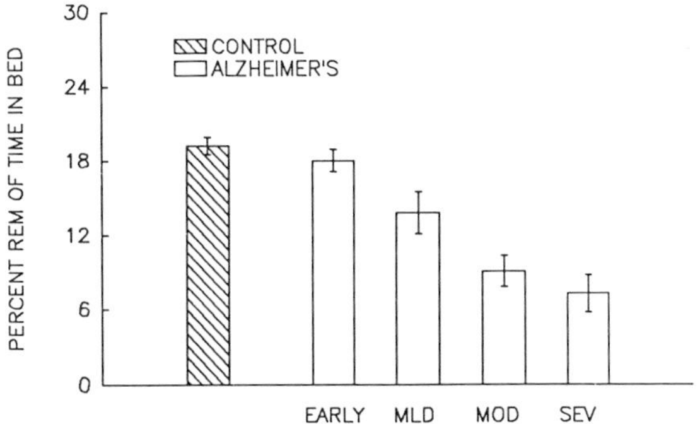

Fig. 3. Mean percent stage REM of ± standard errors of the mean for control and early-stage AD groups (Vitiello et al., 1989), and from mild, moderate and severe AD groups (Prinz et al., 1982a, b) (n = 18, 16 and 10, respectively).

Usefulness of sleep as a biomarker for AD

Sleep/wakefulness changes do, in fact, serve as fairly reliable biomarkers for mild to moderate AD uncomplicated by other disorders, as indicated by our observation that sleep variables classify AD and non-AD patients accurately and predict well for cognitive scores in the mild dementia range (Prinz et al., 1982b; Vitiello et al., 1984b). We used discriminant analyses (DA) to assess the ability of sleep and EEG variables to correctly classify subjects into control or mild dementia groups. When sleep and waking variables were examined in control and mild AD groups, percent waking of time in bed (% W TIB), and percent stage 3 and 4 of time in bed (% 3 – 4 TIB) emerged as the best classifiers, correctly classifying 90% of subjects into mild AD and control groups.

These findings encouraged us to evaluate how well sleep measures might aid in the diagnosis of earlier-stage AD. We examined individuals with a diagnosis of possible or probable AD in the very earliest detectable stages of the disease and compared them with age-, sex- and health-matched control subjects. The demographic and other characteristics of these groups are shown in Table 1, along with sleep/wakefulness results indicating significant changes even in this very early stage of possible AD.

A discriminant analysis using sleep/wakefulness variables to classify AD vs. not-AD status resulted in an overall correct classification of 68% of control and AD subjects. The best predictor was minutes of waking after sleep onset (WASO), a measure of sleep fragmentation (Vitiello et al., 1989). This level of diagnostic predictive power for early AD is not as great as that for later stages of AD. We conclude that other biological variables may classify early AD better than sleep/wakefulness measures.

The coexistence of the various sleep disorders such as sleep apnea or myoclonus syndromes with AD has been studied to a limited extent. An excess amount of sleep apnea activity compared to control subjects has been observed in female but not in male uncomplicated AD patients (Smallwood et al., 1983; Reynolds et al., 1985b; Vitiello et al., 1987). Nocturnal myoclonus occurred to an equal extent in AD and control subject groups (Prinz et al., 1986). Other known causes of sleep pathology have not been studied systematically in AD.

Sleep changes associated with other dementing disorders

Parkinson's disease

Parkinson's disease (PD) is a common neurological, degenerative disorder (Kurtzke, 1984) characterized by tremor, rigidity and bradykinesia, and caused in part by degeneration of dopaminergic cells in the substantia nigra (Hassler, 1984). Dementia occurs more commonly in PD than in a comparable population (Rajput, 1984), with estimates ranging from 20 to 80% (Benson, 1984). It has been argued that the dementia of PD is of the subcortical type (Benson, 1984), while others have considered AD, a cortical dementia, to be causative (Boller, 1980; Hakim, 1979) in the dementing features of PD.

The earliest studies of PD were concerned with the activity of motor tremors in sleep (Tassinari, 1965; April, 1966; Stern; 1968). These studies were in agreement that the tremor of PD is rare in sleep, but can occur in any stage, and when occurring seemed to be related to gross body movements or slight EEG arousals. In 1969 Traczynska-Kubin studied 14 Parkinsonians, aged 38 to 68, with overnight recordings and found a correlation between a low %REM and increased motor rigidity. Other early studies reported reduced total sleep time (including reduced REM and stage 3 – 4 sleep) and increased nighttime wakefulness in Parksinson's patients (Wilson, 1969; Bricolo, 1970; Kales, 1971; Kendel, 1972). Numerous other studies have also reported that sleep is impaired in PD (Bergonzi, 1974; Vardi, 1979; Rabey, 1978; Mouret, 1975; Schneider, 1974). In a more systematic and controlled study Friedman (1980) studied 25 patients, aged 40 to 62, and compared their sleep to that of 10 age-matched control subjects. The patients were kept drug-free for 4 days before the recordings. The mildly affected cases were unchanged from control subjects. However, both the moderately affected and the severely affected patients showed significant increases in WASO, and decreases in %REM, and had increased sleep latencies. The 'severe' patients also showed less stage 3 and 4. Severity of the Parkinsonism was correlated with time awake, minutes of REM and average time of a single REM period.

This relationship between severity of PD and degree of sleep disturbance has also been noted in other studies. In a large questionnaire study involving both patients and their housemates or spouses, Nausieda and coworkers (Nausieda et al., 1984) reported that 74 of 100 PD patients reported sleep disturbances. Patients with sleep complaints were the same age, had had the disease for the same duration, and had taken anticholinergic medication for the same duration as the patients without sleep complaints. However, longer treatment with L-dopa (6.2 yrs vs. 4.2) distinguished the two groups. The prevalence of all complaints increased for each year of L-dopa usage. The most common complaints were insomnia, excessive daytime sleepiness, altered dream events, night terrors and nocturnal vocalizations and hallucinosis. The patients with hallucinosis also had higher sleep disruption scores. Parkinsonian symptomatology (dyskinesias and the on/off phenomenon) were more common in the group who had sleep complaints, suggesting that the more serious sleep complaints are associated with more severe Parkinsonian symptoms and/or with L-dopa-induced changes. Schneider et al. (1974) reported on 26 patients, aged 43 to 74, and found a relationship between severity of clinical signs of PD and the delay in sleep onset, prolonged waking periods and reduction of light synchronous sleep. They found a correlation between pathological results in reaction time and tests of mood and intellect with a reduction in REM sleep. Long-term administration of L-dopa resulted in an increase in REM and NREM sleep, and was interpreted as being the result of improved mobility.

L-Dopa is commonly used in the treatment of Parkinson's patients, and early studies of its effects on sleep indicated a beneficial therapeutic effect. Askenasy and Yahr (1985) recorded the sleep of five Parkinson patients of moderate severity who had complaints of sleep disturbance. They were monitored for sleep and all-night tremor or myoclonus in a drug-free baseline and again after Pergolide and/or L-dopa therapy had resulted in clinical improvement. After clinical improvement, the mean sleep efficiency increased from 66.8 to 73.8%, and the number of elementary phasic motor events per minute decreased from 8.1 to 3.9, both statistically significant. However, even after clinical improvement, the patients were still below the reported norms for sleep efficiency and stages 3 and 4. No stage 4 sleep was recorded either before or after treatment. The authors related the improvement in sleep patterns to the improvement in motor state caused by L-dopa and reflected in the reduced number of elementary phasic motor events. Other studies in this field are in general agreement that L-dopa improves sleep in parallel with its amelioration of clinical symptomatology (Kendel, 1972; Bricolo, 1970; Bergonzi, 1975). This beneficial effect of L-dopa may not continue with chronic long-term use of the drug; a recent report (Nausieda et al., 1984) has correlated many of the sleep complaints of Parkinson's patients with chronic use of the drug.

Whether L-dopa has a direct, therapeutic effect on sleep has been a matter of controversy. Wyatt (1970) noted that L-dopa at bedtime resulted in a statistically significant decrease in REM sleep time and an increase in REM latency, with a tendency for REM rebound later in the night. In a later study (Gillin, 1973), this same group of investigators infused L-dopa intravenously into sleeping depressives. If the drug was given before an REM period, the REM period was delayed. If given at REM onset, the length of the REM period was shortened. These observations indicate that L-dopa's direct effects on sleep may be disruptive, and generally support the notion that L-dopa's beneficial effects on sleep (if any) are mediated by factors related to clinical amelioration of the Parkinsonian disorder.

The frequency of various sleep disorders such as sleep apnea syndrome and restless leg syndrome in

PD has not been well studied. Apps et al. (1985) observed minimal sleep apnea in 12 patients with idiopathic PD, all of whom showed the typical sleep disturbances of PD. More extensive study of this question is needed.

In summary, the vast majority of studies of nocturnal sleep in PD have shown abnormality, most consistently an increased amount of time awake during the night. Decreased slow-wave sleep or REM sleep is also observed in more advanced stages of the disease. These changes are similar to those occurring in AD. In AD, the acetylcholine system deficiency predominates, whereas the dopamine system is preferentially affected in PD. One might therefore expect a sleep pattern change that differs in these two conditions. The lack of sleep changes specific to each disease may relate to the fact that a large percentage of Parkinsonian patients show the changes of AD and vice versa (Alvord, 1974; Boller, 1980; Gaspar, 1984; Leverenz, 1986). In this view, sleep pattern disturbances are similar in these two diseases as a result of these overlapping neuropathological changes. It is also possible that disturbed sleep is a nonspecific outcome resulting from a variety of degenerative pathologies which affect differing brain structures. This interpretation would be strengthened by observations of a similar sleep pattern change in various other degenerative dementias.

Alcohol and alcoholic dementia

Numerous studies have assessed the effects of alcohol and alcohol withdrawal on the sleep of normals and alcoholics (Williams, 1981; Wagman, 1975; Gross, 1973a,b; Lester, 1975; Adamson, 1973; Johnson, 1970; Zarcone, 1983). In general, acute alcohol intake has a sedative effect, with a brisk sleep onset, decreased REM stage and enhanced slow-wave sleep in the first half of the night followed by impaired sleep in the second half of the night. Alcohol withdrawal is characterized by marked fragmentation of sleep stages, decreased stages 3 and 4, increased wake time and increased REM. Chronic abstinent alcoholics have less deep (stage 3 – 4) sleep than normals, and Williams (1981) has shown that changes in the sleep of alcoholics can persist for up to 21 months following abstinence.

The association of sleep disturbance with chronic alcoholism is well-recognized, but few studies have associated this with possible thiamine deficiency, either overt or subclinical, or with chronic Korsakoff's syndrome (KS). Martin and coworkers (Martin et al., 1986) have reported the results of all-night sleep recordings in groups of KS and AD dementia patients, and 9 normal control subjects. The dementia groups were moderately advanced and had similar impairments on Wechsler Memory Scores. The KS and AD patients had similar and significantly reduced amounts of delta sleep (stages 3 and 4 sleep) compared to control subjects. Also, both of the demented groups had a shorter REM latency, but only the KS group compared to control subjects was significant. Intermittent wake time was significantly less in the KS group than the control group. These KS sleep data are generally consistent with the pattern of impaired sleep seen in AD and PD.

Cerebrovascular disorders

While disturbed sleep is a common symptom in acute and chronic stroke of moderate severity, there are almost no polygraphic sleep studies available to quantitate this phenomenon. Multi-infarct dementia (MID) is a progressive dementing disorder caused by multiple diffusely distributed cerebro-vascular pathologies. MID is associated with chronic hypertension and atherosclerosis. Only one study of MID has been reported in the literature. Allen et al. (1987) recently reported the results of 72-hour polygraphic studies in sixteen AD, eight MID and six mixed/unidentified dementia patients. Mean age was over 80 for both control subjects and patients. The demented patients had less stage 2, less REM and more wakefulness, but there were no significant differences between the subgroups of dementia. These data suggest that vascular dementia causes sleep pattern changes similar to those of AD, but this possibility needs to be more thoroughly examined.

Head trauma

Cognitive dysfunction and a dementia syndrome can result from traumatic brain injury. Initial studies examined the similarity of the EEG during coma and sleep, and noted poorly organized sleep stages (Passouant, 1965). Chatrian (1963) studied eleven patients with traumatic coma and stupor, and concluded that EEG patterns resembling those of sleep occurred as the patient improved, and that their presence was a favorable prognostic sign. Bergamasco et al. (1968) and Lessard et al. (1974) reached similar conclusions. Monophasic or biphasic nocturnal patterns were a poor prognostic sign. Harada et al. (1976) concluded from their study of brain-damaged patients of various etiologies that REM sleep was more stable and persistent than stages 3 and 4 in states of cerebral dysfunction. In 1980, Ron et al. reported a study of the sleep of nine head-injured patients and the relationship to the patients' abilities in activities of daily living, locomotion and cognition. They found that the organization of sleep stages approached normal as the patients' rehabilitation progressed. Further, the improvement rate of %REM was correlated with the improvement rate of cognition in seven of the patients. Prigatano et al. (1982) performed single-night recordings in ten closed-head-injury patients 6 to 59 months after injury and found less stage 1 and more awakenings compared to age-matched control subjects. Most writers have postulated that brain injury severe enough to cause cognitive dysfunction may also damage structures involved in sleep.

Pick's disease

Pick's disease is a rare disorder involving neuronal degeneration in frontal brain regions. Perhaps because of its rarity, only one polygraphic sleep study has been published to date. Pawlak et al. (1986) observed that wakefulness was increased, and sleep stages 3 and 4 were decreased significantly in comparison with control subjects. REM sleep was often fragmented, and declined in parallel with reductions in total sleep time.

Huntington's disease (HD)

Huntington's chorea is a genetic disease in which patients develop dementia and choreiform movements (Chase, 1979). Major pathology is in the caudate and putamen, but there is atrophy of the cortical mantle as well (Bruyn, 1979). The dementia of HD is said to be of the subcortical type, with relative preservation of cortical functions such as language (Benson, 1984).

Hansotia (1985) studied seven drug-free HD patients, five of whom were severely affected and two of whom were mild cases without demonstrable dementia. Six normal control subjects were also studied. The mild cases did not report disturbances of sleep, and their overnight studies were normal except for an increase in interspersed wakefulness. There was less %REM, but this did not reach statistical significance. In contrast, the severe group did report sleep maintenance difficulties but not excessive daytime sleepiness. Their records showed increased wakefulness, longer sleep latency, decreased total sleep time, decreased sleep efficiency, increased stages 1 and 2, with decreased stages 3, 4 and REM. In contrast to Sishta et al. (1974), they noted adequate sleep spindles in all records. Iakhno (1985) studied nocturnal sleep in eleven patients and found increased stage 1 and REM with decreased delta (stage 3 and 4) sleep.

Other degenerative disorders

Progressive supranuclear palsy (PSP) is a degenerative neurological disorder which resembles PD but which has relatively more dystonia, dementia and oculomotor dysfunction (Perkin et al., 1978; Steele et al., 1964). Sleep in PSP is greatly disturbed and the degree of disturbance parallels the severity of clinical features. Several studies have documented increased wakefulness and decreased REM sleep in PSP patients (Leygonie et al., 1976; Gross et al., 1978; Laffont et al., 1979). One study observed that central and obstructive sleep apnea activity in PSP patients exceeded control levels (Laffont et al., 1979). In general, EEG changes also occurred in more severely affected PSP patients, obscuring the EEG patterns used to rate sleep stages in some cases (Gross et al., 1978; Leygonie et al., 1976). This phenomenon has also been noted in severe stages in other dementing disorders and may contribute to a positive relationship between sleep disturbance and disease severity.

Another group of degenerative diseases that can cause dementia are the hereditary ataxias (olivopontocerebellar atrophies). There are several reports (Quera Salva and Guilleminault, 1986; Manni et al., 1986; Neil et al., 1980; Osorio and Daroff, 1980) of abnormal sleep patterns in these diseases, most studies indicating abnormalities of REM sleep. There are reports of sleep apnea in these patients as well (Chokroverty et al., 1984). Perret et al. (1979) reported a patient with striatonigral degeneration (another condition resembling PD) who had marked insomnia and no stage 3, 4 or REM sleep. Despite greatly curtailed total sleep in 96 hours of continuous recording, the patient had no disturbance of memory. Lugaresi et al. (1986) reported a 53-year-old man with 'fatal familial insomnia.' This patient and others in his family had a rapidly progressive course of insomnia, no deep (stage 3–4) sleep, disturbances of autonomic function and frequent acting-out of dreams. Neuropathology revealed neuronal loss and gliosis limited to the anterior and dorsomedial thalamic nuclei. Little et al. (1986) reported a similar familial dementia with rapid course and pathology primarily in the dorsomedial and midline thalamic nuclei: six of the seven patients had either daytime somnolence or nighttime insomnia. Although Lugaresi et al.'s patient had deficits of long-term memory and was often in a stuporous state, the authors emphasized his relatively preserved intellect until the final stages of his illness. These cases are similar in clinical aspects, the familial nature and neuropathologically. They emphasize the role of the thalamus in the regulation of the sleep-wake cycle, and the lack of intellectual function decline in spite of severe sleep impairment.

Apnea-myoclonus in the dementing conditions
Many of the progressive dementias involve degenerative pathologies in brainstem regions controlling respiration, muscle tonus or other automatic functions relevant to sleep maintenance. Sleep disorders such as apnea or myoclonus may therefore occur more frequently in these disorders. The number of studies assessing the coexistence of sleep apnea, myoclonus or other sleep pathologies among dementia patient groups is limited. In at least two instances there is evidence that sleep apnea levels are increased compared with control levels: female AD patients (Smallwood et al., 1984; Reynolds et al., 1985b) and progressive supranuclear palsy patients (Laffont et al., 1979; Vitiello et al., 1987). Other sleep disorders which may be exacerbated in dementing disorders include insomnias associated with depression, chronic drug use or other medical, toxic or environmental conditions. Appropriately treated, the sleep disruption due to these secondary sleep disorders can be minimized (Williams and Karacan, 1978).

Summary and conclusion

The general conclusion one can reach from these numerous all-night polygraphic studies is that sleep is impaired in a variety of progressive dementing disorders, each of which has a distinct anatomic pattern of neuronal degeneration and a characteristic pattern of neuropsychological deficit. The nature of the sleep impairment is similar across a wide range of disorders: nighttime wakefulness is increased and deeper stages of sleep (i.e., those with a higher arousal threshold – stages 3 and 4 sleep) are decreased. REM sleep is usually reduced as well. In general, sleep impairment worsens with advancing severity in the various dementing disorders, and is accompanied by increased daytime fatigue and sleepiness. Data reported for other sleep pattern features are limited or inconsistent, including latency to sleep onset and to the first REM period, amount of stages 1 and 2 of sleep and sleep apnea/myoclonus. The nonspecific nature of the sleep pattern changes reported indicates that conventional sleep pattern analysis is not informative in the differential diagnosis of the various dementing disorders. A limited number of studies noted a deterioration in EEG activities associated with sleep (delta waves, spindles, K complexes). More systematic studies are needed to determine whether these or other specific sleep EEG features may serve as better aids in the differential diagnosis of these disorders.

References

Adamson J, Burdick JA: Sleep of dry alcoholics. *Arch. Gen. Psychiatry: 28,* 146, 1973.

Allen SR, Seiler WO, Stahelin HB, Spiegel R: Seventy-two hour polygraphic and behavioral recordings of wakefulness and sleep in a hospital geriatric unit: Comparison between demented and nondemented patients. *Sleep: 10,* 143, 1987.

Alvord EC, Forno LS, Kusske JA, Kauffman RJ, Rhodes JS, Goetowski CR: The pathology of parkinsonism: a comparison of degenerations in cerebral cortex and brainstem. *Adv. Neurol.: 5,* 75 – 193, 1974.

April RS: Observations on parkinsonian tremor in all-night sleep. *Neurology: 16,* 720, 1966.

Apps MCP, Sheaff PC, Ingram DA, Kennard C, Dempsey DW: Respiration and sleep in Parkinson's disease. *J. Neurol. Neurosurg. Psychiatry: 48,* 1240 – 1245, 1985.

Askenasy JJM, Yahr MD: Reversal of sleep disturbance in Parkinson's disease by antiparkinsonian therapy: a preliminary study. *Neurology: 35,* 527 – 532, 1985.

Association of Sleep Disorders Centers: Diagnostic classification of sleep and arousal disorders, First Edition, H.P. Roffwarg, Chairman. *Sleep: 2,* 1 – 137, 1979.

Benson DF: Parkinsonian dementia: cortical or subcortical? *Adv. Neurol.: 40,* 235 – 240, 1984.

Bergamasco B, Bergamini L, Doriguzzi T, Fabiani D: EEG sleep patterns as a prognostic criterion in post-traumatic coma. *Electroencephalogr. Clin. Neurophysiol.: 24,* 374, 1968.

Bergonzi P, Chiurulla C, Cianchetti C, Tempesta E: Clinical pharmacology as an approach to the study of biochemical sleep mechanisms: the action of L-dopa. *Confin. Neurol.: 36,* 5 – 22, 1974.

Bergonzi P, Chiurulla C, Gambi D, Buffait P, Grosslercher JC: L-dopa plus dopa-decarboxylase inhibitor – sleep organization in Parkinson's syndrome before and after treatment. *Acta Neurol. Belg.: 75,* 5 – 10, 1975.

Boller F, Mizutani T, Roessmann U, Gambetti P: Parkinson's disease, dementia, and Alzheimer's disease: clinicopathological correlations. *Ann. Neurol.: 7,* 329, 1980.

Bricolo A, Turella G, Mazza CA, Buffati P, Grosslercher JC: Modificazioni del sonno notturno in parkinsoniani trattati con L-dopa. *Sist. Nerv.: 22,* 181, 1970.

Bruyn GW, Bots GTAM, Dom R: Huntington's Chorea: current neuropathological status. *Adv. Neurol.: 23,* 83 – 94, 1979.

Carlson NR: *Physiology of Behavior,* 3rd edition. Boston: Allyn and Bacon Inc., pp. 351 – 363, 1986.

Chase TN, Wexler NS, Barbeau A: *Huntington's Disease; Advances in Neurology, Vol. 23.* Raven Press: New York, 1979.

Chatrian GE, White LE, Daly D: Electroencephalographic patterns resembling those of sleep in certain comatose states after injuries to the head. *Electroencephalogr. Clin. Neurophysiol.: 15,* 272 – 280, 1963.

Chokroverty S, Sachdeo R, Marden J: Autonomic dysfunction and sleep apnea in olivopontocerebellar degeneration. *Arch. Neurol.: 41,* 926, 1984.

Feinberg I, Carlson VR: Sleep variables as a function of age in man. *Arch. Gen. Psychiatry: 18,* 239, 1968.

Feinberg I, Koresko R, Heller N: EEG sleep patterns as a function of normal and pathological aging in man. *J. Psychiatr. Res.: 5,* 107 – 144, 1967.

Folstein M, Folstein S, McHugh P: Mini Mental State: a practical method of grading the cognitive state of patients for the clinician. *J. Psychiatr. Res.: 12,* 89, 1975.

Friedman A: Sleep pattern in Parkinson's Disease. *Acta Med. Pol.: 21,* 2, 1980.

Gaspar P, Gray F: Dementia in idiopathic Parkinson's disease. *Acta Neuropathol. (Berlin): 64,* 43, 1984.

Gillin JC, Post RM, Wyatt RJ, Goodwin FK, Snyder F, Bunney WE: REM inhibitory effect of L-dopa infusion during human sleep. *Electroencephalogr. Clin. Neurophysiol.: 35,* 181 – 186, 1973.

Gross MM, Goodenough DR, Hastey J, Lewis E: Experimental study of sleep in chronic alcoholics before, during, and after four days of heavy drinking with a nondrinking comparison. *Ann. N.Y. Acad. Sci.: 215,* 254 – 265, 1973a.

Gross MM, Goodenough DR, Nagarajan M, Hastey JM: Sleep changes induced by 4 and 6 days of experimental alcoholization and withdrawal in humans. In Gross MM (Editor), *Alcohol Intoxication and Withdrawal: Experimental Studies.* New York: Plenum, pp. 291 – 304, 1973b.

Gross RA, Spehlmann R, Daniels JC: Sleep disturbances in progressive supranuclear palsy. *Electroencephalogr. Clin. Neurophysiol.: 45,* 16 – 25, 1978.

Hachinski V, Lassen N, Marshall J: Multi-infarct dementia: a cause of mental deterioration in the elderly. *Lancet, 4(2),* 207 – 209, 1974.

Hachinski V, Iliff L, Zilkha E, DuBoulay G, McAllister V, Marshall J, Russell R, Symon L: Cerebral blood flow in dementia. *Arch. Neurol.: 32,* 632 – 637, 1975.

Hakim AM, Mathieson G: Dementia in Parkinson disease: a neuropathologic study. *Neurology: 29,* 1209 – 1214, 1979.

Hansotia P, Wall R, Berendes J: Sleep disturbances and severity of Huntington's disease. *Neurology: 35,* 1672 – 1674, 1985.

Harada M, Minami R, Hattori E, Nakamura K, Kabashima K, Shikai I, Sakai Y: Sleep in brain-damaged patients – an all night sleep study of 105 cases. *Kumamoto Med. J.: 29,* 110 – 127, 1976.

Hassler RG: Role of the pallidum and its transmitters in the therapy of Parkinsonian rigidity and akinesia. *Adv. Neurol.: 40,* 1 – 14, 1984.

Iakhno NN: Disorders of nocturnal sleep in Huntington chorea.

Zhurnal Nevropatol. I Psikhiatrii: 85, 340, 1985.

Johnson LC, Burdick JA, Smith J: Sleep during alcohol intake and withdrawal in the chronic alcoholic. *Arch. Gen. Psychiatry: 22,* 406, 1970.

Jones BE: Basic mechanisms of sleep-wake states. In Kryger MR, Roth T, Dement WC (Editors), *Principles and Practice of Sleep Medicine.* Philadelphia: W.B. Saunders Company, pp. 121–140, 1989.

Kales A, Ansel RD, Markham CH, Scharf MB, Tan TL: Sleep in patients with Parkinson's disease and normal subjects prior to and following levodopa administration. *Clin. Pharmacol. Ther.: 12,* 397–406, 1971.

Kendel K, Beck U, Wita C: Der Einfluf von L-dopa auf den Nachtschlaf bei patienten mit parkinson-syndrom. *Arch. Psychiatr. Nervenkr.: 216,* 82–100, 1984.

Kurtzke JF: Neuroepidemiology. *Ann. Neurol.: 16,* 265–277. 1984.

Laffont F, Autret A, Minz M, Bellevaire T, Gilbert A, Cathala H, Castaigne P: Etude polygraphique du sommeil dans 9 cas de maladie de Steele-Richardson. *Rev. Neurol.: 135,* 127–142, 1979.

Larson E, Lo B, Williams M: Evaluation and care of elderly patients with dementia. *J. Gen. Internal Med.: 1,* 116–126, 1986.

Lessard CS, Sances A, Larson SJ: Period analysis of EEG signals during sleep and post-traumatic coma. *Aerosp. Med.: 45,* 664–668, 1974.

Lester BK, Rundell OH, Cowden LC: Alcohol and sleep in the chronic alcoholic. In Burch N (Editor), *Behavior and Brain Electrical Activity.* New York: Plenum, pp. 55–80, 1975.

Leverenz J, Sumi SM: Parkinson's Disease in patients with Alzheimer's Disease. *Arch. Neurol.: 43,* 662, 1976.

Leygonie F, Thomas J, Degos JD, Bouchareine A, Barbizet J: Troubles du sommeil dans la maladie de Steele-Richardson. *Rev. Neurol.: 132,* 125–136, 1976.

Little BW, Brown PW, Rodgers-Johnson P, Perl DP, Gajdusek DC: Familial myoclonic dementia masquerading as Creutzfeldt-Jakob Disease. *Ann. Neurol.: 20,* 231–239, 1986.

Loewenstein R, Weingartner H, Gillin J, Kaye W, Ebert M, Mendelson W: Disturbances of sleep and cognitive functioning in patients with dementia. *Neurobiol. Aging: 3,* 371–377, 1982.

Lugaresi E, Medori R, Montagna P, Baruzzi A, Cortelli P, Lugaresi A, Tinuper P, Zucconi M, Gambetti P: Fatal familial insomnia and dysautonomia with selective degeneration of thalamic nuclei. *N. Engl. J. Med.: 315,* 997–1003, 1986.

Manni R, Tartara A, Marchioni E, Piccolo B: Polygraphic sleep patterns in hereoataxia: a study of nine cases. *Rev. D'Electroencephalogr. Neurophysiol. Clin.: 16,* 117–121, 1986.

Martin P, Loewenstein R, Kay W, Ebert M, Weingartner H, Gillin J: Sleep EEG in Korsakoff's psychosis and Alzheimer's Disease. *Neurology: 36,* 411–414, 1986.

Mayeux R, Williams JBW, Stern Y, Cote L: Depression and Parkinson's Disease. *Adv. Neurol.: 40,* 241–250, 1984.

McKhann G, Drachman D, Folstein M, Katzman R, Price D, Stadian E: Clinical diagnosis of Alzheimer's disease: report of the NINCDS-ADRDA work group under the auspices of Department of Health and Human Services Task Force on Alzheimer's Disease. *Neurology: 34,* 939–944, 1984.

Mortimer J, Hutton J: Epidemiology and etiology of Alzheimer's disease. In Hutton J, Kenny A (Editors), *Senile Dementia of the Alzheimer Type.* New York: Alan R. Liss, pp. 177–196, 1985.

Mouret J: Differences in sleep in patients with Parkinson's Disease. *Electroencephalogr. Clin. Neurophysiol.: 38,* 653–657, 1975.

Nausieda PA, Glantz R, Weber S, Baum R, Klawans H: Psychiatric complications of Levodopa therapy in Parkinson's Disease. *Adv. Neurol.: 40,* 271–277, 1984.

Neil JF, Holzer BC, Spiker DG, Coble P, Kupfer D: EEG sleep alteration in olivopontocerebellar degeneration. *Neurology: 30,* 660–662, 1980.

Osorio I, Daroff RB: Absence of REM and altered NREM sleep in patients with spinocerebellar degeneration and slow saccades. *Ann. Neurol.: 7,* 277–280, 1980.

Passouant P, Cadilhac J, Delange M, Baldy-Moulinier M, El Kassabgui M: Different electrical stages and cyclic organisation of post-traumatic comas; polygraphic recording of long duration. *Electroencephalogr. Clin. Neurophysiol.: 18,* 720, 1965.

Pawlak C, Blois R, Gaillard J, Richard J: Sleep in Pick's Disease. *Encephale: 12,* 327–334, 1986.

Perkin GD, Lees AJ, Stern GM, Kocen RS: Problems in the diagnosis of progressive supranuclear palsy. *Can. J. Neurol. Sci.: 5,* 167–173, 1978.

Perret JL, Tapissier J, Jouvet M: Insomnie et memoire a propos d'une observation de degenerescence striato-nigrique. *Electroencephalogr. Clin. Neurophysiol.: 47,* 499–502, 1979.

Prigatano GP, Stahl ML, Orr WC, Zeiner HK: Sleep and dreaming disturbances in closed head injury patients. *J. Neurol. Neurosurg. Psychiatry: 45,* 78–80, 1982.

Prinz PN: Sleep patterns in the healthy age: interrelationships with intellectual function. *J. Gerontol.: 32,* 179–186, 1977.

Prinz PN, Peskind E, Vitaliano P, Raskind M, Eisdorfer C, Zemcuznikov N, Gerber C: Changes in the sleep and waking in non-demented and demented elderly. *J. Am. Geriatr. Soc.: 30,* 86–93, 1982a.

Prinz P, Vitaliano P, Vitiello M, Bokan J, Raskind M, Gerber C: Sleep, EEG and mental function changes in mild, moderate and severe senile dementia of the Alzheimer's type. *Neurobiol. Aging: 3,* 361–370, 1982b.

Prinz P, Frommlet M, Vitiello M, Ries R, Williams D: Periodic leg movements are unaffected by mild Alzheimer's Disease. *Sleep Res.: 15,* 200, 1986.

Prinz P, Vitiello M, Bokan J, Kukull W, Russo J, Vitaliano P: Sleep in Alzheimer's Dementia. In von Hahn H, Emser W, Kurtz D, Webb W (Editors), *Interdisciplinary Topics in Gerontology: Vol. 22, Sleep, Aging and Related Disorders.* Basel, Switzerland: Karger, pp. 128–143, 1987a.

Prinz P, Vitiello M, Williams D, Frommlet M, Reis R, Poon L, Wilkie F: Sleep apnea and periodic leg movements in health seniors: Relation to memory. *Sleep Res.: 16,* 409, 1987b.

Quera Salva MA, Guilleminault C: Olivopontocerebellar degeneration, abnormal sleep, and REM sleep without atonia. *Neurology: 36,* 576, 1986.

Rabey J, Vardi J, Glaubman H, Streifler M: EEG sleep study

in Parkinsonian patient under bromocryptine treatment. *Eur. Neurol.: 17,* 345 – 350, 1978.

Rajput A, Offord K, Beard C, Kurland L: Epidemiological survey of dementia in Parkinsonism and control population. *Adv. Neurol.: 409,* 229 – 234, 1984.

Reynolds C, Kupfer D, Taska L, Hoch C, Spiker D, Sewitch D, Zimmer B, Marin R, Nelson J, Martin D: EEG sleep in elderly depressed, demented and healthy subjects. *Biol. Psychiatry: 20,* 431 – 432, 1985a.

Reynolds C, Kupfer D, Taska L, Hoch C, Sewitch D, Restifo K, Spiker D, Zimmer B, Marin R, Nelson J, Martin D, Morycz R: Sleep apnea in Alzheimer's dementia: correlation with mental deterioration. *J. Clin. Psychiatry: 46,* 257 – 261, 1985b.

Reynolds C, Kupfer D, Taska L, Hoch C, Sewitch D, Grochocinski V: Slow wave sleep in elderly depressed, demented and healthy subjects. *Sleep: 8,* 155 – 159, 1985c.

Roffwarg H, Munzio J, Dement W: Ontogenic development of the human sleep-dream cycle. *Science: 152,* 604 – 619, 1966.

Ron S, Algom K, Hary D, Cohen M: Time-related changes in the distribution of sleep stages in brain injured patients. *Electroencephalogr. Clin. Neurophysiol.: 48,* 432 – 441, 1980.

Schneider E, Maxion H, Ziegler B, Jacobe P: Das schlafverhalten von Parkinsonkranken und seine beeinflussung durch L-Dopa. *J. Neurol.: 207,* 95 – 108, 1974.

Siegel JM: Brainstem mechanisms generating REM sleep. In Kryger MR, Roth T, Dement WC (Editors), *Principles and Practice of Sleep Medicine.* Philadelphia: W.B. Saunders Company, pp. 104 – 120, 1989.

Siegel JM, Rogawski MA: A function for REM sleep: regulation of noradrenergic receptor sensitivity. *Brain Res. Rev.: 13,* 213 – 233, 1988.

Sishta SK, Troupe A, Marszalek KS, Kremer LM: Huntington's chorea: an electroencephalographic and psychometric study. *Electroencephalogr. Clin. Neurophysiol.: 36,* 387 – 393, 1974.

Smallwood R, Vitiello M, Giblin E, Prinz P: Sleep apnea: relationship to age, sex and Alzheimer's dementia. *Sleep: 6,* 16 – 22, 1983.

Smallwood R, Giblin E, Ralph D, Vitiello M, Prinz P: An analysis of the 10 sec criterion for apnea-hypopnea scoring: A comparison using 25 sec criterion. *Sleep Res.: 13,* 166, 1984.

Steele JC, Richardson JC, Olzsewski J: Progressive supranuclear palsy. *Arch. Neurol.: 10,* 333 – 359, 1964.

Stern M, Roffwarg H, Duvoisin R: The parkinsonian tremor in sleep. *J. Nerv. Ment. Disord.: 147,* 202, 1968.

Tassinari C, Broughton R, Poire R: An electroclinical study of nocturnal sleep in patients presenting abnormal movements. *Electroencephalogr. Clin. Neurophysiol.: 18,* 95, 1965.

Terry R, Katzman R: Senile dementia of the Alzheimer type. *Ann. Neurol.: 14,* 497 – 506, 1983.

Traczynska-Kubin D, Atzef E, Petre-Quadens O: Le sommeil dans la maladie de Parkinson. *Acta Neurol. Belg.: 69,* 727 – 733, 1969.

Vardi J, Glaubman H, Rabey J, Streifler M: EEG sleep patterns in Parkinsonian patients treated with bromocriptine and L-Dopa: a comparative study. *J. Neural Transm.: 45,* 22, 1979.

Vitiello M, Prinz P: Sleep and EEG studies in Alzheimer's Disease. In Wurtman R, Corkin S, Growdon J (Editors), *Alzheimer's Disease: Advances in Basic Research and Therapies.* Cambridge, MA: Center for Brain Sciences, pp. 625 – 634, 1987.

Vitiello M, Bokan J, Kukull W, Muniz R, Smallwood R, Prinz P: REM sleep measures of Alzheimer's type dementia patients and optimally healthy aged individuals. *Biol. Psychiatry: 19,* 721 – 734, 1984a.

Vitiello M, KuKull W, Prinz P: Sleep/waking and EEG pattern classification of Alzheimer's dementia. *Sleep Res.: 13,* 213, 1984b.

Vitiello M, Smallwood R, Avery D, Pascualy R, Prinz P: Circadian temperature rhythms in young and aged men. *Neurobiol. Aging: 7,* 97 – 100, 1986.

Vitiello M, Prinz P, Williams D, Frommlet M, Ries R: Sleep related respiratory dysfunction in normal healthy aged individuals, Alzheimer's Disease and Major Depressive Disorder patients. *Sleep Res.: 16,* 453, 1987.

Vitiello MV, Prinz PN, Williams DE, Frommlet MS, Ries RK: Sleep is disturbed in patients with mild stage Alzheimer's disease. *J. Gerontol.:* in press, 1989.

Wagman AMI, Allen RP: Effects of alcohol ingestion and abstinence on slow wave sleep of alcoholics. *Adv. Exp. Med. Biol.: 59,* 453 – 466, 1975.

Williams HL, Rundell OH: Altered sleep physiology in chronic alcoholics: reversal with abstinence, *Alcohol. Clin. Exp. Res.: 5,* 318, 1981.

Williams R, Karacan I: *Sleep Disorders: Diagnosis and Treatment.* New York: John Wiley & Sons, 1978.

Williams R, Karacan I, Hursch C: *Electroencephalography of Human Sleep: Clinical Applications.* New York: John Wiley & Sons, 1974.

Wilson WP, Nashold BS, Green RL: Studies of the cortical and subcortical electrical activity during sleep of patients with dyskinesias. In Gillingham J, Donaldson IML (Editors), *Third Symposium on Parkinson's Disease Held at the Royal College of Surgeons of Edinburgh.* Edinburgh: E. and S. Livingstone, pp. 160 – 164, 1969.

Wyatt RJ, Chase TN, Scott J, Snyder F: Effect of L-Dopa on the sleep of man. *Nature: 228,* 999 – 1001, 1970.

Zarcone VP: Sleep and alcoholism. In Chase MH, Weitzman ED (Editors), *Sleep Disorders: Basic and Clinical Research.* SP Medical & Scientific Books: New York, pp. 319 – 325, 1983.

© 1990 Elsevier Science Publishers B.V. (Biomedical Division)
Handbook of Neuropsychology, Vol. 4
F. Boller and J. Grafman (Eds)

CHAPTER 18

Longitudinal studies of aging and age-associated dementias

Martha Storandt

Department of Psychology, Washington University, St. Louis, MO 63130, U.S.A.

Introduction

Although researchers are vocal in calling for longitudinal studies of aging, few exist that cover more than a few years. It is easy to understand why, given the magnitude of the resources that must be devoted to maintaining such efforts. Three such studies that focus on normal aging will be reviewed in this chapter. These are the Seattle Longitudinal Study, the Baltimore Longitudinal Study and the first Duke Longitudinal Study. The first two cover the entire adult life span and are still going on; the third was of later life and is completed. These were chosen because they include variables which are of interest to neuropsychologists, who are often asked to determine whether patterns of psychological performance are 'normal for age' or represent a neuropsychological disorder.

Equally important are longitudinal studies of individuals with neuropsychological disorders. These studies address the issue of the course of the disease and the type of psychological function affected at different stages. There are few such longitudinal studies and those which are available generally cover a limited time span.

Before the discussion of the existing data from longitudinal studies of aging and age-associated neuropsychological disorders, however, a number of methodological issues relating to longitudinal studies will be discussed. It is important to keep these in mind when evaluating the results of both cross-sectional and longitudinal studies.

Methodological concerns

The bulk of information available about the neuropsychology of older people is based on cross-sectional studies. As is often cautioned, cross-sectional studies can address only age differences; they cannot deal with changes in psychological function with age. The age differences observed in cross-sectional studies are suspect primarily because age and cohort are confounded. (Cohort refers to a group of individuals with similar times of birth.) Because age and cohort are both organismic variables and vary together, age differences observed in cross-sectional studies could result from maturation (age) or from environmental and cultural differences that existed at the times successive cohorts were born or matured. For psychologists in the United States the most familiar example of the differences experienced by successive cohorts relates to changes in educational experiences in this century, both positive and negative. Other examples might be physiological in nature (e.g., prenatal care, dietary and nutritional habits).

Because of the necessary confounding of age and cohort in cross-sectional studies, researchers have called for longitudinal studies to answer questions about changes with age. The longitudinal methodology, however, has its problems as well. Just as age and cohort are confounded in cross-sectional studies, age and time of measurement are confounded in longitudinal studies. A common example of a time-of-measurement effect than can distort the study of age changes is the *practice effect.* Positive practice effects confounded with negative age effects can leave the impression of no change. Positive practice effects confounded with incremental age effects can produce overestimates of the impact of maturation. Other combinations lead to other interpretative difficulties.

One way to combat the problem of practice effects in longitudinal studies is to use independent samples at each time of testing. Individuals from the same birth cohort are chosen by random sampling to be tested at different times – some at the first session, some at the second, and so forth. Thus, estimates of performance at successive ages by individuals from the same birth cohort can be used to determine the effects of age uncontaminated by the effects of multiple testing.

Another serious problem often found in longitudinal studies of later adulthood is *selective attrition.* All longitudinal studies are faced with attrition. The reasons for such attrition in studies of later life are generally death, illness, relocation and refusal; thus much of the attrition is not random and individuals who remain in a longitudinal study are those with initially superior performances or scores. Data from the Wechsler Adult Intelligence Scale (WAIS) obtained in the Duke Longitudinal Study (Siegler and Botwinick, 1979) can be used to illustrate this problem. Fig. 1 shows the mean intelligence scores at the first time of testing (Test Session 1) of those individuals who remained in the study at successive times of assessment. Only those people who were tested at all test sessions, up to and including the abscissa test number, were included in the calculation of the successive means of scores at the first time of testing. Curves are shown for three cohorts based on age at the beginning of the study. Each curve shows that those who remained in the study had higher and higher WAIS scores at the beginning of the study. The initially less able were lost to follow-up. Thus, changes based on repeated measures in longitudinal studies of aging represent changes in individuals with superior ability at the beginning and probably underestimate changes in the population.

Some investigators have suggested that the use of independent samples at successive times of testing controls for the effects of attrition. With the exception of those lost to follow-up on the basis of refusal due to boredom or disillusionment with the study, this is not the case. Those who are ill, who have moved away or who have died will not be included in the successive independent samples just as they will not be included in repeated measurements of the same sample.

Other difficulties with longitudinal studies of later life include the more practical matters of sustained funding and maintaining investigator interest over such long periods. Another serious problem is the aging of the methods and theories

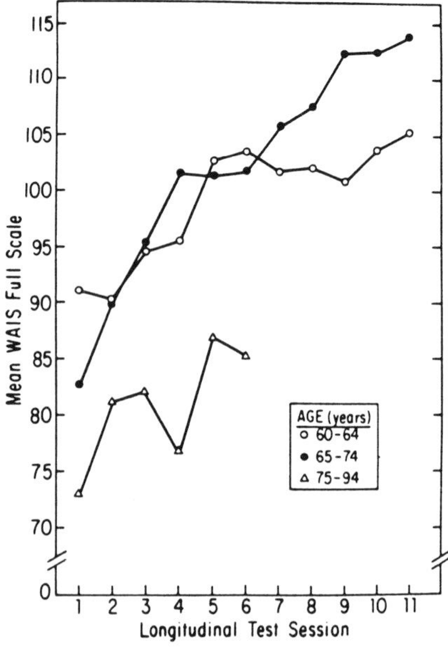

Fig. 1. Mean intelligence test scores at the time of first testing as a function of the number of longitudinal test sessions. Only subjects who were tested on all test sessions, up to and including the abscissa test number, are represented. (From 'A long-term longitudinal study of intellectual ability of older adults: the matter of selective attrition' by I.C. Siegler and J. Botwinick, *J. Gerontol.: 34,* 243, 1979. Copyright 1979 by the Gerontological Society of America. Reprinted with permission.)

which guided the study at its initiation but which become outdated as science advances. All in all, longitudinal studies of aging are useful in that they provide some information about change not available in cross-sectional studies, but they should not be viewed as a panacea. They, too, have their problems.

Normal aging

The Seattle Longitudinal Study

This study of intellectual performance in adulthood was begun by K. Warner Schaie in 1956 as his dissertation research, and published data covering a 28-year span in 7-year intervals are now available. Participants in this study were originally from a large health maintenance organization and are relatively representative of the general population with the exception of the lowest socio-economic classes. The original randomly selected sample comprised 25 men and 25 women in each 5-year birth cohort over the age range of 22 to 70 years. In addition to following these individuals for such a long time, the study has the added advantage in that new samples have been added at each successive time of measurement.

The major focus of the study has been on the Primary Mental Abilities (PMA) test developed as a measure of intelligence in adolescents by Thurstone and Thurstone (1949). This factorially derived test covers five areas:

1. *Verbal Meaning* is a measure of passive vocabulary. It is a four-choice recognition test in which the person chooses the best analogue of the stimulus word.

2. *Space* is a multiple-choice test of spatial orientation. The individual chooses from among the response figures those which are the same, although rotated, as the stimulus.

3. *Reasoning* (also called inductive reasoning) is again a multiple-choice test. The stimulus items form a series based on a rule. The person is to determine the rule and select from among the response choices the item that would come next in the series.

4. *Number* is a true-false test in which the person checks simple addition problems and determines whether each is right or wrong.

5. *Word Fluency* is a measure of verbal recall in which the individual is asked to write as many words as possible beginning with the letter S in 5 min.

All five sections of the PMA are subject to time limits.

Schaie and his colleagues have published numerous articles reporting the results of this valuable research effort (see Schaie, 1983, for a summary of four times of measurement). Given the focus of this handbook, one set of data will be

TABLE 1

Average 21-year age changes estimated from independent samples, in *T*-score points

Age range	n^{a}	Verbal meaning	Space	Reasoning	Number	Word fluency
25 – 46	76/79	– 0.29	– 1.64	– 2.53	– 0.64	– 4.38*
32 – 53	70/77	– 2.01	– 3.93	– 3.49	– 0.31	– 5.79*
39 – 60	71/72	– 1.42	– 4.81*	– 2.86	– 1.16	– 4.47*
46 – 67	65/73	– 6.91*	– 2.76*	– 6.56*	– 3.59	– 8.90*
53 – 74	70/70	– 8.29*	– 5.45*	– 7.36*	– 7.95*	– 12.61*
60 – 81	72/58	– 8.75*	– 5.98*	– 3.54*	– 5.45*	– 8.42*

[a] First number indicates frequency at first age; second number indicates frequency at second age.
* $P < 0.01$.
Abridged from Table 4.14 from Schaie, 1983. Reprinted with permission.

highlighted. Table 1 shows the average 21-year age changes for each of the five PMA factors estimated from independent samples. That is, the age-change estimates are obtained by comparing, for example, the mean of those in the original sample who were 25 in 1956 with the mean of those from the newly added sample from the same population who were 46 in 1977. As described in the previous section, this procedure of comparing independent samples from the same birth cohort controls for practice effects. The entries in the table are differences in *T*-score points. *T* scores with a mean of 50 and a standard deviation of 10 are used in the Seattle Longitudinal Study to obtain comparability across variables and age groups.

Examination of Table 1 reveals declines with age on all PMA scales. Earliest and most pronounced are the age-associated deficits in Word Fluency, the measure of verbal recall ability. Decrements approaching half a standard deviation unit are apparent in the 40s and 50s; decrements of the order of a full standard deviation unit are seen by the 60s and 70s. The other four PMA scales all indicate significant decrements in the 60s and 70s.

The currently most prominent theory of the organization of intelligence is that of Horn and Cattell (1966), which contrasts fluid intelligence with crystallized intelligence. Fluid intelligence reflects the individual's ability to deal with novel information, whereas crystallized intelligence reflects the acculturation process and probably relies more heavily on learned or stored information. It is popularly assumed that fluid intelligence is more susceptible to the aging process and crystallized more resistant.

If the Verbal Meaning factor from the PMA is taken as representative of crystallized intelligence and the Space and Reasoning factors as fluid intelligence (Schaie, 1989), the data from the Seattle Longitudinal Study shown in Table 1 suggest that both types of intelligence decline with age. Fig. 2 shows the mean performance on these three factors of the 88 individuals from Schaie's 1956 total sample who remained to the fifth time of testing, a span of 28 years (Schaie, 1989). Even in this highly select, superior group clear downward trends are apparent at the last two times of testing not only on the Space and Reasoning but also on Verbal Meaning. The age-related decline in crystallized intelligence on the PMA, however, may well involve the effects of test-answering speed.

The relatively early and subsequently large deficits observed on the PMA Word Fluency measure may be of special interest to neuropsychologists. Similar fluency measures are often used in neuropsychological batteries to assess language. Clearly, memory is involved in this task and there is a large body of literature to indicate that memory declines with age. Also the effect of the time limit must be considered. As speculated by Schaie and Hertzog (1983), some portion of the declines seen in the PMA scores may be a function of age changes in perceptual speed. Unpublished analyses (Schaie, personal communication) indicate that taking perceptual speed into consideration moderates, but does not remove, the effect of age on Word Fluency .

The Baltimore Longitudinal Study

As described by Shock and his colleagues (1984), this multidisciplinary study was begun in 1958 and is part of the intramural research efforts of the Na-

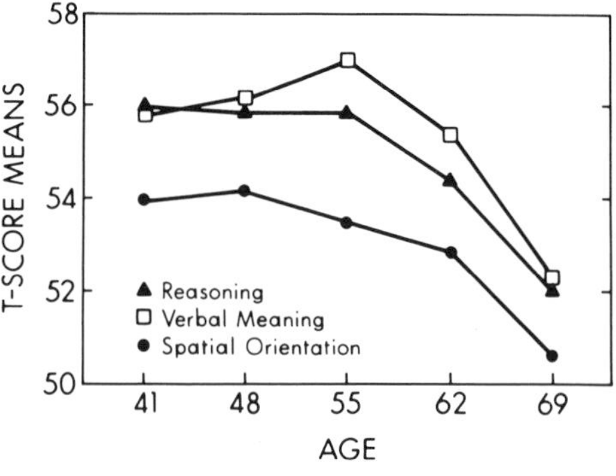

Fig. 2. Age changes over 28 years for the total sample for the abilities of Verbal Meaning, Spatial Orientation and Inductive Reasoning. (Fig. 1 from Schaie, in press. Reprinted with permission.)

tional Institute on Aging. The focus of the study has been on healthy aging in men between the ages of 30 and 80. The participants are, by and large, of high educational and socioeconomic status and in good or excellent health. Over half the sample are government employees. The men in the study are tested every 1 to 2 years (the interval has varied over the course of the study), although not all procedures in this large study are administered at each time of testing. The time interval for many of the psychological tests is 6 years.

Two broad domains of psychological function are assessed: personality and cognition. Only the latter is described here. Because of ongoing recruitment the Baltimore Longitudinal Study, like the Seattle Longitudinal Study, allows the assessment of age changes in independent samples. That is, the performances of men of the same birth cohort tested at earlier and later dates can be compared, thereby eliminating the influence of practice effects.

Learning and memory. Paired-associate and serial learning procedures as well as a nonverbal memory test (the Benton Visual Retention Test) have been included in the Baltimore Study since 1960. Age decrements are clear for all three procedures, often beginning in the midyears and becoming more pronounced in later life (Arenberg, 1983).

Fig. 3 shows data from the 8-item paired associates task administered with a long (3.7 s) anticipation interval. Pairs were consonant-word pairs (e.g., TL-INSANE). The dependent variable is the number of errors to the criterion of one perfect trial. The open circles connected by the dotted line represent the cross-sectional data (n = 165) collected in the early years of the study (1960 to 1964). Many of these men continued in the program, providing repeated-measures longitudinal data at least 6 years later (filled triangles connected by dashed lines). Because enrollment in the longitudinal study was continual, some men were tested for the first time between 1968 and 1974. Estimates of the effects of age free of practice effects can be made by comparing their performances with men from the same birth cohort but tested at an earlier age (solid lines connecting the open and filled circles). The estimates of decline in learning performance are quite similar for the longitudinal and independent sample methodologies.

Similar data for the Benton Visual Retention Test are shown in Fig. 4. The sample sizes are substantial, ranging from 382 in the cross-sectional analysis (263 of whom were re-tested) to 198 in the independent sample. Age-related declines are substantial on this nonverbal memory test.

Intelligence. Although the Baltimore Longitudinal Study clearly demonstrates age decrements in learning and memory, similar analyses of WAIS Vocabulary scores over 6 years revealed minimal change with age (Arenberg, 1978). More recent analyses based on data for men with at least three

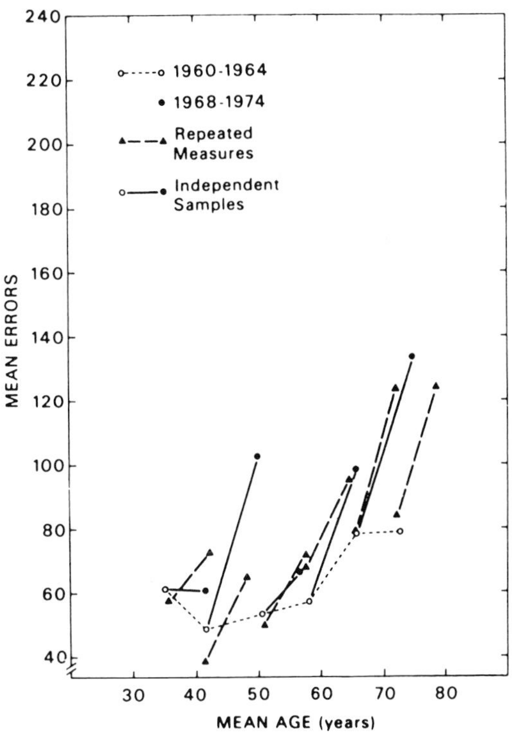

Fig. 3. Pair-associate learning – long interval. (Fig. 2 from Arenberg, 1983.)

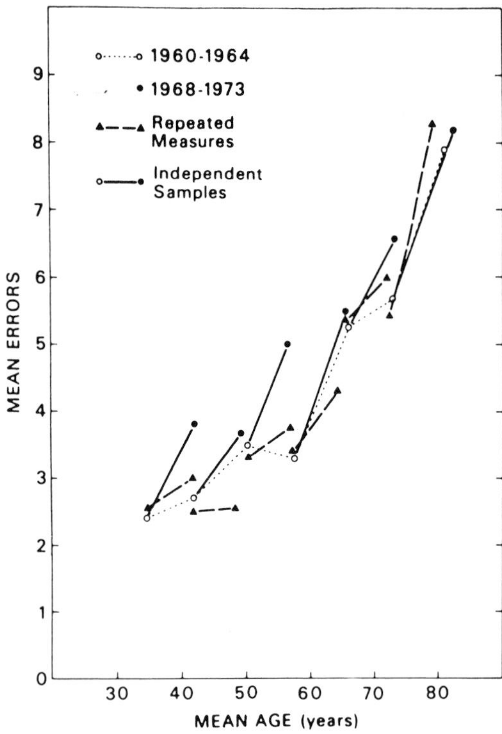

Fig. 4. Benton Visual Retention Test – errors. (Fig. 5 from Arenberg, 1983.)

times of measurement spanning at least 12 years, however, suggest decline for those men initially in their 60s and 70s. The correlation of age with individual measures of slope was −0.41 (Arenberg, personal communication).

Another measure of intelligence, the Southern California Tests of Mental Ability, was administered twice at an average of 6-year intervals to those entering the study between 1959 and 1972, after which time it was discontinued. The results for four of these tests are shown in Fig. 5 (McCrae et al., 1987). These cross-sequential analyses use independent samples from the same birth cohort tested 4 to 8 years apart to control for practice effects. All tests were timed and administered in counterbalanced order. Associational Fluency asks for synonyms, Expressional Fluency requires the person to write sentences with words beginning with designated letters, Ideational Fluency asks the individual to name objects in specific classes, and Word Fluency requests words containing a designated letter. Age decrements can be seen in all four tests. The Word Fluency decrements seen in the Baltimore study are reminiscent of those observed in the Seattle study.

Problem-solving. The Baltimore Longitudinal Study also includes measures of problem-solving. One of these is the 'poisoned foods' task. In the simplest form of the procedure, participants are told that one of eight foods has been poisoned. Their task is to select meals of four food items and

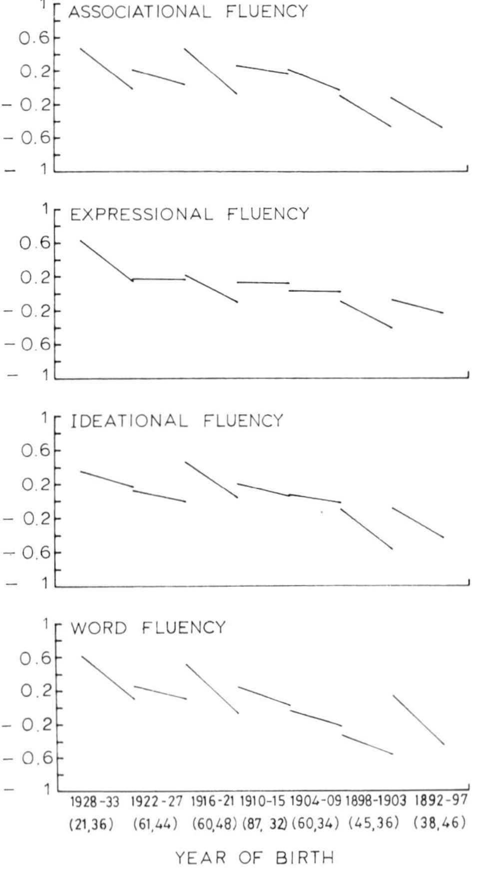

Fig. 5. Cross-sequential plots of standardized fluency test scores for seven birth cohorts tested during two periods of administration. Lines connect means for the same birth cohorts measured during the first and second periods; *n* values are given in parentheses. (Fig. 4 from McCrae et al., 1987.)

identify the poisoned food with as few meal selections as possible by using feedback from the experimenter, who says 'Died' if a meal includes the poisoned food and 'Lived' if it does not. The men were required to write every selection and its designation and to make written notes of their ideas about the solution to minimize the memory load. Further, the task is self-paced. Longitudinal analyses (Arenberg, 1982) over 6 years using both repeated measures and independent samples showed decrements in later life in the oldest cohort (those in their 70s at the beginning of the study). Similar results were obtained using a different experimental paradigm (Arenberg, 1974). It appears that older people experience difficulty in both the analysis and synthesis involved in problem-solving.

The Duke Longitudinal Study

In contrast with the Seattle and Baltimore longitudinal studies, the first Duke Longitudinal Study focused entirely on later life. It is also unlike the Seattle and Baltimore studies in that no additional independent samples were enrolled as the study progressed. Thus, only repeated-measures longitudinal analyses contaminated by practice effects could be conducted.

The study began in 1955 with 270 community volunteers aged 60 to 94. It ended in 1976 after 11 times of data collection and with 44 individuals aged 76 to 102 remaining in the study. Although the sample was not random, it was selected so that its age, race and socioeconomic characteristics reflected those of the Research Triangle community in North Carolina. Men and married individuals were overrepresented.

Only those psychological measures from this multidisciplinary study which are of direct application to neuropsychology are discussed here. There was also a four-wave second Duke Longitudinal Study begun in 1968; however, the psychological measures included in it dealt primarily with personality. (See Siegler, 1983, for a summary of the results of all psychological measures included in the Duke studies.)

Intelligence. Fig. 6 shows the small, but statistically significant, changes in the Performance, Verbal and Full Scale WAIS scaled scores over the first five times of testing (Siegler, 1983). Separate curves are shown for the young-old and old-old cohorts from the sample, divided at Time 1 at age 70, but the patterns are the same. Both the verbal and performance composite measures declined, in this case over an approximately 10-year period. The magnitudes of the decrements are probably underestimated because of selective attrition (Siegler and Botwinick, 1979).

Memory. The three subtests of the Wechsler Memory Scale were added at Time 2. A delayed recall measure of the Logical Memory subtest was also included. The left panel of Fig. 7 shows the 10-year longitudinal data for these measures for the 62 individuals present at each of Times 2 to 6. The right panel illustrates the same data for the 26 people present at Times 2 to 11, covering a period of 16 years. The sample is divided into younger (70

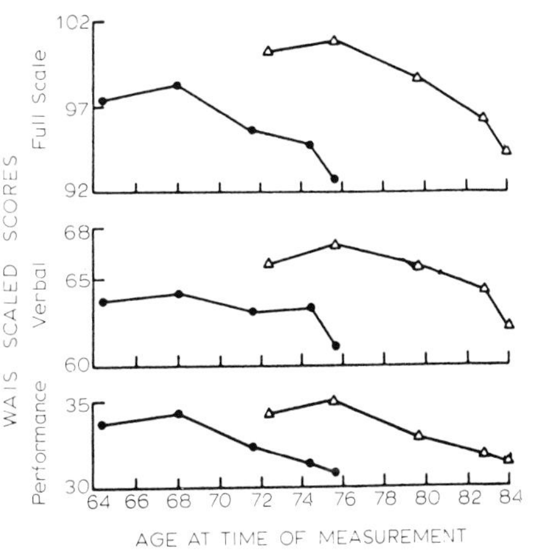

Fig. 6. Verbal, Performance and Full-Scale weighted scores for two groups of subjects, by age. Filled circles are young-old (n = 46); open triangles are old-old (n = 26). (Abridged from Siegler, 1983. Reprinted with permission.)

and under) and older (71 and over) cohorts based on age at Time 2 (McCarty et al., 1982).

These data reveal a longitudinal decline in performance on the Visual Reproduction subtest and longitudinal stability on the easy items from the Associate Learning procedure. The decline in memory for the hard items from the Associate Learning task was statistically significant in the sample present to Time 6 (left panel), but not in those hardy individuals present to the end of the study (right panel). Performance on the Logical Memory subtest was more variable and revealed an

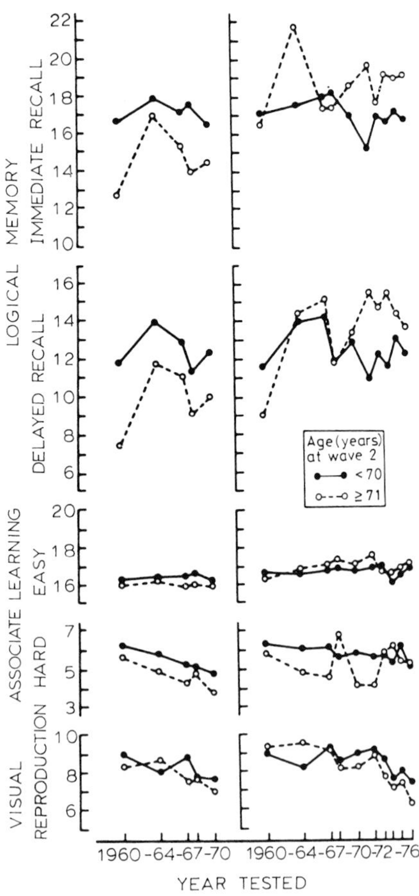

Fig. 7. Longitudinal WMS curves for subjects present at Times 2 – 6 (left) and 2 – 11 (right). (Abridged from 'Cross-sectional patterns of three Wechsler Memory Scale Subtests' by S.M. McCarthy, I.C. Siegler and P.E. Logue, *Journal of Gerontology. 37,* 170, 1982. Copyright 1982 by the Gerontological Society of America. Reprinted with permission.)

initial practice effect. Thus, both verbal and nonverbal memory for new material appear to decline with age for most individuals unless such memory is part of an organized, meaningful whole or involves long-standing strong associations such as those represented by the easy pairs in the Associate Learning subtest. These data also point to the need for alternative forms of the test material in the longitudinal assessment of the recall of meaningful prose.

Speed. Decision time in the choice reaction time procedure included in the Duke Longitudinal Study decreased significantly from 505 ms to 469 ms in 8 years (Siegler, 1983). Movement time (the visuomotor component of the reaction time), however, increased significantly from 360 ms to 450 ms. The net result was no longitudinal change in total reaction time. These longitudinal results are at odds with the widely documented slowing with age found in cross-sectional studies. Further, they are inconsistent with the Birren (1964) hypothesis that a fundamental change associated with aging involves a slowing of the rate at which the individual takes in, processes and responds to information – that is, a slowing of central processes rather than peripheral, motor slowing. Because the other longitudinal studies did not include measures of reaction time, it is difficult to know whether these results from the Duke study are reliable.

Age changes

These three longitudinal studies show decline with age in memory and learning, problem-solving and intelligence, although the rate of decline in crystallized intelligence or the so-called 'hold' verbal tests appears less severe than the rate for fluid intelligence. Some of these changes can be observed as early as the 40s , but they are pervasive in the 60s and 70s for almost all functions. Thus, the pattern of 'normal' aging seen in these longitudinal studies is quite similar to that observed in cross-sectional studies.

The conclusion that age is associated with declines in psychological functions is based on group means. Means can be unduly influenced by some individuals who are declining while others may remain relatively stable. An analysis of the data for 14-year epochs from the Seattle Longitudinal Study indicates, however, that individuals maintain their relative ordering in intelligence as the group means decline, at least through the 70s (Hertzog and Schaie, 1986). This would suggest that the declines in group means reflect decline in many of the people in the sample. This is not to say that there is no variability in the extent or rate of age-associated decline in psychological functions. Analyses of the data from both the Duke (Manton et al., 1986) and Seattle (Schaie, 1989) studies have produced evidence of a number of distinct patterns, including some marked by stability.

The determination of age declines is complicated by the onset of age-associated diseases, such as some of those described in the next section, and physical illnesses which impair performance on psychological tests. It is unknown how many of the individuals who declined in these longitudinal studies had Alzheimer's disease, for example. Further, Manton and his colleagues (1986) found that changes in cognitive status in the Duke study were influenced by race, education and socioeconomic status. The clear answer to the question of changes in cognitive function associated with age is, yes, they occur. What is not clear is why.

Age-associated dementias

A number of neurological disorders are strongly associated with age. The most common is Alzheimer's disease (AD). Although adequate epidemiological data are not available, its prevalence is thought to increase throughout the last half of the life span, being rare in the 40s and 50s and much more common after age 80. Other neurological disorders of later life include dementias associated with cerebrovascular disease and Parkinson's disease as well as rare conditions such as Pick's disease and Jacob-Creuztfeldt disease. As already indicated, there are very few longitudinal studies of these neurological disorders of later life. The first to be described began as a study of healthy aging and only secondarily concerned disease.

The Aging Twins Study

The New York State Psychiatric Institute Study of Aging Twins was begun in 1946 by Franz Kallman and Gerhard Sander. The sample included 268 monozygotic and dizygotic same-sex twins over the age of 60 who lived in or near New York State. A comprehensive review of the analyses of the psychological measures obtained up until 1967 is provided by Jarvik and Bank (1983). Subsequently La Rue and Jarvik (1987) reported longitudinal analyses for 64 survivors who were assessed psychiatrically in 1967, when they ranged in age from 78 to 94. Of these 36 were judged to be healthy; dementia in the other 28 ranged from mild to severe. Unfortunately, type of dementia was unspecified.

Table 2 shows the mean scores on the Vocabulary List 1 from the Stanford-Binet, five subtests of the Wechsler-Bellevue, and a paper-and-pencil tapping test of these 64 demented and nondemented survivors both at the beginning of the study and 20 years later (La Rue and Jarvik, 1987). What is most surprising about these data is they reveal important differences between the demented and nondemented survivors *at the beginning of the study in 1947*. Analyses controlling for age and education showed that those with dementia in 1967 had lower scores 20 years earlier on Vocabulary, Similarities, Digit Symbol, Digits Forward and Block Design. Only Vocabulary showed a significantly greater loss over time for those who developed dementia than those who did not, although the decline in Digits Forward associated with dementia approached significance ($p = 0.07$). The observed initial differences between the two groups did not appear to be associated with confounding variables such as age, education, subsequent degree of dementia, patterns of activity, or physical health.

Two limitations of this study are the mixture of disorders included in the demented group and the lack of neuropathological confirmation of the dementia. With regard to the latter, however, a second psychiatric evaluation 6 years after the 1967 evaluation (Jarvik et al., 1980) confirmed the persistence or worsening of the dementia in all cases included in the analysis. La Rue and Jarvik (1987, p. 87) concluded that 'individuals who develop dementia in old age may experience subtle cognitive declines many years before their cognitive impairment becomes clinically evident'. The obvious question is whether these are the individuals who are declining in the longitudinal studies of 'normal' aging described in the previous section.

Alzheimer's disease

Natural history. Although great research efforts with respect to this most prevalent dementia of later life are now being made, the few published longitudinal studies cover relatively brief periods and the sample sizes are not large (e.g., Berg et al., 1987; Vitaliano et al., 1986). La Rue (1987) described the numerous methodological concerns that plague these efforts. In addition to the problems discussed at the beginning of this chapter, there are questions of the reliability and validity of measures in demented samples as well as accuracy of diagnosis. All these issues must be considered carefully in interpreting the results of longitudinal studies of the natural history of this disease.

Kaszniak and his colleagues (1986) reported the results of three annual examinations of 22 mildly to moderately demented patients compared with 39 age-matched healthy controls. The measures used were from the WMS (Logical Memory and Visual Reproduction) and the Boston Diagnostic Aphasia Examination (Animal Naming, Visual Confrontation Naming, Spoken Commands). The longitudinal repeated measures analyses revealed that the performances of the controls were stable across the 3-year period, whereas those of the patients deteriorated. The magnitude of the decline was greatest on the Spoken Commands test, followed by (in rank order) Visual Confrontation Naming, Visual Reproduction, Animal Naming and Logical Memory.

These researchers pointed out that those tests (e.g., recent memory, verbal fluency) most effective in discriminating mildly demented from healthy individuals are not the measures most useful in tracking the progress of the disease because commonly used tests of these functions are

TABLE 2

Mean scores on cognitive tests in 1947 and 1967 as a function of dementia status in 1967

	No dementia			Dementia		
Test	*n*	1947	1967	*n*	1947	1967
Vocabulary	33	31.36	31.60	26	26.96	24.81
Similarities	33	12.64	10.70	25	8.92	7.32
Digit Symbol	30	34.50	23.73	20	28.05	15.10
Digits Forward	33	6.18	6.12	26	5.88	5.31
Digits Backward	31	4.58	4.10	25	4.28	3.60
Block Design	26	17.23	13.46	17	13.35	8.65
Tapping	30	73.10	51.93	20	66.00	43.05

The numbers of scores differ from subtest to subtest because some participants were unable or unwilling to complete a particular task. Adapted from Table 1, La Rue and Jarvik (1987, p. 84).

generally subject to floor effects as the disease progresses. Data from the Washington University Memory and Aging Project agree in large part with this observation. This program of research, begun in 1979, compares healthy aging with senile dementia of the AD type (SDAT) beginning in the mild stage of the disease. Details of the procedures used in this project can be found in reports of earlier phases of this longitudinal study (Berg et al., 1988; Botwinick et al., 1986, 1988; Storandt et al., 1986). Participants ranged in age from 64 to 81 at time of entry into the study. The diagnosis of AD has been confirmed in all cases that have come to autopsy (Morris et al., 1988).

Table 3 shows the results from longitudinal assessments covering 90 months. To conserve space only data for the first and seventh (most recent) assessments of the healthy controls and for the first, third, fifth and seventh assessments of the SDAT group are shown. Each participant available for follow-up at each time of assessment was seen by the psychometricians. If the person could not perform one or more tasks, a worst score was assigned.

Rather than presenting means and standard deviations, the 25th, 50th and 75th percentiles of each group at each time of testing are shown to illustrate the stability of the performances in the control group and the collapsing of the distributions for the SDAT group toward the floor (or ceiling in the case of the Bender Gestalt and Trailmaking A tests). Parametric statistical analyses are not appropriate for these data. Simple inspection of the table, however, reveals that the progression of AD is associated with pervasive deterioration in all aspects of psychological function measured in this battery of tests. By 34 months 25% or more of the remaining SDAT group were at floor (or ceiling) on all tests except the Forward Digit Span. By 66 months this was true for 75% or more of the demented group for all tests except the Forward Digit Span and the Boston Naming Test. Even on these two tests performances were poor (i.e., 75th percentiles near floor).

The initial performances of the mildly demented individuals were quite similar to those of the healthy control group on the Forward Digit Span (medians of 6 and 7, respectively). As pointed out be Kaszniak and his colleagues (1986), it would be difficult to discriminate mild SDAT from healthy aging on the basis of this measure of primary memory, which appears to be affected, however, as the disease progresses. The revised 60-item Boston Naming test may be useful for both initial discrimination (Storandt and Hill, 1989) and for measuring the progress of the disease, at least through its moderate stage.

Correlates of progression. Rate of behavioral decline appears to be associated with rate of brain atrophy. In a small sample of 10 men with two CT scans less than 2 years apart, on average, Luxenberg and his colleagues (1987) reported that the rate of decline in performance on a neuropsychological test battery correlated with the rates of enlargement in the third and right lateral ventricular volumes (r = 0.67 and 0.83, respectively).

Analyses seeking the effects of selective attrition from longitudinal studies of AD have not found it (Botwinick et al., 1988; Kaszniak et al., 1986). That is, those with poorer performances in the mild stage of the disease are not selectively lost to follow-up. (Attrition in longitudinal studies of AD is primarily due to severe deterioration and subsequent death.) One reason for the lack of selective attrition from initially homogeneous samples of demented individuals may be that the rate of progression of SDAT is highly variable, as illustrated by Fig. 8, which shows the 48-month course for 13 cases in terms of percentage of initial score on a composite dementia scale (Dastoor and Cole, 1985 – 86).

The variability in the course of the disease has led to a search for subtypes and for variables which can predict the rate of deterioration (e.g., Becker et al., 1988). It has been suggested that earlier age of onset (the presenile form) is associated with a more rapid course, but this is not universal. The development of parkinsonism after the onset of AD has also been associated with greater global

TABLE 3

25th, 50th, and 75th percentiles (P) of control and SDAT groups assessed at entry (0) and longitudinally for 90 months

		Control		SDAT			
Measure	P	0	90	0	34	66	90
Wechsler Memory Scale							
Mental Control	75	3	3	2	0	0	0
	50	2	3	2	0	0	0
	25	2	2	0	0	0	0
Logical Memory	75	10	10	3	1	0	0
	50	9	8	1	0	0	0
	25	7	6	0	0	0	0
Digits Forward	75	8	8	7	5	2	3
	50	7	7	6	5	0	0
	25	6	7	5	3	0	0
Digits Backward	75	6	6	4	3	0	0
	50	5	5	3	2	0	0
	25	4	4	2	0	0	0
Associate Learning (recall)							
Easy	75	18	18	14	11	0	0
	50	17	17	11	6	0	0
	25	16	16	8	0	0	0
Hard	75	7	8	0	0	0	0
	50	5	5	0	0	0	0
	25	2	3	0	0	0	0
Associate Learning (recognition)							
Easy	75	6	6	6	6	0	0
	50	6	6	6	5	0	0
	25	6	6	6	0	0	0
Hard	75	4	4	3	2	0	0
	50	4	4	2	1	0	0
	25	4	4	1	0	0	0
Wechsler Adult Intelligence Scale (raw scores)							
Information	75	24	24	14	4	0	0
	50	21	20	8	3	0	0
	25	15	16	5	0	0	0
Comprehension	75	25	25	18	10	0	0
	50	23	22	12	4	0	0
	25	20	19	7	0	0	0
Block Design	75	33	34	24	12	0	0
	50	28	28	12	0	0	0
	25	24	24	2	0	0	0
Digit Symbol	75	51	51	28	12	0	0
	50	45	45	12	1	0	0
	25	39	38	7	0	0	0

TABLE 3 *(continued)*

Measure	P	Control 0	Control 90	SDAT 0	SDAT 34	SDAT 66	SDAT 90
Trails A (secs)	75	54	63	123	180	180	180
	50	40	47	85	180	180	180
	25	32	39	60	121	180	180
Bender Gestalt (errors)	75	3	4	6	12	12	12
	50	2	3	5	7	12	12
	25	2	2	2	5	12	12
Benton Test of Visual Retention (no. correct)							
Recall	75	6	7	3	2	0	0
	50	6	5	2	0	0	0
	25	5	5	1	0	0	0
Copy	75	10	10	9	8	0	0
	50	10	10	9	3	0	0
	25	9	9	7	0	0	0
Boston Naming	75	57	59	44	23	2	4
	50	54	57	27	7	0	0
	25	51	52	15	0	0	0
Word Fluency	75	33	36	19	11	0	0
	50	26	28	12	1	0	0
	25	21	22	6	0	0	0
n		58	38	42	25	18	9

The WAIS and WMS were administered in the standard way. The score on Associate Learning (recall) is the total number of correct responses over three trials; one recognition trial was administered immediately following. A maximum of 3 min was allowed on the Trails A. The maximum number of errors on the Bender Gestalt was 12. The Boston Naming Test was the 60-item revised edition. Word fluency was the number of words beginning with S named in 1 min plus the number of words beginning with the letter P named in 1 min.

neuropsychological deficit and a more rapid course (Morris et al., 1989). Similarly, the presence of aphasia in the mild stage of the disease may be associated with more rapid decline (Faber-Langendoen et al., 1988). The same may be the case for hearing impairment (Uhlmann et al., 1986). Yet Becker and his colleagues (1988) did not find differential rates of progression over 1 year for those with focal lexical/semantic impairment compared with nonfocal patients. At this time variable rates of progression are part of the unexplained individual differences observed in the disease. This will probably continue to be the case until more is known of its mechanisms.

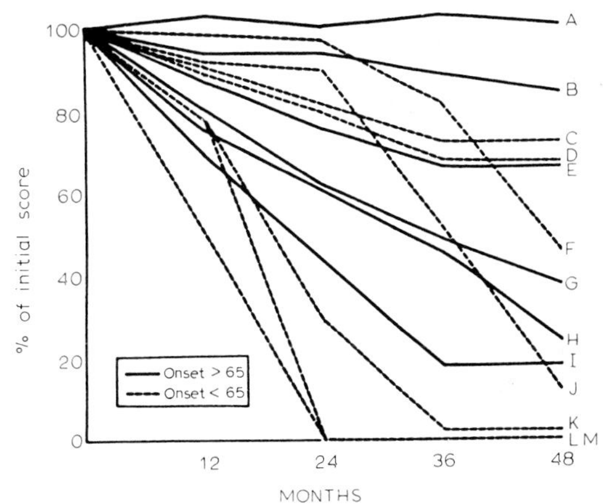

Fig. 8. Course of Alzheimer's disease. (Fig. 1 from Dastoor and Cole, 1985 – 86. Reprinted with permission.)

Vascular dementia

Vascular disease is often said to be the second most common cause of dementia in later life, but its prevalence is still a matter of controversy (Brust, 1988; O'Brien, 1988). There are various types of vascular dementia syndrome described, including the lacunar state, subcortical arteriosclerotic encephalopathy, and multiple cortical and subcortical strokes; however, published material from longitudinal studies is scant. Hershey and her colleagues (1986) conducted a prospective study of seven cases (some of each type just mentioned as determined by MRI) and seven normal controls of similar age. In the 1 to 4 years the participants were followed, none of those with vascular dementia showed stepwise deterioration, often thought to characterize the vascular dementias. Instead, the course fluctuated, perhaps because of careful monitoring and treatment of hypertension in this sample. In fact, scores on the Cognitive Assessment Screening Examination showed improvement over the first year of the study in 4 of the 7 cases and decline in only 1. This pattern is in marked contrast with the decline described in the previous section for patients with AD.

Parkinson's disease

The degree to which Parkinson's disease (PD) is associated with neuropsychological deficits other than motor disabilities is unclear. As with AD, it may be a heterogeneous disorder involving several neurotransmitter systems and their various imbalances. Unlike AD, however, it is even more difficult to study the natural history of the disease because of intervention with levodopa treatment.

Few longitudinal studies of the impact of PD on neuropsychological function are found in the published literature. One study by Mortimer and his colleagues (in press) reported data from two times of testing 1 year apart in 54 patients and 54 matched controls. Of the 17 measures included, significant declines in the PD group over and above those seen in the control group were found on only four (WAIS Vocabulary, Trails A and B, and letter cancellation speed). Two more (WAIS Information and Digit Symbol) approached significance ($p < 0.08$). Four of these measures involved a timed motor response and might be expected in the light of what is known of the pathophysiology of this disease. The other two were of stored information, often described as being a part of crystallized intelligence. Why they should be affected is less clear. If the ability to remember this long-learned information was being affected, other measures from the WMS included in the battery should have declined. All declines were less than two-fifths of a standard deviation, indicating that if cognitive declines do occur with the progression of treated PD they are relatively slow.

Diabetes mellitus

The complications of diabetes mellitus are widespread and some are common in the nervous system (e.g., peripheral neuropathy, retinopathy, stroke). Non insulin-dependent (Type II) diabetes is prevalent among older adults, and clinical experience suggests that some of these individuals may become demented, although the dementia may relate to a coexisting disease (e.g., AD).

The only longitudinal study of the effect of Type II diabetes mellitus on cognitive abilities comes from the Baltimore Longitudinal Study (Robertson-Tchabo et al., 1986). Although, as described in an earlier section of this chapter, the purpose of the Baltimore Longitudinal Study was to examine healthy aging, those with health problems were not ruled out of the study. No evidence was found for a greater rate of decline over either 6 or 12 years in diabetic men than in control groups on either the Benton Visual Retention Test or the WAIS Vocabulary subtest. If diabetes mellitus affects the cognitive abilities of older adults it may do so selectively (i.e., on measures different from those used in this study).

Summary

Longitudinal studies of aging show declines in later life on measures of memory (both verbal and nonverbal), intelligence, verbal fluency, spatial ability, reasoning and problem-solving. The reasons for these declines are not known. One possible explanation is that longitudinal studies include individuals who develop pathological disorders (e.g., dementia) with increasing age. An alternative explanation is that such declines are part of the normal aging process.

There are very few longitudinal studies of dementing disorders in later life. At this time, the best are of AD. These reveal global deterioriation of neuropsychological function.

Acknowledgements

Preparation of this chapter was supported by grants AG 00030, AG 03991 and AG 05681 from the National Institute on Aging. The original research reported in this chapter was supported by grants AG 03991 and AG 05681 from the National Institute of Aging and grant MH 31054 from the National Institute of Mental Health.

References

Arenberg D: A longitudinal study of problem solving. *J. Gerontol.: 29,* 650 – 658, 1974.

Arenberg D: Differences and changes with age in the Benton Visual Retention Test. *J. Gerontol.: 33,* 534 – 540, 1978.

Arenberg D: Changes with age in problem solving. In Craik FIM, Trehub S (Editors), *Aging and Cognitive Processes.* New York: Plenum, Ch. 13, pp. 221 – 235, 1982.

Arenberg D: Memory and learning do decline late in life. In Birren JE, Munnichs MA, Thomae H, Marois M (Editors), *Aging: A Challenge in Science and Society, Vol. 3. Behavioral Sciences and Conclusions.* Oxford: Oxford University Press, Ch. 3, pp. 312 – 322, 1983.

Arenberg D: Analysis and synthesis in problem solving and aging. In Howe ML, Grainerd C (Editors), *Cognitive Development in Adulthood: Progress in Cognitive Development Research.* New York: Springer-Verlag, Ch. 6, pp. 161 – 183, 1988.

Becker JT, Huff J, Nebes RD, Holland A, Boller F: Neuropsychological function in Alzheimer's disease: pattern of impairment and rates of progression. *Arch. Neurol.: 45,* 263 – 268, 1988.

Berg G, Edwards DF, Danziger WL, Berg L: Longitudinal change in three brief assessment of SDAT. *J. Am. Geriatr. Soc.: 35,* 205 – 212, 1987.

Berg L, Miller JP, Storandt M, Duchek J, Morris JC, Rubin EH, Burke WJ, Coben LA: Mild senile dementia of the Alzheimer type: 2. Longitudinal assessment. *Ann. Neurol.: 23,* 477 – 484, 1988.

Birren JE: *The Psychology of Aging.* Englewood Cliffs, NJ: Prentice Hall, 1964.

Botwinick J, Storandt M, Berg L: A longitudinal, behavioral study of senile dementia of the Alzheimer type. *Arch. Neurol.: 43,* 1124 – 1127, 1986.

Botwinick J, Storandt J, Berg L, Boland S: Senile dementia of the Alzheimer type: subject attrition and testability in research. *Arch. Neurol.: 45,* 493 – 496, 1988.

Brust JCM: Vascular dementia is overdiagnosed. *Arch. Neurol.: 45,* 799 – 801, 1988.

Dastoor DP, Cole MG: The course of Alzheimer's disease: an uncontrolled longitudinal study. *J. Clin. Exp. Gerontol.: 7,* 289 – 299, 1985 – 86.

Faber-Langendoen K, Morris JC, Knesevich JW, LaBarge E, Miller JP, Berg L: Aphasia in senile dementia of the Alzheimer type. *Ann. Neurol.: 23,* 365 – 370, 1988.

Hershey LA, Modic MT, Jaffe DF, Greenough PG: Natural history of the vascular dementias: a prospective study of seven cases. *Can. J. Neurol. Sci.: 13,* 559 – 565, 1986.

Hertzog C, Schaie KW: Stability and change in adult intelligence: 1. Analysis of longitudinal covariance structures. *Psychol. Aging: 1,* 159 – 171, 1986.

Horn JL, Cattell RB: Refinement and test of the theory of fluid and crystallized intelligence. *J. Educ. Psychol.: 57,* 253 – 270, 1966.

Jarvik LF, Bank L: Aging twins: Longitudinal psychometric data. In Schaie KW (Editor), *Longitudinal Studies of Adult Psychological Development.* New York: Guilford, Ch. 3, pp. 40 – 63, 1983.

Jarvik LF, Ruth V, Matsuyama SS: Organic brain syndrome and aging: a six-year follow-up of surviving twins. *Arch. Gen. Psychiatry: 37,* 280 – 286, 1980.

Kaszniak AW, Wilson RS, Fox JH, Stebbins GT: Cognitive assessment in Alzheimer's disease: cross-sectional and longitudinal perspectives. *Can. J. Neurol. Sci.: 13,* 420 – 423, 1986.

La Rue A: Methodological concerns: longitudinal studies of dementia. *Alzheimer's Dis. Assoc. Disord.: 1,* 180 – 192, 1987.

La Rue A, Jarvik LF: Cognitive function and prediction of dementia in old age. *Int. J. Aging Hum. Dev.: 25,* 79 – 89, 1987.

Luxenberg JS, Haxby JV, Creasey H, Sundaram M, Rapoport SI: Rate of ventricular enlargement in dementia of the Alzheimer type correlates with rate of neuropsychological deterioration. *Neurology: 37,* 1135 – 1140, 1987.

Manton KG, Siegler IC, Woodbury MA: Patterns of intellectual development in later life. *J. Gerontol.: 41,* 486 – 499, 1986.

McCarty SM, Siegler IC, Logue PE: Cross-sectional and longitudinal patterns of three Wechsler Memory Scale subtests. *J. Gerontol.: 37,* 169 – 175, 1982.

McCrae RR, Arenberg D, Costa PT Jr.: Declines in divergent thinking with age: cross-sectional, longitudinal, and cross-sequential analyses. *Psychol. Aging: 2,* 130 – 137, 1987.

Morris JC, McKeel DW Jr., Fulling K, Torack RM, Berg L: Validation of clinical diagnostic criteria for Alzheimer's disease. *Ann. Neurol.: 24,* 17 – 22, 1988.

Morris JC, Drazner M, Fulling K, Grant EA, Goldring J: Clinical and pathological aspects of parkinsonism in Alzheimer's disease: a role for extranigral factors? *Arch. Neurol.: 46,* 651 – 657, 1989.

Mortimer JA, Jun SP, Kuskowski MA, Warrior AS, Webster DD: Cognitive and affective disorders in Parkinson's disease. In Franks AJ (Editor), *Function and Dysfunction in the Basal Ganglia.* Manchester: Manchester University Press, in press.

O'Brien MD: Vascular dementia is underdiagnosed. *Arch. Neurol.: 45,* 797 – 798, 1988.

Robertson-Tchabo EA, Arenberg D, Tobin JD, Plotz JB: A longitudinal study of cognitive performance in noninsulin dependent (Type II) diabetic men. *Exp. Gerontol.: 21,* 459 – 467, 1986.

Schaie KW: The Seattle Longitudinal Study: A 21-year exploration of psychometric intelligence in adulthood. In Schaie KW (Editor), *Longitudinal Studies of Adult Psychological Development.* New York: Guilford, Ch. 4, pp. 64 – 135, 1983.

Schaie KW: Individual differences in rate of cognitive change in adulthood. In Bengtson VL, Schaie KW (Editors), *The Course of Later Life: Research and Reflections.* New York: Springer Publishing, Ch. 5, pp. 65 – 85, 1989.

Schaie KW, Hertzog C: Fourteen-year cohort-sequential analyses of adult intellectual development. *Dev. Psychol.: 19,* 531 – 543, 1983.

Shock NW, Greulich RC, Andres R, Arenberg D, Costa PT Jr., Lakatta EG, Tobin JD: *Normal Human Aging: The Baltimore Longitudinal Study of Aging* (NIH Publication No. 84 – 2450). Washington, DC: U.S. Government Printing Office, 1984.

Siegler IC: Psychological aspects of the Duke Longitudinal Studies. In Schaie KW (Editor), *Longitudinal Studies of Adult Psychological Development.* New York: Guilford, Ch. 5, pp. 136 – 190, 1983.

Siegler IC, Botwinick J: A long-term longitudinal study of intellectual ability of older adults: The matter of selective attrition. *J. Gerontol.: 34,* 242 – 245, 1979.

Storandt M, Hill R: Very mild senile dementia of the Alzheimer type: II. Psychometric test performance. *Arch. Neurol.: 46,* 383 – 386, 1989.

Storandt M, Botwinick J, Danziger WL: Longitudinal changes: Patients with mild SDAT and matched healthy controls. In Poon LW (Editor), *Handbook for the Clinical Memory Assessment of Older Adults.* Washington, DC: American Psychological Association, Ch. 28, pp. 277 – 284, 1986.

Thurstone LL, Thurstone LG: *Examiner Manual for the SRA Primary Mental Abilities Test.* Chicago: Science Research Associates, 1949.

Uhlmann RF, Larson EB, Koepsell TD: Hearing impairment and cognitive decline in senile dementia of the Alzheimer's type. *J. Am. Geriatr. Soc.: 34,* 207 – 210, 1986.

Vitaliano PP, Russo J, Breen AR, Vitiello MV, Prinz PN: Functional decline in the early stages of Alzheimer's disease. *Psychol. Aging: 1,* 41 – 46, 1986.

Handbook of Neuropsychology, Vol. 4
F. Boller and J. Grafman (Eds)

CHAPTER 19

Statistical practice in aging and dementia research

T. John Rosen

Department of Brain and Cognitive Sciences, Massachusetts Institute of Technology, Cambridge, MA 02139, and Department of Neurology, Massachusetts General Hospital, Boston, MA 02114, U.S.A.

Introduction

This chapter discusses aspects of statistical practice relevant to neuropsychological research, particularly investigations of aging and dementia. The chapter focuses on several recurring statistical problems arising from the frequent presence of 'messy data' in neuropsychological data sets.

Data messiness (Milliken and Johnson, 1984), which is inevitable in clinical research, obscures without necessarily diminishing the scientific value of neuropsychological data. Messiness may take many forms. Problems of assessment, data collection and recording produce unreliable data (measures may be adopted without documentation of their psychometric properties), abundant missing data (subjects drop out of longitudinal studies; incapacitated patients do not or cannot complete demanding tests in cross-sectional studies), violations of assumptions (subjects with heterogeneous brain lesions vary more than do control subjects) and erroneous data (the difficulty of maintaining data accuracy increases with the size of a project). Problems of design and hypotheses may yield poorly matched control groups, extremely multivariate data that innundate the statistician with detailed observations from a few rare subjects, imprecisely defined groups of subjects, and longitudinal data with inconsistent measurement intervals. Messy data problems lack perfect solutions: statistical practice always requires uneasy compromises, and messy data make matters trickier still. I admire the opening comment in Rupert Miller's (1986) excellent book: 'These are the confessions of a practicing statistician. They expose to public view what I am likely to do with a set of data. I may therefore live to regret setting pencil to paper' (page *v*).

Comparisons between groups

An illustrative study exemplifies the most common design in neuropsychological research, which compares groups with different lesions. Suppose that an investigation examines two types of patient, one with Alzheimer's disease (AD) and one with Parkinson's disease (PD), and that each subject takes three tests, one of memory, one of attention and one of language. The purpose of the study is to search for cognitive differences between the AD and PD groups. This groups × measures study superficially resembles an old friend from analysis of variance (ANOVA) classes, the mixed model or split-plot factorial design (Kirk, 1982). Although tests appear to form a repeated factor, the measures are actually fully multivariate rather than repeated because they derive from distinct test instruments.

Within a groups × measures design, the broad concern of 'whether the groups differ' has two separate aspects. First, groups that differ in the same direction on all or most measures differ 'in level', for example, the PD patients generally performing better on most tests than the AD patients.

In generalizing across variables, tests of the level hypothesis depend upon the fact that most behavioral measures in aging and dementia research have a strong evaluative component: most tests evaluate the extent of impairments. Second, groups may have similar or different profiles over the set of behavioral measures; groups with dissimilar profiles differ 'in pattern', for example, the PD patients generally performing worse on some tests and better on other tests than the AD patients. The hypotheses of a groups × measures study concern whether groups differ in level, in pattern, or in both.

Groups × measures studies in neuropsychology often follow the familiar 'double dissociation' research paradigm (Teuber, 1955) in order to identify the specific behavioral capacities subserved by individual brain regions. Because brain lesions in people are fairly rare and individual testing is slow and expensive, neuropsychological studies often compensate for the paucity of subjects by administering many, many tests. (Similar constraints affect studies of aged animals; Olton and Markowska, 1988.) Thus, in practice, the illustrative study could include a dozen tests within each of the domains of memory, attention and language. The result is 'extremely multivariate data' in which the variables may outnumber the subjects, further complicating the problem of group comparisons.

Problems of interpretation

However common the groups × measures design, lack of knowledge about the scales used to measure behavior drastically limits the interpretability of the resulting data. Within the illustrative study, suppose that one wished to test the hypothesis that the 'subcortical dementia' of PD differs in pattern from the 'cortical dementia' of AD (e.g., Cummings and Benson, 1984). Suppose that the PD group generally scored better than the AD group; suppose that the PD group scored much better than the AD subjects on a language measure (said to be a 'cortical' capacity); and suppose that the PD subjects scored only slightly better than the AD subjects on a memory measure (said to be impaired in both dementias). It is tempting to conclude that the data demonstrate pattern differences: the language measure apparently differentiated the AD from PD groups more than did the memory measure. But psychometric and measurement considerations suggest alternative interpretations of the observed differences.

From a psychometric perspective, tests of the pattern hypothesis within a groups × measures design confound differences between groups with differences between measuring instruments. Chapman and Chapman (1973) showed that the magnitude of an observed performance deficit is an increasing function of test reliability. If two tests measure the same attribute but differ in reliability, then patients will display the larger numeric deficit relative to control subjects on the test with the greater reliability. Also, deficit magnitude depends upon the difficulty of the items constituting a test. If multiple groups of subjects are tested on two measures that examine the same behavioral capacity but differ in difficulty, it will appear as if the groups have different patterns of impaired and spared capacities (Olton and Markowska, 1988), resulting in a misleading groups × measures interaction.

From the perspective of measurement theory, the results of a group × measures design best support the hypothesis of pattern differences if the observed scores (e.g., number of items recalled) are linearly related to the theoretical constructs under study (e.g., long-term memory capacity) (Jones, 1983). In part, the magnitude of observed between-group differences reflects nonlinearities in the function relating observed scores to theoretical constructs. Separating the effects of scale properties from the effects of pattern differences may be impossible in the absence of systematic study of the scales.

Psychometric and measurement considerations suggest the possibility that the AD and PD subjects only differed in level, and either the language measure had greater reliability than the memory measure or else characteristics of the scales compressed the groups' memory scores. Conceivably, the opposite pattern of results (larger differences on the memory test than on the language test) might have occurred had other measures been chosen which had different properties. Unless one can distinguish the consequences of scale properties from those of group differences, the groups by measures design fails to test hypotheses about between-group differences in pattern.

Standardization has been tried as a means of eliminating scaling differences (e.g., Filley et al., 1989; Huber et al., 1986). Standardization equalizes means and variances; the related technique of converting raw scores to percentages of maximum scores (e.g., Brandt et al., 1988) equalizes only means. However, the linear transformation used to standardize scales does not correct for differences in reliability or item difficulty, nor does it remove nonlinearities. Similarly, converting quantitative scores to ranks (a nonlinear transformation) may not equate measurement scales. Acquiring the information necessary to rescale a test properly may be difficult or impossible. Chapman and Chapman (1973) suggested matching tests with respect to a control population in which the range of test performance includes the scores earned by the impaired groups, but matching cannot be accomplished should neurologically impaired patients score worse than essentially all control subjects, which commonly occurs in dementia research.

Special circumstances exist in which behavioral data can be used to unambiguously assess the pattern hypothesis. First, the Chapman and Chapman (1973) and Jones (1983) articles discussed how to diminish scaling artifacts in testing hypotheses about pattern effects, although their solutions require more information about scales than is customarily available. The utility of scaling information in clarifying the groups × measures design suggests that neuropsychological researchers should spend more effort studying their behavioral instruments. It is extraordinary that so many neuropsychological research projects depend upon barely studied measuring instruments, which 'measure' behavior only in the sense that rulers with arbitrary and uncalibrated markings 'measure' length. Mere knowledge of a test's reliability and validity does not furnish the necessary information about a scale's linearity and distribution of item difficulty.

Second, administering multiple measures of each behavioral capacity reduces the likelihood that psychometric and measurement artifacts will invalidate tests of the pattern hypothesis. The use of multiple measures is consistent with Campbell and Fiske's (1959) 'multitrait, multimethod' strategy. Suppose that the present hypothetical study had included three separate tests in each of the domains of memory, language and attention, and suppose that the pattern of AD-PD differences had been identical for each of the three measures within a domain. Parallel results across tests would suggest that the results reflected the subjects' underlying capacities rather than the tests' properties. Third, different patterns of results vary in how convincingly they imply dissociation of function (Dunn and Kirsner, 1988) and in their vulnerability to alternative explanations based on scaling artifacts (Jones, 1983). Again referring to the hypothetical experiment, suppose that a true crossover interaction had been observed: AD patients scored better than PD patients on the measure of attention, but PD patients scored better than AD patients on the measure of language. Because scaling artifacts could not account for the reversal in the direction of performance, the psychometric and measurement theory criticisms of the groups × measures design do not apply.

Statistical procedures for groups × measures analyses

The present section focuses on how to analyse data from a groups × measures design, in particular, on tests of pattern differences, which require comparing measures. (Testing level differences is simpler because measures need only be pooled as opposed to compared.) In no way, however, does the present section's computational focus imply the legitimacy of interpretations of results that ignore the psychometric and measurement qualifications previously discussed.

The frequent combination of small samples and multiple behavioral measures limits the applicability of multivariate procedures for testing hypotheses about pattern differences. Even so, tests of pattern differences must incorporate multiple measures. In particular, multiple *t* tests of between-group differences on individual measures (cf. Filley et al., 1989; Huber et al., 1986) cannot validate pattern hypotheses. In ANOVA terminology, multiple tests only examine a series of 'simple main effects', not the critical groups × measures interaction. Observing a significant difference between groups on exactly one of two measures implies neither that the groups differ significantly in pattern nor that they differ more on one measure than on the other.

Because profile analysis (Morrison, 1976) and repeated-measures ANOVA incorporate multiple measures, each can test the level and pattern hypotheses about differences between groups on multiple measures. The contributions of the several variables may be equalized by transforming disparate variables to a common scale. However, neither procedure for studying multivariate group differences is immediately applicable to the analysis of extremely multivariate data. Profile analysis, which is based on multivariate ANOVA, requires 5 or 10 times more subjects than variables and thus is useless with extremely multivariate data. Repeated-measures ANOVA requires strong assumptions which data in a groups × measures design rarely satisfy. The measures must be scaled similarly and have a simple covariance structure possessing the 'sphericity' property (Huynh and Mandeville, 1979); the simplest covariance structure with this property features equal variances for each measure and equal covariances between every pair of measures.

Domain analysis approach. A modified ANOVA performed within a procedure known as 'domain analysis' (Rosen and Corkin, 1986) offers a practical, albeit approximate, method for examining group differences in level and pattern. Domain analysis includes several steps. Power considerations mandate the first in applying domain analysis to extremely multivariate data. Maxwell and Arvey (1982) found that repeated measures ANOVAs lack power if the ratio of subjects to variables is too low, especially if the ratio is less than 1:1. The domain analysis approach then pools variables within domains (e.g., language, memory, attention), and the final analysis uses a single composite measure per domain. As has been discussed, pooling measures into domain scores also minimizes psychometric and measurement barriers to interpreting group differences in pattern.

The next step of domain analysis adapts the raw data to fit a repeated-measures ANOVA by transforming the original variables to a single common scale (e.g., *z* scores), usually based on the distribution of a control sample. Under some circumstances, normalized ranks (Blom, 1958) may be useful; they obviate the necessity for a control sample. Both transformation methods depend upon the existence of a common 'good-bad' dimension that equates the variables in terms of direction. The last step of domain analysis adapts the ANOVA to fit the data by using a Box-type method (Box, 1954; Huynh and Feldt, 1976) of correcting violations of the sphericity assumptions. Observed differences in level correspond to a main effect for groups and differences in pattern correspond to a group × measures interaction.

Domain procedures have been used to compare groups' performance on tests of memory and other cognitive capacities (Corkin et al., 1985). The subjects were 21 amnesic subjects of seven etiologies. The authors concluded that subjects of the four most common etiologies differed in overall performance level but not in pattern of performance.

Classification approach. In a study comparing cognitive impairments of 145 patients with AD to those of 84 patients with Huntington's disease (HD), Brandt et al. (1988) used discriminant analysis 'to determine whether the observed profile differences were sufficiently consistent to classify correctly patients as having AD or HD' (page 556). In general, however, profile analysis appears simpler and more useful than classification methods. The classification approach requires cross-validation because it is difficult to determine the significance of a given degree of accuracy in classification; in contrast, profile analysis immediately generates significance levels. Also, discriminant analysis does not ordinarily distinguish differences in level from differences in pattern. Given that discriminant analysis (which underlies classification methods) and multivariate ANOVA (which underlies profile analysis) have identical computational solutions in the two-group case (Morrison, 1976) and given the advantages of profile analysis, this latter procedure would seem preferable, although like all multivariate methods it requires large sample sizes by neuropsychological standards.

Comparisons between subjects

Neuropsychological studies often examine individuals who experience naturally occurring events such as brain injury, neurological disease or aging. Subjects within a natural lesion group vary considerably in the history, location and severity of pathology, and within-group variation may be as meaningful as comparisons between groups. Existing categories may be too broad; for example, diseases such as AD may result from multiple etiologies. Neuropsychology thus impels reclassification of and comparisons among subjects.

For illustrative purposes, suppose that patients with PD participating in a double-blind, crossover experiment testing recognition memory received scopolamine in one condition and a placebo in the other, and suppose that every patient completed both conditions of the full crossover design twice. The question is whether the patients differ in degree of involvement of the cholinergic system; cholinergic pathology should increase the amnesic effects of scopolamine (Dubois et al., 1987). The statistical problem is how to determine whether the behavioral variation between subjects in the effect of scopolamine is sufficiently large to imply that pathological variation exists. The null hypothesis for the subjects factor states that the observed mean differences among the subjects result only from errors, and the alternative hypothesis states that the subjects genuinely differ.

Replication of the entire crossover design allows an ANOVA F test to determine the significance of differences between the patients. The replications yield two estimates of the difference between the scopolamine and placebo conditions for each patient; the F test compares the variation between patients to that within patients. Rosen et al. (1987) used this procedure to show that a sample of 24 AD patients did not significantly differ in rate of progression of dementia across four clinic visits.

Testing the significance of differences between PD patients corresponds to a common problem in treatment studies, that of distinguishing 'responders' from 'nonresponders,' which is of particular interest in trials assessing a drug's efficacy in syndromes such as AD which may be etiologically diverse. Comparing subjects helps answer the secondary question of whether the drug only aids performance among a subset of subjects (Growdon et al., 1986). Obviously, replication is expensive, demanding on subjects, and decreases the total number of subjects who can be studied. However, should the researcher need to know whether treatment response is homogeneous or heterogeneous across subjects, replication provides the most direct method of comparing subjects.

Researchers often use classification techniques such as cluster analysis to divide an existing subject category (e.g., AD, PD, the aged) into subgroups. Because random variation can produce seemingly fascinating patterns (e.g., fractal-generated 'coastlines', cumulus clouds), one must differentiate random or unreliable classifications from those based on meaningful patterns. For example, Katzman (1985) found that the clinical course of AD differed from patient to patient; some subjects showed extended plateaus (periods without apparent deterioration). Do his observations imply that there exists a subgroup of AD patients who experience periods of stability, or does a random component of mental status scores create patterns out of nothingness? Similarly, El-Awar et al. (1987) used post hoc procedures to differentiate a subgroup of PD patients who manifested a learning impairment from a subgroup who learned normally. Do two patterns of PD exist, or did the subgroups result from arbitrarily dividing a continuum of scores?

Recent papers have presented guidelines for formulating and interpreting classifications of subjects. Jorm (1985, 1989) examined the statistical criteria for inferring the existence of subtypes. Fletcher et al. (1988) argued for a hypothesis-driven approach to classification and presented a detailed framework for conducting classification research. Classification efforts require a thorough appreciation of the relevant statistical issues, but a purely statistical approach to classification would seem inadequate. The major goals of aging and dementia research are to treat impairments and to prevent or halt pathological processes. Because classifications of etiological and pathophysiological significance are most pertinent to disease treatment or prevention, neuropsychological subgroup studies should seek behaviorally based classifications that hold particular promise of corresponding to biological divisions.

The analysis of change

Neither age nor dementia remains constant, and neither can be understood without studying change. The diversity of statistical procedures for analysing changes over time (Plewis, 1985) reflects the difficulties posed by longitudinal data. Papers that have addressed in depth the specific problem of analysing growth or dose-response curves include those by Grizzle and Allen (1969) and Bryant and Gillings (1985).

Questions about change

Extending a paper by Cronbach and Furby (1970), Rogosa et al. (1982) listed several types of question about change. Each type poses different analytic problems.

Individual patterns of change. Studies may examine individual patterns of change. For example, Rosen et al. (1987) found that patients with AD do not develop dementia at individually consistent rates; earlier and later rates of progression showed no correlation.

Change may be decomposed into linear, quadratic and cubic components, each computed individually by means of within-subject regressions (Ghosh et al., 1973; Hand and Taylor, 1987). Each component determines a new variable, which may be analysed by ordinary univariate procedures.

Change within experiments. Studies may determine whether experimentally defined groups differ in rate of change. For example, Heyman et al. (1987) compared the progression of AD patients who did or did not take lecithin over a 6-month period.

True experiments featuring random assignment of subjects to groups pose comparatively little statistical difficulty beyond the problem of how to define change. The main argument in the literature has concerned whether to use regression procedures (e.g., analysis of covariance) to define change (Cronbach and Furby, 1970; Lord, 1963) or whether to use simple difference scores (Rogosa et al., 1982). In part, the argument has focussed on whether difference scores are sufficiently reliable and even whether reliability is desirable (Zimmerman and Williams, 1986). My understanding of this difficult area is that reductions in error variance are desirable and that error variance may decrease if one substitutes a more reliable measure for one that is less reliable, but difference scores are often less reliable than one would like, particularly when the original pre-test and post-test measures are conspicuously unreliable themselves. Should unreliable difference scores weaken significance tests, improving behavioral measures would seem preferable to compensating by means of psychometric wizardry.

Analyses of difference scores should take into account two cautions. First, one should not use difference scores rather than covariance procedures as a means of avoiding restrictive statistical assumptions; analyses of covariance (ANACOVA) and analyses of difference scores do not differ in this regard. Second, difference scores (or estimates of change derived from regression procedures) run into the same measurement problems discussed in a previous section on comparing variables. Suppose that the scores of a patient with AD decreased on a certain measure of memory from 15 to 5 points over a year interval, and that the scores of a less-impaired patient with PD decreased from 25 to 20 points over the same interval. Jorm (1989) pointed out that it is doubtful that the AD patient decreased 'twice' as much as the PD patient. But it is not even obvious that the AD patient decreased 'more' than the PD patient. As Lord (1963) noted, 'Any such comparison of gains for people at different parts of the score scale implies that the score scale is temporarily being treated as if it had 'equal' units over the range involved' (p. 31). Given the dearth of knowledge about scale properties, one can rarely compare changes in the face of initial performance differences.

The problem of interpreting change is of immediate pertinence to treatment studies. Whenever control subjects have superior baseline scores to those of patients, it is extremely difficult to determine whether a pharmacological agent has greater effects on memory among the patients or among the control subjects. The previously cited Dubois et al. (1987) study of the effects of scopolamine in PD avoided ambiguity because (a) PD patients did not perform worse than control subjects in the placebo condition and (b) scopolamine had no effects among control subjects.

Change within correlational designs. Studies may examine factors that correlate with change. For example, Rubin et al. (1987) found that early personality changes in AD were not associated with more rapid progression of dementia. A related design compares changes in non-equivalent groups. For example, Rosen et al. (1987) found that scores on a measure of dementia severity worsened more rapidly among patients with AD than among patients with PD.

Correlating subject characteristics with observed change or comparing change in initially non-equivalent groups raises the specter of the dreaded regression towards the mean artifact. It is difficult to perform and interpret correctly analyses that examine who changes the most as a function of initial characteristics and performance. Lord has written several sobering papers (1963, 1967, 1969) on the regression artifact, focussing on the interpretation of ANACOVAs. Lord showed that individuals who start off with high scores tend to decrease and individuals who start off with low scores tend to increase; however confusing, such observations are 'real' rather than artifactual. Lord also showed that, in attempting to 'partial out' variables or 'equate' groups, covariance procedures address different questions from analyses of means or of individual difference scores. Later papers (Labouvie, 1982; Nesselroade et al., 1980) further emphasized the need for asking specific questions about change, preferably with the aid of a well-defined model.

In practice, confounds between pre-existing differences and subsequent change may limit the interpretability of results. For example, Stern et al. (1987) studied the progression of dementia in AD patients. At entry into the study, patients with extrapyramidal signs (EPS) scored considerably worse on a cognitive measure of mental status than patients without EPS. Change was not studied directly, but a life-table analysis showed that patients with EPS reached a fixed cognitive 'endpoint' sooner than patients without EPS. It is difficult to determine how much of the group differences in time to endpoint can be attributed to the differences at entry into the study.

Type of longitudinal data

Research designs may observe each subject on few or many occasions. Data collection may be structured, having a fixed number of equal measurement intervals, or unstructured, following an arbitrary and variable pattern.

Structured hypotheses about means. Repeated-measures ANOVAs are often used to examine mean differences in structured studies of change, especially when the ratio of subjects to observations is adequately high (Maxwell and Avery, 1982). Sequential data, however, violate ANOVA assumptions. Observations collected closely together in time tend to correlate more than widely separated observations, whereas ANOVA usually assumes a pattern of equal correlations. In particular, trials analyses of learning studies *always* violate ANOVA assumptions (data from adjacent trials correlate more than data from distant trials). The Box-type correction procedures previously described help compensate for violations. In psychological research the use of uncorrected ANOVAs of trials data is rarely challenged (statisticians are less forgiving). The more fastidious may extract and examine separately the linear, quadratic and cubic trends over time (Hand and Taylor, 1987).

Structured studies about variation. Time-series analysis (Gottman, 1981) uses highly structured data to characterize the temporal aspects of variability. Each analysis studies a single subject's data, consisting of a large number (usually at least 30) of observations made at equal intervals. Time-series analysis addresses any of several related questions: whether successive observations are independent, whether shifts in performance over time are cyclical, and how quickly change over time occurs. As shown by the last question, time-series analysis is useful in analysing non-cyclical behaviors. Although rarely used in neuropsychology, time-series analysis could examine the nature of within-subject variation and the efficacy of treatments for memory loss (cf. Gottman, 1973). As an example of the potential of the time-series approach, Gottman (1981) reanalysed data presented by Holtzman (1963) and found that chlorpromazine administered to a single schizophrenic did not change mean scores on a test of the normality of associations, but the patient's scores varied more rapidly over time (scores were more 'erratic') with than without the drug. Other statistical techniques such as randomization tests (Edgington, 1980) also serve to study data from an individual subject, among them procedures for studying the effects of treatments on performance assessed repeatedly over time.

Studies with unstructured data. Research performed in dementia and geriatric medicine clinics generates large quantities of unstructured longitudinal data. Because patient care cannot be compromised in the interests of research, conflicts between the medical and research functions of a clinic may disrupt systematic research protocols. Patients visit the clinic at odd intervals for reasons other than the researcher's convenience; they enroll in research-oriented clinics because of referrals rather than because of reaching a specific stage in a disease; and they quit the clinic for personal reasons, often but not always before entering a nursing home. Unstructured longitudinal data frustrate attempts to align visits across patients; it is unclear whether visits are best matched by age, mental status score, duration of disease, or time since first visit. However messy, clinic data constitute an essential resource for studies of aging and dementia that require substantial numbers of subjects.

Descriptively, raw scores may be plotted as individual time-vs.-score curves, using the same axes for all subjects. The abscissa in these graphs indicates some aspect of time such as date, time since entry into the study, time since start of treatment, or time since disease onset, whatever best clarifies the data; the ordinate indicates scores. Miller (1989) called these 'spaghetti plots' (they look like a handful of slightly crooked pasta). Spaghetti plots may include data from a surprisingly large number of subjects while still remaining legible. Inferentially, an elegant approach to studying change is to estimate and analyse parameters of individual subjects' time-vs.-score curves, by means of either regression or 'area under the curve' analyses.

Regression analyses of change. Unstructured longitudinal data may be analysed through within-subject regression procedures using a non-parametric method developed by Ghosh et al. (1973). Because visits or measurements cannot be aligned over subjects, analyses cannot combine or average raw scores across subjects. Instead, estimates of regression parameters summarizing the time-vs.-score function are derived separately for each subject, and significance tests examine only the derived parameters. Once the within-subject regressions have been completed, the Ghosh et al. procedure requires relatively simple significance tests. Because the variance of parameter estimates depends upon the number and pattern of observations and especially upon the length of time for which subjects are observed, robust or non-parametric significance tests (e.g., the Wilcoxon signed-rank test) must be used.

The Ghosh et al. procedure would be appropriate for comparing the rapidity of the progression of AD among different categories of AD patients, e.g., early vs. late onset, or for determining the long-term effects of a putative treatment relative to a placebo. Although the procedure uses nonparametric statistics, the within-subject regressions assume that the dependent variable (mental status, memory, etc.) is measured on an interval scale. Thus, the current lack of information about the properties of scales severely hampers aging and dementia researchers' ability to study change over time.

Area under the curve analyses. Individual subjects' time-vs.-score functions may be summarized by 'area under the curve' (AUC) methods (Bryant and Gillings, 1985). Suppose that a study is done to determine whether a drug aids memory performance over an extended period. Each subject's time-vs.-score function is plotted after normalization with respect to the pre-test level (usually defined as zero). Memory performance at any follow-up test is indicated by height over the abscissa (time axis), and thus overall memory performance corresponds to the AUC throughout the entire follow-up period. Parametric tests (with structured data) or nonparametric tests (with unstructured data) compare group tendencies. Like methods based on within-subject regression analyses, AUC methods reduce highly multivariate data to one or two measures per subject.

A final note

Two developments during the last few years have changed statistical practice. First, exploratory data analysis (EDA) techniques (Tukey, 1977) provide one's first glimpse of a data set, reveal unexpected patterns, and guide subsequent formal analyses. EDA techniques are graphic (Chambers et al., 1983; du Toit et al., 1986) and informal, and accessible to the researcher as well as to the statistician. Interpretations of neuropsychological data must often take into account individual subjects' characteristics, a task for which EDA techniques are eminently suitable. Similarly, messy data sets such as those collected in studies of aging and dementia routinely contain the unexpected, which EDA helps one find. Second, fully interactive microcomputer programs that implement EDA principles now provide visual access to large data sets. As an example, traditional large statistical packages use tables of mean squares and p values to describe multiple regression results. In sharp contrast, microcomputer programs describe regression relations directly by rotating a three-dimensional scatterplot on a computer screen.

Inevitably, as studies of aging and dementia have increased in size and sophistication, their statistical complexity has increased as well. By enhancing researchers' visualization and understanding of their data, recent developments in

EDA and microcomputer statistical software promise to keep statistical practice closely tied to researchers' concerns.

Acknowledgements

I wish to thank Suzanne Corkin, John Growdon and Victor Henderson, who provided helpful comments on early drafts of this chapter. Preparation of this chapter was supported by USPHS grants AG05134, AG06605 and MH24433.

References

Blom G: *Statistical Estimates and Transformed Beta Variables.* New York: Wiley, 1958.

Box GEP: Some theorems on quadratic forms applied in the study of analysis of variance problems. II: Effects of inequality of variance and of correlation between errors in the two-way classification. *Ann. Math. Stat.: 25,* 484 – 498, 1954.

Brandt J, Folstein SE, Folstein MF: Differential cognitive impairment in Alzheimer's disease and Huntington's disease. *Ann. Neurol.: 23,* 555 – 561, 1988.

Bryant E, Gillings D: Statistical analysis of longitudinal repeated measures designs. In Sen PK (Editor), *Biostatistics: Statistics in Biomedical, Public Health and Environmental Sciences.* Amsterdam: Elsevier, pp. 251 – 282, 1985.

Campbell DT, Fiske DW: Convergent and discriminant validation by the multitrait-multimethod matrix. *Psychol. Bull.: 56,* 81 – 105, 1959.

Chambers JM, Cleveland WS, Kleiner B, Tukey P: *Graphical Methods for Data Analysis.* Belmont, CA: Wadsworth, 1983.

Chapman LJ, Chapman JP: Problems in the measurement of cognitive deficit. *Psychol. Bull.: 79,* 380 – 385, 1973.

Corkin S, Cohen NJ, Sullivan EV, Clegg RA, Rosen TJ: Analyses of global memory impairments of different etiologies. *Ann. N.Y. Acad. Sci.: 444,* 10 – 40, 1985.

Cronbach LJ, Furby L: How should we measure 'change' – or should we? *Psychol. Bull.: 74,* 68 – 80, 1970.

Cummings JL, Benson DF: Subcortical dementia: review of an emerging concept. *Arch. Neurol.: 41,* 874 – 879, 1984.

du Toit SHC, Steyn AGW, Stumpf RH: *Graphical Exploratory Data Analysis.* New York: Springer-Verlag, 1986.

Dubois B, Danze F, Pillon B, Cusimano G, Lhermitte F, Agid Y: Cholinergic-dependent cognitive deficits in Parkinson's disease. *Ann. Neurol.: 22,* 26 – 30, 1987.

Dunn JC, Kirsner K: Discovering functionally independent mental processes: The principle of reversed association. *Psychol. Rev.: 95,* 91 – 101, 1988.

Edgington ES: *Randomization Tests.* New York: Marcel Dekker, 1980.

El-Awar M, Becker JT, Hammond KM, Nebes RD, Boller F: Learning deficit in Parkinson's disease: comparison with Alzheimer's disease and normal aging. *Arch. Neurol.: 44,* 180 – 184, 1987.

Filley CM, Heaton RK, Nelson LM, Burks JS, Franklin GM: A comparison of dementia in Alzheimer's disease and multiple sclerosis. *Arch. Neurol.: 46,* 157 – 161, 1989.

Fletcher JM, Francis DJ, Morris R: Methodological issues in neuropsychology: classification, measurement and nonequivalent group comparisons. In Boller F, Grafman J (Editors), *Handbook of Neuropsychology, Vol. 1.* Amsterdam: Elsevier, pp. 83 – 110, 1988.

Ghosh M, Grizzle JE, Sen PK: Nonparametric methods in longitudinal studies. *J. Am. Stat. Assoc.: 68,* 29 – 36, 1973.

Gottman JM: *N*-of-one and *N*-of-two research in psychotherapy. *Psychol. Bull.: 80,* 93 – 105, 1973.

Gottman JM: *Time-series Analysis: A Comprehensive Introduction for Social Scientists.* Cambridge: Cambridge University Press, 1981.

Grizzle JE, Allen DM: Analysis of growth and dose response curves. *Biometrics: 25,* 307 – 318, 1969.

Growdon JH, Corkin S, Huff FJ, Rosen TJ: Piracetam combined with lecithin in the treatment of Alzheimer's disease. *Neurobiol. Aging: 7,* 269 – 276, 1986.

Hand DJ, Taylor CC: *Multivariate Analysis of Variance and Repeated Measures.* London: Chapman and Hall, 1987.

Heyman A, Schmechel D, Wilkinson W, Rogers H, Krishnan R, Holloway D, Schultz K, Gwyther L, Peoples R, Utley C, Haynes C: Failure of long term high-dose lecithin to retard progression of early-onset Alzheimer's disease. *J. Neural Transm. (Suppl.): 24,* 279 – 286, 1987.

Holtzman WH: Statistical models for the study of change in the single case. In Harris CW (Editor), *Problems in Measuring Change.* Madison: University of Wisconsin Press, pp. 199 – 211, 1963.

Huber SJ, Shuttleworth EC, Paulson GW, Bellchambers MJG, Clapp LE: Cortical vs subcortical dementia: neuropsychological differences. *Arch. Neurol.: 43,* 392 – 394, 1986.

Huynh H, Feldt LS: Estimation of the Box correction for degrees of freedom from sample data in the randomized block and split-plot-designs. *J. Educ. Stat.: 1,* 69 – 82, 1976.

Huynh H, Mandeville GK: Validity conditions in repeated measures designs. *Psychol. Bull.: 86,* 964 – 973, 1979.

Jones GV: On double dissociation of function. *Neuropsychologia: 21,* 397 – 400, 1983.

Jorm AF: Subtypes of Alzheimer's Dementia: a conceptual analysis and critical review. *Psychol. Med.: 15,* 543 – 553, 1985.

Jorm AF: Some pitfalls in data analysis. *Proc. Int. Study Group Pharmacol. Memory Disord. Assoc. Aging: 5,* 63 – 72, 1989.

Katzman R: Clinical presentation of the course of Alzheimer's disease: the atypical patient. *Interdisciplinary Top. Gerontol.: 20,* 12 – 18, 1985.

Kirk RE: *Experimental Design: Procedures for the Behavioral Sciences.* Belmont, CA: Wadsworth, 1982.

Labouvie EW: The concept of change and regression toward the mean. *Psychol. Bull.: 92,* 251 – 257, 1982.

Lord FM: Elementary models for measuring change. In Harris CW (Editor), *Problems in Measuring Change.* Madison: University of Wisconsin Press, pp. 21 – 38, 1963.

Lord FM: A paradox in the interpretation of group comparisons. *Psychol. Bull.: 68,* 304 – 305, 1967.

Lord FM: Statistical adjustments when comparing preexisting groups. *Psychol. Bull.: 72,* 336 – 337, 1969.

Maxwell SE, Avery RD: Small sample profile analysis with many variables. *Psychol. Bull.: 92,* 778 – 785, 1982.

Miller JP: Statistical considerations for quantitative techniques in clinical neurology. In Munsat TL (Editor), *Quantification of Neurologic Deficit.* Boston: Butterworths, pp. 69 – 84, 1989.

Miller RG Jr: *Beyond ANOVA: Basics of Applied Statistics.* New York: Wiley, 1986.

Milliken GA, Johnson DE: *Analysis of Messy Data. Vol. 1: Designed Experiments.* Belmont, CA: Wadsworth, 1984.

Morrison DF: *Multivariate Statistical Methods.* New York: McGraw-Hill, 1976.

Nesselroade JR, Stigler SM, Baltes PB: Regression toward the mean and the study of change. *Psychol. Bull.: 88,* 622 – 637, 1980.

Olton DS, Markowska AL: Within-subjects, parametric manipulations to investigate aging. *Neurobiol. Aging: 9,* 469 – 474, 1988.

Plewis I: *Analysing Change: Measurement and Explanation Using Longitudinal Data.* Chichester: Wiley, 1985.

Rogosa D, Brandt D, Zimowski M: A growth curve approach to the measurement of change. *Psychol. Bull.: 92,* 762 – 748, 1982.

Rosen TJ, Corkin S: On the analysis of disparate variables: assessing quantitative and qualitative group differences. *Proc. Abstr. East. Psychol. Assoc.: 57,* 43, 1986.

Rosen TJ, Growdon JH, Corkin S: Comparison of rates of progression in Alzheimer's disease and Parkinson's disease. *J. Neural Transm. (Suppl.): 24,* 105 – 107, 1987.

Rosen TJ, Growdon JH, Corkin S: Lack of intra-patient consistency in rate of progression in Alzheimer's disease. *Soc. Neurosc. Abstr.: 13,* 1629, 1987.

Rubin EH, Morris JC, Berg L: The progression of personality changes in senile dementia of the Alzheimer's type. *J. Am. Geriatr. Soc.: 35,* 721 – 725, 1987.

Stern Y, Mayeux R, Sano M, Hauser WA, Bush T: Predictors of disease course in patients with probable Alzheimer's disease. *Neurology: 37,* 1649 – 1653, 1987.

Teuber H-L: Physiological psychology. *Ann. Rev. Psychol.: 6,* 267 – 296, 1955.

Tukey JW: *Exploratory Data Analysis.* Reading, MA: Addison-Wesley, 1977.

Zimmerman DW, Williams RH: Note on the reliability of experimental measures and the power of significance tests. *Psychol. Bull.: 100,* 123 – 124, 1986.

Index

Index